b14455481

WITHDRAWN
NDSU

Soil and Water Conservation Advances in the United States

Soil and Water Conservation Advances in the United States

Ted M. Zobeck and William F. Schillinger, Editors

Book and Multimedia Publishing Committee
David Baltensperger, Chair
Warren Dick, ASA Editor-in-Chief
E. Charles Brummer, CSSA Editor-in-Chief
Sally Logsdon, SSSA Editor-in-Chief
Mary Savin, ASA Representative
Hari Krishnan, CSSA Representative
April Ulery, SSSA Representative

Managing Editor: Lisa Al-Amoodi

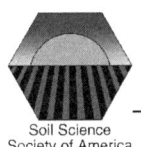

Soil Science Society of America SSSA Special Publication 60

Copyright © 2010 by Soil Science Society of America, Inc.

ALL RIGHTS RESERVED. No part of this publication may be reproduced or transmitted in any form or by any means, electronic or mechanical, including photocopying, recording, or any information storage and retrieval system, without permission in writing from the publisher.

The views expressed in this publication represent those of the individual Editors and Authors. These views do not necessarily reflect endorsement by the Publisher(s). In addition, trade names are sometimes mentioned in this publication. No endorsement of these products by the Publisher(s) is intended, nor is any criticism implied of similar products not mentioned.

Soil Science Society of America, Inc.
677 South Segoe Road, Madison, WI 53711-1086 USA

The U.S. Department of Agriculture offers its programs to all eligible persons regardless of race, color, age, sex, or national origin, and is an equal opportunity employer. Mention of trade names or commercial products is solely for the purpose of providing specific information and does not imply recommendation or endorsement by the USDA-ARS.

ISBN: 978-0-89118-852-0
Library of Congress Control Number: 2010922330

Cover design: Patricia Scullion
Cover photos: (top) Washington State University Holland Library Archives, Pullman, WA; (bottom) Gary Kramer, USDA-NRCS.

Printed in the United States of America.

Contents

Foreword | vii
Preface | ix
Contributors | xi
Conversion Factors for SI and Non-SI Units | xiii

Chapter 1 | 1
Water Conservation for Agriculture
Paul W. Unger, Mary Beth Kirkham, and David C. Nielsen

Chapter 2 | 47
Soil and Water Challenges for Pacific Northwest Agriculture
William F. Schillinger, Robert I. Papendick, and Donald K. McCool

Chapter 3 | 81
Soil and Water Conservation Advances in the Semiarid Northern Great Plains
Donald L. Tanaka, Drew J. Lyon, Perry R. Miller, Stephen D. Merrill, and Brian G. McConkey

Chapter 4 | 103
Major Advances of Soil and Water Conservation in the U.S. Southern Great Plains
B.A. Stewart, R.L. Baumhardt, and S.R. Evett

Chapter 5 | 131
Midwest Soil and Water Conservation: Past, Present, and Future
Douglas L. Karlen, Dana L. Dinnes, and Jeremy W. Singer

Chapter 6 | 163
Historical and Emerging Soil and Water Conservation Issues in the Northeastern USA
Harold van Es

Chapter 7 | 183
Soil and Water Conservation in the Southeastern United States: A Look at Conservation Practices Past, Present, and Future
Warren J. Busscher, Harry H. Schomberg, and Randy L. Raper

Contents

CHAPTER 8 | 201
Soil and Water Conservation in the Mid-South United States: Lessons Learned and a Look to the Future
Martin A. Locke, Donald D. Tyler, and Lewis A. Gaston

CHAPTER 9 | 237
Soil and Water Conservation for California and the Desert Southwest: Past, Present, and Future Trends
A. Toby O'Geen, Michael J. Singer, and William Horwath

CHAPTER 10 | 263
Soil and Water Conservation Advances in the United States— Review and Assessment
Ted M. Zobeck

Subject Index | 293

Foreword

Public awareness of the fragile nature of our soil and water resources has been heightened of late. Given that conservation of soil and water resources is at the heart of a sustainable environment and an adequate world food supply, the Soil Science Society of America (SSSA) is excited and pleased to be able to publish this highly relevant and comprehensive treatise on advances in soil and water conservation in the United States. It contains the "full story" of the scientific papers presented in a Symposium entitled "Major Advances in Soil and Water Conservation" conducted during the Society's Annual Meeting in New Orleans in 2007.

This volume provides an in-depth view of advances in soil and water conservation in the United States. It provides the extensive coverage that readers of our Society's publications have come to expect. The comprehensive nature and high quality of the information was only possible because of the broad experience base of the chapter authors. Drs. Ted Zobeck and William Schillinger are to be commended for the superb job they did in recruiting truly outstanding authors who are at the forefront of research in soil and water conservation. Their expertise brings great credibility to this work.

The Editors skillfully and carefully guided the development of the book, organizing the content by regions of the United States, which makes it an easy to use reference for professors and students. It contains practical application information that will appeal to professional soil scientists and advisors. Authors with experiences specific to their region have done a great job of synthesizing the state of the science in a straightforward and instructive manner. I anticipate this book will be a highly valued resource to soil scientists across the nation.

Gary A. Peterson, Colorado State University
2008 SSSA President

PREFACE

The American Society of Agronomy celebrated 100 years of service to agriculture and science in 2007. Division S-6 of the Soil Science Society of America, Soil and Water Management and Conservation, participated in the celebration by hosting a special symposium on major advances in soil and water conservation for agriculture at the ASA, CSSA, SSSA annual meeting in New Orleans, LA. This publication is comprised of chapters based on papers presented at the symposium, as well as a few additional contributions to fully represent every geographic region of the continental United States.

Productive soils and clean water are essential elements for economic and social prosperity and environmental sustainability. Throughout history, civilizations have thrived or collapsed based on the availability of these vital resources. The lack of arable land and evidence of soil degradation have been identified as causes for the fall of many ancient civilizations, such as those in Mesopotamia, the Anasazi in the western United States, and the Mayans of Central America. The rise and fall of these civilizations is often attributed to accelerated erosion and degradation caused by improper land management or scarce resources. We must understand and remember the lessons of the past, for those who do not heed these lessons are most likely to repeat them.

Approximately 580 million hectares of the continental United States (62% of the total land area) are used for agricultural purposes. This land is used to produce food, fiber, feed, biofuels, and pasture. This land also provides critical ecosystem functions such as nutrient and water cycling, decomposition and detoxification of wastes, and a sink for carbon and greenhouse gases. Scientifically based soil and water conservation and management principles are needed to produce environmentally safe and sustainable outcomes.

Systematic investigation of sound soil and water conservation principles began in response to the dramatic soil erosion produced prior to and during the 1930s Dust Bowl. In 1929, the Buchanan Amendment to the Agricultural Appropriations bill established a nationally coordinated effort providing funding for 10 erosion experiment stations across the United States. The Soil Conservation Act was passed in 1935, placing soil erosion control activities in the Department of Agriculture. The scientific infrastructure available to investigate methods to mitigate the deleterious effects of erosion is now found in national, state, and county-level agencies throughout the country.

Authors of each region of the continental United States were asked to describe the history of soil and water conservation for the last century, the current situation, and suggest the outlook for the future. Each of the regional chapters in this book follows the following format:

- **Introduction.** The authors describe the region and provide an overview of the climate, soils, and agricultural production practices.

- Historic soil and water conservation problems and concerns associated with agricultural practices during the past 100 years. What were the major research findings and recommendations and/or government programs that addressed the problems? Data are shown for major research findings. What conservation practices were readily adopted by farmers? Why were other recommended practices not adopted by farmers? What was the impact of government farm programs on soil and water conservation?

- Recent advances in the past 20 years. How have these advances made a difference for farmers and the environment? Examples and data are provided on how these changes have impacted society.

- Future outlook. Where do we go from here? What are the present research challenges? How do authors visualize agricultural production practices in their region changing in future years to address soil and water conservation concerns?

We feel that this book offers an informative perspective of past issues, methods, and advances in soil and water conservation for each region. The authors are noted experts in soil and water conservation and offer unique insights into the future outlook for their region. The book should be a valuable resource for students and professionals alike.

Appreciation is extended to the authors for their valuable contributions and to the Soil Science Society of America for hosting the symposium in New Orleans and for publication of this book. We hope you find this book informative and useful.

Ted M. Zobeck and William F. Schillinger, Editors

CONTRIBUTORS

Baumhardt, R.L.	USDA-ARS, Conservation and Production Research Lab., P.O. Drawer 10, Bushland, TX 79012 (Louis.Baumhardt@ars.usda.gov)
Busscher, W.J.	USDA-ARS, Coastal Plains Soil, Water, and Plant Research Ctr., 2611 W. Lucas St., Florence, SC 29501-1242 (warren.busscher@ars.usda.gov)
Dinnes, D.L.	USDA-ARS, Natl. Lab. for Agriculture and the Environment, 2110 University Blvd., Ames, IA 50011-3120 (dana.dinnes@ars.usda.gov)
Evett, S.R.	USDA-ARS, Conservation and Production Research Lab., P.O. Drawer 10, Bushland, TX 79012 (Steve.Evett@ars.usda.gov)
Gaston, L.A.	Dep. of Agronomy, Louisiana State Univ., Agricultural Ctr., Baton Rouge, LA 70803 (lagaston@agctr.lsu.edu)
Horwath, W.H.	Dep. of Land, Air, and Water Resources, Univ. of California, One Shields Ave., Davis, CA 95616-8627 (wrhorwath@ucdavis.edu)
Karlen, D.L.	USDA-ARS, Natl. Lab. for Agriculture and the Environment, 2110 Univ. Blvd., Ames, IA 50011-3120 (Doug.Karlen@ars.usda.gov)
Kirkham, M.B.	Dep. of Agronomy, Kansas State Univ., 2004 Throckmorton Plant Sciences Ctr., Manhattan, KS 66506 (mbk@ksu.edu)
Locke, M.A.	USDA-ARS, Water Quality and Ecology Research Unit, Natl. Sedimentation Lab., 598 McElroy, Oxford, MS 38655 (martin.locke@ars.usda.gov)
Lyon, D.J.	Univ. of Nebraska Panhandle Research and Extension Ctr., 4502 Ave. I, Scottsbluff, NE 69361-4939 (dlyon@unlnotes.unl.edu)
McCool, D.K.	USDA-ARS, 253 L.J. Smith Hall, Pullman, WA 99164 (dkmccool@wsu.edu)
McConkey, B.G.	Agriculture and Agri-Food Canada, Agriculture Canada, Box 1030, Swift Current, SK S9H3X2, Canada (mcconkeyb@agr.gc.ca)
Merrill, S.D.	retired, formerly USDA-ARS, P.O. Box 459, Mandan, ND 58554 (steve.merrill@ars.usda.gov)
Miller, P.R.	Dep. of Land Resources and Environmental Sciences, Montana State Univ., Leon Johnson Hall 706, Bozeman, MT 59717 (pmiller@montana.edu)
Nielsen, D.C.	USDA-ARS, Central Great Plains Res. Stn., 40335 County Rd. GG, Akron, CO 80720 (david.nielsen@ars.usda.gov)
O'Geen, A.T.	Cooperative Extension, Dep. of Land, Air, and Water Resources, Univ. of California, One Shields Ave., Davis, CA 95616-8627 (atogeen@ucdavis.edu)
Papendick, R.I.	retired, formerly USDA-ARS, 201 Johnson Hall, Pullman, WA 99164 (papendick@wsu.edu)
Raper, R.L.	USDA-ARS, Dale Bumpers Small Farms Research Ctr., 6883 South State Hwy. 23, Booneville, AR 72927 (Randy.Raper@ars.usda.gov)
Schillinger, W.F.	Dep. of Crop and Soil Sciences, Washington State Univ., Dryland Research Station, Lind, WA 99341 (schillw@wsu.edu)
Schomberg, H.H.	USDA-ARS, J. Phil Campbell, Sr., Natural Resources Conservation Ctr., 1420 Experiment Station Rd., Watkinsville, GA 30677-2373 (Harry.Schomberg@ars.usda.gov)

Singer, J.W.	USDA-ARS, Natl. Lab. for Agriculture and the Environment, 2110 University Blvd., Ames, IA 50011-3120 (jeremy.singer@ars.usda.gov)
Singer, M.J.	Dep. of Land, Air and Water Resources, Univ. of California, One Shields Ave., Davis, CA 95616-8627 (mjsinger@ucdavis.edu)
Stewart, B.A.	Dryland Agriculture Inst., West Texas A&M Univ., WTAMU Box 60278, 2403 Russell Long Blvd., Canyon, TX 70016 (bstewart@wtamu.edu)
Tanaka, D.L.	USDA-ARS-NGPRL, P.O. Box 459, Mandan, ND 58554 (don.tanaka@ars.usda.gov)
Tyler, D.D.	Univ. of Tennessee, Biosystems Engineering and Soil Science, West Tennessee Agricultural Experiment Station, Jackson, TN 38301 (dtyler@utk.edu)
Unger, P.W.	retired, formerly USDA-ARS, Conservation and Production Res. Lab., Bushland, TX; 3603 Thurman St., Amarillo, TX 79109 (pwunger@suddenlink.net)
van Es, H.	Dep. of Crop and Soil Sciences, Cornell Univ., 1005 Bradfield Hall, Ithaca, NY 14853-1901 (hmv1@cornell.edu)
Zobeck, T.M.	USDA-ARS, Wind Erosion and Water Conservation Research, 3810 4th St., Lubbock, TX, 79415-0000 (ted.zobeck@ars.usda.gov)

Conversion Factors for SI and Non-SI Units

To convert Column 1 into Column 2 multiply by	Column 1 SI unit	Column 2 non-SI unit	To convert Column 2 into Column 1 multiply by
		Length	
0.621	kilometer, km (10^3 m)	mile, mi	1.609
1.094	meter, m	yard, yd	0.914
3.28	meter, m	foot, ft	0.304
1.0	micrometer, μm (10^{-6} m)	micron, μ	1.0
3.94×10^{-2}	millimeter, mm (10^{-3} m)	inch, in	25.4
10	nanometer, nm (10^{-9} m)	Angstrom, Å	0.1
		Area	
2.47	hectare, ha	acre	0.405
247	square kilometer, km² (10^3 m)²	acre	4.05×10^{-3}
0.386	square kilometer, km² (10^3 m)²	square mile, mi²	2.590
2.47×10^{-4}	square meter, m²	acre	4.05×10^3
10.76	square meter, m²	square foot, ft²	9.29×10^{-2}
1.55×10^{-3}	square millimeter, mm² (10^{-3} m)²	square inch, in²	645
		Volume	
9.73×10^{-3}	cubic meter, m³	acre-inch	102.8
35.3	cubic meter, m³	cubic foot, ft³	2.83×10^{-2}
6.10×10^4	cubic meter, m³	cubic inch, in³	1.64×10^{-5}
2.84×10^{-2}	liter, L (10^{-3} m³)	bushel, bu	35.24
1.057	liter, L (10^{-3} m³)	quart (liquid), qt	0.946
3.53×10^{-2}	liter, L (10^{-3} m³)	cubic foot, ft³	28.3
0.265	liter, L (10^{-3} m³)	gallon	3.78
33.78	liter, L (10^{-3} m³)	ounce (fluid), oz	2.96×10^{-2}
2.11	liter, L (10^{-3} m³)	pint (fluid), pt	0.473
		Mass	
2.20×10^{-3}	gram, g (10^{-3} kg)	pound, lb	454
3.52×10^{-2}	gram, g (10^{-3} kg)	ounce (avdp), oz	28.4
2.205	kilogram, kg	pound, lb	0.454
0.01	kilogram, kg	quintal (metric), q	100
1.10×10^{-3}	kilogram, kg	ton (2000 lb), ton	907
1.102	megagram, Mg (tonne)	ton (U.S.), ton	0.907
1.102	tonne, t	ton (U.S.), ton	0.907
		Yield and Rate	
0.893	kilogram per hectare, kg ha^{-1}	pound per acre, lb acre^{-1}	1.12
7.77×10^{-2}	kilogram per cubic meter, kg m^{-3}	pound per bushel, lb bu^{-1}	12.87
1.49×10^{-2}	kilogram per hectare, kg ha^{-1}	bushel per acre, 60 lb	67.19
1.59×10^{-2}	kilogram per hectare, kg ha^{-1}	bushel per acre, 56 lb	62.71

Table cont.

To convert Column 1 into Column 2 multiply by	Column 1 SI unit	Column 2 non-SI unit	To convert Column 2 into Column 1 multiply by
1.86×10^{-2}	kilogram per hectare, kg ha^{-1}	bushel per acre, 48 lb	53.75
0.107	liter per hectare, L ha^{-1}	gallon per acre	9.35
893	tonne per hectare, t ha^{-1}	pound per acre, lb acre^{-1}	1.12×10^{-3}
893	megagram per hectare, Mg ha^{-1}	pound per acre, lb acre^{-1}	1.12×10^{-3}
0.446	megagram per hectare, Mg ha^{-1}	ton (2000 lb) per acre, ton acre^{-1}	2.24
2.24	meter per second, m s^{-1}	mile per hour	0.447
		Specific Surface	
10	square meter per kilogram, m^2 kg^{-1}	square centimeter per gram, cm^2 g^{-1}	0.1
1000	square meter per kilogram, m^2 kg^{-1}	square millimeter per gram, mm^2 g^{-1}	0.001
		Density	
1.00	megagram per cubic meter, Mg m^{-3}	gram per cubic centimeter, g cm^{-3}	1.00
		Pressure	
9.90	megapascal, MPa (10^6 Pa)	atmosphere	0.101
10	megapascal, MPa (10^6 Pa)	bar	0.1
2.09×10^{-2}	pascal, Pa	pound per square foot, lb ft^{-2}	47.9
1.45×10^{-4}	pascal, Pa	pound per square inch, lb in^{-2}	6.90×10^3
		Temperature	
1.00 (K − 273)	kelvin, K	Celsius, °C	1.00 (°C + 273)
(9/5 °C) + 32	Celsius, °C	Fahrenheit, °F	5/9 (°F − 32)
		Energy, Work, Quantity of Heat	
9.52×10^{-4}	joule, J	British thermal unit, Btu	1.05×10^3
0.239	joule, J	calorie, cal	4.19
10^7	joule, J	erg	10^{-7}
0.735	joule, J	foot-pound	1.36
2.387×10^{-5}	joule per square meter, J m^{-2}	calorie per square centimeter (langley)	4.19×10^4
10^5	newton, N	dyne	10^{-5}
1.43×10^{-3}	watt per square meter, W m^{-2}	calorie per square centimeter minute (irradiance), cal cm^{-2} min^{-1}	698
		Transpiration and Photosynthesis	
3.60×10^{-2}	milligram per square meter second, mg m^{-2} s^{-1}	gram per square decimeter hour, g dm^{-2} h^{-1}	27.8
5.56×10^{-3}	milligram (H$_2$O) per square meter second, mg m^{-2} s^{-1}	micromole (H$_2$O) per square centimeter second, µmol cm^{-2} s^{-1}	180

Table cont.

Conversion Factors

To convert Column 1 into Column 2 multiply by	Column 1 SI unit	Column 2 non-SI unit	To convert Column 2 into Column 1 multiply by
10^{-4}	milligram per square meter second, mg m^{-2} s^{-1}	milligram per square centimeter second, mg cm^{-2} s^{-1}	10^4
35.97	milligram per square meter second, mg m^{-2} s^{-1}	milligram per square decimeter hour, mg dm^{-2} h^{-1}	2.78×10^{-2}
	Plane Angle		
57.3	radian, rad	degrees (angle), °	1.75×10^{-2}
	Electrical Conductivity, Electricity, and Magnetism		
10	siemen per meter, S m^{-1}	millimho per centimeter, mmho cm^{-1}	0.1
10^4	tesla, T	gauss, G	10^{-4}
	Water Measurement		
9.73×10^{-3}	cubic meter, m^3	acre-inch, acre-in	102.8
9.81×10^{-3}	cubic meter per hour, m^3 h^{-1}	cubic foot per second, ft^3 s^{-1}	101.9
4.40	cubic meter per hour, m^3 h^{-1}	U.S. gallon per minute, gal min^{-1}	0.227
8.11	hectare meter, ha m	acre-foot, acre-ft	0.123
97.28	hectare meter, ha m	acre-inch, acre-in	1.03×10^{-2}
8.1×10^{-2}	hectare centimeter, ha cm	acre-foot, acre-ft	12.33
	Concentration		
1	centimole per kilogram, cmol kg^{-1}	milliequivalent per 100 grams, meq 100 g^{-1}	1
0.1	gram per kilogram, g kg^{-1}	percent, %	10
1	milligram per kilogram, mg kg^{-1}	parts per million, ppm	1
	Radioactivity		
2.7×10^{-11}	becquerel, Bq	curie, Ci	3.7×10^{10}
2.7×10^{-2}	becquerel per kilogram, Bq kg^{-1}	picocurie per gram, pCi g^{-1}	37
100	gray, Gy (absorbed dose)	rad, rd	0.01
100	sievert, Sv (equivalent dose)	rem (roentgen equivalent man)	0.01
	Plant Nutrient Conversion		
	Elemental	Oxide	
2.29	P	P_2O_5	0.437
1.20	K	K_2O	0.830
1.39	Ca	CaO	0.715
1.66	Mg	MgO	0.602

1

Water Conservation for Agriculture

Paul W. Unger
retired, formerly USDA-ARS, Conservation and Production Research Lab., Bushland, TX

Mary Beth Kirkham
Dep. of Agronomy, Kansas State University, Manhattan, KS[1]

David C. Nielsen
USDA-ARS, Central Great Plains Research Station, Akron, CO

The importance of water conservation for agriculture has been recognized for centuries. Bennett (1939), in his book *Soil Conservation*, cited numerous examples from ancient times of countries where canals were developed to convey water to agricultural lands for improved crop production. In addition, reservoirs were constructed for retaining water for later use on agricultural land, terraces were constructed to reduce runoff, plowed fallowing was promoted to conserve water, deep plowing was used in some cases, and contouring was used to retain water on land. Water conservation seldom was the direct object of these practices, but water conservation was achieved by using them.

Water for agriculture is derived from precipitation or from a stream, reservoir, or aquifer where irrigation is practiced. Precipitation frequency in humid regions usually is adequate to provide for plant needs, but even in such regions, precipitation amount and distribution vary considerably from average in any given year. For example, at Watkinsville, GA (all locations and cites mentioned are in the United States unless noted otherwise), where annual precipitation averages 1245 mm, 14-d droughts average three per year, which may severely reduce crop yields. Water conservation, therefore, is important under such conditions (Barnett, 1987). In contrast, excess water is a problem in some situations, and drainage is required for successful crop production.

Precipitation frequency and reliability decrease when going from humid to subhumid, semiarid, and arid regions, thus increasing the importance of water conservation for successful agriculture in the drier regions. Some crops in humid, subhumid, and semiarid regions and most crops in arid regions are irrigated. For successful crop production under all conditions, adequate water must be stored in soil to sustain crops until the next precipitation or irrigation event. Even when using drip or sprinkler irrigation to apply water frequently, water is temporarily held in soil until used by plants.

Even with irrigation, water conservation is important in many cases because supplies are limited or being depleted, with the latter being the case

---
[1] Contribution no. 08-166-B from the Kansas Agric. Exp. Stn.

Soil and Water Conservation Advances in the United States. SSSA Special Publication 60.
T.M. Zobeck and W.F. Schillinger, editors. © 2010. SSSA, 677 S. Segoe Rd., Madison, WI 53711, USA.

for portions of the Ogallala Aquifer in the Great Plains (Stewart, 2003) and for aquifers in China and India (Unger et al., 2006). Water conservation is also important because competition for fresh water is becoming an increasingly important issue among nations, geographical regions, and segments of society, including agricultural, urban, industrial, and recreational users (Unger and Howell, 1999). This is a major issue in some regions where the supply is naturally limited and where the growing needs of other users already often clash with agriculture for available supplies (Kuhn et al., 2007; Levy, 2003; Rothfeder, 2001). Water conservation is also more important than ever because of the increasing amount needed to produce the food, fiber, and fuel for the ever-increasing world population.

Research on water conservation for agriculture has been extensive throughout the past 100 years. It has been conducted at numerous colleges and universities and at state, federal, and private research facilities. The 1907 USDA Yearbook contains a list of "Agricultural Experiment Stations in the United States, Their Locations, Directors, and Principal Lines of Work" (USDA, 1908). The list identifies the main experiment station in the different states, but outlying experiment stations were also established at which agronomic research was conducted in many states. Agronomy is listed as a "principal line of work" at most stations. Although agronomy involves many disciplines related to soils and plants, water is a key factor where these entities meet—that is, water is essential for plants grown in soils. While water conservation and use may not have been the direct object of the agronomic research and, therefore, was not reported, water undoubtedly affected the results in many cases.

Early USDA research involving water in soils or for agriculture was conducted by scientists in the Bureau of Soils and the Bureau of Plant Industry (Landa and Nimmo, 2003). By 1914, the USDA Division of Dryland Agriculture had established 22 dryland experiment stations in the Great Plains (Burnett et al., 1985). The initial research at these stations focused on evaluating crops and crop varieties for suitability to a given area. The vagaries of climate and potential for erosion on many soils were recognized, and the research was directed toward developing crop rotations and management practices to control erosion and maximize dryland crop production. The research often was not on water conservation and usually was not reported as such, but when erosion is controlled, water conservation often is achieved through improved plant growth and reduced runoff. Also, although this research was conducted at dryland stations, the results obtained often were applicable to rainfed agriculture at more humid locations.

In addition to formal research at state, federal, and private facilities, efforts of land managers, namely, farmers, have contributed significantly through individual observations and management strategies to achieve water conservation under various conditions.

Our objectives were to review progress that has been made in our understanding of factors affecting water conservation during the past 100 years and to identify some challenges and opportunities for achieving improved water conservation for agriculture. To illustrate the progress, we review practices developed through the years and comment on their effectiveness for conserving water and achieving greater or more reliable crop production.

Primary Areas of Water Conservation

The principles of water conservation for agriculture are the same whether crop production is under rainfed or irrigated conditions. Water must be captured, retained, and used efficiently for producing a desirable yield. These principles have been recognized for many years. Numerous land, climate, social, and environmental conditions and applied practices affect water conservation (Unger, 2006).

Water Capture

Shaw (1911) and Widtsoe (1920) recognized the need to capture, retain, and efficiently use water derived from precipitation. At that time, however, the primary means of managing water was via plowing. According to Shaw (1911), for example,

> The dominant idea in dry farming is in a sense two-fold. It seeks to secure to the greatest extent practicable the conservation and also the accumulation of moisture in the soil. To accomplish this end, the soil is stirred deeply, whether by the aid of the plow alone or by following the plow with a subsoiler, or by using some other implement, as the deep tilling machine. The ground is compressed subsequent to plowing, and dust mulch is maintained on the soil surface. The increase of organic matter in the soils is also sought.

Although this quotation pertained to "dry farming," the information undoubtedly was applicable to most agriculture at that time.

Water capture is the first step in water conservation, and Shaw (1911) promoted more frequent and deeper plowing, believing that it would increase water storage in soil. Frequent plowing resulted in the surface being devoid of plant residues, and soil crusting after rains was common. Plowing disrupted the crust and possibly reduced runoff at the next rain, but each plowing undoubtedly further aggravated the crusting problem. In the United States, emphasis on plowing to achieve water capture was largely a carryover from practices that settlers had used in their home countries. Plowing also was the primary method of weed control at that time.

Infiltration

Frequent and deep plowing as proposed by Shaw (1911) had potential for capturing and storing water, provided the soil surface was adequately stable to avoid aggregate disintegration, surface sealing, and excessive runoff, thus resulting in favorable water infiltration into soil. Rainfall energy strongly influences aggregate dispersion and surface sealing, thereby also strongly influencing infiltration (Eigel and Moore, 1983; Giménez et al., 1992; Loch, 1989). Bare soil surfaces resulting from frequent and deep plowing as proposed by Shaw (1911) were unprotected against the impact and energy of falling raindrops, which disrupted soil aggregates and thereby undoubtedly led to restricted infiltration. Besides passing through the surface soil, water must penetrate to adequate depths for storage in the zone from which plants use it. Vertical distribution, namely, water penetration to depths below the surface layer, is part of the infiltration process.

Water infiltration into soil is a complex process that involves saturated and unsaturated flow. The initial stage involves unsaturated flow that is driven primarily by the attraction of water to dry soil particles and the surface tension of water held in the spaces between the particles. Gravity and soil solute content also affect unsaturated water flow (Hillel, 1998). Water flow in soil pores due to surface tension is known as *capillarity* and was already recognized in the early 1900s by Briggs and McLane (1907) and Buckingham (1907). Unsaturated flow dominates infiltration as long as the application rate (e.g., precipitation rate) does not cause water ponding on the surface. When the application rate exceeds the unsaturated flow rate, saturated flow becomes dominant. Saturated flow is dominant unless water application (e.g., precipitation) is of low intensity or short duration, or for coarse-textured soils in which water flow is rapid (Baver, 1956).

The loosened soil resulting from frequent and deep plowing as promoted by Shaw (1911) apparently was readily filled with water to the depth of plowing in many cases, but may have adversely affected continued infiltration on some soils. According to Horton (1933), soil surface conditions, namely, at the water–soil contact interface, mainly governs the infiltration rate. Water movement at depths below the surface, however, also is important with respect to infiltration (Baver, 1956; Hillel, 1998; Philip, 1969; Taylor and Ashcroft, 1972; van Bavel and Hanks, 1983). Surface conditions influencing infiltration include soil texture, aggregate size and stability, and water content. Subsurface conditions influencing infiltration include soil texture, water content, structural stability, and horizon characteristics. These influence infiltration through their effect on unsaturated and saturated water flow in the soil profile. When rainfall or irrigation causes water ponding on the surface, entrapped air in soil pores can also reduce infiltration (Dixon, 1966; Wangemann et al., 2000). In contrast, infiltration under ponded water conditions can be greatly enhanced when channels formed by soil fauna (e.g., worms, insects, spiders, etc.) and decayed roots are open to the surface (Cochran et al., 1994; Kladivko, 1994).

Surface Residues

Plowing to "turn under" grasses was used by settlers in the late 1800s and early 1900s to prepare land for crops in the drier regions of the country (e.g., the Great Plains) (Fig. 1–1). Initially, with favorable precipitation, such plowing provided good results, but contributed greatly to the disastrous erosion by wind and dev-

Fig. 1–1. Tillage to "turn under" grasses in preparation for field crop production by early settlers in the Great Plains. Photo: Panhandle-Plains Museum, Canyon, TX.

astation of the land that occurred during the drought of the 1930s (Fig. 1–2). The region most affected was termed the *Dust Bowl* (Bennett, 1939). (Note: For this chapter, we use the Soil Science Society of America [SSSA, 2001] definition of plowing, namely, a tillage operation that is performed to shatter soil with partial or complete inversion at depths usually greater than 20 cm.)

The devastating conditions of the Dust Bowl era led to major land-use changes where the potential for erosion by wind existed, with the realization that crop residues retained on soil were highly effective for controlling erosion. Surface residues also provided water conservation benefits, with Duley and Rus-

Fig. 1–2. (Top) An approaching "dust cloud" during the severe drought of the 1930s in the southern Great Plains. (Bottom) Land devastation caused by severe erosion by wind during the drought of the 1930s. Photos: (top) USDA-NRCS; (bottom) USDA.

sel (1939) being among the first to recognize those benefits. At Lincoln, NE, 54% of rainfall was stored with 4.5 Mg ha^{-1} of flat straw on the soil surface, 34% with straw incorporated into soil, and 20% with a bare surface treatment. Maintaining surface porosity and reducing water flow across the surface with straw were considered major contributors to increased water capture. Duley and Kelly (1939) found that soil surface conditions (cover and aggregate size) affected water infiltration (capture) more than soil surface texture and profile characteristics.

The value of residues for protecting surface aggregates versus their value for reducing water flow across the surface was demonstrated by Borst and Woodburn (1942). In their experiment, plant residues at 4 Mg ha^{-1} were suspended on a screen 25 mm above the surface or placed directly on soil. Runoff of applied water equaled 78% from cultivated, dry, bare (uncovered) soil; 1.7% with residues on the surface; and 1.2% with residues on the screen. They concluded that elimination of raindrop impact on soil aggregates was more important than physical blocking of water across the surface for conserving water. The percentages for the two residue treatments, however, differed only slightly, and flow blocking as considered by Duley and Russel (1939) certainly also was important for conserving water.

When benefits of surface residues for conserving soil and water first became apparent, few tools and techniques were available for producing crops under surface residue conditions. In the 1930s, J. Mack Gowder, a farmer in Georgia, used an implement with a 10-cm-wide chisel point to stir the soil and retain plant residues on the surface. He used the implement, which he called a "bull tongue scooter," in an attempt to mimic the surface cover conditions he observed in a forest on his steeply sloping farm. This method of tillage became known as *stubble-mulch farming*, with that designation being attributed to Dr. H.H. Bennett (Barnett, 1987). Stubble-mulch farming often was (and sometimes still is) referred to as "trash farming" by those who belittled that method of tillage, but it is a highly important practice for conserving soil and water as compared with conditions where clean tillage (i.e., residues plowed under) is practiced.

Stubble-Mulch Tillage

Stubble-mulch tillage (Fig. 1–3) quickly became a recommended conservation practice when the value of keeping the surface covered was recognized. The aim was to keep the soil covered as much of the time as practical to greatly reduce runoff and erosion. Such tillage was the forerunner of today's no-tillage method of farming (Barnett, 1987).

Another Georgia farmer, R. Luther Hardy, used crimson clover (*Trifolium incarnatum* L.) [or ryegrass (*Lolium* spp.)] ahead of summer crops on his good land to achieve soil and water conservation benefits. The clover was partially plowed out in spring to achieve tilled contour strips on which he planted row crops. A 30-cm strip of clover remained between crop rows. Clover was plowed out after setting seed, which provided for a volunteer crop the next year. This tillage system was named the *contour-balk method* and had implications regarding today's method of no-tillage farming (Barnett, 1987). A possible deterrent to using the contour-balk method was competition for water between clover and planted crops (Hendrickson, 1939).

Use of stubble-mulch tillage was promoted primarily for controlling erosion by wind, which was severe during the drought of the 1930s. At that time, the first goal for tillage was to provide a cloddy surface to stop ongoing soil movement

Fig. 1–3. (Top) Stubble mulch tillage being performed after harvest of winter wheat. (Bottom) A sweep on a stubble mulch tillage implement (stubble mulch tillage implements may also have blades instead of sweeps to undercut the soil surface).

by wind. A second goal was use of shallow tillage to control weeds and retain plant residues on the surface to protect the soil from erosion. A third goal was to retain surface residues to reduce runoff, reduce evaporative soil water losses, and conserve more water for the following crop. Various chisel, blade, and sweep implements were developed to achieve these goals (Allen and Fenster, 1986).

When the water conservation (and water capture) benefits of retaining crop residues on the soil surface were recognized (Barnett, 1987; Borst and Woodburn, 1942; Duley and Russel, 1939), extensive research involving stubble-mulch tillage was initiated at many locations, especially in drier regions, and research involving various aspects regarding it continues at some locations. When compared with clean tillage, greater water capture usually was achieved by using stubble-mulch tillage (Black, 1967; Duley and Fenster, 1961; Duley and Russel, 1942; Free, 1953; Greb et al., 1970; McCalla and Army, 1961; Whitfield et al., 1949; Zingg and Whitfield, 1957). The benefits resulted from dissipation of raindrop energy, thus reducing aggregate dispersion and surface sealing; retardation of water flow across the surface, thus providing more time for infiltration; snow trapping; and enhancement of soil organic matter, thus improving soil physical conditions. Infiltration of simulated rainfall increased with increasing organic matter contents and was attributed to increased soil aggregate size (Lado et al., 2004). This demonstrates the importance of favorable soil physical conditions for enhancing water infiltration.

Weed Control

Weed control with chemicals began in the 1800s. Copper sulfate was first used in 1821 (Reinhardt and Ganzel, 2007), and an application of iron sulfate was found to kill broadleaf weeds in 1896 (Tvedten, 2001). The first synthetic organic chemical, namely, 2-methyl-4, 6-dinitrophenol, was introduced in 1932 (Reinhardt and Ganzel, 2007) and a new era of weed control began in 1942 with the development of 2,4-D [(2,4-dichlorophenoxy) acetic acid]. Numerous herbicides are now available, with applications possible before planting or after establishing a crop. Development of effective herbicides has greatly changed crop management practices, which, in turn, has greatly improved water conservation under many conditions. Water conservation resulting from use of herbicides is due to elimination of water use by weeds; less frequent or elimination of tillage for controlling weeds, thus limiting exposure of moist soil to the atmosphere and reducing evaporative water losses; and retaining more crop residues on the surface, thus achieving the water conservation benefits previously mentioned.

Effective weed control, especially during a crop's growing season, is essential for successful crop production. Allowing weed growth, however, can provide protection against erosion under conditions where the soil surface would otherwise be bare, that is, during the interval between crops (Bennett, 1939; Schillinger and Young, 2000). Under such conditions, water conservation could still be achieved through timely termination of weeds (before they produce seed) and their residues may enhance water capture through reduced runoff and improved infiltration. Use of delayed stubble-mulch tillage, which allowed weed growth during part of the fallow period, resulted in soil water contents at wheat planting that were similar to those obtained with use of normal stubble-mulch tillage, which prevented weed growth throughout the entire fallow period (Johnson and Davis, 1972).

Tillage Reduction

With the introduction of herbicides, it became possible to reduce tillage intensity and frequency and sometimes eliminate it for crop production. Systems involving less tillage include limited tillage (McWhorter and Jordan, 1985; Shear, 1985), reduced tillage (Lewis, 1985; Triplett, 1985; Wiese et al., 1985), minimum tillage

(Thomas, 1985; Vyn et al., 1998), ecofallow (Alleman, 1982; Greb, 1978; Wicks et al., 1972), chemical fallow (Fenster et al., 1965; Wiese et al., 1967), and conservation tillage (Allmaras and Dowdy, 1985; Fenster, 1977; Wicks, 1985). *Conservation tillage* is "any tillage sequence, the object of which is to minimize or reduce loss of soil and water; operationally, a tillage or tillage and planting combination which leaves a 30% or greater cover of crop residue on the surface" (SSSA, 2001). Provided the indicated amount of residues remain on the surface, all the above qualify as conservation tillage systems. The ultimate conservation tillage system is *no-tillage*, which is "a procedure whereby a crop is planted directly into the soil with no primary or secondary tillage since harvest of the previous crop; usually a special planter is necessary to prepare a narrow, shallow seedbed immediately surrounding the seed being planted" (SSSA, 2001). With no-tillage (Fig. 1–4), maximum residue amounts remain, thereby potentially providing maximum soil and water conservation benefits.

No-Tillage

No-tillage farming has been used for centuries. For example, Incas in South America planted crops without tillage by making a hole in soil with a stick, putting seeds in soil by hand, and covering seeds with their feet (Derpsch, 1998). The development of effective herbicides through the years encouraged producers to adopt the practice of no-tillage crop production. It achieved a major boost when paraquat [1,1'-dimethyl-(4,4'-bipyridinium)] was developed in the United Kingdom in 1955 (Derpsch, 1998).

Fig. 1–4. (Left) No-tillage grain sorghum after winter wheat under wheat–sorghum–fallow crop rotation conditions. (Right) Grain sorghum approaching maturity under no-tillage conditions as at left. Note the residues from the previous wheat crop remaining on the surface in both photos.

An estimated 25.2 million ha (22.6% of cropland) were used for no-tillage crop production in the United States in 2004 (personal communication, Frank Lessiter, Editor/Publisher, *No-Till Farmer*, June 2007). In 2004, some form of conservation tillage was used on 41% of U.S. cropland. In Argentina, Brazil, and Canada in 1996–1997, no-tillage use in each country was more than 4 million ha, with lesser but significant amounts in several other countries (Derpsch, 1998).

Water conservation generally is improved by using no-tillage, according to numerous reports in the literature, but we will give only a few examples. At Blacksburg, VA, from 1960 to 1965, available soil water content to 15- and 46-cm depths was greater each year with no-tillage than with conventional tillage (Shear, 1985). At Bushland, TX, in the southern Great Plains from 1979 to 1981, soil water contents averaged 149 (c)^2, 179 (b), and 207 (a) mm with moldboard plowing, sweep tillage, and no-tillage treatments, respectively, at planting time for dryland grain sorghum [*Sorghum bicolor* (L.) Moench]. The water storage occurred from the time of wheat harvest in June until sorghum planting in May or June of the following year. Subsequent grain yields averaged 2.6 (b), 2.8 (b), and 3.3 (a) Mg ha^{-1} for the respective treatments (Unger, 1984). For a wheat (*Triticum aestivum* L.)–fallow study in western Nebraska, infiltration of 76 mm of simulated rainfall was 41, 97, and 99% with plow, stubble-mulch tillage, and no-tillage treatments, respectively, during the fallow-after-harvest phase (October) of the cropping system. In the wheat phase at that time in the rotation, wheat plants were 10 cm tall, and infiltration was 42, 66, and 95% with the respective treatments (Dickey et al., 1983).

As indicated by these examples, soil water contents and infiltration amounts were greatest with no-tillage, which retained more residues on the surface than other treatments. No-tillage, however, does not always result in the most infiltration from a given precipitation event (Jones and Popham, 1997; Unger, 1992). Infiltration may be greater into a tillage-loosened soil than a no-tillage soil when precipitation amounts do not exceed the temporary storage capacity of the loosened soil layer. Also, infiltration into a tillage-loosened soil may be greater when the water content of no-tillage soil is already high when precipitation occurs, thereby resulting in limited opportunity for additional water storage, which was the case on Pullman clay loam (fine, mixed, superactive, thermic Torrertic Paleustolls) at Bushland. Even so, soil water contents at planting of winter wheat and grain sorghum were greater with no-tillage than with stubble-mulch tillage (Jones and Popham, 1997).

Although no-tillage provides conditions more conducive for conserving soil and water than other tillage methods, no-tillage with respect to soil water conditions may not be best for all conditions. For example, it generally is not well-suited to poorly drained soils because the additional water aggravates the excess water problem, thus often reducing yields (Amemiya, 1977; Griffith et al., 1977; West et al., 1996). On hardsetting soils, infiltration may be lower with no-tillage than with soil-loosening tillage (Doyle, 1983; Huxley, 1979; Nicou and Chopart, 1979; Wockner et al., 1996).

Deep Soil Loosening

Use of no-tillage involves minimal soil disturbance and effectively conserves water, but soil loosening and even deep loosening as promoted by Shaw (1911)

---

[2] Values followed by the same letter in parentheses are not significantly different at the 5% level, Duncan's Multiple Range Test.

has improved water infiltration and conservation under some conditions. Deep loosening of soil by plowing, vertical mulching, or profile modification received considerable interest starting in the 1960s. Use of these practices improved water capture and/or use on slowly permeable, swelling clay soils (Allen et al., 1994, 1995; Burnett, 1969; Burnett and Hauser, 1967; Burnett et al., 1974; Eck and Taylor, 1969; Hauser and Taylor, 1963, 1964; Musick et al., 1981). Deep plowing or profile modification also improved water capture and/or use on soils that have a fragipan (Bradford and Blanchar, 1977), a shallow clay layer (Greb, 1970), coarse surface materials underlain by a heavy clay (Miller and Aarstad, 1972), hard-setting properties (Mead and Chan, 1988), a claypan (Fehrenbacher et al., 1958), or saline conditions (Bowser and Cairns, 1967; Harker et al., 1977; Travis et al., 1990). Soils having a hardpan, plow pan, indurated horizon, or other compacted condition relatively near the surface usually can be improved with respect to water capture by a less intensive operation such as subsoiling, chiseling, ripping, or paraplowing (Baumhardt et al., 1992; Mahler et al., 2003; McConkey et al., 1990; Mukhtar et al., 1985; Pikul et al., 1992, 1996; Steppuhn et al., 1995). These operations loosen the soil, usually to depths greater than normal tillage or plowing, without inverting the surface layer or causing major mixing of the soil horizons.

The above practices improved water capture by increasing infiltration of rain, irrigation, or snowmelt water. To remain effective, loosened soil must remain "open" at the surface to allow water to readily enter it. Use of deep tillage or profile modification is appropriate only when a known adverse soil condition is present (Unger, 1979). Likewise, subsoiling, chiseling, ripping, or paraplowing are appropriate only when a known adverse condition is present. When profile conditions exist that adversely affect water infiltration and crop production, deep plowing or profile modification may be appropriate if the resulting benefits are long-lasting because performing those operations is costly. For example, the benefits of deep loosening Pullman clay loam were still observed after more than 20 yr. Irrigation water (240 mm) infiltrated an unmodified Pullman profile in 28.6 h as compared with 8.4 and 6.3 h for profiles modified to 0.9- and 1.5-m depths, respectively, 26 yr earlier (Unger, 1993). Likewise, moldboard plowing the Pullman soil 0.4, 0.6, or 0.8 m deep in 1966 was still effective for increasing irrigation water infiltration for winter wheat crops from 1988 to 1992 after loosening the surface layer to a 0.2-m depth (Allen et al., 1995). Also, infiltration was still greater in 2005 for Pullman soil plowed 0.7 m deep in 1971 than for soil not deeply plowed (Baumhardt et al., 2008). The continued benefits indicate that the high cost of deep plowing Pullman soil can be recovered with time.

Soil Surface Alterations

The above tillage practices enhanced water capture mainly by providing conditions conducive to more rapid water infiltration. Another approach is to prevent runoff or reduce the runoff rate, thus providing more time for infiltration, which is achieved in many cases when using conservation tillage, especially no-tillage, or by altering the soil surface.

Longer water retention on the surface can be achieved by a variety of practices. These range from changing tillage direction relative to slope of the land to major operations such as terracing and land leveling (Unger, 2006).

The most basic practice for reducing the runoff rate is *contour tillage* (Janick, 2002), which involves tillage across (perpendicular to) the slope of land (Fig. 1–5).

Fig. 1–5. (Top) cotton growing under contour-tillage conditions. (Bottom) Water retained on ridge-tilled, furrow-diked land under contour-tillage conditions. Photo: O.R. Jones, USDA-ARS, Bushland, TX.

Contour tillage has a long history, and was promoted initially for controlling erosion by water (Bennett, 1939). Its water retention benefits are increased by using tillage methods that create ridges across the slope. *Lister tillage*, which forms relatively high ridges with a tool that turns soil laterally in opposite directions from the furrow being formed, is highly effective for retaining water (Fig. 1–5), but its effectiveness generally greatly decreases after crops are planted or cultivated

Fig. 1–6. Strip tillage is being used in some fields in the photo.

(Bennett, 1939). Use of reduced tillage along with effective herbicides, which is now possible, should help maintain the effectiveness of lister tillage for a longer time. When used in conjunction with contouring, lister tillage effectively retains water on the land. However, because it is a type of clean tillage, soil aggregate dispersion and surface sealing may occur due to raindrop impact, thus resulting in water ponding in the furrows. As a result, much of the retained water may evaporate rather than infiltrate into some soils.

Contour tillage is best suited for use on gently sloping land. A variation of contour tillage that can be used on somewhat more steeply sloping land is *strip cropping*, in which alternate strips of sod and row crops are planted along the contour (Fig. 1–6). Sod strips with their high absorptive capacity help slow runoff (Janick, 2002). This practice probably was brought to the United States by farmers from Europe (Bennett, 1939).

Except on soils having an extremely uniform slope, it is difficult to uniformly retain water throughout the length of lister furrows. More uniform water retention is obtained by using furrow diking (also known as furrow damming, basin tillage, basin listing, tied ridges, or microbasin tillage) along with ridge-forming tillage (Fig. 1–7) (Bennett, 1939; Clark and Jones, 1981; Gerard et al., 1983, 1984; Jones and Clark, 1987; Krishna et al., 1986).

Furrow diking was originally used in the United States in the 1930s, but was generally abandoned by the 1950s because of slow operation of diking equipment, poor weed control, difficulty in performing cultural operations, and limited yield benefits (Jones and Clark, 1987). Interest reoccurred in the 1970s and 1980s when improved equipment and weed control methods became available, which led to its use during the crop growing season rather than mainly during fallow before crop planting and, in turn, to improved water conservation and crop yields (Clark and Jones, 1981; Gerard et al., 1983, 1984; Jones and Clark, 1987; Krishna et al., 1986).

Fig. 1–7. (Top) Water retained on land where furrows are diked and flowing from land from undiked furrows (instrument measures runoff from undiked furrows) (photo source: O.R. Jones, USDA-ARS, Bushland, TX). (Bottom) A furrow-diking implement.

Where use of contour tillage, furrow diking, or strip cropping does not adequately control runoff, some major soil surface alterations may be required to achieve the desired level of runoff control. Undoubtedly, the most widely used such practice worldwide is *terracing*, in which the interval between adjacent terraces is leveled. This is an ancient practice not widely used in the United States, mainly because of the high cost of land leveling. *Conservation bench terraces* (CBTs), developed in the United States, require leveling only a portion of the land between adjacent terraces (Hauser and Zingg, 1959; Zingg and Hauser, 1959). At Bushland, for example, only the lower one-third of the interval between terraces was leveled. Runoff from the unleveled (watershed) area averaged 28 mm and was captured on the leveled area. With the 2:1 watershed/bench area ratio, runoff along with precipitation retained on the bench resulted in an average of 84 mm more water available on bench than on watershed areas. The additional water made annual cropping possible on benches, whereas cropping on watersheds involved fallow between successive crops. Conservation bench terraces having various watershed/bench area ratios have been evaluated at several locations (Armbrust and Welch, 1966; Cox, 1968; Hauser and Cox, 1962; Mickelson, 1968). Effectiveness of CBTs with different ratios depended on the potential for runoff and the infiltration and water holding capacity of the different soils. Because land leveling of large areas is costly, Jones (1981) developed CBTs with benches being equal to one width of tillage equipment, thus decreasing the cost of leveling.

Use of graded and level terraces increases soil water storage relative to that achieved without terracing (Dickson et al., 1940; Finnell, 1944). Use of level terraces with blocked ends in conjunction with contour tillage was especially effective for increasing water storage (Burnett and Fisher, 1956; Dickson et al., 1940; Fisher and Burnett, 1953), but water had to be drained from terraces during wet periods to avoid damage to crops (Harper, 1941). Hauser et al. (1962) found that using open-end level or graded terraces resulted in similar crop yields and, therefore, suggested using open-end level terraces, thus avoiding the need for drainage and for constructing high terrace ridges to retain large volumes of water. Use of graded terraces along with graded furrows slows runoff, thus helping to conserve soil and water (Hauser et al., 1962; Richardson, 1973).

Water harvested from land unsuitable for crops can improve crop production on nearby lands. For example, constructing level pans in broad natural waterways and intercepting and spreading runoff water that normally flowed through them resulted in soil water contents at grain sorghum planting time being 96 mm greater on leveled than on unleveled areas (Mickelson, 1966). At forage sorghum (*Sorghum* spp.) planting time, the increase on leveled areas was 58 mm. In both cases, yields were greater on leveled areas. Although water harvesting results in greater soil water contents and crop yields, it is applicable to relatively small areas and has not been widely adopted for general crop production purposes.

Snow Management

A significant portion of precipitation in northern regions is derived from snow. Where water is limited, as, for example, in the Great Plains, the Pacific Northwest, and the Canadian Prairie Provinces, management to capture snow and snowmelt is highly important with respect to water capture and crop production. Because snow often is accompanied by wind, practices to capture snow are similar to those for controlling erosion by wind. Favorable snow and snowmelt capture have been obtained by using standing crop residues, strip cropping, tall wheatgrass [*Thinopyrum ponticum* (Podp.) Barkworth & D.R. Dewey] barriers, wheat stubble strips, or artificial barriers (Aase et al., 1976; Campbell et al., 1992; Greb, 1975, 1980; Greb and Black, 1971; Maulé and Chanasyk, 1990; McConkey et al., 1997; Nielsen, 1998; Pikul et al., 1996; Steppuhn and Waddington, 1996). Deep soil loosening (ripping) improved water capture from snowmelt on frozen soils (Pikul et al., 1996; Zuzel and Pikul, 1987), but ripping a dry pulverized soil provided little benefit with regard to improving snowmelt infiltration (Pikul et al., 1996). Use of slot mulching, which consisted of packing crop residues into 20-cm wide and 20- to 25-cm deep trenches spaced 2.5 m apart on the contour, reduced runoff from frozen soil compared with that from a no-tillage, non-slotted wheat stubble area (Saxton et al., 1981).

Irrigation Method

In general, practices effective for capturing water from precipitation are effective also for capturing irrigation water. Irrigation methods, however, may strongly influence the amount of applied water that infiltrates the soil.

Irrigation methods are flooding, furrow, sprinkler, Low Energy Precision Application (LEPA) (Fig. 1–8), and drip (surface and subsurface) or some variation of these methods (Howell and Evett, 2005). When using flooding or furrow irrigation, soil permeability and water application rate and duration must be considered to achieve maximum capture of applied water. On moderately and highly permeable soils, water should be applied at a relatively high rate to wet the intended area in a relatively short time. Kemper et al. (1988) used surge irrigation to reduce excessive infiltration into a silty loam. *Surge irrigation* is "a surface irrigation technique wherein flow is applied to furrows (or less commonly, borders) intermittently during a single irrigation set" (SSSA, 2001). Lower application rates and longer times are used on slowly permeable soils, but irrigation efficiencies may be low with furrow irrigation under some conditions (Musick et al., 1988). Furrow irrigation was dominant in the Texas High Plains until 1974 when its use began to decline. Sprinkler irrigation became dominant in the region after 1979 (Musick et al., 1988). Sprinkler irrigation has been dominant in other regions for many years.

With sprinklers, water is applied either with high, medium, or low pressure equipment with various arrangements of the equipment that affect the area

Fig. 1–8. Water being applied to ridge-tilled, furrow-diked land under Low Energy Precision Application (LEPA) conditions.

covered and how water impacts the soil surface (Howell and Evett, 2005). A disadvantage of using high pressure equipment is high evaporative loss of water under some conditions. Spray losses in Kansas were 12% in 1980 and 16% in 1981 (Steiner et al., 1983); they reported losses ranging to 40% at other locations. Spray losses are reduced by using low pressure systems, but because water is applied to a smaller area, runoff may be greater from slowly permeable soils. Use of the LEPA system essentially eliminates runoff and spray losses when used along with furrow diking, but runoff can be high without furrow diking (Howell and Evett, 2005). Application efficiencies of 95 to 98% are attainable by using LEPA along with furrow diking (Bordovsky et al., 1992; Lyle and Bordovsky, 1981, 1983). Spray and runoff losses are eliminated by using surface or subsurface drip irrigation methods, but percolation losses may be high if the soil water content is maintained at a high level (Howell and Evett, 2005).

Major transport losses are possible from the water source to where it is used under irrigated conditions. Losses may be especially high from unlined channels due to seepage and where phreatophytes extract water from irrigation channels or from streams and other waterways (Unger, 2006). Channel linings of cement or flexible membranes and underground pipelines of cement or polyvinyl chloride (PVC) are highly effective for reducing water transport losses. At the point of distribution, use of gated pipes (aluminum, PVC, or flexible materials) can further reduce losses (Unger and Howell, 1999).

Mulching

Mulching is an ancient practice, "perhaps as old as agriculture itself" (Jacks et al., 1955). It affects water conservation through water capture and retention. With respect to water capture, mulches protect the soil surface against raindrop impact, thereby minimizing aggregate dispersion and surface sealing (Loch, 1989). If porous, such mulches allow direct water infiltration into soil or retard water flow across the surface, thereby providing more time for infiltration.

Many different materials have been used as mulches (Bennett, 1939; Bilbro and Fryrear, 1991; Jacks et al., 1955; Unger, 1995). Mulches of crop residues and other plant materials (straw, stover, leaves, corn [*Zea mays* L.] cobs, cotton [*Gossypium hirsutum* L.] gin trash, woodchips, and sawdust) are inexpensive, often readily available, and porous, thus allowing water to readily enter soils. Other porous materials used a mulch are gravel, rocks, coal, bitumen, and similar granular materials (Unger, 1995). In general, mulch effectiveness for increasing water capture increases with the amount on the soil surface (Adams, 1966; Greb, 1979; Mannering and Meyer, 1963; Moody et al., 1963; Unger, 1978, 1995).

Plastic film mulches are used extensively for agricultural crops in some countries and have, for example, increased corn grain yields in the People's Republic of China by 44 to 165% as compared with yields on unmulched areas (Ma, 1988). Their main benefit with respect to water conservation is reduced evaporation, but they do provide water capture benefits if provisions exist for water to enter the soil. In addition, they result in improved water retention by reducing weed competition for water because they effectively control weeds. Mulches of petroleum products (asphalt sprays and resins) improve water capture when untreated sites exist for water to readily infiltrate soils.

Rapid channeling of water into soil is achieved by vertical mulching, which provides a slot in soil filled with crop residues (or other porous materials) that is open to the surface. Use of vertical mulching substantially increased soil water storage (up to 41%) under some conditions (Fairbourn and Gardner, 1972, 1974; Heilman and Gonzalez, 1973; Wendt, 1973). Using a microwatershed (small ridge) between slots, treating the zone between slots with oil, or installing check dams in furrows was important for achieving maximum water capture (Unger, 1995). A variation of vertical mulching is slot mulching (mentioned previously), which has been shown to reduce runoff from frozen soil (Saxton et al., 1981).

Fallowing

In low precipitation regions such as the 17 western U.S. states, fallowing often is practiced to increase soil water storage for the succeeding crop. Haas et al. (1974a) defined summer fallowing "as a farming practice wherein no crop is grown and all plant growth is controlled by cultivation or chemicals during a season when a crop might normally be grown." Such practice forfeits production for one season or year in anticipation of at least a partial increase in production for the next crop.

Although widely used for many years, fallowing has long been a controversial practice because, with respect to water conservation, it often results in low water storage efficiencies (often <25%) (Haas et al., 1974b; Johnson and Davis, 1972; Johnson et al., 1974; Unger, 1972). This is especially the case during the second summer of the fallow period in a wheat–fallow (WF) system (Farahani et al., 1998). In addition, yields usually are not doubled, thereby not compensating for skipping a crop one year (Haas et al., 1974b). Also, the erosion potential, especially by wind, usually is greater on fallowed areas because most crop residues are destroyed where frequent tillage is used for weed control during the fallow period (Haas et al., 1974a). Winter wheat–fallow, however, is still by far the most stable and profitable cropping system in some regions as, for example, in the low precipitation region of the U.S. Inland Pacific Northwest (W.F. Schillinger, personal communication, 2008).

Low water storage efficiency with fallow has received considerable attention with respect to tillage methods and cropping systems used. For example, water storage efficiency with the WF system at several central Great Plains locations averaged 19% with shallow tillage and harrowing and 38% with fall weed control in combination with stubble-mulch tillage (Greb et al., 1974). At Bushland, storage efficiency with the WF system was 10% with one-way disk tillage and 15% with stubble-mulch tillage (Johnson and Davis, 1972). Water storage efficiencies typically are lower in southern regions (southern and central Great Plains) than in northern regions (northern Great Plains and Canadian Prairies) (Unger and Howell, 1999) because of generally higher temperatures and potential evaporation in southern regions.

As compared with the WF system that involves about 15 mo of fallow between successive crops (Fig. 1–9), the wheat–grain sorghum–fallow (WSF) system results in about 11 mo of fallow between successive crops and results in two crops in 3 yr (Fig. 1–9). For a 13-yr study under dryland conditions involving stubble-mulch tillage at Bushland, water storage efficiency was 8% with the WF system and 14% for wheat and 14% for grain sorghum with the WSF system (Unger, 1972). For a WSF study at Bushland, wheat straw was placed on Pullman clay loam at rates ranging from 0 to 12 Mg ha^{-1} at the time of wheat harvest. Tillage was not performed during the fallow period. Water storage during the period between wheat harvest and sorghum planting averaged 46% with 12 Mg ha^{-1} straw and 23%

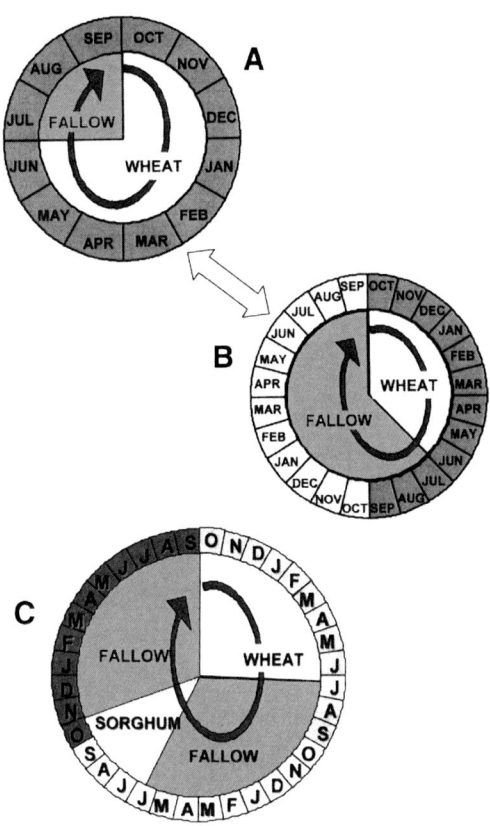

Fig. 1-9. Illustrations of (A) annual wheat, (B) wheat–fallow (one crop in 2 yr), and (C) wheat–sorghum–fallow (two crops in 3 yr) cropping systems. Illustrations provided by R.L. Baumhardt, USDA-ARS, Bushland, TX.

without straw. Grain yields of sorghum planted the spring after wheat harvest averaged 4.0 and 1.8 Mg ha^{-1} for the respective treatments (Unger, 1978).

For a WSF study at Bushland involving irrigated wheat and dryland grain sorghum, water storage efficiencies during fallow after wheat were 35% with no-tillage and 15% with disk tillage. Dryland grain sorghum after fallow yielded 3.1 Mg ha^{-1} with no-tillage and 1.9 Mg ha^{-1} with disk tillage, with the yield increase attributed mainly to the greater water storage with no-tillage (Unger and Wiese, 1979). Jones and Johnson (1983) considered alternate irrigated-dryland cropping systems appropriate for the Texas High Plains because declining water supplies are projected to limit irrigation in the region in the future.

A winter wheat–corn (or grain sorghum)–millet (*Panicum* spp.)–fallow cropping system in the central Great Plains avoids long fallow periods and results in three crops in 4 yr (Wood et al., 1991). For the northern Great Plains, spring wheat–winter wheat–fallow (two crops in 3 yr); safflower (*Carthamus tinctorius* L.)–barley (*Hordeum vulgare* L.)–winter wheat; spring wheat–corn–peas (*Pisum sativum* L.); spring wheat–winter wheat–sunflower (*Helianthus annuus* L.); spring wheat in rotation with soybean [*Glycine max* (L.) Merr.], peas, safflower, sunflower, buckwheat (*Fagopyrum esculentum* Moench), or canola (*Brassica* spp.) systems are being used (Black, 1986; Black and Tanaka, 1996; Unger and Vigil, 1998), thereby reducing the length of fallow periods. Peterson and Westfall (2004) demonstrated that increasing cropping frequency increased the proportion of fallow months that occurred in the fall, winter, and spring months where precipitation storage efficiency was highest and dramatically decreased the proportion of fallow months that occurred in the second summer of the fallow period when no precipitation was stored as soil water.

In general, water storage efficiencies increase with decreases in length of fallow. Storage efficiency generally increases also with decreases in tillage intensity, as with stubble-mulch tillage and especially no-tillage, which result in retaining more crop residues on the surface. Using reduced tillage methods that increase soil water storage and increasing cropping intensity by growing alternative spring and summer crops (less dependence on fallow) to more efficiently use stored water are means by which producers can enhance their profitability (Havlin and Schlegel, 1997).

Other Water Capture Practices

The foregoing practices and conditions having an effect on water capture generally have been extensively researched, and many of them are widely applicable and used. The following practices generally are not widely applicable, but do provide water capture benefits so they are presented briefly.

Chain diking results in a broadcast pattern of 10-cm-deep diamond-shaped basins when used on soil loosened with a chisel, disk, or drill (Fig. 1–10). The basins have little or no effect on subsequent farming operations. The diker (Fig. 1–10), which consists of specially shaped blades welded to a large ship-anchor chain, requires little maintenance and pulling power. The basins help retain water on land, and wheat grain yields were 2.9 and 2.6 Mg ha^{-1} on diked and nondiked areas, respectively (Wiedemann and Smallacombe, 1989). Chain diking also resulted in a threefold increase in grass densities on rangeland as compared with that achieved on nondiked areas.

The surface of some soils is highly unstable, and runoff commonly occurs if the soils are not protected by residues or appropriate runoff control practices. Runoff under field conditions in Israel was reduced sixfold as compared with that from untreated soil when phosphogypsum (PG) at 10 Mg ha^{-1} was applied to a ridged sandy soil (Agassi et al., 1989). When PG at 3.0 Mg ha^{-1} was applied to a clay loam, runoff was less than from untreated bare soil, but greater than with 2.2 Mg ha^{-1} of wheat straw on the surface (Benyamini and Unger, 1984).

Injecting anionic polymers (polyacrylamide [PAM] or starch copolymer solutions) into furrow-irrigation water reduced soil loss in runoff 70% when applied at 0.7 kg ha^{-1} per irrigation. The reduction was 97% when applied at 10 g m^{-3} of water. Net and lateral infiltration was increased by using the treatments, probably because of less sediment movement and surface sealing (Lentz et al., 1992; Trout et al., 1995). A combination treatment of plant residues and PAM in furrows produced greater erosion control and larger infiltration enhancements than those achieved with residues alone (Lentz and Bjorneberg, 2003). Continuously applying PAM in irrigation water, however, decreased infiltration at all concentrations evaluated on some sandy loams in California (Ajwa and Trout, 2006).

A practice similar to contour strip cropping is contour hedging. For a 6-yr study in Peru with contour hedges 4 m apart, average annual water conservation was 287 mm greater with hedges than where rice (*Oryza sativa* L.) and cowpea [*Vigna unguiculata* (L.) Walp.] were grown in rotation without hedges. Soil loss

Fig. 1–10. (Top) Chain diker. (Bottom) Surface depressions from use of a chain diker.

was reduced 73 Mg ha^{-1} annually. Crop yields were not increased in part because hedgerows occupied 22% of the land. More time may be needed to realize the benefits of soil conservation under conditions of the study (Alegre and Rao, 1996). In Iowa, field-saturated hydraulic conductivity within a grass-hedge position was seven times greater than in a row position 7 m upslope from the hedge and 24 times greater that in the deposition position 0.5 m upslope from the hedge. Use of grass hedges increased infiltration relative to that with conventional row crop management (Rachman et al., 2004). In Missouri, a combination of grass barriers and vegetative filter strips decreased runoff by 34% (Blanco-Canqui et al., 2006), indicating the potential for conserving water with such practice. Strips of vetiver grass [*Vetiveria zizanioides* (L.) Nash ex Small] that form dense barriers were also found to be highly effective for trapping sediments and conserving water (Erskine, 1992; Gallacher, 1990).

Cover crops are grown mainly to control erosion, but they can provide water conservation benefits with proper management. Water conservation benefits are derived from the surface cover that improves water infiltration. At Ceres, CA, the presence of cover crops increased the steady infiltration rate by 37 to 41% and cumulative infiltration by 20 to 101% (Folorunso et al., 1992). To achieve water conservation benefits, timely killing of cover crops is essential (Wagner-Riddle et al., 1994). With regard to soil water storage, cover crops may have positive or negative effects. Effects are positive when water capture is increased and negative when they limit water for the following crop or aggravate a wet soil condition. Cover crops generally are better suited for humid and subhumid regions, where precipitation is more reliable, than to semiarid regions, where precipitation is limited (Unger and Vigil, 1998).

Water Retention

After its capture, water must be retained in soil for subsequent use by plants. This is achieved by reducing losses due to evaporation, use by weeds, and deep percolation.

Evaporation

About 70% of the precipitation that falls on the U.S. land area is prevented from moving into storage bodies (including the soil) or streams by evaporation (Hatfield et al., 1992). Water stored in soil is also subject to evaporative losses, with losses occurring before crop establishment and during the growing season.

Soil water evaporation is a highly complex process that involves water potential gradients, soil temperature gradients, and atmospheric conditions. Water potential gradients occur between soil and the atmosphere and in soil itself. Ritchie (1972) recognized two stages of soil water evaporation, and Hillel (1998) and Lemon (1956) recognized three stages, but all agreed the rate was greatest during the first stage, with falling rates occurring in the subsequent stage(s).

Evaporation is greatest when soil is wet (high water potential) and air is dry (low humidity or vapor pressure). The soil water potential changes constantly due to use by plants, deep percolation, or the declining content as evaporation progresses, and increases due to precipitation or irrigation. When surface drying occurs, water must flow to the surface to replenish that lost by evaporation. Flow distances increase with continued evaporation, thereby resulting in increasingly slower liquid or vapor flow to the surface and lower evaporation rates. Eventually, water flow is only in the vapor phase, which results in the lowest rates. Besides changing water potential gradients in soil, water potentials of air constantly change due to climatic changes (temperature, humidity, vapor pressure). Other atmospheric conditions influencing evaporation are solar radiation and windspeed (Hatfield et al., 1992), which also constantly change.

Dust Mulching

According to Widtsoe (1920), dust mulching was the most important method of reducing evaporation to retain water in a soil. Fortier (1909) clearly showed that dust mulch thickness greatly affected soil water evaporation. During 21 d at Davis, CA, evaporation from containers totaled 23% of added water from soil without mulch and 6, 2, and 0.5% from soils covered with 76-, 152-, and 387-mm-thick dust mulches, respectively. Similar reductions in evaporation due to dust mulches also occurred at other locations in the western United States (Fortier, 1909). Whether these results influenced Widtsoe (1920) is not known, but these data showed that dust mulches reduce evaporation and thereby conserve water.

The results reported by Fortier (1909) were based on studies conducted in containers. Under field conditions, dust mulching consists of a granular or powdery soil layer usually produced by tillage at a shallow depth, but it was shown to be largely ineffective for conserving water by the early 1900s, as reported by James (1945). Although it may reduce evaporation, it has not been effective in the Great Plains where precipitation occurs mainly in summer when the potential for evaporation is greatest. Under such conditions, much of the water often evaporated before tillage could be performed to create the mulch. When tillage was performed, it exposed moist soil to the atmosphere that often resulted in soil drying to the depth of tillage. Also, tillage was needed after each significant rain to reestablish the mulch. Such frequent tillage generally resulted in bare soil that was highly susceptible to erosion (Jacks et al., 1955).

Although not effective for reducing evaporation under the above conditions, dust mulching can be effective where trafficability does not unduly delay tillage so that the water already in soil can be retained. Such conditions exist where a distinct dry season follows a distinct rainy season or where water moves to the surface from deeper in soil or from a water table (Jalota and Prihar, 1990; Papendick et al., 1973; Papendick and Miller, 1977). One such region is the Inland Pacific Northwest, where dust mulching for a winter wheat–fallow system is essential for maintaining the seed-zone water content during the dry summer months for subsequent winter wheat establishment. The region receives no precipitation in the summer months.

Other Mulches

Numerous mulching materials mentioned in the Water Capture section may also reduce evaporation. Besides the amount present, crop residue characteristics that influence evaporation are their orientation (standing, flat, or matted), which affects layer thickness and porosity; layer uniformity; reflectivity, which influences the surface radiant energy balance; and aerodynamic roughness resulting from the residues (Van Doren and Allmaras, 1978). Other factors influencing evaporation include residue type, evaporation potential, precipitation characteristics, tillage practices, and soil types (Papendick and Parr, 1989), and wind speed (Tanner and Shen, 1990).

Results of several studies under field conditions clearly illustrated the value of crop residue mulches for reducing evaporation. In Colorado, Smika (1983) measured water losses during a 35-d period without precipitation. Losses were 23 mm from bare soil, 20 mm with flattened wheat straw, 19 mm with 75% flat and 25% standing straw, and 15 mm with 50% flat and 50% standing straw. Straw was 0.46 m tall, and the amount was 4.6 Mg ha^{-1}. Wind speed needed for water loss to begin increased with increases in the amount of standing straw. The loss decreased with increased amounts standing at a given wind speed. Residue orientation (standing or flat) also influenced evaporation through its influence on soil surface temperatures (48, 42, 40, and 32°C with the respective conditions), which influenced vapor pressure of the soil water. Residue height strongly influences evaporation, especially when stem populations are <300 m^{-2}. The height effect decreases with increasing stem populations (McMaster et al., 2000).

Because height of standing residues influences evaporation, a practice that maximizes residue height after harvest of a grain crop such as winter wheat is the use of a stripper header harvesting (SHH) machine (Fig. 1–11). At Bushland, taller residues after SHH reduced mean wind speed and the potential transport of water vapor (evaporation) from wet soil. Irradiant energy at the soil surface was 12% lower under SHH than under platform header harvesting (PHH) conditions. Evaporation estimated with the Bowen ratio-energy balance method was reduced 26% with SHH as compared with PHH, but actual evaporation differences were small because of dry soil conditions during the study (Baumhardt et al., 2002).

The study by Baumhardt et al. (2002) was conducted under no-tillage conditions. No-tillage provides an "in place" mulch that retains most crop residues on the soil surface, thereby improving water capture under many conditions, as indicated in the Water Capture section. The "in place" mulch generally also provides for maximum evaporation control because of residues retained on the surface.

Crop residues for field studies usually are reported on a mass per unit area basis. When evaporation values with wheat straw, grain sorghum stover, and cotton stalks on the surface were compared on a mass basis, distinct crop-specific relationships were obtained. However, when the materials were compared on a thickness (or volume) per unit area basis, differences between the relationships were small and similar to a pooled relationship between residue level and the energy-limited potential evaporation from bare soil (Steiner, 1989). Such relationships can be incorporated into crop growth models to improve water balance prediction for different cropping systems.

Plastic films, which are probably the most commonly used mulching materials other than crop residues, are highly effective for controlling evaporation. With a 100% plastic cover on soil to prevent evaporation and rainwater infiltration, grain sorghum yielded 6.3 Mg ha^{-1} with 178 mm water use from soil. On uncovered plots that were irrigated twice, grain yield was 5.8 Mg ha^{-1}, and water use was 457 mm (Griffin et al., 1966). With 90% of the surface covered with plastic, corn grain yields averaged 4.1 Mg ha^{-1}, and water use averaged 288 mm in a 2-yr study in the northern Great Plains. Without a surface cover, yields averaged 2.4 Mg ha^{-1}, and water use averaged 282 mm (Willis et al., 1963). Clearly, plastic film mulches effectively control evaporation and improve crop production.

Plastic film mulches are not widely used for field crop production in the United States, but are widely used in some countries, and especially in the People's Republic of China. A major reason for their use is water conservation, mainly through reduced evaporation. Ma (1988) reported yield increases ranging from 44 to 165% for corn with plastic mulching as compared with yields from areas not mulched. In Shanzi Province of China, average grain yields were 4.2 Mg ha^{-1} when dryland wheat was planted in three rows in 30-cm-wide furrows separated by 30-cm-wide ridges covered with plastic film. The yields were 65% greater than that of wheat without a plastic cover. The increase was attributed to improved water conservation through both an improved water supply to plants and reduced evaporation (Yang et al., 2000). In the Loess Plateau of China, Fan et al. (2005) achieved greatest plant-available soil water when soil was partially covered with plastic during the fallow before crop planting.

Fig. 1–11. (Top) Harvesting wheat with a combine equipped with a stripper-header. (Bottom) Tall wheat stubble at left is where grain was removed with a stripper-header, and shorter stubble at right is where a cutter-header was used.

Weed Control

Weed control is essential for water conservation purposes because weeds present before crop planting use soil water that could be later used by the crop. Weeds present during a crop's growing season compete directly with it for water, space, light, and nutrients. Weed control usually is achieved by tillage alone, herbicides alone, or a combination of tillage and herbicides. Other control methods are by hand (pulling or hoeing), flame devices, or pest management techniques.

With regard to water retention, timely control is essential because weeds may daily use 5 mm of water from a soil (Wicks and Smika, 1973). When tillage is used, exposing moist soil to the atmosphere may cause losses of 5 to 8 mm for each operation (Good and Smika, 1978). Water losses due to tillage, therefore, must be balanced against water used by developing weeds, which is low in early growth stages. As a result, tillage can be delayed until weeds use as much or slightly more water than that which would be lost by evaporation. The net result of delaying tillage, therefore, is that as much or more water is retained for use by the next crop. Although tillage may immediately stop water use by existing weeds, several operations may be needed to keep weeds under control throughout the cropping period and, thereby, to conserve water (Pressland and Batianoff, 1976). As with tillage, hand-weeding immediately stops water use, but repeated weeding may be needed to achieve the greatest water conservation and crop yield benefits (Twomlow et al., 1997).

To stop water use by weeds, herbicides must enter the weeds and block their physiological activity, thereby causing them to die. Weeds in early growth stages generally are easier to control with herbicides than more mature weeds (Wiese et al., 1966). Large, more mature weeds may be especially difficult to control when stressed for water.

Most crops tolerate some herbicides that can be applied before planting or at various stages during the crop's growing season. Modifications through genetic engineering have greatly expanded the opportunity to use highly effective, quick-acting herbicides to control problem weeds without damaging the planted crops. For example, growing-season weed control is now possible through the development of glyphosate [N-(phosphonomethyl) glycine] resistance in cultivars of cotton, soybean, corn, canola (Moll, 1997; Padgette et al., 1995; Rasche and Gadsby, 1997), and other crops. The widespread availability of glyphosate beginning in the 1980s also greatly facilitated the adoption of conservation-tillage and no-tillage practices.

Some herbicides prevent some weed seeds from germinating and, therefore, eliminate water use by such weeds. Such herbicides, however, also may prevent seed germination of the planted crop. In such cases, some crops can be grown by using "safener-treated" seed (i.e., seed treated to prevent action of the herbicide) and, thereby, achieve effective weed control during the crop's growing season (Jones and Popham, 1997). Some herbicides may not prevent germination of seed of some weeds, which then may become a problem in the planted crop. Under such conditions, careful selection of herbicides is needed to achieve weed control without damaging the crop. Unfortunately, some weeds cannot be controlled with herbicides in some crops. Also, some weeds have become resistant to herbicides, which results in major problems where reduced or no-tillage cropping is practiced (Freebairn et al., 2006), thereby thwarting water conservation efforts.

Cover crops are not classified as weeds, but they use water. Therefore, their management with respect to water retention is important, especially in drier regions where a delay in terminating their growth may result in limited soil water retention for a following crop. As a result, cover crops generally are not recommended for use under dryland conditions, as, for example, in the southern Great Plains (Unger and Vigil, 1998). An exception may be a strip tillage system in the Southern High Plains of Texas where wheat is used as a cover crop where cotton is grown. Wheat is terminated before it has a high demand for water. Evapotranspiration (ET) was similar for such system and a conventional tillage system, but transpiration was a greater part of ET for the strip tillage system (Lascano et al., 1994).

Deep Percolation

Deep percolation occurs when the amount of water entering a soil exceeds its storage capacity, which potentially reduces the amount available for plant use because the water moves to depths beyond the reach of plant roots. Under some conditions, it may be recovered later for irrigation from an aquifer or stream. Deep percolation most frequently occurs on deep porous soils or through preferential flow paths (worm channels, decayed root channels, etc.) on almost any soil.

To reduce the potential for deep percolation losses, crops should be grown that have growing seasons (and their greatest water requirement) corresponding with the time when the potential for percolation is greatest. Other crop management options include early planting to achieve greater root development early in the growing season, growing deep-rooting crops or crop cultivars that extract water from deep in the profile (e.g., sunflower and safflower), and using appropriate fertilization practices to encourage proper root propagation. The potential for deep percolation also can be reduced by deep tillage to enhance deeper plant rooting or to bring materials that retain more water closer to the surface, installing subsurface barriers, and increasing the soil organic matter content.

When considering early planting, the crop's optimum planting time for obtaining favorable yields must be considered. Except that growing certain crops is more profitable than growing others, little or no additional expenses should be incurred when switching to deeper-rooted crops or crop cultivars, or to those having growing seasons that coincide with the time when the deep percolation potential is greatest. This contrasts with the case for deep plowing and installing subsurface barriers for which the potential benefits relative to the cost of performing such operations must be carefully considered.

Freeman silt loam (fine-silty, mixed, superactive, mesic Aquandic Palexeralfs) in eastern Washington and northern Idaho has about a 30-cm-thick A horizon overlying a well-developed A2 horizon at the 30- to 46-cm depth. The underlying B horizon is a dense silty clay loam. Moldboard plowing the soil 90 cm deep resulted in storing 53 mm more water from precipitation in the upper 90 cm of the profile than conventional plowing. Seepage along the A2 horizon may have caused water to be lost from the conventionally plowed soil (Mech et al., 1967).

The surface horizon of Hezel soil (sandy over loamy, mixed, superactive, nonacid, mesic Xeric Torriorthents) in central Washington contains about 70% sand. Moldboard plowing the soil 1 m deep reduced the surface horizon sand content to 40 to 50%. Also, it increased the plant-available water-holding capacity in the upper 30 cm from 36 mm before plowing to 61 mm after plowing (Miller and Aarstad, 1972).

Deep sandy soils generally have high percolation rates that reduce water retention and may result in reduced crop yields. Installing asphalt barriers at about a 60-cm depth in such soils generally increased efficiency of rainfall retention and enhanced crop yields (Erickson et al., 1968; Saxena et al., 1969, 1973; Robertson et al., 1973). Another possibility for reducing deep percolation water losses on sandy soils is to mix a superabsorbent (e.g., PAM) with the soil (Bhardwaj et al., 2007).

Organic materials absorb water readily. Adding large quantities of organic materials will increase the available water storage capacity of soils and in theory should reduce deep percolation losses (Shaxson and Barber, 2003). Adding such materials to soils, however, resulted in variable effects on water retention and, therefore, on percolation losses. For sandy soils, Jamison (1953) found a high positive correlation between water retention and organic matter content. In contrast, Cisse and Vachaud (1988) found that adding organic materials had no effect on the water-holding capacity of degraded sandy soils in Senegal, but it increased plant root development, water absorption, and crop yields. Because water retention by organic materials and fine soil particles (silt and clay) is similar, adding organic materials to fine-textured soils apparently would have little or no effect on water retention. It could, however, improve soil structure and, thereby, increase root proliferation and decrease deep percolation of water. Although improved soil structure, increased root proliferation, and decreased deep percolation are possible, the amount of organic materials required is very high, and applications must be continued for many years to markedly increase soil water retention (Shaxson and Barber, 2003). Also, only the plow layer usually is affected by organic matter additions (Russell, 1988).

Crop Termination Time

Continued water use does not increase yields of grain crops such as corn, wheat, and grain sorghum after they reach physiological maturity, but may improve harvestable yield by delaying plant lodging until harvest is possible. Because yield is not increased, terminating the crop at physiological maturity would stop soil water use and, thereby, conserve some water for a following crop. Some crops such as grain sorghum and cotton have an indeterminate growing season. Where such crops are not terminated by freezing temperatures, terminating their growth immediately after harvest is an alternative method for reducing continued water use. Where second or rattoon crops are possible (e.g., grain sorghum, rice, sugarcane [*Saccharum* spp.]), water use may be less than for the first crop because limited additional plant development may be required (Unger and Howell, 1999).

Efficient Water Use

After water from precipitation has been captured and retained in soil, the amount available must be used efficiently to achieve optimum crop yields and, hence, favorable returns to the producer. Likewise, irrigation water must also be used efficiently to obtain the above results.

Efficient water use in itself usually is not the major goal of producers. Rather, their main goals usually are production level, profitability, and, to some extent, production sustainability. With these goals in mind, production systems based on water availability for crop use become an important consideration for most producers. The amount of water captured and retained, however, as mentioned in previous sections, is influenced by many factors. To achieve a yield that will be profitable to the producer is termed a threshold yield. To attain such yield, a certain amount of water is needed, and such amount under dryland (non-irrigated) conditions may influence the type of cropping system used. For example, systems with long fallow periods may be less efficient regarding precipitation use, but may increase the likelihood of achieving a threshold yield from an economic viewpoint. Fortunately, use of conservation tillage has resulted in achieving both more efficient use of precipitation and the likelihood of acceptable economic threshold yields in many cases.

Scientists have been interested in the amount of water required for successful production of different crops for many years (Briggs and Shantz, 1914; de Wit, 1958; Tanner and Sinclair, 1983). *Water use efficiency* is a term denoting the ratio of plant production to the amount of water used. This term is appropriate for comparing different production systems in detail. However, we mainly discuss practices or options that producers can use to efficiently use water available to them.

Crop Selection

Probably the most important choice a producer of rainfed crops must make is crop (or crop cultivar) selection based on the amount and timeliness of water availability. Foremost, adequate water must be available to support crop establishment and then sustain it throughout the growing season without subjecting it to severe water stress under typical conditions (e.g., average precipitation). Unfortunately, droughts sometimes occur that thwart desired production levels of a given crop. Also, greater than anticipated precipitation sometimes provides more water than required by the crop. Selecting crops on the basis of long-term precipitation averages minimizes adverse results with the crop or crop cultivar selected.

Another important consideration regarding crop selection is crop growing season length relative to the period of adequate water availability. For relatively short periods of water availability, crops with short- or medium-length growing seasons are appropriate, whereas crops with longer growing seasons can be grown when water is available for a longer time. The goal should be to closely match available water supplies with anticipated crop needs, thereby potentially avoiding severe plant water stress or the crop not using water that is available.

A third important consideration is timeliness of adequate water availability relative to when the crop is to be grown (e.g., cool- or warm-season crop). Prevailing temperatures influence what crops can be grown in different seasons.

With irrigation, the above considerations should be applied for using water efficiently. In addition, more options regarding crop selection generally are available with irrigation. For example, with irrigation, cultivars of a given crop having a longer growing season are appropriate. Also, with irrigation, some crops can be grown that cannot be grown without irrigation under some conditions.

Irrigation Management

With respect to efficient water use, the goal for irrigation is to achieve maximum production per unit of water applied. Irrigation scheduling and amount of water to apply are important management factors that influence efficient irrigation water use. Under optimum conditions, crops would be irrigated when they need water. This is accomplished to a large degree by drip (or similar) irrigation methods in which small amounts of water are applied frequently. Under most large-scale field conditions, however, such frequent applications are not practical, and irrigations supply water to soil for later use by crops. The frequency of such irrigations may be influenced by crop water needs, water availability, soil water-holding capacity, equipment limitations, and desired production level. To achieve maximum yields, relatively frequent irrigations that maintain relatively high soil water contents are required. Achieving maximum yields, however, may not result in the most efficient water use. For some crops, use of deficit (or limited) irrigation reduced yields, but also reduced irrigation water use, increased water use efficiency, and improved capture and use of precipitation (Unger and Howell, 1999). Successful use of deficit irrigation strategies generally requires a profile full of soil water at planting.

Irrigation scheduling is influenced by such factors as crop growth stage, crop sensitivity to water deficits, and climatic conditions (precipitation, prevailing temperatures, season of the year, etc.). In addition, a preplant irrigation may be used to increase soil water content, germinate weed seeds before crop planting, leach salts from the profile, or improve conditions for seedbed preparation. Irrigation scheduling decisions can be based on a record of precipitation, knowledge of normal evapotranspiration, reports of evapotranspiration, computer models, or direct sampling to determine the soil water status. The amount of water applied should be such that runoff or deep percolation losses are avoided or minimized. Also, preplant irrigations should be as close as possible to crop needs to avoid excessive losses due to evaporation.

In addition to irrigation scheduling and the amount of water applied, cropping system management also impacts irrigation water use efficiency. As previously mentioned, ET in the southern Great Plains was similar for cotton grown after terminated wheat that was used as a cover crop and with conventional tillage, but transpiration was a greater part of ET where the terminated wheat provided a partial residue cover on the surface (strip tillage was used for managing the wheat residues) (Lascano et al., 1994). In Kansas, corn grain yields were 8.1 and 6.4% greater with strip tillage and no-tillage, respectively, than with conventional tillage, with the yield benefits resulting from less evaporation where surface residues were present (Lamm et al., 2008). Other studies in Kansas showed the benefits of surface residues for suppressing evaporation under irrigated conditions (Klocke, 2004; Lamm and Aiken, 2007; Todd et al., 1991), thereby resulting in evaporation being a smaller part of ET for corn production (Lamm and Aiken, 2007).

Alternate Irrigated–Dryland Cropping

The WSF cropping system for which irrigated wheat is rotated with dryland sorghum (mentioned previously) is an example of alternate irrigated–dryland cropping. The goal for such systems is to grow irrigated and dryland crops under conditions where water for irrigation is limited and where dryland crops can be grown but with generally low yields. After harvesting the irrigated crop, some water from irrigations may remain in the soil. In addition, the following dryland crop benefits also from water stored during the ensuing fallow period. Because dryland crops generally deplete most soil water, some water would be stored during fallow before planting the irrigated crop, and soil conditions usually are favorable for irrigation water infiltration, thus reducing the potential for runoff.

Another example of alternate irrigated–dryland cropping is to grow the same crop alternately under irrigated and dryland conditions on the same land. For winter wheat at Bushland, average grain yields on dryland were 2.3 and 2.1 Mg ha^{-1} after irrigated wheat and for continual dryland wheat, respectively. Grain yields with irrigation were 4.4 and 4.3 Mg ha^{-1} after dryland wheat and for continual irrigated wheat, respectively. Water use efficiencies were slightly greater for alternate irrigated–dryland cropping (Unger, 1977).

Opportunity Cropping

Water availability for crop production without irrigation is highly dependent on precipitation amount and timing, especially in drier regions such as the semiarid Great Plains. Under such conditions, rather rigid cropping systems such as WF and WSF often are used. The goal for using these systems is to increase soil water storage during fallow for the next crop. Precipitation timing and amounts are highly unpredictable, and substantial amounts may occur late in the growing season or soon after a crop is harvested, thus providing little opportunity for storing additional water during the ensuing fallow period. With opportunity cropping (Fig. 1–12), an adapted crop is planted when soil water conditions become favorable, thus eliminating or greatly shortening the length of the fallow period. In the southern Great Plains, for example, short-season grain sorghum can be grown after winter wheat harvest, or winter wheat can be grown after grain sorghum harvest. Other crops evaluated for opportunity cropping at Bushland were triticale (× *Triticosecale* Wittmack), forage sorghum, pearl millet [*Pennisetum glaucum* (L.) R. Br.], oat (*Avena sativa* L.), pinto bean (*Phaseolus vulgaris* L.), fall and spring canola (*Brassica* spp.), and kenaf (*Hibiscus cannabinus* L.) (Unger, 2001). Crops considered suitable for opportunity cropping at the location were winter wheat, grain sorghum, triticale, forage sorghum, pearl millet, and oat. Because opportunity cropping increases cropping intensity relative to fixed systems, precipitation is used more efficiently than with systems involving long fallow periods. Nielsen et al. (2006) showed a 45% increase in economic precipitation use efficiency (i.e., value of crops produced) from a 5-yr study comparing opportunity cropping against set rotations that included fallow in the central Great Plains.

Fig. 1–12. Grain sorghum (foreground) and kenaf (background) being evaluated as opportunity crops.

Avoiding Long Fallow Periods

Some cropping practices, as discussed in the Water Capture section under Fallowing and under Opportunity Cropping, are aimed at avoiding long fallow periods that result in low water use efficiencies under many conditions. With these practices, crops more readily use water from precipitation when it becomes available, thus resulting in generally more efficient water use.

Atmospheric Carbon Dioxide Levels

The increasing concentration of atmospheric CO_2 has potential for affecting the water relations of crops. The concentration increased from 338 ppm in 1980 to 381 ppm in 2006 (Dlugokencky and Schnell, 2007). Studies conducted under controlled environmental conditions have shown that elevated atmospheric CO_2 levels increase water use efficiency (Allen, 1999; Allen et al., 1985). A field study was conducted in the central Great Plains during three growing seasons (1984–1987) with winter wheat (a C_3 crop) under ambient (340 ppm) and elevated CO_2 levels (485, 660, and 825 ppm) (Chaudhuri et al., 1990). Plants were grown in boxes placed in the ground. Water loss was determined by lifting and weighing the boxes. The soil was a silt loam and one-half of the boxes were maintained at a high water level (field capacity; 0.38 m^3 m^{-3}), while the other half were maintained at a low water level (one-half field capacity). Even though it is well known that CO_2 is an antitranspirant (Allen et al., 1985), the amount of water transpired increased as the CO_2 level increased because the elevated CO_2 levels increased growth and leaf area. The amount of water required to produce a gram of grain was calculated from water used and grain yield for each CO_2 level (Chaudhuri et al., 1990). The water requirement (WR), which is the reciprocal of water use efficiency, decreased as CO_2 concentration increased. Under the high water level, the WR was reduced by 29% when the CO_2 level was raised from ambient (3-yr average WR = 642 mL g^{-1}) to 825 ppm (WR = 458 mL g^{-1}). Under the low water level, the WR was reduced by 31% when the CO_2 level was raised from ambient (WR = 797 mL g^{-1}) to 825 ppm (WR = 547 mL g^{-1}). The results indicated that water use by wheat will not decrease as atmospheric CO_2 concentration increases, but that water use efficiency will increase.

Kirkham et al. (1991) determined the effect of CO_2 level on big bluestem grass (*Andropogon gerardii* Vitman) (a C_4 rangeland crop) growing on a silty clay loam kept at a high water level (field capacity; 0.38 m^3 m^{-3}) or a low water level (half field capacity). The CO_2 levels were 337 ppm (ambient) and 658 ppm, about double the ambient level. The WR was calculated by dividing leaf transpiration rate by leaf photosynthetic rate. Elevated CO_2 reduced the WR by 35% for both watering regimes. Other studies, reviewed by Allen (1999) and Allen et al. (1985) for plants such as corn, cotton, and soybean, confirm the findings that, under elevated CO_2 levels, water use efficiency will increase both for C_3 and C_4 crops.

Large increases in water use efficiency under elevated CO_2 levels do not necessarily imply any reduction in crop water requirements per unit area of land (Allen, 1999). As noted by Chaudhuri et al. (1990), water use efficiency for wheat increased under elevated CO_2 levels, but transpiration also increased because of increased plant growth and leaf area. Nevertheless, as CO_2 in the atmosphere increases, farmers should be able to achieve higher crop yields per unit land area with similar amounts of water (Allen, 1999; Robinson et al., 2007). More field data, however, are needed for the major C_3 and C_4 crops, particularly under well-watered and water-stressed conditions (Kimball, 1983), to determine how water use efficiency will change as the atmospheric CO_2 concentration increases.

Future Challenges and Opportunities

The principles of water conservation for agriculture, namely, that water must be captured, retained, and used efficiently for producing a desirable yield, have not changed during the past 100 yr. Although much progress has been made, much water potentially available for agricultural uses is not effectively conserved in many cases. With increasing demands for water by other users and the need for increased agricultural production, it is imperative that continued efforts be made to conserve and use our water supplies effectively and more efficiently. With this in mind, we list and briefly comment on some challenges and opportunities for achieving improved water conservation for agriculture.

1. Develop techniques for reducing crop residue decomposition.
Conservation tillage and especially no-tillage result in crop residues being retained on the soil surface, thereby providing major water conservation benefits under many conditions (Fig. 1–13). Unfortunately, residues decay, thus decreasing their long-term effectiveness. With less decay, greater water conservation should be possible. Possible means for reducing residue decay include using improved harvesting equipment (e.g., using the stripper header), plant breeding to develop sturdier or decay-resistant plant stems, and applying chemicals to retard decomposition.

Fig. 1–13. Crop residues on the surface in a winter wheat–grain sorghum–fallow cropping system under dryland (nonirrigated) conditions. (Left) Standing stubble of winter wheat (the most recent crop) with stalks of the previous sorghum crop lying on the surface. (Right) Standing stalks of grain sorghum (the most recent crop) with stubble of the previous wheat crop lying on the surface.

2. Identify, select, or develop more water-efficient crops or crop cultivars.

Briggs and Shantz (1914) showed major differences in water use to produce a unit yield for different crop species and for different cultivars of a given crop. Crop or cultivar selection is used to achieve efficient water use, but improved efficiency should be possible through genetic engineering techniques, through careful selection of existing crops or cultivars, and through development of improved crops or cultivars for use in a given situation (e.g., region, climatic conditions). For example, genes have been identified that may make it possible to alter corn plants (Setter, 2006), thereby potentially making corn less susceptible to drought and improving water use efficiency for that crop.

3. Determine crop responses to increasing atmospheric CO_2 levels.

Atmospheric CO_2 levels continue to increase. Studies regarding CO_2 level have been conducted, but continued research and plant breeding are warranted to stay abreast of the effect of CO_2 levels on crop productivity and water use efficiency.

4. Develop more effective herbicides or other methods for controlling weeds.

Some herbicides are most effective at a given weed growth stage. With a wider range of effectiveness, generally better weed control should be possible. In addition, some weeds are resistant to herbicides, and improved herbicides or different control methods are needed to adequately control them. Some herbicide-tolerant crops have become available through biotechnology, which has been a major benefit with regard to weed control. This practice is desirable for other crops. Progress in these areas is needed to achieve increased water use efficiency and crop productivity.

5. Develop improved phreatophyte and brush control methods.

Phreatophytes often grow beside canals, streams, or other waterways from which they extract water that could potentially be used for crop production. Brushy plants grow on rangeland and compete with grasses for water. Effective control of such plants is needed to increase the water supply for cropland and rangeland plants.

6. Consider the impacts of ethanol and biofuel production.

Several issues concerning ethanol and biofuel production have implications regarding water conservation for agriculture. In the production process itself, 3.5 to 6 units of water are used for each unit of ethanol produced (Keeney and Muller, 2006). Where grain is used for ethanol production, a large volume of water is used to produce the crop, about 1400 kg water to produce 1 kg corn grain (Stewart and Howell, 2003). Such water requirement for corn grain production results in almost 3400 L of water needed to produce 1 L of ethanol. Where corn is produced under rainfed conditions, such water use may not be of much concern. Under irrigated conditions, especially where the water supply is limited, such water use makes the production of ethanol from corn a questionable activity.

Cellulosic biofuel production also has major implications regarding water conservation. These include crop residue removal effects on water capture (runoff and infiltration effects), water retention (evaporation control), and on the soil itself (surface protection for controlling erosion, organic matter content, structure development). Information regarding these issues is available or being developed

(National Academy of Sciences, 2007; Wilhelm et al., 2007), but readily applicable guidelines or models are needed so that producers or advisors can easily determine the amount of residues needed to avoid harmful consequences at the site under consideration. The use of alternate cellulosic biofuel crops—perennial grasses, brushy plants, fast-growing trees—could reduce the need for using crop residues to produce ethanol.

7. Increase the application of practices known to improve water conservation.

Many studies have shown the value of conservation tillage for improving water conservation and use, but the practice is not used to the extent to which it is applicable. Also, such studies have not been conducted under some conditions where it could be applicable. Additional research and demonstrations involving conservation tillage (especially no-tillage) under a wide variety of cropping systems are needed to develop information so that it can be promoted through education and extension activities to achieve greater acceptance by producers.

8. Conduct interdisciplinary, more comprehensive research.

Much research pertaining to water conservation involves a small number of variables and often is conducted by one or a few researchers. Research and development teams comprised of personnel from several disciplines (e.g., soil, crop, and weed scientists; agronomists; engineers; hydrologists; economists; environmentalists; cropping-system modelers) are needed to simultaneously study more variables and to develop widely applicable, practical, and functional integrated cropping systems. These systems should effectively capture, retain, and efficiently use water; be economically suitable for producers; and help protect the environment.

Summary

The principles of water conservation for agriculture have remained constant during the past 100 years; that is, the water must be captured, retained, and used efficiently to produce a desirable yield. Deep plowing was promoted by Shaw (1911) as the primary method for capturing water in the early 1900s. Deep plowing improves water capture in some soils, but water capture can be achieved also by various less intensive practices, including ridge tillage, stubble mulch tillage, bench terracing, furrow diking, and conservation tillage, which also provide soil conservation benefits. Conservation tillage methods, especially no-tillage, are highly effective for capturing water under many conditions because the surface residues dissipate raindrop energy, thereby minimizing soil aggregate dispersion and surface sealing and maintaining favorable conditions for water infiltration. The residues also reduce the runoff rate, thus providing more time for infiltration.

To retain the captured water, water losses due to evaporation, use by weeds, and deep percolation must be minimized. Dust (soil) mulching, as promoted by Shaw (1911) and Widtsoe (1920), reduces evaporation where a distinct dry season follows a distinct rainy season, as, for example, in the Pacific Northwest. In some other regions, however, effective evaporation control can be achieved with crop residues and other mulches to obtain satisfactory water retention. Numerous herbicides are available to control weeds, and deep percolation losses can be minimized by using appropriate management practices and applying suitable barriers in some cases.

Efficient use of the captured and retained water is largely influenced by management practices being used, including crop selection, irrigation method, and cropping systems.

The development of herbicides; improved tillage methods, including no-tillage; improved irrigation practices; and other related activities have contributed to major advances in water conservation for agriculture during the past 100 years, but challenges and opportunities remain to improve on what has been achieved.

Acknowledgments

The authors thank Cindy Warriner with Crop & Sciences at Washington State University, Ritzville, WA, for her excellent arrangement and preparation of the photos for the book chapter.

References

Aase, J.K., F.H. Siddoway, and A.L. Black. 1976. Perennial grass barriers for wind erosion control, snow management and crop production. p. 69–78. In Proc. Shelterbelts on the Great Plains Symp., Denver, CO. 20–22 Apr. 1976. Journal Ser. 690. Montana Agric. Exp. Stn., Bozeman.

Adams, J.E. 1966. Influences of mulches on runoff, erosion, and soil moisture depletion. Soil Sci. Soc. Am. Proc. 30:110–114.

Agassi, M., I. Shainberg, D. Warrington, and M. Ben-Hur. 1989. Runoff and erosion control in potato fields. Soil Sci. 148:149–154.

Ajwa, H.A., and T.J. Trout. 2006. Polyacrylamide and water quality effects on infiltration in sandy loam soils. Soil Sci. Soc. Am. J. 70:643–650.

Alegre, J.C., and M.R. Rao. 1996. Soil and water conservation by contour hedging in the humid tropics of Peru. Agric. Ecosyst. Environ. 57:17–25.

Alleman, R. 1982. Ecofallow catches on in wheat country. Farm J. May, p. D-4.

Allen, L.H., Jr. 1999. Evapotranspiration responses of plants and crops to carbon dioxide and temperature. p. 37–70. In M.B. Kirkham (ed.) Water use in crop production. The Haworth Press, Inc., New York.

Allen, L.H., Jr., P. Jones, and J.W. Jones. 1985. Rising atmospheric CO_2 and evapotranspiration. p. 13–27. In Advances in evapotranspiration. Proc. Natl. Conf. on Advances in Evapotranspiration. ASAE, St. Joseph, MI.

Allen, R.R., and C.R. Fenster. 1986. Stubble-mulch equipment for soil and water conservation in the Great Plains. J. Soil Water Conserv. 41:11–16.

Allen, R.R., J.T. Musick, and A.D. Schneider. 1994. Deep plowing restrictive-layer soils to improve irrigation infiltration. ASAE Paper 94-2516. ASAE, St. Joseph, MI.

Allen, R.R., J.T. Musick, and A.D. Schneider. 1995. Residual deep plowing effects on irrigation intake for Pullman clay loam. Soil Sci. Soc. Am. J. 59:1424–1429.

Allmaras, R.R., and R.H. Dowdy. 1985. Conservation tillage systems and their adoption in the United States. Soil Tillage Res. 5:197–222.

Amemiya, M. 1977. Conservation tillage in the western Corn Belt. J. Soil Water Conserv. 32:29–36.

Armbrust, D.V., and N.H. Welch. 1966. Evaluation of Zingg conservation bench terraces on Amarillo fine sandy loam soil. J. Soil Water Conserv. 21:224–226.

Barnett, A.P. 1987. Fifty years of progress in soil and water conservation at the Southern Piedmont Conservation Research Center (SPCRC), Watkinsville, Georgia, 1937–1987. Available at ftp://anyone:spc@128.192.164.106/schomberg (verified 1 Oct. 2009).

Baumhardt, R.L., O.R. Jones, and R.C. Schwartz. 2008. Long-term effects of profile modifying deep plowing on soil properties and crop yield. Soil Sci. Soc. Am. J. 72:677–682.

Baumhardt, R.L., R.C. Schwartz, and R.W. Todd. 2002. Effects of taller wheat residue after stripper header harvest on wind run, irradiant energy interception, and evaporation. p. 386–391. In E. van Santen (ed.) Proc. 25th Ann. Southern Conserv. Tillage Conf. for Sustainable Agric., Auburn, AL. 24–26 June 2002. Spec. Rep. 1. Alabama Agric. Exp. Stn., Auburn.

Baumhardt, R.L., C.W. Wendt, and J.W. Keeling. 1992. Chisel tillage, furrow diking, and surface crust effects on infiltration. Soil Sci. Soc. Am. J. 56:1286–1291.

Baver, L.D. 1956. Soil physics. 3rd ed. John Wiley & Sons Inc., New York.

Bennett, H.H. 1939. Soil conservation. McGraw-Hill Book Co., New York.

Benyamini, Y., and P.W. Unger. 1984. Crust development under simulated rainfall on four soils. p. 243–244. *In* 1984 Agronomy Abstracts. ASA, CSSA, and SSSA, Madison, WI.

Bhardwaj, A.K., I. Shainberg, D. Goldstein, D.N. Warrington, and G.J. Levy. 2007. Water retention and hydraulic conductivity of cross-linked polyacrylamides in sandy soils. Soil Sci. Soc. Am. J. 71:406–412.

Bilbro, J.D., and D.W. Fryrear. 1991. Pearl millet versus gin trash mulches for increasing soil water and cotton yields in a semiarid region. J. Soil Water Conserv. 46:66–69.

Black, A.L. 1967. Stubble mulching saves soil water. Montana Farmer-Stockman 54(20):22.

Black, A.L. 1986. Resources and problems in the northern Great Plains area. p. 25–38. *In* Planning and management of water conservation systems, Proc. of a Workshop, Lincoln, NE. October 1985. USDA-SCS Midwest Natl. Tech. Ctr., Lincoln, NE.

Black, A.L., and D.L. Tanaka. 1996. A conservation tillage-cropping systems study in the northern Great Plains of the USA. p. 335–342. *In* E.A. Paul et al. (ed.) Soil organic matter in temperate agroecosystems. Lewis Publ., Boca Raton, FL.

Blanco-Canqui, H., C.J. Gantzer, and S.H. Anderson. 2006. Performance of grass barriers and filter strips under interrill and concentrated flow. J. Environ. Qual. 35:1969–1974.

Bordovsky, J.P., W.M. Lyle, R.J. Lascano, and D.R. Upchurch. 1992. Cotton irrigation management with LEPA systems. Trans. ASAE 35:879–884.

Borst, H.L., and R. Woodburn. 1942. The effect of mulching and methods of cultivation on runoff and erosion from Muskingum silt loam. Agric. Eng. 23:19–24.

Bowser, W.E., and R.R. Cairns. 1967. Some effects of deep plowing a Solonetz soil. Can. J. Soil Sci. 47:239–244.

Bradford, J.M., and R.W. Blanchar. 1977. Profile modification of a Fragiudalf to increase crop production. Soil Sci. Soc. Am. J. 41:127–131.

Briggs, L.J., and J.W. McLane. 1907. The moisture equivalent of soils. USDA Bureau of Soil Bull. 45. U.S. Gov. Print. Office, Washington, DC.

Briggs, L.J., and H.L. Shantz. 1914. Relative water requirement of plants. J. Agric. Res. 3:1–64 (plus 7 plates).

Buckingham, E. 1907. Studies of the movement of soil moisture. USDA Bureau of Soils Bull. 38. U.S. Gov. Print. Office, Washington, DC.

Burnett, E. 1969. Profile modification for improved water intake and storage. Great Plains Agric. Counc. Publ. 34. Vol. 1:59–63.

Burnett, E., G.F. Arkin, and D.L. Reddell. 1974. Deep tillage effects on crop physiological response to water deficit. Paper 74-2533. ASAE, St. Joseph, MI.

Burnett, E., and C.E. Fisher. 1956. Land leveling increases dryland cotton production. Prog. Rep. 1914. Texas Agric. Exp. Stn., College Station.

Burnett, E., and V.L. Hauser. 1967. Deep tillage and soil-plant-water relationships. p. 47–52. *In* Proc. Conf. on Tillage for Greater Crop Production. 11–12 Dec. 1967. ASAE, St. Joseph, MI.

Burnett, E., B.A. Stewart, and A.L. Black. 1985. Regional effects on soil erosion and crop productivity—Great Plains. p. 285–304. *In* R.F. Follett and B.A. Stewart (ed.) Soil erosion and crop productivity. ASA, CSSA, and SSSA, Madison, WI.

Campbell, C.A., B.G. McConkey, R.P. Zentner, F. Selles, and F.B. Dyck. 1992. Benefits of wheat stubble strips for conserving snow in southwestern Saskatchewan. J. Soil Water Conserv. 47:112–115.

Chaudhuri, U.N., M.B. Kirkham, and E.T. Kanemasu. 1990. Carbon dioxide and water level effects on yield and water use of winter wheat. Agron. J. 82:637–641.

Cisse, L., and G. Vachaud. 1988. Influence d'apports de matière organique sur la culture de mil et d'arachide sur un sol sableux du Nord-Sénégal. I. Bilans de consommation, production et développement racinaire. Agronomie 8:315–326.

Clark, R.N., and O.R. Jones. 1981. Furrow dams for conserving rainwater in a semiarid climate. p. 198–206. *In* J.C. Siemens (ed.) Proc. Crop Production with Conservation in the 1980s, Chicago, IL. 1–2 Dec. 1980. ASAE, St. Joseph, MI.

Cochran, V.L., S.D. Sparrow, and E.B. Sparrow. 1994. Residue effects on soil micro- and macroorganisms. p. 163–184. *In* P.W. Unger (ed.) Managing agricultural residues. Lewis Publ., Boca Raton, FL.

Cox, M.B. 1968. Conservation bench terraces in Kansas. Trans. ASAE 11:387–388.

Derpsch, R. 1998. Historical review of no-tillage cultivation of crops. JIRCAS Working Rep. 13:1–18.

de Wit, C.T. 1958. Transpiration and crop yield. Versl. Landbouwk. Onder. 64(6). Inst. of Biol. and Chem. Res. on Field Crops and Herbage, Wageningen, The Netherlands.

Dickey, E.C., C.R. Fenster, J.M. Laflen, and R.H. Mickelson. 1983. Effects of tillage on soil erosion in a wheat-fallow rotation. Trans. ASAE 26:814–820.

Dickson, R.E., B.C. Langley, and C.E. Fisher. 1940. Water and soil conservation experiments at Spur, Texas. Bull. 587. Texas Agric. Exp. Stn., College Station.

Dixon, R.M. 1966. Water infiltration responses to soil management practices. Ph.D. diss. The Univ. of Wisconsin, Madison. Diss. Abstr. 66-5903.

Dlugokencky, E.J., and R.C. Schnell. 2007. Carbon dioxide. Bull. Am. Meteorol. Soc. 88 (Supple. to No. 6):S18–S19.

Doyle, A.P. 1983. Stubble retention. Available at http://www.regional.org.au/au/roc/1983/roc198365.htm (verified 1 Oct. 2009).

Duley, F.L., and C.R. Fenster. 1961. Stubble-mulch farming methods for fallow areas. E C:54–100 Nebraska Ext. Serv., Lincoln.

Duley, F.L., and L.L. Kelly. 1939. Effect of soil type, slope, and surface conditions on intake of water. Res. Bull. 112. Agric. Exp. Stn., Univ. Nebraska, Lincoln.

Duley, F.L., and J.C. Russel. 1939. The use of crop residues for soil and moisture conservation. Agron. J. 31:703–709.

Duley, F.L., and J.C. Russel. 1942. Effects of stubble mulching on soil erosion and runoff. Soil Sci. Soc. Am. Proc. 7:77–81.

Eck, H.V., and H.M. Taylor. 1969. Profile modification of a slowly permeable soil. Soil Sci. Soc. Am. Proc. 33:779–783.

Eigel, J.D., and I.D. Moore. 1983. Effect of rainfall energy on infiltration into bare soil. p. 188–200. *In* Advances in infiltration, Proc. Natl. Conf. on Advances in Infiltration, Chicago, IL. 12–13 Dec. 1983. ASAE, St. Joseph, MI.

Erickson, A.E., C.M. Hanson, and A.J.M. Smucker. 1968. The influence of subsurface asphalt barriers on the water properties and the productivity of sand soils. Trans. 9th Int. Congr. Soil Sci. (Adelaide, Australia) 1:331–337.

Erskine, M.J. 1992. Vetiver grass: Its potential use in soil and moisture conservation in southern Africa. S. Afr. J. Sci. 88:298–299.

Fairbourn, M.L., and H.R. Gardner. 1972. Vertical mulch effects on soil water storage. Soil Sci. Soc. Am. Proc. 36:823–827.

Fairbourn, M.L., and H.R. Gardner. 1974. Field use of microwatersheds with vertical mulch. Agron. J. 66:740–744.

Fan, T., B.A. Stewart, W.A. Payne, Y. Wang, S. Song, J. Luo, and C.A. Robinson. 2005. Supplemental irrigation and water-yield relationships for plasticulture crops in the Loess Plateau of China. Agron. J. 97:177–188.

Farahani, H.J., G.A. Peterson, and D.G. Westfall. 1998. Dryland cropping intensification: A fundamental solution to efficient use of precipitation. Adv. Agron. 64:197–223.

Fehrenbacher, J.B., J.P. Vavra, and A.L. Long. 1958. Deep tillage and deep fertilization experiments on a claypan soil. Soil Sci. Soc. Am. Proc. 22:553–557.

Fenster, C.R. 1977. Conservation tillage in the Northern Plains. J. Soil Water Conserv. 32:37–42.

Fenster, C.R., N.P. Woodruff, W.S. Chepil, and F.H. Siddoway. 1965. Performance of tillage implements in a stubble mulch system: III. Effects of tillage sequences on residues, soil cloddiness, weed control, and wheat yield. Agron. J. 57:52–55.

Finnell, H.H. 1944. Water conservation in Great Plains wheat production. Bull. 655. Texas Agric. Exp. Stn., College Station.

Fisher, C.E., and E. Burnett. 1953. Conservation and utilization of soil moisture. Bull. 767. Texas Agric. Exp. Stn., College Station.

Folorunso, O.A., D.E. Rolston, T. Prichard, and D.T. Louie. 1992. Soil surface strength and infiltration rate as affected by winter cover crops. Soil Technol. 5:189–197.

Fortier, S. 1909. Soil mulches for checking evaporation. p. 465–472. *In* 1908 Yearbook of the USDA. U.S. Gov. Print. Office, Washington, DC.

Free, G.R. 1953. Stubble-mulch tillage in New York. Soil Sci. Soc. Am. Proc. 17:165–170.

Freebairn, D.M., P.S. Cornish, W.K. Anderson, S.R. Walker, J.B. Robinson, and A.R. Beswich. 2006. Management systems in climate regions of the world—Australia. p. 837–878. *In* G.A. Peterson et al. (ed.) Dryland agriculture. 2nd ed. Agron. Monogr. 23. ASA, CSSA, and SSSA, Madison, WI.

Gallacher, R.N. 1990. The search for low-input soil and water conservation techniques. Topics Appl. Resour. Manage. 2:11–37.

Gerard, C.J., P.D. Sexton, and D.M. Conover. 1984. Effect of furrow diking, subsoiling, and slope position on crop yield. Agron. J. 76:945–950.

Gerard, C.J., P.D. Sexton, and D.M. Matus. 1983. Furrow diking for cotton production in the Rolling Plains. Prog. Rep. PR-4174. Texas Agric. Exp. Stn., College Station.

Giménez, D., C. Dirksen, R. Miedema, L.A.A.J. Eppink, and D. Schoonderbeek. 1992. Surface sealing and hydraulic conductances under varying-intensity rains. Soil Sci. Soc. Am. J. 56:234–242.

Good, L.G., and D.E. Smika. 1978. Chemical fallow for soil and water conservation in the Great Plains. J. Soil Water Conserv. 33:89–90.

Greb, B.W. 1970. Deep plowing a shallow clay layer to increase soil water storage and crop yields. PR 70-23. Colorado St. Univ. Exp. Stn., Fort Collins.

Greb, B.W. 1975. Snowfall characteristics and snowmelt storage at Akron, Colorado. p. 45–64. In Proc. Symp. on Snow Management in the Great Plains, Bismarck, ND. 29 July 1975. Great Plains Agric. Counc., Lincoln, NE.

Greb, B.W. 1978. Weeds and water conservation in fallow. Ecofallow Conf., Ogallala, NB. 27 Feb. 1978.

Greb, B.W. 1979. Reducing drought effects on croplands in the west-central Great Plains. USDA Info. Bull. 420. U.S. Gov. Print Office, Washington, DC.

Greb, B.W. 1980. Snowfall and its potential management in the semiarid Central Great Plains. ARM-W-18. USDA, Agric. Res. Sci. and Educ. Admin., Western Region, Oakland, CA.

Greb, B.W., and A.L. Black. 1971. Vegetative barriers and artificial fences for managing snow in the central and northern plains. p. 96–111. In A.O Haugen (ed.) Proc. Snow and Ice in Relation to Wildlife and Recreation Symp., Ames, IA. 11–12 Feb. 1971. Iowa Coop. Wildlife Res. Unit, Iowa St. Univ., Ames.

Greb, B.W., D.E. Smika, and A.L. Black. 1970. Effect of straw-mulch rates on soil water storage during summer fallow in the Great Plains. Soil Sci. Soc. Am. Proc. 31:556–559.

Greb, B.W., D.E. Smika, N.P. Woodruff, and C.J. Whitfield. 1974. Summer fallow in the central Great Plains. p. 51–85. In Summer fallow in the western United States. USDA-ARS Conserv. Res. Rep. 17. U.S. Gov. Print. Office, Washington, DC.

Griffin, R.H., II, B.J. Ott, and J.F. Stone. 1966. Effect of water management and surface applied barriers on yields and moisture utilization of grain sorghum in the southern Great Plains. Agron. J. 58:449–452.

Griffith, D.R., J.V. Mannering, and W.C. Moldenhauer. 1977. Conservation tillage in the eastern Corn Belt. J. Soil Water Conserv. 32:20–28.

Haas, H.J., W.O. Willis, and J.J. Bond. 1974a. Introduction. p. 1–11. In Summer fallow in the western United States. USDA-ARS Conserv. Res. Rep. 17. U.S. Gov. Print. Office, Washington, DC.

Haas, H.J., W.O. Willis, and J.J. Bond. 1974b. Summer fallow in the northern Great Plains (spring wheat). p. 12–35. In Summer fallow in the western United States. USDA-ARS Conserv. Res. Rep. 17. U.S. Gov. Print. Office, Washington, DC.

Harker, D.B., G.R. Webster, and R.R. Cairns. 1977. Factors contributing to crop response on a deep-plowed Solonetz soil. Can. J. Soil Sci. 57:279–287.

Harper, H.J. 1941. The effect of terraces ridges on the production of winter wheat. Soil Sci. Soc. Am. Proc. 6:474–479.

Hatfield, J.L., D.C. Reicosky, J.L. Steiner, and S.B. Verma. 1992. Evaporation in agricultural systems: Implications for natural resource issues. Un-numbered report, NCR-160. Committee on Efficient Use of Water by Vegetation in Great Plains Environments, Ames, IA.

Hauser, V.L., and M.B. Cox. 1962. Evaluation of Zingg conservation bench terrace. Agric. Eng. 43:462–467.

Hauser, V.L., and H.M. Taylor. 1963. Deep tillage of High Plains Hardland soils. Texas Agric. Prog. 9(2):7–8.

Hauser, V.L., and H.M. Taylor. 1964. Evaluation of deep-tillage treatments on a slowly permeable soil. Trans. ASAE 7:134–136, 141.

Hauser, V.L., C.E. Van Doren, and J.S. Robins. 1962. A comparison of level and graded terraces in the southern Great Plains. Trans. ASAE 5:75–77.

Hauser, V.L., and A.W. Zingg. 1959. Conservation benching. Soil and Water 8:12.

Havlin, J.L., and A.J. Schlegel. 1997. Dryland conservation technologies: Enhancing agricultural profitability and sustainability. Ann. Arid Zone 36:291–303.

Heilman, M.D., and C.L. Gonzalez. 1973. Effect of narrow trenching in Harlingen clay soil on plant growth, rooting depth, and salinity. Agron. J. 65:816–819.

Hendrickson, B.H. 1939. Another look at the contour balk method. Soil Conserv. 5(2):36–37, 40.

Hillel, D. 1998. Environmental soil physics. Academic Press, San Diego, CA.

Horton, R.E. 1933. The role of infiltration in the hydrologic cycle. Trans. 14th Ann. Meeting, Am. Geophys. Union 14:446–460.

Howell, T.A., and S.R. Evett. 2005. Pathways to effective applications. p. 84–98. In Proc. 2005 Central Plains Irrig. Conf., Sterling, CO. 16–17 Feb. 2005.

Huxley, P.A. 1979. Zero-tillage at Morogoro, Tanzania. p. 259–265. In R. Lal (ed.) Soil tillage and crop production. Int. Inst. Tropical Agric. (IITA), Ibadan, Nigeria.

Jacks, G.V., W.D. Brind, and R. Smith. 1955. Mulching. Tech. Commun. 49. Commonwealth Bureau of Soil Sci., England.

Jalota, S.K., and S.S. Prihar. 1990. Bare-soil evaporation in relation to tillage. Adv. Soil Sci. 12:187–216.

James, E. 1945. Effect of certain cultural practices on moisture conservation on a Piedmont soil. J. Am. Soc. Agron. 37:945–952.

Jamison, V.C. 1953. Changes in air-water relationships due to structural improvement of soils. Soil Sci. 76:143–151.

Janick, J. 2002. Reading soil. Available at http://www.hort.purdue.edu/newcrop/tropical/lecture_06/ (verified 1 Oct. 2009).

Johnson, W.C., and R.G. Davis. 1972. Research on stubble-mulch farming of winter wheat. USDA Conserv. Res. Rep. 16. U.S. Gov. Print. Office, Washington, DC.

Johnson, W.C., C.E. Van Doren, and E. Burnett. 1974. Summer fallow in the southern Great Plains. p. 86–109. In Summer fallow in the western United States. USDA-ARS Conserv. Res. Rep. 17. U.S. Gov. Print. Office, Washington, DC.

Jones, O.R. 1981. Land forming effects on dryland sorghum production in the southern Great Plains. Soil Sci. Soc. Am. J. 45:606–611.

Jones, O.R., and R.N. Clark. 1987. Effects of furrow dikes on water conservation and dryland crop yields. Soil Sci. Soc. Am. J. 51:1307–1314.

Jones, O.R., and W.C. Johnson. 1983. Cropping practices: Southern Great Plains. p. 365–385. In H.E. Dregne and W.O. Willis (ed.) Dryland agriculture. Agron. Monogr. 23. ASA, CSSA, and SSSA, Madison, WI.

Jones, O.R., and T.W. Popham. 1997. Cropping and tillage practices for dryland grain production in the Southern High Plains. Agron. J. 89:222–232.

Keeney, D., and M. Muller. 2006. Water use by ethanol plants: Potential challenges. Inst. for Agric. and Trade Policy, Minneapolis, MN.

Kemper, W.D., T.J. Trout, A.S. Humpherys, and M.S. Bullock. 1988. Mechanism by which surge irrigation reduces furrow infiltration rates in a silty loam soil. Trans. ASAE 31:821–829.

Kimball, B.A. 1983. Carbon dioxide and agricultural yield: An assemblage and analysis of 430 prior observations. Agron. J. 75:779–788.

Kirkham, M.B., H. He, T.P. Bolger, D.J. Lawlor, and E.T. Kanemasu. 1991. Leaf photosynthesis and water use of big bluestem under elevated carbon dioxide. Crop Sci. 31:1589–1594.

Kladivko, E.J. 1994. Residue effects on soil physical properties. p. 123–141. In P.W. Unger (ed.) Managing agricultural residues. Lewis Publishers, Boca Raton, FL.

Klocke, N.L. 2004. Water savings from crop residue in irrigated corn. p. 133–141. In Proc. Central Plains Irrigation Conf., Kearney, NE. 17–18 Feb. 2004.

Krishna, J.H., G.F. Arkin, J.R. Williams, and J.R. Mulkey. 1986. Modeling furrow dike effects on runoff and crop yields. Paper 86-2016. ASAE, St. Joseph, MI.

Kuhn, T.J., K.W. Tate, D. Cao, and M.R. George. 2007. Juniper removal may not increase overall Klamath River Basin water yields. Calif. Agric. 61(4):166–171.

Lado, M., A. Paz, and M. Ben-Hur. 2004. Organic matter and aggregate size interactions in infiltration, seal formation, and soil loss. Soil Sci. Soc. Am. J. 68:935–942.

Lamm, F.R., and R.M. Aiken. 2007. Tillage and irrigation capacity effects on corn production. Paper 072283. ASABE, St. Joseph, MI.

Lamm, F.R., R.M. Aiken, and A.A. Abou Kheira. 2008. Effects of tillage practices and deficit irrigation on corn. p. 84–100. In Proc. Central Plains Irrigation Conf., Greeley, CO. 19–20 Feb. 2008. CPIA, Colby, KS.

Landa, E.R., and J.R. Nimmo. 2003. The life and scientific contributions of Lyman J. Briggs. Soil Sci. Soc. Am. J. 67:681–693.

Lascano, R.J., R.L. Baumhardt, S.K. Hicks, and J.L. Heilman. 1994. Soil and plant water evaporation from strip-tilled cotton: Measurement and simulation. Agron. J. 86:987–994.

Lemon, E.R. 1956. The potentialities for decreasing soil moisture evaporation loss. Soil Sci. Soc. Am. Proc. 20:120–125.

Lentz, R.D., and D.L. Bjorneberg. 2003. Polyacrylamide and straw residue effects on irrigation furrow erosion and infiltration. J. Soil Water Conserv. 58:312–319.

Lentz, R.D., I. Shainberg, R.E. Sojka, and D.L. Carter. 1992. Preventing irrigation furrow erosion with small applications of polymers. Soil Sci. Soc. Am. J. 56:1926–1932.

Levy, S. 2003. Turbulence in the Klamath River basin. Bioscience 53:315–320.

Lewis, W.M. 1985. Weed control in reduced-tillage soybean production. p. 41–50. *In* A.F. Wiese (ed.) Weed control in limited-tillage systems. Weed Sci. Soc. Am., Champaign, IL.

Loch, R.J. 1989. Aggregate breakdown under rain: Its measurement and interpretation. Ph.D. thesis. Univ. of New England, QLD, Australia.

Lyle, W.M., and J.P. Bordovsky. 1981. Low energy precision application (LEPA) irrigation system. Trans. ASAE 24:1241–1245.

Lyle, W.M., and J.P. Bordovsky. 1983. LEPA irrigation system evaluation. Trans. ASAE 26:776–781.

Ma, S. 1988. Advances in mulch farming in China. p. 510–511. *In* P.W. Unger et al. (ed.) Challenges in dryland agriculture, A global perspective. Proc. Int. Conf. on Dryland Farming, Amarillo/Bushland, TX. 15–19 Aug. 1988. Texas Agric. Exp. Stn., College Station.

Mahler, R.L., F.G. Bailey, S. Norris, and K.A. Loeffelman. 2003. BMPs for erosion control. Available at http://www.uidaho.edu/wq/wqbr/wqbr27.html (revised 3 Jan. 2003; verified 1 Oct. 2009).

Mannering, J.V., and L.D. Meyer. 1963. The effects of various rates of surface mulch on infiltration and erosion. Soil Sci. Soc. Am. Proc. 27:84–86.

Maulé, C.P., and D.S. Chanasyk. 1990. The effects of tillage upon snow cover and spring soil water. Can. Agric. Eng. 32:25–31.

McCalla, T.M., and T.J. Army. 1961. Stubble-mulch farming. Adv. Agron. 13:125–196.

McConkey, B.G., H. Steppuhn, and W. Nicholaichuk. 1990. Effects of fall subsoiling and snow management on water conservation and continuous spring wheat yields in southwestern Saskatchewan. Can. Agric. Eng. 32:225–234.

McConkey, B.G., D.J. Ulrich, and F.B. Dyck. 1997. Snow management and deep tillage for increasing crop yields on a rolling landscape. Can. J. Soil Sci. 77:479–486.

McMaster, G.S., R.M. Aiken, and D.C. Nielsen. 2000. Optimizing wheat harvest cutting height for harvest efficiency and soil and water conservation. Agron. J. 92:1104–1108.

McWhorter, C.G., and T.N. Jordan. 1985. Limited tillage in cotton production. p. 61–76. *In* A.F. Wiese (ed.) Weed control in limited-tillage systems. Weed Sci. Soc. Am., Champaign, IL.

Mead, J.A., and K.Y. Chan. 1988. Effect of deep tillage and seedbed preparation on the growth and yield of wheat on a hard-setting soil. Aust. J. Exp. Agric. 28:491–498.

Mech, S.J., G.M. Horner, L.M. Cox, and E.E. Cary. 1967. Soil profile modification by backhoe mixing and deep plowing. Trans. ASAE 10:775–779.

Mickelson, R.H. 1966. Level pan construction for diverting and spreading runoff. Trans. ASAE 9:568–570.

Mickelson, R.H. 1968. Conservation bench terraces in eastern Colorado. Trans. ASAE 11:389–392.

Miller, D.E., and J.S. Aarstad. 1972. Effect of deep plowing on the physical characteristics of Hezel soil. Circulation 556. Washington Agric. Exp. Stn., Pullman.

Moll, S. 1997. Commercial experience and benefits from glyphosate tolerant crops. p. 931–946. *In* Proc. 1997 Brighton Crop Prot. Conf.—Weeds, Brighton, UK. 17–20 Nov. 1997. British Crop Prot. Counc. (now BCPC), Alton, Hampshire, UK.

Moody, J.E., J.N. Jones, Jr., and J.H. Lillard. 1963. Influence of straw-mulch on soil moisture, soil temperature, and growth of corn. Soil Sci. Soc. Am. Proc. 27:700–703.

Mukhtar, S., J.L. Baker, R. Horton, and D.C. Erbach. 1985. Soil water infiltration as affected by the use of the paraplow. Trans. ASAE 28:1811–1816.

Musick, J.T., D.A. Dusek, and A.D. Schneider. 1981. Deep tillage of irrigated Pullman clay loam—A long-term evaluation. Trans. ASAE 24:1515–1519.

Musick, J.T., F.B. Pringle, W.L. Harman, and B.A. Stewart. 1988. Long-term irrigation trends—Texas High Plains. ASAE Paper SWR 88-103. ASAE, St. Joseph, MI.

National Academy of Sciences. 2007. Water implications of biofuels production in the United States. Report in brief, October 2007. The National Academy of Sciences, Washington, DC.

Nicou, R., and J.L. Chopart. 1979. Water management methods in sandy soils of Senegal. p. 248–258. *In* R. Lal (ed.) Soil tillage and crop production. Int. Inst. Tropical Agric. (IITA), Ibadan, Nigeria.

Nielsen, D.C. 1998. Snow catch and soil water recharge in standing sunflower residue. J. Prod. Agric. 11:476–480.

Nielsen, D.C., M.F. Vigil, and J.G. Benjamin. 2006. Evaluating decision rules for dryland crop selection. *In* Annual Meetings Abstracts [CD]. ASA, CSSA, and SSSA, Madison, WI.

Padgette, S.R., K.H. Kolacz, X. Delannay, D.B. Re, B.J. LaVallee, C.N. Tinius, W.K. Rhodes, Y.I. Otero, G.F. Barry, D.A. Eichholtz, V.M. Peschke, D.L. Nida, N.B. Taylor, and G.M. Kishore. 1995. Development, identification, and characterization of a glyphosate-tolerant soybean line. Crop Sci. 35:1451–1461.

Papendick, R.I., M.J. Lindstrom, and V.L. Cochran. 1973. Soil mulch effects on seedbed temperature and water during fallow in eastern Washington. Soil Sci. Soc. Am. Proc. 37:307–314.

Papendick, R.I., and D.E. Miller. 1977. Conservation tillage in the Pacific Northwest. J. Soil Water Conserv. 32:49–56.

Papendick, R.I., and J.F. Parr. 1989. The value of crop residues for water conservation. *In* Soil, crop and water management in the Sudano-Sahelian zone. Proc. Int. Workshop, ICRISAT Sahelian Center, Niamey, Niger. 7–11 Jan. 1987. ICRISAT, Patancheru, India.

Peterson, G.A., and D.G. Westfall. 2004. Managing precipitation use in sustainable dryland agroecosystems. Ann. Appl. Biol. 144:127–138.

Philip, J.R. 1969. Theory of infiltration. Adv. Hydrosci. 5:215–290.

Pikul, J.L., D.E. Wilkins, J.K. Aase, and J.F. Zuzel. 1996. Contour ripping: A tillage strategy to improve water infiltration into frozen soil. J. Soil Water Conserv. 51:76–83.

Pikul, J.L., Jr., J.F. Zuzel, and D.E. Wilkins. 1992. Infiltration in frozen soil as affected by ripping. Trans. ASAE 35:83–90.

Pressland, A.J., and G.N. Batianoff. 1976. Soil water conservation under cultivated fallows in clay soils of south-western Queensland. Aust. J. Exp. Agric. Anim. Husb. 16:564–569.

Rachman, A., S.H. Anderson, C.J. Gantzer, and A.L. Thompson. 2004. Influence of stiff-stemmed grass hedge systems on infiltration. Soil Sci. Soc. Am. J. 68:2000–2006.

Rasche, E., and M. Gadsby. 1997. Glufosinate ammonium resistant crops: International commercial developments and experiences. p. 941–946. *In* Proc. 1997 Brighton Crop Prot. Conf.—Weeds, Brighton, UK. 17–20 Nov. 1997. British Crop Prot. Counc. (now BCPC), Alton, Hampshire, UK.

Reinhardt, C., and B. Ganzel. 2007. Farming in the 1930s. Available at http://www.livinghistoryfarm.org/farminginthe30s/pests_06.html (verified 1 Oct. 2009).

Richardson, C.W. 1973. Runoff, erosion, and tillage efficiency on graded-furrow and terraced watersheds. J. Soil Water Conserv. 28:162–164.

Ritchie, J.T. 1972. Model for predicting evaporation from a row crop with incomplete cover. Water Resour. Res. 8:1204–1213.

Robertson, W.K., L.C. Hammond, G.K. Saxena, and H.W. Lundy. 1973. Influence of water management through irrigation and a subsurface asphalt layer on seasonal growth and nutrient uptake of corn. Agron. J. 65:866–870.

Robinson, A.B., N.E. Robinson, and W. Soon. 2007. Environmental effects of increased atmospheric carbon dioxide. J. Am. Phys. Surg. 12:79–90.

Rothfeder, J. 2001. Every drop for sale. Penguin Putnam, Inc., New York.

Russell, E.W. 1988. Russell's soil conditions and plant growth. 11th ed. A. Wild (ed.) Longman Group, UK.

Saxena, G.K., L.C. Hammond, and H.W. Lundy. 1969. Yield and water-use efficiency of vegetables as influenced by a soil moisture barrier. Proc. Florida State Hort. Soc. 82:168–172.

Saxena, G.K., L.C. Hammond, and W.K. Robertson. 1973. Effects of subsurface asphalt layers on corn and tomato root systems. Agron. J. 65:191–194.

Saxton, K.E., D.K. McCool, and R.I. Papendick. 1981. Slot mulch for runoff and erosion control. J. Soil Water Conserv. 36:44–47.

Schillinger, W.F., and F.L. Young. 2000. Soil water use and growth of Russian thistle after wheat harvest. Agron. J. 92:167–172.

Setter, T.L. 2006. Identifying genes and their functions for drought tolerance of maize at early kernel development (abstract). *In* Annual Meetings Abstracts [CD]. ASA, CSSA, SSSA, Madison, WI.

Shaw, T. 1911. Dry land farming. The Pioneer Co., St. Paul, MN.

Shaxson, F., and R. Barber. 2003. Optimizing soil moisture for plant production. FAO Soils Bull. 79. FAO, Rome.

Shear, G.M. 1985. Introduction and history of limited tillage. p. 1–14. In A.F. Wiese (ed.) Weed control in limited-tillage systems. Weed Sci. Soc. Am., Champaign, IL.

Smika, D.E. 1983. Soil water change as related to position of straw mulch on the soil surface. Soil Sci. Soc. Am. J. 47:988–991.

Soil Science Society of America. 2001. Glossary of soil science terms. SSSA, Madison, WI.

Steiner, J.L. 1989. Tillage and surface residue effects on evaporation from soil. Soil Sci. Soc. Am. J. 53:911–916.

Steiner, J.L., E.T. Kanemasu, and R.N. Clark. 1983. Spray losses and partitioning of water under a center pivot sprinkler system. Trans. ASAE 26:1128–1134.

Steppuhn, H., and J. Waddington. 1996. Conserving water and increasing alfalfa production using a tall wheatgrass windbreak system. J. Soil Water Conserv. 51:439–445.

Steppuhn, H., J. Waddington, and B.G. McConkey. 1995. Subsoiling to improve snowmelt infiltration and alfalfa yields within tall wheatgrass windbreaks. Can. Agric. Eng. 37:261–268.

Stewart, B.A. 2003. Aquifers, Ogallala. p. 43–44. In B.A. Stewart and T.A. Howell (ed.) Encycl. Water Sci. Marcel Dekker, New York.

Stewart, B.A., and T.A. Howell. 2003. Preface. p. xvii–xviii. In B.A. Stewart and T.A. Howell (ed.) Encycl. Water Sci. Marcel Dekker, New York.

Tanner, C.B., and Y. Shen. 1990. Water vapor transport through a flail-chopped corn residue. Soil Sci. Soc. Am. J. 54:945–951.

Tanner, C.B., and T.R. Sinclair. 1983. Efficient water use in crop production: Research or re-search? p. 1–27. In H.M. Taylor et al. (ed.) Limitations to efficient water use in crop production. ASA, CSSA, and SSSA, Madison, WI.

Taylor, S.A., and G.L. Ashcroft. 1972. Physical edaphology. W.H. Freeman and Co., San Francisco, CA.

Thomas, G.W. 1985. Managing minimum-tillage fields, fertility, and soil type. p. 211–226. In A.F. Wiese (ed.) Weed control in limited-tillage systems. Weed Sci. Soc. Am., Champaign, IL.

Todd, R.W., N.L. Klocke, G.W. Hergert, and A.M. Parkhurst. 1991. Evaporation from soil influenced by crop shading, crop residue, and wetting regime. Trans. ASAE 34:461–466.

Travis, G.R., D.S. Chanasyk, and B.A. Paterson. 1990. Effects of deep plowing on soil water content and drainage of Solonetzic and associated soils. Can. Agric. Eng. 33:231–238.

Triplett, G.B., Jr. 1985. Principles of weed control for reduced-tillage corn production. p. 26–40. In A.F. Wiese (ed.) Weed control in limited-tillage systems. Weed Sci. Soc. Am., Champaign, IL.

Trout, T.J., R.E. Sojka, and R.D. Lentz. 1995. Polyacrylamide effect on furrow erosion and infiltration. Trans. ASAE 38:761–765.

Tvedten, S. 2001. History of pest management—History of the development of organophosphate poisons. Available at http://www.safe2use.com/ca-ipm/01-04-27.htm (verified 1 Oct. 2009).

Twomlow, S., R. Riches, and S. Mabasa. 1997. Weeding—Its contribution to soil water conservation in semi-arid maize production. p. 185–190. In Proc. 1997 Brighton Crop Prot. Conf.—Weeds, Brighton, UK. 17–20 Nov. 1997. British Crop Prot. Counc. (now BCPC), Alton, Hampshire, UK.

Unger, P.W. 1972. Dryland winter wheat and grain sorghum cropping systems—Northern High Plains of Texas. Bull. 1126. Texas Agric. Exp. Stn., College Station.

Unger, P.W. 1977. Tillage effects on winter wheat production where the irrigated and dryland crops are alternated. Agron. J. 69:944–950.

Unger, P.W. 1978. Straw-mulch rate effect on soil water storage and sorghum yield. Soil Sci. Soc. Am. J. 42:486–491.

Unger, P.W. 1979. Effects of deep tillage and profile modification on soil properties, root growth, and crop yields in the United States and Canada. Geoderma 22:275–295.

Unger, P.W. 1984. Tillage and residue effects on wheat, sorghum, and sunflower grown in rotation. Soil Sci. Soc. Am. J. 48:885–891.

Unger, P.W. 1992. Infiltration of simulated rainfall: Tillage system and crop residue effects. Soil Sci. Soc. Am. J. 56:283–289.

Unger, P.W. 1993. Residual effects of soil profile modification on water infiltration, bulk density, and wheat yield. Agron. J. 85:656–659.

Unger, P.W. 1995. Role of mulches in dryland agriculture. p. 241–270. In U.S. Gupta (ed.) Production and improvement of crops for drylands. Oxford & IBH Publ. Co., Pvt. Ltd., New Delhi.

Unger, P.W. 2001. Alternative and opportunity dryland crops and related soil conditions in the Southern Great Plains. Agron. J. 93:216–226.

Unger, P.W. 2006. Soil and water conservation handbook: Policies, practices, conditions, and terms. The Haworth Press, Inc., New York.

Unger, P.W., and T.A. Howell. 1999. Agricultural water conservation—A global perspective. p. 1–36. *In* M.B. Kirkham (ed.) Water use in crop production. The Haworth Press, Inc., New York.

Unger, P.W., W.A. Payne, and G.A. Peterson. 2006. Water conservation and efficient use. p. 39–85. *In* G.A. Peterson et al. (ed.) Dryland agriculture. 2nd ed. Agron. Monogr. 23. ASA, CSSA, and SSSA, Madison, WI.

Unger, P.W., and M.F. Vigil. 1998. Cover crop effects on soil water relationships. J. Soil Water Conserv. 53:200–207.

Unger, P.W., and A.F. Wiese. 1979. Managing irrigated winter wheat residues for water storage and subsequent dryland grain sorghum production. Soil Sci. Soc. Am. J. 43:582–588.

USDA. 1908. Agricultural experiment stations of the United States, their locations, directors, and principal lines of work. p. 507–510. *In* 1907 Yearbook of the USDA. U.S. Gov. Print. Office, Washington, DC.

van Bavel, C.H.M., and R.J. Hanks. 1983. Water conservation: Principles of soil water flow, evaporation, and evapotranspiration. p. 25–34. *In* H.E. Dregne and W.O. Willis (ed.) Dryland agriculture. Agron. Monogr. 23. ASA, CSSA, and SSSA, Madison, WI.

Van Doren, D.M., Jr., and R.R. Allmaras. 1978. Effect of residue management practices on the soil physical environment, microclimate, and plant growth. p. 49–83. *In* W.R. Oschwald (ed.) Crop residue management systems. ASA Spec. Publ. 31. ASA, CSSA, and SSSA, Madison, WI.

Vyn, T.J., G. Opoku, and C.J. Swanton. 1998. Residue management and minimum tillage systems for soybeans following wheat. Agron. J. 90:131–138.

Wagner-Riddle, C., T.J. Gillespie, and C.J. Swanton. 1994. Rye cover crop management impact on soil water content, soil temperature and soybean growth. Can. J. Plant Sci. 74:485–495.

Wangemann, S.G., R.A. Kohl, and P.A. Molumeli. 2000. Infiltration and percolation influenced by antecedent soil water content and air entrapment. Trans. ASAE 43:1515–1523.

Wendt, C.W. 1973. Effects of a minimum tillage-vertical mulch concept on soil moisture and yield of grain sorghum at Lubbock, Texas, 1970–1971. Prog. Rep. PR-3152. Texas Agric. Exp. Stn., College Station.

West, T.D., D.R. Griffith, and G.C. Steinhardt. 1996. Effect of paraplowing on crop yields with no-tillage planting. J. Prod. Agric. 9:233–237.

Whitfield, C.J., C.E. Van Doren, and W. Johnson. 1949. Stubble mulch management for water conservation and erosion control on hardlands of the southern Great Plains. Bull. 711. Texas Agric. Exp. Stn., College Station.

Wicks, G.A. 1985. Weed control in conservation tillage systems– Small grains. p. 77–92. *In* A.F. Wiese (ed.) Weed control in limited tillage systems. Weed Sci. Soc. Am., Champaign, IL.

Wicks, G.A., and D.E. Smika. 1973. Chemical fallow in a wheat-fallow rotation. J. Weed Sci. Soc. Am. 21:97–102.

Wicks, G.A., D.E. Smika, and C.R. Fenster. 1972. Ecofallow—Has its time come? Paper, 1972 Nebraska Wheat Advisory Committee Meeting.

Widtsoe, J.A. 1920. Dry-farming. The MacMillan Co., New York.

Wiedemann, H.T., and B.A. Smallacombe. 1989. Chain diker—A new tool to reduce runoff. Agric. Eng. 70(5):12–15.

Wiese, A.F., T.J. Army, and J.D. Thomas. 1966. Moisture utilization by plants after herbicide treatment. Weeds 14:205–207.

Wiese, A.F., E. Burnett, and J.E. Box, Jr. 1967. Chemical fallow in dryland cropping sequences. Agron. J. 59:175–177.

Wiese, A.F., P.W. Unger, and R.R. Allen. 1985. p. 51–60. *In* A.F. Wiese (ed.) Weed control in limited-tillage systems. Weed Sci. Soc. Am., Champaign, IL.

Wilhelm, W.W., J.M.F. Johnson, D.L. Karlen, and D.T. Lightle. 2007. Corn stover to sustain soil organic carbon further constrains biomass supply. Agron. J. 99:1665–1667.

Willis, W.O., H.J. Haas, and J.S. Robbins. 1963. Moisture conservation by surface and subsurface barriers and soil configuration under semiarid conditions. Soil Sci. Soc. Am. Proc. 27:577–580.

Wockner, G., D. Freebairn, G. Hamilton, and P. Rowlands. 1996. The rough and smooth of rainfall capture in the Maranoa. Available at http://www.regional.org.au/au/asa/1996/poster/731Wockner.htm (verified 1 Oct. 2009).

Wood, C.W., D.G. Westfall, and G.A. Peterson. 1991. Soil carbon and nitrogen changes on initiation of no-till cropping systems. Soil Sci. Soc. Am. J. 55:470–476.

Yang, Q., S. Xue, R. Zhu, and W. Han. 2000. Integrated technique system of dry-farming and water-saving agriculture and mechanization in dry land of China. p. 131–136. *In* D. Niu et al. (ed.) Mechanized dryland and water-saving farming for the 21st century. Proc. China Int. Conf. on Dryland and Water-Saving Farming, Beijing, P.R. China. November 2000. China Agric. Univ. Press, Beijing.

Zingg, A.W., and V.L. Hauser. 1959. Terrace benching to save potential runoff for semiarid land. Agron. J. 51:289–292.

Zingg, A.W., and C.J. Whitfield. 1957. A summary of research experience with stubble-mulch farming. USDA Tech. Bull. 1160. U.S. Gov. Print. Office, Washington, DC.

Zuzel, J.F., and J.L. Pikul. 1987. Infiltration into a seasonally frozen agricultural soil. J. Soil Water Conserv. 42:447–450.

2

Soil and Water Challenges for Pacific Northwest Agriculture

William F. Schillinger
Dep. of Crop and Soil Sciences, Washington State University, Dryland Research Station, Lind, WA

Robert I. Papendick
retired, formerly USDA-ARS, Land Management and Water Conservation Research Unit, Pullman, WA

Donald K. McCool
USDA-ARS, Land Management and Water Conservation Research Unit, Pullman, WA

The focus of this chapter is the Pacific Northwest (PNW) of the United States. We highlight Columbia Basin and Columbia Plateau farmlands in eastern Washington, north-central Oregon, and northern Idaho, also referred to as the Inland PNW (Fig. 2–1). Both dryland and irrigated agriculture are practiced. Dryland farming began first in the higher precipitation region known as the Palouse in southeastern Washington and bordering Idaho in the 1860s by pioneers from Midwest states who sought free and clear title to farmland through the Homestead Act of 1862 (Meinig, 1968). By 1880 settlements were expanding into the low precipitation zones, and by 1907 all available farmland was claimed. Irrigated farming was practiced on a small scale from the earliest days by diverting water from perennial waterways and creeks. In 1905 the Yakima Basin Irrigation Project (Fig. 2–1) was initiated with the building of a series of dams on the Yakima River to divert water for irrigation. Beginning in 1951 large tracts of native desert land in east-central Washington came under crop production from water pumped from behind the Grand Coulee Dam by the federal Columbia Basin Project. Other irrigated farmland was established with water diverted from the Columbia River and its tributaries along the Oregon-Washington border and from deep wells dug mostly in the 1960s. Today, dryland agriculture is practiced on 3,348,000 ha and irrigated agriculture on 646,000 ha in the Inland PNW (Table 2–1).

Wind erosion is a major agricultural concern in the low-precipitation (<300 mm annual) rainfed area (Fig. 2–2) and in the irrigated Columbia Basin and Yakima Basin (Fig. 2–3), where limited crop residue, excessive tillage, drought, poorly aggregated soils with low organic matter content, and high winds combine to cause dust storms that transport suspended soil particulates long distances (Papendick, 2004). Nitrate leaching from irrigated agriculture into domestic groundwater supplies is also a problem. Soils are primarily silts and fine sands

---

Soil and Water Conservation Advances in the United States. SSSA Special Publication 60.
T.M. Zobeck and W.F. Schillinger, editors. © 2010. SSSA, 677 S. Segoe Rd., Madison, WI 53711, USA.

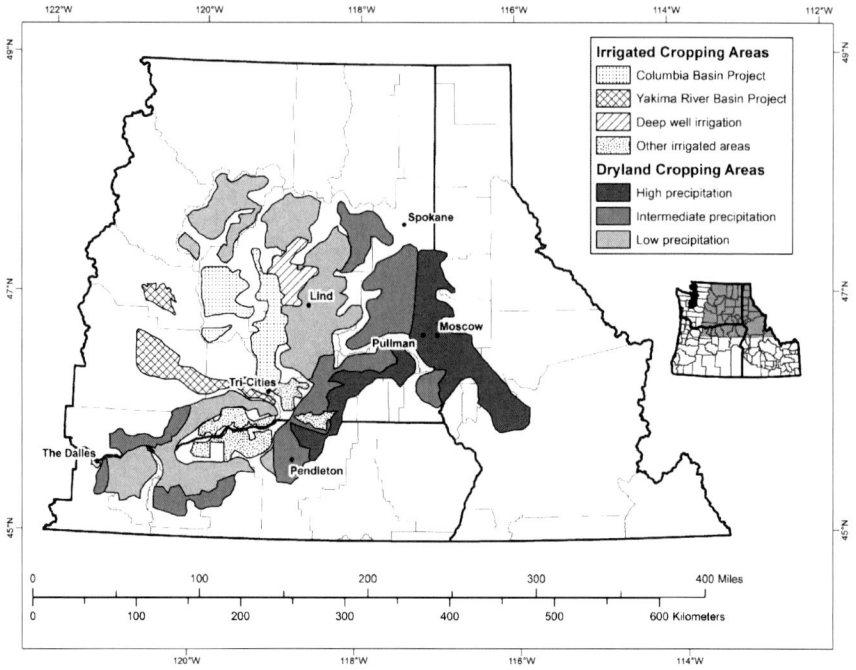

Fig. 2-1. Irrigated and dryland cropping areas of the Inland Pacific Northwest.

Table 2-1. Land area devoted to dryland and irrigated cropping in the Inland Pacific Northwest.

Type of farming	State†	Land area
		ha
1. Dryland		
Low (<300 mm)‡	Washington	1,223,000
	Oregon	334,000
Intermediate (300–450 mm)	Washington	621,000
	Oregon	323,000
	Idaho	25,000
High (450–600 mm)	Washington	382,000
	Idaho	374,000
	Oregon	66,000
2. Irrigation from rivers	Washington	487,000
	Oregon	72,000
3. Irrigation from deep wells	Washington	61,000
	Oregon	26,000

† Total rainfed crop hectares by state in the Inland PNW: Washington 2,226,000; Oregon 723,000; Idaho 399,000. Total irrigated crop hectares by state in the Inland PNW: Washington 548,000; Oregon 98,000.

‡ Numbers in parentheses are average annual precipitation.

Fig. 2–2. Severely wind-eroded summer fallow in Adams county, Washington, in September 1931. Winter wheat grain yield and residue production was low in 1930 following several years of drought. The fields were moldboard plowed to a depth of 13 cm in the spring and then harrowed. Subsequent winds eroded the unprotected soil to plow depth. Here Russian thistle, the most problematic broadleaf weed in the low precipitation zone, provides the only protection from wind erosion, with each thistle holding its quota of soil in lee. Photo: Washington State University Holland Library Archives, Pullman, WA.

Fig. 2–3. Blowing dust from newly planted potato fields in the Columbia Basin in April 1996. Photo: Harold Crose, USDA-NRCS, Ephrata, WA.

that are dominated by particulates <100 μm in diameter and vulnerable to wind erosion by direct suspension (Sharratt et al., 2007).

Water erosion is the primary environmental problem affecting farming and ecology in the intermediate (300–450 mm) and high (450–600 mm) average annual precipitation zones (Fig. 2–4). The highest water erosion rates occur with rapid snowmelt or rain on thawed soil overlying a frozen layer, especially with newly planted winter wheat (*Triticum aestivum* L.) following summer fallow or grain legumes that leave little protective residue cover. We concentrate on Whitman county, WA because it lies in the heart of the high-precipitation Palouse wheat region characterized by steep rolling hills prone to extreme water erosion and where more wheat is produced than in any other county in the United States.

Significant progress in wind and water erosion control and increased water use efficiency has occurred in the past 30 yr. Today's modern tractors, implements, and associated technologies enable farmers to combine field operations in one pass in a timely manner with reduced labor and energy per hectare. Effective use of glyphosate [*N*-([phosphonomethyl)glycine] and other herbicides has greatly reduced the need for tillage and/or eliminated some operations entirely. Numerous research advances and increased technical know-how along with economic incentives (and disincentives) by government farm programs, increased environmental awareness, and escalating input costs have resulted in an ongoing gradual shift to conservation-till, strip-till, and no-till farming.

Description of the Region
Climate

The Mediterranean-like climate of the inland PNW is largely influenced by frontal weather systems moving with prevailing westerly winds from the Pacific Ocean. The Cascade Mountains to the west impose a rain shadow effect. The driest part of the Inland PNW is just east of the Cascade Mountains, where average annual precipitation drops to 125 mm and gradually rises west to east with increase in elevation to 600 mm in the Palouse region.

Dryland agriculture is practiced in areas of south-central Washington that receive as little as 150 mm average annual precipitation, this being among the lowest for dryland wheat production in the world. Precipitation intensities and volumes are low, usually not exceeding 2 to 3 mm h^{-1} and 10 to 20 mm per event. Seventy percent of annual precipitation occurs from October through March, and 25% from April through June. July through September is the driest period. Most vegetation, excluding a few native plants, matures before or is dormant during the dry summer.

Winter weather is cool to cold with mean daily temperature in December and January of −1 and −2°C, respectively, but occasionally dropping to −10°C or lower. During extreme cold, soil that is not covered with snow may freeze to depths of 40 cm, which can lead to heavy water runoff and soil erosion when weather changes bring rain or cause rapid snow melt (Ramig et al., 1983). During summer, high-pressure systems dominate the weather, leading to warm, dry conditions and low relative humidity. Average afternoon temperatures in summer range between 20 and 35°C.

After crop harvest, between 60 and 75% of over-winter precipitation is stored in the soil. These high precipitation storage efficiencies enhance the success of cool-season cereals and legumes. This makes the PNW different from most other

Fig. 2–4. Water erosion in the Palouse on slopes greater than 30%. (Top) Mass failure erosion, where whole portions of saturated soil up to 2 m deep have slipped downward in a field of newly planted winter wheat that lacks surface residue and roots to bind the soil. (Bottom) Severe rill and gully erosion and sedimentation in moldboard plow-based farming. Winter precipitation, steep slopes, thawed surface layers overlying frozen subsurface soils, and rapid snowmelt by chinook wind require that farmland have adequate residue cover throughout the winter. Photos: Washington State University Holland Library Archives, Pullman, WA.

locations with similar annual precipitation, where most precipitation comes as summer rainfall.

Average wind speeds are low throughout the year. However, high winds lasting 24 to 36 h with sustained speeds of 60 to 70 km h^{-1} and gusts up to 125 km h^{-1} that occur with occasional storms when the soil surface is dry are the main cause of wind erosion. These events are relatively isolated and mostly associated with the change of seasons in the fall and spring, but sometimes in the winter. The dust storms can result in annual soil losses of hundreds of megagrams per hectare from susceptible fields and carry dust particulates thousands of kilometers, extending well beyond the boundaries of the PNW.

Soils

Most of the dry farmed soils of the Columbia Plateau are derived from loess deposits, much coming in the last 15,000 years from silty glacial materials carried by cataclysmic outburst floods from Glacial Lake Missoula and released in the path of prevailing westerly winds (McDonald and Busacca, 1988; Busacca, 1989). Many soils have been modified by volcanic depositions and contain, on average, 12% volcanic glass (Busacca et al., 2001). These authors describe the PNW soils as "ash influenced or volcanic influenced" but not volcanic. Farmed soils range in depth from <1 to >7 m in the dry zone and up to 75 m to bedrock where precipitation is higher. Soils are permeable and well drained and in most areas have adequate depth to store winter precipitation. Some that are shallow limit productivity due to low water storage capacity. Where average annual precipitation is >230 mm the soils are primarily Mollisols that originally contained 1.5 to 3.5% soil organic matter. In the drier areas the soils are Aridisols and some Entisols having native organic matter contents of ≤1%. Today after more than 125 years of intensive farming, organic matter contents of most soils have decreased 50 to 60% from original levels (Rasmussen and Parton, 1994).

Soils throughout the Columbia Plateau are predominantly silt loams. However, they grade in sand, clay, and organic matter content in line with the prevailing westerly winds. The soils in the southwestern fringes have the highest sand and lowest organic matter contents and gradually increase in clay and organic matter in the northeasterly direction in trend with prevailing winds and increasing precipitation. Soil textures of the loess soils are generally relatively uniform to the underlying bedrock.

Most soils of the irrigated Columbia Basin are derived from sediments deposited by the same floods 15,000 years ago. These sediments in the presence of an arid climate were winnowed by southwesterly winds and ultimately contributed to the loess deposits in areas of the Columbia Plateau to the north and east (Sweeney et al., 2007). The process resulted in fine sandy soils with very low organic matter content throughout much of the Columbia Basin. The depth, stratification, and permeability of Columbia Basin soils are ideal for irrigated production of grains, vegetables, and fruits adaptable to the Basin's long growing season.

Crops and Cropping Systems
Irrigated Areas

There are two major irrigation projects in the Inland PNW located in central Washington. This land was considered too dry for rainfed agriculture and mostly remained in native bluebunch wheatgrass [*Pseudoroegneria spicata* (Pursh) Á. Löve], basin wildrye [*Leymus cinereus* (Scribn. & Merr.) Á. Löve], needle and thread [*Hesperostipa comata* (Trin. & Rupr.) Barkworth], and other perennial grasses intermixed with shrubs such as big sagebrush (*Artemisia tridentata* Nutt.), gray rabbitbrush [*Ericameria nauseosa* (Pall. ex Pursh) G.L. Nesom & G.I. Baird], and western yarrow (*Achillea millefolium* L.), until broken out for irrigated farming.

The Yakima River Basin Project (Fig. 2–1) was initiated in 1905 by building a series of dams along the Yakima River to capture water from the eastern watershed of the Cascade Mountains that drains an area of 15,940 km^{-2}. The Yakima Basin is one of the most intensively irrigated areas in the United States. Main canals and laterals deliver water to 206,000 ha of cropland along 280 km on both sides of the Yakima River.

The Columbia Basin Project began in 1951 following construction of the Grand Coulee Dam on the Columbia River in 1942. About 3% of the Columbia River's flow is lifted from behind the dam at an average rate of 450 m^3 water s^{-1}. Water is distributed throughout the project via main canals, feeder canals, siphons, and tunnels. The original plan was to irrigate 420,000 ha, but only 263,000 ha has been completed to date (Fig. 2–1) as the second half of the project was postponed due to lack of federal funding. The annual value of crops produced with water from the Yakima River Basin and Columbia Basin Projects exceeds $1 billion (NASS, 2008).

Irrigation water is applied through furrows, high-volume impact sprinklers, low-volume drop nozzle sprinklers, micro-irrigation systems, and drip lines, and there is a corresponding increase in water use efficiency, respectively, with these delivery systems (Howell, 2001). Approximately 20% of cropland in the Columbia Basin and Yakima River Basin Projects is still in furrow irrigation. Furrow irrigation is used exclusively on some high-value seed crops where water droplets on the leaf surface from sprinkler irrigation can elevate fungal diseases of some crops (Troy Peters, Washington State University, personal communication, 2008) and also occasionally interfere with crop pollination.

About 60,000 ha in the uncompleted second half of the Columbia Basin Project is irrigated from deep wells (Fig. 2–1). Most wells were drilled in the 1960s with the intention they would be needed for only 10 to 15 yr until the second half of the Columbia Basin Project was completed. Now, nearly 50 yr later, farmers are still irrigating from deep wells, and the status of the second phase of the Columbia Basin Project remains uncertain. The water table in underground aquifers has declined dramatically since the 1960s, mostly due to this deep well irrigation. Wells for irrigation in the 1960s were drilled to an average depth of 100 m compared to more than 200 m today. The cost of electricity to pump water from 200 m is presently $6 cm^{-1} ha^{-1} (Jeff Schibel, personal communication, 2008). One farmer near Ritzville, WA recently deepened a well to a depth of 880 m at a cost of $650,000. Basalt aquifers in the Columbia Basin are subdivided by a variety of geologic features that limit or block both vertical and lateral groundwater movement. A recent report (Lindsey et al., 2009) showed that no significant recharge of the deeper basalt aquifer system in the Columbia Basin has occurred in more than 10,000 years. Therefore, water pumped from the deep aquifer system is essentially nonrenewable.

About 120,000 ha of irrigated cropland is concentrated in Umatilla and Morrow counties in north-central Oregon and in Benton and Walla Walla counties in Washington (Fig. 2–1). Most of the irrigation water is obtained directly from the

Columbia River or its tributaries, with the remaining 25% pumped from deep wells (Donald Horneck, Oregon State University, personal communication, 2008).

Apple (*Malus domestica* Borkh.), sweet cherry [*Prunus avium* (L.) L.], and pear (*Pyrus communis* L.) are major tree crops. Wine grape production has increased to 12,000 ha in recent years, and many wines produced in the region have an international reputation for high quality. Hops (*Humulus lupulus* L.) are produced on 9000 ha in the Yakima River Basin. Hybrid poplar trees (*Populus deltoides* W. Bartram ex Marshall × *P. nigra* L.) are grown for pulpwood and lumber under drip irrigation on 10,000 ha in north-central Oregon. With their permanent cover, wind and water erosion are not serious concerns with irrigated perennial trees and vines.

Field crops include potatoes (*Solanum tuberosum* L.), corn (*Zea mays* L.), wheat, barley (*Hordeum vulgare* L.), oat (*Avena sativa* L.), alfalfa (*Medicago sativa* L.), and dry bean (*Phaseolus vulgaris* L.). In Washington, average potato tuber yield was 69,400 kg ha^{-1} and corn grain yield 13,200 kg ha^{-1} in 2007 (NASS, 2008). Irrigated wheat grain yields average more than 6700 kg ha^{-1}.

Many vegetable crops such as onion (*Allium cepa* L.) and carrot (*Daucus carota* L.) are grown for direct consumption as well as seed. Several perennial grass species are produced for seed. Due to many available crop options, there are no "set" cropping systems. Farmers rotate crops to reduce pests and diseases, optimize water use, and take advantage of current market opportunities. Wind erosion is a major problem for late-harvested root crops due to lack of residue cover after harvest. This is especially true for potato production that involves a high level of soil disturbance (see Wind Erosion and Air Quality section).

Dryland Areas

Low Precipitation Zone

After a decade of experimenting with annual cropping in the 1880s, pioneer farmers in the low precipitation zone learned that the most stable and economically viable grain yields could be achieved by growing winter wheat with a year of fallow between crops. The 2-yr winter wheat–summer fallow (WW–SF) rotation soon became the dominant crop rotation and has remained so since 1890 because it is less risky and more profitable than other systems tested to date. Average winter wheat (one crop every other year) yields range from 1200 to 3700 kg ha^{-1} with 150 and 300 mm of annual precipitation, respectively. About 1.7 kg of residue is produced for every kg of grain.

Spring wheat and spring barley are planted in lieu of summer fallow on 10% or less of dryland hectares, mostly in years when storage of over-winter precipitation in the soil is ample, for example, when the wetting front extends more than 1 m deep. Grain yield of recrop spring cereals is highly variable, and even with ample over-winter soil moisture storage, timely May and early June rainfall is prerequisite for profitable grain yield. Experience and research have not yet identified any alternative crops or cropping systems that can compete agronomically or economically with winter wheat after summer fallow. However, this situation could change rapidly—in 2008 many farmers accepted contracts that paid $870 Mg^{-1} for yellow mustard (*Brassica hirta* Moench) where earlier the price was $270 Mg^{-1} or less.

Intermediate Precipitation Zone

The standard crop rotations in the intermediate precipitation zone are WW–SF in the dryer portions and a 3-yr winter wheat–spring cereal (either wheat or barley)–summer fallow rotation, where annual precipitation exceeds 350 mm. Some annual cropping is practiced where precipitation is more plentiful or in years when over-winter soil water storage is favorable. There are several crop options other than cool-season cereals, such as yellow mustard, winter and spring canola (*Brassica napus* L. and *B. Campestris* L.), safflower (*Carthamus tinctorious* L.), and dry pea (*Pisum sativum* L.), but currently most farmers plant only winter wheat, spring wheat, and spring barley. Average grain yields range from 3700 to 5400 kg ha^{-1} for winter wheat after summer fallow and 1680 to 3300 kg ha^{-1} for recrop spring wheat and spring barley.

High Precipitation Zone

Annual cropping (i.e., no summer fallow) is generally practiced in this zone. Most farmers have a 3-yr rotation of winter wheat–spring cereal–spring legume, while some others pursue a cereal-only rotation of winter wheat–spring barley–spring wheat (or two spring wheat crops in a row instead of spring barley). Grain yields in the high end (i.e., 600 mm) of this precipitation zone average 6200 kg ha^{-1} for winter wheat, 4100 kg ha^{-1} for spring wheat and spring barley, and 2000 kg ha^{-1} for the spring legume crops lentil (*Lens culinaris* Medik.), dry pea, and chickpea (*Cicer arietinum* L.).

Grain yield of winter wheat is greater following a spring legume crop than after a spring cereal because legumes extract less water from the soil and also provide other presumed positive rotation effects (Paulitz et al., 2002). Some farmers practice a 2-yr winter wheat–spring legume rotation, but control of downy brome (*Bromus tectorum* L.) and jointed goatgrass (*Aegilops cylindrical* Host.), major grass weeds with growth habit similar to winter wheat, are more difficult to control because of the high prevalence of winter wheat compared to 3-yr rotations. Winter wheat effectively extracts soil water to a depth of 1.7 m, but little below this depth. Some innovative farmers grow corn and other deep-rooted crops to make use of deep available soil water (John and Cory Aeschliman, personal communication, 2008).

Wheat is King

Winter wheat has historically been the most stable and profitable dryland crop in all precipitation zones (Papendick, 1996). The price of soft white wheat reached record highs of more than $550 Mg^{-1} (>$15 bushel^{-1}) in 2008 driven by low supply due to global-scale drought and by the increased demand for wheat, barley, corn, and other cereals for human consumption, animal feed, and ethanol production. Despite unprecedented wind and water erosion, wheat grain yields have continued to increase in a linear fashion because of technological advances that include new cultivars with high yield potential and resistance to diseases, the availability of nitrogen fertilizer and herbicides beginning in the 1950s, modern farm equipment, and other agronomic improvements that today allow one farmer to manage 1000 ha or more cropland.

Since 1934, countywide average wheat grain yield in Whitman county, Washington, in the high-precipitation Palouse region has increased from 1630 to 5130 kg ha^{-1} (Fig. 2–5). Grain yield data clearly show that before 1960 wheat cul-

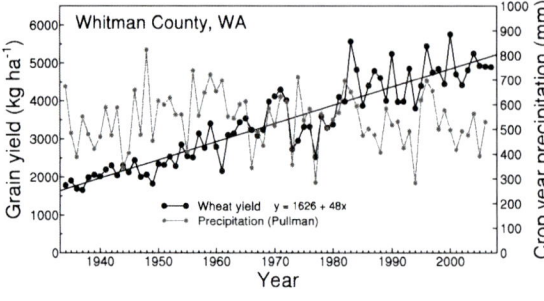

Fig. 2–5. Long-term countywide dryland wheat grain yields in Whitman county, Washington, superimposed with crop-year precipitation from Pullman, WA. Data are a combination of winter and spring wheat called "all wheat" (NASS, 2008). Data show that wheat grain yield has increased by an average of 48 kg ha^{-1} yr^{-1} over 73 yr.

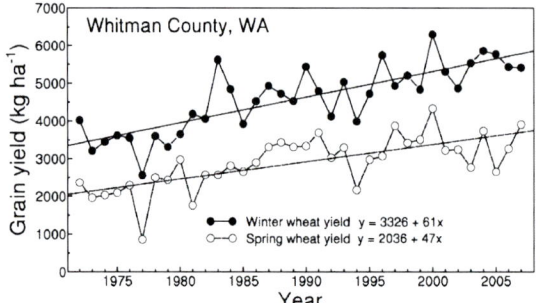

Fig. 2–6. Countywide winter wheat and spring wheat grain yields in Whitman county, Washington, from 1972 to 2007. Data show that winter and spring wheat yields have increased by an average of 61 and 47 kg ha^{-1} yr^{-1}, respectively, over the past 35 yr (NASS, 2008).

tivars could not respond to years of high precipitation because their grain yield potential was low and/or the soil was deficient in nitrogen (Fig. 2–5). Grain yields increased with the widespread availability and use of nitrogen fertilizer (Leggett et al., 1959; Pan et al., 2007) in the 1950s, followed by the release of high-yield-potential semidwarf wheat cultivars in the 1960s (Jones, 2002). By the 1980s and thereafter, countywide average wheat yields continued to increase, despite many years of lower than average precipitation (Fig. 2–5). Grain yield increases also occurred in the low precipitation WW–SF zone in east-central Washington and north-central Oregon (Schillinger and Papendick, 2008).

Separate countywide average winter wheat and spring wheat yield data in Whitman county, Washington, are available beginning in 1972 (NASS, 2008). From 1972 to 2007, winter wheat yield increased by an average of 61 kg ha^{-1} yr^{-1} (3320–5460 kg ha^{-1}, Fig. 2–6). Countywide spring wheat grain yield also increased during this time, at an average rate of 47 kg ha^{-1} yr^{-1} (2040–3680 kg ha^{-1} yr^{-1}, Fig. 2–6). Thus, the grain yield gap between winter wheat and spring wheat in Whitman county has grown from 1280 to 1780 kg ha^{-1} in the last 35 yr.

Available Water and Wheat Grain Yield

Modern wheat cultivars require 6 cm of available water for vegetative growth (before grain production begins), after which each additional centimeter of available stored soil water plus spring (April–June) rainfall will produce an average of 150 and 174 kg grain ha^{-1}, respectively (Schillinger et al., 2008). There is little correlation between rainfall in April and spring wheat grain yield, presumably because surface soils remain relatively wet during April, temperatures are generally cool, and plants are in the seedling stage of development with a small leaf area index that require and use little water. The greatest water use efficiency (i.e., wheat grain yield/centimeters of available water) occurs from rain in May and June (Schillinger et al., 2008). Winter wheat produces more grain per unit of plant-available water than spring wheat for both over-winter precipitation storage in the soil and spring rainfall.

Water Erosion and Off-Site Damages

Irrigated Farming

Most water erosion in irrigated agriculture is caused by excessive and/or inefficient application of water. Eroded soil sediment plugs irrigation drainage systems and road ditches, which must be cleaned at great expense. Annual soil loss from furrow-irrigated fields in the Columbia Basin presently ranges from 35 to 55 Mg ha^{-1} (Harold Crose, USDA-NRCS, personal communication, 2008). The continuing transition from furrow irrigation to more efficient systems, boosted by government cost-share programs such as the Environmental Quality Incentives Program (EQIP)[1], has reduced water erosion from previous levels (see Advances in Soil and Water Conservation section).

Another environmental concern with irrigated agriculture is nitrate leaching below the root zone of crops and into domestic wells. Nitrate levels as high as 55 Mg ha^{-1} in the top 3 m of soil have been recorded from irrigated cropland in the Columbia Basin (Harold Crose, USDA-NRCS, personal communication, 2008). There is general agreement among regulatory agencies and scientists that irrigated agriculture has accounted for the majority of nitrogen loading (Cook et al., 1996). Shallow wells less than 100 m deep are at much greater risk for nitrogen contamination than deeper wells. As most private wells are shallow, a significant portion of domestic well users in the Columbia Basin may be exposed to elevated levels above the 10-ppm nitrate drinking water standard (Cook et al., 1996).

Dryland Farming

Water erosion from rainfed croplands has plagued the region since the inception of farming. Long-term average annual erosion rates in the higher precipitation zones ranged between 22 and 67 Mg ha^{-1} (3 mm of topsoil) with traditional farming practices (USDA, 1978). At these rates some 25 Mg of topsoil are eroded for each megagram of wheat produced. Detailed surveys by the USDA's Soil Conservation Service in the late 1970s in Whitman county, Washington, showed that all of the original topsoil has been eroded from 10% of the land, and one-fourth to three-fourths from an additional 60% of the cultivated area (USDA, 1978). These surveys have not been continued, but since then much more topsoil has been lost and little if any restored. Bare knobs, sparse crop stands, and exposed subsoil on hilltops are evident in fields throughout the Palouse today. Soil loss due to water erosion on newly planted winter wheat fields (i.e., little to no surface cover) in Whitman county in the 43 yr during the winters from 1939–1940 through 1981–1982 was estimated to average 53.8 Mg ha^{-1} yr^{-1} (personal records of Verle G. Kaiser).

Soil slip or mass failure erosion occurs when an entire portion of a hillside becomes saturated with water and slides down the hill (Fig. 2–4, top). Rill erosion, however, is the most common form of erosion and causes the most soil loss, char-

---

[1] EQIP is a USDA-NRCS program that provides farmers incentive payments and cost sharing to implement conservation practices. Incentive payments may be provided for up to 3 yr to encourage farmers to carry out management practices they may not otherwise use without the incentive.

acterized by numerous rivulets along the slope (Fig. 2–4, bottom). Several rills will often concentrate in a low area at the bottom of a hill to form gullies in one season that can be so deep that they must be mechanically filled before they can be crossed by farm implements.

Water erosion is less problematic in the drier zones with its lower precipitation and more gentle slopes; however, it too is accelerated by traditional tillage wheat farming. Annual water erosion rates historically average about 10 Mg ha^{-1} under traditional practices in a mostly WW–SF rotation (USDA, 1978).

Approximately one-third of the eroded sediments are washed by runoff into the region's water bodies, causing incalculable environmental damage in addition to the lost soil resource from millions of hectares (Kok et al., 2009). Eroded sediments are not only a water pollutant; they constitute irreplaceable topsoil from once prime croplands. Lost topsoil reduces the production capacity of croplands, and therefore with time results in reduced water-holding capacity and requires increased levels of costly technological inputs (e.g., nutrients, improved genetics) to sustain grain yields. However, ignoring the cost, these inputs cannot replace the inherent properties of the lost original soil that are crucial to the land's potential productive capacity.

The causes of severe water erosion from tilled soils in the PNW are: (i) winter precipitation climate with high potential for frozen soil runoff, (ii) steep and irregular topography that cannot be easily modified to control erosion, and (iii) lack of surface cover and roughness over winter due to plow-based tillage practices. With traditional plow-based farming two-thirds of the erosion occurs from fall-seeded winter wheat fields that lack protection over winter. The moldboard plow (Fig. 2–7) has historically been the primary tillage tool for grain farming

Fig. 2–7. Inversion of soil to bury heavy winter wheat stubble with a six-bottom moldboard plow in the Palouse circa 1950. Large quantities of winter wheat residue remains a problem for farmers today in the high precipitation region where moldboard plowing is still commonly practiced. However, the trend is toward conservation- and no-till practices. Photo: Washington State University Holland Library Archives, Pullman, WA.

in the high precipitation zone. Its usefulness is credited to residue management, weed control, and seedbed preparation. Plowing was and still is widely used to rid fields of excessive straw residues from high yielding winter wheat that interferes with seedbed preparation, and before the availability of herbicides, was the main method of weed control.

It is now recognized that plow-based tillage is at the root of severe water erosion on much of the wheatlands where it is used. Its primary detrimental effect is burying plant residue needed to protect the surface, disrupting the natural soil structure and beneficial biological soil life (Wuest, 2001) that stabilizes the soil against erosion, and accelerating oxidation of the soil organic matter (Kennedy and Smith, 1995). During the horse and early tractor farming years, soil from moldboard plow tillage furrow was thrown down slope (Fig. 2–7) resulting in "tillage" erosion where topsoil was steadily moved downward by gravitational forces through time (Montgomery et al., 1999). The results of tillage erosion are readily seen throughout the Palouse in abrupt banks or berms up to 3 m or higher along old fence lines, where the soil from the field above had been plowed toward the fence, and in the field below the soil had been plowed away from the fence. Tillage erosion rates increase linearly with depth of downhill moldboard plow tillage (Van Oost et al., 2006). Today's modern tractors have adequate power to throw the moldboard plow furrow upslope to help arrest tillage erosion, but not without additional cost.

More than 80% of water erosion from winter wheat fields occurs from rapid snowmelt or rainfall on thawing soil (Zuzel et al., 1982). Under these conditions the soil surface above the frost layer becomes saturated, and in this fluid or structureless state is readily carried by runoff on bare, sloping land. Soil freezing generally occurs several times during the winter to a depth of 10 cm, and occasionally to 40 cm (Papendick and McCool, 1994). Partial or complete soil thawing frequently occurs between freezing events. Infiltration rates average 15 mm h^{-1} on unfrozen silt loam soils of the region but can approach zero depending on depth of frost and soil water status (Zuzel and Pikul, 1987).

Wind Erosion and Air Quality

Wind erosion is a major problem for irrigated farming in the Columbia Basin and Yakima River Basin as well as for dryland farming in the WW–SF region that receives <300 mm annual precipitation (Fig. 2–1). Several soil types in the Inland PNW are dominated by particles <100 μm in diameter (Saxton et al., 2000) that are readily suspended and transported long distances during windstorms (Kjelgaard et al., 2004). Suspension-size particulates <100 μm in size comprised >90% of eroded sediment from summer-fallowed fields during six high-wind events in Adams county, Washington, in 2003 and 2004 (Sharratt et al., 2007). This indicates that direct suspension, as opposed to saltation and creep, is likely the major source of soil loss during windstorms. These soils also contain many particulates <10 μm in diameter (PM$_{10}$) but only a very small percentage of particulates <2.5 μm in diameter (PM$_{2.5}$) (Sharratt and Lauer, 2006). The small size of PM$_{2.5}$ particulates makes them readily inhalable deep into human lung tissue, whereas particulates >2.5 μm, while also readily inhalable, are deposited in the upper airways and are therefore less of a health concern.

The earliest travelers passing through the low-precipitation region in the days before farming (before the 1880s) wrote of high winds and annoying dust kicked up by horses' hooves (Meinig, 1968), but made no mention of massive dust storms such as those that were frequent after the onset of farming. During the horse farming years (1880–1935), the moldboard plow was used to completely invert the surface soil during primary tillage. Following the plow, a spiked-tooth harrow was used to smooth the soil, control weeds, and to form a "dust mulch" to retain soil moisture during the dry summer (McCall, 1925). This practice created fallow fields devoid of surface residue and roughness and set the stage for recurrent and massive dust storms (Fig. 2–2), as recorded in numerous diaries and local newspaper accounts. Schillinger and Papendick (2008) estimated that 180 Mg ha^{-1} or more of suspended soil was lost in each of such individual 1-d dust storms, 16 times or more the annual tolerable (T value) erosion rate established by the USDA-NRCS. They further speculated that ongoing continual suspended soil emissions during wind storms, along with biological oxidation (Rasmussen and Parton, 1994), is the major reason why soil organic matter has declined by 50% or more in WW–SF systems in the past 125 yr.

When farming converted from horses to tractors in the 1930s, there was a concomitant shift from use of plows to disks or sweep implements that retained more of the crop residue on the surface. The rodweeder with a ground-driven rotating bar replaced the spiked-tooth harrow and became the most widely used secondary tillage implement for controlling weeds in summer fallow. Although the rodweeder with its undercutting action helps to retain residues on the surface, the one to four passes with it during the summer to control Russian thistle (*Salsola iberica* auct.) and spring-germinated downy brome tends to pulverize the soil and make it more susceptible to blowing. Russian thistle weed persists and can root rapidly in the very dry climate after occasional small showers during the spring and summer (Fig. 2–2) and extensively deplete water from the soil.

Water conservation and wind erosion control go hand in hand in some cases and in others they do not. In contrast to other wheat-producing areas, water conservation in the Inland PNW low precipitation zone amounts to more than just maximizing water in the profile from precipitation. Retention of water in the seed zone during the dry summer months for late summer establishment of winter wheat increases crop yields by 30% compared with late-planted wheat that is dependent on fall rains for emergence (Donaldson et al., 2001). Wind erosion is readily controlled with chemical (i.e., no-till) summer fallow where herbicides are used to control weeds, but it is not commonly practiced in the low precipitation zone due to drying of the seed zone. Instead, tillage is widely practiced during fallow to disrupt capillary continuity to retain soil water near the surface (e.g., 10–15 cm) that is adequate for planting winter wheat with deep-furrow drills in late August or early September (Papendick et al., 1973). Without tillage most soils dry out too deeply for early planting to be successful (Hammel et al., 1981).

Air Quality Standards for Agricultural Dust

In 1990, the USEPA mandated provisions in the National Ambient Air Quality Standard (NAAQS) to regulate airborne particles with an aerodynamic diameter of 10 μm or less, commonly referred to as PM_{10}. This was of particular concern in the Inland PNW, where high PM_{10} concentrations at monitoring stations are always strongly correlated with major wind erosion and blowing dust from irrigated and dryland farms. The main provision in the NAAQS affecting agriculture in the Inland PNW was that an average of only one exceedance per year of the PM_{10} threshold of 150 μm m^{-3} per 24-h period was allowed in urban areas with population greater than 100,000. Spokane and the Tri-Cities (Kennewick, Richland, Pasco) in Washington (Fig. 2–1) are the only cities in the affected areas large enough to meet these criteria.

Air quality monitoring sites located at Spokane and the Tri-Cities and observation of field conditions from 1989 through 2008 showed the following:

- There are an average of about two NAAQS exceedances of the PM_{10} standard per year in the Tri-Cities and less than one exceedance per year in Spokane (Fig. 2–8).
- Blowing dust during windstorms has caused all exceedances of the NAAQS standard. PM_{10} concentrations have reached as high 803 μm m^{-3} in Spokane and 1690 μm m^{-3} in the Tri-Cities per 24-h period (Sharratt and Lauer, 2006).
- About 95% of PM_{10} suspended particulates measured in Spokane and the Tri-Cities during windstorms are coarse materials (i.e., $PM_{10-2.5}$), with the remaining particulates less than $PM_{2.5}$. Thus, fine particulates alone have never been the cause of previous 150 μm NAAQS exceedances in the region.
- Many regional farmland soils have significant quantities of coarse particulates, and control measures are required to keep them in place.
- Air quality authorities in Spokane and the Tri-Cities estimate that well over 80% of total particulate emissions during wind storms are derived from agricultural fields. Visual evidence clearly indicates that emissions are especially high from excessively tilled summer-fallowed fields (i.e., no growing crop) that lack protection provided by surface crop residue and/or roughness. New conservation farming practices (see Advances in Soil and Water Conservation section) have reduced this impact.
- Federal research dollars for the Columbia Plateau PM_{10} Project (CP_3) (see Special Grants for Erosion Control Research section) have resulted in the

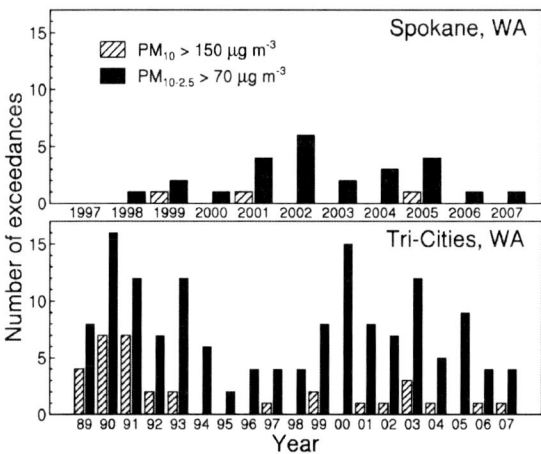

Fig. 2–8. Annual exceedances of the Federal 24-h 150 μm m^{-3} PM_{10} Air Quality Standard (checkered bars) in Spokane, WA and Tri-Cities, WA. The black bars represent exceedances of the 70-μm coarse ($PM_{10-2.5}$) standard proposed by the USEPA in 2006 but not enacted into law. Data courtesy of Ronald Edgar, Spokane County Air Pollution Control Authority, and David Lauer, Benton County Clean Air Authority.

development of several best management practices for improved wind erosion control on farm fields (Papendick, 2004).

- Federal funds have provided incentives for farmers to implement effective wind erosion control measures targeted at meeting the 150 µm m^{-3} standard.
- Because of the high frequency of PM$_{10}$ NAAQS exceedances, eastern Washington is very dependent on the Natural Events Policy (NEP)[2] to avoid urban noncompliance penalties. The NEP excludes airborne particulate matter violations due to natural events provided that best management practices are implemented.
- Urban sources of dust, such as construction sites, are relatively minor. Dust emissions from such sites can be controlled by application of water or cover.

In 2006, the EPA proposed reducing the NAAQS coarse particulate threshold from 150 to 70 µm m^{-3} per 24-h time period and exempting agricultural dust sources (U.S. OFR, 2006). While many farmers readily accepted the proposed exemption, other farmers and scientists argued that dust emissions from farms should be monitored and that farmers should be held accountable for emissions of coarse particulates and given assistance to reduce emissions. If passed into law, the proposed 70 µm m^{-3} standard would have resulted in an average of eight exceedances per year in the Tri-Cities, and more than two in Spokane (Fig. 2–8), largely due to blowing dust from agricultural fields. If exempted, government payments to farmers for wind erosion abatement practices through the EQIP and other programs would have been reduced or eliminated. These programs are very important to the USDA-NRCS who "reward the best" farmers to "motivate the rest." In addition, federal funding for research to develop best management practices for wind erosion control would also have been reduced or eliminated, while recent progress in this area shows a great need for these efforts to be continued and enhanced.

Farmers and scientists further argued that even if emissions from urban sources (e.g., construction sites) were reduced to near zero, numerous and recurrent exceedances of the proposed 70 µm m^{-3} would still occur (Fig. 2–8). These would overwhelm the NEP effectiveness and become unmanageable for state regulatory agencies. The USEPA was urged to realize and account for the fact that agriculture is the major source of urban coarse particulates in the Inland PNW and much of the western United States and that they must provide "workable" thresholds now, not later after facts become more evident, and after ongoing programs targeting dust reduction had been dismantled and could only be restarted with loss of time and at great cost. While USEPA proposed that wind-blown dust from agricultural fields be an exemption, future research may well show it to have associated health risks beyond the "nuisance and episodic" level now acknowledged.

Farmers and scientists had worked together for more than a decade to develop and implement conservation methods for dryland and irrigated farms with the target goal of achieving the 150 µm m^{-3} 24-h clean air standard. These efforts resulted in major reductions of the 150 µm m^{-3} exceedances compared with the late 1980s and early 1990s period (Fig. 2–8). They argued that agriculture must

---

[2] The NEP is an EPA policy wherein high winds are considered natural events if they occur over areas with controls in place for particulate matter. High winds are not considered natural events if they occur over areas where human activities contribute to particulate matter and no controls or best management practices are in place.

continue to be held accountable, not exempted, for dust emissions, and that the NAAQS for these events remain at the existing PM_{10} concentration of 150 μm m^{-3}. The result would be protecting major populations from unnecessary health and nuisance risks, maintaining monitoring and reporting an acceptable level, and continued improvement of farming practices and policies.

It is difficult to determine with certainty how effective the strong opposition from the Inland PNW was to USEPA's proposal (U.S. OFR, 2006) to reduce the NAAQS coarse particulate threshold from 150 to 70 μm m^{-3} and to exempt agricultural dust sources. However, the end result was that USEPA abandoned the proposed change and kept the original standard that holds agriculture accountable for dust emissions.

Modeling Water and Wind Erosion in the Pacific Northwest
Water Erosion

In the early 1930s, Congress provided funding to the USDA to establish a national program on soil erosion research with a mandate to investigate the causes of erosion and determine management practices that would mitigate soil and water losses from agricultural lands. Of the 10 erosion research stations originally established, only the Palouse Conservation Experiment Station, now named the Palouse Conservation Field Station at Pullman, WA was located west of the Rocky Mountains. At each station, standard erosion/runoff plots for various management practices were established. Results from the first 10 yr were published in technical bulletins specific to each station. Results from Pullman were reported by Horner et al. (1944).

There was no developed erosion prediction technology through which the data from the measured sites could be extended to apply to climate, soils, topography, and crop conditions at other locations. The runoff and erosion data from the various studies were collected and analyzed, and in 1965, the empirical Universal Soil Loss Equation (USLE), weighed heavily with data from east of the Rocky Mountains, was developed (Wischmeier and Smith, 1965). The USLE is written as the product of six assumed-to-be independent factors: $A = RKLSCP$, where A is predicted soil loss per unit area, and the six factors are R, rainfall erosivity; K, soil erodibility; L, slope length; S, slope gradient; C, cropping management; and P, erosion-control practice.

Soon after the USLE was developed, it was tested in the Inland PNW with data from the Pullman plots (Horner et al., 1944). It quickly became apparent that the predicted erosion rates were very low compared with observed rates, and the effect of degree of slope seemed quite large for the steep slopes of the region. Also, annual distribution of the rainfall erosivity factor R, based on rainfall kinetic energy and intensity, did not properly account for erosive forces during the winter when surface runoff from low-intensity rainfall and snowmelt dominated the erosion process and accounted for most of the erosion during the year.

In 1972, research was begun to develop regional relationships for the factors in the USLE to enable its use on an interim basis. The original plan was to use data collected during the 1930–1943 period at the Palouse Conservation Field Station to develop regionalized relationships for various USLE factors. The effort was to concentrate on four factors: R, L, S, and C. Soil erodibility, K, relationships from east of the Rocky Mountains (Wischmeier et al., 1971) were accepted on a temporary basis. The support practice, P, relationships for the eastern United States were also tentatively accepted. A major problem quickly developed when, in spite of many searches, the original Palouse Conservation Field Station plot event data could not be found, and to this day are still missing.

The effort shifted to an analysis of end-of-erosion season measurements and visual observations collected over several years from a limited number of fields in Whitman county, Washington,, by the USDA-Soil Conservation Service (SCS) (Verle G. Kaiser, personal communication, 1973). Tentative R, L, and S factor relationships were developed from these data. The first adaptation of the USLE to the Inland PNW was developed in 1973, and field and plot research was initiated to collect the information necessary to develop regionalized relationships for all factors in the USLE. Between 1973 and 1999, sufficient information was collected to regionalize all factors for the USLE. A complete history of this research and many of the results can be found in McCool and Busacca (1999).

In 1985, a group consisting primarily of USDA-ARS researchers and SCS personnel assembled to plan an update, modification, and computerization of the USLE to include results of research data collected since publication of Agriculture Handbook 537 (Wischmeier and Smith, 1978). The Revised Universal Soil Loss Equation (RUSLE1) was the result (Renard et al., 1997). The original USLE form was retained in RUSLE1, but the technology was altered and new data were introduced to evaluate terms for specific conditions. The rainfall-runoff factor R maps were expanded to the western United States, the topographic factors were revised, and the effect of rill to interrill erosion ratio was reflected in the L and S factors. The cover management factor C was altered from seasonal values to a continuous function that is a product of four factors, prior land use, surface cover, crop canopy, surface roughness, and for cropland in the Inland PNW, a fifth factor, the soil moisture factor. For the Inland PNW, the relationships for erodibility K from east of the Rocky Mountains were retained, and all effect of the K and R interaction was placed in the Equivalent R (R_{eq}) factor. Essentially, all the regionalization of factors in the USLE for the Inland PNW was retained in RUSLE1 and accessed through the Equivalent R (R_{eq}) option in the operating program.

The Revised Universal Soil Loss Equation, Version 2 (RUSLE2) (Toy et al., 2002) is more robust and powerful than RUSLE1 and has replaced RUSLE1 for USDA-NRCS conservation planning activities. RUSLE2 is more mathematically based, estimates rill and interrill erosion by solving a set of mathematical equations, and uses site-specific databases for climate, soils, and crops. RUSLE2 retains the regionalized relationships for all factors contained in the USLE version adapted to the Inland PNW. Eastern U.S. erodibility K factors are retained, and all effect of climate and erodibility interaction is placed in the R_{eq} factor. Recent results from analysis of plot data collected at the Palouse Conservation Field Station and elsewhere under natural rainfall conditions indicate very high winter values of soil erodibility. Data collected from winter rainfall events when soil is not snow covered or affected by soil frost indicate erodibility is about eight times the value of standard eastern U.S. K values.

The Water Erosion Prediction Project (WEPP), a project to develop a process-based, continuous simulation hydrologic and erosion model was conceived in 1985 (Flanagan et al., 1995). A complete and validated WEPP hill slope and watershed model was released in 1995 (Flanagan and Nearing, 1995); updates are currently made to the model, interfaces, and databases on an approximately annual basis via the WEPP website.

The WEPP is a process-based, continuous simulation model that predicts erosion by overland water flow due to rainfall excess, snowmelt, or irrigation (Flanagan et al., 1995). The model can simulate soil detachment by raindrops (interrill erosion) and by flowing water in rills (rill erosion), as well as sediment transport and sediment deposition in rills (Foster et al., 1995). Additionally, erosion in larger channels (e.g., ephemeral gullies, earthen channels, grass waterways) can be modeled (Ascough et al., 1995). The WEPP is to be applied to areas where the dominant erosion processes are sheet, rill, and small channel detachment due to overland flow.

Evaluation of the WEPP indicated the winter routines in early versions of this model significantly underpredicted runoff and soil loss when compared with runoff plot data from the Palouse Conservation Field Station (McCool et al., 1998). The WEPP was unable to properly simulate the soil-freezing phenomenon in the Inland PNW. In particular, the simulated freezing duration was much longer than from observed records (Lin et al., 2001). Considerable effort has been invested in modifying the WEPP winter routines to better model snow accumulation and melt, as well as soil frost formation and thaw (Lin and McCool, 2006; Williams et al., 2010). Winter soil erodibility relationships are still under development.

Wind Erosion

The Wind Erosion Equation (WEQ) (Woodruff and Siddoway, 1965) was published the same year as the USLE. Similarly to the USLE, WEQ is an empirical model. It was most successful under Great Plains soil and climate conditions. When applied to the wind erosion–prone areas of the Inland PNW, success was limited due to the silt of soils in the Inland PNW as compared with the soils containing more sand and clay used in the development of WEQ and also due to the influx of fine airborne particulates from upwind sources into fields of the Inland PNW (Stetler and Saxton, 1996). The WEQ used long-term average wind speeds for erosivity, not the event-type high wind speeds that cause most of the erosion. Thus, wind gets averaged out to low values. No sustained attempts were made to regionalize WEQ to the Inland PNW.

The Wind Erosion Prediction System (WEPS) was developed by the USDA-ARS to replace the empirical WEQ. The WEPS is a process-based, daily time-step, continuous simulation computer model that predicts soil erosion through simulation of the physical processes that control wind erosion (Hagen, 1991); wind erosion in WEPS is initiated when wind speed exceeds the threshold velocity for a given soil and biomass condition. After initiation, the duration and intensity of the erosion event depends on the wind speed distribution and the evolution of the surface condition.

Before 2003, WEPS had not been adequately tested in the low-precipitation dryland and irrigated area of the Inland PNW, where direct suspension as opposed to saltation is the dominant process by which particulates are eroded from the soil surface (Kjelgaard et al., 2004). Soil loss associated with suspension, saltation, and creep and PM_{10} emissions were used to validate the WEPS erosion submodel. Erosion from fields managed in a traditional WW–SF rotation was monitored for 2 yr during summer fallow near Washtucna, WA (Feng and Sharratt, 2007). The erosion submodel predicted no erosion for three of six high-wind events. For the remaining three high-wind events, the model overpredicted soil loss (as a result of overestimating creep and saltation) and either overpredicted or underpredicted PM_{10} loss. While the performance of WEPS appears marginal, improvements in modeling efficiency may require better specification of the static threshold friction velocity or additional parameterization of various coefficients that govern emissions, abrasion, and breakage of silt loams on the Columbia Plateau. Indeed, soil and biomass conditions do not necessarily equally govern creep, saltation, and suspension processes. Feng and Sharratt (2005), for example, found that while flat biomass cover and ridge height were the two most important factors affecting creep and saltation, flat biomass cover and soil water content were the two most important factors affecting suspension of particulates and PM_{10} in the PNW.

Plans for a Common Process-Based Wind and Water Erosion Model
In 2004, the USDA-NRCS identified the development of a common physical process-based wind and water erosion model as one of their top priority requests of the USDA-ARS during the next 10 years. The tentatively selected approach is to disintegrate the WEPP and WEPS models into unique stand-alone components (i.e., hill slope water erosion, wind erosion, infiltration, runoff routing) and then incorporate these modules into a model archiving, maintenance, and development tool, the Object Modeling System (OMS) (Ahuja et al., 2004). Additional components from WEPP, WEPS, and other USDA-ARS models will be incorporated within OMS, and the necessary temporal and spatial looping descriptions will be developed to allow for satisfactory water and/or wind erosion simulations. Work on common cropping and management databases and new graphical user interfaces will also be required for the new model. In addition to allowing simulation of either erosion by water or erosion by wind separately, the new model may also have the potential to simultaneously predict combined wind and water detachment, transport, and deposition of soil.

In order for the combined water and wind erosion model to be successful in the PNW, improvements must be made in the predictive capability of WEPP for winter conditions. Modeling the movement of water in the soil in response to freezing action should be improved; modeling of surface effects on infiltration under winter conditions needs additional attention, as currently only crusting is considered. The transient nature of erodibility parameters in response to freezing, thawing, and water tension changes must be addressed. The WEPS will need additional research and modification if dust emissions are to be successfully modeled. Improvements in modeling efficiency may require better specification of the static threshold friction velocity or additional parameterization of various coefficients that govern emissions, abrasion, and breakage of silt loam soils on the Columbia Plateau.

Advances in Soil and Water Conservation
Irrigated Cropland
Conservation strategies for irrigated cropland have focused on residue and cover crop management, making efficient use of water, and eliminating field burning. Conventional farming practices generally involve use of tillage implements, such as the moldboard plow, heavy tandem disk, rotary tiller, and packer, which destroy soil structure and leave the soil smooth, bare, and pulverized.

Land under furrow irrigation is declining each year in the Columbia Basin and Yakima River Basin and across the United States as farmers convert to the more efficient systems (Howell, 2001). Both electric utility companies and the USDA-NRCS offer incentives and cost-share programs to help farmers transition into more efficient methods such as low-pressure drop nozzle sprinklers and drip irrigation systems.

Irrigation methods clearly affect water runoff and erosion in the PNW. Ebbert and Kim (1998) reported that average suspended sediment from nine sampled watersheds in the Columbia Basin ranged from 0.4 kg ha^{-1} d^{-1} in a watershed where sprinklers and drip systems were used (with no furrow irrigation) to 19 kg ha^{-1} d^{-1} in a watershed where the majority of cropland was in furrow irrigation. Water erosion in furrow irrigation systems can be reduced by 90% or more by adding dilute quantities of anionic polyacrylamide (PAM) to irrigation water (Lentz and Sojka, 2000). PAM has been available since 1995 in both dry granules and stock solution to apply to furrow irrigation water at concentrations of 2 kg ha^{-1} (10 ppm) for the initial irrigation and 1 kg ha^{-1} (5 ppm) for subsequent irrigations (Sojka et al., 2007). About 30% of farmers in the Columbia Basin use PAM on their furrow-irrigated land, often with cost-share from EQIP.

Winter cover crops have been shown to improve nitrogen cycling and reduce soil nitrate levels in potato-based crop rotations. In a 2-yr study in the Columbia Basin, cereal and *Brassica* cover crops planted in late August after harvest of corn accumulated between 112 and 142 kg N ha^{-1} (Weinert et al., 2002), but less than 50% of this quantity of nitrogen was accumulated when planting of cover crops was delayed until late September. Over-wintering cover crops significantly reduced soil nitrate levels compared to the bare fallow treatment. The cover crops reduced the potential for nitrate leaching by absorbing and storing nitrogen in plant tissue during the wet winter months and by transpiring water, thus reducing water percolation and nitrate leaching, and also provided significant amounts of available nitrogen to the subsequent potato crop.

Cover crops are a practical means to control wind erosion after harvest of high soil disturbance crops such as potatoes or other crops like dry beans that leave very little surface residue. Winter wheat makes a good cover crop because seed costs are reasonable, it emerges quickly and produces rapid ground cover, is not killed by low temperatures, and withstands sand blasting during windstorms. As a followup on research conducted by Kunch (2001), Kok et al. (2008) created temperature indexes for locations across the Columbia and Yakima River Basins to predict the number of days required to achieve 30% ground cover for winter wheat planted between 1 September and 10 October. Adequate surface cover (i.e., 30%) is not expected at any location for winter wheat planted after 20 October due to insufficient heat units. This guide (Kok et al., 2008) provides valuable information to farmers wanting to implement relatively inexpensive and effective wind erosion control.

Historically, winter cover crops have been incorporated into the soil before planting the spring crop, with the disadvantage being that soil is left vulnerable to wind erosion between spring tillage and crop establishment. Strip-till is a relatively new conservation farming technique where the tillage is confined to narrow strips where seed will be planted. Strip-till is gaining in popularity with farmers using irrigations and is practiced in several crop-rotation scenarios (Andrew McGuire, Washington State University Extension, personal commu-

Fig. 2–9. One pass planting with a 450-horsepower tractor pulling a strip-till cultivator in tandem with a corn planter through alfalfa that has been sprayed with glyphosate herbicide. Liquid fertilizer is delivered via the tanks mounted on the tractor. Photo: Andrew McGuire, Washington State University Extension, Ephrata, WA.

nication, 2008). Corn, beans, and other crops can be strip-tilled into alfalfa in mid-to-late spring after the farmer obtains a first cutting of alfalfa hay. Glyphosate herbicide is used to kill the alfalfa, and a strip-till cultivator and planter are pulled in tandem with a high-horsepower tractor to till, fertilize, and plant in one pass (Fig. 2–9). The strips of undisturbed alfalfa residue provide season-long protection from wind erosion. Where winter wheat is planted as a cover crop following harvest of potatoes, glyphosate is applied to the winter wheat in the spring, and corn or beans are planted using the strip-till machinery and method described. Farmers continue to develop innovative and sometimes elaborate methods (see Fig. 2–10) of strip-till farming that are economically feasible and provide environmental benefits.

Farmers are experimenting with white mustard (*Sinapis alba* Martigena) and oriental mustard (*Brassica juncea* Cutlass) as a biofumigant green manure that provides an alternative to chemicals to control soil-borne pests in potato-based cropping systems. A Columbia Basin farmer developed a wheat/mustard–potato cropping system that allows production of potatoes every other year where traditionally potatoes are grown only once every 4 yr. In this system, mustard is planted no-till or broadcast into newly harvested wheat stubble in mid August, and irrigation is provided. In on-farm tests, mustard produced an average 5730 kg ha^{-1} of dry biomass by late October before first being flail chopped then incorporated into the soil with a tandem disk (Fig. 2–11). Where mustard was used as a green manure water infiltration rates more than doubled compared with the control (McGuire, 2003). Results further showed that mustard green manure suppressed the soil-borne fungus *Verticillium dahliae* Klebahn sufficiently to produce potato yields similar to those following application of metam sodium (sodium methyldithiocarbamate), a commonly used chemical soil fumigant (McGuire, 2003).

Fig. 2–10. Irrigated onion production using strip tillage in the Columbia Basin. A cover crop of winter wheat was planted in the fall after potato harvest. Following emergence, 15-cm-wide strips were sprayed with herbicide, leaving 15 cm-wide strips of growing wheat to protect the soil and scavenge nitrogen during the fall and winter. In the spring, another application of herbicide was used to kill the remaining wheat. (Top) A rototiller machine used to till and apply fertilizer in the bare strips, (Center) followed by an onion planter, leaving the wheat strips intact. (Bottom) The wheat strips protect onions from abrading sand particles and also conserve soil water. Photos: Andrew McGuire, Washington State University Extension, Ephrata, WA.

Fig. 2–11. Mustard green manure is flail-chopped (right) and then incorporated into the soil with a tandem disk with attached packer in late October in the Columbia Basin. Mustard and other *Brassica* crops suppress nematodes, soil fungal pathogens, and weeds to offer farmers effective and less expensive alternatives to chemicals for controlling these pests in potato-based crop rotations. Photo: Andrew McGuire, Washington State University Extension, Ephrata, WA.

Dryland Cropland

Erosion control and water conservation research has been conducted and advocated in the Inland PNW since 1915 (McCall and Holtz, 1921). Systematic and long-term erosion control research began in 1930 with the establishment of the USDA Palouse Conservation Experiment Station at Pullman, WA, this being one of ten USDA soil conservation experiment stations established across the United States at that time. Excellent overviews of major erosion control, water conservation, and conservation tillage research findings through the late 1970s are provided by Horner et al. (1944), Papendick et al. (1983), Ramig et al. (1983), and USDA (1978); these findings are not repeated here.

For the typical WW–SF region, the key question is what management strategies can be used to maximize storage of over-winter precipitation in the soil, conserve seed zone moisture during the summer, and simultaneously effectively control wind erosion? Similarly, in the intermediate and high precipitation zones, the major concern is how to efficiently and profitably farm the land while retaining adequate surface residue over the winter months to control water erosion. Although marked improvements in wind and water erosion control have been made in the past 30 yr, erosion remains an ongoing threat to the resources, environment, and agricultural economy throughout the region.

Kok et al. (2009), Papendick (2004), Schillinger and Papendick (2008), and others have provided overviews of major soil and water conservation accomplishments and findings for dryland farming during the past 30 yr. These include:

- Availability of affordable and effective nonselective herbicides such a glyphosate to control weeds without tillage have made conservation-till and no-till practices possible and practical.
- Volunteer cereals and weeds serve as a disease "green bridge" for newly planted crops and therefore should be completely controlled before planting (Smiley et al., 1992).
- Integrated pest management research in the high-precipitation Palouse demonstrated that diverse 3-yr rotations of winter wheat–spring pea–spring cereal using conservation-till and no-till had less risk and were more profitable than limited rotations using traditional tillage (D.L. Young et al., 1994; F.L. Young et al., 1994).
- Rapid advancement since the mid 1990s in development of no-till grain drills by several implement manufacturers allows precise seed and fertilizer placement in one pass through the field (Fig. 2–12) (Baker and Saxton, 2007). The land area under no-till increases each year in the intermediate and high precipitation zones as farmers gain experience and confidence with this system, being yet further motivated by fuel savings and government farm programs that promote this practice.
- Development of the undercutter method of WW–SF farming is a "win–win" for farmers and the environment. This method uses wide V-blade sweeps that cut beneath soil with minimum surface lifting or disturbance and simultaneously deliver nitrogen during primary spring tillage in April or May (Fig. 2–13, top), followed by as few as one noninversion rodweeding operation (Fig. 2–13, center) during the summer to control Russian thistle and other weeds. With the undercutter method, ample surface residue is retained during the 13-mo fallow period and after planting of winter wheat (Fig. 2–13, bottom) to reduce blowing dust emissions by up to 65% compared to traditional tillage fallow (Sharratt and Feng, 2009). There are no adverse effects on seed-zone water content or winter wheat grain yield (Schillinger, 2001) with the undercutter system, and it is more profitable (Zaikin et al., 2007) than traditional tillage. In 2006, the USDA-NRCS awarded the Washington Association of Wheat Growers a $905,000 Conservation Incentive Grant to cover 50% of the cost of new undercutter implements to farmers wanting to practice this method of WW–SF farming. The undercutter system of WW–SF farming represents the future of wheat farming in the low precipitation zone.
- Long-term cropping systems research in the low-precipitation region showed that spring cereals—wheat, barley, oat, spring oilseeds (canola, yellow mustard, safflower), and recrop winter wheat (i.e., no fallow)—had highly variable grain yields, contained more weeds, and were generally less profitable than WW–SF (Schillinger et al., 2007; Bewick et al., 2008). Grain yield of spring-sown crops ranged from near failure to low when May and June rainfall was not ample, whereas winter wheat after summer fallow better tolerated or otherwise buffered drought during these two critical months (Schillinger et al., 2008). These factors notwithstanding, spring cropping, especially using no-till, provides excellent wind erosion control.
- The Revised Universal Soil Loss Equation (RUSLE2) developed with PNW parameters has become a basic tool for planning conservation farming practices (McCool and Busacca, 1999).
- Runs of the RUSLE2 model by Kok et al. (2009) estimated that annual average water erosion rates from 1975 to 2005 have been reduced by 50% (27–13 Mg ha^{-1}) in the intermediate precipitation zone and by 75% (45–11 Mg ha^{-1}) in the high precipitation zone. Traditional tillage dominated in 1975, but today more than half of the cropland in the high precipitation zone and essentially

Fig. 2–12. No-till planting of spring wheat into standing stubble of the previous winter wheat crop in April 2008 on the John and Cory Aeschliman farm in the Palouse. The residue is left standing and undisturbed to protect the soil from water erosion during the winter. (Top) Farming is conducted on slopes as steep as 45% or more. This 450-horsepower Knudson tractor is equipped with crab steering and a self-leveling cab for operating on steep slopes. (Bottom) The 12-m-wide modified Greats Plains model 3010 air drill has a notched coulter in front of each seed opener to cut through residue and 2-cm-wide shanks to band liquid aqua NH_3–N plus thiosulfate-sulfur about 8 cm below the soil surface. Liquid "starter" fertilizer from a separate tank delivers phosphorus close to the seed that is planted with double-disc openers on 20-cm row spacing. This field has been in continuous no-till for 30 yr. Photos: John Aeschliman, Colfax, WA.

all cropland in the intermediate zone are in some form of conservation tillage. Correspondingly, Kok et al. (2009) reported that the estimated annual soil loss rate from wind erosion in the low precipitation WW–SF zone was reduced by 50% (20–10 Mg ha^{-1}) from 1975 levels due to better retention of surface residues during the fallow period.

- Formation of the Pacific Northwest Direct Seed Association (PNDSA) by farmers in 2000 enabled information exchange and advocacy related to conservation policy issues to promote economically sound and environmentally sustainable conservation farming practices. The annual 2-day PNDSA

Fig. 2-13. The undercutter method of winter wheat–summer fallow conservation farming. (Top) Primary spring tillage plus aqua NH_3–N injection with a Haybuster undercutter V-sweep implement. The narrow pitched and overlapping 80-cm-wide "V" blades slice beneath the soil at a depth of 13 cm to sever soil capillary channels to halt the upward movement of liquid water to retain seed-zone water for late-summer planting of winter wheat. Most residue is left standing for control of wind erosion. (Lower left) A rotating rodweeder is operated 7-to 10-cm below the soil surface to control Russian thistle and other broadleaf weeds during the late spring and summer. (Lower right) Thirty percent or more residue cover at time of planting winter wheat is achieved using the undercutter method. Photos: W.F. Schillinger.

conference is attended by an average of 500 farmers, agricultural industry personnel, extension agents, and scientists.

- Studies in the low precipitation WW–SF region showed that planting in late August to early September into soils with stored water increased grain yield by 30% and straw production by 240% compared to "dusting in" or planting winter wheat at a shallow depth after the onset of fall rains in October (Donaldson et al., 2001). The additional straw produced with early planting of winter wheat is a crucially important resource to combat wind erosion during the fallow period.

- Detailed soil and land use databases are presently being compiled on a grid basis that are compatible with the USDA-ARS Wind Erosion Prediction System (WEPS) dust module for a regional modeling system that will greatly assist in the continuing effort to develop prediction technology for suspension-dominated wind erosion.
- Global positioning satellites, auto-steering tractor systems, infrared remote sensing weed detectors, and related technology have provided a wealth of instrumentation to farmers. These instruments help to eliminate overlap and skips with farm implements, reduce soil compaction by controlling traffic, allow variable rate application of fertilizer and "spot" treatment of individual weeds with herbicides, and other applications that increase farm efficiency and soil conservation.

Special Grants for Erosion Control Research

Extensive research on water and wind erosion in the Inland PNW continues to be conducted by scientists from the University of Idaho, Oregon State University, Washington State University, and the USDA-ARS. Much of this research is made possible by long-term Special Grants authorized by Congress and administered by the USDA–Cooperative States Research and Extension Service.

Solutions to Environmental and Economic Problems (STEEP) is an interdisciplinary research and education program for developing technology for profitable conservation cropping systems, controlling cropland soil erosion, and environmental protection. STEEP was initiated in 1975 with a major focus on controlling water erosion in the Palouse region. A team of innovative farmers and university and USDA-ARS scientists from the three states guide the effort. The main strategy is to shift away from moldboard plow-based tillage toward conservation-till and no-till methods. Numerous research and extension publications from STEEP are available online at http://pnwsteep.wsu.edu (verified 20 Oct. 2009) . Since its inception, funding for STEEP has averaged approximately $500,000 per year. Kok et al. (2009) estimated that the benefits of STEEP had extended over at least 2 million ha since 1975, at a cost of just $15 ha^{-1}, or $0.5 ha^{-1} yr^{-1}.

The Columbia Plateau PM$_{10}$ Project (CP$_3$) was initiated in 1992 by USDA-ARS and Washington State University scientists to develop practical and economically viable solutions for reducing wind erosion and dust emissions from irrigated and rainfed cropland and to assist farmers to implement control practices. Other goals were to research the mechanics of wind erosion and PM$_{10}$ emissions and to develop prediction methods to quantify topsoil loss and effects on downwind air quality. Startup of the CP$_3$ was driven by federal air quality mandates (see Air Quality Standards for Agricultural Dust section) that regulate airborne particulates 10 μm and smaller. More than 100 referred journal articles, plus extension bulletins and videos, have been published by CP$_3$ scientists and extension personnel; these are available online at http://pnw-winderosion.wsu.edu (verified 20 Oct. 2009). Major accomplishments of the CP$_3$ are reported by Papendick (2004).

Needs for Research

Economics, risk reduction, and environmental concerns will likely continue to be the major factors driving policy, research, and farmers' decisions in the future (Upadhyay et al., 2003). The increasing cost of fuel and other inputs in recent years and the availability of environment-related income support by government farm programs such as EQIP favor the ongoing adoption of conservation-till, no-till, and precision farming methods. Priority research needs for soil and water conservation in Inland Northwest agriculture are:

- Develop winter wheat cultivars for late planting (i.e., mid October or later) in chemical summer fallow that can compete economically with early-planted wheat on conservation-till summer fallow in the low precipitation zone.

- Develop winter wheat cultivars with the ability to emerge in 7 to 10 d from deep planting depths of 15 cm or more in dry summer-fallowed soils. These soils often have very low water potential in the seed zone. Successful winter wheat plant establishment from late August to early September planting is presently a prerequisite for achieving the highest potential grain and straw production.

- Develop perennial wheat cultivars that can produce grain for several years before replanting is needed. Perennial wheat will be especially useful in soils with low crop production potential due to rockiness, shallow soil depth, or other limiting characteristics. Many such soils are presently enrolled in the Conservation Reserve Program, and perennial wheat would be a logical "next step" for these lands.

- Determine why wheat straw from different cultivars decomposes at different rates and ultimately breed genotypes with high straw decomposition rates for the intermediate and high precipitation and irrigated regions and slow decomposition rates for the low precipitation zone. It has been known for years that wheat cultivars vary widely in straw decomposition rate. The rate of straw decomposition appears to involve the interaction of several factors and compounds, including the content of hemicellulose, cellulose, lignin, tannins, and nitrogen, as well as the carbon/nitrogen ratio (Stubbs et al., 2009; A.C. Kennedy, personal communication, 2008).

- Develop precision agriculture technologies to allow farmers to make the most efficient use of fuel, fertilizer, herbicides, seed, and other inputs and to deliver inputs at controlled rates on steep topography.

- Maintain strong collaborative relations among research scientists, extension specialists and innovative farmers to develop and evaluate new conservation-till, no-till, and precision agriculture technologies. Provide agency support for farmer-run conservation organizations such as the PNDSA and ensure continued active farmer membership on special research grant steering committees such as STEEP and CP_3.

- Develop a "soil conservation related" research effort for irrigated agriculture. The USDA-ARS and/or concerned land-grant universities should devote more resources for research on high residue farming in diverse irrigated cropping systems.

- Make sure that potential biofuel crops to produce ethanol, biodiesel, and combustible dry biomass can fit into cropping systems in an environmentally sustainable manner.

- Validate the RUSLE2 water and WEPS wind erosion models for Inland PNW conditions to improve prediction of water and wind erosion on the region's diverse cropping systems, soils, and topography. Refine these models under different levels of residue cover, surface roughness, steepness of slopes, and soil types.

- Develop options for flexible and profitable cropping systems that maximize year-round surface cover and take advantage of special climatic conditions such as: (i) late-summer rains that may allow timely planting of alternative crops such as winter canola soon after cereal grain harvest in the intermediate and high precipitation zones or (ii) greater than average over-winter soil water storage that will increase the likelihood of successful spring cropping in typical WW–SF areas.

References

Ahuja, L.R., O. David, and J.C. Ascough II. 2004. Developing natural resource models using the object modeling system: Feasibility and challenges. Trans. 2nd Bienn. Meeting Int. Environ. Modelling and Software Soc., iEMSs. 14–17 June 2004. Osnabrück, Germany.

Ascough, J.C., II, C. Baffaut, M.A. Nearing, and D.C. Flanagan. 1995. Watershed model channel hydrology and erosion processes. p. 13.1–13.20. In D.C. Flanagan and M.A. Nearing (ed.) USDA Water Erosion Prediction Project: Hillslope profile and watershed model documentation. USDA-ARS NSERL Rep. 10. USDA-ARS, West Lafayette, IN.

Baker, C.J., and K.E. Saxton. 2007. No-tillage seeding in conservation agriculture. 2nd ed. UN-FAO, CABI, Cambridge, MA.

Bewick, L.S., F.L. Young, J.R. Alldredge, and D.L. Young. 2008. Agronomics and economics of no-till facultative wheat in the Pacific Northwest, USA. Crop Prot. 27:932–942.

Busacca, A.J. 1989. Long Quaternary record in eastern Washington, U.S.A. interpreted from multiple buried paleosols in loess. Geoderma 45:105–122.

Busacca, A.J., H.M. Marks, and R. Rossi. 2001. Volcanic glass in soils of the Columbia Plateau, Pacific Northwest, USA. Soil Sci. Soc. Am. J. 65:161–168.

Cook, K.V., L. Faulconer, and D.G. Jennings. 1996. A report on nitrate contamination of ground water in the mid-Columbia Basin. Wash. St. Interagency Ground Water Committee Publ. 96-17.

Donaldson, E., W.F. Schillinger, and S.M. Dofing. 2001. Straw production and grain yield relationships in winter wheat. Crop Sci. 41:100–106.

Ebbert, J.C., and M.H. Kim. 1998. Relation between irrigation method, sediment yields, and losses of pesticides and nitrogen. J. Environ. Qual. 27:372–380.

Feng, G., and B.S. Sharratt. 2005. Sensitivity analysis of soil and PM10 loss in WEPS using the LHS-OAT method. Trans. ASAE 48:1409–1420.

Feng, G., and B.S. Sharratt. 2007. Validation of WEPS for soil and PM10 loss from agricultural fields on the Columbia Plateau of the United States. Earth Surf. Processes Landforms 32:743–753.

Flanagan, D.C., J.C. Ascough, II, A.D. Nicks, M.A. Nearing, and J.M. Laflen. 1995. Overview of the WEPP erosion prediction model. p. 1.1–1.12. In D.C. Flanagan and M.A. Nearing (ed.) USDA Water Erosion Prediction Project: Hillslope profile and watershed model documentation. USDA-ARS NSERL Rep. 10. USDA-ARS, West Lafayette, IN.

Flanagan, D.C., and M.A. Nearing. 1995. USDA Water Erosion Prediction Project: Hillslope profile and watershed model documentation. USDA-ARS NSERL Rep. 10. USDA-ARS, West Lafayette, IN.

Foster, G.R., D.C. Flanagan, M.A. Nearing, L.J. Lane, L.M. Risse, and S.C. Finkner. 1995. Hillslope erosion component. p. 11.1–11.12. In D.C. Flanagan and M.A. Nearing (ed.) USDA Water Erosion Prediction Project: Hillslope profile and watershed model documentation. USDA-ARS NSERL Rep. 10. USDA-ARS, West Lafayette, IN.

Hagen, L.J. 1991. A wind erosion prediction system to meet user needs. J. Soil Water Conserv. 46(2):106–111.

Hammel, J.E., R.I. Papendick, and G.S. Campbell. 1981. Fallow tillage effects on evaporation and seed-zone water content in a dry summer climate. Soil Sci. Soc. Am. J. 45:1016–1022.

Horner, G.M., A.G. McCall, and F.G. Bell. 1944. Investigations in erosion control and reclamation of eroded land at the Palouse Conservation Experiment Station, Pullman, Wash., 1931–42. Tech. Bull. 860. USDA, Washington, DC.

Howell, T.A. 2001. Enhancing water use efficiency in irrigated agriculture. Agron. J. 93:281–289.

Jones, S.S. 2002. Wheat in the west. J. West 41:44–46.

Kennedy, A.C., and K.L. Smith. 1995. Soil microbial diversity and the sustainability of agricultural soils. Plant Soil 170:75–86.

Kjelgaard, J., D. Chandler, and K. Saxton. 2004. Evidence for direct suspension of loessial soils on the Columbia Plateau. Earth Surf. Processes Landforms 29:221–236.

Kok, H., R.I. Papendick, and K.E. Saxton. 2009. STEEP: Impact of long-term conservation farming research and education in Pacific Northwest wheatlands. J. Soil Water Conserv. 64:253–264.

Kok, H., R. Papendick, K. Saxton, W. Pan, and R. Bolton. 2008. Planting date guide for winter wheat cover crops to control wind erosion in the Columbia Basin. Wash. St. Univ. Ext. Bull EB2030E.

Kunch, T.K. 2001. Radar assessment and GIS decision support of cover cropping in the Columbia Basin. M.S. thesis, Wash. State Univ., Pullman.

Leggett, G.E., H.M. Reisenauer, and W.L. Nelson. 1959. Fertilization of dry land wheat in eastern Washington. Wash. St. Agric. Exp. Stn. Bull. 602.

Lentz, R.D., and R.E. Sojka. 2000. Applying polymers to irrigation water: Evaluating strategies for furrow erosion control. Trans. ASAE 43:1561–1568.

Lin, C., and D.K. McCool. 2006. Simulating snowmelt and frost depth by an energy budget approach. Trans. ASABE 49:1383–1394.

Lin, C., D.K. McCool, D.C. Flanagan, and B.S. Sharratt. 2001. An energy budget approach to simulate snowmelt and soil frost depth. p. 611–614. In J.C. Ascough and D.C. Flanagan (ed.) Proc. of the Int. Symp. on Soil Erosion Res. for the 21st Century, Honolulu, HI. 3–5 Jan. 2001. ASAE, St. Joseph, MI.

Lindsey, K., W. Burt, J. Porcello, D. Vlassopoulos, M. Karanovic, M. Nielson, and S. Loper. 2009. Basalt aquifer recharge, age, and water level in the Columbia Basin ground water management area of Adams, Franklin, Grant and Lincoln Counties, Washington. Columbia Basin Ground Water Management Area. A summary report to the Washington State Legislature.

McCall, M.A. 1925. The soil mulch in the absorption and retention of moisture. J. Agric. Res. 30:819–831.

McCall, M.A., and H.F. Holtz. 1921. Investigations in dry farm tillage. Bull. 164. Agric. Exp. Stn., State College of Washington, Pullman.

McCool, D.K., and A.J. Busacca. 1999. Measuring and modeling soil erosion and erosion damages. p. 23–56. In E.L. Michalson et al. (ed.) Conservation farming in the United States—The methods and accomplishments of the STEEP Program. CRC Press, Boca Raton, FL.

McCool, D.K., C.D. Pannkuk, C.H. Lin, and J.M. Laflen. 1998. Evaluation of WEPP for temporally frozen soil. Paper 982048. 1998 Annual International Meeting ASAE. Orlando, FL. 12–16 July 1998. ASAE, St. Joseph, MI.

McDonald, E.V., and A.J. Busacca. 1988. Record of pre-late Wisconsin giant floods in the channeled scabland interpreted from loess deposits. Geology 16:728–731.

McGuire, A.M. 2003. Mustard green manures replace fumigant and improve infiltration in potato cropping system. Online. Crop Manage. doi:10.1094/CM-2003-0822-01-RS.

Meinig, D.W. 1968. The Great Columbia Plain: A historical geography, 1805–1910. Library of Congress catalog card 68-11044. University of Washington Press, Seattle.

Montgomery, J.A., D.K. McCool, A.J. Busacca, and B.E. Frazier. 1999. Quantifying tillage translocation and deposition rates due to moldboard plowing in the Palouse region of the Pacific Northwest, USA. Soil Tillage Res. 51:175–187.

NASS. 2008. Idaho, Oregon, and Washington statistics. National Agricultural Statistics Service, USDA, Washington, DC.

Pan, W., W. Schillinger, D. Huggins, R. Koenig, and J. Burns. 2007. Fifty years of predicting wheat nitrogen requirements in the Pacific Northwest USA. p. 10.1–10.6. In T. Bruulsema (ed.) Managing crop nitrogen for weather. International Plant Nutrition Inst., Norcross, GA.

Papendick, R.I. 1996. Farming systems and conservation needs in the northwest wheat region. Am. J. Alternative Agric. 11:52–57.

Papendick, R.I. 2004. Farming with the wind II: Wind erosion and air quality control on the Columbia Plateau and Columbia Basin. Special Rep. XB 1042 by the Columbia Plateau PM_{10} Project. Washington Agric. Exp. Stn., Pullman.

Papendick, R.I., M.J. Lindstrom, and V.L. Cochran. 1973. Soil mulch effects on seedbed temperature and water during fallow in Eastern Washington. Soil Sci. Soc. Am. Proc. 37:307–314.

Papendick, R.I., and D.K. McCool. 1994. Residue management strategies—Pacific Northwest. p. 1–14. In J.L. Hatfield and B.A. Stewart (ed.) Crop residue management. Lewis Publishers. Boca Raton, FL.

Papendick, R.I., D.K. McCool, and H.A. Krauss. 1983. Soil conservation: Pacific Northwest. p. 273–290. In H.E. Dregne and W.O. Willis (ed.) Dryland agriculture. Agron. Monogr. 23. ASA, CSSA, and SSSA, Madison, WI

Paulitz, T.C., R.W. Smiley, and R.J. Cook. 2002. Insights into the prevalence and management of soilborne cereal pathogens under direct seeding in the Pacific Northwest, USA. Can. J. Plant Path. 24:416–428.

Ramig, R.E., R.R. Allmaras, and R.I. Papendick. 1983. Water conservation: Pacific Northwest. p. 105–124. *In* H.E. Dregne and W.O. Willis (ed.) Dryland Agriculture. Agron. Monogr. 23. ASA, CSSA, and SSSA, Madison, WI

Rasmussen, P.E., and W.J. Parton. 1994. Long-term effects of residue management in wheat–fallow: I. Inputs, yield, and soil organic matter. Soil Sci. Soc. Am. J. 58:523–530.

Renard, K.G., G.R. Foster, G.A. Weesies, D.K. McCool, and D.C. Yoder. 1997. Predicting soil erosion by water: A guide to conservation planning with the revised Universal Soil Loss Equation (RUSLE). Agric. Handb. 703. USDA, Washington, DC.

Saxton, K., D. Chandler, L. Stetler, B. Lamb, C. Claiborn, and B.-H. Lee. 2000. Wind erosion and fugitive dust fluxes on agricultural lands in the Pacific Northwest. Trans. ASAE 43:623–630.

Schillinger, W.F. 2001. Minimum and delayed conservation tillage for wheat–fallow farming. Soil Sci. Soc. Am. J. 65:1203–1209.

Schillinger, W.F., A.C. Kennedy, and D.L. Young. 2007. Eight years of annual no-till cropping in Washington's winter wheat-summer fallow region. Agric. Ecosyst. Environ. 120:345–358.

Schillinger, W.F., and R.I. Papendick. 2008. Then and now: 125 years of dryland wheat farming in the Inland Pacific Northwest. Agron. J. 100(Suppl.):S166–S182.

Schillinger, W.F., S.E. Schofstoll, and J.R. Alldredge. 2008. Available water and wheat grain yield relations in a Mediterranean climate. Field Crops Res. 109:45–49.

Sharratt, B.S., and G. Feng. 2009. Windblown dust influenced by conventional and undercutter tillage within the Columbia Plateau, USA. Earth Surf. Processes Landforms 34:1323–1332.

Sharratt, B., G. Feng, and L. Wendling. 2007. Loss of soil and PM_{10} from agricultural fields associated with high winds on the Columbia Plateau. Earth Surf. Processes Landforms 32:621–630.

Sharratt, B.S., and D. Lauer. 2006. Particulate matter concentration and air quality affected by windblown dust in the Columbia Plateau. J. Environ. Qual. 35:2011–2016.

Smiley, R.W., A.G. Ogg, Jr., and R.J. Cook. 1992. Influence of glyphosate on severity of rhizoctonia root rot and growth and yield of barley. Plant Dis. 76:937–942.

Sojka, R.E., D.L. Bjorneberg, J.A. Entry, R.D. Lentz, and W.J. Orts. 2007. Polyacrylamide in agriculture and environmental land management. Adv. Agron. 92:75–162.

Stetler, L.D., and K.E. Saxton. 1996. Wind erosion and PM_{10} emissions from agricultural fields on the Columbia Plateau. Earth Surf. Processes Landforms 21:673–685.

Stubbs, T.L., A.C. Kennedy, P.E. Reisenauer, and J.W. Burns. 2009. Chemical composition of residue from cereal crops and cultivars in dryland ecosystems. Agron. J. 101:538–545.

Sweeney, M.R., D.R. Gaylord, and A.J. Busacca. 2007. Evolution of Eureka Flat: A dust-producing engine of the Palouse loess, USA. Quaternary Int. 162:76–96.

Toy, T.J., G.R. Foster, and K.G. Renard. 2002. Soil erosion: Processes, prediction, measurement, and control. John Wiley and Sons, New York.

Upadhyay, B.M., D.L. Young, H.H. Wang, and P. Wandschneider. 2003. How do farmers who adopt multiple conservation practices differ from their neighbors? Am. J. Alternative Agric. 18:27–36.

USDA. 1978. Palouse cooperative river basin study. SCS; Forest Serv.; and Economics, Statistics, and Coop. Serv. USDA. U.S. Gov. Print. Office, Washington, DC.

U.S. OFR. 2006. National ambient air quality standards for particulate matter; proposed rule. Federal Register (17 Jan.) 71:2619–2708. US Gov. Print. Office, Washington, DC.

Van Oost, K., G. Govers, S. de Alba, and T.A. Quine. 2006. Tillage erosion: A review of controlling factors and implications for soil quality. Prog. Phys. Geogr. 30:443–466.

Weinert, T.L., W.L. Pan, M.R. Moneymaker, G.S. Santo, and R.G. Stevens. 2002. Nitrogen recycling by non-leguminous winter cover crops to reduce leaching in potato rotations. Agron. J. 94:365–372.

Williams, J.D., S. Dun, D.S. Robertson, J.Q. Wu, E. Brooks, D.C. Flanagan, and D.K. McCool. 2010. WEPP simulations of runoff events from small drainages in Northeastern Oregon. J. Soil Water Conserv. (in press).

Wischmeier, W.H., C.B. Johnson, and B.V. Cross. 1971. A soil erodibility nomograph for farmland and construction sites. J. Soil Water Conserv. 26:189–193.

Wischmeier, W.H., and D.D. Smith. 1965. Predicting rainfall erosion losses from cropland east of the Rocky Mountains—A guide for selection of practices for soil and water conservation. Agric. Handb. 282. U.S. Gov. Printing Office, Washington, DC.

Wischmeier, W.H., and D.D. Smith. 1978. Predicting rainfall erosion losses—A guide to conservation planning. Agric. Handb. 537. U.S. Gov. Printing Office, Washington, DC.

Woodruff, N.P., and F.H. Siddoway. 1965. A wind erosion equation. Soil Sci. Soc. Am. Proc. 29:602–608.

Wuest, S.B. 2001. Earthworm, infiltration, and tillage relationships in a dryland pea–wheat rotation. Appl. Soil Ecol. 18:187–192.

Young, D.L., T.J. Kwon, and F.L. Young. 1994. Profit and risk for integrated conservation farming systems in the Palouse. J. Soil Water Conserv. 49:601–606.

Young, F.L., A.G. Ogg, R.I. Papendick, D.C. Thill, and J.R. Alldredge. 1994. Tillage and weed management affects winter wheat yield in an integrated pest management system. Agron. J. 86:147–154.

Zaikin, A.A., D.L. Young, and W.F. Schillinger. 2007. Economic comparison of undercutter and traditional tillage systems for winter wheat–summer fallow farming. Ext. Bull. EB2022E. Washington State Univ., Pullman.

Zuzel, J.F., R.R. Allmaras, and R.N. Greenwalt. 1982. Runoff and soil erosion on frozen soil in northeastern Oregon. J. Soil Water Conserv. 37:351–354.

Zuzel, J.F., and J.L. Pikul, Jr. 1987. Infiltration into a seasonally frozen agricultural soil. J. Soil Water Conserv. 42:447–450.

3

Soil and Water Conservation Advances in the Semiarid Northern Great Plains

Donald L. Tanaka
USDA-ARS, Mandan, ND

Drew J. Lyon
University of Nebraska Panhandle Research and Extension Center, Scottsbluff, NE

Perry R. Miller
Dep. of Land Resour. and Environ. Sci., Montana State University, Bozeman, MT

Stephen D. Merrill
retired, formerly USDA-ARS, Mandan, ND

Brian G. McConkey
Agriculture and Agri-Food Canada, Swift Current, SK, Canada

This chapter deals with the semiarid Northern Great Plains (NGP), which includes parts of Montana, North Dakota, South Dakota, Wyoming, Nebraska, Alberta, and Saskatchewan, designated as Agroecoregions 1, 4, 5, 6, 7, 8, 9, 11, and 12 as described by Padbury et al. (2002) (Fig. 3–1). The purpose of this part of the book is to discuss and illustrate how advances in soil and water conservation technology have evolved to improve precipitation use and to develop sustainable agricultural systems that are resilient for the NGP. The Great Plains has often been referred to as the "Great American Desert," with many early maps showing this area similar to the Sahara desert (Hargreaves, 1957). Captain John Palliser, who conducted the first major natural resource survey of Canadian prairies in 1857, deemed the semiarid portions of Alberta and Saskatchewan too arid for arable agriculture and advised against settlement (Gray, 1967). Not surprisingly, many dryland agricultural practices for North America originated on these plains by necessity. The slogan on the cover of Hardy Campbell's (1907) *Soil Culture Manual* promoted water management in the Great Plains as such—*"The Camel for the Sahara Desert, The Campbell Method for the American Desert."*

Climate of the region is characterized as continental, with annual precipitation typically peaking unimodally in mid to late spring, and 70% of annual precipitation received in the 6-mo period from April to September (Linfield, 1907). Frequency and distribution of precipitation vary considerably from year to year and month to month, in addition to spatial variability in the summer due to con-

Soil and Water Conservation Advances in the United States. SSSA Special Publication 60.
T.M. Zobeck and W.F. Schillinger, editors. © 2010. SSSA, 677 S. Segoe Rd., Madison, WI 53711, USA.

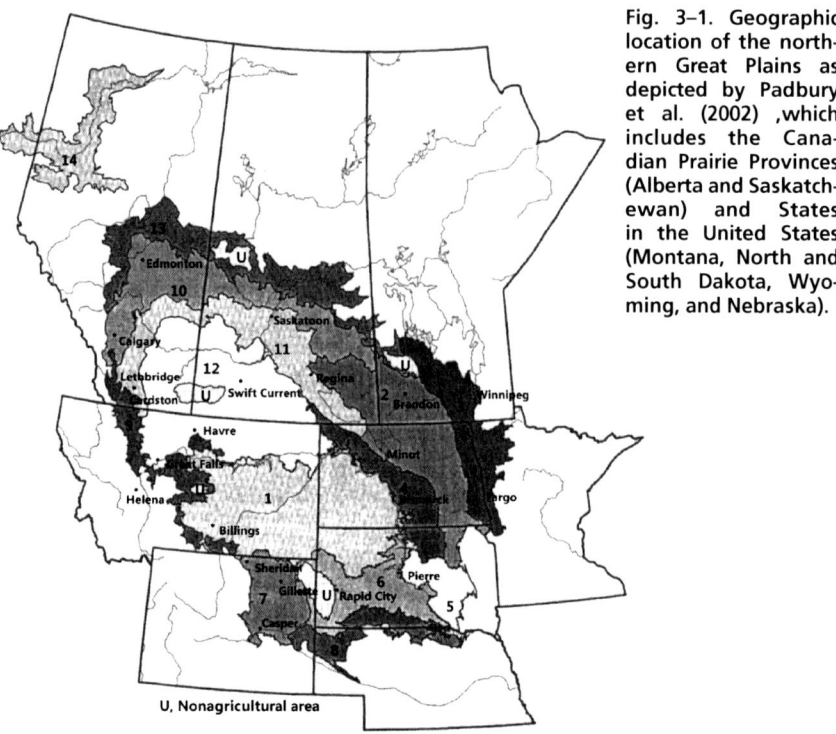

Fig. 3–1. Geographic location of the northern Great Plains as depicted by Padbury et al. (2002) ,which includes the Canadian Prairie Provinces (Alberta and Saskatchewan) and States in the United States (Montana, North and South Dakota, Wyoming, and Nebraska).

vective precipitation systems. Average annual precipitation ranges from 260 mm in the driest production area of north central Montana to more than 400 mm near the transitional boundary to subhumid agroecosystems in northern Nebraska, with a standard deviation near 75 mm. Snow is intermittent and highly variable within this region but may account for 20 to 30% of total precipitation. Key climatic variables were described further by Padbury et al. (2002).

Cultivated soils in the NGP were derived from glacial till and drifts, glacial lake sediments, aeolian sands, loess, residuum, alluvium, and marine sediment parent materials. Glacial till soils are usually north and east of the Missouri River while loess soils dominate the High Plains of Nebraska (Aandahl, 1982). The parent material– native prairie vegetation– climate interactions resulted in soils mostly in the order Mollisols. A relatively small portion of the soils belong to the order Entisols along the region's western edge close to the Rocky Mountains. Mollisols are some of the most productive cultivated dryland soils in North America because the soils have a friable surface soil structure, high cation exchange capacity, high degree of base saturation, and high organic matter content that imparts inherently good fertility (van Riper, 1971).

Historic Soil and Water Conservation
Summer Fallow

Many of the early settlers to the semiarid NGP came from humid places, such as central Canada, Europe, and the U.S. Midwest (Meilicke, 1997; Raban, 1997), spurred by promotion of Northern Pacific, Great Northern, and Canadian Pacific

Fig. 3–2. Settlers to the northern Great Plains brought tillage tools used in areas with greater precipitation.

railways. Settlers brought with them the familiar tillage tools, cropping systems, and seeds that emulated the longer growing season and greater precipitation regions from which they came (Fig. 3–2). They were encouraged to adopt "dry farming" practices, as extolled by Campbell (1907) and fledgling agricultural experiment stations and substations (Bell, 1968). The early settlers to the NGP came during a wet cycle from 1895 to 1915, characterized by above-average precipitation and successful annual crop production (Gray, 1967; Ford and Krall, 1974). When weather conditions changed to a dry cycle, the annual cropping systems were not resilient and were prone to crop failure.

One of the first strategies to help producers stabilize crop yields during drought periods and reduce the risk of crop failure in the NGP was the crop–fallow system (Campbell, 1907; Gray, 1967; Black et al., 1974; Ford and Krall, 1974) (Fig. 3–3). It's impossible to know the origins of crop–fallow and where the practice was first used in the semiarid NGP. The most well-chronicled account places the discovery of summer fallow for the purpose of soil water management near Indian Head, SK in 1886 (Carlyle, 1997). Land idled in 1885 in the Qu'Appelle district of present-day Saskatchewan, yielded very well in the dry season of 1886 while wheat (*Triticum aestivum* L.) grown on stubble yielded very little. As a result, Angus Mackay, an area farmer emigrant from Scotland in 1881, and first head of the Dominion Government Experimental Farm established at Indian Head in 1888, promoted summer fallow vigorously in the Canadian prairies (Phillipson, 2009). In Montana, a drought period from 1917 to 1922 resulted in many farm foreclosures and the entrenchment of summer fallow as a risk management practice by those who remained (Wilson, 1928).

H.W. Campbell's (1907) 316-page textbook, written in a strongly patriarchal style, took great exception to the term *summer fallow*. He referred instead to "summer culture," a sophisticated "system" of timely and more frequent tillage than was typical of early summer fallow, and based ultimately on unsound principles of soil water movement. Campbell's text contains newspaper accounts of the 20-yr history of his summer culture experimentation, beginning around 1885 in

Fig. 3–3. The crop–fallow system was an early strategy to help stabilize crop yields in the northern Great Plains.

Brown county, South Dakota. However, it is unclear when summer fallow was formally entrenched as a key component to his "Scientific Soil Culture" system. A historical bibliography makes reference to his alternating fascination and disinterest in the practice of fallow between 1883 and 1896, but by 1898 Campbell was promoting summer culture with evangelistic zeal (Hargreaves, 1958). His soil management system was promoted by the 1906 Campbell System Farming Association of Denver, CO and in the first (Trans-Missouri) Dry Farming Congress in 1907 in Denver, CO (Campbell, 1907). The third and fourth Congresses were held in Cheyenne, WY and Billings, MT in 1908. During 1906 and 1907 Campbell was employed by the Department of Agriculture in the newly formed Province of Alberta to lecture there, and the Montana Agricultural Experiment Station promoted the "Campbell system" during railway-sponsored Montana Farmers' Institutes in the winter of 1908–1909, designed to embolden settlers about farming prospects in Montana (Hargreaves, 1977). In 1912, the seventh Dry Farming Congress was held in Lethbridge, AB, with promotional assistance from the railways. Given the obvious crop production attributes of summer fallow during a dry year, it would not be surprising if this concept emerged accidentally at many places in the semiarid NGP, coincident with early settlement by farmers, a probability stated by Campbell (1907). Regardless of when and where summer fallow was discovered, and what it was called, it seems certain that there was no greater promoter of this practice than H.W. Campbell.

Summer fallow, the practice of controlling weeds on uncropped land with tillage to store soil water for a later crop, has been practiced for more than a century. Nutrients, principally nitrogen, were also mineralized from soil organic matter during the fallow period and this provided another persuasive benefit (Campbell et al., 2008). Although summer fallow involved a large investment

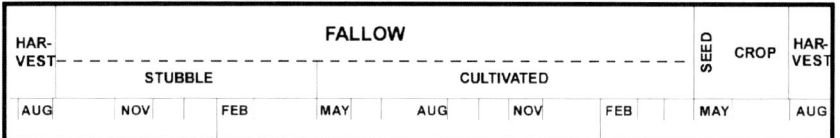

Fig. 3–4. A schematic timeline of a 14-mo winter wheat–fallow system and a 21-mo spring wheat–fallow system. Winter wheat–fallow dominates in the south, and spring wheat–fallow dominates the north of the northern Great Plains.

in land because it required double the area required for an annual crop system, the risk reduction afforded by the extra stored soil water, combined with the agronomic benefits of weed control and soil fertility, made wheat–fallow the predominant crop rotation in the Great Plains during most of the 20th century. Fallow periods in this rotation vary in length from 14 to 21 mo depending on whether it is a winter or spring wheat system, and the actual time wheat plants are growing in the field is only three to 10 mo out of the 24-mo cycle (Fig. 3–4). The 14-mo winter wheat–fallow system dominated in Nebraska, Wyoming, South Dakota, and parts of Montana and Alberta, while the 21-mo spring wheat–fallow system dominated in northeastern Montana, North Dakota, Saskatchewan, and part of Alberta.

Although some wheat was grown following summer fallow in the drier portions of the U.S. Great Plains at the turn of the twentieth century, adoption of fallow by farmers was slow, primarily because satisfactory yields were possible in wet years without summer fallow, and tillage was difficult to accomplish with horse-drawn implements or primitive tractors (Salmon et al., 1953). The general practice of summer fallow became established between 1925 and 1940, with the most widespread adoption during the extended drought in the mid 1930s (Table 3–1). Summer fallow in the NGP peaked in 1971, coincident with the Canadian and U.S. farm programs that favored this practice, and has declined steadily since due to several economic and agronomic factors (Fig. 3–5; Carlyle, 1997).

Early tillage techniques during summer fallow used inversion and mixing implements (i.e., plow and disk) to create a condition known as *dust mulch* fallow (Campbell, 1907; Salmon et al., 1953). Dust mulch fallow created a discontinuity in soil pores to prevent soil water loss during the summer period. Dust mulch not only suppresses soil water evaporation but also disrupts the capillarity that brings stored soil water from below to help crop establishment. The number of tillage operations needed to control weeds and to create a dust mulch ranged from 7 to 15 operations (Salmon et al., 1953). The fine pulverized soil created by dust mulch during summer fallow was vulnerable to wind and water erosion, which became a severe problem culminating in the Dust Bowl era of the 1930s (Hargreaves, 1993) (Fig. 3–6). The Dust Bowl and the Great Depression of 1929

Table 3-1. Historical summer fallow area derived from national census data in four states and two provinces representing the semiarid northern Great Plains.

Year	MT	ND	SD	WY	Year	AB	SK
			ha × 1,000,000				
1925	0.71†	0.67†	0.12†	0.06†	1926	NA	NA
1930	1.12†	0.98†	0.23†	0.08†	1931	1.30	2.80
1935	1.39†	2.09†	1.12†	0.15†	1936	1.73	3.32
1940	1.58†	2.76†	1.00†	0.13†	1941	2.02	3.56
1945	1.28†	1.23†	0.25†	0.08†	1946	2.28	4.56
1950	1.71	2.17‡	0.18	0.12	1951	2.51	5.20
1954	2.02	1.98‡	0.29	0.14	1956	2.87	6.04
1959	2.18	2.37‡	0.40	0.13	1957–60	2.78§	6.00§
1964	2.31	2.81‡	0.63	0.13	1961–64	2.88§	6.88§
					1965–68	2.75§	6.71§
1969	NA	3.52‡	NA	NA	1969–72	2.97§	7.17§
1974	NA	2.68‡	NA	NA	1973–76	2.79§	7.15§
1978	2.25	2.65	0.62	0.14	1977–80	2.62§	6.99§
1981		2.46‡			1981–84	2.06§	6.40§
1987	2.30	2.62‡	0.89	0.13	1986	2.13	5.99
1992	1.97	1.75‡	0.55	0.10	1991	1.77	5.72
1997	1.76	0.93‡	0.36	0.09	1996	1.30	4.01
2002	1.41	1.07‡	0.19	0.06	2001	1.26	3.00
2007	1.37	0.24	0.18	0.05	2007	0.85	2.15

† Includes "idle" land also, which was 4.6, 5.8, 19.2, and 14.8% of "cultivated fallow + idle land" in 1964 in Montana, North Dakota, South Dakota, and Wyoming, respectively.
‡ Periodic 5-yr averages centered on 1951 through 2001, NASS, North Dakota agricultural statistics.
§ Based on 4-yr period averages from Campbell et al. (1986).

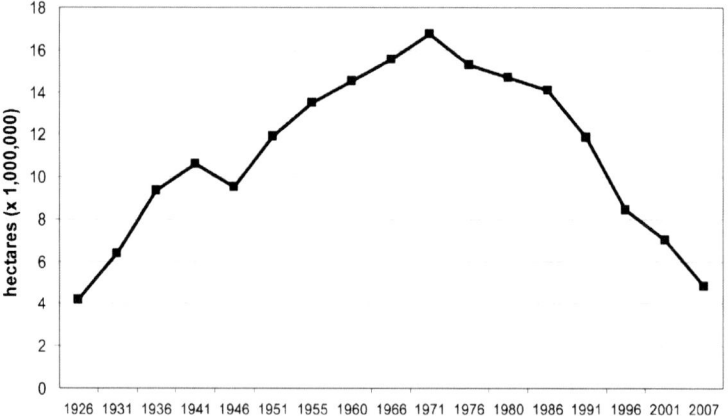

Fig. 3-5. Estimated aggregate summer fallow area in Alberta, North and South Dakota, Saskatchewan, Montana, and Wyoming from 1926 to 2007. Data are derived from annual provincial or state records or national census data available at multiyear (usually five) intervals, corrected to remove otherwise "idled" land in the United States during 1925 to 1945. The median year indicated may involve annual reports including up to 8 yr of data centered on that year used to smooth annual variation between 1949 and 2003.

Fig. 3–6. Dust mulch summer fallow practices resulted in severe wind erosion in the northern Great Plains during the 1930s.

stimulated the first U.S. farm bill, the 1933 Agricultural Adjustment Act (PL 73-10), and the beginning of a tradition for government payments in American agriculture (Cain and Lovejoy, 2004). Because of the need for resource conservation, other acts were established in the mid 1930s, and the Soil Conservation Service (now the Natural Resources Conservation Service) was initiated in 1935 to make funds available to farmers for establishment of soil conservation practices. Similarly, the Prairie Farm Rehabilitation Administration was established in 1935 in the Canadian prairies to further soil and water conservation in response to Dust Bowl conditions (Gray, 1967).

During the late 1930s and early 1940s, farm programs throughout the NGP began to stress resource conservation, and early researchers realized the importance of crop residues on the soil surface for soil water storage and soil conservation (Duley and Russel, 1939; 1942; Chepil, 1944). Using small plot research and manually applying straw, Duley and Russel (1939, 1942) were the first to show the importance of eliminating tillage and maintaining surface residue cover on soil water storage. For the period from late April to early September on a silty clay loam at Lincoln, NE, they were able to attain a fallow efficiency (% of fallow precipitation stored as soil water) of 54% by eliminating tillage and maintaining 2250 kg/ha of winter wheat residue on the soil surface. During the same time period, land that was plowed and had no wheat residue on the soil surface had a fallow efficiency of 21%. With a 2.5-fold increase in soil water storage efficiency and a 10-fold reduction in soil loss from water erosion, the 20- to 40-yr era of stubble-mulch fallow dominated the NGP.

Before 1950, much of the winter wheat land in the NGP was fenced and pastured during the fallow period (C.R. Fenster, personal communication, 2008). Fields were frequently tilled at a shallow depth after harvest to establish volunteer wheat for pasture. The volunteer wheat was pastured during the fall, winter, and into late spring. Tillage for summer fallow began after 1 June. By this time, volunteer wheat and weeds had taken much water from the soil profile. By the mid 1950s, pasturing of summer fallow land was discontinued, and emphasis was placed on tillage systems to store water in the soil profile and retain crop residues on the soil surface to control soil erosion.

Fallow soil water storage efficiency improved as knowledge about residue maintenance and water conservation expanded. Greb (1979) chronicled progress in winter wheat–fallow systems from the early 1900s through 1977 and then projected progress through 1990. Improvements since 1916 in fallow tillage systems increased soil water storage and fallow efficiency, with resulting improvements in winter wheat yield and precipitation use efficiency (PUE = grain yield/total precipitation during entire rotation cycle). The number of tillage operations per fallow period decreased from as many as 7 to 15 in the dust mulch systems of the early 20th century to zero to four operations in modern conservation tillage systems. Precipitation use efficiency doubled from 1916 to 1975, increasing from 1.2 to 2.8 kg of wheat ha^{-1} mm^{-1} (Greb, 1979). This was due to improved fallow-period soil water storage efficiency, which increased from 19 to 33% over the same time period. Greb (1979) projected that fallow efficiency could increase to 40% by 1990, resulting in a PUE of 3.2 kg ha^{-1} mm^{-1}. Unfortunately, there has been little improvement to the 35% storage efficiency Greb achieved for his environment in the early 1970s. Fallow efficiency reports from the 1980s and into the 1990s are generally less than 42%, regardless of the climatic zone where the data were collected (Peterson et al., 1996).

Strip cropping, where crop and fallow occur in narrow alternating strips perpendicular to direction of major eroding winds, was an important soil conservation practice for dust mulch fallow. The development of the practice was attributed to the Koole brothers in 1917 (Gray, 1967). These brothers, who farmed north of Lethbridge, AB, had noticed that wind erosion did not start for many meters downwind of the windward field boundary. By arranging their fields in narrow strips so that fallow strips were always downwind of strips in crop or with recent crop residue, there was major reduction in wind erosion. The width of strips required varied from 10 m in highly erodible sandy soils to 100 m in less erodible clay loam soils (Johnson, 1983), but 50 m or 100 m width became most common, corresponding to either 16 or eight strips per 65-ha (160-ac) field.

Shelterbelts of trees or shrubs were also used for wind erosion control for dust mulch fallow but were never as widely adopted as strip cropping. Reasons included the cost and difficulty of establishing shelterbelts and the problems caused by snow drifts downwind from the shelterbelts, which can aggravate water erosion and salinity and also impede timely weed control and seeding (Johnson, 1983).

Conservation Tillage

Conservation tillage (CT) includes reduced- or minimum-till where the soil surface has 30 to 60% crop residue coverage and no-till where the soil surface has >60% crop residue coverage and minimal soil disturbance occurs only at planting. In the NGP, maintenance of fallow with herbicides and seeding directly into the previous crop stubble represents the penultimate soil conservation practice. No-till systems can be very complex, especially those that strive for large amounts of crop residues on the soil surface while managing high levels of crop diversity (Manitoba–North Dakota Zero Tillage Farmers Association, 1997; Dakota Lakes Research Farm, 2005). Evolution of modern no-till systems required research in many disciplines to overcome early obstacles, as aptly described by Phillips and Young (1973) in their early textbook focused on no-till corn (*Zea mays* L.) production.

According to Phillips and Young (1973), no-till was a logical way to farm that did not incur high wind and water soil erosion. Study of no-till began broadly with private and public research on the concept of non-tilled chemical preparation of the seedbed and was first reported in the early 1950s in Belgium, France, Germany, New Zealand, the U.K, and the USA. Indeed, a monument at the Montana State University Northern Agricultural Research Center near Havre, MT is dedicated to pioneering research into chemical fallow by Torleif Aasheim begun in 1948, claimed as the earliest research on chemical fallow in the United States. Research on chemical fallow on the Canadian prairies began in 1956 (Anderson, 1969). The first no-till adoption by innovative producers began during the 1970s and gradually became a recognized practice during the 1980s. The oldest known continuous no-till farm field in Montana began in 1970 by Arnold Gettel and is located near Power (D. Gettel, personal communication, 2007). A farm field near Indian Head, SK has been under continuous no-till management by the Halford family since 1978 (J. Halford, personal communication, 2009).

The unfulfilled expectation for consistently greater wheat yields with conservation tillage in crop–fallow systems likely delayed farmer adoption in the semiarid NGP, but there were other key factors, such as prohibitively expensive glyphosate [*N*-(phosphonomethyl)glycine] before its international patent expiration 1983–1990 (Baccara et al., 2003) and a lag in engineering technology for efficient and effective no-till seeding. Within the NGP, it is possible to find research reports that conclude both increased (Larney and Lindwall, 1994; Carr et al., 2006; Lafond et al., 2006; Lenssen et al., 2007) and decreased yield (Halvorson et al., 2000; McConkey et al., 2003; Lyon et al., 1998) associated with no-till systems. Important soil N responses related to soil organic matter accumulation in no-till systems have been reported that may limit wheat yield during the period of early conversion of land to no-till management (Halvorson et al., 2000; McConkey et al., 2002; Carr et al., 2006; Huggins and Reganold, 2008). Long-term winter wheat–fallow tillage experiments conducted in western Nebraska for more than 25 yr found no differences in mean grain yields among plow, stubble-mulch, and no-till fallow systems, despite increased soil water in stubble-mulch and no-till systems compared to the plowed system (Lyon et al., 1998). A similar result was found for a fallow–spring wheat system, but not annually cropped systems, at Indian Head, SK (Lafond et al., 2006). Other researchers in the Great Plains have reported similar results (Peterson et al., 1996).

Increased Cropping Intensity

Smika and Wicks (1968) reported that conservation tillage altered the time when water was stored as much as it did total water storage. After 8 mo of fallow (within a total of 14 mo) the plow tillage had stored only 16% of the precipitation (56 mm of water), while the minimum-till and no-till systems had stored 40% (140 mm of water) and 60% (210 mm of water), respectively. For spring wheat–fallow systems, Tanaka and Aase (1987) found that almost 45% of the precipitation (168 mm) was stored during the first 9 mo of fallow, with minimal soil water storage the second winter (Table 3–2). Conservation tillage in spring wheat–fallow systems has improved precipitation storage efficiency values from the low 20s to the upper 30s (Peterson et al., 1996).

Table 3–2. Precipitation storage efficiency for spring wheat–fallow in Canada and the United States as influenced by seasonal segment and tillage practice.

Seasonal segment	Precipitation storage efficiency			
	1939–1950 Staple and Lehane (1952)	1915–1954 Haas and Willis (1962)	1981–1984 Tanaka and Aase (1987) SM CF	
			Stubble-mulch fallow	Chemical fallow
	———————————— % ————————————			
Harvest to May	34.0	33.0	50.7	55.8
May to Sept.	13.0	17.3	19.3	23.2
Second winter	16.0	7.6	8.0	20.0
Total	21.0	19.2	29.9	35.3

As the soil profile begins to fill with water and the surface soil nears field capacity, soil water storage efficiency falls regardless of the tillage system used. Therefore, when using conservation tillage systems, the fallow period could be terminated at an earlier date to allow the planting of a summer crop, as advanced by Peterson et al. (1996) for the central Great Plains. The summer crop will use the stored soil water and rainfall via transpiration rather than the soil losing much of it to evaporation as a result of extending the fallow period another several months. Intensifying the cropping pattern, by shortening the summer fallow period and using the precipitation nearer to the time it is received, creates the potential to increase the overall system precipitation use efficiency and ultimately increase soil productivity via the increased annual amounts of residue added to the soil. However, the strongly unimodal growing season rainfall pattern for much of the semiarid NGP, typically peaking in late spring, limits economic production of most warm-season crops away from the eastern and southern fringes of this region.

Increasing the soil water storage efficiency for summer fallow is not a universally favorable outcome. The additional stored water can aggravate problems with dryland soil salinization because the stored water raises the water table and subsequent evaporation increases salinity of the soil (Christie et al., 1985). Minimizing or eliminating fallow is necessary to prevent and mitigate soil salinization in semiarid climates where the hydrologic and subsoil salt conditions make the land prone to this type of soil loss (Brown et al., 1983).

The elimination of fall tillage, especially when combined with post-harvest herbicides to control weeds that would otherwise regrow in early spring frequently provided an important soil water conservation benefit (Lal and Steppuhn, 1980). This practice, originally intended to improve soil and water conservation on fallow, made recropping in the subsequent spring more attractive. Leaving tall cereal stubble to hold snow provided another mechanism to increase overwinter soil water storage the first winter by 0 to 35 mm (de Jong and Steppuhn, 1983; Caprio et al., 1989; Campbell et al., 1992). Leaving standing cereal stubble over winter is particularly effective for improving soil water storage on sloping land (Lal and Steppuhn, 1980; McConkey et al., 1997). Thus, the benefit of these practices on the common hummocky and rolling landscapes of the NGP may be underestimated from information derived from plots that are located on more level landscapes.

Intensifying cropping systems using no-till and crop sequences such as winter wheat–maize–fallow, winter wheat–maize–proso millet (*Panicum miliaceum* L.)–fallow, and continuous cropping—crops grown include maize, sorghum [*Sorghum bicolor* (L.) Moench], winter wheat, foxtail millet [*Setaria italica* (L.) P. Beauv.], and sunflower (*Helianthus annuus* L.)—has increased annualized grain yield by more than 75% relative to the yield of the winter wheat–fallow system in the central Great Plains (Peterson and Westfall, 2004). These yield increases have translated into 25 to 40% gains in net income for farmers (Kaan et al., 2002). In the central Great Plains, the largest step gain in annualized yield was achieved with the addition of maize or sorghum to the system (i.e., two crops in a 3-yr system). Increasing cropping intensity to three crops in 4 yr only resulted in small yield increases relative to the 3-yr system. Adding diversity to intensified cropping systems has also shown promise for improving weed control in conservation tillage systems (Larney and Lindwall, 1994). However, using warm-season crops to intensify no-till cropping systems in semiarid north central Montana proved disastrous during a recent drought cycle (Miller and Holmes, 2005).

Alternative approaches to using soil water that would otherwise be lost to evaporation during the summer include growing a legume green manure crop. Research into legume green manures in the NGP date back to the early 1900s, but it was generally dismissed as an expensive use of soil water. Legume green manures were similarly regarded until the Zentner et al. (2004) landmark report detailing their economic feasibility when soil water use was identified as a sensible tradeoff for biological N fixation. Subsequent cropping sequence research in Montana (Miller et al., 2006) showed strong promise for pea (*Pisum sativum* L.) green manure as a nitrogen-contributing crop when managed to minimize soil water use. Thus, to make this practice sustainable, intensive management of the legume green manure crop is needed, as well as favorable weather conditions.

Cropping intensification has had positive impacts on soil physical and chemical properties. Cropping system intensification under no-till management decreased bulk density of the surface soil layer, increased total porosity, and increased effective pore space (Shaver et al., 2002). The causal agent for the improvement in physical properties has been the addition of more crop residue biomass to the soil relative to the wheat–fallow system (Shaver et al., 2003). Coupled with the lack of soil disturbance in a no-till environment, the additional residue carbon has promoted aggregation and has increased aggregate stability. This example demonstrates that more intensive agriculture is often more sustainable than low input agriculture.

Recent Advances

Introduction of the "Conservation Title" in the Food Security Act of 1985 represented an important advance in soil and water conservation, setting "conservation compliance" as a future (1995) condition of farm eligibility to receive crop subsidies (Gray, 1986). The Food, Agriculture, Conservation, and Trade Act of 1990 (PL101-624) increased awareness of groundwater pollution, water quality, and probably the most important for the NGP, sustainable agriculture (Cain and Lovejoy, 2004). Sustainable agriculture improved crop diversity, better use of precipitation through annual cropping, and better residue management for soil erosion control and environmental quality. These advancements toward a more sustainable agriculture would not have occurred without conservation-till and no-till residue management techniques to improve use of precipitation.

Changes in U.S. federal farm policy in 1996 decoupled farm support payments from historical base crop production and allowed growers in the Great Plains to plant nonconventional crops like maize, sunflower, dry pea, lentil (*Lens culinaris* Medik), canola (*Brassica napus* L.), crambe (*Crambe abyssinica* Hochst.), chickpea (*Cicer arietinum* L.), buckwheat (*Fagopyrum esculentum* Moench), proso millet, safflower (*Carthamus tinctorius* L.), soybean [*Glycine max* (L.) Merr.], and grain sorghum and adopt cropping intensification without having to give up federal farm payments. In Canada, large-scale diversification started earlier than in the United States because there was a lack of farm policy that supported particular crops, so Canadian farmers diversified to capture crop market opportunities that were underexploited by U.S. farmers whose cropping options were constrained by farm policy. Unlike the wheat–fallow systems, these more intense systems respond positively to the increased soil water storage potential of conservation tillage and effectively deal with the winter annual grass weed problems that hindered many growers from adopting conservation tillage systems in wheat–fallow rotations (Blackshaw et al., 1994). Increased intensification combined with better-designed crop sequences has increased grower interest in conservation tillage, particularly in no-till systems. Rotations that include summer crops such as maize and sorghum in sequence with winter wheat and fallow allow for alternative weed management strategies that reduce weed density, improve effectiveness of herbicides used, and minimize herbicide resistance (Daugovish et al., 1999; Anderson, 2004). However, warm-season crops rely on midsummer growing season precipitation that can be unpredictable in distribution and frequency in much of the NGP, and run a greater risk of negative net economic returns compared with many cool-season crops (Miller and Holmes, 2005).

Pulse crops (annual grain legumes) have revolutionized wheat-based cropping systems in the semiarid NGP more than any other class of annual dicot crops, primarily in Saskatchewan and Alberta, but more recently also in western North Dakota and eastern Montana (Miller et al., 2002a). Area seeded to pulse crops in the semiarid NGP increased 10-fold from 188,000 ha to 2,042,000 ha between 1991 and 2001 and stabilized at greater than two million hectares each year between 2005 and 2008, coincident with effective support of pea and lentil markets in the 2002 U.S. Farm Bill (Fig. 3–7). Pulse crops have important environmental effects on soil N fertility (Walley et al., 2007), soil biology (Lupwayi and Kennedy, 2007), and greenhouse gas emissions (Lemke et al., 2007), and they are important in adaptation of NGP dryland agriculture to climate change (Cutforth et al., 2007). Commercial cultivars of winter types of pea and lentil exist, but the ability of this winter growth habit to extend production of these crops in the semiarid NGP remains uncertain at this time (Chen et al., 2006).

The reductions in price of glyphosate after 1990 in anticipation of and following the end of patent protection (Kappler et al., 2005) resulted in an increase in the use of conservation and no-till cropping systems in the NGP. Before generic glyphosate, farmers could control weeds during fallow more economically with tillage or tillage and glyphosate than with herbicides alone (Wiese et al., 1994; Zentner et al., 2002). With generic glyphosate, no-till became economically feasible for more farmers. Farmers could also cover more ground in less time by spraying than with mechanical tillage, which markedly reduced labor costs per acre,

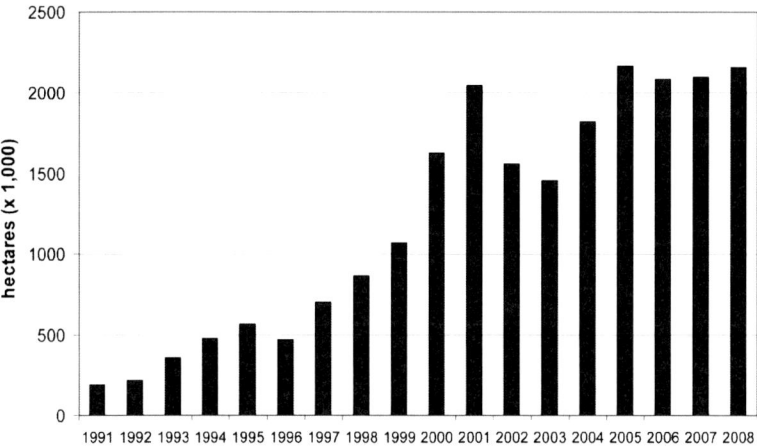

Fig. 3–7. Estimated pea, lentil, and chickpea hectares seeded in semiarid areas of Montana, North Dakota, Alberta, and Saskatchewan (areas delineated by Padbury et al., 2002). Data derived from U.S. Farm Service Agency in Montana and North Dakota and Provincial Statistic Agencies in Alberta and Saskatchewan.

and permitted more timely crop seeding. However, widespread use of glyphosate has resulted in a significant increase in the development of glyphosate-resistant weeds in other regions, which could jeopardize the efficacy of glyphosate and the growth in conservation tillage systems in the NGP in the future (Duke and Powles, 2008). Of equal concern are recent reports of ineffective weed control by glyphosate at increased CO_2 concentrations in controlled environments representing atmospheric concentrations expected to be attained in coming decades (Hatfield et al., 2008). Glyphosate currently represents a fundamental input for no-till systems, so any loss in efficacy can reasonably be expected to have important consequences for soil conservation.

Improved soil and water conservation practices, such as no-till and conservation-till, have helped to reduce the frequency of fallow and have transformed agriculture into large-scale farms that specialize and are energy-intensive systems (Brummer, 1998). Cropping systems that specialize in one or two crops, such as winter wheat or spring wheat, provide minimal or no plant diversity and can ultimately lead to biological and physical soil property degradation of the system and, in many instances, soil chemical property degradation (Kirschenmann, 2002). Many of these cropping systems have had a predetermined crop rotation and were often referred to as "fixed-cropping systems" (Black et al., 1974). Fixed-cropping systems focus on a few crop species; therefore, they lack sufficient crop diversity. The rigidity of the fixed cropping system causes agronomic weaknesses to be reinforced with time, and, in this way, they mimic monoculture systems.

Recent dryland cropping systems research efforts in the NGP have focused on the elimination of summer fallow, with its negative effects on soil quality and its inefficient soil water storage (Miller et al., 2006). The elimination of summer fallow will increase variability in crop response to management, which will make it more difficult for researchers to identify superior management practices, particularly over a short time horizon (Lyon and Peterson, 2005).

Cutforth and McConkey (1997) showed, under conditions of equal total evapotranspiration (ET), there are important improvements in crop water use efficiency (WUE) from no-till planting into standing small grain stubble. Spring wheat planted into 30-cm-tall stubble showed increased WUE of 10 to 15% compared to a cultivated seedbed. This was attributed to improved microclimate for plant growth in standing stubble: evaporation of water from soil surface was reduced, the proportion of ET as transpiration increased, and plant respiration was reduced due to lower wind speeds. Increases in WUE were confirmed for pulse and oilseed crops (Cutforth et al., 2002, 2006). Reduction in wind speeds from standing stubble was discernable even at full crop canopy (Cutforth et al., 2002; 2006). These WUE effects occurred in both years with favorable and unfavorable moisture regimes. Hence, no-till management in semiarid NGP is essential for making the most efficient use of precipitation.

Due to government programs, economic outcomes, and perceived needs among producers and researchers for additional cropping options, the number and diversity of crops in NGP cropping systems increased (Peterson et al., 1996). Annual cropping systems are a viable option for producers and include diverse crops such as oilseeds, pulses, forbs, and forages. The flex-crop systems approach was developed to assist producers in making decisions as to whether to plant a crop or fallow based on soil water status at planting (Brown et al., 1981; Zentner et al., 1993), although this approach has proven impractical to implement on a regional basis. In fact, it appears that stored water at planting of spring crops relates only weakly to wheat yield (Miller, 2006). In a regression analysis containing 402 observations from 10 locations in the central and northern Great Plains during 1907 to 1938 (Cole and Mathews, 1939), only 18% of variance in spring wheat yield was explained by preplanting depth of wet soil (Miller, 2006). Similarly, in a more recent record at Swift Current, SK, including 128 observations during 1967–2002, only 11% of variance in spring wheat yield in continuous wheat was explained by the preplanting amount of soil water, while explained variance increased to 67% when growing season precipitation was added as an additional independent factor in the regression analysis (Miller, 2006). Nevertheless, a flex-crop system based on spring soil water did show increased net returns over rotations with fixed fallow frequency during a 15-yr period at Swift Current, SK (Zentner et al., 2006). Recropping during two significant drought years was successfully avoided, although there were also very low yields during two drought years when spring soil water had exceeded the recropping criteria.

The Food, Agriculture, Conservation, and Trade Act of the 1990s resulted in cropping systems with greater crop diversity (diversity in time) in the NGP. Hence, dryland cropping systems have become more resilient through improved precipitation use efficiency and soil quality (Farahani et al., 1998). Diverse crops in cropping systems provide a "rotation effect," where crop yields usually increase when compared with monoculture systems (Porter et al., 1997). This has been especially true in the semiarid NGP when pulse crops such as pea, lentil, or chickpea are sequenced before wheat or barley (Miller et al., 2002b, 2003; Miller and Holmes, 2005; Carr et al., 2006). The question then becomes how to sequence crops in cropping systems to efficiently exploit soil–microbe–plant–atmosphere interactions that benefit crop production (Tanaka et al., 2005).

Cereal–pulse cropping systems have recently become common in southern Saskatchewan and northeastern Montana and represent a critical first step in improved sustainability beyond cereal–fallow systems (Zentner et al., 2001), but greater crop diversity is desirable in no-till systems to promote crop health, fewer pest problems, and with minimal cost (Manitoba–North Dakota Zero Tillage Farmers Association, 1997; Dakota Lakes Research Farm, 2005). Inclusion of diverse crops in cropping systems creates a crop production environment that is constantly changing, requiring a new cropping system philosophy that is responsive to climatic, biological, and economic agricultural systems dynamics. To promote the advancement of agricultural systems research and better understand soil–plant–environment interactions in cropping systems, Tanaka et al. (2002) defined dynamic cropping systems as "a long-term strategy of annual crop sequencing that optimizes cropping options and the outcome of crop production, economics, and resource conservation goals by using sound ecological management principles." Crop sequence research has been shown to increase spring wheat seed yield by up to 37%, while seed yield of pulse crops, such as chickpea, can be improved by at least threefold through optimal cropping sequence (Tanaka et al., 2007). Crop sequence has also created situations where soil erosion on more fragile soils could be a problem (Krupinsky et al., 2007; van Donk et al., 2008) and, because of the limited quantity of residue remaining after pulses (Blackshaw and Lindwall, 1995; McPhee et al., 1997), creates a special concern for systems that are too reliant on pulse crops.

Management of dynamic cropping systems for soil and water conservation requires responsiveness to environmental conditions, causing a need for timeliness of field and marketing operations, which becomes more difficult as systems increase in complexity. Current research into highly transportable crop decision support systems aims to increase efficiency of management in a spatially explicit manner and should enable better management of complex cropping systems (Ahuja et al., 2002). Presently, agricultural knowledge is generated via multidirectional flow among research, extension, consultants, and producers. To facilitate this knowledge, an interactive computer information product, the Crop Sequence Calculator (available at http://www.mandan.ars.usda.gov, verified 21 Oct. 2009) was developed to help producers assess crop options and sequencing for their cropping systems (Liebig et al., 2008). Use of the Crop Sequence Calculator provides producers options to better manage soil and water resources and provides the tools needed to implement economically viable and environmentally acceptable agricultural systems. The Crop Sequence Calculator is a relatively simple decision support aid, and interest in this tool among farmers shows the need and potential for more extensive development of more robust decision support systems that can optimize economic and environmental outcomes.

Future Outlook

Great challenges lie ahead in agriculture. Recently, soil and water conservation practices coupled with cropping systems have drastically changed, with the advent of no-till farming systems and the associated increases in cropping intensity and diversity. The role of agriculture has expanded to include a fourth "F", fuel from a land base already heavily committed to producing food, feed, and fiber. Retention of crop residues has been crucial to soil protection (Troeh et al., 1999), epitomized in the high residue, low disturbance no-till farming method (D. Beck, personal communication, 2007). Even in the semiarid NGP it is likely that emerging lignocellulosic ethanol production will seek to use soil-protective crop residues. Will a review of existing research show the way forward to optimize crop residue removal, or will important new and long-term lines of research be needed? Insatiable global demand for bio-oils, for food and fuel, will encourage increased production of oilseed crops, which are inefficient in water use and are weakly adapted to the driest parts of the NGP (Miller et al., 2001; Johnston et al., 2002). Will there be a major genetic breakthrough that makes widespread production of oilseed crops more feasible, and what will be the soil consequences of adding more low residue crops in the system? Energy threatens to constrain agricultural activity due to a reliance on fossil fuels. How might energy-efficient cropping systems depart from current economic efficiency? A recent review by Piringer and Steinberg (2006) documented that the major energy input for wheat production in the United States was fertilizer N, accounting for 47% of the total energy input. For dryland wheat production in Saskatchewan fertilizer N accounted for about 60% of total energy input for continuous wheat and about 40% for wheat–fallow (Zentner et al., 1998). Preliminary research in Montana, where high protein wheat is sought in an otherwise low-cost production scheme, shows that fertilizer N may account for more than 70% of the total energy input for wheat production (R. Engel and P. Miller, unpublished data). There are only two significant sources of N for wheat production: application of fossil fuel-derived synthetic N fertilizer and mineralization of soil organic matter. Soil organic matter can be augmented by legume crops via biological N fixation, but knowledge remains surprisingly scant for enhancing soil fertility via legumes, especially in the NGP (Walley et al., 2007). This will require a more thorough understanding of past research, or more likely new research approaches that better capture the spatial and temporal variability in soil N dynamics. Even conventional fertilizer N application appears suspect in Montana, where large volatilization losses (i.e., >30%) have been observed in north-central Montana farm fields under typical N management in winter wheat (R. Engel, personal communication, 2009). The potential of N fixation by bacteria in an associative relationship with nonlegume crops like wheat could fundamentally change the nitrogen fertility situation in the future (Spaepen et al., 2008; Yao et al., 2008).

Perhaps the biggest uncertainty relates to climate change, presenting two principal challenges for farmers. First, increased attention on the environmental footprint of farming is a worldwide phenomena (Nemecek and Erzinger, 2005; Koga et al., 2006; Engstrom et al., 2007) and may result in altered cropping systems or new management strategies that have important interactive effects with soil and water conservation. At this time it is difficult to conceive the exact manner in which farms may need to account for carbon, but effective carbon policy seems certain to promote increased attention on land use and management, including promotion of conservation tillage and decreased N fertilizer application (Paustian et al., 2006; Rosenzweig and Tubiello, 2007). Second, there will be direct effects of climate change on crop and livestock production. Farming systems in the semiarid NGP strive to minimize variability in production under variable and marginal rainfall. Climate in this region is predicted to warm, and increase slightly in precipitation, but the net effect of this warmer and wetter climate on plant growth is uncertain (Backlund et al., 2008). Agricultural adaptation to some degree of altered climate will be required regardless of success with greenhouse gas mitigation initiatives. Is there sufficient knowledge of sound strategies for shifting crop growth patterns through management, or is new research required? Earlier seeding, increased use of crops with winter growth habits, and using a greater diversity of crops seem certain. What technology will be required to enable routinely successful earlier crop establishment in potentially more variable soil and air temperatures? What technology will ensure survival of winter crops with less frequent snow cover? It is likely that these management practices will relate strongly to soil and water management. As energy constrains wheat production, legumes are likely to occupy more land area in the semiarid NGP. The current two million hectares of pulse crops represent approximately 10% of the total dryland annual crop area in semiarid Alberta, Montana, North Dakota, and Saskatchewan, yet 25% of land is occupied by pulse crops in Saskatchewan. What impacts on soil management and water use would this increased pulse crop presence pose for research? If glyphosate were to become increasingly ineffective under elevated atmospheric CO_2 concentrations, what alternative technology will underpin no-till farming? Any reversion from no-till farming methods would have immediate and probably obvious negative effects on soil quality and water use efficiency. Perhaps the most key question of all—will climate change increase production variability in such a way as to restimulate the practice of summer fallow in this semiarid region? The economic conditions that led to the drastic reduction in fallow were those in which the reduction in yield variability with fallow did not compensate for lost total multi-year production for crops whose value was generally decreasing in real terms over time. A reversal of these conditions could cause a return of frequent fallow, namely where frequent fallow reduces the yield variability of a consistently high-value crop without sacrificing much total multiyear production.

To more efficiently use precipitation and energy from the sun in the future, we will need to develop techniques that not only control soil erosion and conserve water, but enhance the soil resource. Currently, soil and water conservation practices and cropping systems rely on extensive use of fertilizer and pesticides. Challenges for the future will be to exploit synergism among crops and cover crops to enhance crop yields and soil quality without additional inputs and to reduce detrimental environmental influences (Kirschenmann, 2002). Future soil and water conservation systems will not only rely on crop sequences to promote synergism, but will need to take advantage of cover crops, interspecies seeding, relay crops, manipulation of the soils and rhizosphere microbial community, and possibly better integration with livestock production (Fig. 3–8). We must learn how to manage these cropping systems to enhance soil and water conservation and learn about the principles and processes involved in interactions of these

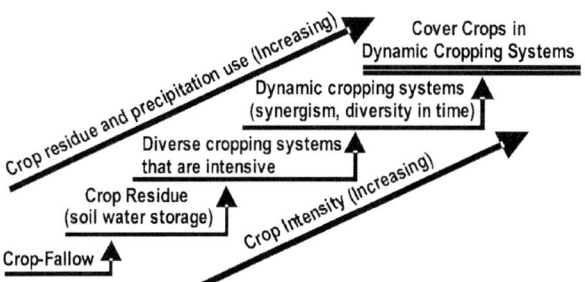

Fig. 3–8. Evolution of soil and water conservation practices in the northern Great Plains as influenced by crop residue, precipitation use, and crop intensity.

complex systems. Most of our current knowledge is from monoculture systems using high inputs such as fertilizers and pesticides (Francis, 1986). We must manage these diverse-multispecies systems to increase total numbers and diversity of soil organisms by obtaining as close to a year-round living food supply as possible. This diversity of plants and soil organisms will not only improve the soil resource, but simultaneously improve soil quality and hence crop production through better use of precipitation.

Acknowledgments

We thank past researchers and agricultural producers for their contributions to soil and water conservation cultural practices that converted a region deemed the "Great American Desert" into the "Bread Basket of the World".

References

Aandahl, A.R. 1982. Soils of the Great Plains: Land use, crops, and grasses. Univ. Nebraska Press, Lincoln.

Ahuja, L.R., L. Ma, and T.A. Howell. 2002. Whole system integration and modelling—Essential to agricultural science and technology in the 21st century. p. 1–8 In L.R. Ahuja et al. (ed.) Agricultural system models in field research and technology transfer. Lewis Publishers, Boca Raton, FL.

Anderson, C.H. 1969. Minimum tillage and chemical fallow. Research Branch soil drifting work planning meeting. 23–24 Sept. 1969. Melfort, Canada.

Anderson, R.L. 2004. Sequencing crops to minimize selection pressure for weeds in the Central Great Plains. Weed Technol. 18:157–164.

Baccara, M., D. Backus, H. Bar-Isaac, L. Cabral, and L. White. 2003. Monsanto's Roundup®. New York Univ. L.N. Stern School of Business, Firms and markets mini-case. 14 July 2003. Available at http://pages.stern.nyu.edu/~lcabral/teaching/monsanto.pdf (verified 22 Oct. 2009). NYU Stern School of Business.

Backlund, P., D. Schimel, A. Janetos, J. Hatfield, M.G. Ryan, S.R. Archer, and D. Lettenmaier. 2008. Introduction. p. 11–20 In The effects of climate change on agriculture, land resources, water resources, and biodiversity in the United States. A report by the U.S. Climate Change Science Program and the Subcommittee on Global Change Research, Washington, DC.

Bell, E.J. 1968. Montana agriculture and the State University 1893–1968. Montana St. Univ. Ext. Serv., Bozeman.

Black, A.L., F.H. Siddoway, and P.L. Brown. 1974. Summer fallow in the northern Great Plains (winter wheat). p. 36–50. In Summer fallow in the western United States. USDA-ARS Conserv. Res. Rep. 17. USDA, Washington, DC.

Blackshaw, R.E., F.O. Larney, C.W. Lindwall, and G.C. Kozub. 1994. Crop rotation and tillage effects on weed populations on the semi-arid Canadian prairies. Weed Technol. 8:231–237.

Blackshaw, R.E., and C.W. Lindwall. 1995. Species, herbicide and tillage effects on surface crop residue cover during fallow. Can. J. Soil Sci. 75:559–565.

Brown, P.L., A.L. Black, C.M. Smith, J.E. Enz, and J.M. Caprio. 1981. Soil water guidelines and precipitation probabilities for barley and spring wheat in flexible cropping systems. Bull. 356 Coop. Ext. Service, Montana State Univ., Bozeman.

Brown, P.L., A.D. Halvorson, F.H. Siddoway, and H.F. Mayland. 1983. Saline-seep diagnosis, control and reclamation. Conservation Rep. 30. USDA, Washington, DC.

Brummer, E.C. 1998. Diversity, stability, and sustainable American agriculture. Agron. J. 90:1–2.

Cain, Z., and S. Lovejoy. 2004. History and outlook for farm bill conservation programs. p. 37–42. Choices, 4th Quarter. Available at http://www.choicesmagazine.org/2004-4/policy/2004-4-09.htm (verified 22 Oct. 2009). USDA-ARS, Mandan, ND.

Campbell, C.A., B.G. McConkey, R.P. Zentner, F. Selles, and F.B. Dyck. 1992. Benefits of wheat stubble strips for conserving snow in southwestern Saskatchewan. J. Soil Water Conserv. 47:112–115.

Campbell, C.A., R.P. Zentner, P. Basnyat, R. DeJong, R. Lemke, R. Desjardins, and M. Reiter. 2008. Nitrogen mineralization under summer fallow and continuous wheat in the semiarid Canadian prairie. Can. J. Soil Sci. 88:681–696.

Campbell, C.A., R.P. Zentner, J.E. Dormaar, and R.P. Voroney. 1986. Land quality, trends and wheat production in western Canada. p. 318–353 In A.E. Slinkard and D.B. Fowler (ed.) Wheat production in Canada. A review. Proc. Can. Wheat Production Symp., Saskatoon, Canada. 3–5 Mar. 1986. Div. Extension and Community Relations, Univ. Sask., SK, Canada.

Campbell, H.W. 1907. Campbell's soil culture manual. 3rd ed. Woodruff-Collins Press Printers and Binders, Lincoln, NE

Caprio, J., G.K. Grunwald, and R.D. Snyder. 1989. Conservation and storage of snowmelt in stubble land and fallow under alternate fallow-strip cropping management in Montana. Agric. For. Meteorol. 45:265–279.

Carr, P.M., G.B. Martin, and R.D. Horsley. 2006. Impact of tillage and crop rotation on spring wheat yield: I. Tillage effect. Crop Manage. doi:10.1094/CM-2006-1018-01-RS.

Carlyle, W.J. 1997. The decline of summer fallow on the Canadian prairies. Can. Geogr. 41:267–280.

Chen, C., P. Miller, F. Muehlbauer, K. Neill, D. Wichman, and K. McPhee. 2006. Winter pea and lentil response to seeding date and micro- and macro-environments. Agron. J. 98:1655–1663.

Chepil, W.S. 1944. Utilization of crop residues for wind erosion control. Sci. Agric. 24:307–319.

Christie, H.W., D.N. Graveland, and C.J. Palmer. 1985. Soil and subsoil moisture accumulation due to dryland agriculture in southern Alberta. Can. J. Soil Sci. 65:805–810.

Cole, J.S., and O.R. Mathews. 1939. Subsoil moisture under semiarid conditions. USDA Tech. Bull. 637. U.S. Gov. Print. Office, Washington, DC.

Cutforth, H.W., S.V. Angadi, and B.G. McConkey. 2006. Stubble management and microclimate, yield and water use efficiency of canola grown in the semiarid Canadian prairie. Can. J. Plant Sci. 86:99–107.

Cutforth, H.W., and B.G. McConkey. 1997. Stubble height effects on microclimate, yield and water use efficiency of spring wheat grown in a semiarid climate on the Canadian prairies. Can. J. Plant Sci. 77:359–366.

Cutforth, H.W., B.G. McConkey, D. Ulrich, P.R. Miller, and S.V. Angadi. 2002. Yield and water use efficiency of pulses seeded directly into standing stubble in the semiarid Canadian prairie. Can. J. Plant Sci. 82:681–686.

Cutforth, H.W., S.M. McGinn, K.E. McPhee, and P.R. Miller. 2007. Adaptation of pulse crops to the changing climate of the northern Great Plains. Agron. J. 99:1684–1699.

Dakota Lakes Research Farm. 2005. The power behind crop rotations. Available at http://www.dakotalakes.com/crop_rotations.htm (verified 22 Oct. 2009). Dakota Lakes Research Farm, Pierre, SD.

Daugovish, O., D.J. Lyon, and D.D. Baltensperger. 1999. Cropping systems to control winter annual grasses in winter wheat (*Triticum aestivum*). Weed Technol. 13:120–126.

de Jong, E., and H. Steppuhn. 1983. Water conservation: Canadian prairies. p. 89–104. *In* H.E. Dregne and W.O. Willis (ed.) Dryland agriculture. Agron. Monogr. 23. ASA, CSSA, and SSSA, Madison, WI.

Duke, S.O., and S.B. Powles. 2008. Glyphosate: A once-in-a-century herbicide. Pest Manage. Sci. 64:319–325.

Duley, F.L., and J.C. Russel. 1939. The use of crop residues for soil and moisture conservation. J. Am. Soc. Agron. 31:703–709.

Duley, F.L., and J.C. Russel. 1942. Crop residues for protecting row-crop land against runoff and erosion. Soil Sci. Soc. Am. Proc. 7:484–487.

Engstrom, R., A. Wadeskog, and G. Finnveden. 2007. Environmental assessment of Swedish agriculture. Ecol. Econ. 60:550–563.

Farahani, H.J., G.A. Peterson, D.G. Westfall, L.A. Sherrod, and L.R. Ahuja. 1998. Soil water storage in dryland cropping systems: The significance of cropping intensification. Soil Sci. Soc. Am. J. 62:984–991.

Ford, G.L., and J.L. Krall. 1974. The history of summer fallow in Montana. Montana Agric. Exp. Stn. Bull. 704. Bozeman, MT.

Francis, C.A. 1986. Potential of multiple cropping systems. p. 137–150. *In* M.A. Altieri and S.B. Hecht (ed.) Agroecology and small farm development. CRC Press, Boca Raton, FL.

Gray, J.H. 1967. Men against the desert. Western Producer Prairie Books, Saskatoon, SK.

Gray, R.J. 1986. Proving out: On implementing the conservation title of the 1985 farm bill. J. Soil Water Conserv. 4:31–32.

Greb, B.W. 1979. Reducing drought effects on croplands in the west-central Great Plains. Agric. Info. Bull. 420. U.S. Gov. Print. Office, Washington, DC.

Haas, H.J., and W.O. Willis. 1962. Moisture storage and use by dryland spring wheat cropping systems. Soil Sci. Soc. Am. Proc. 26:506–509.

Halvorson, A.D., A.L. Black, J.M. Krupinsky, S.D. Merrill, B.J. Wienhold, and D.L. Tanaka. 2000. Spring wheat response to tillage system and nitrogen fertilization within a crop–fallow system. Agron. J. 92:288–294.

Hargreaves, M.W.M. 1957. Dry farming in the northern Great Plains, 1900–1925. Harvard Univ. Press, Cambridge, MA.

Hargreaves, M.W.M. 1958. Hardy Webster Campbell (1850–1937). Agric. Hist. 32:62–65.

Hargreaves, M.W.M. 1977. The dry-farming movement in retrospect. Agric. Hist. 51:149–165.

Hargreaves, M.W.M. 1993. Dry farming in the Northern great plains: Years of readjustment, 1920–1990. Univ. Press of Kansas, Lawrence, KS.

Hatfield, J., K. Boote, P. Fay, L. Hahn, C. Izaurralde, B.A. Kimball, T. Mader, J. Morgan, D. Ort, W. Polley, A. Thomson, and D. Wolfe. 2008. Agriculture. p. 59–60. *In* The effects of climate change on agriculture, land resources, water resources, and biodiversity in the United States. U.S. Climate Change Science Program and the Subcommittee on Global Change Research, Washington, DC.

Huggins, D.R., and J.P. Reganold. 2008. No-till: The quiet revolution. Scientific American. July 2008, p. 70–77. Available at http://www.SciAm.com (posted July 2008, verified 22 Oct. 2009).

Johnson, W.E. 1983. Soil conservation: Canadian prairies. p. 259–272. *In* Dryland agriculture, H.E. Dregne and W.O. Willis (ed.) Dryland Agriculture. Agron. Monogr. 23. ASA, CSSA, and SSSA, Madison, WI.

Johnston, A.M., D.L. Tanaka, S.A. Brandt, D.C. Nielsen, G.P. Lafond, P.R. Miller, and N.L. Riveland. 2002. Oilseed crops for semiarid rotations in the northern Great Plains. Agron. J. 94:231–240.

Kaan, D.A., D.M. O'Brien, P.A. Burgener, G.A.Peterson, and D.G. Westfall. 2002. An economic evaluation of alternative crop rotations compared to wheat-fallow in Northeastern Colorado. Tech. Bull. TB02-1. Agricultural Experiment Station, Colorado State University, Fort Collins.

Kappler, B.F., S.Z. Knezevic, R.N. Klein, D.J. Lyon, A.R. Martin, F.W. Roeth, and G.A. Wicks. 2005. Comparison of glyphosate herbicides in Nebraska. Crop Manage. doi:10.1094/CM-2005-0719-01-RS.

Kirschenmann, F. 2002. Why American agriculture is not sustainable. Renew. Resour. J. 20:6–11.

Koga, N., T. Sawamoto, and H. Tsuruta. 2006. Life cycle inventory-based analysis of greenhouse gas emissions from arable land farming systems in Hokkaido, northern Japan. Soil Sci. Plant Nutr. 52:564–574.

Krupinsky, J.M., S.D. Merrill, D.L. Tanaka, M.A. Liebig, M.T. Lares, and J.D. Hanson. 2007. Crop residue coverage of soil influenced by crop sequence in no-till system. Agron. J. 99:921–930.

Lafond, G.P., W.E. May, F.C. Stevenson, and D.A. Derksen. 2006. Effects of tillage systems and rotations on crop production for a thin Black Chernozem in the Canadian Prairies. Soil Tillage Res. 89:232–245.

Lal, R., and H. Steppuhn. 1980. Minimizing fall tillage on the Canadian prairies- a review. Can. Agric. Eng. 22:101–106.

Larney, F.J., and C.W. Lindwall. 1994. Winter wheat performance in various cropping systems in southern Alberta. Can. J. Plant Sci. 74:79–86.

Lemke, R.L., Z. Zhong, C.A. Campbell, and R.P. Zentner. 2007. Can pulse crops play a role in mitigating greenhouse gases from North American agriculture? Agron. J. 99:1719–1725.

Lenssen, A.W., G.D. Johnson, and G.R. Carlson. 2007. Cropping sequence and tillage system influences annual crop production and water use in semiarid Montana, USA. Field Crops Res. 100:2–43.

Liebig, M.A., D.L. Tanaka, J.D. Hanson, D.W. Archer, J.M. Krupinsky, S.D. Merrill, K.A. Nichols, J.R. Hendrickson, R.L. Anderson, L.D. Charlet, and D.E. Stott. 2008. Crop Sequence Calculator. v. 3. CD. February, 2008. Mandan, ND.

Linfield, F.B. 1907. Dry land farming in Montana. Montana Agric. Coll. Exp. Stn. Bull. 63. Bozeman, MT.

Lupwayi, N.Z., and A.C. Kennedy. 2007. Grain legumes in northern Great Plains: Impact on selected biological soil processes. Agron. J. 99:1700–1709.

Lyon, D.J., and G.A. Peterson. 2005. Continuous dryland cropping in the Great Plains: What are the limits? Agron. J. 97:347–348.

Lyon, D.J., W.W. Stroup, and R.E. Brown. 1998. Crop production and soil water storage in long-term winter wheat-fallow tillage experiments. Soil Tillage Res. 49:19–27.

Manitoba–North Dakota Zero Tillage Farmers Association. 1997. Zero tillage—Advancing the art. Available at http://www.mandakzerotill.org/books/manuals/Advancing%20the%20Art/art-index.html (verified 22 Oct. 2009). Zero Tillage Farmers Association, Bismarck, ND.

McConkey, B.G., D. Curtin, C.A. Campbell, S.A. Brandt, and F. Selles. 2002. Crop and soil nitrogen status of tilled and no-tillage systems in semiarid regions of Saskatchewan. Can. J. Soil Sci. 82:489–498.

McConkey, B.G., F. Selles, P. Miller, and C. Campbell. 2003. Yield and protein of wheat and durum in Brown soil zone as affected by long-term tillage system and crop rotation. *In* Proc. Soils and Crops Workshop. CD. 17–18 Feb. 2003. Univ. Sask., Saskatoon, Canada.

McConkey, B.G., D.J. Ulrich, and F.B. Dyck. 1997. Snow management and deep tillage for increasing crop yields on a rolling landscape. Can. J. Soil Sci. 77:479–486.

McPhee, K.E., S.C. Spaeth, and F.J. Muehlbauer. 1997. Seed yield and residue production of lentil cultivars grown at different slope positions. J. Prod. Agric. 10:602–607.

Meilicke, E.J. 1997. Leaves from the life of a pioneer: Being the autobiography of sometime Senator Emil Julius Meilicke. Can. Plains Res. Ctr., Regina, Canada.

Miller, P. 2006. Crop sequence effects on water and nitrogen: Getting to the root of the matter. p. 4. *In* Proc. Southern Alberta Conserv. Assoc. Annual Conference, Medicine Hat, Canada. 6 Dec. 2006. SACA, Lethbridge, AB, Canada.

Miller, P.R., R.E. Engel, and J.A. Holmes. 2006. Cropping sequence effect of pea and pea management on spring wheat in the northern Great Plains. Agron. J. 98:1610–1619.

Miller, P.R., Y. Gan, B.G. McConkey, and C.L. McDonald. 2003. Pulse crops for the northern Great Plains. 2. Cropping sequence effects on cereal, oilseed and pulse crops. Agron. J. 95:980–986.

Miller, P.R., and J.A. Holmes. 2005. Cropping sequence effects of four broadleaf crops on four cereal crops in the northern Great Plains. Agron. J. 97:189–200.

Miller, P.R., B.G. McConkey, G.W. Clayton, S.A. Brandt, J.A. Staricka, A.M. Johnston, G.P. Lafond, B.G. Schatz, D.D. Baltensperger, and K.E. Neill. 2002a. Pulse crop adaptation in the northern great plains. Agron. J. 94:261–272.

Miller, P.R., C.L. McDonald, D.A. Derksen, and J. Waddington. 2001. The adaptation of seven broadleaf crops to the dry semiarid prairie. Can. J. Plant Sci. 81:29–43.

Miller, P.R., J. Waddington, C.L. McDonald, and D.A. Derksen. 2002b. Cropping sequence affects wheat productivity on the semiarid northern Plains. Can. J. Plant Sci. 82:307–318.

Nemecek, T., and S. Erzinger. 2005. Modelling representative life cycle inventories for Swiss arable crops. Int. J. Life Cycle Assess. 10:68–76.

Padbury, G., S. Waltman, J. Caprio, G. Coen, S. McGinn, D. Mortensen, G. Nielsen, and R. Sinclair. 2002. Agroecosystems and land resources of the Northern Great Plains. Agron. J. 94:251–261.

Paustian, K., J.M. Antle, J. Sheehan, and E.A. Paul. 2006. Agriculture's role in greenhouse gas mitigation. Available at http://www.pewclimate.org/global-warming-in-depth/all_reports/agriculture_s_role_mitigation (verified 22 Oct. 2009). Pew Center on Global Climate Change, Arlington, VA.

Peterson, G.A., A.J. Schlegel, D.L. Tanaka, and O.R. Jones. 1996. Precipitation use efficiency as affected by cropping and tillage systems. J. Prod. Agric. 9:180–186.

Peterson, G.A., and D.G. Westfall. 2004. Managing precipitation use in sustainable dryland agroecosystems. Ann. Appl. Biol. 144:127–138.

Phillipson, D.J.C. 2009. Mackay, Angus. The Canadian Encyclopedia. Available at http://www.canadianencyclopedia.ca/index.cfm?PgNm=TCE&Params=A1ARTA0004923 (verified 22 Oct. 2009).

Phillips, S.H., and H.M. Young, Jr. 1973. No-tillage farming. Reiman Associates, Milwaukee, WI.

Piringer, G., and L.J. Steinberg. 2006. Reevaluation of energy use in wheat production in the United States. J. Industr. Ecol. 10:149–167.

Porter, P.M., J.G. Lauer, W.E. Lueschen, J.H. Ford, T.R. Hoverstad, E.S. Oplinger, and R.K. Crookston. 1997. Environment affects the corn and soybean rotation effect. Agron. J. 89:442–448.

Raban, J. 1997. Bad land. An American romance. Random House, New York.

Rosenzweig, C., and F.N. Tubiello. 2007. Adaptation and mitigation strategies in agriculture: An analysis of potential synergies. Mitig. Adapt. Strat. Global Change 12:855–873.

Salmon, S.C., O.R. Mathews, and R.W. Leukel. 1953. A half century of wheat improvement in the United States. Adv. Agron. 5:1–151.

Shaver, T.M., G.A. Peterson, L.R. Ahuja, D.G. Westfall, L.A. Sherrod, and G. Dunn. 2002. Surface soil properties after twelve years of dryland no-till management. Soil Sci. Soc. Am. J. 66:1296–1303.

Shaver, T.M., G.A. Peterson, L.A. Sherrod, and L.R. Ahuja. 2003. Cropping intensification in dryland systems improves soil physical properties: Regression relations. Geoderma 116:149–164.

Smika, D.E., and G.A. Wicks. 1968. Soil water during fallow in the Central Great Plains as influenced by tillage and herbicide treatments. Soil Sci. Soc. Am. Proc. 32:591–595.

Spaepen, S., S. Dobbelaere, A. Croonenborghs, and J. Vanderleyden. 2008. Effects of Azospirillum brasilense indole-3-acetic acid production on inoculated wheat plants. Plant Soil 312:15–23.

Staple, W.J., and J.J. Lehane. 1952. The conservation of soil moisture in southern Saskatchewan. Sci. Agric 32:36–47.

Tanaka, D.L., and J.K. Aase. 1987. Fallow method influences on soil water and precipitation storage efficiency. Soil Tillage Res. 9:307–316.

Tanaka, D.L., J.M. Krupinsky, M.A. Liebig, S.D. Merrill, R.E. Ries, J.R. Hendrickson, H.A. Johnson, and J.D. Hanson. 2002. Dynamic cropping systems: An adaptable approach to crop production in the Great Plains. Agron. J. 94:957–961.

Tanaka, D.L., R.L. Anderson, and S.C. Rao. 2005. Crop sequencing to improve use of precipitation and synergize crop growth. Agron. J. 97:385–390.

Tanaka, D.L., J.M. Krupinsky, S.D. Merrill, M.A. Liebig, and J.D. Hanson. 2007. Dynamic cropping systems for sustainable crop production in the northern Great Plains. Agron. J. 99:904–911.

Troeh, F.R., J.A. Hobbs, and R.L. Donahue. 1999. Soil and water conservation. Productivity and environmental protection. 3rd ed. Prentice Hall, Upper Saddle River, NJ.

van Donk, S.J., S.D. Merrill, D.L. Tanaka, and J.M. Krupinsky. 2008. Crop residue in North Dakota: Measured and simulated by the wind erosion prediction system. Trans. ASAEBE 51:1623–1632.

van Riper, J.E. 1971. Man's physical world. McGraw-Hill Book Company, New York.

Walley, F.L., G.W. Clayton, P.R. Miller, P.M. Carr, and G.P. Lafond. 2007. Nitrogen economy of pulse crop production in the northern Great Plains. Agron. J. 99:1710–1718.

Wiese, A.F., W.L. Harman, B.W. Bean, and C.D. Salisbury. 1994. Effectiveness and economics of dryland conservation tillage systems in the Southern Great Plains. Agron. J. 86:725–730.

Wilson, M.L. 1928. Dry farming in the north central Montana "Triangle." Bull. 66. Montana Agric. Exp. Stn., Bozeman, MT.

Yao, T., S. Yasmin, and F.Y. Hafeez. 2008. Potential role of rhizobacteria isolated from Northwestern China for enhancing wheat and oat yield. J. Agric. Sci. 146:49–56.

Zentner, R.P., B.G. McConkey, M.A. Stumborg, C.A. Campbell, and F. Selles. 1998. Energy performance of conservation tillage management for spring wheat production in the Brown soil zone. Can. J. Plant Sci. 78:553–563.

Zentner, R.P., C.A. Campbell, V.O. Biederbeck, P.R. Miller, F. Selles, and M.R. Fernandez. 2001. In search of a sustainable cropping system for the semiarid Canadian prairies. J. Sustainable Agric. 18:117–136.

Zentner, R.P., C.A. Campbell, V.O. Biederbeck, F. Selles, R. Lemke, P.G. Jefferson, and Y. Gan. 2004. Long-term assessment of management of an annual legume green manure crop for fallow replacement in the Brown soil zone. Can. J. Plant Sci. 84:11–22.

Zentner, R.P., F.B. Dyck, K.R. Handford, C.A. Campbell, and F. Selles. 1993. Economics of flex-cropping in southwestern Saskatchewan. Can. J. Plant Sci. 73:749–767.

Zentner, R.P., D.D. Wall, D.G. Smith, D.L. Young, P.R. Miller, C.A. Campbell, G.P. Lafond, S.A. Brandt, and A.M. Johnston. 2002. Economics of crop diversification opportunities for the northern Great Plains. Agron. J. 94:216–230.

Zentner, R.P., C.A. Campbell, F. Selles, P.G. Jefferson, R. Lemke, B.G. McConkey, M.R. Fernandez, C. Hamel, Y. Gan, and A.G. Thomas. 2006. Effect of fallow frequency, flexible rotations, legume green manure, and wheat class on the economics of wheat production in the Brown soil zone. Can. J. Plant Sci. 86:413–423.

4

Major Advances of Soil and Water Conservation in the U.S. Southern Great Plains

B.A. Stewart
Dryland Agriculture Institute, West Texas A&M University, Canyon, TX

R.L. Baumhardt and S.R. Evett
USDA-ARS, Conservation and Production Research Laboratory, Bushland, TX

The U.S. Great Plains consist of the broad expanse of prairie and steppe lands that lie east of the Rocky Mountains and cover parts of 10 states—Colorado, Kansas, Montana, Nebraska, New Mexico, North Dakota, Oklahoma, South Dakota, Texas, and Wyoming. While the western boundary is clearly defined by the Rocky Mountain foothills, the eastern boundary occurs along the lower plains of central Texas, Oklahoma, and Kansas, where semiarid dryland production merges into rainfed farming (Baumhardt and Salinas-Garcia, 2006). This chapter will focus on the development of management practices for the combined conservation of water and soil in the southern Great Plains, which includes portions of Colorado, Kansas, Oklahoma, Texas, and New Mexico.

Soils of the southern Great Plains have integrated the effects of time, climate, and geologic factors that formed and exposed current surfaces. Trimble (1980) presented a largely nontechnical description of the geological origin and evolution of the landscape of the Great Plains. Most soils formed from a loess mantle covering the plains after aeolian deposition during the Quaternary period, except where erosion exposed earlier strata including Pliocene alluvial materials along rivers and Permian age residuum on the low or rolling plains (Cronin, 1964). The ~8 million ha of aeolian soils are typically very deep and nearly level Mollisols and Alfisols, featuring mixed high-charge (superactive) clay mineralogy, horizons of accumulated clay and calcium carbonates, and moderate to slow permeability. Soil textures generally vary from silt loams in Kansas, to silty clays in the northern Texas Panhandle, to loamy sands of the Texas South Plains. This general progression is interrupted by exposure and weathering of sediments in the valleys of the river systems crossing the Plains, particularly in the southern Great Plains by the Arkansas River and the Canadian River running eastward and the Pecos River running southward and forming a western boundary to the most southern part of the High Plains. In addition, sandy soils formed on sand hills associated with these valleys. Exposed pre-Quater-

---

Soil and Water Conservation Advances in the United States. SSSA Special Publication 60.
T.M. Zobeck and W.F. Schillinger, editors. © 2010. SSSA, 677 S. Segoe Rd., Madison, WI 53711, USA.

nary sediments in the eastern one-third of the southern Great Plains generally produced fine-textured Alfisols and Inceptisols with variable slopes, although some coarse soils formed from eroded sandstone. Most southern Great Plains soils are located in a semiarid climate or ustic moisture regime, with mesic soil temperatures in Kansas that become thermic when moving southward into Texas and New Mexico. These soils are generally productive when water is available and are well suited for irrigation.

The Great Plains region extends from the provinces of Alberta, Manitoba, and Saskatchewan in Canada southward through the central United States to the southern part of Texas (Fig. 4–1). The annual precipitation for this area varies little from north to south, but consistently decreases from east to west. For example, precipitation ranges from ~500 mm along 100°W to ~350 mm at the eastern edge of the Rocky Mountains. Although the annual precipitation east of the 100th meridian is significantly higher, essentially all of the Great Plains receives less than 700 mm of precipitation annually. Annual potential evaporation is another principal climatic factor that governs plant ecologies and cropping systems. Evaporative demand, as determined from pan measurements, increases from about 1600 mm in the east to >2400 mm along the western boundary of the Great Plains (Farnsworth et al., 1982). Unlike precipitation, however, pan evaporation, temperature, and growing season length exhibit north–south gradients, all of them decreasing from south to north (Baumhardt and Salinas-Garcia, 2006).

Fig. 4–1. The Great Plains of the United States and Canada; the 100th meridian coincides closely with the eastern border of the Texas Panhandle (Miksinski, 1998).

Evaporative demand generally exceeds precipitation by 200 to 500%, a condition that promoted native short grass prairie ecologies, encouraged development of irrigation since prehistorical times, and engendered research that emphasized soil water management on the southern Great Plains.

Development of Irrigation in the High Plains

Before Euro-American settlement, the Great Plains were largely covered with grasses, with no trees except along streams that were few and far apart. During this prehistorical period, as later, the high evaporative demand and uncertain rainfall surely encouraged the first irrigation in the southern Great Plains, which occurred as diversions of surface waters in Kansas (Erhart, 1969) and in the Oklahoma and Texas Panhandles (Thoburn, 1926, 1931). In southern Texas, surface irrigation from canals was already well established along the Rio Grande River when Coronado explored the regions in 1540 (Hutson, 1898). Major Stephen Harriman Long led a military expedition across much of the Great Plains in 1820, and upon completion, Dr. Edwin James, botanist and geologist, reported to Secretary of War, John C. Calhoun, "In regard to this extensive section of the country, I do not hesitate in giving an opinion, that it is almost wholly unfit for cultivation and of course uninhabitable by a people depending on agriculture for their subsistence" (Thwaites, 1905). Nevertheless, early cultivated agriculture developed on the Great Plains in Ellis county, Kansas, which lies immediately east of 100°W (Fig. 4–1) and was the westernmost county when organized in 1867 (Forsythe, 1977). Limited irrigated agriculture was practiced by Hispanic farmers and sheep herders along the Canadian River in Texas near Tascosa in the 1870s (Nostrand, 1996). This was more or less the beginning of historical agriculture in the central and southern Great Plains. During the late 1870s and into the 1880s, agricultural development pushed westward across the prairies into the eastern Dakotas, Nebraska, and Kansas (Hargreaves, 1977). The dry years of the 1880s and early 1890s drove many settlers out; those that remained had largely converted to a subsistence type of mixed agriculture that included ranching. Widespread ranching was aided by the discovery that an accessible aquifer, the Ogallala or High Plains Aquifer (Fig. 4–2), underlay most of the High Plains and could be

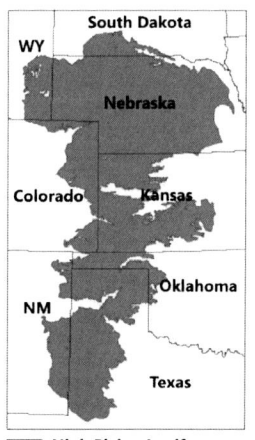

Fig. 4–2. Map of the High Plains Aquifer (USGS, 2008).

accessed by hand dug and drilled wells pumped by windmills. After 1896, however, millions of hectares of land that had been previously considered fit only for ranching because of drought were successfully dryland farmed during a period of favorable precipitation (Norrie, 1977), thus illustrating the cyclical nature of precipitation on the Great Plains. Irrigation from wells also began in semiarid western Texas during this period, with steam or gasoline powered pumps irrigating tracts of from 2 to 400 ha, and windmills irrigating tracts of ~3 ha (Hutson, 1898). Several pumping plants were capable of delivering 10,000 L min^{-1} and irrigating hundreds of hectares (Hutson, 1898).

The potential and rationale for irrigation in the Texas Panhandle were described by Hutson (1898):

> The Llano Estacado has been described as a great plateau having an area of about 90,000 km^2 and with an almost perfectly flat surface, which rises gradually toward the northwest. No rivers cross its surface and at only a few widely scattered localities, and for short distances, is flowing water to be found. The soil is of such character that it readily drinks in the rain which falls on it. This water, or that part of it which is not soon evaporated, percolates downward and is reached by wells of 15 to 60 meters in depth. Many of these wells are capable of furnishing a supply almost inexhaustible to ordinary means of pumping. The soil is too dry to be successfully cultivated without irrigation, and this can be practiced, if at all, only by means of water raised by pumps.

Hutson goes on to state that no more than six locations on the Plains in the Texas Panhandle had areas irrigated by means of pumps and windmills that exceeded the size of house gardens. In addition, two ranches in valleys at the edge of the Plains were irrigating some hundreds of acres at this time. Hutson (1898) assessed the future of irrigation in the Texas Panhandle with these words, "Of the future of irrigation here in general, it may be said that there is opportunity for but the little indicated, at these widely scattered spots, but that this little will prove to be just that small amount needed for rendering practicable the utilization of the High Plains for stock raising, under conditions that will be bearable for those who have to live on these great pasture lands for the conduct of the stock industry." How surprised he would have been to see the great increase of irrigation after 1940, and, how prescient his words may come to be of the future of irrigation in the Texas Panhandle.

At the same time, interest in irrigation was increasing due to the unpredictable rainfall. Large-scale irrigation in Kansas began with diversion of the Arkansas River in the 1880s for surface irrigation (Erhart, 1969). However, problems with erratic stream flow and diversion upstream for the same purpose in eastern Colorado slowed the expansion of irrigation. In 1945 irrigation began to rapidly increase until reaching a plateau of ~1.4 million ha in 1980, then declining to ~1.2 million ha by 2000 (Rogers and Wilson, 2000). Rapid expansion became feasible due to the availability of deep well submersible pumps, modern drilling equipment adapted from oil well drilling technology, internal combustion engines, and the expansion of electrical grids after World War II, and was further motivated by the drought of the 1950s. In the High Plains of Texas, irrigation from wells began in 1911 (U.S. Dep. of Interior, Bureau of Reclamation, 2009), but irrigated areas increased slowly until after the Dust Bowl of the 1930s. Rapid expansion in the Texas High Plains followed the pattern in Kansas, reaching 2.42

million ha in 1974, then declining to 1.59 million ha by 1989 before increasing to 1.87 million ha by 2000 (Colaizzi et al., 2008). Further north in Nebraska and west in the plains of Colorado, diversion of surface waters began in the later 1800s and continued until virtually all surface water flows had been diverted. In some cases, more water was diverted than could be reliably supplied by the river systems, a circumstance that engendered lawsuits and negotiations between the states that continue to have consequences to this day. But, as in Kansas, Oklahoma, and Texas, rapid improvements in drilling and pumping technology were instrumental in the rapid development of irrigation after World War II wherever the aquifer was available and the soil and landforms suitable for irrigation (Ganzel, 2009).

Early Farming Systems

The development of farming in the Great Plains increased dramatically during the first three decades of the 20th century, and H.W. Campbell had perhaps more influence on this than any other individual. Mr. Campbell was a native of Vermont, who homesteaded in Brown county, South Dakota, in 1879 (Hargreaves, 1977). In 1895, he began to promote a system, later named "Campbell's Soil Culture," based on his experience following five successive drought years. Initially, the system consisted of fall plowing, subsurface packing, light seeding, and frequent surface cultivation. The "subsurface packer" was constructed by a blacksmith using a series of wedge-shaped wheels on an axle. The wedges were designed to cut deep into the soil, packing it at the bottom of the cut while loosening the topsoil to form mulch. The basic principle of the Campbell system was packed subsoil covered with loose soil mulch. Although this was often referred to as dust mulching, Mr. Campbell warned that he was not advocating a dust blanket, but rather a soil mulch composed of soil lumps ranging in size from a pin head to a walnut. In his *Soil Culture Manual* (Campbell, 1907), he stated:

> If you would secure the greatest possible benefit from the labor given over to cultivation, you should first provide yourself with some fine-toothed cultivator, so that the soil may be all thoroughly fined, leaving the surface of the firm soil beneath as near level as possible. Great care should be taken to catch your ground in proper condition when excess water has drained, and the soil, to the depth you wish to run your cultivator, is simply moist—neither very wet nor very dry. In this condition the little particles seem to readily separate, one from the other, then your stirred soil is composed of an innumerable number of little, minute lumps, forming a mulch that gives you the highest degree of protection. A mulch made when the soil is in this condition will never blow.

Mr. Campbell was a publicist and promoter, claiming that his farming methods could overcome climatic handicaps in semiarid areas that could not be overcome as well in more humid areas. Campbell (1907) wrote:

> It is stated that the best estimate based on experiments as to the extent of evaporation from the soil in the humid regions shows that fully fifty percent of the rain water which falls is returned to the air directly in vapor. But this is not true of the semiarid region, where a much smaller proportion is returned to the air in that way. And where there is cultivation with a special view to preventing this evaporation from the surface the evaporation is still less....The vital truth is that the so-called semiarid region is almost ideally adapted to

best agriculture. The soil is of the right texture and capable of being handled to the best advantage.

Campbell's methods were promoted by business interests, particularly the railway companies, who were concerned with settlement of the region. Between 1903 and 1907, several nationally circulated periodicals carried accounts of his methods (Hargreaves, 1977). This was the message that invited settlers by the hundreds of thousands onto the Great Plains during the early years of the 20th century. A Dry Farming Congress was held in Denver in 1907, and this was followed by an annual congress for several years (Widstoe, 1911). At the end of the Denver congress that was attended by more than 1000 participants, the acting chairman, J.L. Donahue, a Denver banker, without advance notice, presented a resolution endorsing "the fundamental principles of soil culture as practiced by Professor Hardy W. Campbell" (Hargreaves, 1977). In subsequent congresses, Campbell's views were sharply challenged by representatives of the U.S. Department of Agriculture. They warned at the third Dry Farming Congress that "vastly more data must be gathered before anyone will be warranted in making any broad and sweeping generalizations concerning methods and systems of dry land agriculture" (Hargreaves, 1977). Campbell's influence in the organization thereafter declined sharply.

In retrospect, Mr. Campbell was neither a professor nor a scientist, but he possessed a good knowledge of water movement, capillary flow, and benefits of mulch. He conducted a number of successful demonstration farming operations in several states ranging from south of Amarillo, Texas to South Dakota. His shortcoming was, perhaps, a lack of understanding that the benefits of infiltration and producing a soil mulch of little particles critical to his system decreased sharply with declining organic matter, which resulted from the intensive and numerous tillage operations that were fundamental to his soil culture system.

During the decade of the 1930s, the southern Great Plains faced a crisis of drought and economic depression that had been preceded by favorable annual precipitation 100 mm above average, farm mechanization, and stable European demand for wheat (*Triticum aestivum* L.) (Baumhardt, 2003). The extensive dryland areas that had been successfully farmed for more than three decades became ravished by wind and drought. In 9 of the 12 yr between the years 1929 and 1940, rainfall amounts at Amarillo, TX failed to reach average, and between January 1933 and February 1936 the Amarillo weather bureau reported 192 dust storms (Nall, 1980). This era became known as the infamous Dust Bowl. The most damaged areas in the southern Great Plains were the Texas and Oklahoma panhandles, southwestern Kansas, southeastern Colorado, and northeastern New Mexico. Hugh Hammond Bennett of the Bureau of Chemistry and Soils of USDA in 1933 dispatched H.V. Geib from the erosion investigation station at Temple, TX to conduct a 34 county tour of the region and file a report. Geib reported that the most serious erosion had occurred in patches. He found very little damage in cultivated areas where wheat grew on heavy soils. However, in fields where farmers had planted row crops on silt loams or very sandy soils, Geib found that no less than 13 cm of surface material had been removed (Nall, 1980).

The Dust Bowl era ended with higher than average precipitation for the region, beginning in 1940, that stabilized crop production. Redesigned government programs encouraged diversified cropping systems with rotation sequences that improved precipitation storage when innovative tillage practices from early research were adopted. Another severe drought period occurred from 1950 to 1956 for much of the southern Great Plains, but a rapid expansion of irrigation, improved tillage practices, and relatively good commodity prices prevented another catastrophic crisis like the Dust Bowl.

Early Research Studies: 1900–1940

Research conducted by USDA and the state experiment stations before 1900 was largely by individual investigators. One of the first efforts to conduct coordinated research programs involving federal and state scientists was on dryland agriculture (Quisenberry, 1977). A dryland experiment station was established at Hays, KS in 1901 as the first in the southern Great Plains (Office Technology Assessment, 1981). In October 1903, the USDA initiated research at the XIT Ranch at Channing, TX located about 60 km northwest of Amarillo (Nall, 1973). The XIT Ranch was formed in 1879 in the Texas High Plains on 1.2 Mha (3 million acres) of unsettled land sold by the Texas Legislature to finance a new state Capitol building. Although the focus of the ranch was cattle, ranch personnel began experimenting with crops in the 1890s. The station at Channing was short-lived because in 1905 the personnel and operations were transferred to the Amarillo Experiment Station established in 1904. In 1906, the Office of Dry Land Agriculture was established by USDA, and by 1910, 20 stations were in operation. Eventually, 30 stations were involved (Office Technology Assessment, 1981). Dryland cropping experiments were conducted at 22 locations in the Great Plains from 1903 to 1938 by USDA and state agricultural experiment stations (Fig. 4–3). Although many of these stations have been closed, several continue today. The Amarillo loca-

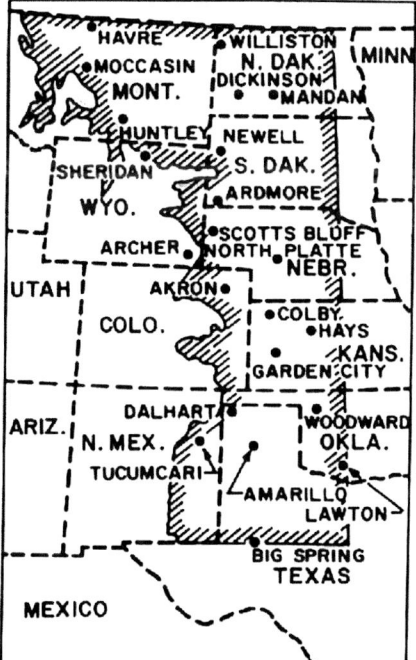

Fig. 4–3. Locations where dryland cropping experiments were conducted from 1903 to 1938 by USDA and State Agricultural Experiment Stations (Burnett et al., 1985).

tion was closed in 1938 and should not be confused with the present USDA-ARS Conservation and Production Research Laboratory at Bushland (15 km west of Amarillo) established in 1938.

Early research studies focused on determining the type of crops that would grow best in the region. Since most farmers had moved to the Great Plains from the more humid farming regions east of the Mississippi River, they brought with them their tools, seeds, and perhaps more importantly, their culture. An integral part of their culture was excessive tillage, and this, along with the widely publicized soil culture system promoted by H.W. Campbell that included frequent tillage certainly played a role in creating the conditions that led to the Dust Bowl during the drought years of the 1930s. Scientists at many of the dryland experiment stations (Fig. 4–3) warned farmers about possible consequences of frequent tillage to incorporate crop residues and refine the soil surface, which degraded the soil's natural cohesiveness and structure (Baumhardt, 2003), but high yields and favorable prices of wheat and other crops during the early years of cultivation were more important to farmers. The high yields were due to above-average rain from 1918 to 1929 (Johnson and Davis, 1972), the very favorable soil physical properties of the newly plowed lands, and the high fertility resulting from the decomposition and mineralization of the soil organic matter. Few farmers realized the high fertility was coming at the expense of declining soil organic matter, and that the declining soil organic matter was making their land less receptive for rainfall and less able to store water for subsequent crops. Moreover, farmers did not understand the effect that organic matter had on holding soil particles together in aggregates, nor the connection between aggregates and erosion, particularly by wind. The Dust Bowl was a time of reckoning, and it became clear that major changes in tillage practices had to be made if farming in the region was going to be sustainable in the future.

Research Studies: 1940–1975

Studies during and immediately following the Dust Bowl era of the 1930s focused on controlling wind erosion. The primary implements used were those invented by farmers as they struggled to protect their land resources. In 1933, Fred Hoeme, a farmer from Hooker, OK, developed a heavy-duty chisel plow. Mr. Hoeme got the idea from a piece of equipment used for road construction that was left in his field. The tool had been used to scarify the roadbed during construction; upon removal, the tool was then dragged for quite a distance through the field. Mr. Hoeme observed that the subsequent wheat crop was much better where the tool had been dragged. Thus, he began experimenting with various materials to build a chisel plow, that later became recognized by many as the "Plow that Saved the Plains." The focus of the chisel plow was to leave crop residues on the field's surface, protecting the soil from erosion and increasing water storage. An early version of the plow along with a marker was dedicated in 2000 as a Historic Landmark of Agricultural Engineering (American Society of Agricultural and Biological Engineers, 2000) at the USDA-ARS Conservation and Production Research Laboratory in Bushland, TX for permanent display. Hoeme and his sons manufactured and sold about 2000 plows from their homestead before selling the manufacturing and distribution rights to W.T. Graham in Amarillo, TX, who marketed the plow worldwide as the Graham-Hoeme plow.

The second plow developed during the Dust Bowl was by Charles Noble, an Alberta, Canada, farmer near Lethbridge. He was a leader in declaring that cultural methods had to be changed and was one of the first to condemn burying residue with dust mulch or clean summer fallow as advocated by H.W. Campbell (MacEwan, 1983). Although Mr. Noble tried for many years to develop new cultural methods for reducing tillage, he had limited success until 1935 when he got the idea for the Noble blade that became widely used throughout the Great Plains. On a trip to California, while he was still dreaming about a new type of cultivator, Noble happened to see a California farmer using a straight blade tool as an aid to cut into the subsoil to loosen his sugar beets and lift them out. The blade was heaving the soil and disturbing the plants without making much change in the general appearance of the field. Noble was instantly excited; wasting no time, he built the first prototype of the Noble blade in a friend's garage in California. The first model was a straight blade mounted on wheels; it was tested in a California orange grove. Excited with the results, Noble shortened his planned stay in California, loaded the prototype on a trailer, and returned to Canada. Prototypes of Noble blades were constructed in 1936, and shortly thereafter Mr. Noble cooperated with many scientists and organizations to evaluate the new plow (MacEwan, 1983). Later models of the Noble blade were mostly V-shaped (Fig. 4–4).

Interest in the Noble blade in the United States significantly increased in 1938 when the newly formed USDA Soil Conservation Service purchased 19 of them for testing, and the famous team of USDA scientists, F.L. Duley and J.C. Russell, then working at the University of Nebraska in Lincoln, became involved in researching the Noble blades. Mr. Noble also promoted the implement by traveling extensively throughout the Great Plains with a blade implement in tow behind his car. He traveled as far south as the Texas Panhandle (MacEwan, 1983). As with the chisel plow developed by Mr. Hoeme, the concept of the Noble Blade was to leave as much crop residue as feasible on the soil surface to prevent wind erosion and increase water storage. The term *stubble-mulching* was coined to describe these cultural practices. Although the original Noble blade design consisted of a single blade, stubble-mulching was later practiced with ganged V-shaped sweep plows (Fig. 4–5), ranging from 75 to 150 cm in width, with only about 15% of the residue being

Fig. 4–4. A later version of the Noble blade first developed in 1936.

Fig. 4–5. Example of a sweep plow used in stubble-mulch tillage for weed control and retention of residues at the soil surface for soil and water conservation.

buried by a single operation (Fig. 4–5). The Noble blade and the Graham-Hoeme implements have both been recognized as Historic Agricultural Engineering Landmarks by the American Society of Agricultural and Biological Engineers.

Bushland, Texas Study

Stubble-mulching played an important role in the southern Great Plains for controlling wind erosion. Johnson et al. (1974) reported that 30 yr of study in Bushland, TX showed that stubble-mulch tillage was very effective in protecting against wind erosion and should be used routinely in place of clean tillage on summer-fallowed land. The study at Bushland was conducted from 1942 to 1970 and compared stubble-mulch tillage with soil inverting, one-way disk plowing for continuously cropped wheat (with ~3 mo between crops) and for a wheat–fallow rotation (one crop every 2 yr with ~15 mo between crops). An additional wheat–fallow treatment with delayed tillage was used in which weeds and volunteer wheat were allowed to grow after harvest until the following spring before stubble-mulch tillage.

As a general rule, a single tillage operation with a one-way plow buries about 60% of the wheat residue compared with only about 15% for a sweep plow (Steiner et al., 1994). Although stubble-mulch tillage was primarily developed to control wind erosion, Johnson et al. (1974) showed that it also conserved more water during the period between annual wheat crops. The 30-yr study showed the average amounts of plant-available soil water in the 1.5-m soil profile at time of seeding was 103 mm for stubble-mulch tillage compared with 91 mm for one-way tillage. The increased soil water also increased grain yield from 600 kg ha^{-1} to 700 kg ha^{-1}. For the wheat–fallow system, plant-available soil water at seeding was 154 mm for stubble-mulch tillage compared with 128 mm for one-way tillage, and the respective grain yields were 1070 and 950 kg ha^{-1}. Somewhat surprising was that the delayed tillage treatment with weeds and volunteer wheat growth for about 8 to 9 mo following harvest also stored 144 mm plant-available soil water at seeding time, which was only 10 mm less than the stubble-mulched plots. This treatment also yielded similarly to stubble-mulch tillage at 1040 kg ha^{-1}, which illustrates that extending the fallow period is not very efficient for increasing soil water storage.

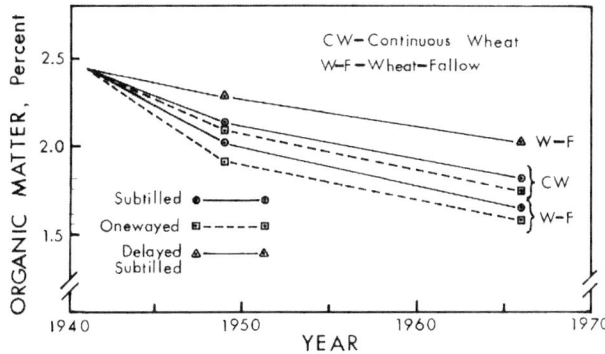

Fig. 4–6. Organic matter content, 0 to 15 cm, of tillage plots as related to cropping system (Johnson et al., 1974).

Another important finding of the long-term study reported by Johnson et al. (1974) involved the rapid decline in soil organic matter for all treatments, which was greater for one-way tillage than for stubble-mulch tillage and more for wheat–fallow than for continuous wheat (Fig. 4–6). Soil organic matter declined the least in the delayed tillage plot because of the large amounts of vegetation produced before tillage. Although the results of the delayed tillage treatment were mostly favorable, the treatment was not considered acceptable because of weed seed and uncontrolled vegetation. The decline of soil organic matter was further verified by the presence of large amounts of nitrate-nitrogen in the soil profile. At the end of the study, 210 kg ha^{-1} of nitrate N were in the 180 cm profile of the one-way tilled plots, and 131 kg ha^{-1} were in the stubble-mulched plots. More than 60% of these amounts were in the lower half of the profiles. In comparison, only 35 kg were in the delayed tillage plots, and less than 50% was in the lower half.

The wheat–fallow cropping system used in this long-term study developed from annual wheat sequences when precipitation between harvest and planting was insufficient to establish another crop (Fig. 4–7). The resulting default fallow period in a wheat–fallow sequence stabilized subsequent wheat establishment

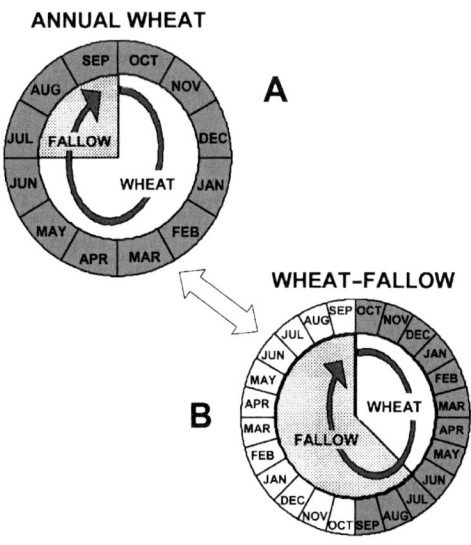

Fig. 4–7. The annual (A) wheat and (B) wheat–fallow cropping sequences diagramed as a 1- or 2-yr cycle. In both sequences, wheat is established in October (top) and harvested about 10 months later in July. Annual wheat crop establishment depends on soil water stored during the typically low precipitation months of July through September. Insufficient moisture often results in an additional 12-mo fallow period to become the wheat–fallow sequence, which stores fallow period precipitation as soil water to stabilize production of one wheat crop in 2 yr (Baumhardt and Anderson, 2006).

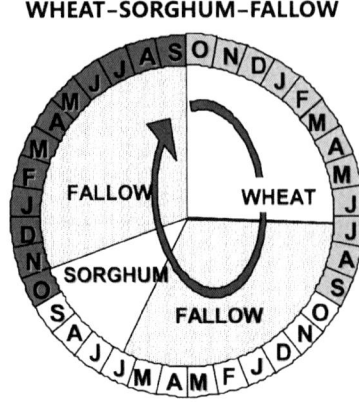

Fig. 4–8. The wheat–sorghum–fallow (WSF) rotation diagramed as a 3-yr cycle beginning with wheat establishment in October (top). Wheat is harvested 10 months later in July, and the soil is fallowed until June of the second year (11 mo) when grain sorghum is grown using soil water stored during fallow to augment summer rainfall. After sorghum harvest in November of the third year the soil is again fallowed for 10 months, when wheat is planted and the cycle repeated (Baumhardt and Anderson, 2006).

and grain yield. It has largely been replaced in the southern Great Plains, however, with a wheat–sorghum [*Sorghum bicolor* (L.) Moench]–fallow cropping system that results in two crops in 3 yr, with 11 mo between the crops (Fig. 4–8). Stewart and Robinson (1997) presented a brief comparison of these systems; it showed that nearly as much water was stored in the soil profile during 11 mo of fallow as during the almost 16 mo of fallow between crops in the wheat–fallow system.

Akron, Colorado Study

Another long-term study showing the beneficial effects of stubble-mulch tillage for controlling wind erosion, increasing soil water storage, and enhancing wheat yields was reported by Greb et al. (1979). They summarized more than 60 yr of progress in wheat production for a wheat–fallow cropping system that produced one wheat crop every 2 yr, with about 16 mo of fallow between crops (Table 4–1). The fallow efficiency (fallow period water stored in the soil divided by precipita-

Table 4–1. Progress in wheat–fallow cropping systems at Akron, CO.†

Years	Tillage	Number tillage operations	Fallow wheat storage		Wheat yield
			mm	% of precipitation	Mg ha⁻¹
1916–1930	Maximum tillage: plow, harrow (dust mulch)	7–10	102	19	1.07
1931–1945	Conventional tillage: shallow disk, rodweeder	5–7	118	24	1.16
1946–1960	Improved conventional tillage: begin stubble-mulch in 1957	4–6	137	27	1.73
1961–1975	Stubble-mulch: begin minimum tillage with herbicides in 1969	2–3	157	33	2.16
1976–1990	Minimum tillage (projected estimate): begin no-tillage in 1983	0–1	183	40	2.69

† Adapted from Greb et al. (1979).

tion and multiplied by 100) was less than 20% when frequent and intensive tillage was used but increased to approximately 30% with stubble-mulch tillage and to 40% with minimum tillage aided by herbicides for weed control. As a result of the improved water storage during the fallow period, wheat yield increased more than twofold. The positive effects accumulated with time because higher yields resulted in more crop residues, thus further enhancing soil water storage and increasing yields, creating an upward spiral. Soil physical properties are also generally improved because soil organic matter concentrations tend to increase as more crop residues are left on the soil surface and tillage is reduced.

The more than twofold increase in grain yields was due to several improved technologies. Greb (1979) attributed the credit of various technologies as follows: water conservation, 45%; improved cultivars, 30%; improved harvesting equipment, 8%; better seeding equipment, 8%; and fertilizer practices, 5%. The reason for the low impact of fertilizer was because of the long fallow period (16 mo) between crops that generally resulted in sufficient mineralization of nutrients to meet dryland crop demand. Fertilizer effects have become much more important in recent years as yields have increased and organic matter concentrations have declined to the levels that the need for fertilizers to supply adequate nutrients has greatly increased. Although Greb (1979) gave water conservation only 45% of the credit, we emphasize that without the increased water, the other technologies would have been of little or no value to a failing crop. In semiarid regions, water is typically the first limiting factor and must be addressed before other improved technologies can be of significance. The relationships shown in Fig. 4–9 illustrate how the amount of water available to the crop impacts the benefit of technologies on grain yield, but the degree of impact will be site-specific (Koohafkan and Stewart, 2008).

Before 1945, irrigation research in the United States was primarily focused on the arid western states where the federal Desert Land Act encouraged irriga-

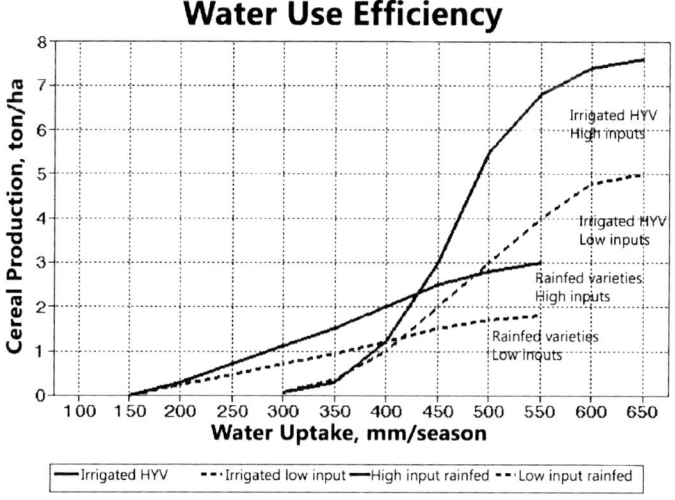

Fig. 4–9. Effects of added inputs, including high yield varieties (HYV), on the water use efficiency of cereal production (Koohafkan and Stewart, 2008).

tion as early as 1877. This was followed by the Carey Land Grant Act of 1984. This act transferred land to the western states if they provided for irrigation of those lands. For example, the Irrigation Experiment Station, which is still in existence, was established at Prosser, WA in 1919. In addition, California appointed a State Engineer to study irrigation as early as 1878. As irrigation in the Great Plains increased rapidly after 1940, research interest in the region also increased (Robins, 1959). In 1940, surface irrigation by flood, furrow, or between borders prevailed, and much of the water applied either ran off the field or percolated more deeply than plant roots could reach, leading to less availability of water for crop growth and yield production, and low overall water use efficiencies (amount of yield per unit of water applied). Since distribution was by gravity flow in mostly unlined canals and ditches, much of the water was also lost through seepage. Water logging of plants near canals was also common. Distribution in furrows was by V-notches cut into the earthen ditch or subditch walls, leading to uneven flow in the furrows. The siphon tube was invented to overcome this problem, and the first plastic siphon tube manufacturer began business in Nebraska in 1945 (Ganzel, 2009).

Siphon tubes had two problems. Setting the tubes was laborious, and the technology only worked with open canals. Research was showing how much water was lost in canals, prompting the installation of piping to eliminate seepage losses. The availability of water under pressure led to the development of gated pipe, which due to the abundance of aluminum after World War II soon became a popular alternative to siphon hoses for regulating delivery of water to furrows. The move toward pressurization of irrigation systems began in earnest at this time. Today more than 52% of the irrigated area in the United States is supplied by pressurized systems, which helps to eliminate conveyance losses.

In 1948, irrigation through sprinklers mounted on pressurized pipes in the field was already known, though not widely used in the Great Plains, when Frank Zybach in Nebraska invented the center pivot sprinkler irrigation system. The center pivot solved two problems; the labor shortage that developed during World War II and continued thereafter due to rapid urbanization of the American population, and the deep percolation losses inherent in furrow or border gravity flow irrigation systems. Adoption of center pivot systems was steady thereafter, such that today more than 70% of the irrigated area in the Southern High Plains is served by such systems (Colaizzi et al., 2008; Rogers and Wilson, 2000).

Research Studies: 1975 to Present

A second major paradigm shift in tillage began in the 1970s following the 1973 formation of the Organization of Petroleum Exporting Countries (OPEC) that sharply raised energy prices. This had a dramatic effect on agriculture because modern U.S. agriculture had been built on energy. Energy was used to plow the fields, produce fertilizer, pump water, and harvest the crops. More importantly, energy had been relatively inexpensive. From 1950 to the time that OPEC was formed, one bushel of wheat (27.3 kg) would buy about one barrel (167 L) of oil. Therefore, the cost of tillage was a small component of the cost of crop production. Although herbicides were available during much of this time period, they were generally expensive in comparison to tillage. Following the formation of OPEC, however, tillage costs increased significantly and the 1:1 wheat/oil ratio increased to as high as 20:1 in some years. This change coupled with increasing concerns about enhancing the environment, resulted in a major shift in research, extension, and industry activities to develop and implement conservation tillage and no-tillage systems. This extended to amplify efforts to increase irrigation efficiency to reduce pumping costs and losses of water and soluble fertilizers to deep percolation. One of the results of this effort was the invention of cablegation in 1980 (Kemper et al., 1981). Cablegation used the pressure of water to move a plug down a gated pipe using a clocking mechanism to regulate the rate of movement and thus the times at which flow was turned on to each furrow. Although research continued on this method into the 1990s, and cablegation became one of several distribution options used on the smaller fields typical in Europe (de Sousa et al., 1999; Renault, 1988), by 1990 only about 100 systems had been installed in the USA (Trout and Kincaid, 1994).

Bushland, Texas Studies

Unger and Baumhardt (1999) summarized more than 40 yr of studies at Bushland, Texas, evaluating the effect of tillage on available soil water storage at grain sorghum planting (Fig. 4–10). The amounts of soil water at time of seeding after the early 1970s were dramatically more than in earlier years. The mean amount of stored soil water at seeding time from 1956 to 1969 was 102 mm compared with 173 mm from 1970 to 1997 or approximately 36 and 49% of the corresponding 10-mo fallow precipitation. Before 1970, research mainly involved clean or stubble-mulch tillage to control weeds during the fallow period between crops. Yields resulting from use of herbicides for dryland cropping were poor during that period (Wiese et al., 1960, 1967). Following the 1973 formation of OPEC, there was a major shift in research and technology transfer to practices that used less tillage and more herbicides during fallow periods. As a result, more residues remained on the soil surface as mulch; this largely accounts for the 71-mm increase in the average amount of stored soil water at time of seeding grain sorghum after 1969 (Fig. 4–10). The average 71-mm increase in stored soil water at time of seeding increased the average grain sorghum yield 1500 kg ha^{-1}, which was 21 kg ha^{-1} mm^{-1} of additional plant-available soil water at seeding. Stewart and Steiner

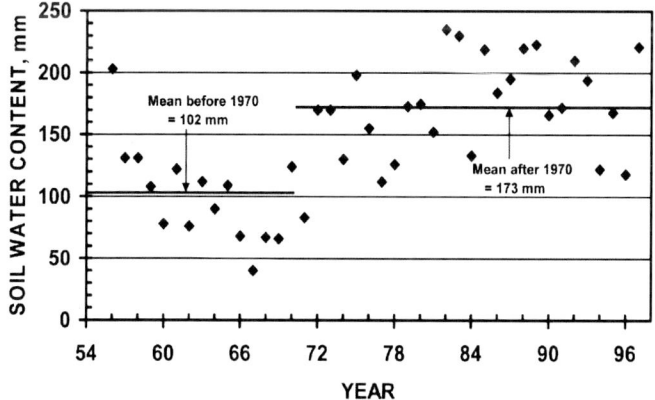

Fig. 4–10. Average annual volumetric soil water content at planting time for dryland grain sorghum in studies conducted from 1956 to 1997 at the USDA-ARS Conservation and Production Research Laboratory, Bushland, TX (Unger and Baumhardt, 1999).

(1990) summarized several studies conducted at Bushland and showed that each millimeter of additional evapotranspiration increased grain yields 15.5 kg ha^{-1} above the threshold value of 127 mm required before any grain was produced. This finding agrees closely with those of Unger and Baumhardt (1999) because it generally showed that a unit of stored plant-available soil water at time of seeding has more benefit than a unit of precipitation received during the growing season. Of course, there are exceptions to this general conclusion because some precipitation events can be particularly timely.

In response to rapidly increasing use of irrigation in the Southern High Plains, an irrigation research program was established at the USDA experiment station in Bushland, TX in 1948 to study irrigation requirements of crops and methods of water application. A sprinkler irrigation research program was begun in 1954, but did not really involve field trials in the Panhandle until 1971. Work with gated pipe began in 1964, and surge flow research began in 1982. Gravimetric and neutron moisture meter measurements were used to measure the crop soil water balance in nearly every irrigated and dryland experiment (Hauser, 1959). Bushland was involved in the trials and development of the meters by 1959. By the 1970s, research results involving tailwater retention and utilization for furrow irrigation (Schneider, 1976), limited tillage of irrigated wheat (Allen et al., 1976), and reduction of evaporative losses by retention of surface crop residues (Unger, 1976; Unger and Wiese, 1979) had been disseminated to farmers. The effect of all these methods of water conservation was to increase the yields produced per unit of water pumped.

Irrigation methods improved during the 1980s. One improvement was that alternate furrow irrigation was shown to reduce water applications but not yields of corn (*Zea mays* L.) and sorghum and to increase water use efficiency (WUE) (Musick and Dusek, 1982). This was due to the reduction in evaporative loss of water from the soil when every other furrow was wetted. Additionally, yields and water table depths continued to decline. However, limited irrigation of sorghum and sunflower (*Helianthus annuus* L.), sometimes in conjunction with dryland farming, was shown to improve the overall water use efficiency, as a result of both reduction of evaporative losses and more effective conjunctive use of rainfall (Stewart et al., 1983; Unger, 1983). Results with corn and soybean [*Glycine max* (L.) Merr.] were not positive (Eck, 1986; Eck et al., 1987).

Inefficiency in furrow irrigation was still a problem, leading to research on furrow compaction to reduce deep percolation losses (Musick et al., 1985; Musick and Pringle, 1986). During the period from 1974 through 1984, average irrigation applications declined from 404 to 347 mm yr^{-1} because of increased sprinkler irrigation, adoption of surge-flow technology with graded furrows, increases in alternative furrow irrigation and conservation tillage, decreased tailwater runoff losses, reductions in preplant irrigations, and some shifts to crops that were more successful with limited irrigation (Musick and Walker, 1987).

Musick et al. (1994) summarized 178 crop seasons of irrigated and dryland wheat data from Bushland, TX in terms of grain yield, water use, and WUE. Maximum yields required 650 to 800 mm of water, a quantity that was only available through irrigation. The WUE for irrigated production was about double that for dryland production, and the curvilinear relationship for WUE in relation to yield showed that high yields were necessary for efficient water use (Fig. 4–11). The contrast between WUE of irrigated versus dryland production was so distinct that

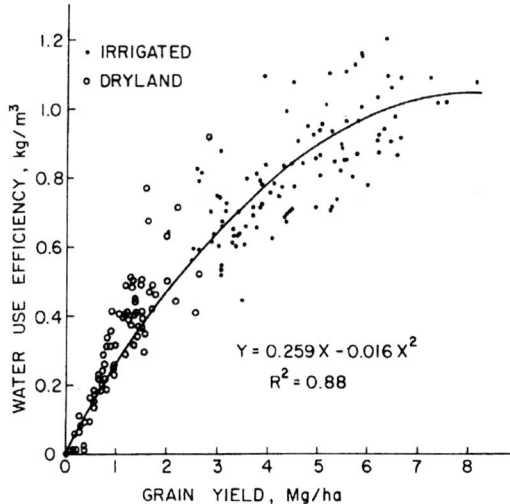

Fig. 4–11. Water use efficiency of irrigated and dryland wheat from 178 crop seasons at Bushland, TX (Musick et al., 1994).

only for a handful of seasons was the WUE of dryland production comparable to that achieved with irrigation. Tillage system studies on irrigated winter wheat–dryland sorghum rotations showed considerable improvement in both yield and WUE for no-tillage as contrasted with disk, sweep, and other tillage methods (Unger and Wiese, 1979; Unger, 1984).

In the late 1980s, a USDA-ARS research program dedicated to high accuracy crop water use determination under both irrigated and dryland production began with the installation of four large weighing lysimeters for direct crop water use measurements at Bushland (Marek et al., 1988). In subsequent years, a team led by Terry Howell determined the crop water use and WUE of fully and deficit irrigated alfalfa (*Medicago sativa* L.), corn, cotton (*Gossypium hirsutum* L.), sorghum, soybean, and winter wheat; for some the dryland water use was determined as well (Evett et al., 2000b; Howell et al., 1997b, 1998, 2004). In a partnership led by Tom Marek of Texas AgriLife (Texas A&M University), USDA-ARS cooperated with the university to establish and support networks of weather stations covering the Panhandle to provide the weather data necessary to establish daily crop water use estimates for all producers and all major crops in that region. Today, what has become the 19-station Texas High Plains Evapotranspiration Network stretches from Pecos at the southwest edge of the Plains, to Munday and Chillicothe in the Rolling Plains in the east, and to Dalhart and Perryton in the north. The network provides daily crop water use estimates for the major crops currently growing in the region, with separate values of evapotranspiration (ET) for three to four planting dates (for annual crops) and with growth stage estimates. The data are made available online, by email, and by fax. Predictions of crop ET are based on the paradigm of a daily reference ET value calculated from weather data using the Penman Monteith equation (Allen et al., 2005) multiplied by a daily crop coefficient that varies with growing degree days (Evett et al., 2000b; Howell et al., 1997b, 1998, 2004). The crop coefficients were determined by the USDA-ARS team, which also made important contributions to the American Society of Civil Engineers (ASCE) Penman Monteith standardized reference ET equations.

More efficient irrigation application methods had been studied since the beginning of sprinkler irrigation research in the 1950s. However, rapid progress did not ensue until the mid 1980s when furrow diking (creating small dikes across furrows to impede water flow) and low-energy precision application (LEPA) technology were introduced for moving irrigation systems. Stationary sprinkler systems were replaced by moving systems; by 1984, 37% of the total irrigated area was irrigated by moving systems (Musick and Walker, 1987). By the end of the 1980s, LEPA technology on moving systems became important as surface irrigated area continued to decline, particularly on more permeable soils of the region (Musick et al., 1988), and the percentage of sprinkler irrigated land rose to 44%, mostly in the northern Texas Panhandle (Musick et al., 1990). Irrigation application efficiencies increased from ~56% achieved with surface irrigation to ~82% with low-impact sprinklers in the Texas Panhandle, with similar values being recorded in Oklahoma (Musick et al., 1988). Application efficiencies achieved with LEPA systems in furrow-diked fields were consistently better than 95% (Lyle and Bordovsky, 1983). Improvements in application efficiency translated into increases in overall WUE. This is an improvement in water conservation, but not directly a reduction in water pumped, as this quote from New (1986) suggests, "center pivots improve water application efficiency enough to irrigate 20% to 25% more acreage than can be covered with furrow irrigation with the same water." As a result of continued irrigation, by 1989 the amount of water stored in the aquifer underlying the High Plains was estimated to have declined by 30% from predevelopment levels (Musick et al., 1990).

In the 1990s, irrigation research reflected the search for more efficient application methods, and the use of these to reduce evaporative losses and increase the ratio of transpiration (*T*, which reflects yields) to total water use or ET (Schneider and Howell, 1993, 1994, 1995, 1998, 1999). Much of this work focused on LEPA systems (Schneider, 2000; Schneider et al., 2000), but increasingly it compared spray, LEPA, and subsurface drip irrigation methods (Colaizzi et al., 2004; Schneider et al., 2001). Interest in drip irrigation, also known as microirrigation, began near Lubbock, TX, in the cotton industry, but drip irrigation was also studied for corn in the Texas and Kansas High Plains (Howell et al., 1997a; Lamm et al., 1995; Lamm and Trooien, 2003). Drip irrigation was shown to be more efficient and to improve T/ET because of the smaller wetted soil surface area (Evett et al., 1995).

Howell (2006) summarized the challenges in increasing WUE in irrigated agriculture, citing examples from the Texas High Plains. Irrigation scheduling to meet the needs of the crop without water loss to overirrigation is key, and probably as important as the choice of application technology. Although information provided by networks, like the Texas High Plains ET Network, allow farmers to make appropriate irrigation application decisions, success still depends on farmer adoption. Since the early 1990s, automatic irrigation scheduling and control systems have been the subject of research at both Bushland and Lubbock, TX (Evett et al., 1996; Wanjura et al., 1992). The systems have been applied to both drip irrigation (Evett et al., 2000a) and center pivot irrigation (Evett et al., 2006; Peters and Evett, 2008). These systems have shown the ability to incrementally improve yields and WUE over those achievable with soil water balance–based irrigation scheduling using the neutron moisture meter, which itself is superior to scheduling based on ET estimates from weather station networks. Although still not fully available in the commercial sector, some aspects of these systems are available commercially and may be part of the next wave of improvements in overall water use efficiency in the Great Plains.

There are also factors other than water that impact grain yields, as was previously discussed (Fig. 4–9). Unger and Baumhardt (1999) showed that average annual grain sorghum yields increased from 800 kg ha^{-1} in 1939 to 3800 kg ha^{-1} in 1997. Yields increased 139% during the 1956 to 1997 time period, or about 50 kg ha^{-1} annually. The authors attributed 46 of those percentage units to the use of improved hybrids, based on results of a uniformly managed 40-yr study. The remaining 93% units were attributed primarily to soil water at time of planting and other factors. The increases in soil water at planting, as already stated, were mainly due to the adoption of improved crop residue management practices after the early 1970s. Growing-season precipitation averaged 270 mm, and total annual precipitation averaged 475 mm, but both were highly variable among years. For example, growing-season precipitation ranged from 76 mm in 1940 to 503 mm in 1960, and total precipitation ranged from 240 mm in 1970 to 828 mm in 1941, but there was no change in the mean precipitation over the long term.

Tribune, Kansas Studies

Tribune, KS is located about 375 km north of Bushland, TX in the northernmost part of the southern Great Plains. The average annual precipitation is 440 mm at Tribune compared with 475 at Bushland, but the potential evapotranspiration is significantly less at Tribune, resulting in a greater evaporation minus precipitation deficit for Bushland (Baumhardt and Salinas-Garcia, 2006). Stone and Schlegel (2006) summarized yield–water supply relationships for grain sorghum and winter wheat for studies conducted from 1974 to 2004. In the 30 years of research, various levels of tillage and/or herbicides were used during noncrop periods for weed control, including conventional, stubble-mulch (sweep) tillage with no herbicides, reduced tillage (herbicides and tillage), and no-till (herbicides exclusively). Grain sorghum yields increased an average of 22.1 kg ha^{-1} for each additional millimeter of plant-available water stored in the soil profile at time of seeding. This is very similar to the 21 kg ha^{-1} shown by Unger and Baumhardt (1999) for studies at Bushland. Likewise, Stone and Schlegel (2006) showed an increase of 16.6 kg ha^{-1} mm^{-1} of growing season water supply (i.e., plant-available soil water at seeding plus growing season precipitation) above a threshold value of 136 mm when data for all tillage systems were included. These values are very close to the 15.5 kg ha^{-1} yield increase value and the 127-mm threshold value reported by Stewart and Steiner (1990) for Bushland studies.

Stone and Schlegel (2006), however, went further in that they separated yield data from no-till, conventional till, and reduced-till treatments to identify some striking differences in grain sorghum yields associated with water supply (Fig. 4–12). For the no-tillage system, an additional millimeter of water increased grain yield 18.4 kg ha^{-1} after a threshold of 157 mm, compared with only 12.9 kg ha^{-1} after a threshold value of 102 mm for conventional and reduced tillage systems. They concluded that mulch increased the amount of precipitation stored in the soil during the fallow period, so more plant-available water was present at time of seeding. They also concluded that the mulch resulted in more efficient use of growing season precipitation.

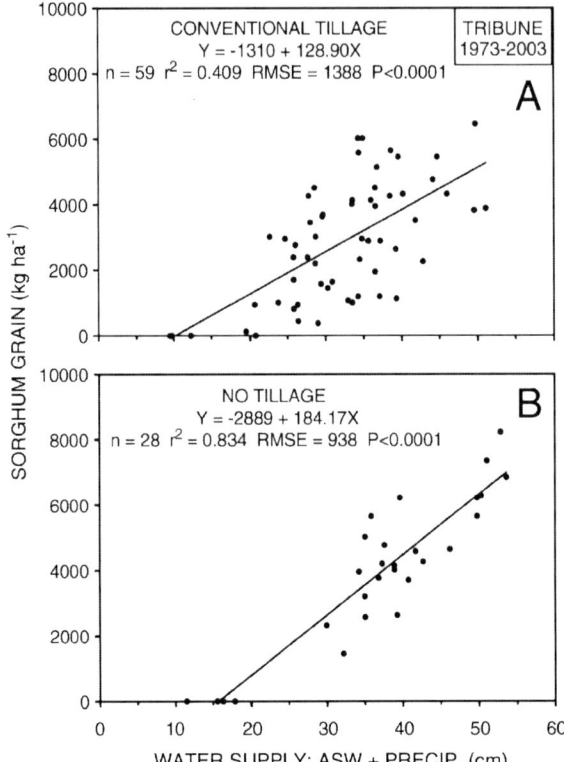

Fig. 4–12. Grain sorghum yield at Tribune, KS associated with water supply (plant-available soil water at emergence plus growing-season precipitation) for dryland conventional tillage (Section A) and for no-till (Section B) treatment groups (Stone and Schlegel, 2006).

Future Trends—Manipulating Plants to Increase Water Use Efficiency

In spite of the significant gains in storing more precipitation as soil water during fallow periods and increasing the use efficiency of growing season precipitation by leaving crop residues on the soil surface, future research must address the fact that dryland crops in the southern Great Plains are severely constrained by scarcity of growing season precipitation. Limited water during the latter growth stages becomes particularly critical for grain crops such as wheat and grain sorghum. The latter stages are the reproductive and grain-filling stages, and without water during this time, yield and quality are drastically reduced. Craufurd et al. (1993) reported that water stress during booting and flowering stages resulted in grain yield reduction of up to 85% for grain sorghum.

The studies discussed above agree that the amount of plant-available soil water at time of seeding is extremely important, and that the amount can be increased by management. An abundant supply of plant-available soil water at time of seeding can result in excellent germination and plant establishment. This is often followed by excessive vegetative growth that cannot be sustained. The challenge is to keep some of the early growing season precipitation and soil water for use during the critical grain production period. Strategies such as reduced plant populations, different spacing between rows, and skip row configurations have been tried by many researchers with mixed results. The mixed results occur because no two growing seasons in semiarid regions are ever the same. That is, the amount, intensity, and timeliness of precipitation during the growing season are so erratic that successful cultural practices for 1 yr often fail in subsequent years. Loomis (1983) stated, in principle, that plant spacing can be varied in a way that influences the time when stored water is used. Roots can explore all of the soil volume earlier in the season with a regular spacing than with a clumped pattern. Where plants are closely spaced within rows, but widely spaced between rows, roots may reach interrow soil much later in the season. That dependence on root extension rate has the effect of spreading the use of stored water over a longer time and, for crops like grain sorghum that have developmental phases, conserving water until after anthesis.

That is the theory, although results have not always been definitive (Blum and Naveh, 1976; Bond et al., 1964). Reducing plant density is the primary management practice that scientists and farmers have relied on to conserve stored soil water for use during latter growth stages. Extension specialists and scientists have recommended planting populations as low as four plants per square meter. Even with these low plant populations, however, severe water stress occurred in most years. One explanation is that corn and particularly sorghum have the ability to produce tillers under favorable growing conditions to compensate for low plant populations and that these tillers offset the desired effect of reducing populations to conserve water. Although the formation of tillers is highly complex and affected by many factors (Bennett and Leyser, 2006; McSteen and Leyser, 2005), it is well understood that plants tiller more when they are thinly spaced and have good growing conditions. It is also well documented, under water stress conditions, that most tillers either fail to produce ears or panicles, or the number and size of grains of tiller panicles or ears are smaller (Bandaru et al., 2006; Gerik and Neely, 1987). Therefore, much of the expected benefit of a lower plant density is often negated by an increased number of tillers that utilize soil water and nutrients for vegetative growth, but contribute little or nothing to grain yield. As with practically all other findings in semiarid areas, however, there are exceptions because of the extreme variability in time, intensity, and distribution of precipitation.

Loomis (1983) stated that crop manipulations involve variations in choice of species and cultivar, timing of events, plant density, fertility status, provision for irrigation, and other factors. Loomis generalized that where soil resources are nonlimiting, uniform cropping will provide the greatest efficiency in light interception and photosynthesis. On the other hand, when soil resources are as limiting as water is in semiarid regions, nonuniform treatment of the land or the crop can be advantageous.

Relatively few scientific principles, let alone practices, are available to increase the efficient use of precipitation in semiarid areas. A maximum proportion of the evapotranspiration should be used for transpiration, with minimum losses to evaporation, drainage, and runoff. Drainage is minimal, in most cases, in semiarid regions, and runoff can be minimized or controlled by good cropping and management practices. Maximizing transpiration while minimizing evaporation during the growing season is more challenging, but usually involves establishing a full canopy as quickly and for as long as practical to minimize evaporation. This strategy works well in humid areas or irrigated conditions where water is generally not limiting. Loomis (1983) presented work from the late 1800s that applied 1 m of water to 1, 2, or 4 ha sown to various crops to determine the best "economy-of-water." He reported that although the experiments did not detect subtle differences due to mild plant stress, deep rooting, etc., they did provide the general answer that the best water economy was obtained through practices that minimized severe stress, a result reflected in the irrigated versus dryland winter wheat study of Musick et al. (1994).

The transpiration rate decreases with an increase in humidity, and in general the humidity within a crop canopy increases with its thickness. With adequate precipitation or supplemental irrigation, narrow rows and high plant populations produce the highest yields and water use efficiencies. In the 1960s, Iowa farmers planted about 40,000 seeds ha^{-1}, and the optimum in 2007 was considered to be 85,000 (Iowa State Agronomy Extension, 2007). Since 2001, Iowa farmers have increased planting density more than 1000 plants ha^{-1} each year. Therefore, there are clearly advantages to keeping plants close together.

Mutual shading could be a factor in increasing water use efficiency. Loomis (1983) discussed the possible effects of cloud cover, screen shelters, and windbreak shelters on water use efficiency and the contributions of increased plant populations on these characteristics. Where water is limiting, however, these practices are seriously handicapped because there is not sufficient water to develop and maintain a complete canopy cover and strategies, such as low plant populations, wide row spacing, and skip row systems often expose large areas of bare soil. Not only is there more bare ground, which increases the portion of evapotranspiration attributable to evaporation, but the plants are further apart, thereby resulting in thinner canopies that allow more air to circulate, which lowers the humidity and increases the transpiration rate.

The development of approaches to manipulate plants to increase water use efficiency seems a promising area for continued research. Bandaru et al. (2006) hypothesized that growing plants in clumps would result in fewer tillers and less vegetative growth so that more soil water would be available during the grain-filling period. Results from a 3-yr study at Bushland, TX and a 1-yr study at Tribune, KS showed that planting grain sorghum in clumps of three to six plants reduced tiller formation to about one per plant, compared with about three for uniformly spaced plants. Grain yields were increased with clump planting by as much as 100% when yields were in the 1000 kg ha^{-1} range and 25 to 50% in the 2000 to 3000 kg ha^{-1} range, but when uniformly planted sorghum yields exceeded 5000 kg ha^{-1}, the clump planted sorghum yields were similar or even slightly decreased. There were also marked differences in plant architecture (Bandaru et al., 2006). That is, uniformly spaced plants produced more tillers and the leaves on both the main stalk and tillers grew outward, exposing essentially all of the leaf area to sunlight and wind. In contrast, clumped plants grew upward, with the leaves partially shading one another and reducing the effect of wind, thereby reducing water use. These results suggest that under semiarid environments where plant populations must be kept low to prevent severe water stress, growing plants in clumps rather than in uniformly spaced rows might enhance grain yields. This strategy is somewhat similar to growing plants in skip rows because skip rows also keep plants closer together than uniformly spacing the plants in all rows. In both of these strategies, however, shading of the soil surface is reduced because the plants are concentrated over a smaller area of the soil surface. Therefore, the evaporation portion of evapotranspiration will likely be higher, particularly if there are numerous small precipitation events during the growing season. This effect could be minimized by using these strategies in a no-till cropping system, so the mulch would decrease soil evaporation during the growing season.

Summary

Soil and water conservation in the Southern High Plains are being achieved in both dryland and irrigated agricultural systems, and increasingly in combinations of these systems. The move to limit tillage and increase the retention of crop residues on the surface has not only engendered major reductions in wind erosion, but it has reduced the evaporative loss of water, making more water available for plant growth and yield formation in both dryland and irrigated systems. Irrigation application efficiencies have steadily improved with the move from surface to pressurized systems and with the ongoing improvements in reduction of evaporative losses in pressurized systems due to the introduction of LEPA and drip irrigation technologies. Irrigation scheduling methods and technologies, including automation, have reduced losses of water to runoff and deep percolation and reduced yield loss due to underirrigation, leading to overall improvement in water use efficiency. However, improvements in irrigation management, methods, and technologies can only improve the efficiency with which water is used for crop production; they cannot reduce pumping of the mostly nonrenewable water resource in the High Plains aquifer. In the end, either energy costs will make pumping noneconomical, the aquifer will be pumped until it can supply no more, or the people of the High Plains will decide to institute policies and regulations that limit pumping to sustainable levels.

References

Allen, R.R., J.T. Musick, and A.F. Wiese. 1976. Limited tillage of furrow irrigated winter wheat. Trans. ASAE 19(2):234–236, 241.

Allen, R.G., I.A. Walter, R.L. Elliott, T.A. Howell, D. Itenfisu, M.E. Jensen, and R.L. Snyder (ed.) 2005. The ASCE standardized reference evapotranspiration equation. ASCE, Reston, VA.

American Society of Agricultural and Biological Engineers. 2000. Graham-Hoeme chisel plow. Available at http://www.asabe.org/awards/historic2/38.html (verified 28 Oct. 2009). ASABE, St. Joseph, MI.

Bandaru, V., B.A. Stewart, R.L. Baumhardt, S. Ambati, C.A. Robinson, and A. Schlegel. 2006. Growing dryland grain sorghum in clumps to reduce vegetative growth and increase yield. Agron. J. 98:1109–1120.

Baumhardt, R.L. 2003. The Dust Bowl era. p. 187–191. In B.A. Stewart and T.A. Howell (ed.) Encyclopedia of water science. Marcel-Dekker, New York.

Baumhardt, R.L., and R.L. Anderson. 2006. Crop choices and rotation principles. p. 113–139. In G.A. Peterson et al. (ed.) Dryland agriculture. 2nd ed. Agron. Monogr. 23. ASA, CSSA, and SSSA, Madison, WI.

Baumhardt, R.L., and J. Salinas-Garcia. 2006. Mexico and the U.S. southern Great Plains. p. 341–364. In G.A. Peterson et al. (ed.) Dryland agriculture. 2nd ed. Agron. Monogr. 23. ASA, CSSA, and SSSA, Madison, WI.

Bennett, T., and O. Leyser. 2006. Something on the side: Axillary meristems and plant development. Plant Mol. Biol. 60:843–854.

Blum, A., and M. Naveh. 1976. Improved water use efficiency in dryland grain sorghum by promoted plant competition. Agron. J. 97:935–942.

Bond, J.J., T.J. Army, and O.R. Lehman. 1964. Row spacing, plant populations and moisture supply as factors in dryland grain sorghum production. Agron. J. 56:3–6.

Burnett, E., B.A. Stewart, and A.L. Black. 1985. Regional effects of soil erosion on crop productivity—Great Plains. p. 285–304. In R.F. Follett and B.A. Stewart (ed.) Soil erosion and crop productivity. ASA, CSSA, and SSSA, Madison, WI.

Campbell, H.W. 1907. Campbell's 1907 soil culture manual. H.W. Campbell, Lincoln, NE.

Colaizzi, P.D., A.D. Schneider, S.R. Evett, and T.A. Howell. 2004. Comparison of SDI, LEPA, and spray irrigation performance for grain sorghum. Trans. ASAE 47:1477–1492.

Colaizzi, P.D., P.H. Gowda, T.H. Marek, and D.O. Porter. 2008. Irrigation in the Texas High Plains: A brief history and potential reductions in demand. Irrig. Drain. doi:10.1002/ird.418.

Craufurd, P.Q., D.J. Flower, and J.M. Peacock. 1993. Effect of heat and drought stress on sorghum (Sorghum bicolor). I. Panicle development and leaf appearance. Exp. Agric. 29:61–76.

Cronin, J.G. 1964. A summary of the occurrence and development of ground water in the Southern High Plains of Texas with a section on artificial recharge studies by B.N. Meyers. U.S. Geological Survey Water-Supply Paper 1693.

de Sousa, P.L., L.L. Silva, and R.P. Serralheiro. 1999. Comparative analysis of main on-farm irrigation systems in Portugal. Agric. Water Manage. 40(2–3):341–351.

Eck, H.V. 1986. Effects of water deficits on yield, yield components, and water use efficiency of irrigated corn. Agron. J. 78:1035–1040.

Eck, H.V., A.C. Mathers, and J.T. Musick. 1987. Plant water stress at various growth stages and growth and yield of soybeans. Soil Field Crops Res. 17:1–16.

Erhart, A. 1969. A page out of irrigation history: Early Kansas irrigation. Irrigation Age. February, p. 20-CNI–20-CN4.

Evett, S.R., T.A. Howell, and A.D. Schneider. 1995. Energy and water balances for surface and subsurface drip irrigated corn. p. 135–140. In F.R. Lamm (ed.) Microirrigation for a changing world: Conserving resources/preserving the environment. Proc. Fifth International Microirrigation Congress. ASAE, St. Joseph, MI.

Evett, S.R., T.A. Howell, A.D. Schneider, D.R. Upchurch, and D.F. Wanjura. 1996. Canopy temperature based automatic irrigation control. p. 207–213. In C.R. Camp et al. (ed.) Proc. International Conference Evapotranspiration and Irrigation Scheduling, San Antonio, TX.

Evett, S.R., T.A. Howell, A.D. Schneider, D.R. Upchurch, and D.F. Wanjura. 2000a. Automatic drip irrigation of corn and soybean. p. 401–408. In R.G. Evans et al. (ed.) Proc. 4th Decennial Natl. Irrig. Symp., Phoenix, AZ. 14–16 Nov. 2000.

Evett, S.R., T.A. Howell, R.W. Todd, A.D. Schneider, and J.A. Tolk. 2000b. Alfalfa reference ET measurement and prediction. p. 266–272. In R.G. Evans et al. (ed.) Proc. 4th Decennial National Irrig. Symp., Phoenix, AZ. 14–16 Nov. 2000.

Evett, S.R., R.T. Peters, and T.A. Howell. 2006. Controlling water use efficiency with irrigation automation: Cases from drip and center pivot irrigation of corn and soybean. p. 57–66. In Proc. 28th Annual Southern Conservation Systems Conference, Amarillo TX. 26–28 June 2006.

Farnsworth, R.K., E.S. Thompson, and E.L. Peck. 1982. Evaporation atlas for the contiguous 48 United States. NOAA Tech. Rep. NWS 33. USDC, NOAA, National Weather Service, Washington, DC.

Forsythe, J.L. 1977. Environmental considerations in the settlement of Ellis County, Kansas. Agric. Hist. 51:38–50.

Ganzel, B. 2009. Irrigation rushes in. Wessels Living History Farm web site. Available at http://www.livinghistoryfarm.org/farminginthe40s/water_01.html (verified 28 Oct. 2009). The Ganzel Group Communications, Lincoln, NE.

Gerik, T.J., and C.L. Neely. 1987. Plant density effects on main culm and tiller development of grain sorghum. Crop Sci. 27:1225–1230.

Greb, B.W. 1979. Technology and wheat yields in the Central Great Plains: Commercial advances. J. Soil Water Conserv. 34:269–273.

Greb, B.W., D.E. Smika, and J.R. Welsh. 1979. Technology and wheat yields in the central Great Plains: Experiment station advances. J. Soil Water Conserv. 34:264–268.

Hargreaves, M.W.M. 1977. The dry-farming movement in retrospect. Agric. Hist. 51:149–165.

Hauser, V.L. 1959. Estimates of precision of moisture measurements made with the d/M gage neutron moisture meter during 1959. USDA-ARS, Western Soil & Water Management Research Branch, Southwestern Great Plains Field Station, Bushland, TX.

Howell, T.A. 2006. Challenges in increasing water use efficiency in irrigated agriculture. In International Symposium on Water and Land Management for Sustainable Irrigated Agriculture, Adana, Turkey. (CD-ROM) 4–8 April 2006.

Howell, T.A., S.R. Evett, J.A. Tolk, and A.D. Schneider. 2004. Evapotranspiration of full-, deficit-irrigated, and dryland cotton on the Northern Texas High Plains. J. Irrig. Drain. Eng. 130(4):277–285.

Howell, T.A., A.D. Schneider, and S.R. Evett. 1997a. Subsurface and surface microirrigation of corn Southern High Plains. Trans. ASAE 40(3):635–641.

Howell, T.A., J.L. Steiner, A.D. Schneider, S.R. Evett, and J.A. Tolk. 1997b. Seasonal and maximum daily evapotranspiration of irrigated winter wheat, sorghum, and corn Southern High Plains. Trans. ASAE 40(3):623–634.

Howell, T.A., J.A. Tolk, A.D. Schneider, and S.R. Evett. 1998. Evapotranspiration, yield, and water use efficiency of corn hybrids differing in maturity. Agron. J. 90:3–9.

Hutson, W.F. 1898. Irrigation systems in Texas. U.S. Department of the Interior, Water-Supply and Irrigation Paper of the USGS 13. U.S. Gov. Print. Office, Washington, DC.

Iowa State Agronomy Extension. 2007. Evaluate seeding rate relative to seed cost. Iowa State Univ. Ext., Ames.

Johnson, W.C., and R.G. Davis. 1972. Research on stubble-mulch farming of winter wheat. Conserv. Res. Rep. 16. USDA-ARS, Washington, DC.

Johnson, W.C., C.E. Van Doren, and E. Burnett. 1974. Summer fallow in the southern Great Plains. p. 86–109. In Summer fallow in the western United States. Conservation Research Rep. 17. USDA-ARS, Washington, DC.

Kemper, W.D., W.H. Heinemann, D.C. Kincaid, and R.V. Worstell. 1981. Cablegation: 1. Cable controlled plugs in perforated supply pipes for automatic furrow irrigation. Trans. ASAE 24:1526–1532.

Koohafkan, P., and B.A. Stewart. 2008. Water and cereals in drylands. FAO, Rome and Earthscan, Sterling, VA.

Lamm, F.R., H.L. Manges, L.R. Stone, A.H. Khan, and D.H. Rogers. 1995. Water requirement of subsurface drip-irrigated corn in northwest Kansas. Trans. ASAE 38(2):441–448.

Lamm, F.R., and T.P. Trooien. 2003. Subsurface drip irrigation for corn production: A review of 10 years of research in Kansas. Irrig. Sci. 22(3–4):195–200.

Loomis, R.S. 1983. Crop manipulations for efficient use of water: An overview. p. 345–374. In H.M. Taylor et al. (ed.) Limitations to efficient water use in crop production. ASA, CSSA, and SSSA, Madison, WI.

Lyle, W.M., and J.P. Bordovsky. 1983. LEPA irrigation system evaluation. Trans. ASAE 26(3):776–781.

MacEwan, G. 1983. Charles Noble: Guardian of the soil. Western Producer Prairie Books, Saskatoon, SK, Canada.

Marek, T.H., A.D. Schneider, T.A. Howell, and L.L. Ebeling. 1988. Design and construction of large weighing monolithic lysimeters. Trans. ASAE 31:477–484.

McSteen, P., and O. Leyser. 2005. Shoot branching. Annu. Rev. Plant Biol. 56:353–374.

Miksinski, T.A., Jr. 1998. The Great Plains and prairies. In S.S. Birdsall and J. Florin. United States Information Agency.

Musick, J.T., and D.A. Dusek. 1982. Skip-row planting and irrigation of graded furrows. Trans. ASAE 25(1):82–87, 92.

Musick, J.T., O.R. Jones, B.A. Stewart, and D.A. Dusek. 1994. Water–yield relationships for irrigated and dryland wheat in the U.S. Southern Plains. Agron. J. 86:980–986.

Musick, J.T., and F.B. Pringle. 1986. Tractor wheel compaction of wide-spaced irrigated furrows for reducing water application. Appl. Eng. Agric. 2(2):123–128.

Musick, J.T., F.B. Pringle, W.L. Harman, and B.A. Stewart. 1990. Long-term irrigation trends– Texas High Plains. Appl. Eng. Agric. 6(6):717–724.

Musick, J.T., F.B. Pringle, and P.N. Johnson. 1985. Furrow compaction for controlling excessive irrigation water intake. Trans. ASAE 28(2):502–506.

Musick, J.T., F.B. Pringle, and J.D. Walker. 1988. Sprinkler and furrow irrigation trends—Texas High Plains. Appl. Eng. Agric. 4(1):46–52.

Musick, J.T., and J.D. Walker. 1987. Irrigation practices for reduced water application—Texas High Plains. Appl. Eng. Agric. 3(2):190–195.

Nall, G. 1973. Panhandle farming in the "Golden Era" of American Agriculture. p. 68–93. In Panhandle-Plains Historical Review XLVI. Panhandle Plains Museum, Canyon, TX.

Nall, G. 1980. The struggle to save the land. p. 26–45. In D.W. Whisenhunt (ed.) The depression in the Southwest. Kennikat Press, Port Washington, NY.

New, L.L. 1986. Center pivot irrigation systems. Texas Agric. Ext. Serv. Leaflet 2219.

Norrie, K. 1977. Dry farming and the economics of risk bearing: The Canadian prairies. Agric. Hist. 51:134–148.

Nostrand, R.L. 1996. The Hispano homeland. University of Oklahoma Press, Norman.

Office of Technology Assessment. 1981. The role and development of public agricultural research. p. 29–52. In An assessment of the United States food and agricultural research system. NTIS PB-82-170572. Office of Technology Assessment, Congress of the United States, Washington, DC.

Peters, R.T., and S.R. Evett. 2008. Automation of a center pivot using the temperature-time-threshold method of irrigation scheduling. J. Irrig. Drain. Eng. 134(3):286–291.

Quisenberry, K. 1977. The dry land stations: Their missions and their men. Agric. Hist. 51:218–228.

Renault, D. 1988. Modernization of furrow irrigation in the South-East of France automation at field level and its implications. Irrig. Drain. Syst. 2(3):229–240.

Robins, J.S. 1959. Conducting successful irrigation research. Soil Sci. Soc. Am. J. 23:249–250.

Rogers, D., and B.B. Wilson. 2000. Kansas irrigation systems and cropping trends. An atlas of the Kansas High Plains Aquifer. Available at http://www.kgs.ku.edu/HighPlains/atlas/index.html#Atlas_Directory (verified 28 Oct. 2009). Kansas Geological Survey, Lawrence.

Schneider, A.D. 1976. Irrigation tailwater loss and utilization equations. J. Irrig. Drain. Div. Proc. ASCE 102(IR4):461–464.

Schneider, A.D. 2000. Efficiency and uniformity of the LEPA and spray sprinkler methods: A review. Trans. ASAE 43(4):937–944.

Schneider, A.D., G.W. Buchleiter, and D.C. Kincaid. 2000. LEPA irrigation developments. p. 89–96. In R.G. Evans et al. (ed.) Proc. 4th Decennial Symposium, National Irrigation Symp. ASAE, St. Joseph, MI.

Schneider, A.D., and T.A. Howell. 1993. Sprinkler application methods and sprinkler system capacity. ASAE Paper 93-2053. Available at http://www.cprl.ars.usda.gov/wmru/pdfs/Sprinkler%20Application%20Methods%20and%20Sprinkler%20System%20Capacity.pdf (verified 28 Oct. 2009). ASAE, St. Joseph, MI.

Schneider, A.D., and T.A. Howell. 1994. Methods, amounts and timing of sprinkler irrigation for winter wheat. ASAE Paper 94-2590. ASAE, St. Joseph, MI.

Schneider, A.D., and T.A. Howell. 1995. LEPA and spray irrigation in the Southern High Plains. p. 1718–1722. In W.H. Espey, Jr. and P.G. Combs (ed.) Vol. 2. Water Resources Engineering. Am. Soc. Civil. Eng., New York.

Schneider, A.D., and T.A. Howell. 1998. LEPA and spray irrigation of corn Southern High Plains. Trans. ASAE 41:1391–1396.

Schneider, A.D., and T.A. Howell. 1999. LEPA and spray irrigation for grain crops. J. Irrig. Drain. Eng. 125(4):167–172.

Schneider, A.D., T.A. Howell, and S.R. Evett. 2001. Comparison of SDI, LEPA and spray irrigation efficiency. Paper 012019. ASAE Annual International Meeting, Sacramento, CA, 29 July–1 Aug. ASAE, St. Joseph, MI.

Steiner, J.L., H.H. Schomberg, and J.E. Morrison, Jr. 1994. Measuring surface residue and calculating losses from decomposition and redistribution. p. 21–32. In Crop residue management to reduce erosion and improve soil quality. Conservation Research Rep. 37. USDA-ARS, Washington, DC.

Stewart, B.A., J.T. Musick, and D.A. Dusek. 1983. Yield and water use efficiency of grain sorghum in a limited irrigation-dryland farming system. Agron. J. 75:629–634.

Stewart, B.A., and C.A. Robinson. 1997. Are agroecosystems sustainable in semiarid regions? Adv. Agron. 60:191–228.

Stewart, B.A., and J.L. Steiner. 1990. Water-use efficiency. p. 151–173. In R.P. Singh et al. (ed.) Dryland agriculture: Strategies for sustainability. Adv. Soil Sci. 13. Springer-Verlag, New York.

Stone, L.R., and A.J. Schlegel. 2006. Yield-water supply relationships of grain sorghum and winter wheat. Agron. J. 98:1359–1366.

Trimble, D.E. 1980. The geologic story of the Great Plains. Geological Survey Bull. 1493. U.S. Gov. Print. Office, Washington, DC.

Thoburn, J.B. 1926. A progress report on Oklahoma archeology. Proc. Oklahoma Acad. Sci. 6(2):369–371.

Thoburn, J.B. 1931. Ancient irrigation ditches on the Plains. Chron. Oklahoma 9(1):56–62.

Thwaites, R.G. (ed.) 1905. Edwin James's account of S.H. Long's expedition, 1819–1820. Early Western Travels 17:147. Arthur H. Clark Company, Glendale, CA.

Trout, T.J., and D.C. Kincaid. 1994. Cablegation evaluation methodology. Appl. Eng. Agric. 9:523–528.

Unger, P.W. 1976. Surface residue, water application, and soil texture effects on water accumulation. Soil Sci. Soc. Am. J. 40:298–300.

Unger, P.W. 1983. Irrigation effect on sunflower growth, development, and water use. Field Crops Res. 7:181–194.

Unger, P.W. 1984. Tillage and residue effects on wheat, sorghum, and sunflower grown in rotation. Soil Sci. Soc. Am. J. 48:885–891.

Unger, P.W., and R.L. Baumhardt. 1999. Factors related to dryland grain sorghum yield increases: 1939 through 1997. Agron. J. 91:870–875.

Unger, P.W., and A.F. Wiese. 1979. Managing irrigated winter wheat residue for water storage and subsequent dryland grain sorghum production. Soil Sci. Soc. Am. J. 43:582–588.

U.S. Dep. of Interior Bureau of Reclamation. 2009. Canadian River Project, Texas. Available at http://www.usbr.gov/projects/Project.jsp?proj_Name=Canadian%20River%20Project (verified 20 Jan. 2010 . U.S. Dep. of Interior, Bureau of Reclamation, Austin TX.

USGS. 2008. Map of the High Plains Aquifer. Available at http://water.usgs.gov/ogw/aquiferbasics/ext_hpaq.html (verified 28 Oct. 2009). U.S. Department of the Interior, USGS.

Wanjura, D.F., D.R. Upchurch, and J.R. Mahan. 1992. Automated irrigation based on threshold canopy temperature. Trans. ASAE 35:153–159.

Widstoe, J.A. 1911. Dry farming: A system of agriculture for countries under a low rainfall. Macmillan, New York.

Wiese, A.F., J.J. Bond, and T.J. Army. 1960. Chemical fallow in the southern Great Plains. Weeds 8:284–290.

Wiese, A.F., E. Burnett, and J.E. Box, Jr. 1967. Chemical fallow in dryland cropping sequences. Agron. J. 59:175.177.

5

Midwest Soil and Water Conservation: Past, Present, and Future

Douglas L. Karlen, Dana L. Dinnes, and Jeremy W. Singer
USDA-ARS National Laboratory for Agriculture and the Environment, Ames, IA

The earliest written records about the Midwest are from explorers such as De Soto, Nicolet, La Salle, Marquette, Joliet, and Perrot, who wrote of diverse cultures nestled within landscapes of native flora and fauna. They described the area as having dense woodlands, seas of tall grasses, and mosaics of wetlands—La Salle discovered these were the most difficult to traverse (Severin, 1968). With regard to soil and water conservation, this great diversity was a patchwork of prairie, savannah, forest, wetland, riparian areas, streams, and lakes that were intimately intertwined. Surface and groundwater hydrology connected each of these ecosystems from the upper basins to the lower reaches, ultimately terminating in either the Great Lakes or Gulf of Mexico and creating the flowing roads that those explorers wrote about.

The Midwest has a temperate, subhumid climate, except along the western edge where it becomes similar to that found in the Great Plains. Weather patterns vary significantly from east to west and north to south. Average annual rainfall varies on a consistent gradient from roughly 1000 mm in the eastern and southern states (Ohio, Indiana, and Missouri) to just under 700 mm in the northwest (Minnesota). Annual average temperatures exhibit a similar gradient ranging from 10.4, 13.7, and 12.4°C in Ohio, Indiana and Missouri, respectively, to 6.3°C in Michigan and 5.1°C in Minnesota.

Dramatic weather events are not uncommon in the Midwest, particularly fast-moving cold fronts with high winds in the fall. The Great Lakes' first ever bulk carrier, La Salle's the *Griffin*, and centuries later the *SS Edmund Fitzgerald*, both fell prey to such storms in late September 1679 and early November 1975, respectively. Midwest wind storm disasters were not limited to the waters of its Great Lakes. On October 8, 1871, a similar cyclonic wind storm ripped through the Midwest on the heels of a severe drought (Haines and Sando, 1969). That date is most frequently remembered for the Chicago Fire that killed approximately 300 people and destroyed more than 17,000 homes and buildings across an area of approximately 800 ha (Pauly, 1984). But while Chicago burned, the deadliest forest fire in our nation's history raged in rural northeast Wisconsin on the same date. The Peshtigo Fire was much more disastrous than the Chicago Fire in almost every respect, claiming 1200 to 2400 lives and burning more than 600,000

Soil and Water Conservation Advances in the United States. SSSA Special Publication 60.
T.M. Zobeck and W.F. Schillinger, editors. © 2010. SSSA, 677 S. Segoe Rd., Madison, WI 53711, USA.

ha (State Historical Society of Wisconsin, 1971; Hipke, 2008; Travel and History, 2008). Michigan also had a catastrophic forest fire sweep across the "lower peninsula" at the same time; 200 people died and 486,000 ha were burned. According to the Sanilac County history, it was "A sky of flame, of smoke a heavenful, the earth a mass of burning coals, the mighty trees, all works of man between and living things trembling as a child before a demon in the gale. To those who have seen, the picture needs no painting" (Absolute Michigan, 2009). Described as "The Fiery Fiend," fires endangered towns across the state, destroying the city of Holland and threatening Muskegon, South Haven, Grand Rapids, Wayland, and the agricultural college in Lansing, reaching the outskirts of Big Rapids. In 1881, Michigan was again hit by a major fire that killed 282 people and burned 400,000 ha.

Tradition attributes the Chicago fire to Mrs. O'Leary's cow, but some suggest that multiple fires occurred at the same time because the earth moved through the tail of a comet (Thunderbolts.info, 2006). With no doubt, fuel for the fires was created by a number of events. Drought and abnormally high temperatures had dried up wetlands, leaving peat exposed on the dry surface (Haines and Sando, 1969). The lumber industry was booming in the area, and normal practices for the time left about one-quarter of the tree biomass as slash, or waste, on the land (Boise State University, 2008). Once cleared of its forest, some areas were converted to agricultural crops by piling slash in heaps (Travel and History, 2008). So great was the fire that it created its own, powerful internal winds, ripping roofs off homes and producing "tornadoes of fire" or firewhirls that were on the leading edge of the advancing fire (State Historical Society of Wisconsin, 1971; Boise State University, 2008). The native conditions had been altered by logging, creating an abundant fuel source that, when combined with severe drought and cyclonic wind storm, had deadly consequences for many throughout the Midwest.

The USDA-NRCS Agricultural Handbook 296 (2006) listed 38 different major land resources areas (MRLA) and 7 of the 12 soil orders in the Midwest—Alfisols, Mollisols, Entisols, Inceptisols, Spodosols, Histosols, and Ultisols. Alfisols, formed under deciduous forest and significantly weathered from high rainfall and warm temperatures, are the dominant soil order across Ohio, Indiana, Michigan, Wisconsin, Illinois, and Missouri. They have medium to high fertility and are frequently used for agricultural crops (USDA-NRCS, 1999). Mollisols, having a thick, dark-colored surface horizon, high organic matter content, and very good fertility, were formed under prairie vegetation and are the predominant soil order in western and southern Minnesota, all of Iowa, northwest Missouri, north-central Illinois and northwestern Indiana. Although very fertile, poor internal drainage is common, so many of these areas required artificial drainage before they could be used for row crop production.

The remaining five soil orders are less common throughout the Midwest, but are important within small areas. Histosols that developed in native prairie and forest wetlands are primarily found in northern Minnesota, northern Wisconsin, and Michigan's Upper Peninsula. These soils have unique properties that are both advantageous and enigmas when used for agricultural and nonagricultural purposes. Entisols are young soils that lack development of horizons due to relatively recent or frequent depositions of eolian or fluvial sand or silt. The Loess Hills in western Iowa and Central Sands in Wisconsin are the predominant Entisols in the Midwest, with smaller areas across northern Minnesota, Wisconsin, and Michigan. Inceptisols, formed under forest vegetation, are also young soils, but they have some evidence of weathering and horizon development. These are found primarily in northeast Minnesota's forested region, with smaller areas in northwest Ohio and scattered across Indiana and Michigan. Spodosols, developed from sandy parent material and occurring under coniferous forest, are very infertile and are acidic due to leaching of conifer litter. Most are found in northern Michigan and northern Wisconsin, typically under second-growth conifer forest. Ultisols in the Midwest are found primarily in southern Missouri, southern Indiana, and southeast Ohio. These soils also formed under deciduous forest, but are more weathered and have lower inherent fertility than Alfisols (USDA-NRCS, 1999).

Many factors influenced settlement patterns in the Midwest. For example, during the early 1800s, in the same writings that were used to spark social change, Mark Twain also introduced the typical lifestyles and agricultural practices of the Midwest to the rest of the world. The increased knowledge of fertile lands and the Midwest's favorable climate for crop production attracted eastern U.S. residents and immigrants seeking a better life. Those factors fueled an explosion of pioneers who wanted to begin new lives in this region. Between 1800 and 1900, entire landscapes of the Midwest were cleared of native vegetation and/or large fauna and replaced by agricultural crops and livestock. Although native prairie grasses and forbs were not always removed from pastured areas, intensive livestock grazing also altered these ecosystems. Overgrazed pastures created denuded areas where European plants, whether brought intentionally or by accident, became established and sometimes invasive (DiTomaso, 2000). This displacement of native prairie, savannah, and forest vegetation occurred on a more intensive and broader scale in areas tilled for agricultural crops or cut for the lumber to build new homes, barns, and rapidly expanding towns and cities.

In an undisturbed state, native midwestern ecosystems were able to withstand extreme climatic events. They protected soil, water, and air resources by functioning as natural sponges and reservoirs, quickly absorbing and storing rainfall, slowing runoff, reducing channel cutting, and preventing flooding by lowering the kinetic energy of the water (Allen, 1993; Sparks et al., 1998; Knox, 2001). Peak rainfall events posed little risk of severe flooding because prairie soils had high amounts of water-absorbing soil organic matter (SOM) that accumulated from dense perennial grass root systems. With both cool- and warm-season species, prairies were actively growing and made highly efficient use of available water during all but the coldest winter months (Dinnes, 2004; Sparks et al., 1998). Forest lands functioned in a similar manner, although once disturbed it took longer for them to regain mature population dynamics through species succession.

This chapter examines Midwest soil and water conservation during three eras defined as the past (settlement–1945), recent past (1945–2005), and present and future (2005–beyond). The time periods were selected based on major events—technological, political, and societal—with the goals being to examine what happened in the past, recognize the current natural resource conditions in the Midwest, and use that knowledge to develop more economically, environmentally, and socially sustainable farming systems for the future.

The Past: Settlement to 1945

Exact boundaries of the Midwest vary according to who you ask, but for this chapter we included the following states based on their official entry into the

United States: Ohio, 1803; Indiana, 1816; Illinois, 1818; Missouri, 1821; Michigan, 1837; Iowa, 1846; Wisconsin, 1848; and Minnesota, 1858. Early settlement by aspiring independent farmers in the eastern portion of this region was difficult due to actions of speculators and "land grabbers." This frustration became so severe at times that vigilante groups even encouraged "hanging land grabbers from trees in a good Christian-like manner" (Timmons, 1948). Federal legislation followed that strongly encouraged resident ownership of the nation's farms through both the Preemption Act of 1841 and Homestead Act of 1862. The latter enabled a person to "freehold" 65 ha (160 acres) and later receive a deed/title to the land if they remained on the property for 5 yr, built a tenement of at least 3.7 by 4.3 m (12 by 14 feet), and grew crops (Potter and Schamel, 1997).

Land Tenure

Following initial settlement by homesteaders, the Midwest saw volatile times and trends in farmland ownership. On the cultural side, the norm was for farm families to be very large. Many children helped meet the high labor requirements needed to operate a farm. When parents passed away, farmland was often bequeathed entirely to the eldest son if there was not enough land to support more than a single family. This practice enabled land to remain owned and operated within the family, although potentially at the expense of other siblings' livelihoods. Despite these cultural practices and the presence of the Homestead Act, the first agricultural census in 1880 showed that 25% of the nation's farmers were tenants (Timmons, 1948). Turner (1927) revealed in his 1920 survey of 85 counties in the U.S. North Central region (states generally the same as the Midwest, but not identified by the survey) that there was essentially no change between 1900 and 1920 in the percentage of farms or in the county area owned by landlords who did not reside in that county and operated their holdings as rented land parcels. He reported that 26% of all rented land and 30 to 31% of rented areas in each county were owned by absentee landlords.

While most of the country prospered through the early and mid 1920s, the farm economy suffered. Many faced a combination of debts from purchased farm equipment and land improvements that were made to increase production in response to increased demand and higher prices during World War I (Alston, 1983). Farm exports were significantly reduced following World War I as a result of tariff barriers between the United States and other countries. Resultant low commodity prices put many farmers at risk, and farm debt accelerated quickly to equal nearly 50% of the nation's farm value. When the Great Depression began in the late 1920s, farmers burdened with heavy debt were in serious financial trouble. One of every four U.S. farms was foreclosed on and ownership passed from owner-operators to corporate and absentee land owners. It was estimated in 1935 that more than 40% of all farmers were tenants and that more than 50% of the nation's farmland was owned by absentee landlords and other non-farming entities (Timmons, 1948).

Farm economies improved during World War II, and these trends were reversed by 1945. The 1945 agricultural census revealed that for the entire nation, famers were once again gaining ownership of the lands they worked (Timmons, 1948). The national census showed that 67.6% of farmers owned all or part of the land they farmed and that the proportion of tenant farmers dropped to 31.7%, the lowest level since 1890. These national trends were similar throughout the Midwest in 1943, although nearly 45% of the farmland was still under lease (Penn, 1943).

Natural Resource Conditions

From settlement through 1945, erosion rates throughout the Midwest were variable and highly dependent on land use and management. Areas of considerable slope were often maintained as pasture or woodland pasture for grazing. The condition of these areas varied depending on the intensity of grazing. Areas with low stocking rates were relatively stable and experienced little erosion. Areas with high stocking rates often experienced high rates of erosion, especially those with fragile soils or when livestock were not removed during rainy periods or spring snowmelt. Crop rotations were highly diversified and often included meadows that did not require annual tillage. Once established, they produced continuous ground cover and generally had little erosion.

Moldboard plowing was generally used across the entire region to prepare soils and the seedbed for planting. This left very little plant residue and barren soil that was highly vulnerable to wind and water erosion (Fig. 5–1). Additionally, in-season cultivation was commonly performed several times throughout the growing season to manage weed populations in row crops. On sloping landscapes, where annual row crops and small grains dominated, erosion rates were among the highest in recorded history (Follett and Stewart, 1985). Clearing of native vegetation and tillage increased erosion losses and sediment delivery by several orders of magnitude (Novotny, 1999).

By the mid 1930s, the Iowa State Planning Commission's Natural Resources Board concluded that because the state's prairies were plowed, 40% of the land had lost 50 to 75% of its surface soil, and lakes were filling with silt (Chase, 1936). The 1938 USDA Yearbook of Agriculture (USDA, 1938) also presented data from the Ohio Experiment Station showing that where corn (*Zea mays* L.) was grown continuously from 1894 through 1935, soil loss averaged 4 cm and carried with it 63% of the SOM. For areas including oat (*Avena sativa* L.) crops, soil loss was 2.6 cm, and SOM was reduced by only 36% (Turner and Rabalais, 2003). Studies from

Fig. 5–1. Moldboard plowing, such as here in Monona County, Iowa in 1940, was the typical primary tillage operation to prepare fields for planting of all crops across the Midwest at that time. This practice left loose, barren soil highly at risk to losses from wind and water erosion. Photo courtesy of the USDA-NRCS.

Fig. 5–2. Hugh Hammond Bennett, first chief of the USDA Soil Conservation Service (now Natural Resources Conservation Service, USDA-NRCS), inspects a site of farmland wind erosion near Ottawa County, Michigan. Photo courtesy of the USDA-NRCS.

the early 1930s reported that soil erosion from portions of Major Land Resource Area (MLRA) 105 (Driftless Area) in southwest Wisconsin, southeast Minnesota, and northeast Iowa were as high as 33.4 Mg ha^{-1} yr^{-1} (14.9 tons a^{-1} yr^{-1}) (Argabright et al., 1996).

These effects of soil and crop management are often overlooked because during the 1930s intensive tillage, coupled with periods of drought and national financial stress extending into the farm economy, led to the devastating Dust Bowl (Schubert et al., 2004; Egan, 2006) that destroyed vast farming areas in the Great Plains. Eroded soil was carried by wind storms that were so immense they were called "black blizzards" (Helms, 1990). The combined effects of wind and water erosion throughout the nation, coupled with persuasive arguments of Hugh Hammond Bennett motivated Congress to create the Soil Erosion Service, predecessor to the Soil Conservation Service (SCS), in 1935 and to name Mr. Bennett as its first Chief (Fig. 5–2). The function of the SCS was to implement government policies that promoted and aided in establishment of practices on private lands to conserve both soil and water resources and to conduct soil surveys in each state.

Artificial Drainage Effects

The process of installing artificial drainage began in the mid 1800s in the eastern portion of the Midwest and in the late 1800s for the western portion. Federal law supported artificial drainage in this area through the Swamp Land Acts of 1850 and 1860 and again almost 100 years later with the Flood Control Act of 1944. One focus of the Swamp Land Acts was to promote conversion of wetlands to tillable croplands, a challenge that was overwhelmingly accomplished. Each of these laws intentionally encouraged drainage activities, including tiling, ditching, and channelization to prevent flooding (Wooten and Jones, 1955). Implementing these practices may have reduced flooding in the upper portions of watersheds, but often at the expense of greater flood risk to lower portions of the watersheds (Allen, 1993; Galloway, 2005). Unfortunately, it was not understood that improving landscape water storage capacity was really a better practice to manage flooding and that efforts to speed water flow simply increased flood risk downstream (Allen, 1993; Sparks et al., 1998; Knox, 2001; Dinnes 2004).

Stream channelization (Fig. 5–3) also began in the late 1800s and continues today such that larger streams in Iowa have decreased in length by nearly 45% (Zaimes et al., 2006). Tile drain installation and digging of drainage ditches also increased the length, drainage density, and channel frequency of intermittent

Fig. 5–3. Artificial drainage and channelization of streams were major factors changing the hydrology and landscape characteristics of the Midwest.

streams in the headwater areas of watersheds (Zaimes et al., 2006). The overall impacts of artificial drainage on landscape hydrology across the Midwest included a decreased capacity to store water and shorter water residence times that subsequently increased stream flow during peak rainfall events (Holden et al., 2004). The increased stream flow translated into increased energy in the waters that further eroded and transported sediments, causing even greater stream bank erosion and channel incision (Menzel, 1983; Schumm, 1999; Zaimes et al., 2006).

Cropping Systems

As artificial drainage expanded throughout the Midwest, the cultivated area increased and crop sequence changed. Poorly drained areas that were previously either completely avoided or occasionally cut for their "wild hay" were plowed and converted from native prairie and wetlands to rotations of row, vegetable, small grain, and meadow crops (Hewes and Frandson, 1952). Fields with irregular boundaries that had been managed using site-specific strategies for optimizing production by placing different crop types on the areas for which they were best suited, were gradually replaced with larger fields with straight and uniform boundaries (square or rectangular). The new management philosophy was to alter the site-specific soil conditions to meet the selected crops' needs. While this strategy worked fairly well during times of favorable weather, Mother Nature often reclaimed the poorly drained areas during peak rainfall events and turned them back into wetlands, destroying the agronomic crops or preventing essential field operations.

From settlement to 1945, farms in the Midwest were highly diversified, with livestock, grain, and forage production. Principal crops included corn, wheat (*Triticum aestivum* L.), oat, rye (*Secale cereale* L.), clovers (*Trifolium* spp.), grasses, alfalfa (*Medicago sativa* L.), garden vegetables, sorghum [*Sorghum bicolor* (L.) Moench], and tobacco (*Nicotiana tabacum* L.). This reflected the U.S. average of five different commodities for all farms in 1900 and between four and five in 1945 (Dimitri et al., 2005). Crop rotation and integration of livestock were needed to maintain production because off-farm fertilizer inputs were generally not available and rarely affordable. Soil fertility was maintained by rotating grain and legume crops and applying livestock manure. Crop rotations also helped break insect and disease cycles. Grain and forage were fed to livestock, which included animals for mechanical draft power as well as food. Common livestock included beef and dairy cattle, swine, sheep, poultry, and draft horses and mules. During early settlement years and before a transportation infrastructure was developed, farms and farmers were focused more on livestock than crop production (Willham, 2000). Converting grain into meat was more viable than moving grain directly into commercial markets.

Animal Production Systems

Beef cattle, dairy cattle, and swine numbers in the Midwest generally increased between 1870 and 1945 (Fig. 5–4). Beef production nearly tripled from about 9 million to more than 26 million head, while the number of dairy cattle increased from less 3 million to more than 10 million by 1945. In 1870, there were more than 18 million swine in the Midwest, and by 1945 this number had nearly doubled to 36 million. On-farm poultry populations doubled from 1880 to 1890, showed a slight decline by 1900, and then increased steadily until 1940. After a drop in poultry numbers in 1940, wartime needs brought farm poultry to a new high of more than 170 million birds in 1945. Sheep production was at its peak in 1870 at just over 11 million head. It then declined by 35% over the next 20 yr before rebounding slightly to about 10 million, where it stayed fairly constant through 1945.

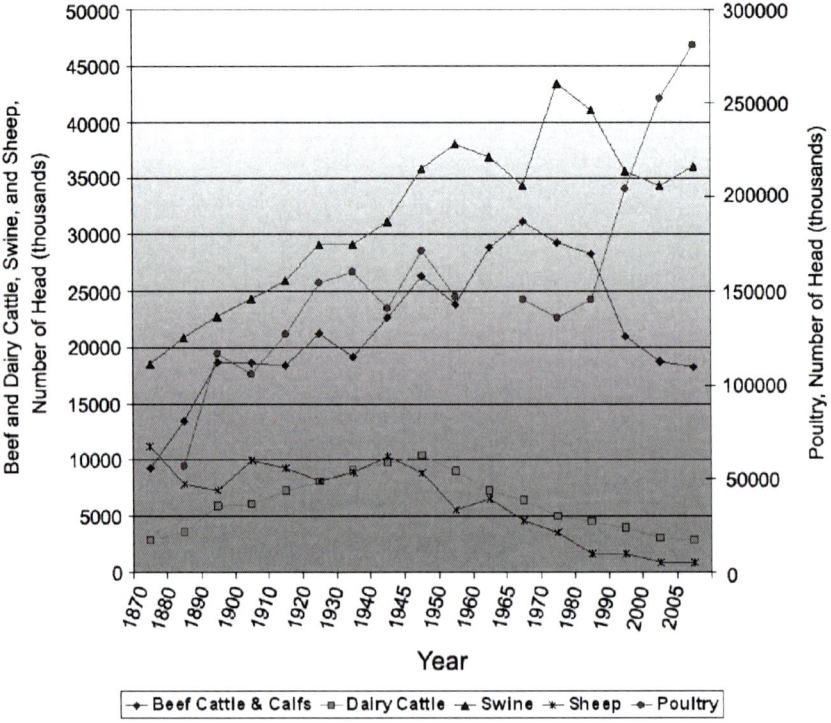

Fig. 5–4. Midwest commodity, on-farm livestock populations, 1870–2005. Data compiled for respective years from USDA-NAL Yearbooks of Agriculture, U.S. Census of Agriculture, USDA-NASS and USDA-NASS Illinois Field Office. *Due to missing data, turkey numbers for total poultry were estimated for Wisconsin in 1990–2005, based on average of 1980 and 1985 ratio of that state's production to the remaining Midwestern States.

Fig. 5–5. Farming operations in the early 1900s commonly required mechanical and animal power, and many human hands and labor hours. The forage threshing here on one of the author's grandfather's farmstead shows 15 people working the operation that currently requires just one person using large baling equipment and tractors. Photo courtesy of Dana L. Dinnes.

Mechanization

Farming before 1945 required many people and draft animals to till, plant, cut, bale, thresh, and transport crops (Fig. 5–5), even though early versions of the modern day tractor began to appear in the Midwest during the late 1800s. One of the first "traction engines" was built by a custom thresher, John Froelich, in 1892, who started the Waterloo Gasoline Traction Engine Company in Waterloo, IA. He built four working models, but his initial efforts were unsuccessful, and the company was sold twice, eventually to Deere and Company, before it achieved success (Hilliard, 1972).

With increased mechanization, Midwest farmers were able to manage more land in an efficient manner, thus contributing to an increase in row crops. Following World War II, off-farm inputs to manage soil fertility, disease, weeds, and insects also became much more available. The relatively quick adoption of these new technologies ushered in a new period of agriculture that again brought many changes affecting soil and water conservation.

1945 to the Present

During the past 60 yr, agriculture in the Midwest and around the world has undergone major changes that have brought many improvements, including greater crop yields, highly efficient animal production enterprises, new products, and a global marketing system. However, there has been a consistent, steady decline in the number and diversity of crops being grown throughout the Midwest, with soybean [*Glycine max* (L.) Merr.] emerging as the primary crop grown in rotation with corn. These changes helped ensure a consistent, uniform commodity supply for agricultural industries and many new products being developed primarily from corn and soybean grain. With regard to soil and water conservation, these cropping changes have raised many concerns, including longer periods of time when soils are "biologically active" but lack living plants to capture sunlight, water, and available nutrients. Being biologically active means that N is being cycled from decaying plant tissues and made available for uptake. Rainfall and snowmelt are also occurring and filling up the pore space, but with only one crop each year there are several months in late autumn and early spring when excess water either runs off or leaches through the profile, carrying the nutrients into surface and groundwater. This contributes to eutrophication and other water quality concerns, such as Gulf hypoxia.

Increased corn and soybean production throughout the Midwest also resulted in a separation of crop and animal production enterprises, raising concerns about odor, managing manure, water quality, and animal welfare. These issues are discussed under the rubrics of "livestock effects" and "environmental consequences," but in general show that as crop and animal production enterprises became specialized and separated, animals were raised in more confined and consolidated operations, sometimes with less space and freedom than some felt was appropriate for animal welfare. Animal consolidation also resulted in manure being stored for longer periods of time in pits, lagoons, or other confined spaces, contributing to stronger odors because of anaerobic storage conditions and occasionally leaking into surface water or groundwater resources. For more information, readers are encouraged to consult the volumes that have been written about these topics (e.g., Ritter and Shirmohammadi, 2001).

Hydrologic Changes

Hydrologic response to land use change is complex. Before the Midwest was cleared by settlers, the dominant fate for precipitation was infiltration. After land was cleared of native vegetation, the dominant processes were shifted to surface runoff and soil erosion (Anderson, 2000). Natural water storage characteristics of the prairies and forest were changed to a condition that could store far less precipitation than before settlement (Allen, 1993; Knox, 2001). Many of the wetlands were artificially drained by ditches and shallow underground tile systems. Streams were straightened or channelized and riparian vegetation removed to allow for increased areas of row crops and ease of machinery operations (Sparks et al., 1998; Knox, 2001; Dinnes et al., 2002). Overall, the effect on hydrology was reduced surface and near-surface water residence time. This increased the speed of water movement from land to streams and resulted in "flashier" streamflows that subsequently led to more frequent and greater flood events (Allen, 1993; Galloway, 2005).

Drainage activities also started and accelerated the processes of dewatering, oxidation, and subsidence on large acreages of organic soils ("mucks" as they are called locally) in the upper Midwest. These organic soils (Histosols) are very productive sites for high quality vegetable crops, including celery (*Apium graveolens* L.), parsnip (*Pastinaca sativa* L.), carrot (*Daucus carota* L.), radish (*Raphanus sativus* L.), potato (*Solanum tuberosum* L.), and onion (*Allium cepa* L.), as well as corn, soybean, and sugarbeet (*Beta vulgaris* L.) (Fig. 5–6). They have also been literally mined (i.e., dug up and sold) in the past for use as a garden amendment (peat moss) for greenhouse planter boxes and home gardens.

Clearing and cultivating organic soils has created several unique and interesting challenges. Most organic soils are black, and when exposed to direct

Fig. 5–6. Radish production on organic soils in Michigan. Note dark soil color and pivot irrigation system. Photo courtesy of NRCS, 2008.

sunlight, surface soil temperatures often increase more than in mineral soils, burning young seedlings and sensitive crops in a process called burnoff. Excess soil acidity in organic soils also causes crop problems like forked roots in sugarbeets (Lucas, 1982), and in many areas the water depth must be regulated to meet plant needs while allowing mechanical planting and harvesting operations.

Currently, many Histosols in the Upper Midwest have only a small fraction of their original thickness and actually may no longer be classified as Histosols. These organic soils are in danger of extinction during the next generation if measures are not taken to reestablish earlier groundwater levels and reinstall wind breaks. Reduction in thickness of these "mucks" is demonstrated by the fact that many fields have been tiled up to three times during the past hundred years because buried drainage tile end up on the soil surface as these soils subside and erode (Lucas, 1982). This reduction in organic soil thickness has been accentuated by wind erosion related to the removal of wind breaks and other current management practices. Because of their low bulk density, water erosion is also a problem on organic soils. Surface irrigation (pivots and hand lines) is available on many drained fields and used to supply crop water requirements and in some cases to provide moisture to soils before wind events to control wind erosion.

Overall, hydrologic processes are reflective of landscape management. Using data from 11 gauging stations located throughout Iowa, Schilling and Libra (2003) reported that annual baseflow and baseflow percentage increased significantly in nearly all watersheds during the second half of the 20th century. This increased baseflow means that more water was moving through the soil profile and into streams and rivers rather than being used by plants. The authors speculated that multiple factors were contributing to an increase in baseflow, including greater use of conservation practices, increased installation of artificial drainage, increased row crop production in contrast to forage or grass crops, channel incision, and longer periods during spring and autumn when soils were bare and there was no living vegetation transpiring water from the soil.

Crop Production

From 1945 to the present, small amounts of native land in the Midwest continued to be converted to agricultural production, especially with artificial drainage, but the primary driver for increased crop production was intensification or producing

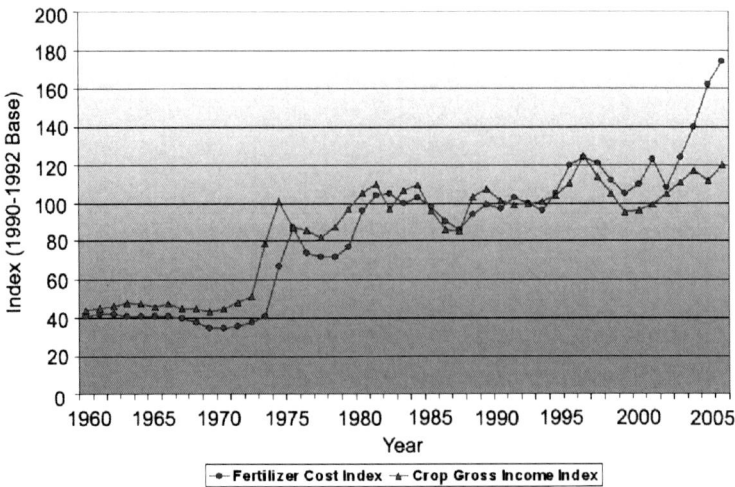

Fig. 5–7. Trends in U.S. farm fertilizer cost and crop gross income with 1990–1992 statistics as an index base (100), years 1960–2006. Data from USDA-ERS, 2007.

more per unit area. Also, chemical advances during and after World War II led to new industries that supplied farmers with commercial fertilizers and pesticides. These products allowed farmers to simplify crop rotations by using purchased inputs to address soil fertility, disease, and insect pressures. This change also had profound effects on soil and water conservation. For example, a comparison of inputs for a 2-yr corn–soybean and 4-yr corn–soybean–oat–alfalfa rotation showed that beneficial yield effects of 4-yr rotations could be replaced by external inputs of fertilizers and pesticides, but the total value (i.e., nutrient cycling, stabilization of soil structure, stimulating microbial populations) of expanded crop rotations was often lost (Porter et al., 2003). Use of off-farm inputs increased variable production costs, but it allowed farmers to raise cash grain crops on the same fields each year and often provided greater short-term profits. More subtle effects of management on soil properties such as soil organic matter levels, water-holding capacity, compaction, infiltration, and runoff were rarely assessed.

Figure 5–7 shows trends in U.S. fertilizer cost and crop gross income for 1960 through 2006, using 1990 to 1992 data as an index (100). There is variation among individual years, but gross income from crops was generally greater than fertilizer cost (USDA-ERS, 2007). Beginning in 1994, this trend reversed and showed a dramatic increase for 2003 to 2006, as fertilizer costs began to increase faster than crop values.

Land Tenure

Changes in farm economics since 1945 also changed demographics and relationships of farm tenancy and ownership. As the number of farms declined, the average size of surviving operations and prevalence of rented land rose steadily. This change affects decisions related to soil and water conservation. When land is rented, there is often no guarantee of a long-term commitment for either party. This often reduces both incentives and capital for long-term investments in practices that sustain soil resources compared with situations where land is owned and there is a desire to pass it on to the next generation. Figure 5–8 shows that Midwest farm numbers decreased by approximately 60%, with the loss of nearly 1.1 million farms from 1950 to 2005 (USDA-NASS, 2007). Using 1950 data as a base, this increased the average Midwest farm size from 100 to more than 200 ha, although this average value is confounded by a substantial increase in the number of very small "hobby farms" for which most family income is derived from nonfarm sources.

Many farmers in the Midwest began to rent additional farmland to keep up with narrowing agricultural profit margins. The result, just as Penn (1943) noted for an earlier era, is that once again the Midwest has more than 50% of its farmland owned by off-farm landlords (Forster, 2006). This is consistent with the national trend for 1993 showing 8% of off-farm landlords owned more than one-half of all rental lands in the nation (U.S. Department of Commerce, Bureau of the Census, 1993). According to the 2002 U.S. Census of Agriculture (USDA-NASS, 2002), rented farmland at the county level was often 40% or more (Fig. 5–9). Duffy (2004) reported that within Iowa, rented land, excluding that in government programs, increased from 43 to 59% from 1982 to 2002. Furthermore, the type of lease contracts shifted from half of rented land being in share crop status in 1982 to more than two-thirds (69%) being under cash rent in 2002 (Duffy, 2004). Farmland lease contracts are rarely written for periods longer than two or three years. This short-term nature further increases the pressure on rental operators and ultimately affects land use decisions, especially long-term investments required for soil and water conservation.

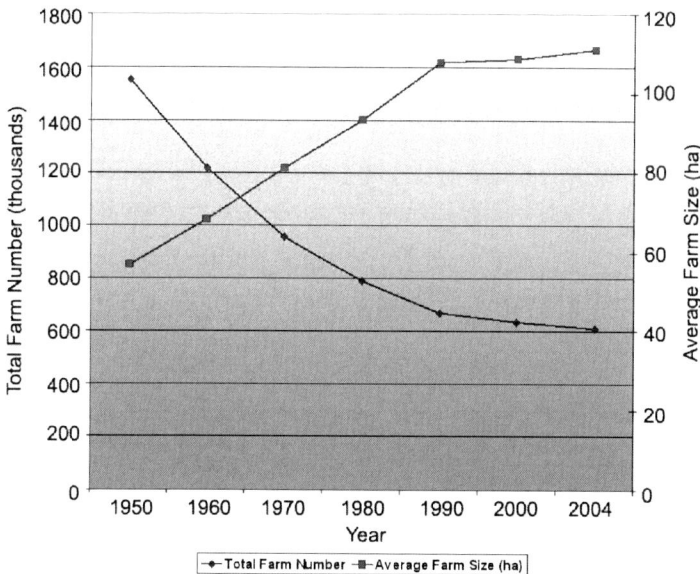

Fig. 5–8. Trends in Midwest farm numbers and average farm area, 1950–2005. Data from USDA-NASS.

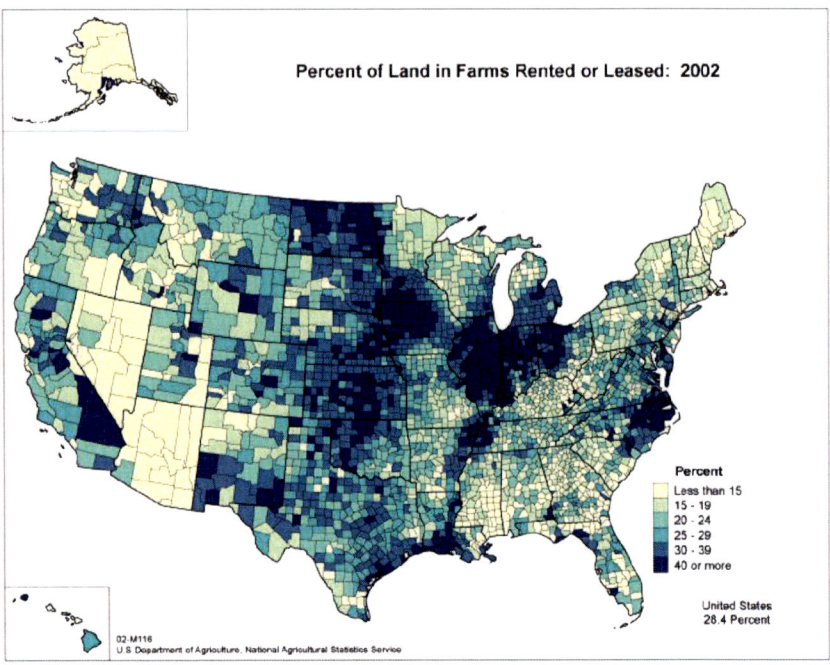

Fig. 5–9. Percentage of non-operator owned farm lands in the United States at the county scale, 2002. Data and graphic from USDA-NASS (2002).

Livestock Effects

Increased concentration of animals has required practices that were not used in the past, creating new environmental challenges. For animals to survive and grow quickly under confined conditions, vitamins, antibiotics and hormones are added to their feed rations. Consequently, some of these materials are passed through with animal waste. In addition, although manure has always accumulated, been odorous, and presented risks of *E. coli*, *Cryptosporidium* and other fecal pathogens, management has become a more important issue as the size of animal confinement operations grew.

Traditionally, livestock numbers for individual operations were relatively small, and manure was collected and distributed across the landscape in frequent but small volumes throughout the year. Because of weather, time, equipment, and other factors, it was not uncommon for more manure to be spread on areas close to barns and feeding areas than on fields further away. However, as the size of operations grew, manure lagoons, pits, and slurry stores containing millions of liters of manure for a single production site were not uncommon. Changes in cropping systems eliminated summer application, and with larger equipment, it became most efficient to transport manure in large tanks that weigh several tons when loaded. Thus, manure applications are now possible only under suitable, dry field conditions in spring and fall when crops are not present. These less frequent manure applications have caused contamination to become a more serious water quality concern (Campagnolo et al., 2002; Kolpin et al., 2002).

A direct soil and water conservation effect of these changes in livestock operations is that manure management plans now must meet regulated requirements throughout the Midwest, with guidelines based on a minimum number of animal units housed at an individual site. Most midwestern states have instituted phosphorus indices to guide manure applications and thus minimize the risk of having manure entering water resources (Mallarino et al., 2002; and Bundy et al., 2008).

Crop Yield Response

Crop yields during the past 60 yr have increased significantly (USDA-NASS, 2007): Corn yield increased nearly fourfold from ~2.5 to ~9.3 Mg ha^{-1}. Soybean and wheat yield tripled (~1.1 to ~3.0 Mg ha^{-1} and ~1.4 to ~4.0 Mg ha^{-1}, respectively). Hay yield doubled from ~3.2 to ~6.3 Mg ha^{-1}. Oat increased 60% (1.5–2.4 Mg ha^{-1}). Potato yield increased more than sixfold, from 6.4 to 39.3 Mg ha^{-1}. For the first several decades, use of fertilizer and pesticide inputs made field conditions more favorable for crop growth, and improvements in crop breeding led to crop varieties better suited for regional climate and soil differences (e.g., water stress tolerance for sandy soils) and with enhanced disease resistance. In latter decades, biotechnology and better crop genetic information led a new era in crop improvement. Insertion of *Bacillus thuringiensis* (Bt) genes that produce a crystal protein that is toxic to many crop insect pests greatly reduced potential yield losses and reduced the need for insecticides. Other genetic modifications created new crop varieties that were tolerant to specific types of herbicides [e.g., glyphosate; *N*-(phosphonomethyl)glycine], thus reducing weed competition for water and nutrients. Improvements in cultural practices such as row spacing, fertilizer placement, drainage, irrigation, and soil and water conservation practices, such as terracing, no-tillage, and strip-tillage have also contributed to increased crop yields.

Environmental Consequences

A number of unintended environmental consequences have resulted from the combined effects of short-term land leases, small profit margins, high input costs, increased debt payments, and increased production of annual row crops. First, the average number of commodities produced per farm fell from four to five in 1945 to less than two by 2002 (Dimitri et al., 2005). Corn and soybean production has become the dominant land use at the expense of all other crops, and by using more purchased inputs, agronomic benefits of extended crop rotations have gradually vanished. Furthermore, although soybean generally does not receive N fertilizer, it, like corn, is an annual row crop with a relatively short growing season. One of the unintended consequences associated with this simple rotation is that it has become a significant source of sediment, nutrient, and chemical contaminants to Midwest water resources (Kanwar et al., 1996, 2005; Randall et al., 1997; Jaynes et al., 1999; Dinnes et al., 2002; Kanwar et al., 2005; Bakhsh and Kanwar, 2007). Increased leaching of nitrate N (NO$_3$–N) into ground and surface waters emerged as a major environmental problem for all agricultural row-crop areas.

Numerous studies and papers have documented that both corn and soybean fields are major contributing areas of NO$_3$–N, soluble herbicides, and their metabolites to water resources, especially from tile drained soils (Willrich, 1969; Baker et al., 1975; Baker and Johnson, 1981; Kladivko et al., 1991; Buhler et al., 1993; Jayachandran et al., 1994; Randall et al., 1997; Jaynes et al., 1999; Randall and Mulla, 2001; Dinnes et al., 2002). To better understand the magnitude of these off-site effects, Zucker and Brown (1998) estimated that nearly 21 million ha of midwestern farmland had been artificially drained by 1987, a trend that has continued to the present (Fig. 5–10). Subsequently, the Midwest was identified as a major source area of NO_3–N contamination in the Gulf of Mexico and that leaching from this area has played a large part in the growth of hypoxic conditions and has caused economic damage to the fishing industry near the mouth of the Mississippi River (Rabalais et al., 1996; USEPA, 2008).

Water quality issues are important, but accelerated soil erosion, driven by both natural and human-induced forces is the most widespread soil degradation process not only in the Midwest, but throughout the world. Whether induced by water, wind, tillage, or irrigation, soil erosion results in permanent loss of effective rooting depth, pollution of water resources, and emission of greenhouse gases (GHGs) from soils (Lal et al., 2004). During the past 75 yr, tremendous efforts have been made to reduce soil erosion, and volumes far beyond the scope of this chapter have been written about it (e.g., Follett and Stewart, 1985; Lal, 1999). However, it would be remiss in a chapter about soil and water conservation in the U.S. Midwest not to mention that much of the early development of tools includ-

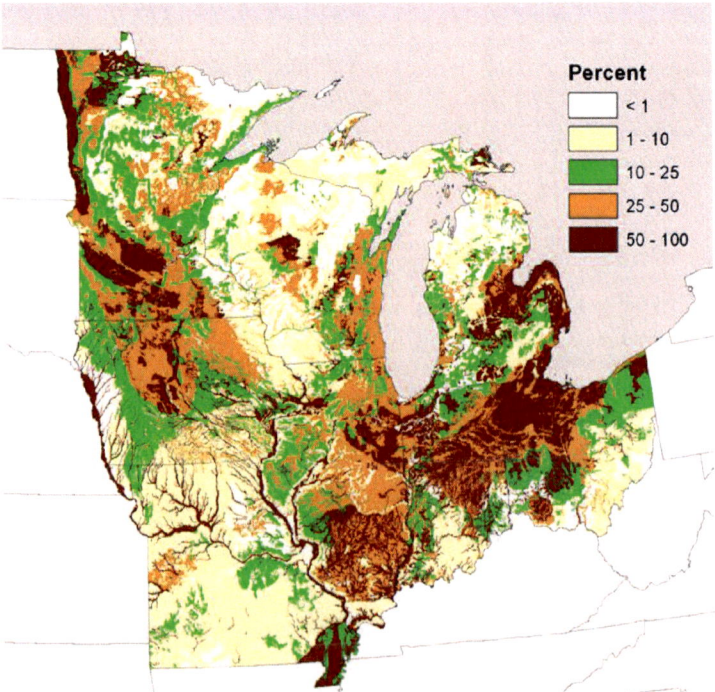

Fig. 5–10. Current percentage of soils with installed artificial drainage practices, 2005. Graphic adapted from Jaynes, D.B. and D.E. James, no date given. The extent of farm drainage in the United States. Available at http://www.ars.usda.gov/SP2UserFiles/Place/36251510/TheExtentofFarmDrainageintheUnitedStates.pdf (verified 19 Nov. 2009).

ing the Universal Soil Loss Equation (USLE), Soil Loss Tolerance Standard (T), Revised Universal Soil Loss Equation (RUSLE), Water Erosion Prediction Project (WEPP), and Wind Erosion Equation (WEQ) occurred in this region. These tools have helped land managers make much better management decisions and have significantly reduced erosion, but they do not address the full range of ecosystem services provided by soils (Soil and Water Conservation Society, 2008).

Not all Midwest cropping system changes have resulted in environmental quality problems. Some have had very positive benefits. For example, advances in conservation and best management practices (BMPs), such as reduced- or no-tillage, have improved soil conditions where they have been adopted. Two key Midwest research pioneers who led these efforts are Drs. Glover Triplett and Dave Van Doren. They led the development of crop production techniques that would reduce soil erosion and save labor and time. In doing so, they established the oldest continuously maintained comparison in the world between no-tillage and plow tillage. Long-term data from the site near Wooster, OH shows that after 18 and 36 yr, the amount of carbon stored in soil is much greater for no-tillage than plow tillage (Mahboubi and Lal, 1998). Carbon is the basic component of soil humus, and increased carbon concentrations significantly improve the quality of soil for crop production. It is now clear that no-tillage and crop rotation systems are excellent technologies for maintaining high crop yields and sustaining soil quality.

The USDA-NRCS defines conservation tillage as any tillage practice that leaves at least 30% crop residue on the soil surface after the tillage operation has been completed. Reduced tillage leaves between 15 and 30% residue cover, while conventional tillage leaves less than 15% residue cover. No-tillage can mean different things to different people, but we define no-tillage as using practices that only minimally disturb the soil to achieve good seed placement and soil–seed contact. Strip-tillage, an evolving version of no-tillage, incorporates one additional soil disturbing operation. A narrow shank is drawn through the soil directly beneath the "row" where a planter will eventually place the crop seed (Fig. 5–11a, 5–11b). The narrow, disturbed zone is commonly about 7 cm wide. It accommodates fertilizer placement beneath the row and can help disrupt in-row compaction that may have occurred during harvest.

Any soil management practice that reduces soil disturbance and leaves more surface residue cover reduces the risk of soil erosion and transport, thereby offering an opportunity for improved soil and water quality (Dinnes, 2004). This is well documented for areas where such practices have been adopted at an appreciable scale (e.g., Argabright et al., 1996). Unfortunately, although these alternative tillage practices began to be tested and adopted more than 40 yr ago, midwestern tillage practice data monitoring its growth is only available since 1989. According to Conservation Technology Information Center (2007) data (Fig. 5–12), there has been a shift toward no-tillage practices from 1990 to 2004, with an increase of approximately 19%. For the same time period, reduced tillage decreased by 5% and conventional tillage decreased by nearly 13%. These trends are encouraging and indicate improvements are being made in agricultural soil management. However, these improvements in tillage management may not be sufficient to overcome losses due to other cropping system changes. Figure 5–13 shows that during the 1990s more land was converted from diversified forage-based cropping systems into cultivated row crops in the Upper Mississippi River and Ohio

Fig. 5–11. (a) A strip-tillage unit showing residue spreaders, cutting coulter, tillage shank, and covering disks (photo courtesy of Yetter Farm Equipment). (b) Appearance of a Midwest corn field following autumn strip tillage (photo courtesy of Dr. Mahdi Al-Kaisi, Iowa State University).

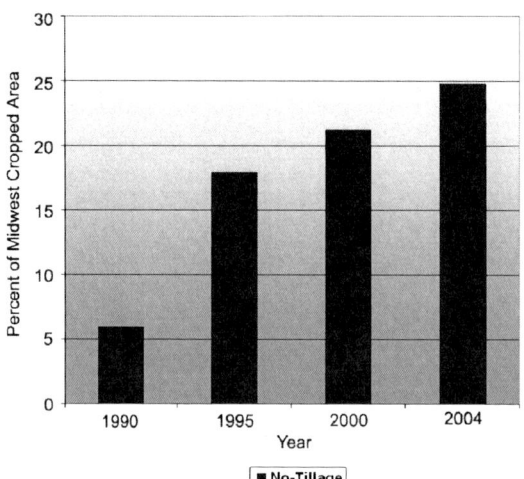

Fig. 5–12. Midwest tillage trends for 1990–2004.

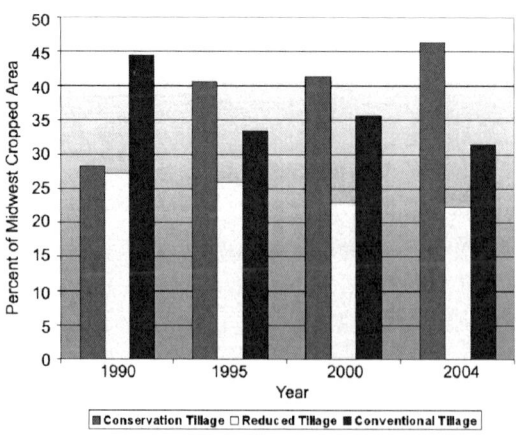

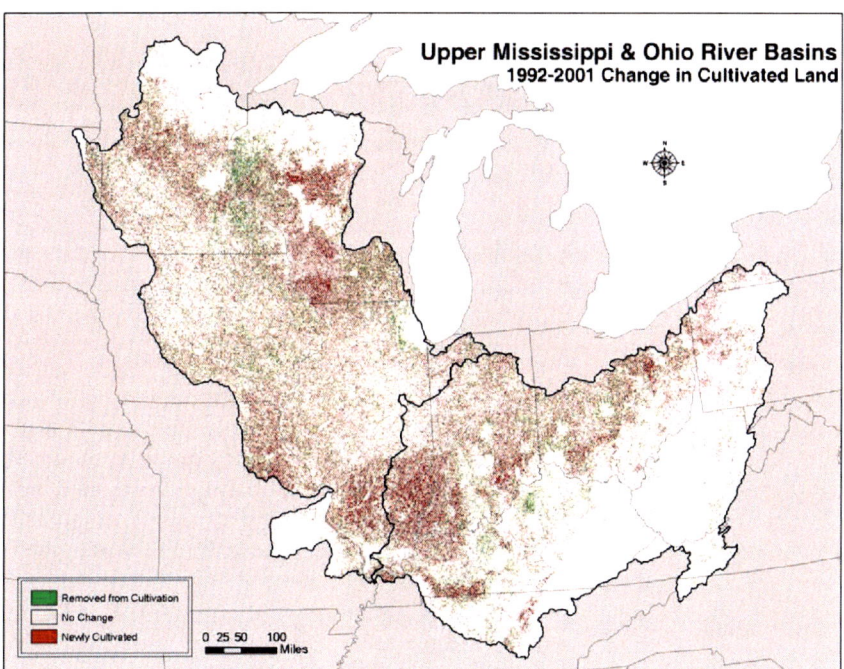

Fig. 5–13. Changes in land use across the Upper Mississippi River and Ohio River Basins between 1992 and 2001. Graphic courtesy of Dr. Bill Crumpton, Iowa State University.

River Basins between 1992 and 2001, especially in the southern portions of Illinois and Indiana, northeastern Ohio and Missouri, and southwestern Wisconsin.

Having examined the past and present eras, we can now look back and see the many gains that were achieved and challenges that were either created or simply discovered. Technologies advanced dramatically and enhanced our abilities to detect specific elements and compounds in soil, water, plants, and air. Another major change was the energy crisis of the 1970s, which has reemerged during the first decade of the 21st century. This has rekindled interest in conservation tillage and harvesting crop residues and other materials as feedstock for biofuel production, a practice that could have major implications for the midwestern landscape. With regard to soil and water conservation, wide-scale production of biofuel from plant biomass is a relatively unknown management scenario that will change rapidly as technologies for biochemical and thermochemical processing develop. Decisions must be made regarding the optimum feedstock, where it should be grown, and how it should be processed. Within the Midwest, the long-term environmental and sustainability impacts will vary dramatically depending on the pathways that emerge to provide energy independence and increased security.

The Future
Crops

The Midwest will undoubtedly remain a major crop production area because all of the crops currently produced are needed for feed, food, fiber, and now fuel production. Use of conservation tillage will undoubtedly increase because of its ability to save time and energy. Another benefit of conservation tillage is the increased infiltration and decreased soil erosion from fields where it is being used. However, the increased infiltration must be balanced against increased baseflow. Schilling (2005) reported that increases in baseflow in Iowa were directly related to increasing row crop intensity. They concluded that a 13 to 52% increase in the amount of row crops draining into 11 of Iowa's rivers during the 60 to 70 yr period ending in 2000 increased baseflow by 33 to 135 mm or 7 to 31%. Increased infiltration reduces the potential for runoff and soil erosion, but without careful nutrient management the increase can have unintended negative consequences since the dominant pathway for NO_3–N to enter surface waters is via natural baseflow and subsurface drainage tiles that hasten drainage. Preliminary evidence indicates that the shift to row crop dominated cropping systems within the Cedar and Raccoon River systems in Iowa has contributed to increasing NO_3–N concentrations with time. Using the soil and water assessment tool (SWAT) to study changes in the landscape within the Raccoon River watershed in Iowa, Jha et al. (2007) showed that as the percentage of land enrolled in the Conservation Reserve Program (CRP) increased to about 50%, nitrate loading also decreased by about 50%.

Clearly, enrolling 50% of the Midwest in a CRP-type land use is not immediately practical, but the Jha et al. (2007) study does identify potential improvements in natural resource conservation that are possible by using soil and water conservation practices to change agricultural landscapes. In-field conservation practices such as the use of annual or perennial cover crops can also markedly reduce nutrient loss. In Iowa, growing a rye cover crop reduced nitrate N concentration and load in subsurface drainage water by 59% and 61%, respectively, (Kaspar et al., 2007). When planted where swine manure was injected at a target rate of 212 kg N ha^{-1}, rye accumulated 65 kg N ha^{-1} in shoots compared to only 35 kg N ha^{-1} without manure (Singer et al., 2008). Undoubtedly, use of cover crops can enhance nutrient cycling and reduce the potential for offsite movement of nutrients, but between 2001 and 2005 only 11% of Midwest farmers used cover crops (Singer et al., 2007). Fortunately for soil and water resources, approximately 56% of farmers in this region indicated that they would plant cover crops if cost-sharing was available.

Midwest agriculture could also be diversified by incorporating crops such as winter triticale (× *Triticosecale rimpaui* Wittm.) into current corn and soybean rotations (Gibson et al., 2007). Grown for forage, grain, or as a cover crop winter triticale could provide several advantages to Midwest cropping systems. Like rye, it can capture and use N left in the soil profile by previous crops (Kessavalou and Walters, 1999), prevent soil erosion during periods of high rainfall (Kessavalou and Walters, 1997; Strock et al., 2004), provide valuable forage (Schwarte et al., 2005) or grain for feeding swine (Hale et al., 1985; Myer et al., 1990) or cattle (Hill and Utley, 1989; Smith et al., 1994), and straw for either bedding or possibly bioenergy production. Studies in Iowa showed that N uptake by winter triticale ranged from 39 to 133 kg ha^{-1} without additional N fertilizer (Gibson et al., 2007). Nitrogen uptake increased with each 33 kg ha^{-1} increment of additional N fertilizer. For N rates of 0 to 90 kg ha^{-1}, winter triticale captured 47 to 82 kg of soil N ha^{-1} in addition to that supplied as fertilizer. This reduced profile NO_3–N by an average of 33 to 53 kg ha^{-1} in central Iowa and by 46 to 53 kg ha^{-1} in southwest Iowa (Nance et al., 2007).

Livestock

For livestock production, it's doubtful whether current trends for fewer farmers producing more animals will change in the foreseeable future. This underscores the need for good soil and water conservation efforts, because large volumes of manure increase the risk for water quality problems. Furthermore, there are also limited fiscal and human resources to ensure there is comprehensive monitoring for proper manure management.

One animal production practice that could have increasing soil and water conservation effects if feed and transportation costs remain high is an increase in winter grazing of corn stover. This may occur because providing feed can account for more than one-half of the total cost of managing a beef cow herd (Clark et al., 2004). Although grazing corn stover is one option for decreasing production expenses, there are some concerns among producers that cattle trampling can negatively affect soil physical properties by increasing soil compaction and subsequently decreasing crop yields. Most studies evaluating soil compaction and cattle grazing have been conducted during summer months, and the results may not be relevant to grazing corn crop residues when soils are frozen. Studies in Iowa (Clark et al., 2004) showed that soil bulk density was not affected, but penetration resistance to a depth of 10 cm increased in paddocks grazed in October and November. Cattle grazing had no effect on subsequent soybean plant population, but yield decreased with increasing soil penetration resistance (r^2 = 0.36). As the proportion of time soil temperature was below 0°C during the grazing period increased, soybean yield increased (r^2 = 0.72). The authors concluded that effects of grazing corn crop residues on subsequent soybean yield will be minimal if grazing is restricted to periods when soils are frozen or if the soils are disked before planting soybean.

Environmental Effects

Long-term sustainability of corn–soybean rotations from an environmental perspective has been questioned because of greater soil erosion, greater and more rapid (flashy) loss of runoff water (surface and subsurface) compared to cropping systems containing alfalfa and grass perennials, and greater loss on NO_3–N to ground and surface waters (Randall, 2003). Others have stated that continuous corn and corn–soybean rotations are not sustainable cropping systems because both require substantial additions of fertilizers and pesticides (Heichel, 1978; Pimentel et al., 1978). Reincorporating forage crops into corn and soybean rotations will result in more agronomically sustainable systems, but farmers will be hesitant to adopt extended rotations without incentives and markets that encourage production of forages and other crops (Karlen et al., 2006).

Biofuel Feedstock Production

Current U.S. biofuel production is dominated by ethanol made from corn grain, and biodiesel made predominantly from soybean. However, second-generation biofuels will be developed using cellulosic feedstocks rather than grain or oilseed crops that can also be used for food and feed. This transition is poised to have significant soil and water conservation effects because it will create the markets and incentives needed to diversify cropping systems across the landscape. Biofuels made from these renewable feedstocks are also an attractive alternative to gasoline because they can decrease the net release of GHGs from the transportation sector (Perlack et al., 2005).

Corn stover, the aboveground material left in fields after corn grain harvest, was identified as a primary biomass source in the Billion Ton Report (Perlack et al., 2005). However, emphasizing corn stover as the predominant cellulosic feedstock for biofuel production could further promote what's already known to be an environmentally leaky system and further stress soil and water resources. Continuous corn and corn-soybean rotations are described as being "environmentally leaky" because of the increased potential for causing runoff and leaching discussed previously. These losses, however, do not stop at the edge of fields, and can accentuate hypoxia or "dead zones" in the Gulf of Mexico and elsewhere (Donner and Kucharik, 2008). Erosion associated with increased row crop production can further degrade soil resources (Blanco-Canqui and Lal, 2007), and as experienced with the Southern Corn Blight [*Bipolaris maydis* (Y. Nisik. and C. Miyake) Shoemaker] increased monoculture can also increase a region's vulnerability to plant diseases that can spread quickly and travel over long distances.

Many farmers and small rural communities argue that development of ethanol plants created greater local demand for commodity crops and higher prices for corn and soybean. One result was that local investment and control of ethanol and biodiesel plants reinvigorated many small Midwest communities by providing well-paying jobs. Others, however, argue that the number of jobs added to local economies has been overestimated (Low and Isserman, 2009).

With regard to soil and water conservation, price and demand projections for corn-only ethanol plants have suggested that to meet increased demand for ethanol, the area devoted to corn would have to increase by 7.3 million ha (Elobeid et al., 2006). Considering that corn-soybean rotations lose only three quarters as much N as continuous corn, Elobeid et al. (2006) and Wisner (2007) concluded that a 7.3 million ha increase in corn production could increase annual N loss by 7.5 kg ha^{-1}.

It has been suggested that about one-half of the increased corn production area could come from conversion of CRP land, pasture, or hay land to row crops (Wisner, 2007). However, most CRP and other perennial cover areas are in those land uses because they are ill-suited for row crop production. Many of these soils are environmentally fragile and classified as highly erodible lands. Converting such lands to corn production will likely result in losses of N, P, pesticides and sediments that greatly exceed those from current corn and soybean fields. For example, Simpson et al. (2008) concluded that depending on site-specific conditions and weather patterns, annual N loss to water resources from corn fields could increase by 37% (117 million kg N yr^{-1}) and P losses could increase by 25% (9 million kg P yr^{-1}) compared with current levels. Similarly, Sands (2006) calculated that at current grain ethanol conversion rates (0.4 L kg^{-1} or 2.84 gal bu^{-1}) and an average corn grain yield of 10.9 Mg ha^{-1}, each liter of ethanol costs 2.5 kg of soil (21 lb soil gal^{-1} ethanol) if soil erosion in corn fields occurred at the USDA Natural Resources Inventory average value (10.98 Mg ha^{-1} yr^{-1}) for Iowa cropland.

To be sustainable, harvesting corn residue as a feedstock for biofuel production must be approached carefully and with close monitoring of several soil and water conservation indicators (Wilhelm et al., 2004). Among those indicators are total soil organic carbon (SOC) and various C fractions, including microbial biomass, water-soluble organic compounds, and stabilized forms of soil carbon (Johnson et al., 2006a; Stevenson, 1994). One management practice that can help meet biofuels feedstock needs and sustain soil resources is the use of no-tillage practices. This suggestion was supported by Mann et al. (2002) who calculated that one-half of the stover from a corn field under no-tillage management could be removed without increasing soil erosion beyond that associated with using chisel or disk-chisel systems and returning all crop residues in the same field. However, the full measured impact of wide-spread harvesting of crop residues on soil resources remains to be determined.

In a review of several research studies that estimated the amount of aboveground residue required to maintain SOC, Johnson et al. (2006a) reported that moldboard plow systems required 2.5 ± 1.0 Mg C ha^{-1} while no-tillage and chisel plow systems required 1.8 ± 0.4 Mg C ha^{-1}, to sustain current SOC levels. When comparing crop rotations for systems using moldboard tillage, Johnson et al. (2006b) calculated that those based on corn required 3.0 ± 1.0 Mg C ha^{-1}, while wheat-based rotations required only 2.2 ± 1.1 Mg C ha^{-1} to maintain SOC. They attributed this difference to lower rainfall and temperatures in wheat production zones and potentially slower C turnover than in corn production areas.

In another study on tillage and corn stover mass interactions, Johnson et al. (2006b) determined that to maintain soil C in continuous corn (CC) and corn–soybean (CS) rotations using chisel plow or no-tillage (CNT) versus moldboard plowing (MP) would require 7.6, 5.3, 12.5, and 7.9 Mg ha^{-1} of corn stover to be returned for CC-MP, CC-CNT, CS-MP, and CS-CNT treatments, respectively. Those data were based on a 0.53 Harvest Index (HI) for corn grain at 155 g kg^{-1} water content, and a 0.46 HI for soybean at 2.3 Mg ha^{-1} and a water content of 130 g kg^{-1}. Using the same HI and grain moisture values, the minimum corn grain yield to produce enough corn stover to maintain soil C for those four treatments would be 9.9, 6.9, 16.8, and 10.3 Mg ha^{-1} for CC-MP, CC-CNT, CS-MP, and CS-CNT, respectively. To put those grain yields in perspective, the 2008 national average for corn grain was 9.7 Mg ha^{-1}, while the 2003 to 2008 average for the five Midwest states (IA, IL, IN, MN, and OH) producing the most corn grain was 10.1 Mg ha^{-1}, and the high-yield average for those states between 2003 and 2008 was 10.7 Mg ha^{-1}. To consistently produce 16.8 Mg ha^{-1}, corn grain yields will have to increase by at least 40% in the five high-yielding Midwest states. Furthermore, it is also important to remember that fields are not uniform and to maintain effective soil and water conservation, the amount of harvested corn residue will need to vary spatially according to landscape position and inherent soil productivity.

Producing cellulosic-derived ethanol from perennial biomass crops has the potential to significantly improve water quality (Simpson et al., 2008), provide more net energy and reduce GHG emissions (McLaughlin and Walsh, 1998). This is feasible because perennial biomass crops (1) provide year-round ground cover that intercepts rain and reduces erosion, (2) develop plant root systems at greater soil depths and more extensively than annual crops– thus stabilizing the soil, and (3) capture a greater quantity of nutrients, reduce leaching volume, improve water infiltration, reduce water runoff, and increase soil organic matter (McLaughlin and Walsh, 1998; Mann and Tolbert, 2000; Lewandowski et al., 2003; Dinnes, 2004; Glover, 2004; Cox et al., 2006). Perennial feedstock may also require less fertilizer and pesticide inputs than current row crops (Lewandowski et al., 2003; Crews,

2005; Perlack et al., 2005). This process could produce bio-oil, syngas, and charcoal, the latter of which may be returned to the field to recycle nutrients, sequester C, and improve soil, water and air quality (Laird, 2008).

Global Climate Change

A general circulation model developed in the Geophysical Fluid Dynamic Laboratory at Princeton University was used to produce estimates of temperature and precipitation changes at various levels of CO_2. It projected that at twice the current amount of atmospheric CO_2, the central U.S. would experience winter temperatures that were about 5°C warmer than the current average, while other seasons would be about 3°C warmer (Wendland, 1994). Precipitation estimates for the Midwest varied from present levels to about 20% less. Based on these model projections, current U.S. crop zones could shift north and east by approximately 500 km. This would shift the Corn/Soybean Belt in the Great Lakes area to soils that are not as favorable for corn and soybean production (Wendland, 1994).

Climate change effects in the Midwest have also been examined using the Environmental Policy Integrated Climate (EPIC) model (formerly known as the Erosion Productivity Impact Calculator). Lee et al. (1996) estimated that a precipitation increase of 20% in the Midwest would increase runoff by 40% and erosion by 37%. O'Neal et al. (2005) also ran a series of model scenarios for crop production, climate change, and subsequent runoff and soil loss effects in five of the eastern Midwest states (Illinois, Indiana, Michigan, Ohio, and Wisconsin). Their calculations showed that in comparison to 1990 through 1999, runoff from a large portion of the study area would increase by 10 to 310%, while soil loss would increase by 33 to 274% between 2040 and 2059. Increased precipitation and decreased temperature stress were major factors contributing to these increases.

A Landscape Vision

Even in the absence of climate change, global food, feed, fiber, and energy demands from a soil and water conservation perspective will continue to exert forces on the Midwest landscape that will require new approaches, policies, and visions to ensure sustainability of the region's production capacity. One approach is to develop a landscape or agroecoregion plan that utilizes soil and plant diversity to achieve more sustainable systems for both rural and urban residents. To demonstrate this approach, Brezonik et al. (2001) used a model that considers several factors (e.g., temperature, precipitation, soil resources) associated with ecoregions and agricultural management factors associated with MLRAs to select soil and crop management practices. However, their approach may be difficult to implement because each watershed, MLRA, or ecoregion consists of a complex mix of soil types, climate regimes, landscapes, land use characteristics, and agricultural production practices. The physical attributes are generally captured in soil mapping units, but when merged with ownership and management plans, the units differ in scale, and their boundaries rarely match. In another effort, Hatch et al. (2001) suggested integrating watershed and agroecoregion information to better identify critical source areas of nonpoint pollution in agricultural watersheds. This would enable users to prioritize and target proper management practices, thus optimizing the use of funds for soil and water quality improvement.

With the advent of global positioning systems (GPS), geographic information systems (GIS), remote sensing, auto-control equipment, and other technologies, future soil and water conservation practices can be implemented using precision or site-specific mapping and management to improve both production and profitability. Such technologies have already been used to manage fertilizers and pesticides (Giles and Slaughter, 1997; Tian et al., 1999; Ferguson et al., 2002; Khosla et al., 2002; Robert, 2002), optimize placement of terraces, drainage tile, and both in-field and field-edge conservation practices (Zhang et al., 2002; Dinnes, 2004; Berry et al., 2003). Recently, they have also been used to help select crops, crop rotations, and tillage for entire fields (Kitchen et al., 2005; Lerch et al., 2005).

When applied to questions associated with production of bioenergy and bioproducts, site-specific technologies offer an excellent opportunity to increase net environmental benefits of agriculture. By once again diversifying Midwest landscapes and incorporating annual, perennial, and intercropping mixtures into future farming operations, many problems can be solved—erosion, carbon sequestration, rural community employment and outmigration, transportation corridors, wildlife habitat, general aesthetics in rural areas, and soil, water, and air quality. Implementing a landscape-scale vision such as this is also one way to address many of the biofuel concerns being raised by several authors (e.g., Doornbosch and Steenblik, 2007; Ernsting and Boswell, 2007; Fargione et al., 2008; Searchinger et al., 2008).

Some may question how such a vision could be implemented in a free-market society with multiple land owners and operators. One approach would be to first identify land tenure and community access rights, drainage patterns, soil quality status, crop rotation and distribution patterns, economic conditions, conservation practices, wildlife and human restrictions, and community concerns at scales of 10 to 30 m^2. This was recently demonstrated by Williams et al. (2008) using a GIS-driven methodology to delineate critical agroecozones and agroecoregions and then identifying the most suitable crops for those areas. Their procedure relied completely on digital databases and was thus much more objective than previous methods (Kitchen et al., 2005). Resolution of the Williams et al. (2008) procedure was 1 km, which is coarser than the procedures used by Kitchen et al. (2005) for an individual field. Yan et al. (2007) described an objective, GIS database-driven methodology that has similarities to that of Williams et al. (2008), but was conducted at the single-field scale to delineate zones for differing management practices for individual crops. We suggest blending all of these technologies and developing new methodologies for site-specific management of landscape-scale areas. This would in essence combine the field-scale goals of Lerch et al. (2005) and Kitchen et al. (2005) with the landscape techniques of Yan et al. (2007) and Williams et al. (2008). Ultimately, individual management areas and fields would be blended into well-managed landscapes that provide multiple ecosystem services and benefits for everyone. The decision to take advantage of the benefits derived from these systems, however, will still reside with the land manager.

Using biofuel production as the driver for increased ecosystem services, the landscape-scale management plan that we propose might include establishing woody species (e.g., *Populus* spp.) near streams as buffers and long-term biomass sources. Next, *Miscanthus* (*Miscanthus* × *giganteus* J.M. Greef & Deuter ex Hodk. & Renvoize), reed canarygrass (*Phalaris arundinacea* L.), or eastern gammagrass (*Tripsacum dactyloides* L.), or diverse mixtures of these and similar species, could be used at slightly higher landscape positions to both benefit from and reduce leaching of NO_3–N and to sequester C as soil organic matter. Slightly higher on the landscape, diverse mixtures of warm-season grasses and cool-season legumes could produce biomass and store organic carbon in soils. In autumn, these perennials would provide a source of biomass, thus addressing at least three of the landscape problems (e.g., biomass production, C sequestration, and water quality). Moving up the landscape, a diversified rotation of annual and perennial crops would be used to meet food, feed, and fiber needs. Erosion could be partially mitigated by using cover crops and/or living mulches. Intensive row crop production areas could be established using BMPs with the awareness that if fertilizer recovery was less than desired, there would be a substantial buffer/lignocellulosic production area lower on the landscape to capture residual nutrients and sediment. By adapting recommendations from Kitchen et al. (2005) and Dinnes (2004) to this landscape vision, we propose a step by step approach that includes:

- Using georeferenced technologies and methods to identify landscape attributes
- Identifying critical production and conservation issues within the area
- Delineating critical areas that require different crops and management practices
- Identifying suitable crops, rotations and conservation practices for each area
- Developing a landscape-scale precision agriculture system
- Applying policies, education and programs that address social and economic concerns currently limiting adoption and implementation of landscape-scale precision agriculture systems
- Monitoring yield, soil, water, and air quality indicators to document system performance toward achieving production and conservation goals
- Reevaluating and making adaptive changes to improve its performance

Public Conservation Policy

The ultimate driver for implementing soil and water conservation practices is the attitude of the people sharing in decision making regarding how natural resources should be managed. Recognizing the importance of attitude toward natural resources is not new and has been articulated very eloquently by authors such as Leopold (1989) and Hillel (1991). The passion and commitment shown by these authors will be needed to shift agricultural policies and public perception to ensure adoption of improved and more sustainable agricultural practices.

As stated by Power (1994), "… a major obstacle to changing cropping systems has been created by the government commodity programs in place these last several decades … these programs have rewarded those who maintained monocultures on their base feed grain acres by assuring these producers a particular price for their product." They also stated that farmer adoption of sustainable agriculture practices may require financial incentives and education to assist them in the conversion processes. If a landscape vision is successfully implemented, future land management decisions can be based on ecologically and economically sound information, and not on emotional appeals by special interest groups that either lack a sound scientific basis (Power, 1994) or simply seek to maintain practices that have been proven to be unsustainable.

Finally, in addressing public perception, McIsaac (1994) described a set of requirements and processes needed to attain adoption of sustainable farming practices. He explained,

Developing and implementing sustainable land uses within a particular ecological setting will likely involve cooperative efforts in several different spheres: technological, social, cultural, and moral. Bringing people together to deliberate constructively over values, risks, uncertainties, alternative technologies and visions for a more sustainable agriculture will require leadership and ... integrative power ... organizing for a more sustainable agriculture should attempt to integrate people based on their unselfish interests, such as intra- and intergenerational ethics, morality, altruism, loyalty, and love.

Undoubtedly, to serve society and the environment in the Midwest or elsewhere better, the best recommendation is to strive for improved communication that recognizes the importance of long-term soil and water conservation. Understanding complex interactions between management decisions, productivity, and environmental consequences is essential to prevent society from traveling in a wrong direction on the pathway to sustainability.

References

Absolute Michigan. 2009. The Great Michigan Fire of 1871. Available at http://www.absolutemichigan.com/dig/michigan/the-great-michigan-fire-of-1871/ (verified 18 Nov. 2009).

Allen, W.H. 1993. The great flood of 1993. BioScience 43(11):732–737.

Alston, L.J. 1983. Farm foreclosures in the United Stated during the Interwar Period. J. Econ. Hist. 43(4):885–903.

Anderson, K.L. 2000. Historic alteration of surface hydrology on the Des Moines Lobe. Iowa Geology 25. Iowa Dep. Natural Resources, Geological Survey Bureau, Iowa City, IA.

Argabright, M.S., R.G. Cronshey, J.D. Helms, G.A. Pavelis, and H.R. Sinclair, Jr. 1996. Historical changes in soil erosion, 1930–1992: The Northern Mississippi Valley Loess Hills. Historical Notes 5. USDA-NRCS, Washington, DC.

Baker, J.L., K.L. Campbell, H.P. Johnson, and J.J. Hanway. 1975. Nitrate, phosphorus, and sulfate in subsurface drainage water. J. Environ. Qual. 4:406–412.

Baker, J.L., and H.P. Johnson. 1981. Nitrate-nitrogen in tile drainage as affected by fertilization. J. Environ. Qual. 10:519–522.

Bakhsh, A., and R.S. Kanwar. 2007. Tillage and N application rates affect on corn and soybean yields and NO_3–N leaching losses. Trans. ASABE. 50:1189–1198.

Berry, J.K., J.A. Delgado, R. Khosla, and F.J. Pierce. 2003. Precision conservation for environmental sustainability. J. Soil Water Conserv. 58(6):332–339.

Blanco-Canqui, H., and R. Lal. 2007. Soil and crop response to harvesting corn residues for biofuel production. Geoderma 141:355–362.

Boise State University. 2008. Disasters: Firestorms of 1871. Available at http://www.boisestate.edu/history/ncasner/hy210/peshtigo.htm (verified 12 Nov. 2009).

Brezonik, P.L., K.W. Easter, L. Gerlach, L. Hatch, D. Mulla, and J.A. Perry. 2001. Integrating modeling and management of agriculturally-impacted watersheds: Issues of spatial and temporal scale. Tech. Rep. 141. Univ. of Minnesota, St. Paul.

Buhler, D.D., G.W. Randall, W.C. Koskinen, and D.L. Wyse. 1993. Atrazine and alachlor losses from subsurface tile drainage of a clay loam soil. J. Environ. Qual. 22:583–588.

Bundy, L.G., A.P. Mallarino, L.W. Good, P. Nowak, J. Norman, and D.J. Mulla. 2008. Field-scale tools for reducing nutrient losses to water resources. p. 171–187. In The Upper Mississippi River Sub-basin Nutrient Committee. Final Report: Gulf Hypoxia and Local Water Quality Concerns Workshop. ASABE, St. Joseph, MI.

Campagnolo, E.R., K.R. Johnson, A. Karpati, C.S. Rubin, D.W. Kolpin, M.T. Meyer, J.E. Esteban, R.W. Currier, K. Smith, K.M. Thu, and M. McGeehin. 2002. Antimicrobial residues in animal waste and water resources proximal to large-scale swine and poultry feeding operations. Sci. Total Environ. 299:89–95.

Chase, S. 1936. Rich land, poor land: A study of waste in the natural resources of America. Whittlesey House, McGraw-Hill, New York.

Clark, J.T., J.R. Russell, D.L. Karlen, P.L. Singleton, W.D. Busby, and B.C. Peterson. 2004. Soil surface property and soybean yield response to corn stover grazing. Agron. J. 96:1364–1371.

Conservation Technology Information Center. 2007. CRM Survey. Available at http://www.conservationinformation.org (verified 12 Nov. 2009). CTIC, West Lafayette, IN.

Cox, T.S., J.D. Glover, D.L. Van Tassle, C.M. Cox, and L.R. DeHaan. 2006. Prospects for developing perennial grain crops. BioScience 56(8):649–659.

Crews, T.E. 2005. Perennial crops and endogenous nutrient supplies. Renew. Agric. Food Syst. 20(1):25–37.

Dimitri, C., A. Effland, and N. Conklin. 2005. The 20th century transformation of U.S. agriculture and farm policy. USDA-ERS Econ. Info. Bull. 3. Available at http://www.ers.usda.gov/publications/eib3/eib3.pdf (verified 12 Nov. 2009). USDA-ERS, Washington, DC.

Dinnes, D.L. 2004. Assessments of practices to reduce nitrogen and phosphorus nonpoint source pollution of Iowa's surface waters. Available at ftp://ftp.nstl.gov/pub/NPS/NPS%20Nutrient%20Pollution%20Assessments%20of%20Conservation%20Practices.pdf (verified 29 April 2009). Iowa Dep. of Natural Resources, Des Moines and USDA-ARS Natl. Soil Tilth Lab., Ames, IA.

Dinnes, D.L., D.L. Karlen, D.B. Jaynes, T.C. Kaspar, J.L. Hatfield, T.S. Colvin, and C.A. Cambardella. 2002. Nitrogen management strategies to reduce nitrate leaching in tile-drained midwestern soils. Agron. J. 94:153–171.

DiTomaso, J.M. 2000. Invasive weeds in rangelands: Species, impacts, and management. Weed Sci. 48:255–265.

Donner, S.D., and C.J. Kucharik. 2008. Corn-based ethanol production compromises goal of reducing nitrogen export by the Mississippi river. Proc. Natl. Acad. Sci. USA 105:4513–4518.

Doornbosch, R., and R. Steenblik. 2007. Biofuels: Is the cure worse than the disease? Available at http://www.oecd.org/dataoecd/15/46/39348696.pdf (verified 12 Nov. 2009). SG/SD/RT(2007)3. OECD, Paris.

Duffy, M.D. 2004. Trends in Iowa farmland ownership. Iowa St. Univ. Ext. Available at http://www.iowafarmlands.com/trends.html (verified 12 Nov. 2009).

Egan, T. 2006. The worst hard time: The untold story of those who survived the great American dust bowl. Houghton Mifflin Company, Boston.

Elobeid, A., S. Tokgoz, D.J. Hayes, B.A. Babcock, and C.E. Hart. 2006. The long-run impact of corn-based ethanol on the grain, oilseed, and livestock sectors: A preliminary assessment. Briefing Paper 06-BP 49. Center of Agriculture and Rural Development, Ames, IA.

Ernsting, A., and A. Boswell. 2007. Agrofuels: Towards a reality check in nine key areas. Biofuelwatch. Available at www.biofuelwatch.org.uk (verified 12 Nov. 2009).

Fargione, J., J. Hill, D. Tillman, S. Polasky, and P. Hawthorne. 2008. Land clearing and the biofuel carbon debt. Science 319(5867):1235–1238.

Ferguson, R.B., G.W. Hergert, J.S. Schepers, C.A. Gotway, J.E. Cahoon, and T.A. Peterson. 2002. Site-specific management of irrigated maize: Yield and soil residual nitrate effects. Soil Sci. Soc. Am. J. 66:544–553.

Follett, R.F., and B.A. Stewart (ed.) 1985. Soil erosion and crop productivity. ASA, CSSA, and SSSA, Madison, WI.

Forster, D.L. 2006. An overview of U.S. farm real estate markets. Ohio State Univ. Extension, Working paper: AEDE-WP-0042-06. The Ohio State Univ., Columbus.

Galloway, G.E., Jr. 2005. Corps of Engineers responses to the changing national approach to floodplain management since the 1993 Midwest Flood. J. Contemp. Water Res. Educ. 130:5–12.

Gibson, L.R., C.D. Nance, and D.L. Karlen. 2007. Winter triticale response to nitrogen when grown after corn or soybean. Agron. J. 99:49–58.

Giles, D.K., and D.C. Slaughter. 1997. Precision band sprayer with machine-vision guidance and adjustable yaw nozzles. Trans. ASAE 40(1):29–36.

Glover, J.D. 2004. The necessity and possibility of perennial grain production systems. Renew. Agric. Food Systems 20(1):1–4.

Haines, D.A., and R.W. Sando. 1969. Climatic conditions preceding historically great fires in the North Central Region. USDA-Forest Service Research paper NC-34.

Hale, O.M., D.D. Morey, and R.O. Myer. 1985. Nutritive value of Beagle 82 triticale for swine. J. Anim. Sci. 60:503–510.

Hatch, L.K., A. Mallawatantri, D. Wheeler, A. Gleason, D. Mulla, J. Perry, K.W. Easter, R. Smith, L. Gerlach, and P. Brezonik. 2001. Land management at the major watershed–agroecoregion intersection. J. Soil Water Conserv. 56(1):44–51.

Heichel, G.H. 1978. Stabilizing agricultural energy needs: Role of forages, rotation, and nitrogen fixation. J. Soil Water Conserv. 33:279–282.

Helms, D. 1990. Conserving the Plains. The Soil Conservation Service in the Great Plains. Agric. Hist. 64(2):58–73.

Hewes, L., and P.E. Frandson. 1952. Occupying the wet prairie: The role of artificial drainage in Story County, Iowa. Ann. Assoc. Am. Geogr. 42:24–50.

Hill, G.M., and P.R. Utley. 1989. Digestibility, protein metabolism and ruminal degradation of Beagle 82 triticale and Kline barley fed in corn-based cattle diets. J. Anim. Sci. 67:1793–1804.

Hillel, D. 1991. Out of the Earth: Civilization and the life of the soil. University of California Press, Berkley.

Hilliard, S.B. 1972. The dynamics of power: Recent trends in mechanization on the American farm. Technol. Cult. 13(1):1–24.

Hipke, D.C. 2008. The Great Peshtigo Fire of 1871. Available at http://www.peshtigofire.info (verified 12 Nov. 2009).

Holden, J., P.J. Chapman, and J.C. Labadz. 2004. Artificial drainage of peatlands: Hydrological and hydrochemical process and wetland restoration. Prog. Phys. Geogr. 28(1):95–123.

Jayachandran, K., T.R. Steinheimer, L. Somasundaram, T.B. Moorman, R.S. Kanwar, and J.R. Coats. 1994. Occurrence of atrazine and degradates as contaminants of subsurface drainage and shallow groundwater. J. Environ. Qual. 23:311–319.

Jaynes, D.B., J.L. Hatfield, and D.W. Meek. 1999. Water quality in Walnut Creek watershed: Herbicides and nitrate in surface waters. J. Environ. Qual. 28:45–59.

Jha, M.K., P.W. Gassman, and J.G. Arnold. 2007. Water quality modeling for the Raccoon River watershed using SWAT. Trans. ASABE 50:479–493.

Johnson, J.M.-F., R.R. Allmaras, and D.C. Reicosky. 2006a. Estimating source carbon from crop residues, roots, and rhizodeposits using the national grain-yield database. Agron. J. 98:622–636.

Johnson, J.M.-F., D. Reicosky, R. Allmaras, D. Archer, and W. Wilhelm. 2006b. A matter of balance: Conservation and renewable energy. J. Soil Water Conserv. 63(4):121–125.

Kanwar, R.S., R.M. Cruse, M. Ghaffarzadeh, A. Bakhsh, D.L. Karlen, and T.B. Bailey. 2005. Corn/soybean and alternate farming systems effects on water quality. Appl. Eng. Agric. 21(2):181–188.

Kanwar, R.S., D.L. Karlen, C.A. Cambardella, T.S. Colvin, and C. Pederson. 1996. Impact of manure and N-management systems on water quality. p. 65–77. *In* Proc. Annu. Integrated Crop Manage. Conf., 8th, Ames, IA. 19–20 Nov. 1996. Iowa State Univ. Ext., Ames.

Karlen, D.L., E.G. Hurley, S.S. Andrews, C.A. Cambardella, D.W. Meek, M.D. Duffy, and A.P. Mallarino. 2006. Crop rotation effects on soil quality at three northern corn/soybean belt locations. Agron. J. 98:484–495.

Kaspar, T.C., D.B. Jaynes, T.B. Parkin, and T.B. Moorman. 2007. Rye cover crop and gamagrass strip effects on NO_3 concentration and load in tile drainage. J. Environ. Qual. 36:1503–1511.

Kessavalou, A., and D.T. Walters. 1997. Winter rye as a cover crop following soybean under conversation tillage. Agron. J. 89:68–74.

Kessavalou, A., and D.T. Walters. 1999. Winter rye cover crop following soybean under conservation tillage: Residual soil nitrate. Agron. J. 91:643–649.

Khosla, R., K. Fleming, J.A. Delgado, T.M. Shaver, and D.G. Westfall. 2002. Use of site-specific management zones to improve nitrogen management for precision agriculture. J. Soil Water Conserv. 57(6):513–518.

Kitchen, N.R., K.A. Sudduth, D.B. Myers, R.E. Massey, E.J. Sadler, and R.N. Lerch. 2005. Development of a conservation-oriented precision agriculture system: Crop production assessment and plan implementation. J. Soil Water Conserv. 60(6):421–430.

Kladivko, E.J., G.E. Van Scoyoc, E.J. Monke, K.M. Oates, and W. Pask. 1991. Pesticide and nutrient movement into subsurface tile drains on a silt loam soil in Indiana. J. Environ. Qual. 20:264–270.

Knox, J.C. 2001. Agricultural influence on landscape sensitivity in the Upper Mississippi River Valley. Catena 42:193–224.

Kolpin, D.W., E.T. Furlong, M.T. Meyer, E.M. Thurman, S.D. Zaugg, L.B. Barber, and H.T. Buxton. 2002. Pharmaceuticals, hormones, and other organic wastewater contaminants in U.S. streams, 1999–2000: A national reconnaissance. Environ. Sci. Technol. 36:1202–1211.

Laird, D.A. 2008. The charcoal vision: A win-win-win scenario for simultaneously producing bioenergy, permanently sequestering carbon, while improving soil and water quality. Agron. J. 100:178–181.

Lal, R. (ed.) 1999. Soil quality and soil erosion. CRC Press, Boca Raton, FL.

Lal, R., T.M. Sobecki, T. Iivari, and J.M. Kimble (ed.) 2004. Soil degradation in the United States: Extent, severity, and trends. Lewis Publishers, Boca Raton, FL.

Lee, J.L., D.L. Phillips, and R.F. Dodson. 1996. Sensitivity of the U.S. Corn Belt to climate change and elevated CO_2: II. Soil erosion and organic carbon. Agric. Syst. 52:503–521.

Leopold, A. 1989. A Sand County almanac and sketches here and there. A Special Commemorative edition. Oxford Univ. Press, New York.

Lerch, R.N., N.R. Kitchen, R.J. Kremer, W.W. Donald, E.E. Alberts, E.J. Sadler, K.A. Sudduth, D.B. Myers, and F. Ghidey. 2005. Development of a conservation-oriented precision agriculture system: Water and soil quality assessment. J. Soil Water Conserv. 60(6):411–421.

Lewandowski, I., J.M.O. Scurlock, E. Lindvall, and M. Christou. 2003. The development and current status of perennial rhizomatous grasses as energy crops in the U.S. and Europe. Biomass Bioenergy 25:335–361.

Low, S.A., and A.M. Isserman. 2009. Ethanol and the local economy: Industry trends, location factors, economic impacts, and risks. Econ. Dev. Q. 23(1):71–88.

Lucas, R.E. 1982. Organic soils (Histosols) formation, distribution, physical and chemical properties and management for crop production. Res. Rep. 435 Farm Science. Michigan State University and Cooperative Extension Service in Cooperation with the Institute of Food and Agricultural Sciences, Agricultural Experiment Stations, University of Florida. MSU Bull. Off., East Lansing, MI.

Mahboubi, A.A., and R. Lal. 1998. Long-term tillage effects on changes in structural properties of two soils in central Ohio. Soil Tillage Res. 45:107–118.

Mallarino, A.P., B.M. Stewart, J.L. Baker, J.D. Downing, and J.E. Sawyer. 2002. Phosphorus indexing for cropland: Overview and basic concepts of the Iowa phosphorus index. J. Soil Water Conserv. 57(6):440–447.

Mann, L., and V. Tolbert. 2000. Soil sustainability in renewable biomass plantings. Ambio 29(8):492–498.

Mann, L., V. Tolbert, and J. Cushman. 2002. Potential environmental effects of corn (*Zea mays* L.) stover removal with emphasis on soil organic matter and erosion. 2002. Agric. Ecosyst. Environ. 89:149–166.

McIsaac, G. 1994 Sustainable agriculture: Weaving the pieces together into a coherent system. p. 254–283. *In* G. McIsaac and W.R. Edwards (ed.) Sustainable agriculture in the American Midwest: Lessons from the past and prospects for the future. Univ. of Illinois Press, Chicago and Urbana.

McLaughlin, S., and M. Walsh. 1998. Evaluating environmental consequences of producing herbaceous crops for bioenergy. Biomass Bioenergy 14(4):317–324.

Menzel, B.W. 1983. Agricultural management practices and the integrity of instream biological habitat. p. 305–329. *In* F.W. Schaller and G.W. Bailey (ed.) Agricultural management and water quality. Iowa State Univ. Press, Ames.

Myer, R.O., G.E. Combs, and R.D. Barnett. 1990. Evaluation of three triticale cultivars as potential feed grains for swine. Proc. Soil Crop Sci. Soc. Fla. 49:155–158.

Nance, C.D., L.R. Gibson, and D.L. Karlen. 2007. Reducing soil nitrate leaching potential with winter triticale. Soil Sci. Soc. Am. J. 71:1343–1351.

Novotny, V. 1999. Diffuse pollution from agriculture—A worldwide outlook. Water Sci. Technol. 39(3):1–13.

O'Neal, M.R., M.A. Nearing, R.C. Vining, J. Southworth, and R.A. Pfeifer. 2005. Climate change impacts on soil erosion in Midwest United States with changes in crop management. Catena 61:165–184.

Pauly, J.J. 1984. The Great Chicago Fire as a national event. Am. Q. 36(5):668–683.

Penn, R.J. 1943. Tenure situation in the North Central Region: 1940–1944. J. Land Public Utility Econ. 19(3):370–376.

Perlack, R.D., L.L. Wright, A.F. Turhollow, R.L. Graham, B.J. Stokes, and D.C. Erbach. 2005. Biomass as feedstock for a bioenergy and bioproducts industry: The technical feasibility of a billion-ton annual supply. Available at http://feedstockreview.ornl.gov/pdf/billion_ton_vision.pdf (verified 12 Nov. 2009). Oak Ridge Natl. Lab., Oak Ridge, TN.

Pimentel, D., J. Krummel, D. Gallahan, J. Hough, A. Merrill, I. Schreiner, P. Vittum, F. Koziol, E. Back, D. Yen, and S. Fiance. 1978. Benefits and costs of pesticide use in U.S. food production. BioScience 28(12):772–784.

Porter, P.M., D.R. Huggins, C.A. Perillo, S.R. Quiring, and R.K. Crookston. 2003. Organic and other management strategies with two- and four-year crop rotations in Minnesota. Agron. J. 95:233–244.

Potter, L.A., and W. Schamel. 1997. The Homestead Act of 1862. Social ed. 61(6):359–364.

Power, J.F. 1994. Sustainable cropping systems. p. 144–162. In G. McIsaac and W.R. Edwards (ed.) Sustainable agriculture in the American Midwest: Lessons from the past and prospects for the future. Univ. of Illinois Press, Chicago and Urbana.

Rabalais, N.N., W.J. Wiseman, R.E. Turner, B.K. Sen Gupta, and Q. Dortch. 1996. Nutrient changes in the Mississippi River and system responses on the adjacent continental shelf. Estuaries 19:386–407.

Randall, G.W. 2003. Present-day agriculture in southern Minnesota—Is it sustainable? Available at http://sroc.cfans.umn.edu/research/soils/publications/Present-Day%20Agriculture.pdf (verified 12 Nov. 2009). Univ. of Minnesota, Southern Research and Outreach Center, Waseca.

Randall, G.W., D.R. Huggins, M.P. Russelle, D.J. Fuchs, W.W. Nelson, and J.L. Anderson. 1997. Nitrate losses through subsurface tile drainage in conservation reserve program, alfalfa, and row crop systems. J. Environ. Qual. 26:1240–1247.

Randall, G.W., and D.J. Mulla. 2001. Nitrate nitrogen in surface waters as influenced by climatic conditions and agricultural practices. J. Environ. Qual. 30:337–344.

Ritter, W.F., and A. Shirmohammadi (ed.) 2001. Agricultural nonpoint source pollution: Watershed management and hydrology. CRC Press, Boca Raton, FL.

Robert, P.C. 2002. Precision agriculture: A challenge for crop nutrition management. Plant Soil 247:143–149.

Sands, D. 2006. A soil conservationist's view of ethanol. Iowa Natural Heritage Found. Mag. Available at http://www.inhf.org/2006fallmag/articles/2006fallmag-environmentalpolicy.htm (verified 12 Nov. 2009).

Schilling, K.E. 2005. Relation of baseflow to row crop intensity in Iowa. Agric. Ecosyst. Environ. 105:433–438.

Schilling, K.E., and R.D. Libra. 2003. Increased baseflow in Iowa over the second half of the 20th century. J. Am. Water Res. 39:851–860.

Schubert, S.D., M.J. Suarez, P.J. Region, R.D. Koster, and J.T. Bacmeister. 2004. On the cause of the 1930s Dust Bowl. Science 303(5665):1855–1859.

Schumm, S.A. 1999. Causes and controls of channel incision. p. 19–33. In S.E. Darby and A. Simon (ed.) Incised rivers. John Wiley and Sons, Chichester, U.K.

Schwarte, A.J., L.R. Gibson, D.L. Karlen, M. Liebman, and J.L. Jannink. 2005. Planting date effects on winter triticale dry matter and nitrogen accumulation. Agron. J. 97:1333–1341.

Searchinger, T., R. Heimlich, R.A. Houghton, F. Dong, A. Elobeid, J. Fabiosa, S. Tokgoz, D. Hayes, and T.-H. Yu. 2008. Use of U.S. Croplands for biofuels increases greenhouse gases through emissions from land use change. Science 319(5867):1238–1240.

Severin, T. 1968. Explorers of the Mississippi. A.A. Knopf, Inc. New York.

Simpson, T.W., A.N. Sharpley, R.W. Howarth, H.W. Paerl, and K.R. Mankin. 2008. The new gold rush: Fueling ethanol production while protecting water quality. J. Environ. Qual. 37:318–324.

Singer, J.W., C.A. Cambardella, and T.B. Moorman. 2008. Enhancing nutrient cycling by coupling cover crops with manure injection. Agron. J. 100:1735–1739.

Singer, J.W., S.M. Nusser, and C.J. Alf. 2007. Are cover crops being used in the U.S. Corn Belt? J. Soil Water Conserv. 62:353–358.

Smith, W.A., G.S. du Plessis, and A. Griessel. 1994. Replacing maize grain with triticale grain in lactation diets for dairy cattle and fattening diets for steers. Anim. Feed. Sci. Technol. 49:287–295.

Soil and Water Conservation Society. 2008. Beyond T: Guiding sustainable soil management. SWCS, Ankeny, IA.

Sparks, R.E., J.C. Nelson, and Y. Yin. 1998. Naturalization of the flood regime in regulated rivers: The case of the Upper Mississippi River. BioSci. 48(9):706–720.

State Historical Society of Wisconsin. 1971. The Great Peshtigo Fire: An eyewitness account (Rev. Peter Pernin). Available at http://library.wisc.edu/etext/WIReader/WER2002-0.html (verified 12 Nov. 2009). State Historical Society of Wisconsin, Madison. Reprinted from Wisc. Mag. Hist. 54:246–272.

Stevenson, F.J. 1994. Humic chemistry: Genesis, composition, reactions. 2nd ed. John Wiley and Sons, New York.

Strock, J.S., P.M. Porter, and M.P. Russelle. 2004. Cover cropping to reduce nitrate loss through subsurface drainage in the northern U.S. Corn Belt. J. Environ. Qual. 33:1010–1016.

Thunderbolts.info. 2006. The comet and the Chicago Fire. Available at http://www.thunderbolts.info/tpod/2006/arch06/060206chicagofire.htm (verified 18 Nov. 2009).

Tian, L., J.F. Reid, and J.W. Hummel. 1999. Development of a precision sprayer for site-specific weed management. Trans. ASAE 42(4):893–900.

Timmons, J.F. 1948. Farm ownership in the United States: An appraisal of the present situation and emerging problems. J. Farm Econ. 30(1):78–100.

Travel and History. 2008. Disasters: Great Peshtigo Fire. Available at http://www.u-s-history.com/pages/h2113.html (verified 12 Nov. 2009).

Turner, H.A. 1927. Absentee farm ownership in the United States. J. Land Public Utility Econ. 3(1):48–60.

Turner, R.E., and N.N. Rabalais. 2003. Linking landscape and water quality in the Mississippi River Basin for 200 years. Bioscience 53(6):563–572.

USDA. 1938. Soils and men. Yearbook of Agriculture 1938. 75th Congress, 2d Session. House Doc. 398. Superintendent of Documents, Washington, DC.

USDA-ERS. 2007. Data sets: U.S. fertilizer use and price. Available at http://www.ers.usda.gov/Data/FertilizerUse/ (verified 12 Nov. 2009).

USDA-NASS. 2002. Census of Agriculture: 2002. Available at http://www.agcensus.usda.gov/Publications/2002/Ag_Atlas_Maps/Operators/ (verified 12 Nov. 2009). Census publications, Washington, DC.

USDA-NASS. 2007. Data and statistics. Available at http://www.nass.usda.gov/Data_and_Statistics/Quick_Stats/index.asp (verified 29 April 2009). USDA-NASS, Washington, DC.

USDA-NRCS. 1999. Soil taxonomy, a basic system of soil classification for making and interpreting soil surveys. Available at http://soils.usda.gov/technical/classification/taxonomy/ (verified 29 April 2009)

USDA-NRCS. 2006. Land resource regions and major land resource areas of the United States, the Caribbean, and the Pacific Basin. Available at http://soils.usda.gov/survey/geography/mlra/ (verified 12 Nov. 2009).

U.S. Department of Commerce, Bureau of the Census. 1993. Who owns America's farmland? Statistical Brief SB/93-10. Available at http://www.census.gov/apsd/www/statbrief/sb93_10.pdf (verified 12 Nov. 2009). Bureau of the Census, Washington, DC.

USEPA. 2008. Hypoxia in the Northern Gulf of Mexico: An update by the EPA Science Advisory Board. Available at http://yosemite.epa.gov/sab/sabproduct.nsf/C3D2F27094E03F90852573B800601D93/$File/EPA-SAB-08-003complete.unsigned.pdf (verified 12 Nov. 2009).

Wendland, W.M. 1994. Paleoclimates—A guide to climates of the future. p. 215–230. In G. McIsaac and W.R. Edwards (ed.) Sustainable agriculture in the American Midwest: Lessons from the past and prospects for the future. Univ. of Illinois Press, Chicago and Urbana.

Wilhelm, W.W., J.M.-F. Johnson, J.L. Hatfield, W.B. Voorhees, and D.R. Linden. 2004. Crop and soil productivity response to corn residue removal: A literature review. Agron. J. 96:1–17.

Willham, R.L. 2000. Partners: Livestock in western civilization. Iowa State Univ. Printing Dep. Ames.

Williams, C.L., W.W. Hargrove, M. Liebman, and D.E. James. 2008. Agro-ecoregionalization of Iowa using multivariate geographical clustering. Agric. Ecosyst. Environ. 123:161–174.

Willrich, T.L. 1969. Properties of tile drainage water. Completion Rep. Proj. A-013-IA. Iowa State Water Resources Res. Inst., Iowa State Univ., Ames.

Wisner, R. 2007. Ethanol drives up food costs. Food Technol. 61(3):124.

Wooten, H.H., and L.A. Jones. 1955. The history of our drainage enterprises. p. 478–498. In The Yearbook of Agriculture, 1955. USDA, Washington, DC.Yan, L., S. Zhou, L. Feng, and L. Hong-Yi. 2007. Delineation of site-specific management zones using fuzzy clustering analysis in a coastal saline soil. Comput. Electron. Agric. 56:174–186.

Zaimes, G.N., R.C. Schultz, and T.M. Isenhart. 2006. Riparian land uses and precipitation influences on stream bank erosion in Central Iowa. J. Am. Water Res. Assoc. 42(1):83–97.

Zhang, N., M. Wang, and N. Wang. 2002. Precision agriculture—A worldwide overview. Comput. Electron. Agric. 36(2–3):113–132.

Zucker, L.A., and L.C. Brown. 1998. Agricultural drainage: Water quality impacts and subsurface drainage studies in the Midwest. Ext. Bull. 871. The Ohio State Univ., Columbus.

6

Historical and Emerging Soil and Water Conservation Issues in the Northeastern USA

Harold van Es
Department of Crop and Soil Sciences, Cornell University, Ithaca, NY

The geographical focus of this chapter is the area from Maine in the North to West Virginia and Maryland in the South and includes the regions commonly referred to as New England and the Mid-Atlantic. The northern extent of the region, including the New England states and New York, consists of forest-associated glaciated soils (mostly Alfisols) with high soil variability due to complex depositional patterns of glacial till, outwash, and lacustrine parent materials. Post-glacial depositions occurred in river valleys, which are now generally used intensively for agriculture and urban development. The nonglaciated areas are generally to the South of the 41 and 42° N latitudes (approximately the latitude of New York City) and primarily consist of coarse-textured Coastal Plain sediments along the shore and loamy Piedmont soils further inland, and mixed soil types in the mountainous Appalachian region (Piedmont, Ridge-and-Valley, and Allegheny).

The region experiences a continental climate, with oceanic influences along the coastal areas. Annual precipitation is in the 600- to 1000-mm range and is generally distributed evenly during the year (Northeast Regional Climate Center, 2009). Potential evaporation is usually negligible during winter months and increases to about 200 mm per month in the summer. The growing season varies within the region depending on latitude and elevation and is generally 6 to 8 months long.

Agricultural production is adapted to the soils and climate, as well as the proximity to major urban centers. Dairy production accounts for the largest fraction of agricultural receipts, and is especially important in Pennsylvania, New York, and Vermont. It is also associated with significant imports of feed supplements from grain production areas, which create environmental concerns because of nutrient accumulations from net surpluses in farm nutrient balances. Cash grain production occurs in areas that allow for large-scale crop production such as western New York and the Coastal Plain region. Recently, intensive poultry production has become a significant industry, especially in eastern Maryland and Delaware. Fruit and vegetable production has traditionally served the urban

---

Soil and Water Conservation Advances in the United States. SSSA Special Publication 60.
T.M. Zobeck and W.F. Schillinger, editors. © 2010. SSSA, 677 S. Segoe Rd., Madison, WI 53711, USA.

centers and is now experiencing an expansion into specialty crop production systems, including small organic farms.

Many of the lands in the region are seasonally wet (imperfectly drained) and are often artificially drained to improve crop production. Irrigation is limited to high-value fruit and vegetable crops for most of the region using either surface or groundwater sources. Larger scale irrigation systems are used on field crops on droughty Coastal Plain soils in the southern part of the region, mostly using groundwater sources.

Agriculture and Land Use History

Population densities in the pre-colonial era were low, and agricultural land use was sparse and concentrated along rivers, lakes, and ocean shores. Draft animals were absent in pre-colonial America, and the early inhabitants generally grew crops with human labor. The "three sister" cropping system was widely used in the Northeast, involving intercrops of indigenous maize (*Zea mays* L.), bean (*Phaseolus vulgaris* L.), and squash (*Cucurbita pepo* L.), often on raised "hills" to improve microdrainage. This system, with limited tillage and the inclusion of a legume, provided relatively sustainable crop production.

Colonial agriculture rapidly expanded in the 1600s from several centers: English settlements along the southeastern and southern New England coasts, the Chesapeake Bay and Delaware Valley, and a Dutch colony in the Hudson Valley (until 1664, when it also fell under British control). French colonial influence was mostly limited to trade settlements and did not involve extensive land clearing in the current U.S. territory. The southern region became the focus of a large export industry oriented around tobacco (*Nicotiana tabacum* L.) production (Montgomery, 2007).

Most of the land was owned as large estates, in many cases with absentee landowners, which promoted extractive land use. The global British Empire was expanding and consolidating in the 1700s, which required extensive quantities of timber for ship building and dwelling construction. With the old country's forest resources depleted, the new colonies were deforested to meet the growing demand (Montgomery, 2007). With the exception of a few areas, most lands in New England and along the coastal strip were eventually deforested by the 1800s. The highly profitable production of tobacco in the southern part of the region, mostly Maryland and Virginia, involved intensive tillage and lacked rotation with soil-building crops. This resulted in very rapid soil degradation, abandonment, and expansion onto new lands (Montgomery, 2007). Agriculture in other areas of the region mostly consisted of grain and feed production based on the European system. This involved plowing with draft animals and the "open field" method of rotation, which included cereal grains and one fallow year out of three (Stoll, 2002). The often intense and erosive rainfall in the colonies created much higher erosion and land degradation rates than experienced in Western Europe. Also, unlike Europe, the new colonies had an abundance of land coupled with a shortage of labor, which promoted extensive land use and a philosophy of "farm, deplete, and abandon" (Stoll, 2002).

After the Revolutionary War, the remaining virgin lands of the Northeast, including the fertile lake plains of western New York, were developed through sales or donated to war veterans whose military services were paid with land ownership. The Erie Canal, completed in 1825, and the railroads a few decades later provided efficient transportation to the western parts of the region and allowed better access to the Great Lakes and to new lands further west. Western New York and southeastern Pennsylvania, with naturally fertile loam soils, became breadbaskets for the Northeast, with excess grain production supplying the East Coast cities.

In the early 1800s much of the region was involved in the "Merino Madness," involving sheep with high-quality fleece brought from Spain. Embargo following the War of 1812 left the United States cut off from textile trade with Britain, and the Merino sheep provided a domestic supply of wool (Stoll, 2002). Moreover, the hardy sheep allowed the marginal hilly lands, which had been deforested during previous decades, to be productively used through grazing. By the 1830s New York farmers grazed 4.3 million Merinos and even the small state of Vermont had a population of 1.7 million sheep, one sheep per 1.5 acre (Stoll, 2002). The Merino boom was eventually followed by a bust after trade resumed with the British, and much of the marginal hilly lands were no longer used for agriculture.

In the early 1800s a new philosophy emerged on land use and farming that was promoted by people who were identified as "improvers" (Stoll, 2002). They promulgated the idea of improving land to increase sustainability of existing farms, as opposed to the "emigrant" who exhausted land and moved on to new lands in the Midwest. James Madison was, among others, a strong advocate for improvement. Some northeastern farmers adopted better soil management practices, including use of manure and rotations with perennial sod crops to improve soil fertility, as well as other practices that were promoted by English agriculturalist Jethro Tull and others. Although abusive land use remained widespread, land improvement eventually allowed for more stable agriculture in the region.

The first commercial fertilizer was imported to the region in 1824 when Peruvian guano arrived in Baltimore (Montgomery, 2007). By the 1850s guano was imported at the rate of about a 0.5 million Mg yr^{-1}. It is believed that the extensive use of guano during that time triggered the first eutrophication concerns in the Chesapeake Bay. As with other regions of the United States, artificial fertilizer became widely adopted in the Northeast during the middle of the 20th century, which reduced organic matter cycling and exacerbated soil organic matter losses from tillage. In addition, nutrient accumulation became a serious concern in the region as livestock-based farms started to import large amounts of feed supplement from the Midwest through new transportation networks. The additional feed added nutrients to normal farm nutrient cycles (soil–crop–feed–animal–manure and back to the soil), resulting in nutrient surpluses and accumulation in soils.

Changing Land Use

Soil conservation, through land retirement, arrived early in the Northeast as a result of economic forces, which is illustrated by the change in the area of land in farms (Table 6–1). In 1850, the earliest date of an agricultural census, much of New Hampshire's land base was actively used for agricultural production (911,852 ha). By 1890, agricultural activities had declined by a quarter to about 700,000 ha, as land was abandoned and forests naturally regenerated on the marginal lands after sheep production became unprofitable. This decline continued, and by 1978 only about 70,000 ha of New Hampshire was in active agricultural use. This further decreased in recent decades to only about 52,000 ha, a 94% decline from its

Table 6-1. Acres of improved land in crop production for New Hampshire, New York, and Maryland from 1850 to 2007 (Source: U.S. Census of Agriculture).

Year	New Hampshire	New York	Maryland
		ha	
1850	911,852	5,025,630	1,133,152
1890	699,591	6,637,699	1,382,228
1978	69,964	2,406,016	732,939
2007	52,219	1,747,556	569,204

peak. At present, agriculture in New Hampshire is primarily limited to the fertile valleys and mostly involves livestock and horticultural systems.

New York's agricultural land area peaked in 1890 at about 6.6 million ha but declined thereafter. Current agricultural land is only one quarter of the 1890 peak. Maryland followed a similar pattern but currently still retains about 40% of its 1890 peak, presumably due to a larger fraction of relatively level and productive land that is suitable for mechanized agriculture.

Most of the loss in agricultural lands resulted in increased forest cover, often through government-sponsored reforestation programs. Many farms on the marginal lands were not competitive for the commodities shipped by new railroads from the more productive Midwest (Montgomery, 2007). The reforestation in essence was a massive soil conservation effort as it substituted erosive agricultural land uses with trees. However, the loss of agricultural lands is not universally considered as a societal benefit due to the loss of open space. Also, agricultural land in the past century was lost due to aggressive expansion of large urban areas, especially after World War II. This often resulted in loss of highly productive agricultural land. For example, New York's Long Island soils provided a significant part of the food needs for the nearby city. Most of Long Island is now urbanized, except for the eastern part, which is still used to produce high-value horticultural crops.

Recent and Current Issues

Despite its areal downsizing, agriculture in the Northeast remained diverse and now includes profitable livestock, grain, and horticultural farms. Most counties established Soil and Water Conservation Districts in the 1940s after national awareness was raised during the Dust Bowl era. Early emphasis was on the implementation of state and federal soil erosion control programs and promotion of water management, especially artificial soil drainage. Starting in the late 1980s soil and water conservation programs evolved rapidly due to three major changes in program emphases. First, the 1985 Food Security Act, especially the conservation compliance and conservation reserve provisions, inserted regulatory components to soil and water conservation programs that were until then purely voluntary. Conservation compliance compelled farmers to bring erosion rates on their lands to tolerable levels to avoid losing federal benefits, and the conservation reserve program provided incentives to take lands out of active crop production and maintain them as unharvested meadows. Second, new federal wetland protection regulations put a sudden and near-complete end to wetland drainage efforts. Third, programs shifted toward off-site impacts of land management, especially related to water quality, and became more targeted toward high-risk areas in a watershed-based approach.

On-Site versus Off-Site Costs

The Northeast experiences less soil erosion than most other regions of the United States (Table 6–2). This is in part the result of less erosive rainfall patterns and the fact that many erodible soils are no longer used for crop production. However, most soils in the region are forest-derived and have thin surface horizons. They have low tolerable soil loss values as well as a higher penalty to soil productivity for a given unit of soil loss (Table 6–2).

The off-site costs of soil erosion and associated pollutants involve water quality damages, as well as off-stream impacts such as flood damage, water treatment needs, etc. (Clark et al., 1985). The most recent estimates of off-site costs by Hansen and Ribaudo (2008; Table 6–2) are based on a benefit model that includes (i) proximity to a recreational area affected by soil and associated chemical losses, (ii) the economic damage incurred from a decrease in environmental quality, (iii) replacement cost for the damage, and (iv) averting expenditures (those incurred to reduce risk before actual costs are incurred, like flood protection). Note: Table 6–2 expresses cost in terms of benefit per ton of avoided erosion. The off-site costs of soil erosion are unevenly distributed across different regions of the country (Table 6–2), and the Northeast experiences the highest total cost per ton of soil eroded ($7.12). This is mainly attributed to the high population density and the large number of people who use water resources for recreational and municipal services. Expensive soil and water conservation efforts, often organized through watershed-based initiatives, can therefore be justified based on the high cost of the off-site damages. Recent federal legislation, including the Safe Drinking Water Act and the Concentrated Animal Feeding Operations provisions under the authority of the Clean Water Act, as well as several state laws have affected

Table 6–2. Benefits from a 1-yr reduction in water erosion and associated off-site damages by Farm Production Region (Hansen and Ridaudo, 2008).

Region	Erosion†	Benefits			
		Soil productivity	Marine recreational fishing	Municipal and industrial use	Total water erosion related
	Gg	$ Mg^{-1}			
Northeast	168,000	1.27	1.57	1.45	7.12
Delta States	212,000	0.43	0.02	0.68	2.76
Appalachia	439,000	0.57	0.01	0.43	2.47
Lake States	164,000	1.21	0.00	1.36	4.68
Southeast	227,000	0.41	0.00	0.48	2.51
Corn Belt	880,000	1.01	0.00	0.21	2.77
Pacific	607,000	0.40	0.49	0.17	3.54
Southern Plains	444,000	0.37	0.41	0.28	3.61
Mountain States	910,000	0.26	0.00	0.21	3.37
Northern Plains	609,000	0.41	0.00	0.07	1.46

† Estimates from Ribaudo (1986).

agricultural nutrient and soil management practices. Some current programs are highlighted in the following sections.

Source Protection of Drinking Water

The region has high demands for drinking water from surface and subsurface sources. Nutrient and pathogen losses from livestock farms and high fertilizer usage in horticultural and urban regions pose threats to water resources. Municipalities that depend on groundwater from unconfined aquifers often require careful nutrient management in wellhead protection areas.

New York City presents an unusual scenario, as it obtains 5 billion liters per day of unfiltered drinking water for about 9 million people (New York State Department of Environmental Conservation, 2009) from watersheds in the upstate New York area (Fig. 6–1). The 1989 Safe Drinking Water Act required the city to provide assurance for high water quality, especially related to possible pathogen contamination from livestock (e.g., *Giardia lamblia* Kofoid and Christiansen and *Cryptosporidium Parvum* Tyzzer, which reproduce in the intestinal tracts of animals and humans). To avoid expensive filtration, the city initiated an extensive and far-reaching watershed agricultural program to reduce pathogen and phosphorus transport to the reservoirs. Programs have targeted a range of practices, including animal and barnyard management, nutrient management plans, and erosion and sediment control.

Coastal Estuaries

The estuaries along the Atlantic Coast provide unique ecological, fishery, and recreational services to large populations (Poe, 1999). The North Atlantic estuaries are the least impacted by water quality concerns in the nation (Bricker et al., 2007). This may be attributed to the fact that they are generally deep and well flushed by tidal flows and have limited agricultural activities in the watersheds. The Mid-Atlantic estuaries, on the other hand, are the most impacted in the

Fig. 6–1. Map of watersheds in the Hudson Valley and Catskills regions that provide New York City drinking water supplies. Source: New York City Dep. of Environmental Protection.

nation as they are relatively large, shallow, and less flushed. They also have more urban and agricultural activities on the contributing lands. The latter include the Long Island Sound, Peconic Bay, Delaware Bay, and Chesapeake Bay. These estuaries are primarily threatened by nutrients and sediment (for a comprehensive report on Northeast estuaries, see Bricker et al., 2007). Nitrogen loading is a significant concern as it results in eutrophication problems and affects aquatic plants and animals. Phosphorus is also a concern in estuaries that include freshwater components. The Chesapeake Bay has been the focus of many studies and remediation programs because of its size (the nation's largest), the uniqueness of its ecosystem, and proximity to large urban centers. High water column N levels were diagnosed as a major concern for the Bay ecosystem in the 1980s, with associated increases in both plankton and epiphyte algal growth (Malone et al., 1993). The central focus on efforts to restore the Bay has been on reducing nutrient loading. In the Coastal Plain area, N from agricultural land primarily reaches the Bay through groundwater seepage, while the other areas mainly load the estuary through surface waters. Nutrient loading is also unevenly distributed in contributing watersheds (Fig. 6–2), and targeting programs to the main areas of concern provides more effective use of limited resources for conservation programs. For example, N loading in the Susqueahanna River Basin, the most significant N contributor to the Chesapeake Bay, is highly concentrated in southeastern Penn-

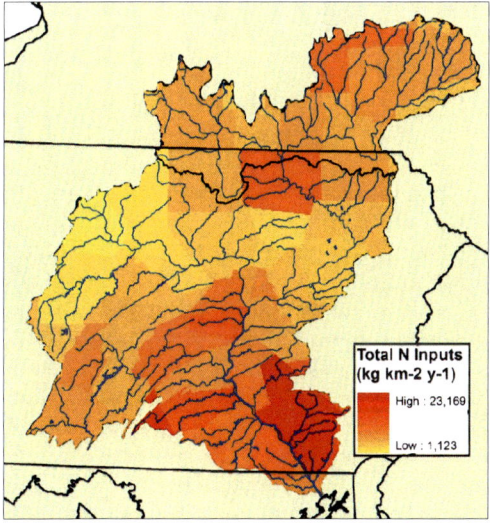

Fig. 6–2. Map of net anthropogenic nitrogen inputs to the Susquehanna River Basin in Southern New York, Pennsylvania, and Maryland developed using the Scientific Committee on Problems of the Environment-Net Sum of Anthropogenic Nitrogen Inputs (SCOPE-NANI) model. Deposition was estimated based on data from CASTNET (Clean Air Status and Trends Network) and NADP (National Atmospheric Deposition Program) monitoring stations and modeled estimates for regions and species that are not monitored. Fertilizer application rates within counties were obtained from the literature. Nitrogen fixation was derived from crop area data from the Census of Agriculture multiplied by N fixation rates from the literature. Net N import in food and feed were derived from crop and animal data from the Census of Agriculture and data from the literature on crop and feed N contents and animal and human N requirements. Courtesy of Peter Woodbury, Dennis Swaney, and Robert Howarth, Cornell University.

sylvania, where intensive agriculture and high livestock densities are especially of concern (Fig. 6–2).

Many efforts have been developed to reduce nutrient loading. The state of Maryland asserted its interest in the health of the Chesapeake Bay by adopting strict nutrient management regulations (State of Maryland, 2000). Detailed plans based on university nutrient management recommendations are required for all farms with more than 4 ha receiving nutrient applications. Delaware implemented a nutrient management act that requires nutrient management planning for livestock farms with more than eight animal equivalent units (Sims, 1999). Pennsylvania, which drains large areas into the Chesapeake Bay through the Susquehanna River (Fig. 6–2), passed legislation that requires farms with high animal density (two animal equivalent units per acre) to develop nutrient management plans (Beegle, 2007). Several northeastern states also have cost-share programs related to water quality protection from agricultural lands, in addition to various federal programs.

Freshwater Lakes

Another major concern with off-site impacts is associated with the many freshwater lakes, especially in the northern glaciated area. These water bodies are highly responsive to P inputs, which cause eutrophication, including algal blooms and nuisance aquatic vegetation. Soil P levels have generally increased in northeastern soils, especially on livestock farms as a result of feed imports. In an analysis of historical soil test data, Ketterings et al. (2005) determined that New York's statewide P levels remained constant from 1957 to 1980, but steadily increased after 1980. Forty-seven percent of the soil samples currently test equal to or higher than the critical agronomic soil test value. On vegetable and fruit farms, high soil P levels are often associated with high fertilizer applications or excessive use of compost on organic farms (Thomas Morris, personal communication). On dairy farms, soil P accumulation is primarily associated with manure applications based on estimated N availability. Since half the manure N may be lost through leaching and volatilization, and the manure P remains absorbed on soil particles, a gradual increase in soil P levels is observed (Magdoff and van Es, 2009). Soil P saturation in turn poses risks for runoff losses on sloping lands (Kleinman et al., 2000), as well as leaching losses in soils with low P sorption capacity and shallow groundwater, especially on the Coastal Plain in Delaware and Maryland (Maguire and Sims, 2002). Both nutrient management and soil erosion control are critical to reducing P loading. In response to concerns about eutrophication in Lake Champlain bays, the State of Vermont adopted the Accepted Agricultural Practice Rules, which address nutrient and pesticide applications, including a prohibition on manure spreading between December 15 and April 15, and guidelines on soil erosion control, use of buffer zones, and groundwater protection (Vermont Agency of Agriculture, 2006).

Soil and Nutrient Management Tools

Soil water erosion control efforts are currently implemented with the use of the Revised Universal Soil Loss Equation tool (Renard et al., 1991), similar to other regions of the country. Nutrient management tools provide guidance on the timing, rates, and application methods related to nutrients. These tools vary somewhat among the states, in part due to the use of different soil nutrient extraction methodologies and nutrient management guidelines. The northeastern states have coordinated the development of a phosphorus index (Lemunyon and Gilbert, 1993). Most states use the nitrate leaching index first proposed by Williams and Kissel (1991), although New York has expanded the interpretations, especially related to concerns about nutrient losses from fall manure applications (van Es et al., 2002).

Future Issues and Opportunities

Bioenergy and Greenhouse Gas Emissions

Climate change as a result of the accumulation of greenhouse gases is expected to result in an increase in extreme weather conditions, posing greater risk for drought, runoff, and erosion (Nearing et al., 2004). These concerns are likely to induce changes in land use and soil and water conservation practices in the Northeast. As discussed earlier, the region has experienced significant conversion of agricultural land to forest since the mid to late 1800s (Table 6–1), and approximately 35 million acres are currently tree covered (Smith et al., 2001). The extensive reforestation of the region has contributed to large amounts of carbon stocks sequestered in both soil and forest floor. Since 1900, the Northeast is estimated to have sequestered 300 Tg of C in soil and forest floor stocks, while all other regions in the United States have experienced net emissions during that period (Woodbury et al., 2007; Fig. 6–3). In fact, sequestration of C in the relatively small Northeast region offset about one-half the accumulated emissions from the other areas in the continental United States. The sequestration will be asymptotically stabilizing in the near future, as land conversion is reaching its limits and the accumulation rate of C stocks decreases with increasing forest maturity.

Increasing interest in the use of biomass for energy may generate an increase in three major sources of bioenergy:

Woody Biomass

The accumulation of tree biomass on forested lands in the Northeast provides a large stock of bioenergy. Some is currently used for home heating (e.g., wood stoves, especially in rural areas), and some limited power generation is achieved with wood. The economic parameters need to shift considerably for the use of wood biomass to become more widely adopted, but the 100-plus years of accu-

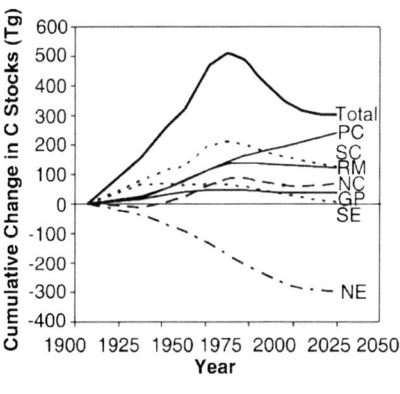

Fig. 6–3. Estimated cumulative change in carbon stock in forest floor and soil as a result of land use conversions from 1900 to 2050 by U.S. region. Positive values indicate emission; negative values indicate sequestration. Region abbreviations: PC, Pacific Coast; SC, South Central; RM, Rocky Mountain; NC, North Central; GP, Great Plains; SE, Southeast; NE, Northeast. Source: Woodbury et al., 2007; reproduced with permission.

mulated photosynthetic energy remains a resource that may ultimately be used to help meet the region's energy demands. Foresters and soil and water conservation specialists need to ensure sustainable utilization of this resource.

Biomass from newly planted willow (*Salix* spp.) trees is also a promising source of bioenergy (Volk et al., 2004). Many marginal lands in the region are poorly drained, and water-loving willows can fill a landscape niche with positive benefits for soil and water conservation (e.g., as riparian buffer strips) and landscape aesthetics. Short-rotation willow biomass provides a potential source of income for farms, as field activities primarily occur outside the growing season, when labor availability is greater (Downing et al., 2005).

Crop Biomass

Grasses and grain crop residues can potentially provide significant amounts of biomass energy (Fig. 6–4). The proximity to population centers and the large energy consumption associated with home heating in the region provides opportunities for use of these plant materials, especially when directly combusted. Cellulosic conversion to liquid biofuel may also have potential, but technological breakthroughs are still needed to make it economically viable. Maize grain ethanol is not likely to become a major source of bioenergy in the Northeast, as the region already is a net importer of grains.

The removal of crop residues can be readily adopted on grain farms with current land use and farm equipment, but poses potential concerns for soil qual-

Fig. 6–4. Two sources of agricultural bioenergy: (top) maize stover may provide a sustainable source of bioenergy if combined with no-tillage; (bottom) grass biomass allows for sustainable use of marginal lands (photo by Jerry Cherney).

ity. Moebius et al. (2008), however, concluded that a significant fraction of maize stover can be sustainably removed when using no-tillage. Under plow-tillage, stover removal results in significant soil degradation.

The cool and humid Northeast climate is highly suitable to grass production (Cherney et al., 1991; Cherney, 2006). Additionally, the region has extensive areas of hilly and marginal lands adapted to low-input production of grass biomass, similar to the use of these lands for sheep production in the early 1800s. This may provide an important source of income in economically challenged hilly regions, and may also conserve open space and soil.

Other Energy Sources

The livestock-intensive Northeast region produces a large amount of manure and food waste, making the generation of biogas from anaerobic digesters an attractive option. Methane capture in digestors combined with the evolution of a carbon market will make this technology increasingly attractive as a source of income for farmers through carbon credits. The emphasis will be on larger farms and may coincide with more sophisticated manure handling systems that also facilitate better land application of nutrients.

Also, increasing interest in wind energy and construction of wind farms may cause concerns about soil and water conservation. Many wind farms are placed on ridges in mountainous regions that are currently forested or used for agriculture. Water erosion, runoff, disruption of wildlife, and landslides are possible concerns and conservation practices need to be implemented to ensure that off-site damage remains limited.

Soil Quality/Health Management

Like the efforts of the "improvers" in the early 1800s, soil quality has again emerged as an important focus for soil and water management in the Northeast. With farmers and lay audiences, the term *soil health* is often preferred when referring to the dynamic soil quality concept because it connotes a holistic approach to soil management (Idowu et al., 2008). *Soil quality* has been defined as the capacity of soil to function for specific purposes (Karlen et al., 1997). Soil quality integrates physical, chemical, and biological components and processes and the interactions among them (Karlen et al., 2001). The physical structure of soil plays an integral role in controlling chemical and biological processes (Dexter and Czyz, 2000), and it also affects infiltration, aeration, and drainage, as well as root penetration and proliferation. Alternatively, biological and chemical processes, such as root growth, organic matter accumulation and decomposition, macrofauna activity, and bacterial and fungal proliferation influence pore size distribution, density, and stability of the soil's structure (Wright and Upadhyaya, 1998). Soil-impacting practices such as tillage, traffic, plant cover systems, and organic and inorganic inputs (accidental or deliberate) strongly influence all components of soil quality and, thus, ecological functioning (Doran and Parkin, 1996).

Soil quality can be measured in the field, but interpretations are very limited by large sources of variability, such as field moisture conditions, timing, and unsophisticated measurement equipment. A holistic laboratory soil test has been developed that provides an integrated assessment of the triad of soil quality domains—physical, biological, and chemical (Idowu et al., 2008). The Cornell Soil Health Test (CSHT; Table 6–3) employs soil quality indicators that represent

Table 6–3. Soil quality indicators included in the Cornell Soil Health Test, and associated processes.

Soil indicator	Affected soil process
Physical	
Soil texture	all
Aggregate stability	aeration, infiltration, shallow rooting, crusting
Available water capacity	water retention
Surface hardness	rooting at depth, internal drainage
Biological	
Organic matter content	energy/C storage, water and nutrient retention
Active C content	organic material to support biological functions
Potentially mineralizable N	ability to supply N
Root rot rating	soil-borne pest pressure
Chemical-standard	
pH	toxicity, nutrient availability
Extractable P	P availability, environmental loss potential
Extractable K	K availability
Minor element contents	micronutrient availability, elemental imbalances, toxicity

processes relevant to soil functions and also provides information that is useful for practical soil management (Gugino et al., 2007). Unlike the standard approach that focuses on soil chemical amendments like fertilizers, soil quality management needs to be approached from a holistic perspective within the context of the constraints of the soil and the farm (e.g., attitude to change, equipment availability, cropping system, availability of organic sources). Management practices listed in Table 6–4 provide opportunities for improving soil quality and also reduce runoff, erosion, and chemical losses. Managing for enhanced soil quality can provide societal benefits (Poe, 1999) by promoting advantages to land managers in terms of soil productivity.

Soil Quality and Climate Change

Climate change will likely impose greater stresses on soils (Nearing et al., 2004). Higher quality soils are more resilient to weather extremes, which are expected to be more frequent as a result of climate change. For example, long-term experiments have shown that plant-available water capacity in the surface horizon increased by up to 34% with no-tillage compared with plow tillage (Moebius et al., 2008), significantly reducing drought sensitivity. When plow pans are present, new methods like zone tillage, which loosens subsoils in narrow slots, make subsoil water more accessible to roots.

Increased soil water availability impacts water management in the humid Northeast, where supplemental irrigation is used to reduce drought stress between rainfall events. Increased plant water availability extends the time period until the onset of drought stress and greatly reduces the probability of stress occurrence. For example, higher water retention capacity and deeper rooting may increase the crop drought stress-free period from 7 to 12 d. For a typical

Table 6–4. Linking soil health test measurements to general management solutions through short-term and long-term strategies (Magdoff and van Es, 2009).

	Suggested management practices	
	Short term or intermittent	Long term
Physical concerns		
Low aggregate stability	fresh organic materials (shallow-rooted cover/rotation crops, manure, green clippings)	reduced tillage, surface mulch, rotation with sod crops
Low available water capacity	stable organic materials (compost, crop residues high in lignin, biochar)	reduced tillage, rotation with sod crops
High surface density	limited mechanical soil loosening (e.g., strip tillage, aerators); shallow-rooted cover crops, biodrilling, fresh organic matter	shallow-rooted cover/rotation crops; avoid traffic on wet soils; controlled traffic
High subsurface density	targeted deep tillage (zone building, etc.); deep-rooted cover crops	avoid plows/disks that create pans; reduced equipment loads and traffic on wet soils
Biological concerns		
Low organic matter content	stable organic matter (compost, crop residues high in lignin, biochar); cover and rotation crops	reduced tillage, rotation with sod crops
Low active C	fresh organic matter (shallow-rooted cover/rotation crops, manure, green clippings)	reduced tillage, rotation
Low mineralizable N	N-rich organic matter (leguminous cover crops, manure, green clippings)	cover crops, manure, rotations with forage legume sod crop, reduced tillage
High root rot rating	disease-suppressive cover crops, disease breaking rotations	disease-suppressive cover crops, disease breaking rotations, integrated pest management practices
Chemical concerns		
Low CEC	stable organic matter (compost, lignaceous/cellulosic crop residues, biochar), cover and rotation crops	reduced tillage, rotation
Unfavorable pH	liming materials or acidifier (e.g., S)	repeated applications based on soil tests
Low P, K	fertilizer, manure, compost, P-mining cover crops, mycorrhizae promotion	repeated application of P/K materials based on soil tests, increased application of sources of organic matter, reduced tillage
High salinity	subsurface drainage and leaching	reduced irrigation rates, low-salinity water source, water table management
High Na	gypsum, subsurface drainage, and leaching	reduced irrigation rates, water table management

Northeast climate condition, this reduces the probability of drought stress at any time in the month of July from 1 in 20 (5%) to 1 in 100 (1%; Magdoff and van Es, 2009). Therefore, a higher quality soil allows crops to be grown with no water stress for longer dry periods, thereby reducing the need for irrigation and increases resilience to climate extremes.

Water Quality Impacts of Land Use and Management

Despite many efforts to reduce problems in the region's estuaries due to high nutrient loading from the contributing watersheds, water quality improvements have been mixed. Phosphorus loading to reservoirs in the New York City water supply watersheds has decreased due to aggressive implementation of conservation management practices, including stream-bank fencing, precision feeding, and the use of cover crops with silage corn (Bryant et al., 2008). However, in the past 20 years, the health of the Chesapeake Bay in terms of dissolved oxygen and chlorophyll-a has not shown improvement (Fig. 6–5), despite extensive agricultural and urban nutrient management programs in the contributing watersheds. This may be attributed to the slowness of the reduction in groundwater N loading from the Coastal Plain area because of the long travel time of deep groundwater from agricultural areas to the Bay, as well as an apparent failure to significantly reduce nutrient loading from the rivers. Arguably, future efforts may need to go beyond a simple reduction of agricultural nutrient use based on plans that focus on agronomic optimums (Staver, 2001).

The establishment of Total Maximum Daily Load (TMDL) regulatory standards for impaired water under the Clean Water Act will promote far-reaching nutrient and sediment reduction efforts in most of the northeastern coastal watersheds. The Chesapeake Bay and Peconic Estuary Programs have recently set specific reduction targets for nutrient loading from the contributing watersheds that require more stringent controls on the land. This will drive further soil and nutrient conservation efforts in the near future.

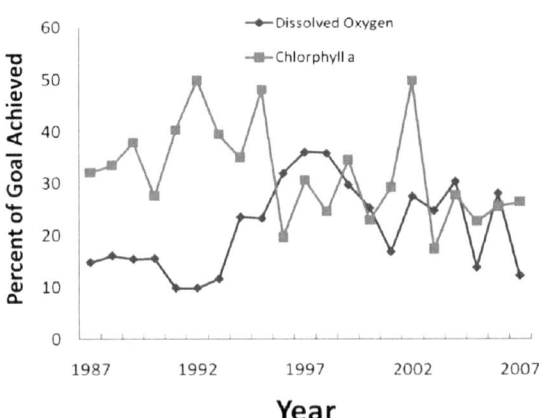

Fig. 6–5. Chesapeake Bay health assessment (percent of goal achieved) for dissolved oxygen and chlorophyll a for the period 1987 to 2007. Data source: USEPA Chesapeake Bay Program; http://www.chesapeakebay.net/status_bayhealth.aspx?menuitem=15048, verified 25 Nov. 2009.

New Practices

It is expected that soil and water conservation efforts in the Northeast United States will continue their emphasis on a diversity of management approaches. The following practices are expected to receive greater promotion and adoption, mostly in the context of efforts to increase soil productivity and reduce off-site environmental impacts:

Risk-Based Management of Nutrients

The use of P indexing allows for evaluating relative risk of P loss at the farm and watershed scales. This risk is in part based on the principle of "infiltration excess" runoff that occurs during infrequent extreme precipitation events when the rainfall rate exceeds the soil's capacity for intake. In many watersheds in the Northeast, surface runoff is generated by "saturation excess," which generally occurs in low-lying wet areas as a result of the concentration of subsurface lateral flow from higher elevations. It varies in space and time and has larger contributing areas during wet periods (Gburek and Sharpley, 1998). GIS-based water-routing models that estimate contributing areas can be combined with soil test information and P loss indexing to improve estimates of P loss risk (Sharpley et al., 2008). This will be facilitated by the emerging use of digital landscape-scale data (e.g., digital elevation models, digital soil maps), as well as georeferenced soil test information and nutrient application records.

Similarly, recent studies have shown that N management, especially in systems involving organic N sources, needs greater consideration of timing and rates of application. For example, sod plowing and fall manure application generate very high N losses, and these practices need to be carefully considered in cases where N contamination is a concern (van Es et al., 2002). Many northeastern livestock farms have significant excesses of nutrients that are either lost through leaching and denitrification (N) or that accumulate and may subsequently be lost in runoff (P). Current concerns about water quality and greenhouse gas emissions have not yet generated very strict regulatory actions, mostly as a result of a desire to limit negative economic impacts. There is still considerable potential for reducing environmental nutrient losses, but these will require greater investments through education, government cost sharing, and overall de-intensification of animal-based agriculture in certain areas (e.g., southeastern Pennsylvania; Fig. 6–2). Also, internalization of the environmental costs through higher food prices allows for a more realistic expression of the true societal cost of agriculture.

Adaptive Nitrogen Management

Adaptive management refers to the concept of adjusting management practices based on local conditions and knowledge. Soil fertility testing is a relatively simple example of such an approach.

Current approaches to estimating optimum N fertilizer rates in the Northeast are mostly based on mass balances and expected economic returns. However, local soil conditions and weather impact soil N and affect economic optimum N rates (van Es et al., 2007). Notably, wet or dry conditions can greatly influence the optimum N rate. Higher precision in N management for maize may be achieved through adaptive in-season N applications that are based on information of early-season soil, crop, and weather information. Increased climate variability will make the need for adaptive N management more compelling. Adaptive N man-

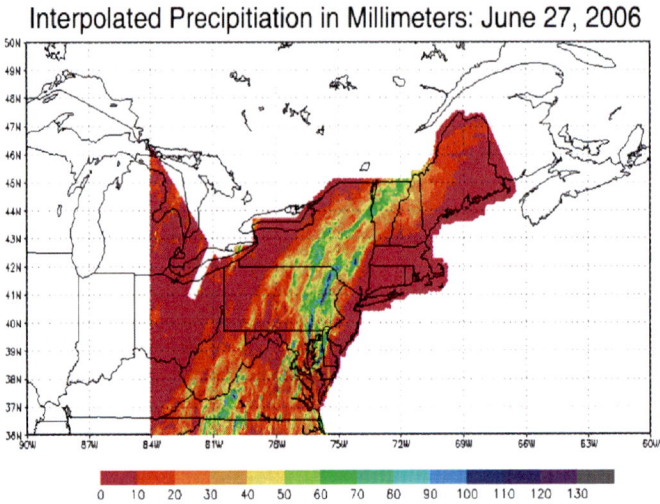

Fig. 6–6. High-resolution precipitation data based on corrected radar estimates for the U.S. Northeast (4 by 4 km gridded daily totals) allow for more spatially explicit modeling of soil–plant–atmosphere processes. Courtesy of Northeast Regional Climate Center.

agement approaches using computer models and high resolution climate data have recently been developed (Melkonian et al., 2007). The use of information technologies and higher quality input data, such as the recently developed 4-km gridded daily climate data (Fig. 6–6), are expected to be increasingly employed for soil, water and nutrient management.

Cover Crops

Cover crops provide multiple benefits for soil quality enhancement, nutrient scavenging, erosion and runoff control, and pest suppression. Farmers and researchers are exploring opportunities to incorporate them into their cropping systems and in some cases have experimented with the use of cover crop mulches where winter grains and legumes are rolled and mulched within a no-tillage system (Fig. 6–7). This provides excellent nutrient cycling, improved soil quality, good weed control, and virtual elimination of erosion concerns.

Fig. 6–7. Rolled rye cover crop is being prepared for row-crop planting using a zone builder. Photo by Anu Rangarajan.

Fig. 6–8. Strip tillage results in a narrow tilled zone that leaves most of the soil surface undisturbed. Photo by Robert Schindelbeck.

Restricted Tillage Systems

No-tillage cropping systems have been widely adopted on the well-drained and warmer soils of the Coastal Plain. The remainder of the Northeast, however, has lagged behind other areas in the nation, primarily due to the cold, wet, and more compacted soils that prevail in the region. Zone and strip tillage appear to be better adapted to the soils and climate of northern parts of the region and are now being rapidly adopted by grain, vegetable, and dairy farmers. Zone tillage (Fig. 6–8) involves the use of narrow tillage tools that create loosened bands that extend into the subsoil (30–40 cm depth). This is followed by a row crop planter, typically with multiple fluted coulters mounted on the front. It creates a fine seedbed approximately 15 cm wide by 10 cm deep and moves residue away from the row. This "vertical tillage" approach promotes deeper root growth and water movement. Zone tillage provides soil quality improvements similar to no-tillage, but is more energy intensive.

Strip tillage uses a similar approach, but the tillage shanks are shallower (typically about 20 cm), thereby reducing energy consumption. In the Northeast region, zone and strip tillage are either performed in the fall or early in the spring to allow for soil settling before planting. Some farmers inject fertilizers with the tillage operations, thereby reducing the number of passes on the field.

Compaction Prevention and Controlled Traffic

Soil compaction is a serious concern in the Northeast, since field traffic on wet soils is difficult to avoid given the humid climate. One of the most promising practices for reducing soil compaction is the use of controlled traffic lanes in which all field operations are limited to the same lanes (Fig. 6–9). The primary benefit of controlled traffic is the prevention of compaction for most of the field at the expense of limited areas that receive all the compaction. Because the degree of soil compaction doesn't necessarily accumulate with each equipment pass (i.e., most of the compaction occurs with the heaviest loading and does not greatly increase beyond it), damage in the traffic lanes is not much more severe than that occurring on the whole field in a system with uncontrolled traffic. Controlled traffic lanes may actually have an advantage in that the consolidated soil is able to bear greater loads, thereby better facilitating field traffic. Compaction also can be reduced significantly by maximizing traffic of farm trucks along the field bound-

Fig. 6–9. Controlled traffic farming in strips with precision satellite navigation: 12-row corn–soybean strips with traffic lanes between the fourth and fifth row from the strip edge.

aries and using planned access roads, rather than allowing them to randomly travel over the field.

Controlled traffic systems require adjustment of field equipment to ensure that all wheels travel in the same lanes and also require discipline from equipment operators. For example, planter and combine widths need to be compatible, although not necessarily the same, and wheel spacing may need to be expanded. A controlled traffic system is most easily adopted with row crops in zone, ridge, or no-till systems (not requiring full-field tillage) because crop rows and traffic lanes remain recognizable year after year. Ridge tillage, in fact, requires controlled traffic, as wheels should not cross the ridges. Adoption of controlled traffic is expected to expand with the availability of real-time kinematic (RTK) satellite navigation. These advanced global positioning systems provide centimeter-level accuracy, which facilitates precision steering of field equipment. Controlled traffic lanes can therefore be laid out with unprecedented accuracy.

Conclusion

In the previous centuries, the U.S. Northeast has undergone dramatic land use changes, from mostly virgin land at the beginning of the colonial era to deforestation and exhaustive land use in the 1600s to 1800s, to partial land abandonment, and reforestation from the mid to late 1800s until the present. Agriculture has remained viable but became more geographically concentrated and intensive. Soil and water conservation efforts have increasingly focused on the off-site impacts of agricultural land use, reflecting the high societal costs to nearby urban populations. Future soil and water conservation programs will likely remain focused on off-site impacts, but are also expected to address bioenergy needs, soil quality enhancement, and improved production efficiency.

Greater challenges are associated with the structure of agriculture and whether society can address the broken cycle of nutrient flows on farms and the problem of regional nutrient accumulations. Ultimately, accomplishments in soil and water conservation in the United States are based on the willingness of farmers to be stewards of these resources, which requires production economics that provide incentives for conservation. The United States will need to consider the full costs of agriculture and food production and find win–win solutions that allow for progress toward environmental conservation. Undoubtedly, the market place is inadequately equipped to accomplish this, and the use of regulations and financial incentives will remain part of the landscape.

References

Beegle, D. 2007. Pennsylvania's nutrient management act (Act 38). Who is affected? Agronomy Facts 54. Pennsylvania State University, University Park.

Bricker, S., B. Longstaff, W. Dennison, A. Jones, K. Boicourt, C. Wicks, and J. Woerner. 2007. Effects of nutrient enrichment in the nation's estuaries: A decade of change. NOAA Coastal Ocean Program Decision Analysis Ser. 26. Available at http://ccma.nos.noaa.gov/publications/eutroupdate/ (verified 24 Nov. 2009). National Centers for Coastal Ocean Science, Silver Spring, MD.

Bryant, R.B., T.L. Veith, P.J.A. Kleinman, and W.J. Gburek. 2008. Cannonsville Reservoir and Town Brook watersheds: Documenting conservation efforts to protect New York City's drinking water. J. Soil Water Conserv. 63:339–344.

Cherney, J.H. 2006. Grass biomass in the Northeast USA. 2006. Bioenergy Information Fact Sheet 1. Available at http://www.grassbioenergy.org/downloads/Bioenergy_Info_Sheet_1.pdf (verified 24 Nov. 2009). Cornell Univ. Coop. Ext., Ithaca, NY.

Cherney, J.H., K.D. Johnson, J.J. Volenec, and D.K. Greene. 1991. Biomass potential of selected grass and legume crops. Energy Sources 13:283–292.

Clark, E., II, J. Haverkamp, and W. Chapman. 1985. Eroding soils: The off-farm impacts. The Conservation Foundation, Washington, DC.

Dexter, A.R., and E.A. Czyz. 2000. Soil physical quality and the effects of management. p. 153–165. *In* M.J. Wilson and B. Maliszewska-Kordybach (ed.) Soil quality, sustainable agriculture, and environmental security in central and eastern Europe. Published in cooperation with NATO Scientific Affairs Division. Kluwer Academic Publ., Dordrecht, The Netherlands.

Doran, J.W., and T.B. Parkin. 1996. Quantitative indicators of soil quality: A minimum data set. p. 25–37. *In* J.W. Doran and A. Jones (ed.) Methods for assessing soil quality. SSSA Spec. Publ. 49. SSSA, Madison, WI.

Downing, M., T.A. Volk, and D. Schmidt. 2005. Development of new generation cooperatives in agriculture for renewable energy research, demonstration, and development projects. Biomass Bioenergy 28:425–434.

Gburek, W.J., and A.N. Sharpley. 1998. Hydrologic controls on phosphorus loss from upland agricultural watersheds. J. Environ. Qual. 27:267–277.

Gugino, B.K., O.J. Idowu, R.R. Schindelbeck, H.M. van Es, D.W. Wolfe, B.N. Moebius-Clune, J.E. Thies, and G.S. Abawi. 2007. Cornell soil health assessment training manual. Version 1.2. Available at http://www.hort.cornell.edu/soilhealth/extension/manual.htm (verified 24 Nov. 2009). Cornell University, Geneva, NY.

Hansen, L., and M. Ribaudo. 2008. Economic measures of soil conservation benefits. USDA-ERS Tech. Bull. 1922.

Idowu, O.J., H.M. van Es, G.S. Abawi, D.W. Wolfe, J.I. Ball, B.K. Gugino, B.N. Moebius, R.R. Schindelbeck, and A.V. Bilgili. 2008. Farmer-oriented assessment of soil quality using field, laboratory, and VNIR spectroscopy methods. Plant Soil 307:243–253.

Karlen, D.L., S.S. Andrews, and J.W. Doran. 2001. Soil quality: Current concepts and applications. Adv. Agron. 74:1–40.

Karlen, D.L., M.J. Mausbach, J.W. Doran, R.G. Cline, R.F. Harris, and G.E. Schuman. 1997. Soil quality: A concept, definition, and framework for evaluation. Soil Sci. Soc. Am. J. 61:4–10.

Ketterings, Q.M., J. Kahabka, and W.S. Reid. 2005. Trends in phosphorus fertility of New York agricultural land. J. Soil Water Conserv. 59:10–20.

Kleinman, P.J.A., R.B. Bryant, W.S. Reid, A.N. Sharpley, and D. Pimentel. 2000. Using soil phosphorus behavior to identify environmental thresholds. Soil Sci. 165:943–950.

Lemunyon, J.L., and R.G. Gilbert. 1993. Concept and need for a phosphorus assessment tool. J. Prod. Agric. 6:483–486.

Magdoff, F.R., and H.M. van Es. 2009. Building soils for better crops: Sustainable soil management. 3rd ed. Sustainable Agric. Research and Education Outreach, Beltsville, MD.

Maguire, R.O., and J.T. Sims. 2002. Soil testing to predict phosphorus losses. J. Environ. Qual. 31:1601–1609.

Malone, T.C., W. Boynton, T. Hortin, and C. Stevenson. 1993. Nutrient loading to surface water: Chesapeake Bay case study. p. 8–38. *In* M.F. Uman (ed.) Keeping pace with science and engineering. National Academy Press, Washington DC.

Melkonian, J., H.M. van Es, A.T. DeGaetano, J.M. Sogbedji, and L. Joseph. 2007. Application of dynamic simulation modeling for nitrogen management in maize. p. 14–22. *In* T. Bruulsema (ed.) Managing crop nutrition for weather. Int. Plant Nutrition Inst. Publ., Norcross, GA.

Moebius, B.N., H.M. van Es, J.O. Idowu, R.R. Schindelbeck, D.J. Clune, D.W. Wolfe, G.S. Abawi, J.E. Thies, B.K. Gugino, and R. Lucey. 2008. Long-term removal of maize residue for bioenergy: Will it affect soil quality? Soil Sci. Soc. Am. J. 72:960–969.

Montgomery, D. 2007. Dirt: The erosion of civilizations. Univ. of California Press, Berkeley.

Nearing, M.A., F.F. Pruski, and M.R. O'Neal. 2004. Expected climate change impacts on soil erosion rates: A review. J. Soil Water Conserv. 59:43–50.

New York State Department of Environmental Conservation. 2009. New York City Watershed Program. Available at http://www.dec.ny.gov/lands/25599.html (verified 24 Nov. 2009).

Northeast Regional Climate Center. 2009. Comparative climate data for the United States. Available at http://www.nrcc.cornell.edu/page_ccd.html. (verified 24 Nov. 2009).

Poe, G.L. 1999. Maximizing the environmental benefit per dollar expended: An economic interpretation and review of agricultural environmental benefits and costs. Soc. Nat. Res. 12:571–598.

Renard, K.G., G.R. Foster, G.A. Weesies, and J.P. Porter. 1991. RUSLE Revised Universal Soil Loss Equation. J. Soil Water Conserv. Soc. 46:30–33.

Ribaudo, M. 1986. Reducing soil erosion: Offsite benefits. USDA-ERS AER-561.

Sharpley, A.N., P.J.A. Kleinman, A.L. Heathwaite, W.J. Gburek, J.L. Weld, and G.J. Folmar. 2008. Integrating contributing areas and indexing phosphorus loss from agricultural watersheds. J. Environ. Qual. 37:1488–1496.

Sims, J.T. 1999. Delaware's state nutrient management program: An overview of the 1999 Delaware nutrient management act. NM-01. Univ. of Delaware, Newark.

Smith, W.B., J.S. Vissage, D.R. Darr, and R.M. Sheffield. 2001. Forest resources of the United States, 1997. North Central Res. Stn., For. Serv., USDA, St. Paul, MN.

State of Maryland. 2000. Nutrient and commercial fertilizer applicattion requirement for agricultural land and land including state property, not used for agricultural purposes. Code of Maryland 15.20.06. Available at http://www.mda.state.md.us/pdf/nmregs06.pdf (verified 24 Nov. 2009).

Staver, K.W. 2001. Increasing N retention in Coastal Plain agricultural watersheds. The Scientific World 1(s2):207–215.

Stoll, S. 2002. Larding the lean earth, soil and society in nineteenth century America. Hill and Wang, New York.

van Es, H.M., K.J. Czymmek, and Q.M. Ketterings. 2002. Management effects on N leaching and guidelines for an N leaching index in New York. J. Soil Water Conserv. 57(6):499–504.

van Es, H.M., B.D. Kay, J.J. Melkonian, and J.M. Sogbedji. 2007. Nitrogen management under maize in humid regions: Case for a dynamic approach. p. 6–13. In T. Bruulsema (ed.) Managing crop nutrition for weather. Int. Plant Nutrition Inst. Publ., Norcross, GA.

Vermont Agency of Agriculture. 2006. Accepted agricultural practice regulations. Available at http://www.vermontagriculture.com/ARMES/awq/AAPs.htm (verified 25 Nov. 2009).

Volk, T.A., T. Verwijst, P.J. Tharakan, L.P. Abrahamson, and E.H. White. 2004. Growing energy: Assessing the sustainability of willow short-rotation woody crops. Frontiers Ecol. Environ. 2(8):411–418.

Williams, J.R., and D.E. Kissel. 1991. Water percolation: An indicator of nitrogen-leaching potential. p. 59–83. In R.F. Follet, D.R. Keeney, and R.M. Cruse (ed.) Managing nitrogen for groundwater quality and farm profitability. SSSA, Madison, WI.

Woodbury, P.B., L.S. Heath, and J.E. Smith. 2007. Effects of land use change on soil carbon cycling in the conterminous United States from 1900 to 2050. Global Biogeochem. Cycles 21:GB3006 doi:10.1029/2007GB002950.

Wright, S.F., and A. Upadhyaya. 1998. A survey of soils for aggregate stability and glomalin, a glycoprotein produced by hyphae of arbuscular mycorrhizal fungi. Plant Soil 198:97–107.

7

Soil and Water Conservation in the Southeastern United States: A Look at Conservation Practices Past, Present, and Future

Warren J. Busscher
USDA-ARS, Coastal Plains Soil, Water, and Plant Research Center, Florence, SC

Harry H. Schomberg
USDA-ARS, J. Phil Campbell Sr. Natural Resource Conservation Center, Watkinsville, GA

Randy L. Raper
USDA-ARS, Dale Bumpers Small Farms Research Center, Booneville, AR

Soil and water conservation in the southeastern United States has changed over the years, and new challenges will call for more changes in the future. The first conservationists were Native Americans, followed by early European settlers. Both groups conserved the land by rotating fields in and out of crop production. As demands for agricultural output increased, producers began to crop the land continuously, and this caused the soil to deteriorate. In the Piedmont, soils eroded into the streams and lakes, where they still reside today. In the Coastal Plains, soils became compacted, infertile, and held little water available for crop growth. Today, many soils in these areas require stringent management to be productive. New management systems have been developed that rely on the use of cover crops in combination with reduced tillage. These systems have been shown to increase organic matter near the soil surface, which improves fertility and physical properties, increasing infiltration for plant use. Irrigation was introduced to maximize productivity and help offset high labor and input costs; irrigation filled in the gaps of unevenly timed rainfall. Recently, these new management practices are being challenged by the demand for organic matter to make fuel and the demand for water to meet the needs of industry and a growing population. These new challenges have to be met with research on new production systems, carbon sequestration management, irrigation management that uses less water, and new water storage sites that can satiate population and industrial growth while satisfying ecological, hydrological, and political expectations.

The Piedmont and Coastal Plain regions of the southeastern USA have subtropical climates, with hot, humid summers and mild to chilly winters. This climate typically occurs in subtropical latitudes at the southeastern side of continents.

Soil and Water Conservation Advances in the United States. SSSA Special Publication 60.
T.M. Zobeck and W.F. Schillinger, editors. © 2010. SSSA, 677 S. Segoe Rd., Madison, WI 53711, USA.

Weather patterns typically move from west to east, with significant precipitation year-round. Summer rains come in the form of thunderstorms, tropical storms, and hurricanes. In the southeastern USA, much of the rainfall comes from water vapor that is carried north and east from the Gulf of Mexico along weather frontal boundaries. The coldest month is above 0°C, the warmest month is above 22°C, and the least mean monthly rainfall is 60 mm (McKnight and Hess, 2000).

Average annual rainfalls in the southeastern USA range from 1000 to 1700 mm, with fairly uniform mean distribution throughout the year (SERCC, 2007). These averages suggest abundant water, but they do not reflect the large fluctuations of drought and excess rain that occur over time (Fig. 7–1) and space (Fig. 7–2). The fluctuations affect not only soil water contents and irrigation for agriculture, but they also affect dependability of water supplies for industries, municipalities, and power plants (Davis, 2002; Foskett et al., 2007). Water supplies are being overtaxed during summer growing seasons, and surpluses are dwindling as the population increases and droughts grip the region (Auchmutey, 2007; Morris, 2007). Water shortage fears plague southeastern states, and lawsuits abound over the diminishing supplies (Henderson, 2007; WRLB News, 2007), while there is little action to increase storage (Pittman, 2007). In recent times, the Southeast has gained only one desalinization plant and few regional reservoirs or aquifer storage/recovery units.

Coastal Plain soils were generally formed from sandy marine sediments in a warm, wet climate. They have kandic or oxic horizons that are similar to argillic horizons but have low activity clays (Soil Survey Staff, 1999). Inceptisols and entisols can be found in the alluvial areas around the rivers. Many soils need to be drained to be productive (see http://www.soilinfo.psu.edu, verified 30 Nov. 2009). Further inland, the Piedmont (Virginia into Alabama) is an erosional landscape with gently rolling uplands and moderate to steep valley slopes that grade down to adjacent streams. In this region, soils developed from residuum that is several meters thick. Soil nutrient contents are low because most weatherable minerals

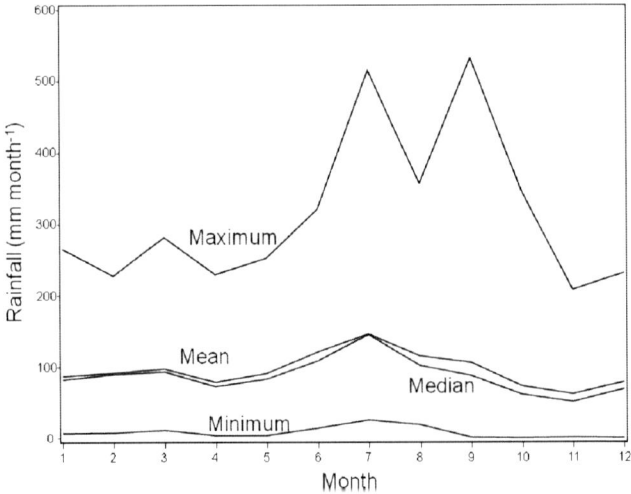

Fig. 7–1. Rainfall statistics for Florence, SC for the years 1892 to 1992.

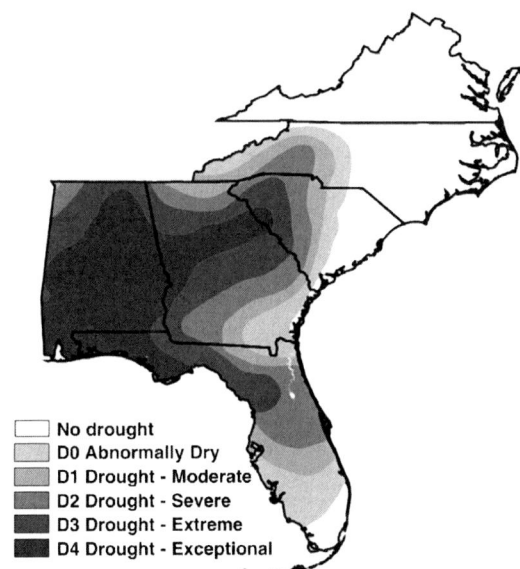

Fig. 7–2. Palmer Drought Severity Index for the southeastern USA averaged from January 1999 to January 2000. The image was provided by the NOAA/ESRL Physical Sciences Division, Boulder, CO, from their web site at http://www.cdc.noaa.gov/ (verified 1 Dec. 2009).

- No drought
- D0 Abnormally Dry
- D1 Drought - Moderate
- D2 Drought - Severe
- D3 Drought - Extreme
- D4 Drought - Exceptional

that were present in the original igneous and metamorphic rocks have leached from the upper soil horizons. Alfisols and entisols form on ridgetops, on steep slopes, in clayey deposits, and in alluvial materials along the rivers.

Most land in the Southeast is privately owned. Much of it is forested and managed for timber, recreation, and, near the cities, for development. Land cleared for cropping has declined over the past century, particularly in the piedmont. Much of it has reverted to forests, while cropland continues to be viewed as the easiest to develop for home and commercial interests. On a county-wide basis, cropped land consists of anywhere from 5 to 30% of the area. Most counties have less than 15% cropland, but this adds up to 8 to 16 × 10^6 ha (http://usda.mannlib.cornell.edu/, verified 30 Nov. 2009). Because soils are not as fertile as many other parts of the country, they require more management and higher energy inputs.

Farming Trends in the Southeastern Coastal Plain

The average Coastal Plain farm is less than 200 ha (NASS, 2002). The number of farms and the number of hectares farmed are decreasing as a result of drought, urbanization, and the economics of large farm sizes. Eighty-five percent of the farms are operated by families or individuals, and the majority of producers list something other than farming as their primary occupation. Farm production runs the economic gamut, with net incomes from less than $10,000 to more than $200,000 (NASS, 2002). Although the incomes quoted are net, gross receipts and expenses can run into the millions, even for operations of modest size. Because of the warm wet weather and sandy soils, producers spend more than the U.S. average on pest control and fertilizers. Producers generally irrigate to supplement rainfall rather than using it as a primary crop water source; this accounts for low irrigation rates compared to other parts of the United States. However, dependency on irrigation and sophisticated management continue to grow.

Farming Trends in the Southern Piedmont

The Piedmont has about 5.7 million ha of agricultural land. About 1.5 million ha are used for crop production. The rest is used for forage or hay production (NASS, 2002). Most Piedmont farms are small, with an average size of 49 ha and median size of 29 ha. The number of farms and amount of farmland has declined, while farm size has increased. A decline in farm production is attributed to poor soil productivity and urbanization. The greatest amount of harvested Piedmont agricultural land is in North Carolina, with 486,000 ha; Alabama has the least, with 27,000 ha. North Carolina produces 65, 77, 76, and 68% of the corn (*Zea mays* L.), cotton (*Gossypium hirsutum* L.), soybean [*Glycine max* (L.) Merr.], and wheat (*Triticum aestivum* L.), respectively, grown in the Piedmont. Beef cattle, dairy, and poultry contribute substantially to Piedmont farm incomes.

Most Piedmont cropland is used to grow soybean, wheat, corn, and cotton. These four crops are grown on 36, 19, 16, and 11%, respectively, of the row-cropped land. Corn acreage in the region is expected to increase because of the greater demand for its use in ethanol production. Other crops grown in the region include sorghum [*Sorghum bicolor* (L.) Moench], tobacco (*Nicotiana tabacum* L.), sweet potato [*Ipomoea batatas* (L.) Lam.], bean (*Phaseolus vulgaris* L.), orchard crops, and vegetables. The vegetable industry has grown rapidly in the past 10 yr because of urban markets in Atlanta, Charlotte, Raleigh-Durham, and Greenville-Spartanburg. This trend is expected to continue as high transportation costs discourage shipping from the West to eastern cities. Typically, vegetables are produced using conventional practices, but adoption of cover crops and conservation tillage systems has increased. A variety of vegetables are produced in the region including sweet corn, tomato (*Solanum lycopersicum* L.), squash (*Curbita* spp.), and pea (*Pisum sativum* L.) in the summer; and broccoli (*Brassica oleracea* L. var. *italica* Plenck), cauliflower (*Brassica oleracea* L. var. *botrytis* L.), cabbage (*Brassica oleracea* L.), winter squash (*Cucurbita maxima* Duchesne), and pumpkin (*Cucurbita pepo* L.) in the fall. The Piedmont relies less on farm program crops or dairy products than other areas of the United States. The Piedmont has the highest proportion of farmers with full-time off-farm jobs. Farming provides less than the average portion of total household income. Full-time farmers make up only a small fraction of the rural population.

Historical Perspective

The first agriculturalists in the southeastern United States were the Native Americans. As archeologists are beginning to discover, the Native Americans had a greater influence on the environment than was earlier believed. They were descendants of Paleo-Americans (Mann, 2005), who crossed the land bridge from Siberia over 14,000 yr ago. As the southeastern United States changed from paraglacial to a more temperate climate and populations increased, the Native Americans changed from hunter-gatherers to urban societies with Mississippian characteristics (King, 2002) imported from the west. The settled Native American societies, as seen by Desoto in the middle 1500s, grew crops on fields where several plants such as maize, beans, and squash were cultivated together; this type of planting scheme was capable of sustaining large populations with nutritious food. Crops were planted on cleared land for 2 yr, and then the land was allowed to rest for 8 yr (Mann, 2005). As these societies died out due to disease and war, European settlers entered the area.

During the decline of the Native American society and before the Europeans moved in, the southeastern Piedmont was described as having clear, clean streams and deep, dark soils (Harper, 1998; Trimble 1974). Closer to the coast, soils were wet and sandy but productive. The area was ripe for settlement. After attempts with several crops, early European settlers found rice (*Oryza sativa* L.) and indigo (*Indigofera hirsuta* L.) to be profitable along the coast (New York Times, 1901). With time, settlements moved inland, and the rice–indigo combination along with cotton, cattle, tobacco, and timber set the stage for the arguably "idyllic" antebellum south that benefited a few select landowners (Boyle, 1996).

During the early years of European settlement, producers practiced shifting cultivation where part of the land would be cleared and farmed for a few years until the soil was depleted. Then more land would be cleared and farmed while the depleted land rested. This farming practice was similar to that used by Native Americans and by farmers in some areas of Europe. During the late 1700s, settlers moved into the North Carolina and Virginia Piedmont and continued to practice shifting cultivation. In the early 1800s, settlers from North Carolina and Virginia moved into the Georgia Piedmont (Trimble, 1974). They cleared land and grew tobacco, corn, cotton and other crops. Cotton served as a cash crop, while corn was grown for consumption by farm animals, such as mules for plowing, cows for dairy, swine for meat, and poultry for eggs. Based on the agricultural data from that time (Brown, 2002), many growers were subsistence farmers. Small farmers were usually tenants who had little incentive to conserve soil because they often stayed only through one or two cropping seasons. Poor land management practices during the cotton-farming era (1820–1930) left the surface of the sloping Piedmont soils bare for long periods of time, which exposed them to the erosive forces of rainfall. Significant erosion occurred, with cumulative losses of 14 to 24 cm throughout the region (Trimble, 1974). Soil eroded from the uplands into reservoirs, floodplains, and stream bottoms (Jackson et al., 2005), where much of it is predicted to remain for several millennia. It is not surprising that Hugh Hammond Bennett, the Father of Soil Conservation came from the southeastern Piedmont (USDA-NRCS, 2009), where he personally witnessed the devastating impacts of soil erosion.

In the early 20th century, eroded soil, the boll weevil [*Anthonomus grandis* (Boheman)], and low cotton prices abruptly ended cotton cultivation in the Southeast (Fig. 7–3 and 7–4). Cotton was replaced by tobacco, peanut (*Arachis hypogaea*

Fig. 7–3. Cotton after defoliation. Photo by David Nance, USDA-ARS Image Gallery.

Fig. 7–4. Dedicated in 1919, the Boll Weevil Monument, in Enterprise, AL, is symbolic of just how important the boll weevil was in the South. Photo from the USDA History Collections, National Agricultural Library.

L.), corn, and soybean (Haney et al., 1996), all of which can leave the surface relatively bare and prone to erosion. Crop productivity in the Piedmont is still limited today by the almost total loss of topsoil from fields as a result of previous mismanagement. Losses included not only the topsoil but also its nutrients, organic matter, fertility, and water-holding capacity. Many Piedmont soils today consist of exposed subsurface soil horizons that are dense because of their high clay content and that restrict plant production because of high exchangeable Al contents. Soil productivity problems of the region would not be this severe if early on we could have developed greater wisdom and foresight, a stronger land ethic, and a desire to use better management practices (Trimble, 1974).

As bad as the situation may have been in the Southeast, soil conservationists could not attract the attention of the public and government until the Dust Bowl of the 1930s when dense clouds of eroded soil blackened midwestern skies. This led to the establishment of the Soil Conservation Service (SCS) as an agency within USDA (Helms, 1990). It was led by the strong conservation advocate Hugh Hammond Bennett. The SCS (now Natural Resources Conservation Service), along with other USDA agencies, developed and continue to develop modern methods of soil and water conservation for use in the Southeast and other areas of the country. Practices like terracing (Fig. 7–5), contouring, and cover crops, along with conversion of land to permanent cover, reduced soil loss by more than an order of magnitude. As the majority of Piedmont row-crop agriculture moved to the flatter, less-erodible soils of the Coastal Plains, Piedmont land production shifted to forestry and pasture, resulting in even less soil loss. Trimble (1974) estimated that a relative erosive factor of 1 applied to row-crop land in 1920 to 1930

Fig. 7–5. Building terraces in the Piedmont. Photo from the archives of the USDA-ARS, J. Phil Campbell, Senior, Natural Resource Conservation Center, Watkinsville, GA.

Fig. 7–6. Mule and disk. Photo from the archives of the USDA-ARS, National Soil Dynamics Laboratory, Auburn, AL.

would now be 0.45 due to improved production and conservation practices. But row crops were not the only problem; agricultural mechanization and soil management both helped and hindered the restoration of southeastern soils.

Over the years, soil management and crop production systems have advanced with corresponding advances in mechanization. Because Native Americans did not have draft animals, they developed, maintained, and harvested their fields by hand. Draft animals were introduced by the Europeans. By the late 1800s, mules (Fig. 7–6) were the standard method of providing power for plows and other field operations. With mules, land could be plowed almost to the stream bank as wet alluvial soils drained in late spring. Plowing and in-season cultivation resulted in erosion, and, in the Piedmont, sediments filled stream channels. In the Coastal Plain, sediment-laden streams took on braided channel patterns, turning lowlands into riparian wetlands with ill-defined stream channels, decreasing land area that could be used for crops.

As the 20th century dawned, agricultural mechanization began to develop. In the early 1900s, tractors made their way to the farm. But they were not readily adopted until the 1920s when competition among manufacturers forced prices down to about $400 (Leffingwell, 1994), not too far above the cost of an automobile (Fig. 7–7 and 7–8). In the early 1930s, rubber tires were introduced to tractors (Macmillan and Jones, 1988). Tires provided more power and the ability to move tractors quickly between fields. Two and three bottom plow tractors provided a relatively quick and easy method to prepare large tracts of land or multiple small tracts. Tractor weights prevented their use in poorly and somewhat poorly drained areas; low-lying areas that had subsurface water necessary to sustain

Fig. 7–7. Early Minneapolis-Moline tractor. Photo courtesy of Brian Rukes, http://www.angelfire.com/ok/mmreg/book.html.

Fig. 7–8. Early cotton harvester. Photo from the archives of the USDA-ARS, National Soil Dynamics Laboratory, Auburn, AL.

plant growth during dry summer months had to be abandoned. Tractors also permitted deeper plowing than was possible with mules. As a result, subsoil was mixed into the now erosion-thinned surface layer bringing to the surface acidity and reduced organic-matter soil. This mixing degraded the quality of soil needed for crops, especially crops that were grown without the benefit of much added lime and fertilizer.

More recently, equipment companies have focused on efficiency and speed of operation. As a result, agricultural equipment has increased in size and cost. This increase is perhaps most evident at the Nebraska Tractor Tests. In their 1948 tests, vehicles weighed less than 4500 kg; now, a 170-kw (225 hp) tractor weighs about 9000 kg, although some can weigh more than 25,000 kg. Increased vehicle size leads to increased pressure on soils and deterioration of compaction-susceptible soils like those of the Southeast. Increased compaction then leads to more dependence on large machinery to break up the hard soil—a vicious cycle. Increased tillage leads to increased erosion, reduced organic matter, and reduced productivity. These debilitating effects are being reversed by newer reduced tillage systems, controlled traffic, and organic residue and carbon management. Indeed, agricultural compaction problems of the area might have been solved by modern no-till or reduced-tillage management if it had not been for new challenges.

Recent Advances
Coastal Plains, Plant Water Availability
Except for years of drought, which can be devastating for the southeastern Coastal Plain (Sheridan et al., 1979), rainfall is abundant. Yet, almost every year, water is the limiting growth factor because the sandy soils have low water-holding capacities (0.08 g g^{-1}), and crops normally experience periods of no rain for 2 wk or more (Sheridan et al., 1979), which causes yield-reducing stress (Sadler and Camp, 1986). More water can be made available to the plant by opening up the soil profile to root growth through deep tillage.

Coastal Plain Tillage
Deep tillage helps many Coastal Plain soils remain productive by physically disrupting its massive structure. Soil horizons, especially the eluviated (E) horizon just below the Ap, can have strengths high enough to reduce or prevent root growth (Busscher et al., 2002), even when soil water contents are at field capacity (Campbell et al., 1978). Deep tillage disrupts the E horizon (Fig. 7–9), increasing root growth, water uptake, and yield (Busscher et al., 2002; Raper et al., 2000).

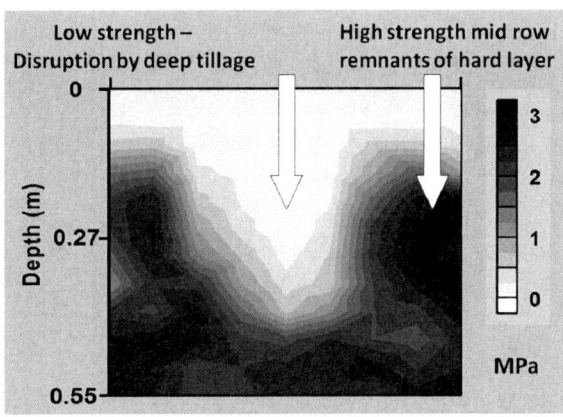

Fig. 7–9. Soil strength pattern for noninversion tillage in the Coastal Plains. The hard layer is basically the E horizon.

Once the roots penetrate the tilled E horizon, they can grow below it into the B horizon that generally has weak blocky structure. Even when the B horizon hardens as it dries, roots can grow along the fracture planes, that is, the faces of the aggregated structural units.

With time, the loosening effects of tillage diminish as the soil reconsolidates (Raper et al., 2000; Shukla et al., 2003), causing reduced crop yields (Arvidsson et al., 2001; Radford et al., 2000). Although the effects of deep tillage can be seen for years (Busscher et al., 2002; Munkholm et al., 2001), incomplete reconsolidation reduces yield from one growing season to the next as soil strength increases enough to restrict root growth. As a result, deep tillage for these soils is recommended annually (Threadgill, 1982; Porter and Khalilian, 1995). On the negative side, deep tillage is expensive; it requires large tractors (14–20 kw per shank), 20 to 40 min ha^{-1} of labor, and 20 to 25 L ha^{-1} of fuel (Karlen et al., 1991). On the positive side, deep tillage is noninversion; several deep tillage implements can disrupt the soil without disturbing much of the surface, thus, leaving residue to protect the surface from erosion.

Piedmont Region

Current Piedmont conservation tillage is based on practices that started in the 1970s. These practices, such as reduced tillage and the use of cover crop residues, improve soil physical, chemical, and biological properties through the beneficial effects of added organic matter. The most apparent improvement is with water. When organic matter is not incorporated, it can act as surface mulch, reducing runoff from rainfall, increasing infiltration, and improving plant water uptake and growth (Bruce et al., 1988; Freese et al., 1993; Raczkowski et al., 2002; West et al., 1991).

System Response to Adoption of Reduced Tillage

Changes in soil properties associated with reduced or conservation tillage and increased biomass inputs were the keys to improving crop productivity and sustainability of agriculture in both the Coastal Plan and Piedmont regions. Bruce et al. (1995), using data from a series of studies, illustrated how increasing biomass and reducing tillage altered the distribution of carbon within the soil profile and improved soil surface physical properties that regulated water infiltration and availability. Conservation tillage was the critical management factor required to keep residues on the soil surface (Reeves, 1997). The beneficial effects were more apparent in systems that rely on high-residue producing crops (corn, sorghum, small grains) and in double-crop systems. Using a wheat–sorghum double-crop system in Georgia, Langdale et al. (1984) demonstrated that soil C in the top 1 cm increased 57% in a no-till system compared with a conventional tillage system. Carbon from crop residues was critical for improving aggregate stability and water infiltration (Langdale et al., 1990; Bruce et al., 1992). Measurable changes in soil physical and biological properties usually required 3 to 5 yr to demonstrate because of the large variability in most soil properties. However, yield changes could often be seen in the first year, depending on producer experience and management, soil physical factors, and environmental conditions.

Although early conservation studies demonstrated little or no yield advantage (Brown et al., 1985; Langdale et al., 1984), improvements in planters, residue management accessories, and development of best management practices (BMPs) increased the success of conservation systems by optimizing edaphic factors affecting seed germination and vigor. For example, soil temperature, soil water, crop rotation sequence, and cover crops directly impact seed germination through influences on root pathogens and allelopathy. A critical lesson learned was the value of cover cropping for high residue production. The lack of tillage alone created problems, but lack of tillage coupled with cover crops produced large amounts of residue for weed suppression and water conservation. This coupling allowed conservation tillage to have immediate positive effects on yields. The benefits of improved BMPs were illustrated in several recent studies from Alabama.

In a study in the sand mountain region, Schwab et al. (2002) showed that cotton yields were the same or better for conservation tillage systems with and without noninversion subsoil tillage compared with conventional tillage. Using the same soil, Raper et al. (2000) observed a need for some type of in-row disruption of the shallow hard pan in the first year, whereas in subsequent years the presence of a cover crop resulted in equal or greater yields for the no-till system compared with the conventional tillage system. Siri-Prieto et al. (2007a) worked in an integrated winter-annual grazing cotton–peanut–cotton cropping system on a Coastal Plain soil in south Alabama and found that the best tillage system for optimum infiltration, cone index, and bulk density was paratilling without disking. After 3 yr, this system increased SOC and total N at the soil surface (0–5 cm) by 38 and 56%, respectively. In addition, paratilling without disking resulted in the highest seed cotton and peanut yields (Siri-Prieto et al., 2007b).

Terra et al. (2006) showed an immediate yield response for cotton in a corn–cotton conservation tillage system. During the first 3 yr, yields were 10, 24, and 14% greater in the conservation system than in the conventional system. In the first 2 yr (dry seasons), greater yields with the conservation system were attributed to improved soil water use efficiency (Lascano et al., 1994; Reeves, 1994). The third year was a wet year, and yield advantages for the conservation system again may have been related to greater water use efficiency although the authors did not speculate. In the same study, after one rotation cycle (30 mo), no-till increased soil organic C (0–5 cm; 0–2 in depth) by approximately 50% compared with conventional tillage (7.34 and 7.62 vs. 5.02 Mg ha^{-1}, respectively). Conservation systems had greater soil organic C increases relative to conventional systems at low soil quality landscape positions. They concluded that the potential was great to sequester C using high-residue producing conservation systems for degraded soils throughout the southeastern United States.

Soil Amendments and Soil Productivity

Because Piedmont soils have low organic matter, limited amounts of basic cations, low cation exchange capacity, and predominance of 1:1 clays, they are prone to surface sealing by crust formation. Crusts can form during rainfall events and can dramatically increase runoff and erosion. Zhang and Miller (1996) showed that soil cover, gypsum, or a combination of the two were effective in significantly reducing crusting and increasing infiltration rates in a Cecil sandy loam compared with the control (no treatment). Infiltration rates increased 26% for either cover or gypsum and 132% for the combined treatment. Soil cover and gypsum treatments were effective in modifying both chemical (dispersion) and physical (raindrop impact) forces critical in crust and seal formation. Also using gypsum, Sumner (1993) demonstrated its beneficial effects on reduction of subsurface Al toxicity. Reducing Al in the subsoil allowed roots to extract water and nutrients from a greater volume of soil, improving crop productivity. These effects could last for many years, as indicated by Toma et al. (1999). Sixteen years after application of gypsum, soil profile Ca and SO_4, were increased and exchangeable Al was decreased compared to the untreated control soil profile. The addition of gypsum improved corn and alfalfa (*Medicago sativa* L.) yields by 25 to 50%.

Other amendments beneficial to soils came from animal byproducts. Manure and litter provide additional nutrients and positively influence soil properties important for soil and water conservation. Researchers from Alabama (Kingery et al., 1994) studied the impact of long-term (15 yr) land application of broiler litter on environmentally related soil properties and found soil pH was 0.5 higher to a depth of 0.6 m under littered vs. unlittered soils because of the Ca and Mg in the manure. Litter additions were found to significantly increase organic matter. After 3 yr of additions, Nyakatawa et al. (2001) reported organic matter increases of 55 to 80% in silt loam soils of northern Alabama. Increases were due to both the manure and greater plant growth in response to nutrients.

Manure additions promoted formation of water-stable aggregates important for maintaining soil structure (Haynes and Naidu, 1998). Manure applied to soils increased the protected pools of C in small macroaggregates (Aoyama et al., 2000) and microaggregates (Kapkiyai et al., 1999); this helped maintain aggregate stability. When compared with the control, up to 22.4 Mg ha^{-1} of poultry litter applied to bare plots on a sandy loam Piedmont soil decreased runoff and soil loss (Giddens and Barnett, 1980) by as much as 50%. Dairy manure also reduced soil losses on corn plots (Mueller et al., 1984).

Adding poultry litter in conservation tillage management (Endale et al., 2002) resulted in a positive synergistic effect on cotton yields. In no-till treatments, poultry litter improved yields 35 to 50% over conventionally tilled and fertilized cotton. Apparently, poultry litter provided slow release of nutrients and increased water availability, which provided a superior condition for cotton production. More recently, when Endale et al. (2008) compared no-tillage management with conventionally tilled and fertilized corn, no-till increased grain yield by 11%, poultry litter increased grain yield by 18%, and the combination increased grain yield by 31%.

Future Outlook

Water Storage

Although three-fourths of our planet is covered with water, most of it is tied up in saline oceans or ice (USGS, 2009), leaving less than 1% for human, animal, and crop plant use. In humid regions, much of that 1% is renewed by annual rainfall. It flows in perennial streams, moves through aquifers, and is taken up by plants for transpiration. In the Southeast, the perennial streams are relatively short, typically 500 linear (nonmeandering) km (300 miles) or less. This limits our ability to use and reuse water before it enters the ocean. The Floridan aquifer ranges from southern South Carolina to eastern Mississippi. It is a productive aquifer whose water is used extensively by industry, agriculture, and municipalities in the coastal plains (USGS, 2008). Aquifer water is replenished from its overlying surficial aquifer or from rainfall in areas where the surficial aquifer is thin or absent. Plants take up water mainly throughout the summer growing season when evapotranspiration exceeds rainfall. During this time, shallow water tables fall until the weather turns cold, leaves drop from trees, and winter rains replenish the soil.

Because of high rainfall rates in the Southeast, consumptive water use is only about 3% of the total renewable water supply (USGS, 1984). We consume 0.23 of 8.86×10^{11} L (6 of 234 billion gallons) per day. With this amount of water, there does not appear to be a deficit—yet crops wilt, municipalities regularly request voluntary water restrictions, and states argue about how much water they and their neighbors can take from various rivers (Rowles et al., 2008). Water systems are being taxed by increasing population, urbanization, and industrialization. New water capture and storage facilities are needed to slow water flow from the Piedmont to the ocean and retain winter/early spring rains. Building new surface water storage facilities proceeds at a slower pace than needed because of legal, social, political, engineering, hydrological, and environmental hurtles. Other than conservation, new facilities are the only option for water-hungry areas, especially the Piedmont, where groundwater is not as plentiful as on the Coast.

Even though the Coastal Plain has the highly productive Floridan Aquifer, overpumping of groundwater has been seen in areas with large populations, heavy industrial use, and extensive irrigation. Although groundwater in these areas is recharged, the recharge area is often some distance inland from the area that needs recharge. Excessive drawdown and salt water intrusion force Coastal areas to depend more and more on surface waters. In the Atlantic coastal area of Georgia alone, more than 60,000 human-made structures are used to supply water to farms, cities, industry, and golf courses. More or larger facilities will be needed as the population of the area continues to grow.

Soil Organic Matter

For the past decades, soil scientists and producers have been trying to increase organic matter in southeastern soils to improve fertility, water-holding capacity, and production. But, now that fuel prices have soared, organic matter residue in the form of cellulose may be removed from fields to produce ethanol. How much residue can southeastern soils afford to lose before soil properties and/or production are affected? To determine this, research has begun, again—research was started during a previous fuel crisis, but because the crisis (Margolis and

Kammen, 1999) did not continue, the research priority decreased and funding ceased. Previous results (Karlen et al., 1984) showed that some residue could be removed from cropping systems on southeastern soils provided that nutrients were replaced with fertilizer, but fertilizer production requires large amounts of energy (Williams et al., 2005). More research needs to be done to determine if an acceptable level of removal can be found that is economical and sustainable.

Fuel and Deep Tillage

For proper soil management, deep tillage of many coastal soils is required to loosen subsurface compacted horizons. Because deep tillage requires more than 20 L ha^{-1} of fuel, it is becoming prohibitively expensive as diesel prices increase. Deep tillage needs to be replaced by other forms of management. One management system attempted in the past with some success is irrigating the soil with drip tubes buried just above the hard layer to keep it soft and supply crop water needs (Fig. 7–10). However, this requires careful management to avoid overwatering or underwatering. Overwatering prevents roots from penetrating a flooded layer, while underwatering does not loosen the hard layer. It is likely that both will occur simultaneously between and at the buried tubes or between and at emitters along the tubes (Camp et al., 2000). Because water is not at the soil surface, this type of irrigation can create risks during stand establishment for years with dry early seasons.

Deep tilling on a multiple-year rotation has also been studied. In many cases, not tilling every year reduces yield to levels that may be acceptable given the increase in fuel costs. For some crops, such as cotton, annual deep tillage may not be necessary to maintain yields. Deep tilling every 2 to 3 yr may be just as efficient as deep tilling annually (Busscher and Bauer, 2003). This will depend on the variety grown (Kasperbauer and Busscher, 1991) and on the amount of rainfall that recompacts the soil between seasons (Busscher et al., 2002).

Subsoiling is often performed at a standard depth, while the compacted layer's depth varies throughout a field. If subsoiling is based on the deeper zones of the compacted layer, its disruption is too deep for the zones of the field where the compacted layer is shallow. If subsoiling is based on the shallower zones of the compacted layer, it will not disrupt the whole compacted layer, leaving hard zones that will limit root growth. Technologies are now available that allow subsoiling to vary with the depth of the compacted layer. This can save energy without sacrificing crop yields. A 4-yr experiment was conducted in southern Alabama to evaluate the concept of site-specific depth of subsoiling. Site-specific subsoiling produced yields equivalent to those produced by the uniform deep

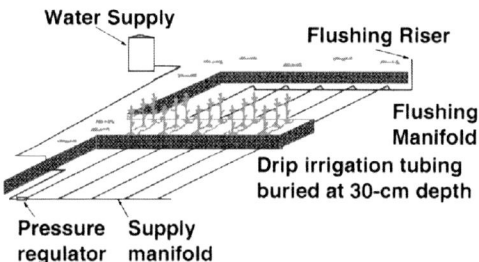

Fig. 7–10. Buried microirrigation tubes that keep the hard layer wet and soft.

subsoiling, while reducing draft forces, drawbar power, and fuel use (Raper et al., 2005; Raper et al., 2007).

Another way to reduce energy demand is to amend the soil so that deep tillage would be drastically reduced or eliminated. Two potential amendments are polyacrylamide (PAM) and biochar. Older formulations of PAM were used as soil conditioners in the early 1950s (Weeks and Colter, 1952). They improved plant growth by stabilizing aggregates in the surface 30- to 40-cm depths. Hundreds of kilograms of PAM per hectare were needed, limiting PAM use to high value crops and nurseries. By the 1980s, polymer formulations and purity improved, making them more effective at lower concentrations. In the 1990s, water-soluble environmentally safe anionic PAM was identified as an effective erosion-preventing and infiltration-enhancing polymer when applied at 1 to 10 mg L^{-1} in furrow irrigation water (Lentz et al., 1992; Sojka and Lentz, 1997). For PAM to be effective deeper in the profile, larger amounts are needed and deeper mixing will cost several hundred dollars per hectare. But given the high cost of fuel, this might be economically feasible if the PAM could last multiple years. Current estimates are that PAM breaks down at a rate of 10% per year (Azzam et al., 1983; Tolstikh et al., 1992; Entry et al., 2008).

Another amendment that has attracted attention in the past few years is biochar. It gained prominence as a result of archeologists finding charcoal-amended soils in the Amazon and other historically old areas that are more productive than expected (Mann, 2005). If biochar is effective in improving productivity for long periods of time, it could be an economically feasible soil amendment, especially if the amendment would eliminate or reduce tillage for extended periods. Biochar's effectiveness depends on its source material, how it is produced, and how it is activated during its production.

Conservation Organizations

There are many conservation organizations and societies, such as the Sierra Club, Ducks Unlimited, the Soil and Water Conservation Society, and the Soil Science Society of America, that work toward the betterment of our environment. One governmental organization that developed out of the Dust Bowl conservation movement was the local conservation district. In 1937, President Franklin Roosevelt wrote every governor recommending state legislation that would allow local landowners to form conservation districts. Because of the recent Dust Bowl, legislation was passed by every state, and today the country has nearly 3000 conservation districts. Districts are run by local boards of commissioners or supervisors who are either elected or appointed. Board members are local citizens who are concerned about the conservation of soil, water, and other natural resources in their region. Boards are supported by small administrative and/or natural resource professional staffs. Board members and their staffs draw on help from various state and federal such as the USDA-NRCS; NGOs, including the National Association of Conservation Districts (NACD, www.nacdnet.org, verified 1 Dec. 2009) or their respective State Association of Conservation Districts; and professional organizations, such as the Soil and Water Conservation Society. Because districts are local, board members have knowledge of and experience with their specific conditions; and because they have national/state governmental support systems, board members can make informed decisions on local management of natural resources. Local districts were initially developed to support rural resource conservation, but because urban land issues increased and resource problems developed there, the districts have had to widen their scope of involvement. Regardless of whether concerns are rural or urban, conservation management systems that the districts implement are voluntary, incentive-driven programs aimed at benefiting all citizens. As populations increase in the Southeast and as we make more demands on our resources, organizations like the local conservation district and the state associations of districts, as well as the NACD will be challenged more and require more of the population, both rural and urban, to become educated and involved for our own wellbeing and that of our environment.

Conclusions

Southeastern conservation practices have had to keep pace with progress and current events, starting with the Native Americans and early European settlers clearing the land to support growing populations, continuing with the adaptation of management systems to larger farms and mechanized agriculture, and now continuing with reduced tillage systems that maintain surface cover. But new challenges will make us rethink our current paradigm. Recent rapidly escalating fuel prices have challenged our practices of noninversion tillage. Increasing population has challenged agriculture's access to water and created a demand for more water storage. And the need for fuel cellulose is beginning to question how much organic residue we need on the surface for erosion control and sustainable development while maintaining the quality of the soil.

If we would have had more foresight, we might have developed erosion control techniques earlier than we did to prevent the loss of topsoil from thousands of productive hectares. We could have researched and developed more water storage sites for our growing populations. We could have developed more energy efficient crop management systems to save fuel. But that did not happen. As a result, research on these and other problems may be more important than today than ever—research to save and conserve our soil and water resources for our use and the use by future generations.

References

Aoyama, M., D.A. Angers, A. N'Dayegamiye, and N. Bissonnette. 2000. Metabolism of C-13-labeled glucose in aggregates from soils with manure application. Soil Biol. Biochem. 32:295–300.

Arvidsson, J., A. Trautner, J.J.H. van den Akker, and P. Schjønning. 2001. Subsoil compaction caused by heavy sugarbeet harvesters in southern Sweden: II. Soil displacement during wheeling and model computations of compaction. Soil Tillage Res. 60(1–2):79–89.

Auchmutey, J. 2007. Atlanta's population surpasses five million. The Atlanta-Journal Constitution. 22 Mar. 2007.

Azzam, R., O.A. El-Hady, A.A. Lofty, and M. Hegela. 1983. San-RAPG combination simulating fertile clayey soils, parts I–IV. Int. Atomic Energy Agency. SM-267(15):321–349.

Boyle, C.C. 1996. Rise of the Georgetown rice culture. Available at www.ego.net/us/sc/myr/history/rise.htm (accessed Dec. 2007).

Brown, R.H. 2002. The greening of Georgia: The improvement of the environment in the twentieth century. Mercer Univ. Press, Macon, GA.

Brown, S.M., T. Whitwell, J.T. Touchton, and C.H. Burmester. 1985. Conservation tillage systems for cotton production. Soil Sci. Soc. Am. J. 49:1256–1260.

Bruce, R.R., A.W. White, Jr., A.W. Thomas, W.M. Snyder, G.W. Langdale, and H.F. Perkins. 1988. Characterization of soil-crop yield relations over a range of erosion on a landscape. Geoderma 43:99–116.

Bruce, R.R., G.W. Langdale, L.T. West, and W.P. Miller. 1992. Soil surface modification by biomass inputs affecting rainfall infiltration. Soil Sci. Soc. Am. J. 56:1614–1620.

Bruce, R.R., G.W. Langdale, L.T. West, and W.P. Miller. 1995. Surface soil degradation and soil productivity restoration and maintenance. Soil Sci. Soc. Am. J. 59:654–660.

Busscher, W.J., and P.J. Bauer. 2003. Soil strength, cotton root growth and lint yield in a southeastern USA coastal loamy sand. Soil Tillage Res. 74(2):151–159.

Busscher, W.J., P.J. Bauer, and J.R. Frederick. 2002. Recompaction of a coastal loamy sand after deep tillage as a function of subsequent cumulative rainfall. Soil Tillage Res. 68(1):49–57.

Camp, C.R., P.J. Bauer, and W.J. Busscher. 2000. Subsurface drip irrigation for cotton with conservation tillage. ASAE Paper 00-2184. ASAE, St. Joseph, MI.

Campbell, R.B., D.C. Reicosky, and C.W. Doty. 1978. Physical properties and tillage of Paleudults in the southeastern Coastal Plains. J. Soil Water Conserv. Soc. 29:221–224.

Davis, J. 2002. Georgia's water crisis. The Atlanta Journal-Constitution. 14 July 2002.

Endale, D.M., M.L. Cabrera, J.L. Steiner, D.E. Radcliff, W.K. Vencil, H.H. Schomberg, and L. Lohr. 2002. Impact of conservation tillage and nutrient management on soil water and yield of cotton fertilized with poultry litter or ammonium nitrate in the Georgia Piedmont. Soil Tillage Res. 66:55–68.

Endale, D.M., H.H. Schomberg, D.S. Fisher, M.B. Jenkins, R.R. Sharpe, and M.L. Cabrera. 2008. No-till corn productivity in a southeastern USA Ultisol amended with poultry litter. Agron. J. 100:1401–1408.

Entry, J.A., R.E. Sojka, and B.J. Hicks. 2008. Carbon and nitrogen stable isotope ratios can estimate anionic polyacrylamide degradation in soil. Geoderma 145:8–16.

Foskett, K., M. Newkirk, and S. Shelton. 2007. Georgia's water crisis: The power of water. The Atlanta Journal-Constitution. 18 Nov. 2007.

Freese, R.C., D.K. Cassel, and H.P. Denton. 1993. Infiltration in a Piedmont soil under three tillage systems. J. Soil Water Conserv. 48:214–218.

Giddens, J., and A.P. Barnett. 1980. Soil loss and microbiological quality of runoff from land treated with poultry litter. J. Environ. Qual. 9:518–520.

Haney, P.B., W.J. Lewis, and W.R. Lambert. 1996. Cotton production and the boll weevil in Georgia: History, cost of control, and benefits of eradication. Res. Bull. 429. The Georgia Agric. Exp. Stn., College of Agric. and Environ. Sci., The Univ. of Georgia, Athens.

Harper, F. (ed.) 1998. The travels of William Bartram. Naturalist ed. Univ. of Georgia Press, Athens.

Haynes, R.J., and R. Naidu. 1998. Influence of lime, fertilizer and manure applications on soil organic matter content and soil physical conditions: A review. Nutr. Cycl. Agroecosyst. 51:123–137.

Helms, D. 1990. Conserving the Plains: The soil conservation service in the Great Plains. Agric. Hist. 64:58–73.

Henderson, B. 2007. Fear of water shortage pits NC against SC. The Charlotte Observer. 8 June 2007.

Jackson, C.R., J.K. Martin, D.S. Leigh, and L.T. West. 2005. A southeastern piedmont watershed sediment budget: Evidence for a multi-millennial agricultural legacy. J. Soil Water Conserv. 60:298–310.

Kapkiyai, J.J., N.K. Karanja, J.N. Qureshi, P.C. Smithson, and P.L. Woomer. 1999. Soil organic matter and nutrient dynamics in a Kenyan nitisol under long-term fertilizer and organic input management. Soil Biol. Biochem. 31:1773–1782.

Karlen, D.L., W.J. Busscher, S.A. Hale, R.B. Dodd, E.E. Strickland, and T.H. Garner. 1991. Drought condition energy requirement and subsoiling effectiveness for selected deep tillage implements. Trans. ASAE 34:1967–1972.

Karlen, D.L., P.G. Hunt, and R.B. Campbell. 1984. Crop residue removal effects on corn yield and fertility in a Norfolk sandy loam. Soil Sci. Soc. Am. J. 48:867–872.

Kasperbauer, M.J., and W.J. Busscher. 1991. Genotypic differences in cotton root penetration of a compacted subsoil layer. Crop Sci. 31:1376–1378.

King, A. 2002. Mississippian period: Overview. *In* The New Georgia Encyclopedia. University of Georgia, Athens.

Kingery, W.L., C.W. Wood, D.P. Delaney, J.C. Williams, and G.L. Mullins. 1994. Impact of long-term land application of broiler litter on environmentally related soil properties. J. Environ. Qual. 23:139–147.

Langdale, G.W., W.L. Hargrove, and J.E. Giddens. 1984. Residue management in double-crop conservation tillage. Agron. J. 76:689–694.

Langdale, G.W., R.L. Wilson, Jr., and R.R. Bruce. 1990. Cropping frequencies to sustain long-term conservation tillage systems. Soil Sci. Soc. Am. J. 54:193–198.

Lascano, R.J., R.L. Baumhardt, S.K. Hicks, and J.L. Heilman. 1994. Soil and plant water evaporation from strip-tilled cotton: Measurement and simulation. Agron. J. 86:987–994.

Leffingwell, R. 1994. Classic John Deere tractors. Motorbooks Int. Publ., Osceola, WI.

Lentz, R.D., I. Shainberg, R.E. Sojka, and D.L. Carter. 1992. Preventing irrigation furrow erosion with small applications of polymers. Soil Sci. Soc. Am. J. 56:1926–1932.

Macmillan, D., and R. Jones. 1988. John Deere tractors and equipment. Volume one: 1837–1959. ASAE, St. Joseph, MI.

Mann, C.C. 2005. 1491: New revelations of the Americas before Columbus. Vintage and Anchor Books, New York.

Margolis, R.M., and D.M. Kammen. 1999. Underinvestment: The energy technology and R&D policy challenge. Science 285:690–692.

McKnight, T.L., and D. Hess. 2000. Climate zones and types: The Köppen system. p. 200–201. *In* Physical geography: A landscape appreciation. Prentice Hall, Upper Saddle River, NJ.

Morris, M. 2007. Extreme heat has contributed to exceptional drought. The Atlanta Journal-Constitution. 23 Aug. 2007.

Mueller, D.H., R.C. Wendt, and T.C. Daniel. 1984. Soil and water losses as affected by tillage and manure application. Soil Sci. Soc. Am. J. 48:896–900.

Munkholm, L.J., P. Schjønning, and K.J. Rasmussen. 2001. Non-inversion tillage effects on mechanical properties of a humid sandy loam. Soil Tillage Res. 62:1–14.

NASS. 2002. 2002 Census of Agriculture. Maps and cartographic resources. Agricultural atlas of the united states: Map index. Available at http://www.nass.usda.gov/research/atlas02/ (accessed May 2008, verified 1 Dec. 2009). NASS, Washington, DC.

New York Times. 1901. Rice, silk, indigo. Available at http://query.nytimes.com/mem/archive-free/pdf?_r=1&res=9C0CEEDD1F38E733A25751C1A9639C946097D6CF&oref=slogin (verified 1 Dec. 2009).

Nyakatawa, E.Z., K.C. Reddy, and G.F. Brown. 2001. Residual effect of poultry litter applied to cotton in conservation tillage systems on succeeding rye and corn. Field Crops Res. 71:159–171.

Pittman, C. 2007. Desal plant: Trick or treat, The St. Petersburg Times. 21 Aug. 2007.

Porter, P.M., and A. Khalilian. 1995. Wheat response to row spacing in relay intercropping systems. Agron. J. 87:999–1003.

Raczkowski, C.W., G.B. Reddy, M.R. Reyes, G.A. Gayle, W.J. Busscher, P.J. Bauer, and B. Brock. 2002. No-tillage performance on a Piedmont soil. p. 273–276. *In* E. van Santen (ed.) Making conservation tillage conventional: Building a future on 25 years of research. Proc. 25th Annual Southern Conservation Tillage Conf. for Sustainable Agriculture, Auburn AL. 24–26 June 2002.

Radford, B.J., B.J. Bridge, R.J. Davis, D. McGarry, U.P. Pillai, J.F. Rickman, P.A. Walsh, and D.F. Yule. 2000. Changes in the properties of a Vertisol and responses of wheat after compaction with harvester traffic. Soil Tillage Res. 54:155–170.

Raper, R.L., D.W. Reeves, C.H. Burmester, and E.B. Schwab. 2000. Tillage depth, tillage timing, and cover crop effects on cotton yield, soil strength, and tillage energy requirements. Appl. Eng. Agric. 16:379–385.

Raper, R.L., D.W. Reeves, J.N. Shaw, E. vanSanten, and P.L. Mask. 2005. Using site-specific subsoiling to minimize draft and optimize corn yields. Trans. ASAE 48:2047–2052.

Raper, R.L., D.W. Reeves, J.N. Shaw, E. vanSanten, and P.L. Mask. 2007. Site-specific subsoiling benefits for cotton production in Coastal Plains soils. Soil Tillage Res. 96:174–181.

Reeves, D.W. 1994. Cover crops and rotations. p. 125–172. *In* J.L. Hatfield and B.A. Stewart (ed.) Crops residue management. Adv. Soil Sci. Lewis Publ. Boca Raton, FL.

Reeves, D.W. 1997. The role of soil organic matter in maintaining soil quality in continuous cropping systems. Soil Tillage Res. 43:131–167.

Rowles, K., D. Wilson, and M. Masters. 2008. Georgia Water Planning and Policy Center Agricultural water policy outreach. Paper 2008-002. Georgia Water and Planning Policy Center, Albany, GA.

Sadler, E.J., and C.R. Camp. 1986. Crop water use data available from the southeastern USA. Trans. ASAE 29:1070–1079.

SERCC. 2007. Number of days with precipitation equal to or above 0.01 inches for selected cities in the Southeast. Available at http://www.sercc.com/climateinfo/historical/meanprecip.

html (verified 1 Dec. 2009). Southeastern Regional Climate Center, Univ. of North Carolina, Chapel Hill.

Schwab, E.B., D.W. Reeves, C.H. Burmester, and R.L. Raper. 2002. Conservation tillage systems for cotton in the Tennessee Valley. Soil Sci. Soc. Am. J. 66:569–577.

Sheridan, J.M., W.G. Knisel, T.K. Woody, and L.E. Asmussen. 1979. Seasonal variation in rainfall and rainfall-deficit periods in the Southern Coastal Plain and Flatwoods Regions of Georgia. Georgia Agric. Exp. Stn. Res. Bull. 243.

Shukla, M.K., R. Lal, and M. Ebinger. 2003. Tillage effects on physical and hydrological properties of a typic argiaquoll in central Ohio. Soil Sci. 168:802–811.

Siri-Prieto, G., D.W. Reeves, and R.L. Raper. 2007a. Tillage systems for a cotton-peanut rotation with winter-annual grazing: Impacts on soil carbon, nitrogen and physical properties. Soil Tillage Res. 96:260–268.

Siri-Prieto, G., D.W. Reeves, and R.L. Raper. 2007b. Tillage requirements for integrating winter-annual grazing in cotton production: Plant water status and productivity. Soil Sci. Soc. Am. J. 71:197–205.

Soil Survey Staff. 1999. Soil taxonomy, A basic system of soil classification for making and interpreting soil surveys. 2nd ed. USDA-NRCS. USDA Agric. Handb. 436. U.S. Gov. Print. Office, Washington, DC.

Sojka, R.E., Lentz, R.D. 1997. Reducing furrow irrigation erosion with polyacrylamide (PAM). J. Prod. Agric. 10:1–2, 47–52.

Sumner, M.E. 1993. Gypsum and acid soils: The world scene. Adv. Agron. 51:1–32.

Terra, J.A., J.N. Shaw, D.W. Reeves, R.L. Raper, E. van Santen, E.B. Schwab, and P.L. Mask. 2006. Soil management and landscape variability affects field-scale cotton productivity. Soil Sci. Soc. Am. J. 70:98–107.

Threadgill, E.D. 1982. Residual tillage effects as determined by cone index. Trans. ASAE 25:859–863.

Tolstikh, L.I., N.I. Akimov, I.A. Golubeva, and I.A. Shvetsov. 1992. Degradation and stabilization of polyacrylamide in polymer flooding conditions. Int. J. Polymeric Mater. 17:177–193.

Toma, M., M.E. Sumner, G. Weeks, and M. Saigusa. 1999. Long-term effects of gypsum on crop yield and subsoil chemical properties. Soil Sci. Soc. Am. J. 39:891–895.

Trimble, S.W. 1974. Man-induced soil erosion on the Southern Piedmont: 1700–1970. Soil Conservation Society of America, Ankeny, IA.

USDA-NRCS. 2009. Biography of Hugh Hammond Bennett. Available at http://www.nrcs.usda.gov/ABOUT/history/bennett.html (verified 30 Nov. 2009).

USGS. 1984. National water summary 1983—Hydrologic events and issues. USGS Water-Supply Paper 2250 (updated in 1995). USGS, Washington, DC.

USGS. 2008. Ground water atlas of the United States, Alabama, Florida, Georgia, South Carolina, HA 730-G, Floridan Aquifer System. Available at http://pubs.usgs.gov/ha/ha730/ch_g/G-text6.html (accessed Oct. 2008, verified 30 Nov. 2009).

USGS. 2009. Water science for schools. Available at http://ga.water.usgs.gov/edu/ (verified 30 Nov. 2009).

Weeks, L.E., and W.G. Colter. 1952. Effect of synthetic soil conditioners on erosion control. Soil Sci. 73:473–484.

West, L.T., W.P. Miller, G.W. Langdale, R.R. Bruce, J.M. Laflen, and A.W. Thomas. 1991. Cropping system effects on interrill soil loss in the Georgia Piedmont. Soil Sci. Soc. Am. J. 55:460–466.

Williams, J.R., R.G. Nelson, and M.L. Langemeier. 2005. The impact of higher energy prices on Great Plains crop farm expenditures. Great Plains Res. 15:135–152.

WRLB News. 2007. Columbus may join Georgia, Alabama, Florida water war. 19 June 2007.

Zhang, X.C., and W.P. Miller. 1996. Physical and chemical crusting processes affecting runoff and erosion in furrows. Soil Sci. Soc. Am. J. 60:860–865.

8

Soil and Water Conservation in the Mid-South United States: Lessons Learned and a Look to the Future

Martin A. Locke
USDA-ARS, Water Quality and Ecology Research Unit, National Sedimentation Laboratory, Oxford, MS

Donald D. Tyler
University of Tennessee, Biosystems Engineering and Soil Science, West Tennessee Agricultural Experiment Station, Jackson, TN

Lewis A. Gaston
Department of Agronomy, Louisiana State University Agricultural Center, Baton Rouge, LA

The culture and politics of the Mid-South region of the United States at the beginning of the 20th century were largely driven by a powerful agrarian sector. Over the last one hundred years, major social, economic, technological, and demographic changes have reshaped the agricultural landscape of the Mid-South and its regional and national influence. Although other economic sectors in the Mid-South have gained importance, agriculture, in many ways, is still the forefront, and urban centers within this region are hubs for agricultural commerce.

The Mid-South region as defined here includes Arkansas, Louisiana, Mississippi, southeastern Missouri (Mississippi alluvial plain known as the Bootheel), western Tennessee (area west of the Highland Rim), and eastern Texas (area roughly east of Austin) (Fig. 8–1). What commonalities do these states share that provide a distinct and coherent theme for discussion? The label "Deep South" might loosely apply, although this term generally casts a wider net. Certainly, these states, or portions thereof, possess a culture and history that can be described as "southern." All the states have the Mississippi River as a border, with the exception of Texas, which can claim to be part of the vast drainage system of the lower Mississippi River because of the Red River Valley in the eastern part of the state. The convenience of geographic proximity is the simplest rationale for linking these states together within the Mid-South region. They are all located in the southern, central area of the continental United States.

The evolution of soil conservation awareness and management in the last century is interwoven with social, technological, and political changes. For example, consider the impacts of government programs on implementation of conservation management, the adoption of sustainable practices enhanced by the

Soil and Water Conservation Advances in the United States. SSSA Special Publication 60.
T.M. Zobeck and W.F. Schillinger, editors. © 2010. SSSA, 677 S. Segoe Rd., Madison, WI 53711, USA.

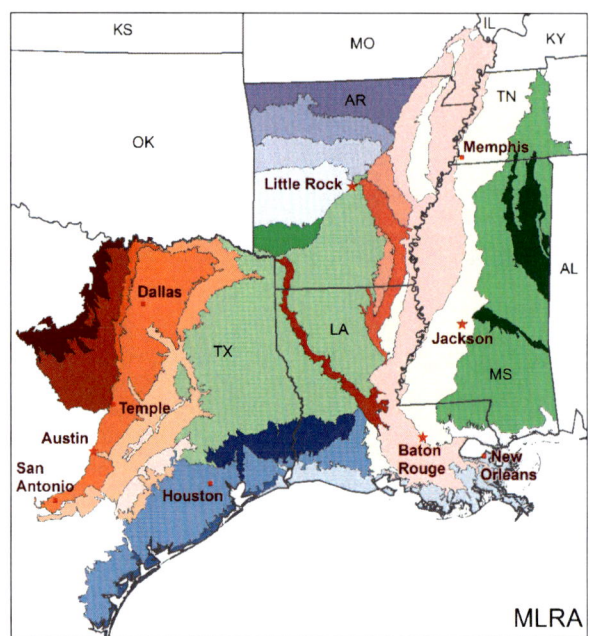

Fig. 8–1. Major Land Resource Areas (MLRA) in the Mid-South region of the United States (USDA-NRCS, 2006).

knowledge from county extension agents, the adoption of tractors rather than mules, and, in stark contrast, the effects of widespread use of transgenic crops on conservation tillage. These are but a few examples of the progress made in preserving and improving soil fertility and productivity. In this chapter we provide an account of the last one hundred years of conservation agriculture in the Mid-South of the United States, with the goal that lessons learned are applied to ensure continued sustainability of soil as a vital natural resource.

Physiography and Demographics of the Mid-South

The Mid-South area included in this chapter is bounded on the east by the Tennessee River and the eastern border of Mississippi (Fig. 8–1). The northern edge includes the northern border of Arkansas and six counties in the southeast corner of Missouri, while the southern edge is the Gulf Coast of Mexico. The western boundary of the Mid-South region stretches to the edge of the great prairie region of Central Texas. Total area for the Mid-South is 709,104 km^2, or about 7.5% of the area in the United States (Table 8–1). The topography varies from level to nearly level in the coastal plain and delta plains to the steep hills of northern Arkansas. The elevation of the Mid-South region ranges from 2.44 m below sea level in New Orleans to 839 m above sea level at Mount Magazine in Arkansas.

The climate across the Mid-South can be described as warm and humid, with more temperate regimes in areas to the north and subtropical conditions nearer the Gulf Coast. Climatic variation within the Mid-South generally trends from wetter to drier as one moves from the east to the west or south to north, while temperatures increase from north to south. Mean annual temperature ranges from 14.4 to 16.6°C in the northern portion of the Mid-South to 20.0 to 24.4°C in the southern portion (USDA-NRCS, 2006). Mean annual precipitation for the Mid-South trends from 762 to 1143 mm moving northwest, and 1524 to 2286 mm moving southeast.

The population of the Mid-South in 2000 was 28,935,382, almost a fourfold increase from the 1900 census (U.S. Census Bureau, 1900, 2000). The population as a percentage of the total U.S. population has remained at approximately 10% from 1900 to the present (Table 8–1). The population increase for the Mid-South is in large part due to the dramatic growth of urban centers, particularly in Texas. The population of the Mid-South near the beginning of the 20th century was predominantly rural (<50% of the population living in metropolitan areas), but by 2000, this was

Table 8–1. Total area and population of Mid-South states. Source: U.S. Census Bureau, 1900, 2000.

State	Total area	1900 Population	2000 Population	2006 est. Population
	km^2			
Arkansas	134,856	1,311,564	2,673,400	2,810,872
Louisiana	112,825	1,381,625	4,468,976	4,287,768
Mississippi	121,489	1,551,270	2,844,658	2,910,540
Southeast Missouri†	8,866	94,699	156,516	154,346
West Tennessee‡	28,252	602,055	1,499,802	1,526,816
East Texas§	302,816	2,752,535	17,292,030	19,608,818

† Six counties in Southeast Missouri.
‡ 21 counties in West Tennessee.
§ 133 counties in East Texas.

only true of Arkansas and Mississippi (Hobbs and Stoops, 2002). Similar to 1900, major urban centers at present are Little Rock, AR; New Orleans, LA; Jackson, MS; Memphis, TN; Houston, TX; Dallas-Fort Worth, TX; and Austin, TX. Comparing the figures from the 1900 and 2000 census, population density (persons per square kilometer of total area) increased in the Mid-South from 12 to 38, reflecting the growth of metropolitan areas. Increased urbanization is reflected in how the land is used. The number of farms has decreased in the last century (Fig. 8–2), while the farm sizes have increased (Fig. 8–3) (U.S. Census Bureau, 1900, 2000).

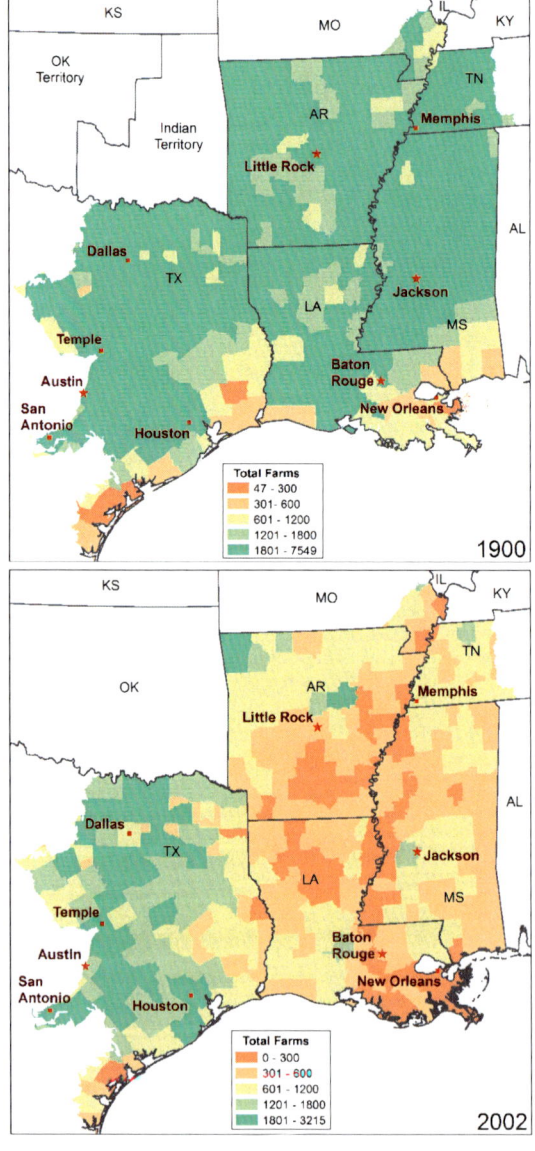

Fig. 8–2. Total number of farms in the Mid-South region of the United States, 1900 and 2002 (Minnesota Population Center, 2004; U.S. Census Bureau, 1900, 2002; University of Virginia, Geospatial and Statistical Data Center, 2004).

Geology and Topography

The Mississippi Embayment located near the center of the continental United States is a trough formed when the continent began to divide, but failed (Fenneman, 1938). The resulting weakened crustal plate down-warped, allowing seas to form and subside in several cycles throughout geological time. The Mississippi Embayment gradually filled with deposition of marine sediment, emerged from the sea, and now provides a channel for the Mississippi River. West Tennessee, the Missouri Bootheel, most of Mississippi, and eastern Arkansas are within the Mississippi Embayment.

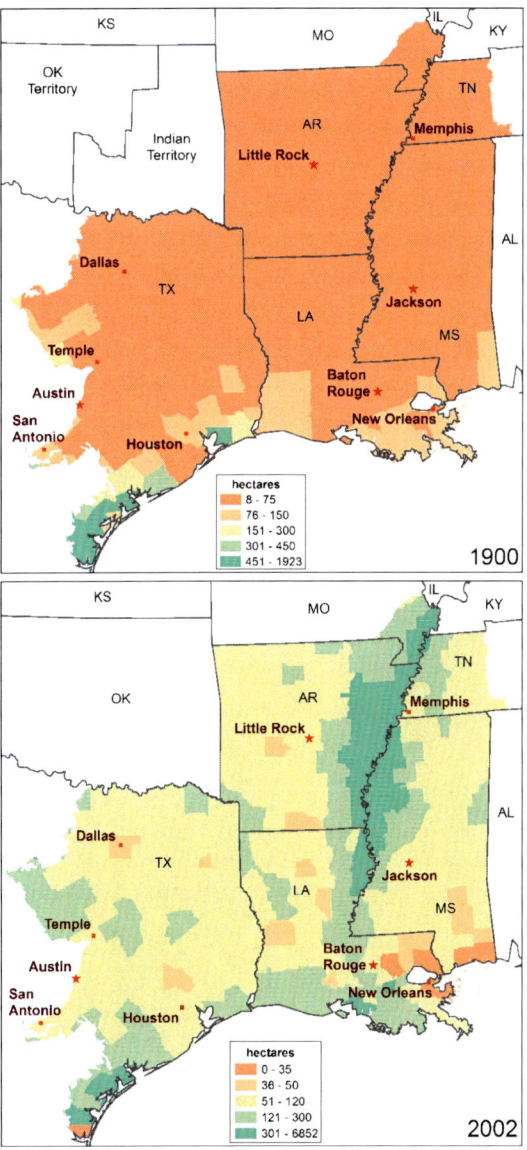

Fig. 8–3. Average farm size in the Mid-South region of the United States, 1900 and 2002. (Minnesota Population Center, 2004; U.S. Census Bureau, 1900, 2002; University of Virginia, Geospatial and Statistical Data Center, 2004).

At the center of the Mid-South region, meanders of the Mississippi River and tributaries shaped the relatively flat topography of the "Delta" regions in northeast Arkansas, Louisiana, Mississippi, and Missouri, overlaying the marine sediments with alluvial sediments. To the south and west, marine sediment deposition formed southwestern Arkansas, Louisiana, most of Mississippi, West Tennessee, and East Texas. The highlands of northwest Arkansas, consisting of the Ouachita Mountains and Boston Mountains of the Ozark Plateau, are part of the Piedmont to the east, but are separated from the Piedmont by the Mississippi Embayment. On the western edge of the Mid-South, the topography of the Blacklands of Texas is characterized by a nearly level to gently sloping, dissected plain.

Soil and Land Resource Areas

In the early 20th century, scientists were in the process of defining and establishing the discipline of soil science; soil surveys were conducted to classify and group soils according to prescribed criteria. In a treatise on southern soils, Bennett (1921) characterized soils in the Mid-South as Mississippi Bluffs and Silt Loam uplands, Coastal Plain, Stream Bottoms and Second Bottoms, Appalachian Mountains and Plateaus, and Limestone Valleys and Uplands. Reflecting the region's geology, Jenny (1941) described parent materials of soils in the (i) Mississippi Embayment as river alluvium and loess from unconsolidated rocks, predominantly of Pleistocene origin; (ii) Arkansas uplands as limestones, sandstones, and shales from consolidated rocks; and (iii) Gulf Coastal Plain areas of Louisiana, Mississippi, and Texas as sands, clays, and limestones from unconsolidated rocks of variegated origin. Later, soil classifications grouped the Mid-South subregions as Coastal Plain, Loess-covered Coastal Plain, Mississippi Alluvial Plain, and Piedmont (Southern Regional Soil Research Committee, 1959). According to the U.S. Comprehensive Soil Classification System, the soils of the Mid-South include 7 of the 12 taxonomic soil orders, excluding Andisols, Aridisols, Gelisols, Oxisols, and Spodosols (Soil Survey Staff, 1999) (Fig. 8–4). Another useful and more recent geographic classification of areas is that of land resource regions and areas, i.e., a physiographic area that is similar in climate, topography, water resources, land use, and pattern of soils (USDA-NRCS, 2006). This will be the primary basis used here for describing the physiography and land use in the Mid-South, but other sources are used as well (Carter, 1931; Fraps and Fudge, 1937; Godfrey et al., 1968; Krusekopf, 1962; Logan, 1916; Moore, 1916; Nelson et al., 1923; Springer and Elder, 1980; Vanderford, 1975). The Mid-South is comprised of 5 of the 20 land resource regions of the continental United States: East and Central Farming and Forest Region; Mississippi Delta Cotton and Feed Grains Region; South Atlantic and Gulf Slope Cash Crops, Forest, and Livestock Region; Atlantic and Gulf Coast Lowland Forest and Crop Region; and Southwestern Prairies Cotton and Forage Region (Fig. 8–1). Each of these five land resource regions is further subdivided into major land resource areas (MLRAs).

Arkansas is the only Mid-South state in the East and Central Farming and Forest Region, and four MLRAs in Arkansas are applicable to this region: Boston Mountains, Ozark Highlands, Arkansas Valley and Ridges, and Ouachita Mountains (USDA-NRCS, 2006). The Boston Mountains and Ozark Highland areas in northwestern Arkansas are characterized by forested rolling hills and valleys and steep and rugged mountains. Soils in this area were formed under deciduous forest vegetation from weathered residuals of underlying sedimentary rock.

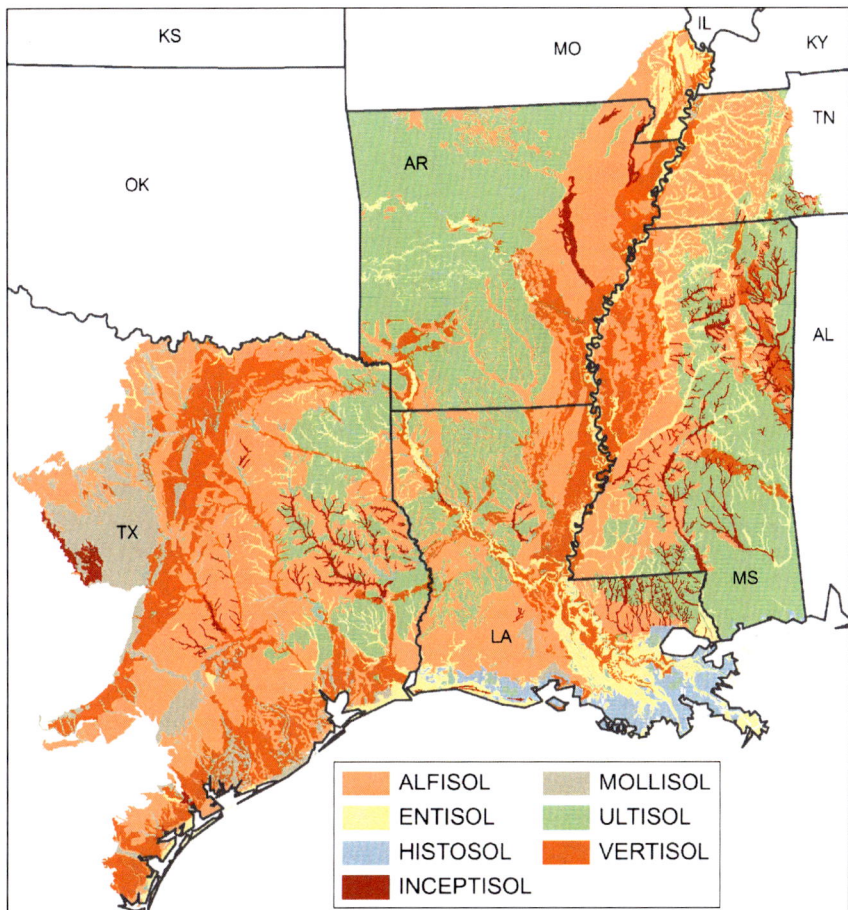

Fig. 8–4. Distribution of major soil orders in the Mid-South region of the United States (USDA-NRCS Soil Survey Staff, 2010; USDA-NRCS, 2010).

The soils are low in fertility, and many have a relatively high chert content that renders them difficult to till, but resistant to erosion. Soils are primarily Alfisols and Ultisols, and the soil series include Captina, Clarksville, and Mountainburg. (See Table 8–2 for descriptions of the soil series mentioned in the chapter.) The Arkansas Valley and Ridges area is aptly described by its name and consists primarily of grassland (48%) and forest (34%). Soils are primarily Ultisols, such as Linker and Nella, with some Inceptisols in river valleys. The Ouachita Mountains occupy the area of north-central to western Arkansas, and this subregion is characterized by rugged terrain, which is more than 60% forested. Soils were developed from sandstones and shales and are medium textured; predominant soil orders are Ultisols and Inceptisols (e.g., Zafra and Bismarck). Relatively little cropping occurs in the aforementioned upland and highland MLRAs (1–6% of the land area), and major management concerns are erosion control in crop and forest production areas and sustainability or improvement of soil productivity.

Table 8–2. Soil series and descriptions for some of the soils of the region.

Series	Description
Ariel	coarse-silty, mixed, active, thermic fluventic Dystrudepts
Austin	fine-silty, carbonatic, thermic udorthentic Haplustolls
Bastrop	fine-loamy, mixed, active, thermic udic Paleustalfs
Billyhaw	very-fine, smectitic, thermic typic Hapluderts
Bismarck	loamy-skeletal, mixed, semiactive, thermic, shallow typic Dystrudepts
Boswell	fine, mixed, active, thermic vertic Paleudalfs
Bowie	fine-loamy, siliceous, semiactive, thermic plinthic Paleudults
Branyon	fine, smectitic, thermic udic Haplusterts
Brenham	fine-silty, carbonatic, thermic udic Calciustolls
Bruno	sandy, mixed, thermic typic Udifluvents
Bunyan	fine-loamy, mixed, active, nonacid, thermic typic Ustifluvents
Burleson	fine, smectitic, thermic udic Haplusterts
Cadeville	fine, mixed, active, thermic albaquic Hapludalfs
Calhoun	fine-silty, mixed, active, thermic typic Glossaqualfs
Captina	fine-silty, siliceous, active, mesic typic Fragiudults
Clarksville	loamy-skeletal, siliceous, semiactive, mesic typic Paleudults
Coarsewood	coarse-silty, mixed, superactive, calcareous, thermic udic Ustifluvents
Collins	coarse-silty, mixed, active, acid, thermic aquic Udifluvents
Coushatta	fine-silty, mixed, superactive, thermic fluventic Eutrudepts
Crawford	fine, smectitic, thermic leptic udic Haplusterts
Doss	loamy, carbonatic, thermic, shallow typic Calciustolls
Dowling	very-fine, smectitic, nonacid, thermic vertic Endoaquepts
Dundee	fine-silty, mixed, active, thermic typic Endoaqualfs
Eastwood	fine, smectitic, thermic chromic vertic Hapludalfs
Eddy	loamy-skeletal, carbonatic, thermic, shallow typic Ustorthents
Eufaula	siliceous, thermic psammentic Paleustalfs
Forestdale	fine, smectitic, thermic typic Endoaqualfs
Gillsburg	coarse-silty, mixed, active, acid, thermic aeric Fluvaquents
Grenada	fine-silty, mixed, active, thermic oxyaquic Fraglossudalfs
Houston	very-fine, smectitic, thermic oxyaquic Hapluderts
Houston Black	fine, smectitic, thermic udic Haplusterts
Iuka	coarse-loamy, siliceous, active, acid, thermic aquic Udifluvents
Kirvin	fine, mixed, semiactive, thermic typic Hapludults
Leeper	fine, smectitic, nonacid, thermic vertic Epiaquepts
Lewisville	fine-silty, mixed, active, thermic udic Calciustolls
Linker	fine-loamy, siliceous, semiactive, thermic typic Hapludults
Mantachie	fine-loamy, siliceous, active, acid, thermic fluventic Endoaquepts
Marietta	fine-loamy, siliceous, active, thermic fluvaquentic Eutrudepts
Memphis	fine-silty, mixed, active, thermic typic Hapludalfs
Mountainburg	loamy-skeletal, siliceous, subactive, thermic lithic Hapludults
Natchez	coarse-silty, mixed, superactive, thermic typic Eutrudepts
Nella	fine-loamy, siliceous, semiactive, thermic typic Paleudults
Oktibbeha	very-fine, smectitic, thermic chromic Dystruderts
Portland	very-fine, mixed, superactive, nonacid, thermic vertic Epiaquepts
Providence	fine-silty, mixed, active, thermic oxyaquic Fragiudalfs
Ruston	fine-loamy, siliceous, semiactive, thermic typic Paleudults
Sharkey	very-fine, smectitic, thermic chromic Epiaquerts
Ships	very-fine, mixed, active, thermic chromic Hapluderts
Shubuta	fine, mixed, semiactive, thermic typic Paleudults
Stephen	clayey, mixed, active, thermic, shallow udorthentic Haplustolls
Vaiden	very-fine, smectitic, thermic aquic Dystruderts
Weswood	fine-silty, mixed, superactive, thermic udifluventic Haplustepts
Whitesboro	fine-loamy, mixed, superactive, thermic cumulic Haplustolls
Wrightsville	fine, mixed, active, thermic typic Glossaqualfs
Zafra	loamy-skeletal, siliceous, semiactive, thermic typic Hapludults

The Mississippi Delta Cotton and Feed Grains Region consists of four MLRAs, and is almost entirely within the confines of the Mid-South, which includes portions of Arkansas, Louisiana, Mississippi, Southeast Missouri, and western Tennessee (USDA-NRCS, 2006). The Southern Mississippi River Alluvium is the largest of these MLRAs, and, as the name implies, is comprised of a narrow floodplain on either side of the Mississippi River from the Gulf of Mexico in Louisiana through Arkansas, Mississippi, and West Tennessee to southeast Missouri. Likewise, the Arkansas River Alluvium and the Red River Alluvium areas located in Arkansas and Louisiana derived from the Arkansas River and Red River, respectively. The generally fertile soils in these three MLRAs developed from alluvium and are very deep and highly variable, and the topography is nearly level to gently undulating (Krusekopf, 1962; Logan, 1916; Vanderford, 1975). Predominant soil orders in these alluvial soils are Alfisols (Dundee, Forestdale), Entisols (Bruno), Inceptisols (Coushatta, Dowling, Portland), and Vertisols (Sharkey). Although these alluvial plains were once covered with hardwood forests and cypress swamps, much of the land was cleared and drained in the early part of the 20th century. Cropland in the MLRAs ranges from 37% in the Red River Alluvium to 70% of the area in the alluvial plains of the Arkansas and Mississippi rivers. The Southern Mississippi Terraces is the fourth MLRA in the Mississippi Delta Cotton and Feed Grains Region and is contained within Arkansas and Louisiana. Soils in this MLRA are mostly Alfisols (e.g., Forestdale, Grenada), and the topography varies from level to gently sloping and steep along terrace escarpments. Cropland (42%) and forest (47%) are the primary uses of the land. The generally fertile loess soils have significant silt contents and are highly erodible in their native level to steep topography.

The South Atlantic and Gulf Slope Cash Crops, Forest, and Livestock Region has five MLRAs and includes parts of Arkansas, Louisiana, Mississippi, West Tennessee, and East Texas (USDA-NRCS, 2006). The Southern Coastal Plain is the largest MLRA in the United States and claims parts of Louisiana, Mississippi, and West Tennessee. The topography is variable and ranges from nearly level and undulating valleys to steep uplands. Soils are derived from marine sediment, consist of sands, clays, shale, and some gravel, and are weathered and low in fertility (Carter, 1931; Logan, 1916; Moore, 1916). The predominant soil orders in this MLRA are Alfisols (Cadeville), Entisols (Iuka), Inceptisols (Mantachie), and Ultisols (Ruston, Shubuta) (Springer and Elder, 1980; USDA-NRCS, 2006; Vanderford, 1975). Most of the land is in forest (64%), with only 17% in cropland. The Western Coastal Plain is almost entirely (99%) contained within areas of Arkansas, Louisiana, and east Texas (known as the East Texas Timberlands), and consists of level to steep uplands, with some flood plains and terraces along streams. Primary soil orders are Alfisols (Eastwood, Wrightsville) and Ultisols (Bowie, Ruston). This MLRA is largely in forest (69%) and grassland (18%), with only 2% in cropland. About 90% of the land area in the Southern Mississippi Valley Loess MLRA is in the Mid-South (Arkansas, Louisiana, Mississippi, southeast Missouri, and West Tennessee). Soils in this area are deep and mantled with loess of varying thickness underlain by unconsolidated gravel, sand, silt, and clay (Carter, 1931). Major soil orders are Alfisols (Calhoun, Memphis), Entisols (Collins, Gillsburg), Inceptisols (Ariel, Natchez), and Ultisols (Providence) (Springer and Elder, 1980; USDA-NRCS, 2006; Vanderford, 1975). The topography is variable, ranging from nearly level on flood plains to sloping to steep on ridge tops and side slopes. Land use is almost equal in cropland (36%) and forest (40%), with 13% in grassland. The Mid-South portion of the Alabama and Mississippi Blackland Prairie MLRA is in Mississippi. Important soil orders are Inceptisols (Leeper, Marietta) and Vertisols (Houston, Oktibbeha); the terrain ranges from nearly level to hilly (Logan, 1916; Vanderford, 1975). Forest (48%) and grassland (29%) are the major uses of land, with 16% of the area being used as cropland. Arkansas is the only Mid-South state in the Cretaceous Western Coastal Plain MLRA. The topography is nearly level flood plains and uplands to moderately sloping uplands. The soils are moderately deep, with the major soil orders being Alfisols (Boswell, Vaiden) and Inceptisols (Leeper). Forest (63%) and grassland (25%) are primary uses of land, with only 5% in cropland.

The Atlantic and Gulf Coast Lowland Forest and Crop Region includes portions of the coastal states of Louisiana, Mississippi, and Texas (USDA-NRCS, 2006). The Mid-South segment of this region is comprised of five MLRAs: Gulf Coast Prairie, Gulf Coast Saline Prairie, Gulf Coast Marsh, Eastern Gulf Coast Flatwoods, and Western Gulf Coast Flatwoods. This region is characterized by low-lying, flat to gently sloping topography. The soils were developed from marine sediment on coastal lowlands, coastal plains, drowned estuaries, tidal marshes, and beaches (Carter, 1931; Logan, 1916). Dominant soil orders are Alfisols, Entisols, and Ultisols, and this is the only part of the Mid-South where Histosols and Spodosols have developed. The Gulf Coast Prairie (32% cropland, 40% grassland, 5% forest) and Gulf Coast Marsh (16% cropland, 6% grassland, and 8% forest) are the only MLRAs with any significant cropland. Salinity inhibits crop production in the Gulf Coast Saline Prairie, and most land use is for grassland (34%). The Eastern and Western Gulf Coast Flatwoods MLRAs are primarily in forest (67–74%).

The portion of the Southwestern Prairies Cotton and Forage Region that includes the Mid-South is entirely in Texas (USDA-NRCS, 2006). The seven MLRAs from this region that are in Texas are West Cross Timbers, East Cross Timbers, Grand Prairie, Texas Blackland Prairie (Northern and Southern Parts), and Texas Claypan Area (Northern and Southern Parts). Grassland (68%) used for pasture and rangeland is the primary use of land in the West Cross Timbers area of north central Texas. Topography ranges from nearly level to undulating, and soils are predominantly Alfisols (Chaney, Nimrod) and Entisols (Pulexas). The East Cross Timbers area in north-central Texas includes Fort Worth, and 25% of the area is urban. The largest use of land is grassland (51%) in this area of gently sloping to rolling landscape. Major soil orders are Alfisols (Bastrop, Eufaula), Entisols (Bunyan), and Mollisols (Whitesboro). The Grand Prairie area in north-central Texas has a gently rolling to hilly landscape. The deep soils in this area are underlain by limestone and shales; the dominant soil orders are Mollisols (Doss, Lewisville) and Vertisols (Branyon, Crawford). A majority of the area is in grassland (75%). The northern part of the Texas Blackland Prairie in central Texas consists of nearly level to gently sloping dissected plains and includes several major urban areas. Dominant soil orders are Entisols (Eddy), Mollisols (Austin, Stephen), and Vertisols (Burleson, Houston Black); the soil is moderately to very deep, and is underlain by chalk, claystone, marl, and shale (Carter, 1931). Land use in this MLRA is a mixture of cropland (29%) and grassland (49%). The southern part of the Texas Blackland Prairie in east-central Texas has similar gently sloping topography underlain by calcareous clays, sandstones, and marls. The deep to very deep soils include Entisols (Coarsewood), Inceptisols (Weswood), Mollisols (Brenham), and Vertisols (Ships). Most of the area is in grassland (80%), with only 9% used for cropland. The southern part of the Texas Claypan Area in south-central Texas consists of level to gently sloping plains dissected by river valleys. Major soil orders are Alfisols, Entisols, Mollisols, and Vertisols. Soils are deep to very deep and range from excessively drained to somewhat poorly drained. Grassland as pasture or livestock grazing dominates the landscape (80%), with a minor portion of the area developed as cropland (7%). The northern part of the Texas Claypan Area in northeastern Texas is characterized by nearly level to gently sloping, dissected plains. Soil orders of importance are Alfisols (Wrightsville), Ultisols (Kirvin, Ruston), and Vertisols (Billyhaw). Land use is mixed, with 54% grassland, 27% forest, and 8% cropland.

Historical Perspectives of Soil Conservation in the Mid-South: 1900–1980

Agriculture, Society, and Soil Erosion in the Mid-South

Since the settlement of the United States, there have been numerous mentions of soil erosion and the potential problems that resulted from erosion (McDonald, 1941). Predominant farming practices during the 19th century in the United States involved the "pioneering ax and plow," which meant removing trees, clearing stumps, and intensive tillage (Fig. 8–5). Very severe erosion resulted from this activity (Bennett and Lowdermilk, 1938; Fite, 1984; Maddox, 1915). In some cases, land was abandoned after moderate to severe erosion. The land continued to erode as farmers moved to adjacent fields. It was reported that the practice in the Mid-South became particularly important after the Civil War. In some areas of Tennessee and Mississippi, these abandoned areas were not allowed to naturally revegetate, but instead were kept clean by burning, presumably to make it easier to reuse the abandoned gullied land.

The aftermath of the Civil War of the United States profoundly impacted the economy and agriculture of the Mid-South, and those effects were still evident at the beginning of the 20th century. During the period following the Civil War, state agricultural experiment stations were established by the Hatch Act of 1887, and by the early 1900s were providing local research recommendations to farmers.

The era beginning in the early 20th century was known as the Progressive Era; an active period for agriculture in the largely rural Mid-South region. The Smith Lever Act of 1914 provided federal support for county extension agents. Agricultural organizations such as the Farmers Union in Arkansas, Louisiana, Mississippi, and Texas, and respective state Farm Bureaus emerged as spheres of influence. Drainage of the low-lying delta areas of Mississippi, Arkansas, Louisiana, and Missouri completely transformed the agricultural landscape, and the formation of drainage districts provided local control over the use of water. A variety of agricultural commodities were tried in new areas; for example, rice (*Oryza sativa* L.) began to emerge as an important commodity crop in Arkansas.

During the first two decades of the 20th century, the agricultural industry faced setbacks. World War I depleted the agricultural work force. Soil resources in the Mid-South were exhausted from overuse and poor management. Some farmland reverted to forests. Boll weevil [*Anthonomus grandis* (Boheman)] was a scourge to the cotton (*Gossypium hirsutum* L.) industry. Water-induced erosion following

Fig. 8–5. Early mechanical tillage methods and equipment, Mississippi Delta. Source: Delta Branch Experiment Station, Stoneville, MS.

tillage was ruining soils, and proponents of conservation were warning that common practices, such as clear cutting, tilling, and cropping hilly land, had ruinous impacts in terms of nutrient depletion and erosion (Bennett, 1921; Maddox, 1915).

While early southern agricultural leaders such as Nicholas Sorsby warned of the destructive impacts of erosion (McDonald, 1941), the widespread recognition of soil erosion as a societal problem had been almost completely ignored by many until the early 1900s. There was little mention of soil erosion in the Yearbooks of Agriculture from 1894 to 1913. This may have been due, in part, to the arrangement of the books themselves, in that they contain individual chapters dealing with very specific subjects of interest during the time. The 1913 Yearbook has an article dealing with the economic wastes that occurred from soil erosion (Davis, 1913), and another article, "Farms, Forest, and Erosion" (Dana, 1916) appeared in the Yearbook of Agriculture, 1916. Initial concerns about soil erosion in the early 1900s as a national problem came from the Bureau of Soils in the USDA. As a result of the county-based soil surveys that began in approximately 1900, more attention was directed toward soil erosion (Helms, 2009). Meanwhile, farmers of the Mid-South continued practices that were destructive to the land, and a coordinated national effort to address erosion was yet to come.

Although there were some technological improvements, including the use of pesticides against the boll weevil and the use of fertilizers to replenish soil resources (U.S. Census Bureau, 1930), agricultural decline in the Mid-South escalated during the 1920s. Many small farmers lost their lands, resulting in larger areas of farmland in fewer hands (Fig. 8-2, 8-3). Increasingly, tenants and sharecroppers operated a larger proportion of farms. Farms operated by tenants increased from 55% in 1910 to 65% in 1930 (U.S. Census Bureau, 1910, 1920, 1930). Although there was some diversification of agricultural commodities, cotton was still an important crop, and a fall in cotton prices devastated the economy throughout the Mid-South. High drainage taxes in the Delta areas were prohibitive, and high tariffs that benefitted northern industry hurt agriculture in the South. Highways and automobiles improved, varying transportation options, but the rural population began to decline. The Mississippi River flood of 1927 had a profoundly negative effect on the agricultural economies of the states bordering the river.

During this period, Hugh Hammond Bennett, a legendary observer of the soil erosion problem, noted that in some of the loess soils of the South, farming had been virtually abandoned due to severe gully erosion (Bennett, 1927). He drew national attention to the erosion problem with a publication about soil erosion in 1928 (Bennett and Chapline, 1928).

In one stark example of erosion in the Mid-South, Lentz et al. (1929) described the condition of a Mississippi farm near Oxford settled in the 1830s, relative to observations in the late 1920s. They noted the speed at which gullies formed using the observations in an area called Linder's Pasture. The area was reported in 1884 to be a level cotton field free of gullies. By 1929, the field had become a "maze of deep gullies and washes." One particular gully was approximately 18 m deep and was rapidly growing wider as the sides slumped, filling in the bottom. The soil materials in this area are loess, windblown-silty deposits, over lenses of sand, clay, and gravel that are rapidly removed with subsequent collapse of the overlying loess, increasing the rapidity of severe deep gully formation (Fig. 8-6). This same process was occurring in similar loess soils in western Tennessee, resembling the "badlands of the Dakotas" (Wells, 1933). Gullies 15 m deep or more were reported in 1933, and the surface form of this area was referred to as the "hills of erosion" (Wells, 1933).

Unfortunately, the 1930s brought the Depression Era, and the agricultural economy worsened. Population shifts occurred, and depletion of the rural pop-

Fig. 8–6. Gully formation on a cultivated loess hill slope in Western Tennessee. Photo credit Don Tyler, University of Tennessee, circa 1970s.

ulation continued. Many farmers abandoned eroded or drought-stricken lands, resulting in migrations westward. Cotton prices fell even further, and people lost their farms. Landowners lost their land for not paying taxes, and became tenants or sharecroppers.

Along with the rest of the nation, the Mid-South had its share of documented erosion during this time. In addition to the erosion problems reported for loess hill areas, less rolling surface forms in the Southeastern Uplands (Pearson and Ensminger, 1957) and Mississippi Delta Region (Grissom, 1957) also had serious erosion problems documented from the 1930s. In Tyler, TX, on gentle slopes with annual rainfall of 1016 mm, clearing and tillage increased runoff by a factor of 23 and soil loss by a factor of 239 for a 4-yr period as compared to the original soil with native vegetation (Utz et al., 1938). Annual soil losses were 63 Mg ha^{-1} on the cultivated areas compared to 0.2 Mg ha^{-1} in areas of dense soil surface cover (Bennett and Lowdermilk, 1938). Level areas of the Coastal Plain and Mississippi Valley generally had almost no soil erosion, but even in the flatter Delta regions of the Mid-South, soil movement in fields under cultivation was high during periods of flooding from December of 1931 to January of 1932, resulting in soil losses of 76 Mg ha^{-1} (Utz et al., 1938). Even now, a general distinction is sometimes made that soil is removed from flat areas but at slower rates, and that in some cases the soil lost in river bottom areas is replaced by sediment added during floods. This soil movement on and off the land can have tremendous impacts on water quality. The rolling areas of the Black Belt soils of Mississippi, and the rolling parts of the larger Black Belt of central Texas also experienced severe topsoil removal. In Rockwall County in Texas, 14% of the Houston clay was mapped as an eroded phase in 1931 (Bennett, 1931). The surface color in many cases was gray or white because the underlying chalk was exposed.

The interface of societal problems of the Great Depression and the acknowledgment of land degradation and poverty was noted by Hambridge (1938), providing an initial insight into the various consequences of the Depression and the role of government in regulating land use. Williams (1964) summarized these consequences and connected the beginning of the Great Depression in 1929, the severe droughts of the early 1930s, the Dust Bowl, and the pleas from Bennett (Bennett and Chapline, 1928) as major reasons for increased coordinated national emphasis on the soil erosion problem. The initial pleas of Bennett resulted in the Buchanan Amendment of the 1929 Agricultural Appropriations Bill, which provided funding for 10 erosion experiment stations across the United States, including two in the Mid-South located in Tyler and Temple, TX (Bennett, 1939; Harmel et al., 2007). In 1935, the Soil Conservation Act was passed, placing most of the erosion control activities in the Department of Agriculture (Helms, 2009). The 1936 Soil Conservation and Domestic Allotment Act provided funds to help reduce surpluses and conserve soil by shifting to alternative crops, such as legumes and grasses, which helped to improve soil quality.

During the late 1930s and into the period during and after World War II, profound technological advances in farming methods were beginning to transform U.S. agriculture into the breadbasket of the world. Mules gave way to tractors (Fig. 8–5). Men were drafted into the armed forces, leading to labor shortages. The mechanical cotton picker was introduced, but because of initial inefficiencies it did not gain popularity until the 1960s. Thus, laborers were still needed to pick cotton. Sharecroppers in the Mid-South were becoming less needed, but there was an increased demand for day laborers. With increasingly fewer tenant farmers (reduced from 65% in 1930 to 42% in 1950; U.S. Census Bureau, 1930, 1950), major population shifts continued in the Mid-South, particularly among African Americans, who moved to northern cities in huge numbers.

During the 1950s and 1960s, great strides in agricultural technology were made with new machinery and fertilizer formulations and the introduction of pesticides and crop varieties. Demand for agricultural commodities continued to increase. Farmers began to clear and use more and more marginal, erodible land. Heavier tillage equipment was used, further contributing to the destructive effects of erosion. During this time, the Soil Bank Program was established as part of the Agricultural Act of 1956, which had a conservation reserve component that funded the removal of marginal and erodible land from crop production, primarily to address farm surpluses. Such land was diverted toward conservation practices. As part of this program, millions of acres of trees were planted in the Mid-South. Although the Soil Bank Program was repealed by the Food and Agriculture Act of 1965, it was a model for future legislation establishing the current Conservation Reserve Program.

Environmental issues came to the forefront again during the 1970s. Grain exports from the United States increased, and commodity prices rose sharply. Twenty-four million hectares of new cropland were subsequently brought into cultivation from 1972 to 1982. Some of this land was much more erodible than that previously used for cropland. This was the situation that existed before the passage of the Food Security Act of 1985, one of the first attempts to connect commodity price support programs with soil conservation. Under this legislation, farmers who did not apply Soil Conservation Service (SCS, now known as NRCS) conservation plans would be out of compliance and would be denied some farm program benefits. The SCS was the agency responsible for writing the appropriate farm plans for necessary action on conservation practices. In much of the Mid-South these plans involved cropping systems that included no-tillage (NT) and maintenance of surface residue cover. The Food Security Act also created the Conservation Reserve Program (CRP), which provided incentives for removing highly erodible land out of production for a period up to 10 yr (Helms, 2009) (Fig. 8–7).

Fig. 8–7. (Left) Soybean cropland (summer 2001) that was converted to CRP in 2004. (Right) The same area under CRP in 2009. Beasley Lake Watershed, Sunflower County, Mississippi. Photo credits: (left) Martin Locke, (right) John Massey; USDA-ARS.

Early Efforts to Reduce Soil Erosion

Much of the literature on soil and water conservation from the first half of the 20th century can be found in state experiment station bulletins. Erosion experiment stations were established in 1929 as a result of the Buchanan Amendment to the Agricultural Appropriations Bill, and a nationally coordinated effort was begun to document the effects of agricultural practices on erosion and runoff. The erosion stations in Texas at Temple and Tyler represented some of the soils in the Mid-South. The Flood Control Act of 1944 provided funds for the USDA to work with the U.S. Corps of Engineers in implementing emergency runoff measures and for developing water resources in 11 watersheds throughout the United States, four of which are in the Mid-South (Little Tallahatchie, Middle Colorado River, Trinity River, and Yazoo River) (USDA-FS, 1988). The USDA-ARS National Sedimentation Laboratory was established at Oxford, MS in 1958 to address erosion and conservation of loess soils. For similar reasons, the University of Tennessee Research and Education Center at Milan was organized in 1962.

Terracing, Contouring, and Strip-Cropping

Terracing was one of the earliest practices used to attempt to control erosion in the Mid-South (Bennett and Lowdermilk, 1938; Ramser, 1929). Extension bulletins, such as that published in Mississippi by Carpenter and Gross (1918), provided stepwise instructions on the installation of terraces. In the mid-19th century, Sorsby published recommendations for hillside ditching and horizontal plowing based on his studies on farms in Alabama and Mississippi (McDonald, 1941). Bennett was a strong opponent of using terracing as a single erosion control practice, pointing out that terracing is an "important measure in the control of erosion," but that "used, improperly, it may do more harm than good" (Bennett and Lowdermilk, 1938). They continued this discussion with a farmer survey of the perceived effects of terracing alone, with most finding it unsatisfactory in many fields. Bennett and Lowdermilk (1938) promoted a combination of practices such as strip-cropping, crop rotation, winter cover crops, contour plowing, and removing land from cultivation to restore critically eroding areas. These practices were discussed elsewhere in the 1938 Yearbook of Agriculture (Enlow and Musgrave, 1938; Kell, 1938; Nichols and Chambers, 1938), including a discussion on the coordination of practices (Utz, 1938). Researchers at that time were beginning to look at systems of practices. For example, Garin and Gabbard (1941) conducted an analysis in the Trinity River Basin in Texas of a coordinated watershed approach using a combination of terraces, cultivated land retired to pasture or meadow, and strip-cropping to control erosion. In research at the erosion station in Temple, TX, Smith et al. (1954) showed that contouring and strip-cropping consistently reduced runoff and erosion, particularly on fields with higher slopes.

Limited Tillage, Herbicides, and No-Tillage

Little research on conservation tillage was conducted in the Mid-South in the early part of the 20th century. Problems with excessive tillage became more apparent, and evidence supporting the need to protect and reclaim the land slowly accumulated. In an article on gullied lands of western Tennessee, Maddox (1915) recognized the land as "one of our indispensible natural resources" and that, of the processes that will "injure the soil surface and reduce the productive area, erosion is perhaps the greatest." In a review of the literature on tillage,

Sewell (1919) noted conflicting information on the benefits of plowing and cultivation, other than for weed control. A single study from the Mid-South, located in Welborn, TX, was mentioned in the review; however, Lee in Georgia was cited in the review concluding that "tillage ... especially in the southern States, impaired the natural fertility of the soil" (Sewell, 1919).

With the observed negative erosive effects of tillage, some research focused on critically analyzing the benefits of tillage. Some called into question the use of dust mulch and frequent cultivation to prevent water runoff and concluded that cultivation is mainly important for weed control to prevent weed water use and crop competition. Early research at the Jackson Station in western Tennessee found no response to machine-powered mechanically cultivating weeds versus using a hoe to remove weeds (University of Tennessee, 1915). Later work on depth of soil tillage and mechanical cultivation versus hand hoeing for cultivation was done by Mooers (1944) on soils across Tennessee. He compared different plowing depths and mechanical cultivation versus hand hoeing alone. On some soils, hand hoeing gave equal yields to cultivation, while on other soils, yields were slightly lower. Initial plowing depth had no effect on crop yield on any of the soils. Research by Harris (1964) in Mississippi showed a yield and profit decline when cotton was hand hoed and cultivated with machine power compared with hand hoeing alone. In addition, the possibility of limiting the degree of tillage and depth while still maintaining yield was verified on silty and clayey soils in Arkansas (Phillips, 1968).

The reduction in tillage soon led to consideration of doing no seedbed preparation but instead planting into the existing soil cover with proper equipment and using herbicides for weed control. This could result in optimum erosion protection. In the late 1950s and early 1960s chemical weed control to replace cultivation was becoming more feasible and economical (Goddard and Lard, 1965). Eventually better herbicides and equipment became available (Denton and Tyler, 2002). Soon after, NT cropping research became common in most areas of the Mid-South (Melville and Rabb, 1976; Hinkle, 1975, Graves et al., 1980, Tyler and Overton, 1982).

Research on NT was extensive during the 1960s and 1970s and was summarized by Blevins et al. (1994) and Tyler et al. (1994) for parts of the Mid-South. A number of research studies were conducted on the effects of NT and cover crops relative to water quality. Some examples include studies by Shelton et al. (1983) and a summary of a large number of studies in Mississippi during this period (McGregor et al., 1996). Dramatic reductions in runoff and soil erosion from NT cropping and residue management were shown in most studies.

Cover Crops

Keeping the soil covered was recognized by Bennett et al. (1919) as the only feasible way of adequately controlling soil erosion on steeper slopes in the soil survey map of Shelby County, TN, which lies in the same loess belt as Lafayette County, MS (Lentz et al., 1929). Bennett observed that gully erosion was still severe, even on much of the sloping land where contoured farming was used. In some cases, he thought terracing would help, but on many fields, conversion to grasses and clover (*Trifolium* spp.) or permanent pasture was the only solution.

At SCS experiment stations (predecessors of the USDA, Agricultural Research Service experiment stations) across the nation, including those in the Mid-South

(Tyler and Temple, TX), early soil loss measurements demonstrated the importance of soil coverage. Summarizing early research at these stations, Bennett (1939) reported that "without exception...annual soils losses from the areas devoted to clean-tilled crops are many times greater than the corresponding losses from the areas heavily covered with protective vegetation." Twenty years after research at the Tyler station began, Smith et al. (1954) reported that rotation of sweetclovers and small grains tended to have less soil loss than continuous small grain. Soils where crops were grown with sweetclover and native grasses with no top growth removed accumulated organic matter and nutrients.

In Arkansas, Bartholomew et al. (1939) measured less runoff and soil loss with a winter cover crop of vetch (*Vicia* spp.), and negligible soil loss was observed from Bermuda grass (*Cynodon dactylon* L.) sod. They also found that soil loss in corn (*Zea mays* L.) rotated with oats (*Avena sativa* L.) and clover was less than that in continuous corn. Differences in soil loss were attributed to an improved ability of rotated soils to absorb water.

In a Lafayette County, Mississippi study, Lentz et al. (1929) noted that terraces, which were considered impractical, and cover crops were seldom used for the production of cotton and corn. They did observe that soil coverage, even with only honeysuckle (*Lonicera japonica* Thunb.) or broomsedge (*Andropogon* spp.), was quite effective in stabilizing gullies and preventing further erosion. Less erosion was also observed with inferior covers of scrubby undergrowth of burned-over hardwood stands when compared with adjacent abandoned fields. Other plants promoted for cover to reclaim eroded soils in the Mid-South included kudzu [*Pueraria montana* (Lour.) Merr.] and black locust (*Robinia pseudoacacia* L.), and loblolly pine (*Pinus taeda* L.) (McGinnis, 1933; O'Brien and Skelton, 1946).

In addition to using cover crops to protect the soil from erosion, considerable research was done in many Mid-South states on the use of cover crops to improve soil productivity. Cover crops were used in rotation with row crops or as winter legumes (Baird and Knisel, 1971; Brown, 1945; Davis et al., 1940; Fox, 1907; Grissom, 1950; Haddon, 1953; Long and Overton, 1963; Mississippi Agricultural Experiment Station, 1934; Mooers and Hazelwood, 1945; Nelson, 1944; Offutt, 1970; Patrick et al., 1957; Reynolds et al., 1950, 1958; Smith et al., 1954). Data from these studies indicated great promise for the use of winter cover crops to provide additional soil cover, enhance crop yields, increase soil organic matter, and, with legumes, potentially supply fixed nitrogen to the following row crop.

Soil and Water Conservation Trends in the Mid-South: 1980 to Present

Improved Soil Conservation, Continued Water Quality Problems

Data from the Natural Resources Inventory (NRI) for states in the Mid-South show substantial reduction in water erosion of cropland per hectare from 1982 to 2003 (Table 8–3; USDA-NRCS, 2000, 2007b). Within this time, acreage in cropland decreased (Table 8–4; USDA-NRCS, 2000, 2007a), in part due to establishment of the CRP. Thus, recent advances in soil and water conservation may be summarized as reduced water erosion per acre on reduced acreage. The per acre reduction in water erosion from remaining cropland during the past quarter century (Table 8–3) reflects increased conservation management. Major in-field

Table 8–3. Estimated average water erosion (sheet and rill) from cropland by year for states in the Mid-South (USDA-NRCS, 2000, 2007b).

State	Year				
	2003	1997	1992	1987	1982
	Mg ha^{-1}				
Arkansas	6.9	7.6	7.6	8.3	8.3
Louisiana	6.9	7.4	7.8	9.2	10.5
Mississippi	10.3	11.9	12.8	14.8	17.2
Missouri	9.2	12.5	14.8	18.8	24.4
Tennessee	8.1	17.2	20.4	24.2	24.6
Texas	5.6	5.8	5.8	5.8	5.8

Table 8–4. Trends in cropland and CRP acreage by year for the states in the Mid-South (USDA-NRCS 2000, 2007a).

State	Year									
	2003		1997		1992		1987		1 982	
	Crop	CRP	Crop	CRP	Crop	CRP	Crop	CRP	Crop	CRP
	1000 ha									
Arkansas	3046	59	3088	93	3131	95	3230	39	3281	0
Louisiana	2201	81	2292	57	2419	582	2548	17	2596	0
Mississippi	2015	320	2168	324	2319	315	2699	118	3003	0
Missouri	5540	592	12859	650	5406	649	5826	231	6075	0
Tennessee	1924	94	1881	151	1967	178	2177	70	2265	0
Texas	10353	1617	10910	1582	11446	1609	12636	641	13496	0

management changes include wider use of some form of conservation tillage/residue management and cover crops. Edge-of-field or predischarge practices, such as hedges (Dabney et al., 1995; Meyer et al., 1995) and filter strips (Sanderson et al., 2001), intended to limit input of eroded soil into water bodies have also been adopted to some degree (Lovell and Sullivan, 2006).

However, use of conservation management is not universal. State-compiled water quality inventories provided to the USEPA include lists of impaired water bodies, i.e., 303(d) lists, which commonly cite soil disturbance by agricultural practices as a suspected cause for impairments such as turbidity and low dissolved oxygen due to enrichment in O_2–consuming substances. Watershed restoration plans typically prescribe better soil conservation by wider adoption of best management practices to meet total maximum daily loads.

The Mid-South also has larger-scale water quality problems due to sediment-bound and dissolved nutrients. Real or potential enrichment of surface water with P from soils fertilized with poultry waste is a problem in the Mid-South, particularly in Arkansas (USDA-NRCS, 2006). A rather large eutrophic-hypoxic zone in the northern Gulf of Mexico off the Louisiana coast is believed to result from enrichment in nutrients, presumably drained from the Upper Mississippi River Valley (Rabalais et al., 1996); however, inputs from the Mid-South may also contribute (Southwick et al., 2002). Control of nutrient loading depends on soil conservation as well as nutrient management.

Early-Stage Transition to Conservation Tillage

By 1980, the foundation of conservation tillage/residue management in the Mid-South had largely been established by research attempting to quantify their benefits and refine production methods to meet or exceed yield and profitability under conventional practices. While some work in the Mid-South on reduced tillage dates to about 1960 (Phillips, 1968), the rationale was not of soil and water conservation for those Delta soils, although Dendy (1981) and Murphree and McGregor (1991) later showed soil loss of 11 to 27 Mg ha^{-1} on flat Delta soils. Within the decade, however, concern about erosion and degradation of loessial, fragipan soils—later confirmed and explained by Rhoton (1990) and Rhoton and Tyler (1990) and further substantiated by Cullum et al. (2002) and McGregor et al. (1992, 1999b)—led to initiation of work on the efficacy and practicability of NT soybeans [*Glycine max* (L.) Merr.], rotations with corn, and double cropping with wheat (McGregor et al., 1975). There had been tentative success with NT elsewhere by that time (Triplett and Dick, 2008).

Intermediate- and long-term soil erosion losses from NT soybeans were 0.10 or less than those from conventional-tillage (CT) (McGregor et al., 1975; Mutchler and Greer, 1984). Data for corn were equally impressive (McGregor and Greer, 1982; McGregor and Mutchler, 1983). Furthermore, yields were not compromised. Commonly this was not the case, but rather than an inherent limitation of the system, Shelton and Bradley (1987) acknowledged lack of experience as a major factor behind early poor yields from NT compared to CT. With increased experience, NT yields were more often equal to or superior to CT yields.

Cover Crops and Related Systems

Leading into recent times, the traditional use of cover crops as a green manure had waned in favor of commercial fertilizers despite its recognized value for soil conservation. Nevertheless, research and demonstration on cover crops in the Mid-South persisted (Millhollon and Melville, 1991) or had been initiated with low-residue cotton (Scott et al., 1990; Keisling et al., 1994) (Fig. 8–8). Results for the above Red River and Mississippi Delta soils showed increased yields or reduced need for N fertilization. Besides building soil organic C (SOC), a rye (*Secale cereale* L.) and vetch cover also improved soil physical properties beneficial to plant growth (Scott et al., 1990; Keisling et al., 1994). Studies with planted cover crops in NT or reduced-tillage cotton to further improve soil retention (Mutchler and McDowell, 1990) were started at Holly Springs, MS, following initial research by Mutchler et al. (1985). No-tillage reduced erosion to about 1 Mg ha^{-1} from 72 Mg ha^{-1} for CT (Mutchler et al., 1985). Planting vetch or wheat further reduced erosion from this system, and the effect of the cover crop was much greater for the most erosive system, CT, reducing erosion by approximately 25% (Mutchler and McDowell, 1990).

Data from the cotton erosion studies at Holly Springs, MS, also suggested a residual effect from previous management. For example, erosion from CT cotton on previous NT soil was about one-half that of the same system but with long CT history (Mutchler et al., 1985). Erosion was least from NT cotton grown on previously double-cropped wheat–soybean soil. Later work by Dabney et al. (2004) and Wilson et al. (2004) on the tillage history confirmed the previous findings for NT, but the residual effect due to wheat–soybean is less clear. However, work with NT wheat and wheat–soybean (Dou and Hons, 2006; Franzluebbers et al., 1994, 1995)

Fig. 8–8. Mississippi Delta cotton production under reduced tillage (top) with, and (bottom) without a rye cover crop. Stoneville, MS. Photo by Wade Steinriede, 2009, USDA-ARS.

showed greater accumulation of SOC with greater cropping intensity, including accumulation of organic C extending into subsurface soil (Wright et al., 2007a). Among NT sorghum [*Sorghum bicolor* (L.) Moench], soybean, and wheat, wheat produced a higher accumulation of organic C and greater proportion of macroaggregates (Wright and Hons, 2005), both associated with better water infiltration, and less runoff and erosion (Rhoton et al., 2002). Furthermore, subsurface accumulation of C for the monocultures was greater for wheat and sorghum than for soybean (Wright et al., 2007b). Long-term erosion data in the Texas Blackland Prairie (Harmel et al., 2006) are consistent with such benefits of small grain cover, especially during the wetter parts of the year.

Cover crops produce a much greater mass of residue than native winter annuals, particularly a nonlegume like wheat where soil N fertility is high ($\sim$4 Mg ha^{-1}; Boquet et al., 2004a,b), providing good protection of the surface soil. Since harvesting a wheat cover offers direct return, double-cropped wheat systems were developed throughout the Mid-South about 25 yr ago. Some initial yields were good with NT for sorghum (Gerik and Morrison, 1984; Viator and Marshall, 1981) and soybean (Griffin et al., 1983; Rabb and Melville, 1984), and some were not (for sorghum Hairston et al., 1984; Howard, 1987; for soybean Boquet et al., 1982; Boquet and Walker, 1984; Shelton et al., 1982). However, Boquet and Walker (1984) and Shelton and Bradley (1987) offered several explanations, including height of wheat stubble and lower soil moisture at later planting with NT. Regardless, double-cropped wheat systems help conserve soil, particularly with CT. Shelton and

Bradley (1987) reported only 25% as much erosion with wheat–soybean compared with CT soybean.

Understanding Conservation Tillage Systems Better

Studies quantifying soil and water conservation with no- and reduced-tillage continued beyond the early work with soybean, corn, cotton, double crops, and cover crops (Fig. 8–9). This research continued some of the earlier work (Mutchler and McDowell, 1990; McGregor et al., 1999b; Cullum et al., 2002) and initiated new studies, as with sorghum (McGregor and Mutchler, 1992). Data on the full suite of systems was necessary for predictive modeling (e.g., Universal Soil Loss Equation, USLE, Wischmeier and Smith, 1978; Revised Universal Soil Loss Equation, RUSLE, Renard et al., 1997) because of differing crop growth habits and amount of crop residue. As an example of the latter, McGregor et al. (1990) found that erosion rates from conventionally tilled soil increased in the order: wheat < corn < fallow residue. Results of Dabney et al. (2004) indicated that surface cover is equally important to holding erosion in check as the development of physicochemical conditions in NT soil that favor infiltration and oppose particle detachment and loading into runoff. Furthermore, development of these conditions is slow and crop-dependent (Rhoton, 2000). Thus, different and long-term studies were needed for better expression of soil biological, chemical, and physical changes under NT that affect soil and water conservation, and agronomic responses. An example of the latter is long-term yield data for soybean that showed steady yields from NT but decreasing yields from conventional tillage due to progressive erosion (McGregor et al., 2006). Long-term tillage and cover crop studies were begun throughout the Mid-South during this time to monitor time-dependent soil and agronomic changes (discussed below).

Fig. 8–9. Reduced tillage soybeans. Beasley Lake Watershed, Sunflower County, Mississippi. Photo by Martin Locke, 2005, USDA-ARS.

Given data from the Mid-South region and elsewhere showing that NT worked to reduce erosion and conserve soil (i.e., ~ an order of magnitude or more in better soil conservation), the first objective was to develop and demonstrate systems that matched economic yields of the status quo. Plots were also incubators for changes in soil properties that affect plant growth/yield, soil erosion and other parameters of water quality. Where runoff and erosion were monitored, it made sense to also measure tillage effects on losses of nutrients and other agrochemicals.

Agronomic Studies

No-tillage has been generally successful with major crops of the Mid-South except rice and sugarcane (*Saccharum officinarum* L.), but it is more challenging with heavier textured soils (Triplett and Dick, 2008) and not always an initial success. As examples of the latter, initial yields of cotton were significantly reduced with NT on a silt loam in Mississippi, but the trend reversed after 2 yr (Dabney et al., 1995), particularly with wheat cover crop (Dabney, 1995; Triplett et al., 1996). Keisling (1993) found significantly reduced cotton yields with NT on a loessial soil in Arkansas, and later (Keisling et al., 1995) compared types of reduced-tillage systems for silt loam and clay soils. However, at least in some years there were no differences in cotton yields between CT and NT (Govindasamy et al., 1996). Pettigrew and Jones (2001) had similarly disappointing results for 2 yr of cotton in the Mississippi Delta.

In some cases, yields never suffered with conversion to conservation tillage. For example, Hutchinson and Shelton (1990) had no cotton yield loss with NT on a Louisiana loessial soil and up to 90% less erosion if combined with wheat cover crop (Hutchinson et al., 1991). These results were confirmed with longer-term cotton studies (Boquet et al., 2004a,b). Similarly, there was no difference between NT and CT sorghum with subsurface banded N fertilizer (Locke and Hons, 1988a). Bradley (1995) summarized cotton yields for studies in Tennessee that began in 1981, reporting no yield loss with NT. Having found no yield problem for cotton with NT, much of the work with NT focused on N (Howard et al., 2001c), P, or K (Howard et al., 1997, 1998, 2001a,b) fertilization, and lime requirements (Cochran et al., 2007). Unlike with cotton, however, placement affects N use efficiency in sorghum (Locke and Hons, 1988b) or corn (Howard and Tyler, 1989), particularly where lime is surface-applied (Howard and Essington, 1998).

Even on heavy-textured soil, NT has been shown to work. Boquet and Coco (1991) found no cotton yield reduction with no- or reduced-tillage on a clay soil in Louisiana and a yield advantage with hairy vetch cover crop regardless of tillage system (Boquet et al., 1995). Early data from Texas were mixed, with Morrison and Chichester (1994) finding no differences in corn, sorghum, or wheat yields between NT and CT, but Potter et al. (1996) reporting a yield reduction in corn but not sorghum with NT. Later, highest yields of corn on a Texas Blackland Prairie clay soil (Torbert et al., 2001) were obtained using NT and wide, raised beds (Morrison et al., 1990) at the highest N rate, 168 kg ha^{-1}.

Rice floodwater discharge may degrade downstream water quality. Studies have shown that NT, particularly compared to the practice of tilling or leveling the soil surface under water to control red rice, greatly reduces the loss of suspended sediment (e.g., Feagley et al., 1991). However, yields are reduced and returns poorer (e.g., Pearce et al., 1999), leading to its limited use (Leon et al., 2008;

Snipes et al., 2005). No-tillage following rice harvest and retention of winter rainfall behind levees helps reduce overall soil loss, while increasing waterfowl habitat (Hite et al., 2003), but water quality in such ponds may be highly variable (Maul and Cooper, 2000).

For perennial sugarcane, tillage before planting, spring tillage, and burning of combine harvest residue are traditionally used for best yields; however, chemical control of weeds and old cane during fallow has been shown to be as effective as tillage (Etheredge et al., 2008). Yields with NT equaled those with spring tillage, and returns increased (Judice et al., 2006). No yield loss was observed when residue was swept off row tops rather than burned (Judice and Griffin, 2008).

Effects on Soil Properties

With time, interrelated biological, chemical, and physical changes consistent with improved soil and water quality and conservation were expected to develop in conservation tillage soils. This was shown in numerous studies from the Mid-South (e.g., Rhoton, 1990). Perhaps the most evident change was an increase in SOC under NT (e.g., Dou and Hons, 2006; Franzluebbers et al., 1994, 1995; Locke et al., 2005; Potter et al., 1998; Potter and Chichester, 1993; Salinas-Garcia et al., 1997a,b; Wright et al., 2007a,b; Zablotowicz et al., 2000; Zibilske and Bradford, 2007). However, the effect was mostly limited to about the upper 5 cm of soil, although deeper with some rotations (Locke et al., 2005; Wright et al., 2007a,b; Zablotowicz et al., 2000). As expected, N content paralleled C content (Salinas-Garcia et al., 1997a,b; Wright and Hons, 2004, 2005; Wright et al., 2007a,b; Zibilske and Bradford, 2007). Microbial biomass C and N followed the same trends (Franzluebbers et al., 1994, 1995; Salinas-Garcia et al., 1997a,b). Together, these measures of soil quality showed that conservation tillage was beneficial. They have also led to physical conditions more favorable to water infiltration and retention (Wright and Hons, 2004; Wright and Hons, 2005; Zibilske and Bradford, 2007). The increase in organic C in the surface soil may also reduce free Al via complexation and increase solubility of K and Si, tending to alter mineralogical transformations in the surface soil (Karathanasis and Wells, 1989), which might further the nutrient stratification that develops under NT (Howard et al., 1999; Potter and Chichester, 1993).

Effects on Water Quality

Early studies showed that reduced tillage, especially NT, lowered total runoff losses of N and P by decreasing soil erosion but increased the losses of these nutrients in dissolved form, especially P (McDowell and McGregor, 1984), the latter apparently a function of the mass of crop residue at the soil surface. Shelton and Mote (1989) reported a similar shift in nutrient loss with NT soybean to more bioavailable, dissolved forms. Chichester and Richardson (1992), however, found no greater loss of dissolved N or P from a NT clay soil on paired watersheds, but nearly 10 times lower loss of sorbed forms. Besides N and P, loss of C (as a substrate for microbial activity) affects water quality. Thus, the effect of tillage on runoff biological oxygen demand appears to be negligible (Schreiber and Neumaier, 1987), with reduced amount of particle-bound C under NT offset by increased dissolved forms. Similarly, Viator et al. (2008) found no season-long benefit of retaining, rather than burning, sugarcane residue on several measures of water quality, including biological oxygen demand. Regardless of uncertain effects on various water quality parameters, conservation tillage is successful for its initial purpose, soil conservation and the resulting decrease in suspended solids in runoff (Fig. 8–10).

While much of the conservation research in the Mid-South has involved plot studies, in the past 20 yr, there has been increasing emphasis placed on field or watershed-scale evaluations. In the early 1990s, USDA established a network of studies in a project called the Management System Evaluation Areas (MSEA) to assess the effects of conservation practices on water quality at watershed scales. Early MSEA project research was in the Midwestern states, but the Mississippi Delta MSEA (MD-MSEA) project was established in 1994. Effects of conservation practices on water quality in three oxbow lake watersheds were evaluated for 10 yr (Nett et al., 2004; Zablotowicz et al., 2006). In 2003, USDA-NRCS and USDA-ARS partnered, along with other state and federal organizations, to conduct watershed studies quantifying the effects of NRCS conservation practices. This ongoing national research effort was called the Conservation Effects Assessment Project (CEAP). Fourteen watersheds across the United States were selected to participate in the CEAP watershed assessment studies, and four of these were in the Mid-South (Beasley Lake, MS; Goodwin Creek, MS; Leon River, TX; and Little Toposhaw River, MS). Initial results from these watersheds have been reported (Harmel et al., 2008; Kuhnle et al., 2008; Locke et al., 2008b; Wilson et al., 2008; Yuan et al., 2008).

Fig. 8–10. Effects of vegetative buffers on water quality of runoff from fields in the Mississippi Delta: (a) low sediment in runoff from a field with a vegetative buffer; (b) significant sediment observed in runoff discharged from a plowed field with no vegetative buffer. Photo credits: (a) Wade Steinriede, 2005, USDA-ARS; (b) John Massey, 2009, USDA-ARS.

What are the Lessons from the Past? Where Are We Going in the Future?

Efforts in the early 20th century to control soil erosion lacked national coordination and funding, although many farmers and scientists recognized the negative effects that popular farm practices had on soil productivity. However, realization that erosion was a problem with widespread ramifications that needed to be addressed at a national level did not occur until the disastrous effects of the Dust Bowl era. Legislation by Congress provided the impetus for a concerted and coordinated effort to conduct research to counter soil erosion. The erosion stations established in the Mid-South and elsewhere began to provide the database needed to give substance to conservation recommendations being made to farmers. Other legislation provided funding for the USDA to implement programs to promote soil conservation. Nationally, as well as in the Mid-South, federal and state experiment stations worked with the newly established USDA-SCS in the 1930s and 1940s to evaluate and promote conservation practices. These efforts continued throughout the remainder of the 20th century, and a proliferation of research was published throughout the Mid-South during this time.

Farming in the Mid-South underwent major transformations in the 20th century (Fig. 8–2, 8–3), and conservation methods adapted accordingly. Conservation tillage and renewed use of cover crops, together with edge-of-field controls for nonpoint source agricultural inputs, and enrollment in the CRP have improved soil and water conservation in the Mid-South. However, environmental concerns continue to persist at local and regional scales. While soil loss was the primary focus for the first half of the century, attention has also turned to the loss of agrichemicals in runoff and their effects of water quality and habitats. Furthermore, issues such as hypoxia in the Gulf of Mexico have rekindled the call for nationally coordinated efforts to promote soil conservation.

Where should future efforts in soil and water conservation in the Mid-South be directed? Advances in information technology enable better utilization of large databases and enhance model improvements. Remote sensing could be used to monitor agricultural effects on soil erosion and to develop databases describing soil conditions. At smaller field scales, modeling may aid design of precision fertilizer and pesticide programs by considering various scenarios for off-site transport. Improvement in climate models may provide better information to agricultural producers with decisions to perform operations affecting soil erosion and water quality. Improvements need to be made with field- and watershed-scale models to evaluate the integrated impact of practices on soil erosion, such as in evaluating the use of a combination of practices to control sheet and rill, gully, and channel erosion. Results from simulation modeling (e.g., AnnAGNPS; Yuan et al., 2002, 2008) suggest that certain combinations of conservation practices and their use at more vulnerable sites could improve overall soil and water conservation, reducing sediment loads by up to about 70%. Further refinement in watershed-scale modeling to account for hydrologic details missed in digital elevation models (DEMs), within source area spatial variability, etc. may lead to greater confidence and wider application of this approach. This may improve efforts to target vulnerable sites within a watershed and to ensure minimal site-specific impacts to the soil. At a much larger scale, systematic, detailed modeling (and changes in practices based on results) may make progress toward mitigating more widespread problems, such as hypoxia in the Gulf of Mexico.

The retirement of highly erodible land into the CRP is effective in reducing erosion and improving soil and water quality (FAPRI, 2007), and in some cases even shifts the focus of water quality to channel erosion and its control (Kuhnle et al., 2008; Wilson et al., 2008). However, a significant portion of the remaining cropland in the Mid-South is still under conventional tillage management. Therefore, although there are direct and coordinated efforts for improved soil and water conservation, serendipity has and may continue to play an important role, and expansion of research is needed on emerging and innovative conservation practices that produce multiple benefits. Examples include genetically modified crops, environmentally friendly biofuel crops, and integrating wetlands into the agricultural landscape.

Widespread and heavy reliance on genetically modified crop cultivars leads to the interesting observation that technology introduced for better, cheaper, and more flexible weed control—herbicide-resistant crops—benefits soil and water conservation by facilitating adoption of conservation tillage (Cerdeira and Duke, 2006; Roberts et al., 2006; Locke et al., 2008a,b). Data from a long-term study on water quality in Mississippi oxbow lakes, for example, showed decreases in suspended sediment, nutrients, and pesticides that paralleled joint adoption of herbicide-resistant varieties and conservation tillage management (Zablotowicz et al., 2006; Locke et al., 2008a). However, it is uncertain what effects the emergence of herbicide-resistant weeds will have on this positive trend. Herbicide programs are being developed to address the problem (Gustafson, 2008). Further, long-term effects of herbicide-resistant crops on soil quality in conservation systems have not been adequately assessed (Locke et al., 2008b).

Crops such as corn and sugarcane that are currently promoted in the Mid-South for biofuel production require large management inputs such as fertilizer and irrigation that may be at odds with efforts to improve the environment. Second generation biofuel crops are needed that not only require less input, but also provide environmental benefits such as improved erosion control. There are many areas in the Mid-South where marginal land is used for row crop production. However, marginal lands are the consensus sites for growing switchgrass (*Panicum virgatum* L.), miscanthus (*Miscanthus* × *giganteus* J.M. Greef & Deuter ex Hodk. & Renvoize), or other perennial biofuel crops. Data for the performance of switchgrass (Meyer et al., 1995; Sanderson et al., 2001) and miscanthus (Cullum et al., 2007; McGregor et al., 1999a) in controlling erosion are positive. Thus, if these crops prove economically viable (Popp, 2007) and environmentally sound, conversion of substantial acreage in the Mid-South from tilled crops to non-tilled perennials may have an effect analogous to conversion to CRP.

Natural and constructed wetlands, widely used for hunting and fishing, provide valuable habitat for wildlife. Conservation practices such as buffers can be used to integrate wetlands into the agricultural landscape for sediment, pesticide, and nutrient trapping and processing (e.g., Moore et al., 2009). Vegetation in ditches draining agricultural areas can increase retention time of runoff with subsequent reduction in pollutant loss in outflow (Kröger et al., 2009). Retention ponds adjacent to agricultural fields might similarly be used (Dendy and Cooper, 1984; Cooper and Knight, 1990). Temporary wetlands might be created if drainage outlets to fields were plugged during the fallow seasons to allow accumulation of field runoff.

In the last 20 yr, experimental plot studies for soil erosion have been reduced and concentrated to fewer experiment stations throughout the Mid-South. There is still a need for these smaller-scale studies as well as field- and watershed-scale studies such as CEAP to study the impact of loadings from soil and water conservation practices downstream. Coordinated and integrated plot studies need to be expanded to study emerging practices on the various soils and climatic zones throughout the region. Techniques need to be developed to track and identify the source of sediment loadings within watersheds to target the placement of appropriate practices.

A systematic approach to implementing practices that address and integrate soil, water, chemical, energy, and global climate change issues would provide effective economical and environmental conservation measures to address all these issues. Conservation research in the Mid-South should continue to adapt to changing needs and priorities. Based on past experience, local and national resources should be pooled to provide widely coordinated efforts that are still sensitive to more region-specific needs.

Acknowledgments

Thanks to Darlene Wilcox for developing maps of the Mid-South and to Pam Locke for helping with the pictures. We thank Ron Bingner and Robert Wells for insightful comments.

References

Baird, R.W., and W.G. Knisel. 1971. Soil conservation practices and crop production in the blacklands of Texas. Conserv. Res. Rep. 15. USDA-ARS, U.S. Gov. Print. Office, Washington, DC.

Bartholomew, R.P., D.G. Carter, W.C. Hulburt, and L.C. Kapp. 1939. Influence of rainfall, cropping, and cultural methods on soil and water losses. Arkansas Agric. Exp. Stn. Bull. 380. Univ. of Arkansas, Fayetteville.

Bennett, H.H. 1921. Soils and agriculture of the southern states. MacMillan, New York.

Bennett, H.H. 1927. What's new in agriculture. p. 591–593. In 1927 Yearbook of agriculture. U.S. Gov. Print. Office, Washington, DC.

Bennett, H.H. 1931. Cultural changes in soils from the stand point of erosion. J. Am. Soc. Agron. 23:434–454.

Bennett, H.H. 1939. Soil conservation. McGraw-Hill, New York.

Bennett, H.H., and W.R. Chapline. 1928. Soil erosion: A national menace. USDA Circ. 33. U.S. Gov. Print Office, Washington, DC.

Bennett, H.H., and W.C. Lowdermilk. 1938. General aspects of the soil-erosion problem. p. 581–607. In 1938 Yearbook of agriculture: Soils and men. U.S. Gov. Print. Office, Washington, DC.

Bennett, H.H., R.T. Allen, J.V. Davis, and C.R. Watkins. 1919. Soil survey of Shelby County Tennessee. U.S. Gov. Print. Office, Washington, DC.

Blevins, R.L., W.W. Frye, M.G. Wagger, and D.D. Tyler. 1994. Residue management strategies for the Southeast. p. 63–76. In J.L. Hatfield and B.A. Stewart (ed.) Crop residue management. CRC Press, Boca Raton, FL.

Boquet, D.J., G.A. Breitenbeck, and A.B. Coco. 1995. Cotton yield and growth responses to tillage intensity and cover crops. p. 39–44. In M.R. McClelland et al. (ed.) Conservation tillage systems for cotton: A review of research and demonstration from across the Cotton Belt. Arkansas Agric. Exp. Stn. Spec. Rep. 169. Univ. of Arkansas, Fayetteville.

Boquet, D.J., and A.B. Coco. 1991. Tillage and cover crop systems for cotton on clay soil. Louisiana Agric. 30:23–24.

Boquet, D.J., R.L. Hutchinson, and G.A. Breitenbeck. 2004a. Long-term tillage, cover crop, and nitrogen effects on cotton: Yield and fiber properties. Agron. J. 96:1436–1442.

Boquet, D.J., R.L. Hutchinson, and G.A. Breitenbeck. 2004b. Long-term tillage, cover crop, and nitrogen effects on cotton: Plant growth and yield components. Agron. J. 96:1443–1452.

Boquet, D.J., and D.M. Walker. 1984. Wheat–soybean doublecropping: Stubble management, row spacing and irrigation. Louisiana Agric. Exp. Stn. Bull. 760. Louisiana State Univ., Baton Rouge.

Boquet, D.J., D.M. Walker, J.L. Bartleson, and R.L. Hutchinson. 1982. Adapting wheat–soybean double-cropping to Louisiana. Louisiana Agric. 26:20–21.

Bradley, J.F. 1995. Success with no-till cotton. p. 46–48. *In* M.R. McClelland et al. (ed.) Conservation tillage systems for cotton: A review of research and demonstration from across the Cotton Belt. Arkansas Agric. Exp. Stn. Spec. Rep. 169. Univ. of Arkansas, Fayetteville.

Brown, H.B. 1945. Effect of certain summer and winter legume crops in improving corn yield in South Louisiana. Louisiana Bull. 396. Louisiana State Univ., Baton Rouge.

Carpenter, J.W., and E.R. Gross. 1918. The terrace in Mississippi. Ext. Dep. Mississippi Agric. Mech. Coll. Ext. Bull. 9. Mississippi Agric. Mech. College, Mississippi State.

Carter, W.T. 1931. The soils of Texas. Texas Agric. Exp. Stn. Bull. 431. Texas Agric. Mech. College, College Station.

Cerdeira, A.L., and S.O. Duke. 2006. The current status and environmental impacts of glyphosate-resistant crops: A review. J. Environ. Qual. 35:1633–1658.

Chichester, F.W., and C.W. Richardson. 1992. Sediment and nutrient loss from clay soils as affected by tillage. J. Environ. Qual. 21:587–590.

Cochran, R.L., R.K. Roberts, J.A. Larson, and D.D. Tyler. 2007. Cotton profitability with alternative lime application rates, cover crops, nitrogen rates, and tillage methods. Agron. J. 99:1085–1092.

Cooper, C.M., and S.S. Knight. 1990. Nutrient trapping efficiency of a small sediment detention reservoir. Agric. Water Manage. 18:149–158.

Cullum, R.F., K.C. McGregor, C.K. Mutchler, J.R. Johnson, and D.L. Boykin. 2002. Soybean yield response to tillage, fragipan depth, and slope length. Trans. ASAE 43:563–571.

Cullum, R.F., G.V. Wilson, K.C. McGregor, and J.R. Johnson. 2007. Runoff and soil loss from ultra-narrow row cotton plots with and without stiff-grass hedges. Soil Tillage Res. 93:56–63.

Dabney, S.M. 1995. Cover crops in reduced tillage systems. p. 58–60. *In* M.R. McClelland et al. (ed.) Conservation tillage systems for cotton: A review of research and demonstration from across the Cotton Belt. Arkansas Agric. Exp. Stn. Spec. Rep. 169. Univ. of Arkansas, FayettevilleDabney, S.M., L.D. Meyer, W.C. Harmon, C.V. Alonso, and G.R. Foster. 1995. Depositional patterns of sediment trapped by grass hedges. Trans. ASAE 38:1719–1729.

Dabney, S.M., C.E. Murphee, G.B. Triplett, E.H. Grissinger, L.D. Meyer, L.R. Reinschmiedt, F.E. Rhoton, and W.M. Lipe. 1995. No-till cotton production on silty uplands. p. 49–52. *In* M.R. McClelland et al. (ed.) Conservation tillage systems for cotton: A review of research and demonstration from across the Cotton Belt. Arkansas Agric. Exp. Stn. Spec. Rep. 169. Univ. of Arkansas, Fayetteville.

Dabney, S.M., G.V. Wilson, K.C. McGregor, and G.R. Foster. 2004. History, residue, and tillage effects on erosion of loessial soil. Trans. ASAE 47:767–775.

Dana, S.T. 1916. Farms, forest, and erosion. p. 107–134. *In* 1916 Yearbook of agriculture, What's new in agriculture. U.S. Gov. Print. Office, Washington, DC.

Davis, F.L., C.G. Hobgood, and C.A. Brewer, Jr. 1940. Growing legumes in Louisiana. Louisiana Bull. 318. Louisiana State Univ. Agric. Exp. Stn., Baton Rouge.

Davis, R.O.E. 1913. Economic waste from soil erosion. p. 207–220. *In* 1913 yearbook of agriculture. U.S. Gov. Print. Office, Washington, DC.

Dendy, F.E. 1981. Sediment yield from a Mississippi Delta cotton field. J. Environ. Qual. 10:482–486.

Dendy, F.E., and C.M. Cooper. 1984. Sediment trap efficiency in a small reservoir. J. Soil Water Conserv. 39:278–280.

Denton, H.P., and D.D. Tyler. 2002. Making no-till "conventional" in Tennessee. p. 53–58. *In* E. van Santeen (ed.) Making conservation tillage conventional: Building a future on 25 years of research. Proc. 25th Annual Southern Conservation Tillage Conference for Sustainable Agriculture, Auburn, AL. Alabama Agric. Exp. Stn., Auburn University, AL.

Dou, F., and F.M. Hons. 2006. Tillage and nitrogen effects on soil organic matter fractions in wheat-based systems. Soil Sci. Soc. Am. J. 70:1896–1905.

Enlow, C.R., and G.W. Musgrave. 1938. Grass and other thick growing vegetation in erosion control. p. 615–633. *In* Yearbook of agriculture: Soils and men. U.S. Gov. Print. Office, Washington, DC.

Etheredge, L.M., Jr., J.L. Griffin, and M.E. Salassi. 2008. Alternatives to tillage/herbicide programs in fallowed sugarcane field. Louisiana Agric. 51:30–32.

FAPRI. 2007. Estimating water quality, air quality, and soil carbon benefits of the Conservation Reserve Program. FAPRI-UMC Report 01-07. Available at www.fapri.missouri.edu/outreach/publications/2007/FAPRI_UMC_Report_01_07.pdf (verified 14 Dec. 2009). Food and Agriculture Policy Research Institute (FAPRI), University of Missouri, Columbia.

Feagley, S.E., G.C. Sigua, R.L. Bengtson, P.K. Bollich, and S.D. Linscombe. 1991. Effects of different management practices on surface water quality from rice fields in south Louisiana. J. Plant Nutr. 15:1305–1321.

Fenneman, N.M. 1938. Physiography of the eastern United States. McGraw-Hill, New York.

Fite, G.C. 1984. Cotton fields no more: Southern agriculture 1865–1980. The Univ. Press of Kentucky, Lexington.

Fox, J.W. 1907. Report of work at the Delta Station for 1907–08. Mississippi Agric. Exp. Stn. Bull. 129. Mississippi Agric. Mech. College, Mississippi State.

Franzluebbers, A.J., F.M. Hons, and D.A. Zuberer. 1994. Long-term changes in soil carbon and nitrogen pools in wheat management systems. Soil Sci. Soc. Am. J. 58:1639–1645.

Franzluebbers, A.J., F.M. Hons, and D.A. Zuberer. 1995. Soil organic carbon, microbial biomass, and mineralizable carbon and nitrogen in sorghum. Soil Sci. Soc. Am. J. 59:460–466.

Fraps, G.S., and J.F. Fudge. 1937. Chemical composition of soils of Texas. Texas Agric. Exp. Stn. Bull. 549. Texas Agric. Mech. College, College Station.

Garin, A.N., and L.P. Gabbard. 1941. Land use in relation to sedimentation in reservoirs, Trinity River Basin, Texas. Texas Agric. Exp. Stn. Bull. 597. Texas Agric. Mech. College, College Station.

Gerik, T.J., and J.E. Morrison, Jr. 1984. No-tillage of grain sorghum on a shrinking clay soil. Agron. J. 76:71–76.

Goddard, R., and C.F. Lard. 1965. No cultivation vs. limited cultivation of cotton. Tenn. Farm Home Sci. Progress Rep. 53. Univ. Tennessee Agric. Exp. Stn., Knoxville.

Godfrey, C.L., C.R. Carter, and G.S. McKee. 1968. Land resource areas of Texas. Texas Agric. Exp. Stn. Bull. B-1070. Texas Agric. Ext., College Station.

Govindasamy, R., M.J. Cochran, J. Sharma, M. McClelland, and C. Smith. 1996. Conventional tillage vs. conservation tillage in cotton: An economic analysis. p. 4–12. In M. McClelland and T. Keisling (ed.) Conservation technology in Arkansas agriculture. Arkansas Agric. Exp. Stn. Research Ser. 449. Univ. Arkansas, Fayetteville.

Graves, C.R., T. McCutchen, L.S. Jeffrey, J.R. Overton, and R.M. Hayes. 1980. Soybean–wheat cropping systems: Evaluation of planting methods, varieties, raw spacing, and weed control. Bull. 597. Univ. Tennessee Agric. Exp. Stn., Knoxville.

Griffin, J.L., R.W. Taylor, and R.J. Habetz. 1983. Conservation tillage for double-cropped soybeans in southwest Louisiana. J. Soil Water Conserv. 39:78–80.

Grissom, P.H. 1950. Soil fertility practices for cotton production in the Yazoo-Mississippi Delta. Mississippi Agric. Exp. Stn. Bull. 473. Mississippi State Univ., Mississippi State.

Grissom, P.H. 1957. The Mississippi Delta Region. p. 524–531. In 1957 Yearbook of agriculture: Soil. U.S. Gov. Print. Office, Washington, DC.

Gustafson, D.I. 2008. Sustainable use of glyphosate in North American cropping systems. Pest Manage. Sci. 64:409–416.

Haddon, C.B. 1953. Experiments with legumes at the Northeast Louisiana Experiment Stn. Louisiana Bull. 477. Louisiana State Univ., Baton Rouge.

Hairston, J.E., J.O. Sanford, J.C. Hayes, and L.L. Reinschmiedt. 1984. Crop yield, soil erosion, and net returns from five tillage systems in the Mississippi Blackland Prairie. J. Soil Water Conserv. 39:391–395.

Hambridge, G. 1938. Soils and men—A summary. p. 1–44. In 1938 Yearbook of agriculture: Soils and men. U.S. Gov. Print. Office, Washington, DC.

Harmel, R.D., J.V. Bonta, and C.W. Richardson. 2007. The original USDA-ARS experimental watersheds in Texas and Ohio: Contributions from the past and visions for the future. Trans. ASABE 50:1669–1675.

Harmel, R.D., C.W. Richardson, K.W. King, and P.M. Allen. 2006. Runoff and soil loss relationships for the Texas Blackland Prairies ecoregion. J. Hydrol. 331:471–483.

Harmel, R.D., C.G. Rossi, T. Dybala, J. Arnold, K. Potter, J. Wolfe, and D. Hoffman. 2008. Conservation Effects Assessment Project research in the Leon River and Riesel watersheds. J. Soil Water Conserv. 63:453–460.

Harris, V.C. 1964. Production of cotton without postemergence cultivation or hand hoeing. 1964. Mississippi State Univ. Agric. Exp. Stn. Bull. 685. Mississippi State Univ., Mississippi State.

Helms, D. 2009. Hugh Hammond Bennett and the creation of the Soil Erosion Service. J. Soil Water Conserv. 64:68A–74A.

Hinkle, D.A. 1975. Use of no-tillage in double-cropping wheat with soybean or grain sorghum. Rep. 223. Univ. Arkansas Agric. Exp. Stn., Univ. Arkansas, Fayetteville.

Hite, D., W. Intarapapong, F. Kari, and T. Maupin. 2003. Economic and environmental benefits of rice production in the Mississippi Delta. Mississippi Agric. Forest. Exp. Stn. Bull. 1122.

Hobbs, F., and N. Stoops. 2002. Demographic trends in the 20th century. Census 2000 Spec. Reports. U.S. Census Bureau, Washington, DC.

Howard, D.D. 1987. Nitrogen fertilization effects on grain sorghum in conventional and no-till systems. Tenn. Farm Home Sci. 141:3–5.

Howard, D.D., and M.E. Essington. 1998. Effects of surface-applied limestone on the efficiency of urea-containing nitrogen sources for no-till corn. Agron. J. 90:523–528.

Howard, D.D., M.E. Essington, R.M. Hayes, and W.M. Percell. 2001a. Potassium fertilization of conventional- and no-till cotton. J. Cotton Sci. 5:197–205.

Howard, D.D., M.E. Essington, J. Logan, R.K. Roberts, and W.M. Percell. 2001b. Phosphorus and potassium fertilization of disk-till and no-till cotton. J. Cotton Sci. 5:144–155.

Howard, D.D., M.E. Essington, and D.D. Tyler. 1999. Vertical phosphorus and potassium stratification in no-till cotton soils. Agron. J. 91:266–269.

Howard, D.D., C.O. Gwathmey, M.E. Essington, R.K. Roberts, and M.D. Mullen. 2001c. Nitrogen fertilization of no-till cotton on loess-derived soils. Agron. J. 93:157–163.

Howard, D.D., C.O. Gwathmey, R.K. Roberts, and G.M. Lessman. 1997. Potassium fertilization of cotton on two high testing soils under two tillage systems. J. Plant Nutr. 20:1645–1656.

Howard, D.D., C.O. Gwathmey, R.K. Roberts, and G.M. Lessman. 1998. Potassium fertilization of cotton produced on a low K soil with contrasting tillage systems. J. Prod. Agric. 11:74–79.

Howard, D.D., and D.D. Tyler. 1989. Nitrogen source, rate, and application method for no-tillage corn. Soil Sci. Soc. Am. J. 53:1573–1577.

Hutchinson, R.L., R.C. Aycock, G.P. Boquet, S.M. Cruse, P.A. Miletello, C.L. Pinnell-Alison, R.L. Rogers, and W.W. Russell. 1991. An evaluation of conservation tillage systems for cotton on the Macon Ridge. Louisiana Coop. Ext. Ser. Publ. 2460. Louisiana State Univ., Baton Rouge.

Hutchinson, R.L., and W.L. Shelton. 1990. Alternative tillage systems and cover crops for cotton production on the Macon Ridge. Louisiana Agric. 33:6–8.

Jenny, H. 1941. Factors of soil formation. McGraw-Hill Co., New York.

Judice, W.E., and J.L. Griffin. 2008. To burn or not to burn—Sugarcane crop residue management. Louisiana Agric. 51:37–38.

Judice, W.E., J.L. Griffin, C.A. Jones, L.M. Etheredge, Jr., and M.E. Salassi. 2006. Weed control and economics using reduced tillage programs in sugarcane. Weed Technol. 20:319–325.

Karathanasis, A.D., and K.L. Wells. 1989. A comparison of mineral weathering trends between two management systems on a catena of loess-derived soils. Soil Sci. Soc. Am. J. 53:582–588.

Keisling, T.C. 1993. Reduced tillage for cotton production in Arkansas. p. 18–23. In M. McClelland et al. (ed.) Conservation technology in Arkansas agriculture 1992. Arkansas Agric. Exp. Stn. Research Series 432. Univ. of Arkansas, Fayetteville.

Keisling, T.C., R.F. Ford, and H.D. Scott. 1995. Tillage systems for cotton on Mississippi Delta and Loessial Plains soils. Commun. Soil Sci. Plant Anal. 26:441–452.

Keisling, T.C., H.D. Scott, B.A. Waddle, W. Williams, and R.E. Frans. 1994. Winter cover crops influence on cotton yield and selected soil properties. Commun. Soil Sci. Plant Anal. 25:3087–3100.

Kell, W. 1938. Strip cropping. p. 634–645. In Yearbook of Agriculture: Soils and men. U.S. Gov. Print. Office, Washington, DC.

Kröger, R., M.T. Moore, M.A. Locke, R.F. Cullum, R.W. Steinriede, S. Testa, C.T. Bryant, and C.M. Cooper. 2009. Evaluating the influence of wetland vegetation on chemical residence time in Mississippi Delta drainage ditches. Agric. Water Manage. 96:1175–1179.

Krusekopf, H.H. 1962. Major soil areas of Missouri. Univ. Missouri Agric. Exp. Stn. Bull. B785. University of Missouri, Columbia.

Kuhnle, R.A., R.L. Bingner, C.V. Alonso, C.G. Wilson, and A. Simon. 2008. Conservation practice effects on sediment load in the Goodwin Creek Experimental Watershed. J. Soil Water Conserv. 63:496–503.

Lentz, G.H., J.D. Sinclair, and H.G. Meginnis. 1929. Erosion report. Lafayette Co., Mississippi. USDA Forest Service, Southern Exp. Stn., New Orleans, LA.

Leon, C.T., E.P. Webster, S.L. Bottoms, and D.C. Blouin. 2008. Water management and chemical control of red rice (*Oryza punctata*) in water-seeded imidazolinone-resistant rice. Weed Technol. 22:132–135.

Locke, M.A., and F.M. Hons. 1988a. Fertilizer placement effects on seasonal nitrogen accumulation and yield of no-tillage and conventional tillage sorghum. Agron. J. 80:180–185.

Locke, M.A., and F.M. Hons. 1988b. Tillage effect on seasonal nitrogen accumulation of labeled fertilizer nitrogen in sorghum. Crop Sci. 28:694–700.

Locke, M.A., S.S. Knight, S. Smith, Jr., R.F. Cullum, R.M. Zablotowicz, Y. Yuan, and R.L. Bingner. 2008a. Environmental quality research in the Beasley Lake watershed, 1995 to 2007: Succession from conventional to conservation practices. J. Soil Water Conserv. 63:430–442.

Locke, M.A., K.N. Reddy, and R.M. Zablotowicz. 2008b. Integrating soil conservation practices and glyphosate-resistant crops: Impacts on soil. Pest Manage. Sci. 64:457–469.

Locke, M.A., R.M. Zablotowicz, P.J. Bauer, R.W. Steinriede, and L.A. Gaston. 2005. Conservation cotton production in the southern United States: Herbicide dissipation in soil and cover crops. Weed Sci. 53:717–727.

Logan, W.N. 1916. The soils of Mississippi. Mississippi Agric. Exp. Stn. Tech. Bull. 7. Mississippi Agric. Mech. College, Mississippi State.

Long, O.H., and J.R. Overton. 1963. Button clover as a green manure crop for cotton. Univ. Tennessee Agric. Exp. Stn. Bull. 370. Univ. Tennessee, Knoxville.

Lovell, S.T., and W.C. Sullivan. 2006. Environmental benefits of conservation buffers in the United States: Evidence, promise, and open questions. Agric. Ecosyst. Environ. 112:249–260.

Maddox, R.S. 1915. West Tennessee gullied lands and their reclamation. Resour. Tennessee 5:8–22.

Maul, J.D., and C.M. Cooper. 2000. Water quality of seasonally flooded agricultural fields in Mississippi, USA. Agric. Ecosyst. Environ. 81:171–178.

McDonald, A. 1941. Early American soil conservationists. USDA-SCS Misc. Publ. 449. U.S. Gov. Print. Office, Washington, DC.

McDowell, L.L., and K.C. McGregor. 1984. Plant nutrient losses in runoff from conservation tillage corn. Soil Tillage Res. 4:79–91.

McGinnis, H.G. 1933. Using soil-binding plants to reclaim gullies in the South. USDA Farmers Bull. 1697. U.S. Gov. Print. Office, Washington, DC.

McGregor, K.C., R.F. Cullum, C.K. Mutchler, and J.R. Johnson. 2006. Long-term no-till and conventional-till soybean yields. Mississippi Agric. Forest. Exp. Stn. Bull. 1146.

McGregor, K.C., S.M. Dabney, and J.R. Johnson. 1999a. Runoff and soil loss from cotton plots with and without stiff-grass hedges. Trans. ASAE 42:361–368.

McGregor, K.C., and J.D. Greer. 1982. Erosion control with no-till and reduced-till corn for silage and grain. Trans. ASAE 25:154–159.

McGregor, K.C., J.D. Greer, and G.E. Gurley. 1975. Erosion control with no-till cropping practices. Trans. ASAE 18:918–920.

McGregor, K.C., and C.K. Mutchler. 1983. C-factors for no-till and reduced-till corn. Trans. ASAE 26:785–788, 794.

McGregor, K.C., and C.K. Mutchler. 1992. Soil loss from conservation tillage for sorghum. Trans. ASAE 35:1841–1845.

McGregor, K.C., C.K. Mutchler, and R.F. Cullum. 1992. Soil erosion effects on soybean yields. Trans. ASAE 35:1521–1525.

McGregor, K.C., C.K. Mutchler, and R.F. Cullum. 1999b. Long-term management effects on runoff, erosion, and crop production. Trans. ASAE 42:99–105.

McGregor, K.C., C.K. Mutchler, J.R. Johnson, and D.E. Pogue. 1996. USDA and MAFES cooperative soil conservation studies at Holly Springs, 1956–1996. Mississippi Agric. Forest. Exp. Stn. Bull. 1044.

McGregor, K.C., C.K. Mutchler, and M.J.M. Romkens. 1990. Effects of tillage with different crop residues on runoff and soil loss. Trans. ASAE 33:1551–1556.

Melville, D.R. and J.L. Rabb. 1976. Studies with no-till soybean production. Louisiana Agric. 20:3, 16.

Meyer, L.D., S.M. Dabney, and W.C. Harmon. 1995. Sediment-trapping effectiveness of stiff-grass hedges. Trans. ASAE 38:809–815.

Millhollon, E.P., and D.R. Melville. 1991. The long-term effects of winter cover crops on cotton production in northwest Louisiana. Louisiana Agric. Exp. Stn. Bull. 830. Louisiana State Univ., Baton Rouge.

Minnesota Population Center. 2004. National Historical Geographic Information System: Prerelease Version 0.1. Available at http://www.nhgis.org (verified 5 Jan. 2010). Univ. of Minnesota, Minneapolis.

Mississippi Agricultural Experiment Station. 1934. A compilation of experimental and other data on winter legumes. Mississippi Agric. Exp. Stn. Bull. 303. Mississippi Agric. Mech. College, Mississippi State.

Mooers, C.A. 1944. Depth and method of soil preparation and cultivation for corn and cotton. Univ. Tennessee Agric. Exp. Stn. Bull. 191. Univ. Tennessee, Knoxville.

Mooers, C.A., and B.P. Hazelwood. 1945. Sericea as a soil-improving crop for corn. Univ. Tennessee Agric. Exp. Stn. Bull. 197. Univ. Tennessee, Knoxville.

Moore, C.A. 1916. The soils of Tennessee. Resour. Tennessee 5:154–173.

Moore, M.T., C.M. Cooper, S. Smith, Jr., R.F. Cullum, S.S. Knight, M.A. Locke, and E.R. Bennett. 2009. Mitigation of two pyrethroid insecticides in a Mississippi Delta constructed wetland. Environ. Pollut. 157:250–256.

Morrison, J.E., Jr., and F.W. Chichester. 1994. Tillage system effects on soil and plant nutrient distributions on vertisols. J. Prod. Agric. 7:364–373.

Morrison, J.E., T.J. Gerik, R.W. Chichester, J.R. Martin, and J.M. Chandler. 1990. A no-tillage farming system for clay soils. J. Prod. Agric. 3:219–227.

Murphree, C.E., and K.C. McGregor. 1991. Runoff and sediment yields from a flatland watershed in soybeans. Trans. ASAE 34:407–411.

Mutchler, C.K., and J.D. Greer. 1984. Reduced tillage for soybeans. Trans. ASAE 27:1365–1369.

Mutchler, C.K., and L.L. McDowell. 1990. Soil loss from cotton with winter cover crops. Trans. ASAE 33:432–436.

Mutchler, C.K., L.L. McDowell, and J.D. Greer. 1985. Soil loss from cotton with conservation tillage. Trans. ASAE 28:160–163, 168.

Nelson, M. 1944. Effect of the use of winter legumes on yields of cotton, corn, and rice. Arkansas Exp. Stn., Bull. 451. Univ. Arkansas, Fayetteville.

Nelson, M., W.H. Sachs, and R.H. Austin. 1923. The soils of Arkansas. Arkansas Agric. Exp. Stn. Bull. 187. Univ. Arkansas, Fayetteville.

Nett, M.T., M.A. Locke, and D.A. Pennington (ed.) 2004. Water quality assessments in the Mississippi Delta: Regional solutions, national scope. ACS Symp. Ser. 877. American Chemical Society, Washington, DC.

Nichols, M.L., and T.B. Chambers. 1938. Mechanical measures of erosion control. p. 646–665. In Yearbook of Agriculture: Soils and men. U.S. Gov. Print. Office, Washington, DC.

O'Brien, R.E., and D.W. Skelton. 1946. The production and utilization of kudzu. Mississippi Agric. Exp. Stn. Bull. 438. Mississippi State Univ., Mississippi State.

Offutt, M.S. 1970. Winter legume trials in Arkansas, 1959 to 1967. Univ. Arkansas Agric. Exp. Stn. Bull. 755. Univ. Arkansas, Fayetteville.

Patrick, W.H., Jr., C.B. Haddon, and J.A. Hendrix. 1957. The effect of longtime use of winter cover crops on certain physical properties of Commerce Loam. Soil Sci. Soc. Am. Proc. 21:366–368.

Pearce, A.D., C.R. Dillion, T.C. Keisling, and C.E. Wilson, Jr. 1999. Economic and agronomic effects of four tillage practices on rice produced on saline soils. J. Prod. Agric. 12:305–312.

Pearson, R.W., and L.E. Ensminger. 1957. Southeastern Uplands. p. 578–594. In 1957 Yearbook of agriculture: Soil. U.S. Gov. Print. Office, Washington, DC.

Pettigrew, W.T., and M.A. Jones. 2001. Cotton growth under no-till production in the lower Mississippi River Valley alluvial flood plain. Agron. J. 93:1398–1404.

Phillips, R.E. 1968. Minimum seedbed preparation for cotton. Agron. J. 60:437–441.

Popp, M.P. 2007. Assessment of alternative fuel production from switchgrass: An example from Arkansas. J. Agric. Appl. Econ. 39:373–380.

Potter, K.N., and F.W. Chichester. 1993. Physical and chemical properties of a vertisol with continuous controlled-traffic, no-till management. Trans. ASAE 36:95–99.

Potter, K.N., J.E. Morrison, Jr., and H.A. Torbert. 1996. Tillage intensity effects on corn and grain sorghum growth and productivity on a Vertisol. J. Prod. Agric. 9:385–390.

Potter, K.N., H.A. Torbert, O.R. Jones, J.E. Matocha, J.E. Morrison, Jr., and P.W. Unger. 1998. Distribution and amount of soil organic C in long-term management systems in Texas. Soil Tillage Res. 47:309–321.

Rabalais, N.N., R.E. Turner, D. Justic, Q. Dortch, W.J. Wiseman, Jr., and B.K. Sen Gupta. 1996. Nutrient changes in the Mississippi River and system responses on the adjacent continental shelf. Estuaries 19(2B):386-407.

Rabb, J.L., and D.R. Melville. 1984. Double cropping soybeans and wheat in northwest Louisiana. J. Soil Water Conserv. 39:77-78.

Ramser, C.E. 1929. The prevention of the erosion of farm lands by terracing. J. Am. Soc. Agron. 21:430-432.

Renard, K.G., G.R. Foster, G.A. Weesies, D.K. McCool, and D.C. Yoder. 1997. Predicting soil erosion by water: A guide to conservation planning with the Revised Universal Soil Loss Equation (RUSLE). Agric. Handb. 703. USDA-ARS, U.S. Gov. Print. Office, Washington, DC.

Reynolds, E.B., P.R. Johnson, and H.F. Morris. 1950. Hairy vetch, bur clover, and oats as soil-building crops for cotton and corn in Texas. Texas Agric. Exp. Stn. Bull. 731. Texas Agric. Mech. Univ., College Station.

Reynolds, E.B., H.E. Rea, E. Whiteley, P.A. Rich, and J.E. Roberts. 1958. Legumes for soil improvement for cotton and corn. Texas Agric. Exp. Stn. Bull. 901. Texas Agric. Mech. Univ., College Station.

Rhoton, F.E. 1990. Soybean yield response to various depths of erosion on a fragipan soil. Trans. ASAE 54:1073-1079.

Rhoton, F.E. 2000. Influence of time on soil response to no-till practices. Soil Sci. Soc. Am. J. 64:700-709.

Rhoton, F.E., M.J. Shipitalo, and D.L. Lindbo. 2002. Runoff and soil loss from midwestern and southeastern U.S. silt loam soils as affected by tillage practice and soil organic matter content. Soil Tillage Res. 66:1-11.

Rhoton, F.E., and D.D. Tyler. 1990. Erosion-induced changes in the properties of a fragipan soil. Soil Sci. Soc. Am. J. 54:223-228.

Roberts, R.K., B.C. English, Q. Gao, and J.A. Larson. 2006. Simultaneous adoption of herbicide-resistant and conservation-tillage cotton technologies. J. Agric. Appl. Econ. 38:629-643.

Salinas-Garcia, J.R., F.M. Hons, and J.E. Matocha. 1997a. Long-term effects of tillage and fertilization on soil organic matter dynamics. Soil Sci. Soc. Am. J. 61:152-159.

Salinas-Garcia, J.R., F.M. Hons, J.E. Matocha, and D.A. Zuberer. 1997b. Soil carbon and nitrogen dynamics as affected by long-term tillage and nitrogen fertilization. Biol. Fert. Soils 25:182-188.

Sanderson, M.A., R.M. Jones, M.J. McFarland, J. Stroup, R.L. Reed, and J.P. Muir. 2001. Nutrient movement and removal in a switchgrass biomass-filter strip treated with dairy manure. J. Environ. Qual. 30:210-216.

Schreiber, J.D., and E.E. Neumaier. 1987. Biochemical oxygen demand of agricultural runoff. J. Environ. Qual. 16:6-10.

Scott, H.D., T.C. Keisling, B.A. Waddle, R.W. Williams, and R.E. Frans. 1990. Effects of winter cover crops on yield of cotton and soil properties. Arkansas Agric. Exp. Stn. Bull. 324. Univ. Arkansas, Fayetteville.

Sewell, M.C. 1919. Tillage: A review of the literature. J. Am. Soc. Agron. 11:269-290.

Shelton, C.H., and J.F. Bradley. 1987. Controlling erosion and sustaining production with no-till systems. Tenn. Farm Home Sci. 141:18-23.

Shelton, C.H., and C.R. Mote. 1989. Soil erosion and related water quality. Tenn. Farm Home Sci. 152:26-31.

Shelton, C.H., F.D. Tompkins, and D.D. Tyler. 1982. Soil erosion from five soybean tillage systems in west Tennessee. Tenn. Farm Home Sci. 122:14-18.

Shelton, C.H., F.D. Tompkins, and D.D. Tyler. 1983. Soil erosion from five soybean tillage systems. J. Soil Water Conserv. 38:425-428.

Smith, R.M., R.C. Henderson, and O.J. Tippit. 1954. Summary of soil and water conservation research from the Blackland Experiment Station, Temple, Texas 1942-53. Texas Agric. Exp. Stn. Bull. 781. Texas Agric. Mech. Univ., College Station.

Snipes, C.E., S.P. Nichols, D.H. Poston, T.W. Walker, L.P. Evans, and H.R. Robinson. 2005. Current agricultural practices of the Mississippi Delta. Mississippi Agric. Forestry Exp. Stn. Bull. 1143. Mississippi State Univ., Mississippi State.

Soil Survey Staff. 1999. Soil taxonomy, a basic system of classification for making and interpreting soil surveys. 2nd ed. USDA-NRCS Agric. Handb. 436. U.S. Gov. Print. Office, Washington, DC.

Southern Regional Soil Research Committee. 1959. Certain properties of southeastern United States soils and mineralogical procedures for their study. Southern Regional Bull. 61.

Cooperative Regional Research Project S-14. Virginia Agric. Exp. Stn., Virginia Polytech. Inst., Blacksburg.

Southwick, L.M., B.C. Grigg, T.S. Kornecki, and J.L. Fouss. 2002. Potential influence of sugarcane cultivation on estuarine water quality of Louisiana's Gulf coast. J. Agric. Food Chem. 50:4393–4399.

Springer, M.E., and J.A. Elder. 1980. Soils of Tennessee. Univ. Tennessee Agric. Exp. Stn. Bull. 596. Univ. Tennessee, Knoxville.

Torbert, H.A., K.N. Potter, and J.E. Morrison, Jr. 2001. Tillage system, fertilizer nitrogen rate, and timing effect on corn yields in the Texas Blackland Prairie. Agron. J. 93:1119–1124.

Triplett, G.B., S.M. Dabney, and J.H. Siefker. 1996. Tillage systems for cotton on silty upland soils. Agron. J. 88:507–512.

Triplett, G.B., Jr., and W.A. Dick. 2008. No-tillage crop production: A revolution in agriculture. Agron. J. 100:S153–S165.

Tyler, D.D., and J.R. Overton. 1982. No-tillage advantages for soybean seed quality during drought stress. Agron. J. 74:344–347.

Tyler, D.D., M.G. Wagger, D.V. McCracken, and W.L. Hargrove. 1994. Role of conservation tillage in sustainable agriculture in the southern United States. p. 209–229. In M.R. Carter (ed.) Conservation tillage in temperate agroecosystems. CRC Press, Boca Raton, FL.

University of Tennessee. 1915. Twenty-seventh annual report of the agricultural experiment station of the University of Tennessee for 1914. Univ. Tennessee, Knoxville.

University of Virginia, Geospatial and Statistical Data Center. 2004. Historical Census Browser. Available at http://fisher.lib.virginia.edu/collections/stats/histcensus/index.html. (verified 5 Jan. 2010).

U.S. Census Bureau. 1900. Census of population and housing: 1900 Census. Available at www.census.gov/prod/www/abs/decennial/1900.htm (verified 14 Dec. 2009). U.S. Census Bureau, Washington, DC.

U.S. Census Bureau. 1910. Census of population and housing: 1910 Census. [Online]. Available at www.census.gov/prod/www/abs/decennial/1910.htm (verified 14 Dec. 2009). U.S. Census Bureau, Washington, DC.

U.S. Census Bureau. 1920. Census of population and housing: 1920 Census. [Online]. Available at www.census.gov/prod/www/abs/decennial/1920.htm (verified 14 Dec. 2009). U.S. Census Bureau, Washington, DC.

U.S. Census Bureau. 1930. Census of population and housing: 1930 Census. [Online]. Available at www.census.gov/prod/www/abs/decennial/1930.htm (verified 14 Dec. 2009). U.S. Census Bureau, Washington, DC.

U.S. Census Bureau. 1950. Census of population and housing: 1950 Census. [Online]. Available at www.census.gov/prod/www/abs/decennial/1950.htm (verified 14 Dec. 2009). U.S. Census Bureau, Washington, DC.

U.S. Census Bureau. 2000. U.S. Census 2000. Available at www.census.gov/main/www/cen2000.html (verified 14 Dec. 2009). U.S. Census Bureau, Washington, DC.

U.S. Census Bureau. 2002. Census of agriculture—2002 census of agriculture. Vol. 1, Chap. 2 County level data. Available at http://www.agcensus.usda.gov/Publications/2002/Volume_1,_Chapter_2_County_Level/index.asp (verified 5 Jan. 2010). U.S. Census Bureau, Washington, DC.

USDA-FS. 1988. Yazoo-Little Tallahatchie flood prevention project—A history of the Forest Service's role. U.S. Forest Service Forestry Rep. Feb; R8-FR 8:63.

USDA-NRCS. 2000. Summary report, 1997 national resources inventory (rev. December 2000). [Online]. Available at www.nrcs.usda.gov/technical/NRI/1997/summary_report/report.pdf (verified 14 Dec. 2009).

USDA-NRCS. 2006. Land resources regions and major land resource areas of the United States, the Caribbean, and the Pacific Basin. Agric. Handb. 296. Available at http://soils.usda.gov/survey/geography/mlra/ (verified 5 Jan. 2010). U.S. Gov. Print. Office, Washington, DC.

USDA-NRCS. 2007a. National resources inventory, 2003 annual NRI, land use. Available at www.nrcs.usda.gov/technical/NRI/2003/Landuse-mrb.pdf (verified 14 Dec. 2009).

USDA-NRCS. 2007b. National resources inventory, 2003 annual NRI, soil erosion. Available at www.nrcs.usda.gov/technical/NRI/2003/SoilErosion-mrb.pdf (verified 14 Dec. 2009).

USDA-NRCS. 2010. Distribution maps of dominant soil orders. Available at http://soils.usda.gov/technical/classification/orders/ (verified 8 Jan. 2010).

USDA-NRCS Soil Survey Staff. 2010. U.S. general soil map (STATSGO). Available at http://soildatamart.nrcs.usda.gov (verified 5 Jan. 2010).

Utz, E.J. 1938. The coordinated approach to soil erosion control. p. 666–678. *In* Yearbook of agriculture: Soils and men. U.S. Gov. Print. Office, Washington, DC.

Utz, E.J., and E.C. Kellogg, E.H. Reed, J.H. Stallings, and E.N. Munns. 1938. The problem: The nation as a whole. p. 84–110. *In* Yearbook of agriculture: Soils and men. U.S. Gov. Print. Office, Washington, DC.

Vanderford, H.B. 1975. Soil and land resources of Mississippi. Mississippi Agric. Forest. Exp. Stn., Mississippi State Univ., Mississippi State.

Viator, H.P., R. Bengston, S. Hall, L. Gaston, M. Selim, J. Wang, B. Legendre, T. Hymel, J. Flanagan, J. Hoy, C. Kennedy, and J. Prudente. 2008. Influence of sugarcane post-harvest residue management on yield, water quality. Louisiana Agric. 51:39–40.

Viator, H.P., and J.G. Marshall. 1981. No-till grain sorghum production following wheat. Louisiana Agric. 25:16–17.

Wells, F.B. 1933. Ground-water resources of western Tennessee. Water-supply paper 656. Tennessee Div. of Geology. U.S. Gov. Print. Office, Washington, DC.

Williams, D.A. 1964. Grass in soil and water conservation. USDA-SCS, Washington, DC.

Wilson, G.V., S.M. Dabney, K.C. McGregor, and B.D. Barkoll. 2004. Tillage and residue effects on runoff and erosion dynamics. Trans. ASAE 47:119–128.

Wilson, G.V., F.D. Shields, Jr., R.L. Bingner, R. Reid-Rhoades, D.A. DiCarlo, and S.M. Dabney. 2008. Conservation practices and gully erosion contributions in the Topashaw Canal watershed. J. Soil Water Conserv. 63:420–429.

Wischmeier, W.H., and D.D. Smith. 1978. Predicting rainfall erosion losses—A guide to conservation planning, USDA Agric. Handb. 537. U.S. Gov. Print. Office, Washington, DC.

Wright, A.L., F. Dou, and F.M. Hons. 2007a. Crop species and tillage effects on carbon sequestration in subsurface soil. Soil Sci. 172:124–131.

Wright, A.L., F. Dou, and F.M. Hons. 2007b. Soil organic C and N distribution for wheat cropping systems after 20 years of conservation tillage in central Texas. Agric. Ecosyst. Environ. 121:376–382.

Wright, A.L., and F.M. Hons. 2004. Soil aggregation and carbon and nitrogen storage under soybean cropping sequences. Soil Sci. Soc. Am. J. 68:507–513.

Wright, A.L., and F.M. Hons. 2005. Soil carbon and nitrogen storage in aggregates from different tillage and crop regimes. Soil Sci. Soc. Am. J. 69:141–147.

Yuan, Y., S.M. Dabney, and R.L. Bingner. 2002. Cost effectiveness of agricultural BMPs for sediment reduction in the Mississippi Delta. J. Soil Water Conserv. 57:259–267.

Yuan, Y., M.A. Locke, and R.L. Bingner. 2008. Annualized agricultural non-point source model application for Mississippi Delta Beasley Lake watershed conservation practices assessment. J. Soil Water Conserv. 63:542–551.

Zablotowicz, R.M., M.A. Locke, L.A. Gaston, and C.T. Bryson. 2000. Interactions of tillage and soil depth on fluometuron degradation in a Dundee silt loam soil. Soil Tillage Res. 57:61–68.

Zablotowicz, R.M., M.A. Locke, L.J. Krutz, R.N. Lerch, R.E. Lizotte, S.S. Knight, R.E. Gordon, and R.W. Steinriede. 2006. Influence of watershed system management on herbicide concentrations in Mississippi Delta oxbow lakes. Sci. Total Environ. 370:552–560.

Zibilske, L.M., and J.M. Bradford. 2007. Soil aggregation, aggregate carbon and nitrogen, and moisture retention induced by conservation tillage. Soil Sci. Soc. Am. J. 71:793–802.

9

Soil and Water Conservation for California and the Desert Southwest: Past, Present, and Future Trends

A. Toby O'Geen, Michael J. Singer, and William Horwath
Department of Land, Air, and Water Resources, University of California, Davis, CA

The four southwestern states described in this chapter—Arizona, California, Nevada, and New Mexico—reflect a vast diversity in landscapes. The region extends across 1600 km of longitude and 965 km of latitude, with a great variation in precipitation and temperature. Areas suitable for cropland within this region have in common low rainfall and high temperatures during the summer, and high diversity of soils. In California, Arizona, and parts of New Mexico, rapid population growth puts pressure on agricultural land uses.

General physiographic regions important to agriculture in the Southwest include: (i) the Sonoran, Colorado, and Mojave Deserts in Arizona, California, and Nevada; (ii) the Basin and Range in eastern California, Nevada, southwestern New Mexico, and southern and western Arizona; (iii) the Colorado Plateau in northern and eastern Arizona and northwestern New Mexico; (iv) the Great Plains in eastern New Mexico; and (v) the Central Valley, Salinas Valley, and Imperial Valley in California. The Southwest contains several large mountain ranges, including the Rocky Mountains, Sierra Nevada, Coast Ranges, and Cascade Mountains, which serve as important watersheds for environmental, recreational, urban, and agricultural uses.

The agricultural landscape is equally diverse. Rangeland occupies the largest spatial extent of any land use. The combined irrigated land of New Mexico, Arizona, and Nevada is about 971,000 ha compared to 3.2 million hectares in California (Table 9–1). The combined irrigated area in the four states is approximately 18% of the total irrigated agriculture in the United States (USDA Census of Agriculture, 2007). Common crops in New Mexico and Nevada include alfalfa hay (*Medicago sativa* L.), cotton (*Gossypium hirsutum* L.), and wheat (*Triticum aestivum* L.). Arizona has a more diverse crop mix, including cotton, nuts, wheat, barley (*Hordeum vulgare* L.), vegetables, and fruits. California has the most diverse suite of agricultural commodities, with a mixture of more than 300 crops, and supplies more than half of the nation's fruits, nuts, and vegetables. Common products grown almost exclusively in California include almonds [*Prunus dulcis* (Mill.) D.A. Webb], artichokes (*Cynara cardunculus* L.), dates (*Phoenix dactylifera* L.), figs (*Ficus carica* L.), kiwifruit [*Actinidia deliciosa* (A. Chev.) C.F. Liang & A.R. Ferguson],

---

Soil and Water Conservation Advances in the United States. SSSA Special Publication 60.
T.M. Zobeck and W.F. Schillinger, editors. © 2010. SSSA, 677 S. Segoe Rd., Madison, WI 53711, USA.

Table 9–1. Summary of cropland in production in the Southwest.

State	Cropland†	Irrigated land†	Water erosion‡
	——————— ha ———————		t yr^{-1} × 10^3
California	3,830,207	3,244,024	3,178 ± 943
New Mexico	944,544	335,908	1,238 ± 231
Arizona	487,818	354,569	547 ± 122
Nevada	305,019	279,650	32.6 ± 19

† USDA Census of agriculture (2007).
‡ USDA-NRI (2003).

olives (*Olea europaea* L.), pistachios (*Pistacia vera* L.), prunes (*Prunus domestica* L.), raisins (*Vitis vinifera* L.), and walnuts (*Juglans* spp.)

The diversity in terrain and current and past climates makes generalizing the soils difficult. Most agricultural soils are located in valley settings (with the exception of wine grapes and some tree crops) and hence are derived from alluvium. Mollisols, Alfisols, Inceptisols, Entisols, Aridisols, Vertisols, and Histosols are the main soil orders in production. Most of the productive farmland (Fig. 9–1, generalized as Land Capability Classes I–III) exists in Ustic and Aridic moisture regimes in Arizona and New Mexico and Xeric and Aridic moisture regimes in Nevada and California (Fig. 9–2). Similarly, most of the farmland throughout the Southwest is located in areas with thermic soil temperature regimes, with areas of lesser extent in hyperthermic and mesic soil temperature regimes (Fig. 9–3). The arid and semiarid conditions that are representative of most of the cultivated agriculture in these four states present some common challenges for agriculture, including water supply and quality, salt and sodium-affected soils, drainage, wind and water erosion, and urban expansion. This chapter considers each of these challenges and the conservation strategies developed to address them. Much of the data discussed in this chapter are from research from California because of its vast land area in production (Table 9–1).

In California, precipitation varies with elevation, latitude, and proximity to the coast. The winter growing season is as important as summer. In many instances we use California's Central Valley as a case study to demonstrate the issues surrounding soil and water conservation in the Southwest. The Central Valley is made up of the Sacramento River and San Joaquin River and Tulare Lake basins. The San Joaquin Valley is located in the southern half of the Central Valley. It contains more than 500,000 ha of land, much of which consists of irrigated agriculture (Letey et al., 2002).

The long growing season, availability of water associated with large infrastructure improvements, and fertile soils make the Central Valley one of the most important agricultural regions in the world. Precipitation ranges from 130 mm in the south to 380 mm in the north and occurs mostly during the winter. Precipitation is not adequate in amount or timing for growing most crops; thus, irrigation is required for high productivity, which is the case for most of the Southwest. Massive investments in water supply infrastructure and the perceived resistance to soil erosion have translated to very few efforts to conserve water and soil during most of the late 19th and 20th centuries.

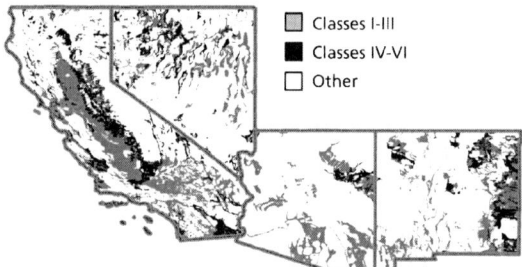

Fig. 9-1. Land capability class for the southwest. Classes 1 through 3 represent productive irrigated land. Classes 4 through 6 represent marginal and erosive land with the potential to support perennial tree crops. USDA-NRCS STATSGO database.

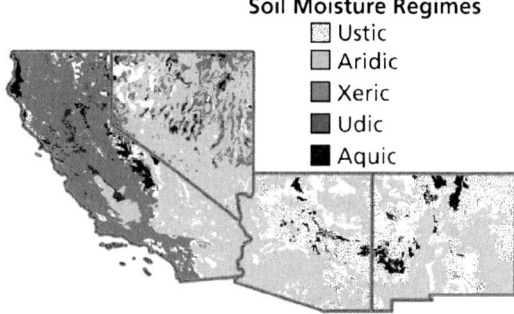

Fig. 9-2. Dominant soil moisture regimes in the Southwest. Soil temperature regimes are generally defined as follows: Aridic (desert climate)—soil is dry in all parts for more than half the year and is never moist more than 90 consecutive d during the growing season; Ustic (monsoonal climate)—soil is dry more than 90 but fewer than 180 cumulative days, but is not dry during the growing season; Xeric (Mediterranean climate)—soil is dry more than 45 consecutive days during the growing season and is moist more than 45 consecutive days in winter; Udic (humid climate)—soil is not dry for as many as 90 cumulative days; Aquic (wetland environment)—soil is saturated long enough during the year to produce reducing conditions. USDA-NRCS STATSGO database.

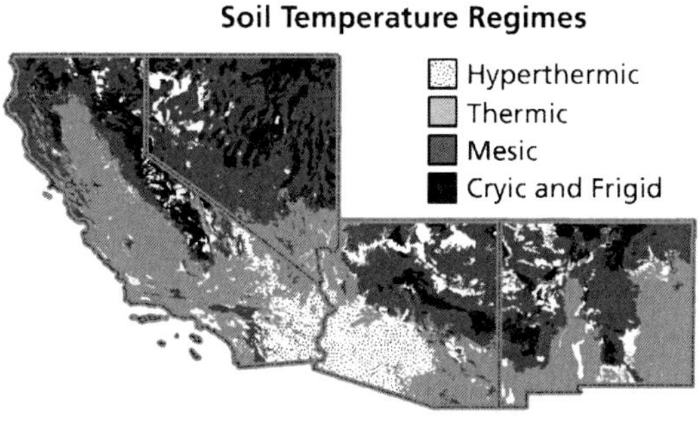

Fig. 9-3. Dominant soil temperature regimes in the southwest. Mean annual soil temperature regimes are measured at 50-cm depth and are generally defined as: Hyperthermic >22°C; Thermic 15–22°C; Mesic 8–15°C; Frigid <8°C with warm summers; Cryic <8°C with cold summers. USDA-NRCS STATSGO database.

Historical Perspective of Soil and Water Conservation

Prehistoric agriculture in the Southwest was complicated by the extreme aridity common to most low-elevation settings and the short growing season indicative of uplands. Maize (*Zea mays* L.), beans (*Phaseolus vulgaris* L.), squash (*Cucurbita pepo* L.), and bottle gourd [*Lagenaria siceraria* (Molina) Standl.] were the first crops grown in the Southwest. These crops, however, were not adapted to the climatic conditions of the Southwest. Paleoenvironmental studies indicate that the introduction of these cultivars took place between 3500 and 2400 BP (Wills, 1988). The initiation of agriculture in the Southwest may have coincided with a period of wetter and cooler climate (Hevly, 1983), which may explain agriculture's first foothold in this region.

The Gold Rush had a substantial impact on agriculture, particularly in California. By the 1850s many miners abandoned their search of gold for a new golden treasure, wheat. The proximity to shipping ports and willingness to adopt mechanized, labor-saving technologies transformed agriculture in California into large-scale operations that were part of the global economy (Olmstead and Rhode, 2001). By the early 1900s large-scale grain production switched to smaller-scale fruit production in California. For example, between 1859 and 1929 the number of farms increased by 700%, yet the average farm size decreased from 180 to 90 ha (Olmstead and Rhode, 2001).

Water Supply

In the Southwest, most farmland was confined to the arid and semiarid valleys in which irrigation was developed. Most of the issues surrounding soil and water conservation focused on infrastructure development and land reclamation. According to Jelinek (1979), the four historical developments that made agriculture possible in California, and the larger Southwest, were irrigation, development of crop cultivars, labor supply, and marketing. Jelinek (1979) makes no mention of conservation issues in his book. The availability of water was of utmost importance because evapotranspiration (ET) far exceeds precipitation during the growing season. As with most arid and semiarid regions, fresh water supply is available in localized areas, often at great distances relative to farmland or at great cost associated with pumping of groundwater. Most farmland in the Southwest is irrigated from major infrastructure improvement projects on rivers and associated reservoirs, such as the Colorado, Salt (Arizona), Gila (Arizona), Sacramento (California), and Rio Grande (New Mexico) Rivers, and the Sacramento–San Joaquin River Delta (California).

The earliest irrigation schemes in California were initiated by the Spanish Padres, who built dams, reservoirs, and aqueducts to bring water to cultivated areas (Jelinek, 1979). Before the development of widespread irrigation, California agriculture was mostly free-range cattle and sheep production. No assessment of the damage to soils or native vegetation produced by this land use has been made. Following the Gold Rush period from 1848 to 1872, the demand for California wheat vastly increased the area under dryland cultivation. Jelinek (1979) refers to the period from 1872 to 1902 as the "wheat era." During this period, wheat production in the region was the most mechanized in the world, and early literature suggests that soil conservation was not a high priority (Horn, 1976).

Irrigation began in California's Central Valley at the end of the 19th century and was limited to gravity-fed diversions from the San Joaquin River. Citrus cultivation began in 1873 with the introduction of the navel orange [*Citrus sinensis* (L.) Osbeck] from Brazil. In the 1920s, the extent of irrigated land expanded with increased groundwater pumping. This somewhat unsustainable practice was mitigated through the Central Valley Water Project and the State Water Project. These massive infrastructure investments transformed California by diverting its abundant water supply in the northern portion of the state to the irrigated land in the south (Howitt and Sunding, 2003).

By the 1940s, the effects of intensive agriculture were starting to be understood. In a brief report developed by the State of California Agriculture Conservation Association, USDA (1947) reported that in the previous 100 years, 75% of the topsoil had been eroded on 100,000 ha, 25 to 75% on 1 million ha, and there was slight but increasing erosion on 1.4 million ha.

The development of irrigation systems in California and other states has greatly increased the value of farm products produced for export and domestic consumption, but it has also caused vast changes to the hydrology of the state. These developments have had the unintended consequences of severe land subsidence in parts of California due to groundwater pumping, and the near fatal decrease in some fish populations due to diversion of stream flows from their natural courses. Many of these issues have been addressed during the later quarter of the 20th century as the demand for water for urban and agricultural uses has put enormous strain on water resources in the region. However, the challenges associated with degradation of water quality (surface and groundwater) via nonpoint-source pollution still threaten the sustainability of water resources in the Southwest.

Land Evaluation and Reclamation

The first hundred years of California agriculture began with the arrival of Mexican cattle in 1769 (Adams 1946). Within a few years, the first wheat crop was sown in the San Diego River Valley. The early Spanish missionaries were very aware of soil resources and often mapped their soils according to a simple classification system. Soils were rated as first-, second-, and third-rate soils. First-rate soils were used for vegetable gardens. Other soils were used for fruits and nuts and included almost all commercial species grown today. The other states in the Southwest began agriculture later as water resources along the Colorado River and other river systems were developed in the late 19th and early 20th centuries.

By 1919, 60% of California farmlands had a soil survey (Horn, 1976). Today, all of California's cultivated land has had at least one soil survey and some have had three generations of surveys. These surveys clearly showed that many of California's older soils had strongly developed subsoils, which imposed limitations for planting many crops (especially tree crops). Soil surveys in Arizona, Nevada, and New Mexico found similar subsoils. The solution to the drainage and rooting problems associated with these strongly developed subsoils was subsoiling, which was first initiated in the 1920s in California (Kaddah, 1976).

Various kinds of cemented horizons and clay-rich B horizons limit root growth and downward water movement (Fig. 9–4). The solution was (and still is) to remove the offending layers. In the early 20th century one common method of mitigating these restrictive horizons was by dynamite to prepare holes for plant-

Fig. 9–4. Spatial extent of soils with root and water restrictive horizons that require deep tillage. USDA-NRCS STATSGO database.

ing trees and vines. As equipment became larger and more powerful, horizons are now "ripped" or "slip-plowed" (Fig. 9–5). Either process destroys or disrupts the natural soil horizonation and creates a more uniform plant growth medium. In parts of the San Joaquin Valley one can see stone walls made from bits of hardpan removed from fields that have been ripped. Ripping brought the pan fragments to the soil surface. A modern concern with this practice is that much of the natural soil in intensively farmed regions has been lost and the remaining natural soils are now "rare and endangered" (Amundson et al., 2003). Land leveling is another common modification practice implemented to maintain uniform application of irrigation water that has resulted in major alteration to soils.

In California, soil plowing began in earnest following the Gold Rush (Jenny, 1946). The Stockton Gang Plow became popular on what was considered tule and adobe land, i.e., poorly drained, often clay-rich soils. In the late 1860s, wheel plows or sulkies and gang plows were common in the California coastal areas. These were shallow plows used for cultivating wheat. By 1879, California ranked seventh among all states in wheat production at almost 800,000 metric tons annually (Wilson, 1984). As water resources were developed and more crop cultivars were introduced, deep tillage and clean and frequent plowing was adopted. The first field experiments were on the comparative effects of shallow and deep plowing and were undertaken at the University of California by Hilgard in 1875 (Jenny, 1946).

Fig. 9–5. Photograph of a slip plow used to modify soils with restrictive horizons. Photo by Bill Wildman.

Possibly one of the largest soil reclamation projects in the Southwest was the agricultural development of the Sacramento–San Joaquin Delta, a 2978-km^2 region that was reclaimed for agricultural use in the late 1800s and early 1900s. Levee construction to prevent flooding and a network of drainage systems have supported crops valued in excess of $375 million annually in these peat soils.

"Reclamation" of the delta islands through levee construction has resulted in rapid decomposition of the organic soils. Land surfaces are now as much as 10 m below sea level. The levees are in poor condition, and their failure is of concern to water managers because the water supply for agriculture and urban uses south of the delta depends on their continued maintenance (Lund et al., 2008). One of the unmet challenges for soil management is how to maintain the islands in their current condition and eventually rebuild the organic matter levels.

Salinity and Sodicity

Soils of arid and semiarid areas are prone to accumulate soluble salts and sodium because evaporation and plant transpiration far exceed precipitation. Eugene Hilgard, who worked at the University of California from 1874 to 1916, was one of the first to recognize the importance of soil conservation in agriculture and especially to recognize the problems of salinity and sodicity (Horn, 1976). Soluble salts accumulate in soils, leading to plant stress, which is reflected in decreased yields at best and complete loss of crop at worst. This continues to be an issue in the Southwest because irrigation water contributes to the salt load of soils. Without sufficient leaching and an adequate sink for the salty drainage water, agriculture becomes impossible. In California this has reached critical concern because suitable sinks for the salty drain waters do not exist (Hanson and Ayars, 2002; Letey et al., 2002). Many farms now store their drain water on site (Tanji et al., 2002).

Sodicity, known as "black alkali" is a problem of excess sodium on the soil exchange complex. Sodium raises the soil pH to levels unacceptable for healthy plant growth, solubilizes organic matter, and destroys soil structure. Reclamation of sodic soils requires the addition of calcium bearing amendments, such as gypsum, sufficient drainage water, and a sink for the disposal of the drainage water. Salinity and sodicity require drainage that is often provided by ditches or more frequently by perforated pipe buried at a predetermined depth and slope angle to a drain that leads to a final sink. In the early days, the perforated pipe was clay tile, which has now been replaced by perforated plastic pipe (Fig. 9–6).

Fig. 9–6. Tile drain installation in the San Joaquin Valley, California. Image courtesy of Blaine Hanson, University of California, Davis.

Urban Expansion

California has more than 36.7 million inhabitants (USDA-Census of Agriculture, 2007). In 1950, the population was 10.6 million. For the period April 2000 to July 2007 the population increased by 7.9%, which is significantly higher than the average growth rate for the United States. This growth is representative of the increase in population since the end of World War II. Rapid population growth has produced fast and extensive growth of urban and suburban areas throughout California and the Southwest. In the area around San Francisco Bay, high housing prices and strong demand created a housing boom in the San Joaquin Valley that often occurred on high-quality agricultural land. The issue of farmland conversion was a contentious political issue for much of the 20th century and will continue into much of this century. Among the attempts to understand and direct farmland conversion onto soils with lower agricultural potential, the California Land Conservation Act of 1965, often called the Williamson Act, was enacted to provide a mechanism of farmland protection. The Act enables local government units such as counties to enter into long-term contracts with private land owners restricting the land to agricultural use. The land-owner is taxed on the basis of productivity, and the state provides the local government with subvention payments that reduce the tax losses produced by the restrictions on development.

To monitor the conversion of farmland to other uses the state created the Farmland Mapping and Monitoring Program (FMMP) in the Department of Conservation in 1982 (California Department of Conservation, 2009). From 1984 to present, the agency has published reports on changes in agricultural land use for the whole state and by county. A recent summary of land use change published by FMMP showed that in the last 20 yr, approximately 500,000 ha of farmland have been converted to other uses (Table 9–2). These data only include private lands that have been mapped by USDA-NRCS, and the total area included in their study has increased since it was initiated.

Table 9–2. Land use change in California by land use category.†

Land use category	Total change	Avg. annual change
	ha	
Prime farmland	−186,670	−8,485
Farmland of statewide importance	−82,596	−3753
Unique farmland	16,891	768
Farmland of local importance	−54,409	−2,473
Irrigated farmland	−13,183	−599
Nonirrigated farmland	−5,084	−231
Total important farmland	−325,022	−14,773
Grazing land	−172,137	−7,825
Total agricultural land (important farmland + grazing land)	−497,159	−22,598
Urban and built-up land	391607	17,800
Other land	98,653	4484
Water	7131	324

† Data from the California Department of Conservation, Division of Land Resource Protection. Numbers have been rounded in converting from acres to hectares.

Table 9-3. Changes in land use between 2002 and 2004 for 18.5 million hectares in California.†

Land use category	Total area 2002	Total area 2004
	——— ha ———	
Prime farmland	2,086,068	2,054,270
Farmland of statewide importance	1,105,490	1,089,114
Unique farmland	521,671	516,012
Irrigated farmland	219,511	217,236
Nonirrigated farmland	3,673	3,019
Farmland of local importance	1,152,562	1,155,268
Important farmland subtotal	5,088,975	5,034,920
Grazing Land	6,633,144	6,618,005
Agricultural land subtotal	11,722,119	11,652,925
Urban and built-up land	1,326,493	1,367,700
Other land	5,221,308	5,248,682
Water area	285,075	285,688
Total area inventoried	18,554,995	18,554,995

† Data from the California Department of Conservation, Division of Land Resource Protection.

Another recent report, for example, showed that between 2002 and 2004 the amount of urban and built-up land had increased by more than 40,000 ha (Table 9-3).

Wind and Water Erosion

There is little indication in the historical literature that either wind or water erosion were considered major issues in California, in part because much of the cultivated land is on low slopes and precipitation occurs as low-intensity storms. California has few of the high-intensity summer thunderstorms that produce water erosion in the other southwestern states. Perhaps the most devastating erosion in the western states was caused by hydraulic mining in California, where whole hillsides were washed away in the search for gold. This practice resulted in sedimentation of the lower reaches of many streams, and with the present-day decrease in sediment load, streams now tend to downcut, leading to widespread bank erosion.

California has rich forest resources, and some of the more severe water erosion has occurred under this land use, in particular from road building. Little remaining "old growth" forest exists in the region, and forest management now recognizes the importance of careful and minimal road building and careful harvest practices that have reduced water erosion compared to the forest harvesting practices that followed the Gold Rush. There are few data on historical or modern amounts of wind erosion, but conservation efforts have seen a revival due to concerns about poor air quality in the region. Cultivation in the California Delta region has lead to severe wind erosion in the past (California Department of Water Resources, 1980). Many locations in California's Central Valley do not meet USEPA annual average standards of 50 µg m^{-3} for PM_{10}, fine particles with aerodynamic diameter less than 10 µm. Although agricultural operations are only one of many sources, conservation efforts to reduce dust emissions have expanded. Chipping of orchard wood, oiling roads, and conservation tillage are some of the efforts aimed at reducing dust emissions. These initiatives are part of the Environmental Quality Incentives Program in the 2008 Farm Bill. Wind breaks or shelterbelts, lines of vegetation perpendicular to prevailing wind directions, have been installed in parts of the region with some success in reducing wind erosion and dust emissions.

Water Conservation Research Studies
Water Conservation

Irrigation scheduling is an important tool for saving water and managing water deficits, particularly in arid and semiarid agricultural settings. Research on irrigation scheduling spans the last century. Much of the early research focused on irrigation efficiency and relationships between crop water demand and crop yield in the form of crop- and region-specific water production functions (Curry, 1938, 1939; Sammis, 1981). In this approach, water balance methods are used with either measured ET or reference crop ET and crop coefficients to predict yield as a function of ET (Hanson and Ayars, 2002). In California, reference ET is measured directly with weather stations across the state with the California Irrigation Management Information System (CIMIS, http://wwwcimis.water.ca.gov/cimis/welcome.jsp, verified 3 Dec. 2009) that allows growers to schedule irrigation according to actual crop demand. Initiated in 1982, CIMIS has been a major technological advance to aid growers in improving water use efficiency.

Several studies have focused on irrigation scheduling of cotton throughout the Southwest, where approximately 250,000 ha of upland cotton is grown (Steger et al., 1998). A common practice in cotton production is to conserve water by inducing early-season stress to encourage deep rooting. The relationships between fiber yield and excess vegetative growth associated with early irrigations after planting vs. inducing plant stress with delayed early-season irrigations has been studied in California and Arizona (Harris and Hawkins, 1942; Grimes et al., 1978). Yields were highest when cotton was irrigated at leaf water potentials between –1.6 to –2.3 MPa (Grimes and Yamada, 1982). A study in Arizona demonstrated that cotton yields decreased with increasing early season water stress. Yields were highest for treatments where the initial irrigation occurred when midday leaf water potentials reached –1.5 MPa and were slightly lower when irrigated at –2.3 MPa (Steger et al., 1998). In cotton grown on saline soils, Hanson and Kite (1984) scheduled irrigations based on measurements of plant stress via a pressure bomb chamber to reduce the number of irrigations. This approach increased yield by 16% compared to normal practices.

Improving Surface Irrigation

The beneficial use and allocation of water resources has been a concern for all states in the Southwest. Innovative agricultural practices offer opportunities to conserve water and maintain profitability. Upgrading furrow irrigation systems has conserved water by reducing losses from deep percolation. One approach is to reduce field length in combination with shorter irrigation set times, which increases irrigation uniformity by decreasing the water advance time to reach the end of the field. Hanson (1989) found that where field lengths are greater than 400 m, a 50% reduction in field length and a similar reduction in irrigation set time reduced deep percolation by more than 50%. However, the reduced field lengths increased surface runoff despite reduced irrigation set times. Therefore, measures need to be implemented to recover the runoff, such as tailwater recovery systems.

Other irrigation improvements for water conservation include implementation of alternate furrow irrigation or compaction of furrows with torpedoes to improve water advance. Conversion to surge irrigation, where water is applied in pulses that result in wetting and drying cycles during the irrigation event, was found to be an effective water conservation strategy, reducing deep percolation by 30 to 40% in soils with textures ranging from sandy loam to clay loam texture (Goldhamer et al., 1987). Surge irrigation has been shown to reduce the average depth of water infiltration by 31% and increase infiltration uniformity by 37% (Pukey and Wallender, 1989).

Deep percolation has been reduced by increasing irrigation uniformity and irrigation efficiency (Hanson and Fulton, 1994). Improvements of irrigation efficiency and uniformity can be observed through careful irrigation management of existing systems with irrigation scheduling and upgrading existing surface irrigation systems. Converting to pressurized irrigation systems such as hand-move and linear-move sprinklers, low-energy precision applications systems, or drip has also been shown to be effective (Hanson and Fulton, 1994).

Drip Irrigation

Converting from conventional furrow irrigation to drip was an emerging water conservation practice in the early 1970s (Fig. 9–7). The goals were to improve irrigation efficiency, reduce water use, and protect groundwater from nitrate contamination. Conversion from furrow to drip irrigation can have multiple benefits, including increased yield, water savings, reduced fertilizer application, reduced erosion, and less tillage. Drip irrigation improves irrigation uniformity and efficiency by applying water precisely where it is needed, thus limiting water losses via surface runoff and deep percolation. These benefits can only be realized with careful management and need to be evaluated with the costs associated with the infrastructure change, energy use, and maintenance (Hanson et al., 1997).

Fig. 9–7. Example of drip irrigation in perennial crops. Image courtesy of USDA-NRCS.

Benefits associated with the conversion from furrow to drip have been commodity specific in terms of yield differences. For example, in the San Joaquin Valley no difference was found between cotton yields (Howell et al., 1987), where as fresh market tomatoes where found to have higher yields under drip (Schweers and Grimes, 1976). In New Mexico, a comparison of furrow, sprinkler, and drip irrigation showed no difference in lettuce (*Lactuca sativa* L.) yields and higher potato (*Solanum tuberosum* L.) yields under drip (Sammis, 1980).

Field-scale research has shown that significant water savings can occur with drip. In the San Joaquin Valley, California, cotton yields increased by 12% and water use decreased by 9% under drip compared with furrow (Fulton et al., 1991). In the Salinas Valley, California, a field-scale investigation of furrow, surface drip, and buried drip showed little difference in lettuce yield between furrow and subsurface drip, but lower yields for surface drip. Drip irrigation, however, applied much less water than furrow irrigation. In three lettuce crops grown in 1991 and 1992, the applied water from drip ranged from 55 to 149 mm less than furrow irrigation (Hanson et al., 1997).

The disadvantage of using drip in row crops is the need to move and/or avoid drip tape during cultivation and replanting. Deep-buried drip lines can avoid this, but supplemental irrigation is needed to establish the crop. Most field-scale studies show that profitability is significantly higher with furrow irrigation (Hanson et al., 1997) mainly because installation and maintenance costs can range from $1,500 to $2,500 per hectare under drip (Hanson and May, 2003; Hanson et al., 2009). In addition, the focused delivery of water under drip systems can reduce root volume in tree crops.

Pressurized sprinklers and drip irrigation systems save water and can improve yield by improving irrigation efficiency. Grower surveys have shown that the use of high pressure sprinklers and drip systems has increased substantially in California, with an observed decrease in surface irrigation (Edinger-Marshall and Letey, 1997). In California, surface/gravity fed irrigation has decreased by approximately 31% in the last decade (Orang et al., 2008). The use of drip irrigation has increased by 31%. This conversion was due in large part to a decrease in field crop area, which is mainly surface irrigated, and an increase in the extent of orchards and vineyards, which are irrigated by drip (Fig. 9–8a and 9–8b).

Irrigation in Salt-Affected Environments

A large body of research exists that pertains to agricultural production with saline ($4 \leq EC < 30$ dS m^{-1}) and saline–sodic ($4 \leq EC < 30$ dS m^{-1} and $10 \leq SAR < 40$) water supplies. Electrical conductivity (EC) is a measure of the conductivity of electricity through a soil solution extract and is used to estimate the concentration of soluble salts. Sodium adsorption ratio (SAR) describes the relationship between soluble Na and other soluble divalent cations and is used to estimate the exchangeable Na on cation-exchange sites used to identify sodic soils. The Southwest has large regions in agricultural production where salt-affected soils are an issue. Some options exist for agriculture in salt-affected environments, and consideration of these solutions is based on the availability of high quality water, adequate drainage, and crop type. The following management practices have been investigated when water is in short supply or irrigation water is of poor quality: (i) blending water supplies of poor and high quality (Grattan and Oster, 2003), (ii) cyclic reuse of saline and nonsaline waters, and (iii) sequential reuse

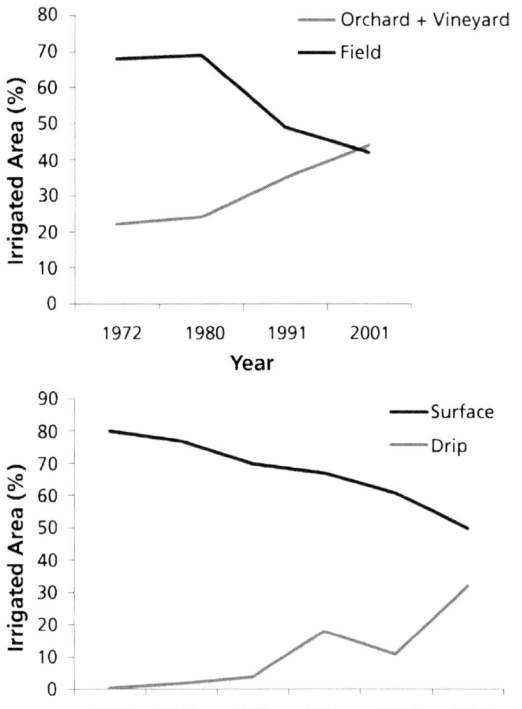

Fig. 9–8. Trends in irrigated area by (a) crop category and (b) irrigation type. Redrawn from Orang et al. (2008), a grower survey in the San Joaquin Valley.

where designated fields receive drainage water collected from other fields to irrigate salt-tolerant crops.

Approximately 610,000 ha of farmland are estimated to be affected by saline, regionally high water tables in the San Joaquin Valley in California (Tanji, 1990). No viable drainage options exist for this region. In the mid 1990s sequential reuse of agricultural drain water was evaluated in California's west side of the San Joaquin Valley as a strategy to safely dispose of saline agricultural discharge. Ideally, sequential reuse of drainage waters can be applied until salinity levels reach 20 to 30 dS m^{-1} and as long as physical properties of soils are not greatly affected when high levels of sodium are supplied. These exceedingly high salinity levels can be tolerated by halophytes such as salt grass [*Distichlis spicata* (L.) Greene], Bermuda grass [*Cynodon dactylon* (L.) Pers.], dwarf saltwort (*Salicornia bigelovii* Torr.), salt bush (*Atriplex* spp.), and salt cedar (*Tamarix* spp.). Sequential reuse was also evaluated on pistachio production, where trees were irrigated with different water applications ranging from 3.5 to 16 dS m^{-1} (Ferguson et al., 2002). No significant differences in pistachio growth parameters (leaf area, increase in trunk diameter, and aboveground biomass) were observed among the lower salinity treatments, but significant decreases were observed with the 12 and 16 dS m^{-1} treatments. Salt-tolerant crops such as grass forages have been successfully grown using saline–sodic drainage waters. These crops have been irrigated with water with EC values of 8 to 12 dS m^{-1} for more than 7 yr in soils with saturated-paste extract electrical conductivity (ECe) of 19 to 13 dS m^{-1} (Suyama et al., 2007).

Reuse of saline drainage waters has been evaluated on salt-tolerant forages as a strategy to reduce areas affected by shallow water tables with high salinity and to decrease the amount of drainage effluent (Grattan et al., 2004). A variety of forages were grown in experimental sand tanks and irrigated with two treatments. Either 15 or 25 dS m^{-1} of irrigation water was applied, and biomass accumulation was measured periodically after salinization. For the 15 dS m^{-1} treatment, biomass production rates were highest for alfalfa 'SW 9720', paspalum 'PI 299042' (*Paspalum vaginatum* Sw.), and alfalfa 'Salado'. Narrow leaf trefoil (*Lotus glaber* Mill.) and Alkali sacaton [*Sporobolus airoides* (Torr.) Torr.] had the lowest biomass accumulation. Broadleaf trefoil 'Big' (*Lotus corniculatus* L.) did not tolerate either of the salinity treatments. Cumulative biomass of the alfalfa cultivars was reduced by more than 50% for the 25 dS m^{-1} irrigation treatment. The salt-tolerant forages were more tolerant to the 25 dS m^{-1} treatment than alfalfa, with biomass reductions ranging from 0 to 20% (Grattan et al., 2004).

Agricultural sustainability in salt-affected regions such as the San Joaquin Valley depends on management practices that maintain a tolerable salt balance in the root zone (Schoups et al., 2005). Recent work has addressed the application of subsurface drip in processing tomatoes grown on salt-affected soils in the west side of the San Joaquin Valley (Hanson et al., 2009). One way drip has been shown to be effective in salt-affected regions is by reducing deep percolation, an effective strategy to maintain shallow, saline groundwater tables to depths below the root zone (Hanson and Fulton, 1994; Hanson et al., 2009). In a setting where productivity is suppressed by marginal soils, subsurface drip increased yield and profitability of processing tomatoes compared with sprinkler irrigation (Hanson and May, 2003). Yields under subsurface drip were 15 to 35% higher than under sprinkler irrigation. Tomatoes grown with drip irrigation also displayed better quality based on color, as determined by commercial graders. Water use was slightly higher under drip because of the need to flush salts out of the root zone, but with higher yields, water savings were realized by planting fewer hectares. Most importantly, drip irrigation has been shown to ensure the sustainability of agriculture in salt-affected regions of the San Joaquin Valley because it allows the manager to irrigate with adequate frequency, amount, and uniformity to leach salts out of the root zone and limit deep percolation and associated rise of the saline water table (Hanson et al., 2009).

Soil Conservation Research Studies

Soil erosion in California did not receive active attention by the University of California until 1930 when interest was stimulated by the federal government to address soil and water conservation across the United States (Jenny 1946). In early years, when winter wheat was a major crop in California, soil was protected from torrential rains by crop cover. As irrigation resources were developed to allow for cultivation of a variety of summer crops, soil erosion became more problematic because the land was often left bare during the rainy season. The construction of extensive irrigation water conveyance systems allowed for agricultural intensification and diversification. The bountiful water supplies from mountain snowmelt fostered a surface conveyance irrigation based on gravity feed. In emerging row crop agricultural systems of the Southwest, furrow irrigation systems were developed utilizing an array of linear soil beds (75–150 cm wide) interspersed with furrows to transport water. In pasture and orchard irrigation systems, units of land referred to as checks are surrounded by small levees (mounded soil) and flood irrigated. Both irrigation systems have water outflows or return to canals of the main conveyance system, which transports sediments from fields. Common soil and water conservation techniques implemented in the early 1900s to prevent wind and water erosion included contour subsoiling, strip cropping, land leveling, and bench-terracing on contours (Wohletz and Dolder, 1952).

There is a perception that water erosion is insignificant on level landscapes common to the semiarid Southwest, however, soil loss on level landscapes often ranges from 300 to 500 kg ha^{-1} yr^{-1} from winter rains and summer irrigation (Horwath, 2009, unpublished data). During winter, precipitation causes significant sediment transport in furrowed fields. In summer, irrigation return from fields can also lead to significant soil loss and cause flow interruption in ditches and canals. An important factor that governs soil erosion in these settings is surface sealing, which decreases infiltration and increases runoff. In a study of 17 medium-textured soils, Le Bissonnais and Singer (1993) found that surface seals did not form in soils with >30 g kg^{-1} organic carbon and >2.4% citrate-bicarbonate-dithionite (CBD)–extractable Fe and Al, and these soils were less susceptible to soil erosion. Thus, conservation practices that maintain soil organic C can reduce erosion. Interestingly, there is evidence to suggest that the use of N fertilizers beginning in the 1950s coincided with a buildup in soil organic C in California croplands through increased biomass production and the sequestration of eroded carbon in valley landscape positions (Harden et al., 1999). Moreover, a California-wide comparison of soils sampled in 1945 and again in 2001 showed that soil quality has not decreased significantly in 60 yr, and properties such as total C, total N, and plant-available P have increased (De Clerck et al., 2003). Practices such as conservation tillage that are observed to increase soil organic carbon elsewhere in the United States do not appear to be effective in California's Mediterranean climate (Veenstra et al., 2007).

Summer fallow fields or recently harvested fields can be susceptible to wind erosion in the arid west (Madden et al., 2009). Though soil losses are generally low, the emissions of fine soil particles are a health concern. Fine soil particles with aerodynamic diameter <10 μm (PM_{10}) have been linked to decreased lung function, cardiac arrhythmia, and heart attacks (USEPA, 2004). The intensive tillage operations used to maintain soil beds have been linked to these particulate emissions. Conservation tillage practices and cover crops may reduce the intensity of the emissions. The increased practice of straw removal for various biomass markets further decreases organic residues on harvested lands of some crops.

Conservation Tillage and Cover Crops

Early on, agronomists observed the positive effects of cover in reducing erosion. The introduction of stubble mulching on winter fallow land gave good results in reducing soil erosion (Jenny, 1946). As farm machinery became more developed to clean out irrigation ditches, less concern was given to soil erosion from winter fallow fields (Rasmussen, 1975; Wik, 1975). This has led to a marked absence of conservation tillage practices in southwestern agriculture. It is estimated that conservation tillage is currently practiced on less than 1% of row crop land area in California's Central Valley (Mitchell et al., 2007). Today, California's State Water Resource Control Board is holding growers accountable for any form of agricultural runoff. This may result in growers considering implementation of conservation tillage practices.

The use of cover crops can also address soil conservation and runoff issues. The use of cover crops in the Southwest is not widely practiced. In many areas, especially California and Arizona, mild winters allow growing of cash crops year round. Cover crops have been used more extensively in perennial systems, such as orchards and vineyards. Planting cover crops in vineyards has been practiced since the early 1990s (McGourty et al., 2008). The use of cover crops in other orchard crops is becoming more common, but overall the adoption of cover crops is less than 5% of agricultural land in the western United States (USDA-NASS, 2003).

Winter cover crops are routinely grown in permanent cropping systems to reduce water erosion during winter months (Fig. 9–9). Vineyards, which were once grown on flat valley bottoms, are now found on steeply sloping ground throughout California. It is common practice to either plant grasses or legumes or to allow natural revegetation between vine rows on hilly terrain. This is an effective practice for minimizing water erosion. Contour farming is not practiced in hilly vineyards of California due to safety concerns associated with the operation of farm equipment. Tractors can tip over easily if operated along contours on steep slopes because the narrow vine-row spacing makes it impossible to use tractors with a wide wheel base.

Growing cover crops can be an essential element of an integrated nutrient and soil organic matter (SOM) management strategy. Cover crops can sustain N availability by adding N through biological N fixation, capturing N through uptake, and retaining N in SOM. Legume cover crops can add up to 100 kg ha^{-1} N through biological nitrogen fixation (Poudel et al., 2001). One of the most important aspects of cover crops is the uptake of residual soil nutrients, especially nitrate, which can significantly reduce nutrient movement off-site either through leaching or runoff. In a study comparing the fate of N in different crop management

Fig. 9–9. Cover crops grown between rows of winegrapes in the San Joaquin Valley, California.

systems receiving similar additions of fertilizer N from various sources, winter cover crops and/or winter wheat significantly reduced soil nitrate levels to <5 mg kg^{-1} to a depth of 2 m compared to a winter fallow field that had in excess of 25 mg kg^{-1} (Poudel et al., 2001). Nonlegumes such as ryegrass (*Lolium multiflorum* Lam.) or Sudan grass [*Sorghum bicolor* (L.) Moench ssp. *drummondii* (Nees ex Steud.) de Wet & Harlan] can also act as "catch crops" to tie up nitrates during winter rains. Mixtures of legume and cereal cover crops can perform both functions.

Cover crops also increase SOM by increasing the amount of biomass added to the soil. The additional biomass of cover crops can be incorporated into the soil as a green manure in standard tillage systems or left on the surface as mulch in conservation tillage systems. When left on the surface, cover crop residues have been shown to effectively control weeds, reduce soil erosion and conserve soil moisture by reducing evaporation (Hartwig and Ammon, 2002; Lu et al., 2000). In California, the combined use of conservation tillage and cover crops together is especially uncommon. Adoption of soil conservation practices such as cover crops and conservation tillage is low because traditional practices are more profitable (Jackson et al., 2003).

Cover crop management for nutrient retention and SOM accrual is effective in all types of cropping systems, ranging from conventional to organic. In the arid Southwest, cover crops can aid in enhancing water infiltration and can lead to additional water storage. In the fall, cover crops may need an initial irrigation to become established. Irrigation water availability following the summer cash crop often makes this option impractical, especially for legume cover crops that need to be established before colder weather sets in. In the spring, excessive cover crop growth can deplete the soil profile of water (Prichard et al., 1989). It is important to terminate the cover crop before excessive growth occurs; however, field entry in the spring depends on climate and soil conditions. A study in the Sacramento Valley, California demonstrated that using cover crops could reduce runoff and increase soil water content. The percentage of rainfall as runoff was significantly higher (19%) in conventional fallow field treatments compared to those with cover (4%) and organically grown (7%). Cover crops increased the water holding capacity of soils to a level as high as 47 mm more than fallow fields, but this increase was only realized when the cover crop was destroyed before the onset of ET as the weather warms in the spring (Joyce et al., 2002). The reduced runoff of precipitation in fields with cover crops significantly lowers erosion potential. However, the adoption of winter cover in the Southwest is extremely low.

Another benefit of cover crops is to promote soil C sequestration. In cropping systems with and without annual winter cover crops, annual cover cropping led to an increase of 3 t C ha^{-1} after 5 yr (Poudel et al., 2001). After 10 yr, no new soil carbon was sequestered, showing the soil carbon had reached equilibrium. The limited potential to sequester soil C is likely related to the warmer conditions often found in the intensive agricultural regions of the Southwest. The study also revealed that maintaining a consistent annual cover crop was required to maintain the soil C levels.

Residue Management

In many agricultural systems, the decline in long-term soil fertility, loss of soil structure, and potential for erosion is often a direct consequence of partial or complete removal of aboveground biomass as food, feed, bedding, fuel, or building materials. The loss of near surface nutrient-rich soil and particulate organic fractions via tillage, erosion, and land modification exacerbates this problem. Growing crops that return a large amount of residue to the soil is an important strategy to recycle nutrients, replenish SOM pools, and reduce the need for other inputs, such as fertilizers, cover crops, or organic amendments (Horwath, 2007). Following the legislative reduction of the burning of rice straw in California, the return of residues eventually reduced the fertilizer N application recommendation by 27 kg N ha^{-1} compared to where residues were removed or burned (Bird et al., 2002). In general, residue management has received little attention, especially in furrow irrigated systems. Crop residues in furrow irrigated fields prevent uniform irrigation water movement in furrows. The use of overhead irrigation and subsurface drip would allow for surface residue management, implementation of conservation tillage practices, and a potential for water savings.

Land Evaluation

Meaningful land evaluation techniques are critical to soil and water conservation efforts, production agriculture, and agricultural sustainability because proper land use and the implementation of best management practices should be guided by soil limitations and terrain attributes. The Storie Index was developed as a semiquantitative method of rating soils based on productivity data collected from major soils in California in the 1920s and 1930s (Storie, 1932; Reganold and Singer, 1979). The Storie Index assesses the productivity of a soil from the following four factors: (A) the degree of soil profile development, (B) surface texture, (C) slope, and (X) other landscape conditions including drainage, microrelief, fertility, acidity, erosion, and salt content. A score ranging from 0 to 100% is determined for each factor, and the scores are then multiplied together to derive an index rating (Storie, 1932, 1978). In an attempt to reduce biases of Storie ratings generated by individuals, the most recent version of the Storie Index is now a model driven in the National Soil Information System (NASIS) that determines factor ratings using fuzzy logic rating curves for selected soil properties (O'Geen et al., 2008). Storie ratings are published in all soil surveys in California to evaluate land use and are also used by the Williamson Act to define prime farmland for preservation. This state legislation provides incentives to owners of prime farmland through property-tax subsidies as a means of protecting agricultural land from urbanization. This application of the Storie Index has major implications for the future of prime farmland and for land use planning throughout the state.

Effects of Land Reclamation

In some instances government programs that supported the drainage of marginal land for agricultural production have had a negative impact on soil conservation. Drainage and cultivation in the Delta has resulted in subsidence of the land surface at long-term average rates of 2.5 to 7.6 cm yr^{-1} (California Department of Water Resources, 1980; Rojstaczer et al., 1991; Rojstaczer and Deverel, 1993; Ingebritsen et al., 2000). Since reclamation, much of the region has subsided from 3 to 6.4 m. A portion of the delta soils has subsided more than 15 m. Delta subsidence is caused by several interrelated factors, including oxidation of SOM, wind erosion, compaction, burning, tectonic activity, and shrinkage by dewatering (Broadbent, 1976). This level of soil loss threatens both agricultural productivity and the stability of the levee system.

Recent Advances in Soil and Water Conservation
Water Conservation

Recent advances in soil and water conservation in the Southwest has gained momentum through concerns about agriculturally derived nonpoint-source pollution. California has taken an unprecedented approach to regulating nonpoint-source pollution. All agricultural dischargers (>22,000 growers) require a waiver of waste discharge, which includes as a condition that growers participate in local water quality monitoring programs and the public availability of monitoring results. If exceedances of water quality constituent standards are identified, then best management practices must be implemented to mitigate pollution. As a result, a wide range of best management practices have been studied to determine their suitability for implementation in California's Mediterranean climate, including vegetative filter strips (Grismer et al., 2006; Tate et al., 2004), tailwater return ponds (Schwankl et al., 2007), constructed and restored wetlands (O'Geen et al., 2007; Maynard et al., 2009), buffer strips (Liu et al., 2008); cover crops (Lu et al., 2000), and orchard and vineyard floor management practices (O'Geen et al., 2007). Many of these efforts have both water and soil conservation benefits and will continue to be implemented to maintain all beneficial uses of the state's water supply.

Availability of water will continue to be a major challenge in the Southwest. California has about 4 million hectare meters of developed water, and more than 80% is used for irrigation. Water that was once allocated to agricultural uses is now increasingly being used for urban and environmental purposes. As more water is allocated to a rapidly expanding urban population and to emerging environmental needs, California will likely see a water shortage of 2.46 billion m^3 in the immediate future (State of California Department of Water Resources, 1998). The availability and cost of water will affect the types of crops planted. It will also place greater pressures on groundwater resources. With increasing urban and environmental demands on western water supplies, irrigation management strategies that save water are of utmost importance.

Regulated deficit irrigation (RDI) is a promising strategy for conserving water in tree crops and vines. Regulated deficit irrigation is a form of irrigation scheduling where water stress is induced by supplying less water than the crop ET demand at certain times of the growing season. A variety of commodities have been studied including pistachio, almond, peach [*Prunus persica* (L.) Batsch], olive, prune, winegrapes, and citrus (Chalmers et al., 1981; Goodwin and Jerie, 1992; Goldhamer and Salinas, 2000; Goldhamer and Viveros, 2000; Goldhamer et al., 2002; Goldhamer and Beede, 2004). Regulated deficit irrigation has been demonstrated to save more than 50% of the consumptive water use (as high as 80% in pistachio) without reducing profits, and in some instances increasing them. Early season stress in almonds resulted in increased profitability by improving nut quality and disease resistance (Goldhamer et al., 2006; Teviotdale et al., 2001). In addition, Regulated deficit irrigation accelerates hull splitting in almonds, which could lead to alternative harvest techniques that would limit dust production and associated wind erosion (Goldhamer et al., 2006). Recently, it was demonstrated that mid-summer regulated deficit irrigation may be profitable for alfalfa production in arid areas, if the water saved can be sold at an adequate price to others where water is in short supply (Ottman et al., 1996; Hanson et al., 2007).

Soil Conservation

The San Joaquin Valley has been designated by the USEPA as a serious nonattainment area for PM_{10}. The region often exceeds Ambient Air Quality Standards for PM_{10} during fall when soils are dry and tillage and harvest occur. This is a problem in areas throughout the Southwest. Agriculture is believed to be a major source of fugitive dust (Cuscino et al., 1981). Among the conservation practices under study are conservation tillage and tillage timing to reduce dust emissions. A number of studies have shown that tillage operations performed at soil moisture contents above permanent wilting point significantly reduce dust emissions (Clausnitzer and Singer, 2000; Madden et al., 2009).

In the United States, conservation tillage practices have increased to occupy approximately 37% of cropland. In California, however, conservation tillage is practiced on only 16% of total cropland and 1% of land in annual row crops (Mitchell et al., 2007). Conservation tillage practices may increase in California in the future as growers seek ways to meet air quality standards. Conservation tillage in a 2-yr cotton–tomato rotation demonstrated a 33% reduction in respirable dust (4 µm in aerodynamic diameter) compared to traditional tillage (Baker et al., 2005). Similarly conservation tillage practices have been shown to decrease emissions in dairy forage rotations by 52 to 93% (Madden et al., 2008). In both studies the reduction was attributed to less mechanical disturbance. Fields under conservation tillage also had higher moisture content and a lower degree of soil pulverization (Madden et al., 2008).

Farmland Protection Programs

Farmland protection programs are intended to minimize the unnecessary and irreversible conversion of farmland to nonagricultural uses. Nationally, the Conservation Reserve Program (CRP) has provided technical and financial assistance to eligible growers and ranchers to address soil, water, and related natural resource concerns. The CRP pays growers and ranchers to convert highly erodible land to grassland. The CRP has reduced soil erosion and sedimentation in streams and lakes, improved water quality, promoted wildlife habitat, and enhanced grassland, forest, and wetland resources. The CRP's objective is to protect highly erodible cropland or other environmentally sensitive land by providing year-round vegetative cover with grasses, wildlife plantings, trees, filterstrips, or riparian buffers. Often, the CRP is used on-farm to address sensitive areas vulnerable to soil disturbance, while maintaining other areas of the farm or ranch for intensive crop or livestock production. In California and New Mexico, CRP land amounts to 0.4 and 1.8% of total registered land in the United States (USDA-FSA 2007). Registered CRP land in Nevada and Arizona is not reported due to confidentiality reasons because less than four land owners in these states participate in the program.

In California The California Land Conservation Act of 1965, commonly referred to as the Williamson Act, allows local governments to contract with private landowners to retain land for agricultural or related open space use. Since 1991, approximately 6.5 million ha of land has been consistently enrolled in the program (California Department of Conservation, 2009). This compares to 10.3 million ha in total farmland in California (USDA Census of Agriculture, 2007). The Williamson Act allows growers to pay a lower tax rate, which presumably allows them to add conservation improvements to their land. Both programs have been popular and are models that promote land stewardship and farm sustainability. Recent shortages in state government receipts, however, may bring about the elimination of funding for the Williamson Act.

Future Outlook

Adaptation and mitigation strategies for climate change will likely affect soil and water conservation in the Southwest. Management practices that limit greenhouse gas emissions, such as conservation tillage to increase carbon storage and reduce CO_2 loss, and improved nutrient management strategies to mitigate N_2O production will likely be employed. Research and management strategies that improve water-use efficiency will continue to be a focus. Infrastructure improvements such as levee repair and development of surface and groundwater stores will be necessary for sustainable water supplies in the future.

The environmental and social benefits of soil and water conservation are required to address the increasing demands for water and reduction in energy inputs. The approaches outlined in the above sections provide the means to sustain agriculture in the Southwest through addressing emerging environmental concerns and maintaining or enhancing the livelihoods of growers and ranchers. The main benefit of adopting soil conservation practices, besides reducing water and energy use, is improved soil health. Healthy soils leads to more sustainable surface and groundwater supplies. Maintaining the quality of groundwater will become increasingly important as we rely on groundwater reserves to address gaps in water supply due to urban and environmental demands and the effects of climate change. The combined benefits of addressing water limitations, energy use, and increasing soil quality will ensure the viability of southwestern agriculture.

A growing problem in parts of the Southwest is the conversion of agricultural land to urban and industrial uses. California's population increased 25% from 1980 to 1990 to more than 30 million people (Charbonneau and Kondolf, 1993). More than 200,000 ha of farmland were converted to urban and developed land uses from 1988 to 2000 (California Department of Conservation, 2009). If these land conversion rates are maintained, approximately 1.5 million hectares could be lost in the next century (California Department of Conservation, 2009). Similarly, this rate of land use conversion in California will lead to a 2.46-billion m³ shortage of water for agriculture annually during normal rainfall years (State of California Department of Water Resources, 1998).

Despite this urban expansion, the net amount of irrigated cropland has remained relatively constant in California because marginal lands have been developed for production. In response to urbanization, farmland development is expanding into the foothills and dissected terraces on the western and eastern margins of the Central Valley, California, which were originally considered rangeland. The loss of prime farmland and the associated conversion of marginal lands to farmland mean that growers are working more erosive landscapes that require more inputs than what was required for prime farmland (Charbonneau and Kondolf, 1993). Thus, soil and water resources will be subjected to added pressures in the future from climate change, agriculture, and urbanization.

Recent studies have shown that the adoption of best management practices by growers increases with exposure to local diffusion networks, which consist of groups such as growers, outreach and education entities, and agricultural organizations, who communicate information about policy through social connections (Lubell and Fulton 2007; Lubell and Fulton, 2008). While growers increasingly face new environmental regulations and policies, funding that maintains these diffusion networks such as the Hatch Act (funding for University Land Grant Agricultural Experiment Stations) and Smith–Lever Act (funding for Cooperative Extension) has increased merely 4.8 and 1.5%, respectively, since 1996 (Lubell and Fulton 2007). These small increases in funding are further marginalized by the severe cuts in state funding to Land Grant Universities in the last decade. Thus, the future outlook for the adoption of soil and water conservation practices is bleak without the support for these organizations.

Increasingly, growers are faced with regulatory incentives to protect natural resources. Successful conservation efforts rely on creative and constructive implementation strategies, which are best encouraged by positive incentives such as subsidies. Currently, a majority of agricultural subsidies allocated via the farm bill are commodity based, and with the exception of dairy and cotton, few of these subsidized commodities are major crops in the Southwest. To achieve agricultural sustainability in the Southwest in the future, state and federal governments must expand subsidies for soil and water conservation practices.

References

Adams, F. 1946. The historical background of California agriculture. p. 1–50. *In* C.B. Hutchison (ed.) California agriculture. Univ. of California Press, Berkeley.

Amundson, R., Y. Guo, and P. Gong. 2003. Soil diversity and land use in the United States. Ecosystems 6:470–482.

Baker, J.B., R.J. Southard, and J.P. Mitchell. 2005. Agricultural dust production in standard and conservation tillage systems in the San Joaquin Valley. J. Environ. Qual. 34:1260–1269.

Bird, J.A., A.J. Eagle, W.R. Horwath, M.W. Hair, E.E. Zilbert, and C. van Kessel. 2002. Long-term studies find benefits, challenges in alternative rice straw management. Calif. Agric. 56(2):69–75.

Broadbent, F.E. 1976. Factors influencing the decomposition of organic soils of the California Delta. Hilgardia 29:600–605.

California Department of Conservation. 2009. Farmland mapping and monitoring program. Available at http://www.conservation.ca.gov/dlrp/fmmp/overview/Pages/background.aspx (verified 7 Dec. 2009).

California Department of Water Resources. 1980. Subsidence of organic soils in the Sacramento–San Joaquin Delta. State of California, Resources Agency, Dep. of Water Resources, Central District.

Chalmers, D.J., P.D. Mitchell, and L.A.G. van Heek. 1981. Control of peach tree growth and productivity by regulated water supply, tree density, and summer pruning. J. Am. Soc. Hortic. Sci. 106(3):307–312.

Charbonneau, R., and G.M. Kondolf. 1993. Land use change in California: Nonpoint source water quality impacts. Environ. Manage. 17:453–460.

Clausnitzer, H., and M.J. Singer. 2000. Environmental influences on respirable dust production from agricultural operations in California. Atmos. Environ. 34:1739–1745.

Curry, A.S. 1938. Consumptive use of water by alfalfa in tanks. New Mexico Coll. Agric. Mech. Arts, and Agric. Exp. Stn. Press Bull. 871.

Curry, A.S. 1939. Use of water by alfalfa. New Mexico Coll. Agric. Mech. Arts, and Agric. Exp. Stn. Press Bull. 904.

Cuscino, T.A., Jr., J. Kinsey, R. Hackney, R. Bohn, and R.M. Roberts. 1981. The role of agricultural practices in fugitive dust emissions. MRI Project .4809-L. California Air Resources Board (CaliforniaRB), Sacramento.

De Clerck, F., M.J. Singer, and P. Lindert. 2003. A 60-year history of California soil quality using paired samples. Geoderma 114:215–230.

Edinger-Marshall, S., and J. Letey. 1997. Irrigation shifts toward sprinklers, drip and microsprinklers. Calif. Agric. 51(3):38–40.

Ferguson, L., J.A. Poss, S.R. Grattan, C.M. Grieve, D. Wang, C. Wilson, T.J. Donovan, and C.T. Chao. 2002. Pistachio rootstocks influence scion growth and ion relations under salinity and boron stress. J. Am. Soc. Hortic. Sci. 127:194–199.

Fulton, A.E., J.D. Oster, B.R. Hanson, C.J. Phene, and D.A. Goldhamer. 1991. Reducing drainwater: Furrow vs. subsurface drip irrigation. Calf. Agric. 45(2):4–8.

Goldhamer, D.A., M.H. Alemi, and R.C. Phene, 1987. Surge vs. continuous flow irrigation. Calif. Agric. 41(9,10):29–32.

Goldhamer, D.A., and R.H. Beede. 2004. Regulated deficit irrigation effects on yield, nut quality and water-use efficiency of mature pistachio trees. J. Hortic. Sci. Biotechnol. 79(4):538–545.

Goldhamer, D.A., and M. Salinas. 2000. Evaluation of regulated deficit irrigation on mature orange trees grown under high evaporative demand. Proc. Intl. Soc. Citrucult. IX Congress 227–231.

Goldhamer, D.A., M. Salinas, C. Crisosto, K.R. Day, M. Soler, and A. Moriana. 2002. Effects of regulated deficit irrigation and partial root zone drying on late harvest peach tree performance. Acta Hortic. 592:343–350.

Goldhamer, D.A., and M. Viveros. 2000. Effects of preharvest irrigation cutoff durations and postharvest water deprivation on almond tree performance. Irrig. Sci. 19:125–131.

Goldhamer, D.A., M. Viveros, and M. Salinas. 2006. Regulated deficit irrigation in almonds: Effects of variations in applied water stress timing on yield and yield components. Irrig. Sci. 24:101–114.

Goodwin, I., and P. Jerie. 1992. Regulated deficit irrigation: From concept to practice. Advances in vineyard irrigation; 10 July 1992; Aust. NZ Wine Ind. J. 258–261.

Grattan, S.R., and J.D. Oster. 2003. Use and reuse of saline-sodic waters for irrigation of crops. p. 131–162. In S.S. Goyal et al. (ed.) Crop production in saline environments: Global and integrative perspectives. Haworth Press, New York.

Grattan, S.R., C.M. Grieve, J.A. Poss, P.H. Robinson, D.L. Suarez, and S.E. Benes. 2004. Evaluation of salt-tolerant forages for sequential water reuse systems. I. Biomass production. Agric. Water Manage. 70:109–120.

Grimes, D.W., W.L. Dickens, and H. Yamada. 1978. Early season water management for cotton. Agron. J. 70:1009–1012.

Grimes, D.W., and H. Yamada. 1982. Relation of cotton growth and yield to minimum leaf water potential. Crop Sci. 22:134–139.

Grismer, M.E., A.T. O'Geen, and D.J. Lewis. 2006. Sediment control with vegetative filter strips (VFSs). UC-DANR Series Publ. 8195. Available at http://ucanr.org/freepubs/docs/8195.pdf (verified 7 Dec. 2009).

Hanson, B.R. 1989. Drainage reduction potential of furrow irrigation. Calif. Agric. 43:6–8.

Hanson, B.R., and A.E. Fulton. 1994. Methods and economics of drainage reduction through improved irrigation. J. Irrig. Drain. Eng. 120:308–321.

Hanson, B.R., and J.E. Ayars. 2002. Strategies for reducing subsurface drainage in irrigated agriculture through improved irrigation. Irrig. Drainage Syst. 16:261–277.

Hanson, B.R., and S.W. Kite. 1984. Irrigation scheduling under saline high water tables. Tans. ASAE 27:1430–1434.

Hanson, B.R., and D.E. May. 2003. Drip irrigation increases tomato yields in salt-affected soil of San Joaquin Valley. Calif. Agric. 57:132–137.

Hanson, B.R., D.E. May, J. Simunek, J. Hopmans, and R.B. Hutmacher. 2009. Drip irrigation provides the salinity control needed for profitable irrigation of tomatoes in the San Joaquin Valley. Calif. Agric. 63:131–136.

Hanson, B.R., D. Putnam, and R. Snyder. 2007. Deficit irrigation of alfalfa as a strategy for providing water for water-short areas. Agric. Water Manage. 93:73–80.

Hanson, B.R., L.J. Schwankl, K.F. Schulbach, and G.S. Pettygrove. 1997. A comparison of furrow, surface drip, and subsurface drip irrigation on lettuce yield and applied water. Agric. Water Manage. 33:139–157.

Harden, J.W., J.M. Sharpe, W.J. Parton, D.S. Ojima, T.L. Fries, T.G. Huntington, and S.M. Dabney. 1999. Dynamic replacement and loss of soil carbon on eroding cropland. Global Biogeochem. Cycl. 13:885–901.

Harris, K., and R.S. Hawkins. 1942. Irrigation requirements of cotton on clay loam soils in the Salt River Valley. p. 421–459. In Ariz. Exp. Stn. Bull. 181.

Hartwig, N.L., and H.U. Ammon. 2002. Cover crops and living mulches. Weed Sci. 50:688–699.

Hevly, R.H. 1983. High-altitude biotic resources, paleoenvironments, and demographic patterns: Southern Colorado Plateaus, A.D. 500–1400. p. 22–40. In J. Winter (ed.) High altitude adaptations in the Southwest. Cultural Resources Management Rep. 2. USDA Forest Service, Albuquerque, NM.

Horn, T.S. 1976. A century of service, Univ. of California 1874–1974. Div. Agric. Sci., Berkeley, CA.

Horwath, W.R. 2007. Carbon cycling and formation of soil organic matter. p. 303–339. In E.A. Paul (ed.) Soil microbiology, ecology and biochemistry. Academic Press, New York.

Howell, T.A., M. Meron, K.R. Davis, C.J. Phene, and H. Yamada. 1987. Water management of trickle and furrow irrigated narrow row cotton in the San Joaquin Valley. Appl. Eng. Agric. 3:222–227.

Howitt, R., and D. Sunding. 2003. Water infrastructure and water allocation in California. In J. Siebert (ed.) California agriculture: Dimensions and issues. Giannini Foundation of Agricultural Economics Information Series Paper IS031. Available at http://repositories.cdlib.org/giannini/is/IS031 (verified 7 Dec. 2009).

Ingebritsen, S.E., M.E. Ikehara, D.L. Galloway, and D.R. Jones. 2000. Delta subsidence in California—The sinking heart of the State. USGS Open-File Rep. FS-005-00.

Jackson, L.E., I. Ramirez, R. Yokota, S.A. Fennimore, S.T. Koike, D.M. Henderson, W.E. Chaney, and K.M. Klonsky. 2003. Scientists, growers assess trade-offs in use of tillage, cover crops and compost. Calif. Agric. 57:48–54.

Jelinek, L.J. 1979. Harvest empire: A history of California agriculture. Boyd & Fraser, San Francisco, CA.

Jenny, H. 1946. Exploring California soils. p. 317–394. In C.B. Hutchison (ed.) California agriculture. Univ. of California Press, Berkeley.

Joyce, B.A., W.W. Wallender, J.P. Mitchell, L.M. Huyck, S.R. Temple, P.N. Brostrom, and T.C. Hsiao. 2002. Infiltration and soil water storage under winter cover cropping in California's Sacramento Valley. Tans. ASAE 45:315–326.

Kaddah, M.T. 1976. Subsoil chiseling and slip plowing effects on soil properties and wheat grown on a stratified fine sandy soil. Agron. J. 68:36–39.

Le Bissonnais, Y., and M.J. Singer. 1993. Seal formation, runoff and interrill erosion from seventeen California soils. Soil Sci. Soc. Am. J. 57:224–229.

Liu, X., X. Zhang, and M. Zhang. 2008. Major factors influencing the efficacy of vegetated buffers on sediment trapping: A review and analysis. J. Environ. Qual. 37:1667–1674.

Lu, Y.C., B. Watkins, J.R. Teasdale, and A.A. Abdul-Baki. 2000. Cover crops in sustainable food production. Food Rev. Int. 16:121–157.

Lubell, M., and A. Fulton. 2007. Local diffusion networks act as pathways to sustainable agriculture in the Sacramento River Valley. Calif. Agric. 61:131–137.

Lubell, M., and A. Fulton. 2008. Local policy networks and agricultural watershed management. J. Public Admin. Res. 18:673–696.

Lund, J., W. Fleenor, E. Hanak, R. Howitt, J. Mount, and P. Moyle. 2008. Envisioning futures for the Sacramento–San Joaquin Delta. Public Policy Inst. of California, San Francisco.

Letey, L., C.F. Williams, and M. Alemi. 2002. Salinity, drainage and selenium problems in the western San Joaquin Valley of California. Irrig. Drainage Syst. 16:253–259.

Madden, N.M., R.J. Southard, and J.P. Mitchell. 2008. Conservation tillage reduces PM_{10} emissions in dairy forage rotations. Atmos. Environ. 42:3795–3808.

Madden, N.M., R.J. Southard, and J.P. Mitchell. 2009. Soil water content and soil disaggregation by disking affects PM_{10} Emissions. J. Environ. Qual. 38:36–43.

Maynard, J.J., A.T. O'Geen, and R.A. Dahlgren. 2009. Bioavailability and fate of phosphorus in constructed wetlands receiving agricultural runoff in the San Joaquin Valley, California. J. Environ. Qual. 38:360–372.

McGourty, G., J. Nosera, S. Tylicki, and A. Toth. 2008. Self-reseeding annual legumes evaluate as cover crops for untilled vineyards. Calif. Agric. 62:191–194.

Mitchell, J.P., K. Klonsky, A. Shrestha, R. Fry, A. Dusalt, J. Beyer, and R. Harben. 2007. Adoption of conservation tillage in California: Current status and future perspectives. Aust. J. Exp. Agric. 47:1383–1388.

O'Geen, A.T., J.J. Maynard, and R.A. Dahlgren. 2007. Efficacy of constructed wetlands to mitigate non-point source pollution from irrigation tailwaters in the San Joaquin Valley California, USA. Water Sci. Technol. 55:55–61.

O'Geen, A.T., S. Southard, and R.J. Southard. 2008. A revised Storie Index for use with digital soils information. UC-ANR 8000 Ser. Publ. 8335.

Olmstead, A.L., and P.W. Rhode. 2001. The red queen and the hard reds: Productivity growth in American wheat, 1800–1940. Agricultural History Center, University of California, Davis.

Orang, M.N., J.S. Matyac, and R.L. Snyder. 2008. Survey of irrigation methods in California in 2001. J. Irrig. Drainage Eng. ASCE 134:96–100.

Ottman, M.J., B.R. Tickes, and R.L. Roth. 1996. Alfalfa yield and stand response to irrigation termination in an arid environment. Agron. J. 88:44–48.

Poudel, D.D., W.R. Horwath, J.P. Mitchell, and S.R. Temple. 2001. Impacts of cropping systems on soil nitrogen storage and loss. Agric. Syst. 68:253–268.

Prichard, T.L., W.M. Sills, W.K. Asai, L.C. Hendricks, and C.L. Elmore. 1989. Orchard water use and soil characteristics. Calif. Agric. 43:23–25.

Pukey, D.R., and W.W. Wallender. 1989. Surge flow infiltration variability. Tans. ASAE 32:894–900.

Rasmussen, W.D. 1975. A postscript: Twenty-five years of change in farm productivity. p. 84–86. In J.H. Schideler (ed.) Agricultural history: Agriculture in the development of the far west. Agricultural History Center, Univ. of California, Davis.

Reganold, J.P., and M.J. Singer. 1979. Defining prime farmland by three land classification systems. J. Soil Water Conserv. 34:172–176.

Rojstaczer, S.A., R.E. Hamon, S.J. Deverel, and C.A. Massey. 1991. Evaluation of selected data to assess the causes of subsidence in the Sacramento–San Joaquin Delta, California. USGS Open-File Rep. 91-193.

Rojstaczer, S.A., and S.J. Deverel. 1993. Time dependence of atmospheric carbon inputs from drainage of organic soils. Geophys. Res. Lett. 20:1383–1386.

Sammis, T.W. 1980. Comparison of sprinkler, trickle, subsurface, and furrow irrigation methods for row crops. Agron. J. 72:701–704.

Sammis, T.W. 1981. Yield of alfalfa and cotton as influenced by irrigation. Agron. J. 73:323–329.

Schoups, G., J.W. Hopmans, C.A. Young, J.A. Vrugt, W.W. Wallender, K.K. Tanji, and S. Panday. 2005. Sustainability of irrigated agriculture in the San Joaquin Valley, California. Proc. Natl. Acad. Sci. USA 102:15352–15356.

Schwankl, L.J., T.L. Prichard, and B.R. Hanson. 2007. Tailwater return systems. Univ. of California Div. of Agriculture and Natural Resources Publ. 8225.

Schweers, V.H., and D.W. Grimes. 1976. Drip and furrow irrigation of fresh market tomatoes on a slowly permeable soil: Part 1. Production. Calif. Agric. 30:8–10.

State of California Department of Water Resources. 1998. The California water plan update. Bull. 160-98. Vol. 1. State of California Department of Water Resources, SacramentoSteger, A.J., J.C. Silvertooth, and P.W. Brown. 1998. Upland cotton growth and yield response to timing the initial postplant irrigation. Agron. J. 90:455–461.

Storie, R. 1932. An index for rating the agricultural values of soils. Bull. 556. Calif. Agric. Exp. Stn., Berkeley.

Storie, R. 1978. Storie Index soil rating. Division of Agricultural Sciences, Univ. of California, Spec. Publ. 3203.

Suyama, H., S.E. Benes, P.H. Robinson, G. Getachew, S.R. Grattan, and C.M. Grieve. 2007. Biomass yield and nutritional quality of forage species under long-term irrigation with saline-sodic drainage water: Field evaluation. Anim. Feed Sci. Technol. 135:329–345.

Tanji, K.K. 1990. Nature and extent of agricultural salinity. Agricultural Salinity Assessment and Management. ASCE Manuals and Reports on Engineering Practice 71. ASCE, New York.

Tanji, K., D. Davis, C. Hanson, A. Toto, R. Higashi, and C. Amrhein. 2002. Evaporation ponds as a drainwater disposal management option. Irrig. Drainage Syst. 16:279–295.

Tate, K.W., M.D. Gracas, C. Pereira, and E.R. Atwill. 2004. Efficacy of vegetated buffer strips for retaining *Cryptosporidium parvum*. J. Environ. Qual. 33:2243–2251.

Teviotdale, B.L., D.A. Goldhamer, and M. Viveros. 2001. Effects of deficit irrigation on hull rot disease of almond trees caused by *Monilinia fructicola* and *Rhizopus stolonifer*. Plant Dis. 85(4):399–403.

USDA. 1947. The agricultural conservation program on California's farms and ranches. Production and marketing administration, California State PMA Committee.

USDA Census of Agriculture. 2007. 2007 Census Report. Available at http://www.agcensus.usda.gov/Publications/2007/Full_Report/index.asp (accessed 10 July 2009, verified 7 Dec. 2009).

USDA-FSA. 2007. Conservation Program Statistics. Available at http://www.fsa.usda.gov/FSA/web app?area=home&subject=copr&topic=rns-css (verified 7 Dec. 2009).

USDA-NASS. 2003. Agricultural Statistics Database. Available at http://www.nass.usda.gov.

USDA-NRI. 2003. National Resources Inventory. 2003 Annual NRI. Available at http://www.nrcs.usda.gov/Technical/nri/2003/nri03landuse-mrb.html (accessed 9 June 2009, verified 7 Dec. 2009).

USEPA. 2004. The particle pollution report: Current understanding of air quality and emissions through 2003. Available at http://www.epa.gov/airtrends/aqtrnd04/pmreport03/pmcover_2405.pdf (verified 7 Dec. 2009). USEPA, Washington, DC.

Veenstra, J.J., W.R. Horwath, and J.P. Mitchell. 2007. Tillage and cover cropping effects on aggregate-protected carbon in cotton and tomato. Soil Sci. Soc. Am. J. 71:362–371.

Wik, R.M. 1975. Some interpretations of the mechanization of agriculture in the Far West. p. 73–83. *In* J.H. Schideler (ed.) Agricultural history: Agriculture in the development of the far west. Agricultural History Center, Univ. California, Davis.

Wills, W.H. 1988. Early agriculture and sedentism in the American Southwest. Evidence and interpretations. J. World Prehist. 2:445–488.

Wilson, J. 1984. Breadbasket of the world: California's great wheat growing era, 1860–1890. Book Club of California, San Francisco.

Wohletz, L.R., and E.F. Dolder. 1952. Know California's Land—A land capability guide for soil and water conservation in California. State of California Department of Natural Resources and USDA-Soil Conservation Service, Sacramento.

10

Soil and Water Conservation Advances in the United States—Review and Assessment

Ted M. Zobeck
USDA-ARS, Wind Erosion and Water Conservation Research Unit, Lubbock, TX

A review and assessment of soil and water conservation in the United States requires the consideration of a country with vast resources and diverse climate. The U.S. land area totals nearly 930 million hectares (2.3 billion acres), 769 million hectares (1.9 billion acres) of which are the continental United States. This chapter focuses on the continental United States. In 2002, agricultural land accounted for 62% of the total continental U.S. land, while the total grazing and pasture area comprised 41% of the total (Lubowski et al., 2006).

The effects of land management on soil resources will depend on many factors that influence the soils, such as climate, relief, and organisms acting through time on the parent material of soil. Thus, an examination of management must be considered in the context of the physical and environmental factors, as well as anthropogenic influences.

The mean annual air temperature (MAT) in the continental United States tends to decrease from south to north and with increasing elevation (Fig. 10–1). The MAT varies from a high of 24°C in southern Florida to about 2°C in the northern United States and at the upper elevations of some of the western mountain ranges (Fig. 10–1). The mean annual precipitation (MAP) varies from a low of 58 mm in Death Valley, California to a high of more than 6000 mm in northwest Washington (Fig. 10–2). The combination of the temperature and precipitation, along with consideration of the temporal distribution and range in values, are summarized by the nine climate zones in the continental United States (Wikipedia, 2009, Fig. 10–3).

This chapter provides a summary of each region described in this book. Each summary presents a brief description of the region's extent, climate, soils, agricultural production, and soil and water conservation issues. This is followed by a description of soil management and assessment techniques and concludes with a look to future soil and water challenges and opportunities in the United States.

Soil and Water Conservation Advances in the United States. SSSA Special Publication 60.
T.M. Zobeck and W.F. Schillinger, editors. © 2010. SSSA, 677 S. Segoe Rd., Madison, WI 53711, USA.

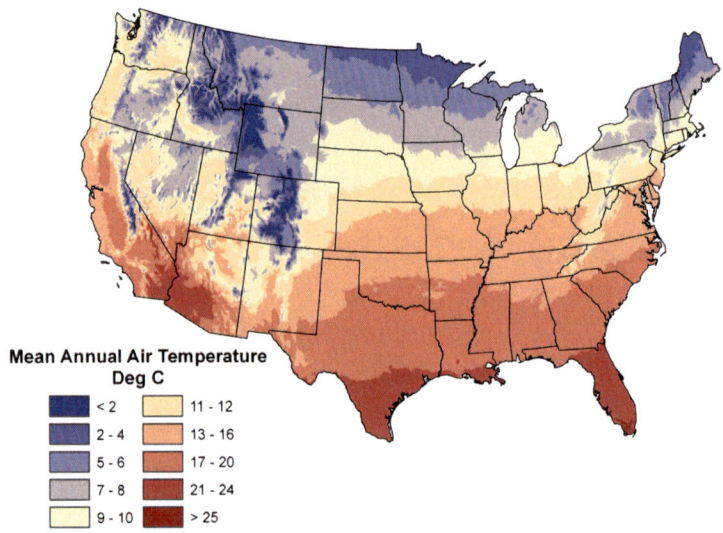

Fig. 10–1. Mean annual air temperature of the continental United States (1971–2000). Modified from data provided, with permission, from the PRISM Group, Oregon State University, http://www.prismclimate.org (verified 17 Dec. 2009).

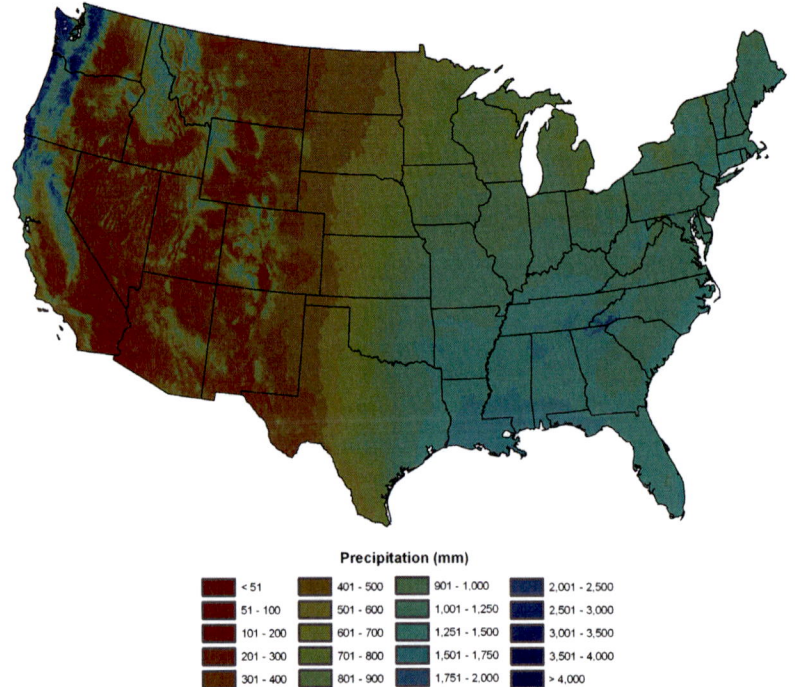

Fig. 10–2. Mean annual precipitation of the continental United States (1971–2000). Modified from data provided, with permission, from the PRISM Group, Oregon State University, http://www.prismclimate.org (verified 17 Dec. 2009).

Climate Zones of the Continental United States

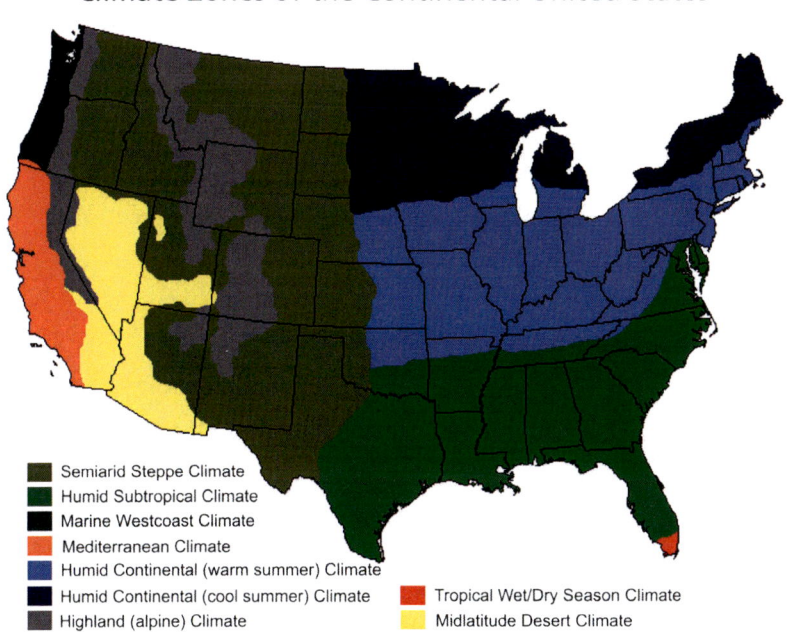

Fig. 10–3. Climate zones of the continental United States. Provided by Wikipedia at http://en.wikipedia.org/wiki/File:Climatemapusa2.PNG (verified 17 Dec. 2009).

Regional Settings and Issues
Inland Pacific Northwest Region—Columbia Basin and Plateau

Soil and water conservation advances in the Inland Pacific Northwest (PNW) region are described in Chapter 2 (Schillinger et al., 2010). This region focuses on the Columbia Basin and Plateau in north-central Oregon, northern Idaho, and eastern Washington with 3,348,000 ha of dryland and 646,000 ha of irrigated cropland. The region has a Mediterranean-like (i.e., winter precipitation) climate with low precipitation volumes and intensities. Annual precipitation ranges from 125 mm just east of the Cascade Mountains and rises from west to east to more than 600 mm in the Palouse region (Fig. 10–2). Winters are cool to cold, with temperatures occasionally dropping to –10°C or lower. Between 60 and 75% of the over-winter precipitation is stored in the soil after crop harvest.

The soils are predominately silt loam Mollisols and Aridisols (Fig. 10–4) developed from loess deposits that have been modified by volcanic material and so are considered to be "ash influenced." The soils tend to have properties that grade in characteristics in the direction of the prevailing winds, with the highest sand and lowest organic matter contents in the southwest and increasing clay and organic matter in the northeasterly direction.

For purposes of discussion, the dryland farming region can be divided into three areas, according to precipitation zones: low (<300 mm), intermediate (300–450 mm), and high (>600 mm). Irrigation is used for crop production in areas that are too dry for rainfed crops (Chapter 2, Fig. 2–1, Schillinger et al., 2010).

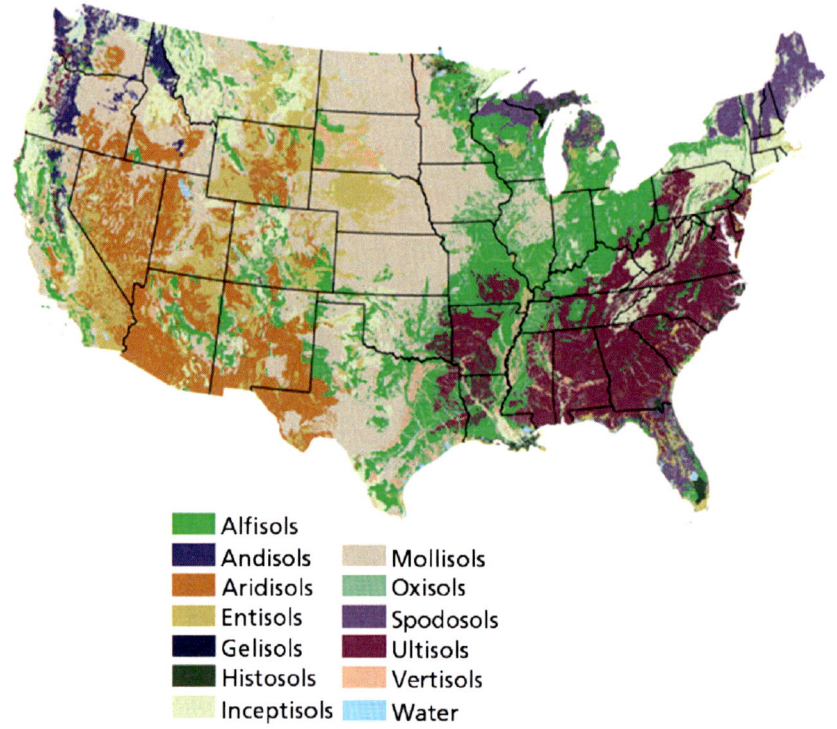

Fig. 10–4. Soil orders of the continental Unites States (USDA-NRCS, 2008).

Cropping systems vary considerably among zones. The irrigated zone supports a wide variety of crops, including fruit and pulpwood trees, wine grapes (*Vitis vinifera* L.), hops (*Humulus lupulus* L.), and a large assortment of field and vegetable crops. The dryland areas have fewer cropping options. The low precipitation zone is generally a 2-yr winter wheat (*Triticum aestivum* L.)–summer fallow (WW-SF) rotation, with spring wheat and spring barley (*Hordeum vulgare* L.) planted in some areas, mostly when over-winter precipitation storage in the soil is abundant. The intermediate precipitation zone has WW-SF in addition to a 3-yr rotation of winter wheat–spring cereal–summer fallow. Annual cropping is generally practiced in the high precipitation zone, with most growers using a 3-yr winter wheat–spring cereal–spring legume or winter wheat–spring barley–spring wheat rotation.

The major environmental concerns in the irrigated zone are water erosion caused by improper application of water, nitrate leaching below the root zone of crops and into domestic wells, and wind erosion in the Columbia and Yakima Basins when surface residues are not available to protect the soil surface. Irrigated agricultural has been identified as the source for the majority of nitrogen loading in the Columbia Basin (Cook et al., 1996). Conservation strategies have focused on promoting residue and cover crops, efficient water use, conservation tillage, and eliminating field burning (Schillinger et al., 2010). Polyacrylamide

(PAM) is used by about 30% of growers in the Columbia Basin on furrow-irrigated land to reduce erosion, often with cost share from government programs. Studies have documented the efficacy of using cover crops to improve nitrogen cycling and reduce nitrate levels in soils and reduce wind and water erosion. An overview of the principal uses and benefits of cover crops and green manures has been provided by Sullivan (2003).

Water erosion can be a problem in all rainfed dryland zones, but it is particularly acute in the high precipitation zone. Severe water erosion occurs when rainfall or snowmelt occurs on steep slopes that lack surface cover or roughness in the winter when they are frozen (Fig. 10–5). The frozen soils do not allow water infiltration and thus the rainfall runs off and carries sediment and chemicals attached to the sediment with it. Mass movement of soils also may occur as entire hill-slopes become saturated and flow downhill (Fig. 10–5).

Movement of soil downhill during tillage (tillage erosion) has also been identified in the PNW. For many years, soil was thrown down slope during moldboard tillage and moved downward by gravity (Montgomery et al., 1999). The USDA-NRCS has documented dropoffs of up to 3 m where the soil from the field above had been plowed toward the fence, and the field below had been plow away from the fence (Montgomery et al., 1999). Development of affordable nonselective herbicides along with new conservation-till and no-till (NT) implements to allow precise placement of seed and fertilizer in one pass have greatly assisted adoption of conservation farming systems that reduce erosion.

Wind erosion is a major problem for the dryland farming region receiving less than 300 mm annual precipitation as well as the irrigated Columbia Basin and the Yakima River Basin (Chapter 2, Fig. 2–1, Schillinger et al., 2010). These areas often produce limited crop residue, have poorly aggregated soils with little roughness due to excessive tillage, and are prone to high winds. Several soils dominated by wind erodible particles are readily suspended and travel great

Fig. 10–5. Soil slip occurs on steep slopes when thawed soil slides over the frozen soil layer below in the Palouse area, Washington. Photo by Tim McCabe, USDA-NRCS photo gallery, http://photogallery.nrcs.usda.gov/ (verified 17 Dec. 2009).

distances (Kjelgaard et al., 2004). Air quality concerns in the Tri-Cities (Kennewick, Richland, Pasco) and Spokane of Washington state have been correlated with wind erosion from cropland. New conservation farming systems have been developed for improved wind erosion control on farm fields (Papendick, 2004). For example, primary tillage using an undercutting wide V-blade that kills weeds with minimal surface disturbance while simultaneously delivering nitrogen has been used in the WW-SF system.

Great Plains Region

The soil and water conservation advances in the Great Plains were described in Chapters 3 (Tanaka et al., 2010) and 4 (Stewart et al., 2010). The Great Plains includes all or portions of 10 U.S. states (Colorado, Kansas, Montana, Nebraska, New Mexico, North Dakota, Oklahoma, South Dakota, Texas, and Wyoming) and three Canadian provinces (Alberta, Manitoba, and Saskatchewan) (Chapter 4, Fig. 4–1).

The climate is characterized as a semiarid steppe (Fig. 10–3), with MAP decreasing from east to west from 500 to 350 mm, with little variation north to south. Temperature and length of growing season decrease from south to north (Baumhardt and Salinas-Garcia, 2006). The northern part of the region was topographically smoothed by continental glaciations and blanketed by undulating till and lacustrine deposits (USDA-NRCS, 2006a). The central and southern part of the region is a level to gently rolling fluvial plain with entrenched (dissected) streams in the southern section. Most of the region has been affected by aeolian (wind) processes due to strong and persistent winds during the spring season. The natural vegetation is grassland with some trees along drainage ways, leading to the development of Mollisols with dark, relatively organic rich soil surfaces (Fig. 10–4). However, significant areas of Alifisols, Inceptisols, and Entisols also occur. Less well developed Inceptisols and Entisols are found in the sandy, wind-blown soils of some areas.

The cropping systems in the region must be adapted to relatively low precipitation and strong spring winds. In areas with ample groundwater resources, irrigation is used to supplement rainfall. The High Plains Aquifer is the principal source for irrigation in this region (Fig. 10–6). The Ogallala Aquifer, which underlies about 80% of the High Plains, is the principal geologic unit forming the aquifer (U.S. Dep. of the Interior, USGS, 2007) and the principal groundwater source for irrigation. Growers in dryland cropping areas often use a fallow period to store moisture in wheat–fallow and wheat–sorghum [*Sorghum bicolor* (L.) Moench]–fallow systems in the High Plains. The principal irrigated crops in the north and central portions of the region include corn (*Zea mays* L.), soybean [*Glycine max* (L.) Merr.], alfalfa (*Medicago sativa* L.), and seed crops, while cotton (*Gossypium hirsutum* L.), peanut (*Arachis hypogaea* L.), and sorghum are the principal irrigated crops in the southern High Plains (USDA-NRCS, 2006a).

Irrigation has been used in the Great Plains since the late 1800s to improve crop productivity. Details of the development of irrigation in the Great Plains are provided in Chapter 4 (Stewart et al., 2010). Early crop irrigation was provided by flooding the field, which led to inefficiencies due to water loss from deep percolation past the root zone, inadvertent loss from the field, or excessive evaporation. Methods were developed to alleviate these problems by regulating the flow of water down the furrows using pressurized gated pipe in a method called *cablegation* (Kemper et al., 1981) or in intermittent applications of water to the furrows

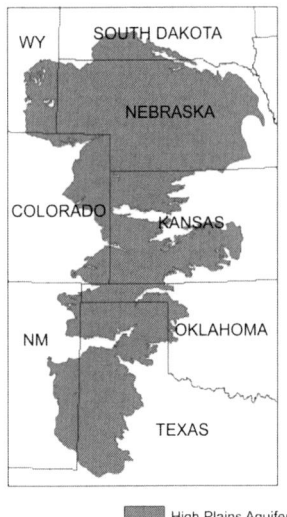

Fig. 10–6. High Plains Aquifer. Adapted from USGS Fig. 1 at http://co.water.usgs.gov/nawqa/hpgw/SETT.html (verified 17 Dec. 2009).

called *surge flow*. The center pivot pressurized sprinkler system, first invented by Frank Zyback in Nebraska in 1948, has now been widely adopted in the Great Plains (Stewart et al., 2010). For example, more than 70% of the irrigated area in the Southern High Plains is served by center pivot irrigation systems (Colaizzi et al., 2008). Improvements in center pivot irrigation systems include the use of furrow diking to retain water in the furrows while water is applied using a low-energy precision application (LEPA) method with various options of water application (Schneider et al., 2000). Subsurface drip irrigation (SDI), also called *microirrigation*, using permanently buried drip lines to irrigate the crop at or immediately below the root zone (Bordovsky and Porter, 2008) is also becoming widely accepted. A detailed monograph on recent scientific advances and principles of irrigation was presented by Lascano and Sojka (2007).

Wind and water erosion (Fig. 10–7) are significant management issues if the soils are not protected. Conservation cropping systems have been developed that maintain crop residue on the soil surface to better control erosion and enhance environmental quality (Tanaka et al., 2010). Recent advances in the northern Great Plains includes the reduction and even the elimination of the fallow and more intensive cropping by including diverse crops in annual cropping systems. Advances in reduced and NT management techniques, including the development of genetically modified crops that have herbicide resistance, offer new opportunities to reduce tillage and retain more crop residue on the soil surface. In addition, changes in U.S. federal farm policy in 1996 that decoupled farm support payments from historical base crop production has allowed growers to plant a variety of nonconventional crops, generally improving profitability compared to wheat–fallow while increasing grower interest in conservation-tillage systems (Tanaka et al., 2010). Advances in the southern High Plains include the development of conservation-till and NT systems and improvement in water use efficiency of plants (Stewart et al., 2010). For example, recent studies have shown growing sorghum plants in clumps enhanced stored water availability during the grain-filling period and improved crop water use efficiency.

Fig. 10–7. Dust storm approaching Ransom Canyon in Texas, June 18, 2009. Photo courtesy of John Stout.

Midwest Region

The soil and water conservation advances in the Midwest region of the United States were described in Chapter 5 (Karlen et al., 2010). The region encompasses Michigan, Minnesota, Wisconsin, Ohio, Indiana, Illinois, Iowa, and Missouri and is very diverse, with 38 different Major Land Resource Areas (USDA-NRCS, 2006a).

The Midwest has a temperate, humid, continental climate with cool summers in the north (Minnesota, Wisconsin, and most of Michigan) and warm summers in the south (Fig. 10–3). The MAT decreases from south to north, from 16°C in Missouri to 2°C in northern Minnesota (Fig. 10–1), and MAP varies from roughly 1000 mm in the southern and eastern states to a low of about 700 mm in northwest Minnesota (Fig. 10–2).

The soils of the region have generally developed from glacial sediments, loess, or residual bedrock originally under forests and grasslands. Alfisols formed under deciduous forests, have medium to high fertility, and are the dominant soils in Ohio, Indiana, Michigan, Wisconsin, Illinois, and Missouri (Fig. 10–4). Mollisols formed under prairies, have thick dark surfaces high in organic matter, high fertility and are the predominant soil order in Iowa, northwestern Missouri, north-central Illinois, western Minnesota, and northwestern Indiana (Fig. 10–4). Histosols, developed from wetland areas, are locally important soils in some areas (Fig. 10–8).

In many areas of the Midwest, the soils are poorly drained, with seasonal water tables near the soil surface. Artificial drainage of wetland soils began in the 1800s. Federal laws were enacted in 1850 and 1860 to promote the conversion of wetlands to tillable croplands (Karlen et al., 2010). These efforts greatly increased the tillable acres in the Midwest and promoted rotations of row crops, vegetables, small grain, and meadow crops (Hewes and Frandson, 1952).

Cropping systems have varied considerably through time. Before about 1945, the cropping systems were highly diversified, with livestock, grain, and forage production. Crop rotations and livestock were needed to maintain production because off-farm fertilizer and other inputs were not available and/or not afford-

Fig. 10–8. (Left) lettuce growing on organic soil; (right) subsidence post showing subsidence of organic soil in Florida.

able. Many changes in agriculture have occurred since 1945. The development of commercial chemical fertilizers and pesticides has allowed growers to simplify and/or remove rotations and yet address fertility, disease, and insect pressures. Recent advances in biotechnology and crop genetics have introduced plants with inbred protection against certain insects and tolerance to specific types of herbicides. These changes have produced significant advances and fostered much greater acceptance of conservation-till and NT cropping systems.

The major environmental concerns in the Midwest include water erosion and concomitant increases in nutrient and chemical contamination of water resources (Kanwar et al., 2005). Of particular concern is the leaching of nitrate N into ground and surface waters in agricultural row-crop areas. Conservation practices using annual or perennial cover crops have markedly reduced nitrate concentration and load in subsurface drainage water (Kaspar et al., 2007) and reduced soil erosion. In addition, management practices that reduce soil disturbance and leave more residue on the soil surface, such as conservation and NT practices, reduce the risk of soil erosion and transport that contribute to degradation of soil and surface water resources. Recent data by the Conservation Technology Information Center show an increase of 19% in Midwest cropland in NT since 1990 (Chapter 5, Fig. 5–12).

Northeast Region

The soil and water conservation advances in the Northeast region of the United were described in Chapter 6 (van Es, 2010). This region includes the area from Maine in the north to West Virginia and Maryland in the south. This highly diversified area includes sections in four Land Resource Areas: the northeastern forage and forest regions, the northern Atlantic slope diversified farming region, and portions of the east and central farming and forest regions, and Atlantic and Gulf Coast lowland forest and farming region (USDA-NRCS, 2006a).

The MAT of the region varies from 5°C in Maine to 15°C in Maryland (Fig. 10–1), and MAP ranges from 600 to slightly more than 1500 mm (Fig. 10–2). The region has a humid continental climate, with cool summers in the north and warm summers in the south (Fig. 10–3).

The soils are dominantly Entisols and Spodosols in the northeastern area from Maine to New York, and northern Pennsylvania and New Jersey; Alfisols, Ultisols, and Inceptisols in the northern Atlantic area of Pennsylvania, New Jersey, Maryland, and western West Virginia; Ultisols in the Atlantic and Gulf Coast lowland forests and crop regions of New Jersey and Maryland; and Ultisols and Inceptisols in the Alleghany Plateau areas of West Virginia and western Pennsylvania (Fig. 10–4; USDA-NRCS, 2006a).

Agricultural production is highly diversified and adapted to the climate and soils of the region. Dairy production accounts for the largest fraction of agricultural receipts and is associated with significant imports of feed supplements and nutrient surpluses that create environmental concerns (van Es, 2010). Poultry is a significant industry in Maryland and Delaware. Grain crops, mainly corn, soybean, and small grains, are grown in areas where large-scale crop production is possible. Specialty crops are grown on small farms, including organic farms, and fruit and vegetable production are particularly important near urban centers. Many soils have poor internal drainage and have artificial subsurface drainage.

Recent conservation issues in the Northeast focus on the effects of management on soil and water quality. Although the Northeast has less soil erosion than most other areas of the country, it experiences the highest cost per ton of soil eroded (Hansen and Ribaudo, 2008). The high cost of erosion relates to costs associated with the proximity of recreation areas affected by soil loss and associated chemical pollution, decreases in environmental quality, replacement costs for the damage, and costs of practices to avoid damage.

Those in urban centers are concerned about pollution of drinking water sources. Mid-Atlantic estuaries are often large, shallow, and easily impacted by nearby urban and agricultural activities (Fig. 10–9). Many freshwater lakes of the region are also susceptible to urban and agricultural activities and are particularly sensitive to eutrophication due to excessive nutrient additions.

Scientists in the Northeast have been proactive in the development of soil and nutrient management tools to assess effects of management on the land. These tools include a phosphorus index (Lemunyon and Gilbert, 1993), expanded interpretations for a nitrate leaching index (van Es et al., 2002), and a protocol for assessing soil health (Schindelbeck et al., 2008).

Fig. 10–9. Estuaries provide unique ecological services within short distances of populations centers. Photo courtesy of Earth Observatory, NASA.

Southeast Region
Piedmont and Coastal Plains

The soil and water conservation advances in the southeastern U.S. Piedmont and Coastal Plains were described in Chapter 7 (Busscher et al., 2010). The climate of the Southeast Region is humid subtropical, with hot, humid summers and mild to cool winters (Fig. 10–3). Rainfall occurs throughout the year and may come in the form of thunderstorms, tropical storms, and hurricanes.

The soils in the Coastal Plains have generally formed from sandy marine sediments and developed into Ultisols (Fig. 10–4), forming subsurface layers with low cation exchange capacity to clay ratios (Soil Survey Staff, 1999). The Piedmont is an erosional landscape, with rolling uplands to steep valley slopes west of the Coastal Plains and soils developed from the weathered bedrock into Alfisols and Entisols (Busscher et al., 2010). In general, Piedmont soils have low organic matter and are low in basic cations and exchange capacity and nonexpansive clays. These soils are prone to surface crusting, which reduces water infiltration and increases runoff and erosion. Surface crusting is reduced using cover crops and amendments such as gypsum, manure, PAM, biochar, or other amendments.

Compaction is a significant soil management issue in the Southeast, especially on many Coastal Plain soils, because it can reduce root development, water retention, and crop growth. Deep tillage is used to alleviate the problem when feasible. Although deep tillage requires large tractors that use considerable fuel, this practice does not invert the soil, so residues are left on the surface (Busscher et al., 2010). Site-specific subsoiling methods are available that result in equivalent yields to those produced by uniform subsoiling, while reducing draft forces, drawbar power, and fuel use (Raper et al., 2007).

Conservation tillage and cover crops (Fig. 10–10) are often used in the Coastal Plain and in the Piedmont, where water erosion is a significant problem. Studies have shown that organic matter from crop residues is critical for improving aggregate stability and water infiltration (Bruce et al., 1992). Although measurable changes in soil physical and biological properties may take 3 to 5 yr to become evident, yield changes in crops have been observed in the first year, depending on grower experience and other factors.

Fig. 10–10. Planting maize (*Zea mays* L.) into standing cereal rye (*Secale cereale* L.) cover crop in the southeastern Coastal Plains. Photo courtesy of Don Watts, USDA-ARS, Florence, SC.

Florida

Northern Florida has the climate, soils, and soil management issues similar to the Coastal Plain region described above. However, central and southern Florida, about two-thirds of the state's land area, differs and is identified as the Florida Subtropical Fruit, Truck Crop, and Range Region (USDA-NRCS, 2006a). More than one-half of the region consists of swamps and marshes, with only 10% in cropland. The climate is humid subtropical in the north and tropical with a wet and dry season in the south (Fig. 10–3). Total average rainfall ranges from 1120 to 1525 mm, with 60% occurring from June through September (Fig. 10–2). The maximum average annual temperature varies from 18 to 21°C in the north and from 23 to 25°C in the southern peninsula and in the Keys (Fig. 10–1).

Florida generally consists of low, flat coastal plains. The soils are Entisols and Spodosols, with significant areas of Alfisols and Histosols (Fig. 10–4). Ultisols occur in the northern part of the state. Management of Histosols is of particular concern because of significant soil loss caused by subsidence and wind erosion. A concrete post buried 2.7 m in the soil at the Everglades Research and Education Center in Belle Glade in 1924 had been exposed 1.8 m by March 2008, averaging about 2.2 cm of subsidence per year (Fig. 10–8). The rate of subsidence is closely related to the height of the groundwater table (Lucas, 1982). Subsidence occurs as the water table is drained and the soils are exposed to oxidation and erosion. Recent management to control the water table level has been successful in slowing the rate of subsidence, although it is still substantial in many areas.

Agricultural production in Florida is quite diverse. The long growing season and subtropical climate allow production of citrus, sugarcane (*Saccharum arundinaceum* Retz.), a variety of fruits and nuts, vegetables, melons, potato (*Solanum tuberosum* L.), floriculture, sod, and peanut (USDA-NASS, 2008). Although wind and water erosion are generally low in Florida (USDA-NRCS, 2006b), wind erosion can be locally severe on organic soils when the soils are bare during planting season. Water table management is important during the summer, but many crops require some irrigation during the generally dry fall and winter (USDA-NRCS, 2006a). Groundwater and surface water quality also are concerns in Florida.

Mid-South Region

The soil and water conservation advances in the Mid-South were described in Chapter 8 (Locke et al., 2010). In this book, the Mid-South region includes Arkansas, Louisiana, Mississippi, southeastern Missouri (Mississippi alluvial plain known as the Bootheel), western Tennessee (area west of the Highland Rim), and eastern Texas (area roughly east of Austin). This region is part of the drainage system for the lower Mississippi River.

The climate of the region is humid subtropical (Fig. 10–3), with MAT ranging from 14 to 24°C (Fig. 10–1) and MAP ranging from 760 to 2300 mm (Fig. 10–2). Eight of the twelve soil orders recognized by the Soil Survey Staff (1999) have been identified in the Mid-South: Alfisols, Entisols, Histosols, Inceptisols, Mollisols, Spodosols, Ultisols, and Vertisols (Fig. 10–4). Chapter 8 (Locke et al., 2010) describes the distribution of the soils within each major land resource area of the Mid-South.

Recent advances in conservation measures on cropland in the Mid-South have substantially reduced water erosion (Chapter 8, Table 8–2, Locke et al., 2010), particularly in Mississippi, Missouri, and Tennessee. Much of the reduction is attributed to land placed in grassland under the USDA Conservation Reserve Program (CRP). In this program, the amount of highly erodible cropland planted to protective grasses and shrubs increased from 1.1 million hectares in 1983 to about 2.8 million hectares in 2003 (Chapter 8, Table 8–3, Locke et al., 2010).

Significant changes in farming practices include adoption of some form of conservation tillage system and residue management, particularly using cover crops. In addition, edge-of-field practices and practices designed to limit the input of eroded sediment into water bodies have been adopted to some extent (Locke et al., 2010). Early research demonstrated great reduction in water erosion in loessial, fragipan, and other soils with NT on soybean, rotations with corn, and double-cropped with wheat (McGregor et al., 1975; Mutchler and Greer, 1984). More recent work on modern cropping systems using new cultivars with different growth habits and amounts of residue confirm earlier studies and add new information needed for development of predictive erosion models. No-till management physically protects the soil with residue and improves the physical and chemical properties of the soil that make soil aggregates more stable and resistant to dispersion and transport and enhance infiltration of water, reducing runoff. Work by Dabney et al. (2004) indicated that surface cover is equally important as the development of soil physicochemical conditions in NT soil that favor infiltration and oppose particle detachment and transport into runoff (Locke et al., 2010).

No-till systems have had some difficulties on Mid-South soils with higher clay and silt contents (sometimes called heavy soils). For example, Pettigrew and Jones (2001) had disappointing grain yields after 2 yr of cotton in Mississippi River valley alluvial flood plain soils. Many other studies report favorable yields after conversion to NT systems on heavy soils. For example, highest yields of corn on a Texas clay soil were obtained using NT on raised beds (Torbert et al., 2001).

Overall, research in the Mid-South has shown that the conversion to conservation tillage, particularly to NT, has improved soil properties conducive to crop production and improved water quality as erosion and runoff are reduced. Numerous studies have shown an increase in the surface soil organic C and N content, microbial biomass, water infiltration and retention, and reduced losses of N and P by soil erosion, although dissolved forms of N and P have increased (Locke et al., 2010).

Southwest Region

The soil and water conservation advances in the Southwest were described in Chapter 9 (O'Geen et al., 2010). In this book, the U.S. Southwest includes the states of Arizona, California, Nevada, and New Mexico, a region of great variation in climate, soils, and cropping systems. This region includes parts of the Sonoran, Mojave, and Chihuahuan deserts (all states); the Colorado Plateau in Arizona and New Mexico; and the Central, Salinas, and Imperial valleys of California. Much of the variation in climate and soils in the region can be attributed to the great regional variation in topography as well as proximity to the coast. California includes the lowest point in the United States, Death Valley, with an elevation of 84 m below sea level, and Mt. Whitney, the highest peak in the continental United States, at an elevation of 4418 m above sea level. The MAT (Fig. 10–1) varies from a low of −3°C in the White Mountains of California to a high of 24°C in Death Valley; MAP (Fig. 10–2) ranges from a high of 2600 mm near the northern coast of California to 58 mm in Death Valley.

Four climate zones are found in the region. A Mediterranean-type climate with hot dry summers and cool wet winters is found in much of California (Fig. 10–3). A mid-latitude desert climate occupies much of Nevada, southeast California, and western Arizona. Semiarid steppe climate is found in northeast Arizona and much of New Mexico. Alpine climate is found in the higher elevations in all states.

Soils reflect the variation in topography and climate in the region. Aridisols and Entisols dominate the deserts and semiarid areas (Fig. 10–4). Inceptisols, Alfisols, and Mollisols are found at higher elevations and in areas with more humid conditions where precipitation is more effective to promote vegetative growth and soil development. Flood plains are dominated by Entisols and Inceptisols. Gelisols and Ultisols occur at high elevations in mountain areas of California. Alfisols, Aridisols, Entisols, Mollisols, and Vertisols are soil orders found in valleys of central California (USDA-NRCS, 2006a).

Approximately 2.2 million hectares of cropland are found in the Southwest. The cropland areas generally have high temperature and low rainfall and require irrigation for crop production. About 76% of the region is irrigated (USDA-NASS, 2007), and California accounts for 77% of the irrigated cropland. More than 85% of the cropland in California is irrigated.

A long growing season, ample irrigation water, and fertile soils allow for production of a great variety of crops, especially in California. More than 300 crops are grown across the region, including citrus and tropical fruit crops, nuts, vegetables (Fig. 10–11), rice (*Oryza sativa* L.), sugarbeet (*Beta vulgaris* L.), cotton, cereal grains, and hay (USDA-NRCS, 2006a). Dairy and beef cattle production on feedlots and rangeland is also important.

The soil and water conservation issues of the region are generally focused on infrastructure development for irrigation and land reclamation (Jelinek, 1979). Most farmland is irrigated from major infrastructure improvement projects on rivers and associated reservoirs. Some of these large projects have had unforeseen consequences. For example, severe land subsidence has occurred in parts of California as a result of groundwater pumping and near fatal decreases in some fish populations have occurred due to diversions of stream flows (O'Geen et al., 2010). Severe wind erosion and air quality concerns have occurred in the Owens Valley area at Owens (dry) Lake in California as water was diverted for urban use and irrigation (Gill and Cahill, 1992; Reheis, 2009).

Research on more efficient and effective irrigation systems has been reported since the 1930s (Curry, 1938). Current research continues to develop innovative practices that conserve soil and water and maintain profitability. Recent advances have been made to improve furrow irrigation (i.e., by modifying field lengths, set times, and furrow irrigation patterns), improve surge irrigation, and other efforts to reduce deep percolation and water loss. Conversion from furrow to drip irrigation in this region needs to be evaluated with the costs associated with the infrastructure change, energy use, and maintenance costs and efforts (Hanson et al., 1997). Some crops seem to have higher yields under drip irrigation [potato, tomato (*Solanum lycopersicum* L.)], while others show no difference in yield [cotton and lettuce (*Lactuca sativa* L.)] (O'Geen et al., 2010).

Fig. 10–11. Lettuce crop in central California. Photo by Gary Kramer, USDA-NRCS photo gallery, http://photogallery.nrcs.usda.gov/ (verified 17 Dec. 2009).

Salt-affected soils are an issue in some areas of this region. Salt-affected soils include saline soils that have an electrical conductivity of the soil solution between 4 and 30 dS m^{-1} and saline-sodic soils that are saline and also have sodium absorption ratio between 10 and 40. Solutions to solve these issues rely on the availability of high-quality water, adequate drainage, and suitable crops. Soil management practices must be designed to maintain a tolerable level of salt in the root zone (Schoups et al., 2005). Recent work has shown that subsurface drip irrigation provides sufficient control of irrigation frequency, amount, and uniformity to leach salts out of the root zone and limit deep percolation and the associated rise in the saline water table (Hanson et al., 2009).

Wind erosion is a concern in some areas of the arid Southwest where recently harvested or recently tilled fields can be susceptible to erosion by wind, and tillage and other cultural practices can cause the release of fugitive dust (Madden et al., 2008; Madden et al., 2009). Conservation tillage has been used to reduce fine dust emissions in some cropping systems (Madden et al., 2008).

Soil Management Assessment

Soil and water conservation efforts in the United States have had significant impact on the natural resources of each region. The distinctive environment of each region presents unique challenges that have been met with inimitable solutions. Recent methods of measuring and characterizing the effect of soil and water conservation efforts on soil and water resources are presented in the following sections.

National Resource Inventory

One index of the overall success of soil conservation efforts in the United States would be a measure of national trends in estimated soil erosion (also called soil loss). Soil erosion is usually defined as the detachment, transport, and subsequent deposition of soil particles under the influence of water, wind, and gravity. Soil erosion on cropland is of particular interest because of its on-site impacts on soil quality and crop productivity, and its off-site impacts on water quantity and quality, air quality, and biological activity (USDA-NRCS, 2007).

Each year the USDA-NRCS, in cooperation with the Iowa State University's Center for Survey Statistics and Methodology, collects information for use in a National Resources Inventory (NRI) of non-Federal farmland in the United States. This land includes privately owned lands, tribal and trust lands, and lands controlled by state and local governments. The NRI is a longitudinal sample survey based on statistical principles and procedures designed to assess conditions and trends of soil, water, and related resources (Mausbach and Dedrick, 2004). Details about the NRI are found at http://www.nrcs.usda.gov/technical/NRI/ (verified 16 Dec. 2009). The NRI was conducted in 5-yr cycles from 1982 to 1997. The last NRI reported in 2003 was based on data collected during 2000 through 2003. The data reported here represent only the continental United States. The NRI includes estimates for water (sheet and rill) erosion and wind erosion (Fig. 10–12). The NRI also provides information on surface area by land cover/use and wetlands by land use. Erosion is computed using scientific models that predict long-term average annual soil loss based on climatic data for the sampling sites and specific soil and site characteristics as well as cropping system information gathered during the NRI inventory. Soil and site characteristics considered include information on soil texture, land steepness, field length, and so on. Important cropping information includes crops grown, tillage system employed, and conservation structures in place.

Water erosion is estimated in the NRI using the Revised Universal Soil Loss Equation (RUSLE). The RUSLE (Renard et al., 1991) is an empirical and process-based model that predicts long-term soil loss from sheet and rill erosion from specific field slopes under specified cover and management conditions (USDA-NRCS, 2002). RUSLE is a revised version of the Universal Soil Loss Equation (USLE) developed by Wischmeier and Smith (1978). Soil loss is expressed in the USLE as the following equation:

$$A = f(RKLSCP) \qquad [1]$$

where A is the predicted soil loss, f indicates a nonlinear functional relationship among the variables R, a rainfall factor; K, a soil erodibility factor; LS, a topographic factor considering slope length and steepness; C, a crop cover and management factor; and P, a conservation practice factor. The RUSLE expresses the information of USLE in a user-friendly computer environment, provides estimates of erosion for shorter time periods than provided by USLE, and considers many interactions of the factors not considered in USLE (Laflen, 1998). The RUSLE was originally provided in a MS DOS environment but has recently been upgraded to a Windows environment in RUSLE2 (USDA-NRCS, 2009). RUSLE2 uses the basic formulation of RUSLE but computes values on a daily basis. In addition, a new ridge subfactor has been added, the deposition equation has been extended to consider sediment characteristics and how deposition changes with these characteristics, and new relationships for describing residue processes have also been added (USDA-ARS, 2009).

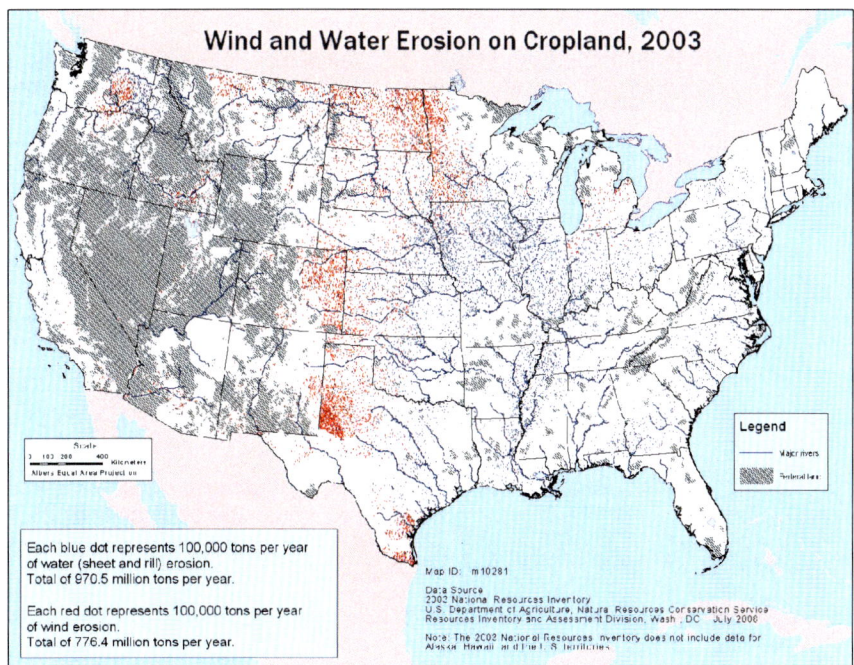

Fig. 10–12. Estimated average annual wind and water erosion on cropland in the United States, according to the 2003 National Resources Inventory (USDA-NRCS, 2007).

The Wind Erosion Equation (WEQ) is currently used in the NRI to compute the soil loss by wind erosion. The WEQ was designed to predict long-term average annual soil erosion by wind based on a specific set of climatic and field conditions. It can also be used to predict erosion for specific time periods when using the appropriate factors in the equation. The WEQ is determined using the following equation:

$$E = f(IKCLV) \qquad [2]$$

where E is the estimated annual soil loss, f indicates a nonlinear functional relationship among the variables I, a soil erodibility index; K, a soil surface roughness factor; C, a climatic factor; L, represents the unsheltered distance; and V, a vegetative cover factor. The USDA-NRCS National Agronomy Manual (USDA-NRCS, 2002) has detailed instructions on the use of WEQ and a spreadsheet version of WEQ for use in the United States has been provided by Sporcic et al. (1998).

The key findings of the NRI have been presented by the NRCS (USDA-NRCS, 2007). Between 1982 and 2003, soil erosion on U.S. cropland decreased by 43%. Estimated water erosion was 2.2 billion Mg yr^{-1} (an average of 5.8 Mg ha^{-1} yr^{-1}) and erosion due to wind was 1.7 billion Mg yr^{-1} (an average of 4.7 Mg ha^{-1} yr^{-1}). The total mass of erosion by wind and water erosion estimated in 2003 is presented in Fig. 10–12. Approximately 28% of all cropland was eroding above the soil loss tolerance levels set by the USDA, down from an estimated 40% eroding above the tolerance level in 1982. These trends in declining soil loss are encouraging and suggest conservation efforts have been making significant impacts on the soils resource.

Conservation Effects Assessment Project

While the NRI reports on conditions and trends of soil, water, and related resources, it does not specifically quantify the environmental benefits of conservation practices. The Conservation Effects Assessment Project (CEAP) was initiated by the USDA-ARS, USDA-NRCS, and the Extension Service (CREES) in response to a call for better accountability of societal benefits from the Farm Security and Rural Investment Act of 2002, referred to as the 2002 Farm Bill (Duriancik et al., 2008; Mausbach and Dedrick, 2004). CEAP was designed to quantify the environmental benefits of conservation practices at the national and watershed scale using a mix of data collection, model development, model application, and research (Mausbach and Dedrick, 2004). The national assessment provides modeled estimates of conservation benefits for annual reporting and the watershed-scale component quantifies the benefits at the watershed scale.

CEAP activities are organized into three interconnected efforts (Duriancik et al., 2008):

1. Bibliographies, literature reviews, and workshops were conducted to establish what is known about the environmental effects of conservation practices and to determine what still needs to be done. The USDA National Agricultural Library has developed six bibliographies of existing literature on the effects of conservation practices and programs (USDA-NAL, 2009). Several subject area specialists were also enlisted to provide additional synthesis of the current state of knowledge of conservation practice effects, including identifying areas needing additional research. The literature reviews included studies of the benefit of conservation on cropland (Schnepf and Cox, 2006) and to fish and wildlife (Haufler, 2005, 2007).

2. Watershed-scale studies were established to quantify water quality and soil quality effects of conservation practices. Forty-one watersheds were established since the inception of CEAP (Fig. 10–13). The watersheds fall into three general groups:

   - Fourteen USDA-ARS benchmark watersheds were identified that are the subjects of long-term research on soil quality and water quality effects of conservation systems on rain-fed cropland.
   - CSREES competitive grants were established for 16 retrospective studies (3-yr) on watersheds to determine the effects of conservation practices on water quality and quantity, the effects of timing and location of practices, and to explore socioeconomic factors related to adoption and maintenance of conservation practices. This list includes three new watersheds for grazing lands (L. Duriancik, personal communication, March 2009).
   - USDA-NRCS special emphasis studies were established on 11 watersheds using 3-yr studies to address special issues such as land application of animal waste, soil erosion, drainage management, and water conservation.

3. National and regional assessments using scientifically based models will be used to estimate the environmental benefits of conservation practices implemented each year. The assessments will include consideration of croplands, wetlands, grazing lands, and wildlife.

Although much still needs to be done, a thorough review of the current status and accomplishments of each assessment category of CEAP after the first 5 yr was provided by Duriancik et al. (2008).

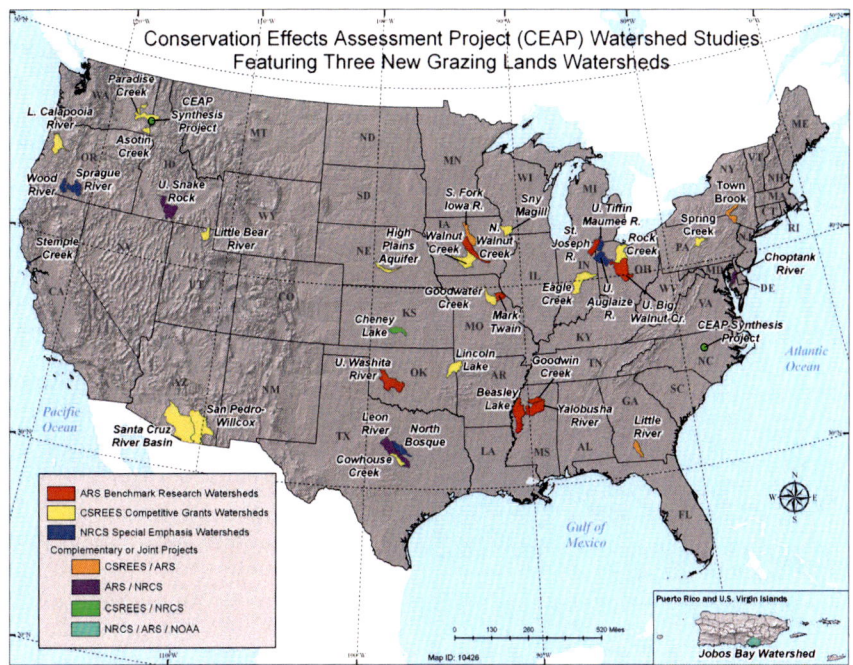

Fig. 10–13. Conservation Effects Assessment Project (CEAP) watershed study sites.

Soil Quality Indexes

A variety of specialized tools have been developed to assess the effects of land management on soil resources. The capacity of the soil to function for specific purposes has been defined as soil quality (SQ) (Karlen et al., 1997). It is critical to understand that soils need to be evaluated for a specific purpose because soils that function well for one purpose may function very poorly for another purpose. For example, a soil that functions well for growing crops may function very poorly as a filter for septic systems. In other words, an appropriate SQ assessment tool measures changes in soil function in response to management within the context of the soil use (Andrews et al., 2004). A review of the past, present, and future of soil quality assessment was provided by (Karlen et al., 2008a). In this section I will briefly review four SQ assessment tools currently in use.

Soil Conditioning Index

The USDA-NRCS has adopted the Soil Conditioning Index (SCI) (USDA-NRCS, 2002) as a tool to estimate the effects of crop management on soil organic matter, (SOM = soil organic carbon × 1.7). The SCI was not designed to evaluate the current SOM level but to assess whether or not the current management will cause the SOM to increase, decrease, or remain stable. Determination of the SCI is required for several USDA-NRCS practice standards, such as the Conservation Crop Rotation Practice Standard 328. The SCI is also specified for use in the Conservation Security Program of the Farm Security and Rural Investment Act of 2002.

The SCI estimates qualitative changes in SOM in the soil surface based on the combined and weighted effects of organic material (OM) returned to the soil, field operations (FO), and wind and water induced erosion (ER) based on the following equation (USDA-NRCS, 2003):

$$SCI = [OM \times (0.4)] + [FO \times (0.4)] + [ER \times (0.2)] \qquad [3]$$

This equation shows that OM and FO each accounts for 40% of the final SCI value, while wind and water erosion accounts for 20% of the final value. Negative values of SCI indicate decreasing levels of SOM; positive values indicate increasing SOM. This index assumes field operations reduce SOM by stimulating organic matter breakdown as tillage buries residues and mixes the soil. Maintaining organic residues will maintain and increase SOM levels. The amount of reduction of SOM due to field operations depends on the native level of SOM that may be sustained for a given site.

The SCI is determined using RUSLE2 (USDA-NRCS, 2003). Specific field sampling and laboratory analyses are not required, but knowledge of the field location, soil type, and crop management systems used at the site is needed to determine the SCI. Other information needed to determine SCI is provided in RUSLE2. However, RUSLE2 can be modified to provide field-specific values of some factors, such as residue and yield values that will improve SCI estimates. An evaluation of SCI using nine long-term C studies found that positive trends in C followed positive trends in SCI, and negative SCI trends were associated with negative C trends (Hubbs et al., 2002). An evaluation of SCI for a wide variety of southern High Plains agroecosystms in grasslands and cropped (grower) fields (Zobeck et al., 2007) found the SCI more related to more labile forms of soil organic matter such as particulate organic matter carbon than more stable forms of organic matter.

Soil Management Assessment Framework

The Soil Management Assessment Framework (SMAF) is a SQ assessment tool based on the effects of soil management practices on dynamic soil properties and overall soil function (Andrews et al., 2002; Karlen et al., 2006). To develop a SQ index value, SMAF uses laboratory and field data of a set of soil properties (called SQ indicators in SMAF) that will be evaluated against a set of scoring curves. Cropping systems are evaluated using a group of SQ indicators that represent properties that have the greatest sensitivity for the soil function under consideration. The indicators include soil physical, chemical, and biological data. The scoring curves indicate the potential of the soil to function for specific purposes. The users of SMAF do not need extensive knowledge of the relationship between soil indicators and management. The crop and soils information are used by SMAF to adjust the scoring curves for the effect of inherent soil properties, climate, and crop response (Wienhold et al., 2006). The soil indicator scoring curves vary from 0 to 1, where 1 represents the highest potential for a given use and that the indicator is nonlimiting for the use (Andrews et al., 2004). The SMAF has been tested in Georgia, Iowa, California, and the Pacific Northwest (Andrews et al., 2002, 2004); Iowa and Wisconsin (Karlen et al., 2006); and the U.S. Great Plains (Wienhold et al., 2006; Zobeck et al., 2007, 2008). A web-based tool to use SMAF to assess soil quality is found at http://soilquality.org/tools/smaf_intro.html (verified 16 Dec. 2009).

Agroecosystem Performance Assessment Tool

The Agroecosystem Performance Assessment Tool (AEPAT) employs a computer program using multiobjective analysis principles to assess agroecosystem performance (Liebig et al., 2004). This approach is similar to SMAF in that indicators representative of specific agroecosystem functions are evaluated. The AEPAT is designed for agricultural researchers working with long-term agroecosystem experiments (Liebig and Varvel, 2003) and has been used for numerous teaching applications (M. Liebig, personal communication, March 2009). In AEPAT, the indicators are assigned to specific agroecosystem functions, such as food production or nutrient cycling, and are compared based on their difference from a standard or optimum value. The user must also provide information used to develop the scoring curve for each indicator. The functions are weighted by the users, and the individual scores are combined into an overall index.

The input demands of AEPAT require that the user have a thorough understanding of how indicators relate to management goals (Wienhold et al., 2006). The AEPAT can be obtained at the USDA-ARS Northern Great Plains Research Laboratory website at http://www.ars.usda.gov/Services/docs.htm?docid=10644 (verified 17 Dec. 2009).

Cornell Soil Health Test

The Cornell Soil Health Team has developed a cost-effective protocol for assessing the health status of soils in New York and the U.S. Northeast (Gugino et al., 2007; Schindelbeck et al., 2008). The team looked at 39 potential soil physical, biological, and chemical property indicators, considering factors such as cost and response to management, and evaluated them for their use to rapidly assess soil health. The protocol emphasizes the integration of soil biological measurements with soil physical and chemical measurements (Gugino et al., 2007). A list of properties used in the protocol includes those measured in the field (such as using a field penetrometer) and laboratory (such as soil nutrient content). Work continues to identify the most promising indicators (Moebius et al., 2007). Similar to SMAF and AEPAT, scoring curves that vary from 1 (poorest) to 10 (highest), developed separately for the major soil groups in the region, are also used to convert the value for a specific indicator to a rating value. Details about Cornell soil health test are provided at http://soilhealth.cals.cornell.edu/ (verified 17 Dec. 2009).

Comparing Indexes

The Cornell Soil Health Test is a relatively new test, and comparisons with other indexes are not available. Wienhold et al. (2006) compared AEPAT and SMAF in an evaluation of cropping systems in the Great Plains. Since the input requirements of SMAF and AEPAT are different, a high degree of correlation between the two indexes was not expected and was considered inappropriate. However, since both tools were designed for assessing management on soil function, general agreement was expected (Wienhold et al., 2006). There was general agreement between the two assessment tools when they were used to compare management practices, with generally higher soil quality found for the conservation systems tested. The study also demonstrated that all soil properties observed exhibited temporal variation, which was likely related to weather, previous crop in the rotation, and the dynamic nature of the many properties measured. Testing through time was recommended to determine the direction of change.

A comparison of SMAF and SCI for a watershed in north-central Iowa showed a positive correlation of the indexes in a comparison of four crop sequences (Karlen et al., 2008a,b). The SCI values were all positive, indicating SOM accumulation, and showed good agreement with the SQ values of SMAF for comparisons of tillage and landscape groups. A potential advantage of using SMAF rather than SCI is that SMAF is designed to evaluate several SQ indicators to assess the effects of management on the combined biological, chemical, and physical effects on soil resources (Karlen et al., 2008a).

An evaluation of SMAF and SCI using a controlled, replicated study that included NT and conventionally tilled corn, and NT corn with rotations including barley, soybean, and dry bean (*Phaeseolus vulgaris* L.) at three levels of nitrogen varying from 0 to 224 kg N ha^{-1} (0–200 lb ac^{-1}) found that both SQ indexes clearly separated the plots with very high levels of N from plots with no N (Zobeck et al., 2008). However, for the SQ index of SMAF (SQI), the mid-level of N was statistically the same as both extreme levels. Statistical differences were observed among all N levels for the SCI (Fig. 10–14). The SQI also seemed to make more detailed differentiation among crop management systems than the SCI. The SQI separated the cropping systems into three groups with decreasing SQI value as tillage intensity increased and as lower residue crops were introduced into the cropping system (Fig. 10–15). The SQI allowed overlap among cropping groups not recognized by SCI. Selection of the most appropriate SQ index seems to be a tradeoff between data requirements, resolution required, and the desired use of the evaluation tool.

A Look to the Future

Each region described in this book represents a wide variety of crops, soils, climates, and social environments that impact and limit soil management options. For example, water is an essential ingredient for crop production and human habitation. In some regions, such as the Great Plains, Columbia Basin, and the Southwest, precipitation often needs to be supplemented through irrigation for profitable production. This need has been met by diverting water from rivers through large irrigation projects or through the use of valuable and often nonrenewable groundwater. In other parts of the United States, such as the Northeast and Midwest, excess water must be removed from the soil by artificial drainage to allow crop production. In all regions, competition for water among urban and rural uses is an issue.

This competition for water among contending rural and urban interests takes several forms. Sometimes, such as in the Southwest, competition for water may be direct. Water is needed for this rapidly urbanizing region to support urban centers, while at the same time, water is needed to grow high-value crops. In other regions, as in the Northeast, the interaction of urban and agricultural land use is more indirect. The watershed producing the water for New York City is located in the upstate area (van Es, 2010) and is used in part for agricultural production. An extensive and successful watershed protection program was initiated by the city to reduce pollutants contributed to the watershed by agricultural activities. Future challenges for water are expected and will require careful consideration of all alternatives to develop sustainable solutions.

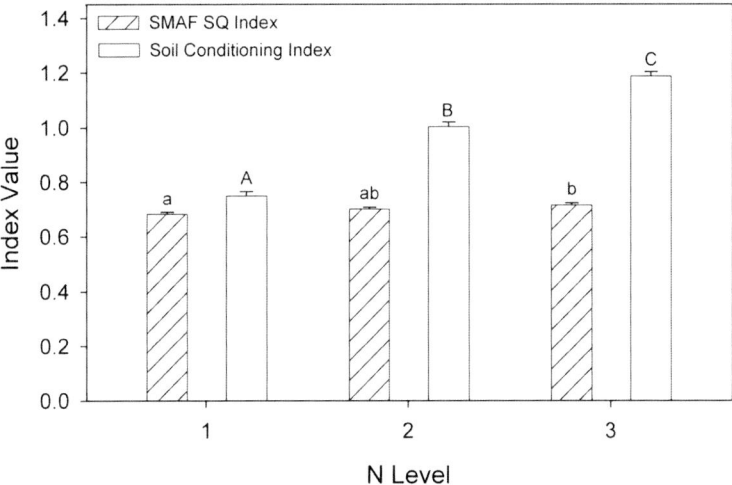

Fig. 10–14. Effect of nitrogen level on the Soil Management Assessment Framework (SMAF) soil quality index and soil conditioning index. Adapted from Zobeck et al., 2008; used with permission.

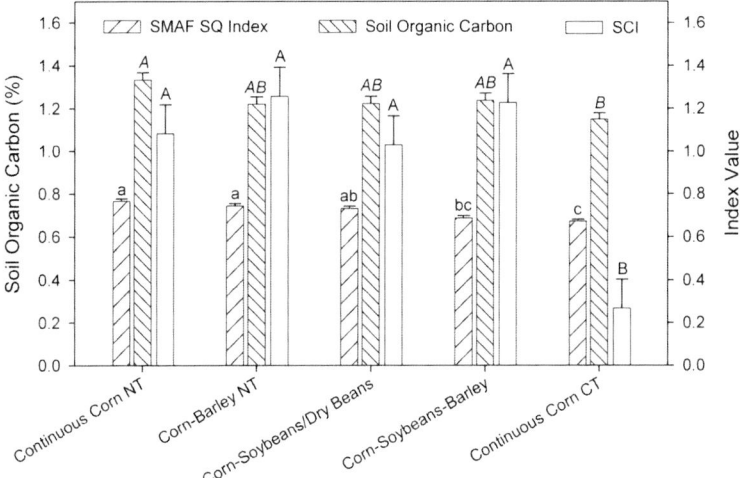

Fig. 10–15. Comparison of SMAF soil quality index and soil conditioning index values with soil organic carbon content.

Some soil conservation issues may be important in some regions but not in others. For example, compaction is a significant problem in Coastal Plains soils, and practices such as deep tillage have been developed to mitigate this problem. However, compaction is not a significant problem on the silty loess soils of the Columbia Basin and Plateau, where wind erosion of exposed fallow fields is the major challenge, and conservation systems have been designed to meet this need. Other soil and water conservation issues have a broad impact that affect several regions.

Energy production via biofuels in the United States is an area that has become, and will continue to be, of considerable interest and activity (Karlen et al., 2010). Biofuels are produced directly using crops to generate ethanol or biodiesel and indirectly using cellulosic materials. The use of crop residues for biofuels production may pose significant challenges for soil conservation and soil quality. Removal of all crop residues will expose the soil to wind and water erosion and reduce the amount of carbon returned to the soil needed to maintain soil organic carbon necessary to produce high soil quality for sustainable agricultural production (Johnson et al., 2007). Recent research has determined the amount of aboveground residue needed to maintain soil organic carbon for sustainable crop production (Johnson et al., 2006a,b; Wilhelm et al., 2007). Similar research will be needed in all regions since crops differ in their decomposition rates, particularly given different climatic conditions and soils.

Biofuels production will not be equally desirable or feasible for every region. It may seem reasonable in regions that receive ample precipitation to produce a crop. However, growing crops to produce fuel may not be sustainable or economically feasible in regions that require irrigation for crop production. Careful consideration of all costs (economics, social, and environmental) must be considered. If groundwater is used for irrigation, the cost of pumping and the opportunity costs for the use of the water for other competing uses must be considered.

A detailed analysis of the technical feasibility, costs, and environmental issues related to the production of biofuels has been reported by the National Research Council (2009). The report stresses that to provide sustainable biomass production we must ensure it has a low impact on global food, feed, and fiber production and that it does not aggravate other critical challenges, including soil, water, and air quality; carbon sequestration; greenhouse-gas emissions; rural development; and wildlife habitat.

Soil erosion continues to be an issue in all regions (Fig. 10–12). The type and amount of soil erosion differs among regions. Wind erosion is a particular concern in the Great Plains and in some areas of the Southwest and Northwest where strong winds blow and low crop residues do not sufficiently protect the soil surface. Water erosion is of greater concern in eastern U.S. regions. However, NT and cover crops are two practices that several regions often use to address issues of soil erosion and to improve soil quality.

Future soil and water management decisions may also be significantly impacted by expected impending changes in the U.S. climate. A study commissioned by the U.S. Global Change Research Program (Karl et al., 2009) summarizes the science of climate change and the impacts of climate change on the United States now and in the future. The report states that precipitation and runoff are likely to increase in the Northeast and Midwest in winter and spring, and decrease in the West, especially the Southwest, in spring and summer. Climate change will place additional burdens on an already stressed water system. Soil water erosion rates may be expected to change for a variety of reasons, including changes in the erosive power of rainfall (Pruski and Nearing, 2002) and changes in plant biomass (Nearing et al., 2004). The mechanisms by which climate change will modify plant biomass and subsequent erosion and runoff are complex. Nearing et al. (2004) provided a review of the expected climate change impacts on soil erosion rates.

Fig. 10–16. No-till soybeans planted in the residue of a wheat crop in Arkansas. Photo by Tim McCabe, USDA-NRCS photo gallery, http://photogallery.nrcs.usda.gov/ (verified 17 Dec. 2009).

Adoption of NT for crop production (Fig. 10–16) confers many benefits on the soil, including reduced soil erosion and sedimentation, improved soil tilth, carbon sequestration, reduced fuel consumption, increased soil moisture, and more (Fawcett and Towery, 2002). Recent developments in biotechnology to produce herbicide- and insect-tolerant crops and new NT implements that allow precise seed placement in residues have promoted adoption of NT in all regions. Surveys by the Conservation Tillage Information Center show that from 1990 to 2002, although the total acreage of conservation tillage seemed to have reached a plateau, adoption of NT continued to increase (Fawcett and Towery, 2002). In fact, NT rose from about 16.5 million hectares in 1995 to about 22.4 million hectares in 2002, representing a growth of 35%. Since NT saves on average 36 L of fuel per hectare per year, adoption of NT continues to increase. Unfortunately, NT has not increased substantially in all regions. Adoption has been limited in some regions, such as the Southwest and southern Great Plains, due to the cost of irrigation needed to maintain a cover crop or other issues. Future work is needed to overcome these limitations.

Cover crops protect the soil surface from the erosive effects of water and wind, reduce nitrate concentration and load in subsurface drainage water (Kaspar et al., 2007), improve aggregate stability and water infiltration (Bruce et al., 1992), and increase carbon sequestration. Use of cover crops has been particularly successful in the Midwest, Southeast, and Mid-South region, where precipitation is abundant and erosion is a persistent problem. Use and development of new cover crops will remain an important feature in future soil conservation systems.

Discussion of future soil and water conservation systems would not be complete without considering how to evaluate these systems. The National Resources Inventory (USDA-NRCS, 2007) has been used to estimate annual wind and water erosion since 1982. The NRI statistically samples soil and site characteristics of many locations and uses the data in erosion models to estimate erosion on farm fields. This information is used to identify the type, amount, and location of soil erosion (Fig. 10–12). The limitations of this approach to estimate erosion were discussed by Trimble and Crosson (2000). They suggest that a comprehensive national system of monitoring soil erosion and consequent downstream sediment movement and/or blowing dust is critical. CEAP will provide additional data to compare with NRI estimates as it quantifies the environmental benefits of conservation practices at the national and watershed scale. The data in CEAP will include a mix of data collection, model development and application, and new research (Mausbach and Dedrick, 2004).

The efforts mentioned above quantify the effects of soil management at the national and regional level. New tools are now available to quantify the effects of farming practices under specific climates, soils, and site characteristics. Some tools, such as the SCI, provide estimates of changes in single factors, in this case organic carbon content. Other tools such as the SMAF and the Cornell soil health test are based on the effects of soil management practices on dynamic soil properties and assess the soil quality for specific soil functions. A recent study of the SCI and SMAF as tools to provide comprehensive soil assessment by the Soil and Water Conservation Society (Soil and Water Conservation Society, 2008) pointed out the strength and weaknesses of each tool but suggested they still fall short of an ideal system. They suggested the development of a suite of existing or developing tools linked through a common interface with geographic information system capability may well be the most efficient approach to building an ideal system. In addition, they suggested developing a coordinated plan to create this system, led by the USDA, in collaboration with partners in academia, federal, state, and local agencies, as well as nonprofit and for-profit entities. Such a collaboration will accelerate acceptance and use of the tools and help refine the tools for use in diverse settings and for diverse purposes (Soil and Water Conservation Society, 2008).

So much work still needs to be done. Different regions in the United States have unique resource concerns and issues that demand clear solutions tailored to their specific environment and anticipated changes in climate. New initiatives such as biofuels and difficult issues created by competing interests for scarce resources (e.g., water) continue to challenge soil conservation and land use specialists. New tools have been and continue to be developed to help us assess and improve management systems. The goal is the development of sustainable, energy efficient agricultural systems to provide high-quality, safe food and other agricultural products for the United States and the world.

References

Andrews, S.S., D.L. Karlen, and C.A. Cambardella. 2004. The soil management assessment framework: A quantitative soil quality evaluation method. Soil Sci. Soc. Am. J. 68:1945–1962.

Andrews, S.S., D.L. Karlen, and J.P. Mitchell. 2002. A comparison of soil quality indexing methods for vegetable production systems in Northern California. Agric. Ecosyst. Environ. 90:25–45.

Baumhardt, R.L., and J. Salinas-Garcia. 2006. Dryland agriculture in Mexico and the U.S. southern Great Plains. p. 341–364. In G.A. Peterson et al. (ed.) Dryland agriculture. 2nd ed. Agron. Monogr. 23. ASA, CSSA, and SSSA, Madison, WI.

Bordovsky, J.P., and D.O. Porter. 2008. Effect of subsurface drip irrigation system uniformity on cotton production in the Texas High Plains. Appl. Eng. Agric. 24(4):465–472.

Bruce, R.R., G.W. Langdale, L.T. West, and W.P. Miller. 1992. Soil surface modification by biomass inputs affecting rainfall infiltration. Soil Sci. Soc. Am. J. 56:1614–1620.

Busscher, W.J., H.H. Schomberg, and R.L. Raper. 2010. Soil and water conservation in the southeastern United States: A look at conservation practices past, present, and future. p. 183–200. In T.M. Zobeck and W.F. Schillinger (ed.) Soil and water conservation advances in the United States. SSSA Spec. Publ. 60. SSSA, Madison, WI.

Colaizzi, P.D., P.H. Gowda, T.H. Marek, and D.O. Porter. 2008. Irrigation in the Texas High Plains: A brief history and potential reductions in demand. Irrig. Drainage 58:257–274.

Cook, K.V., L. Faulconer, and D.G. Jennings. 1996. A report on nitrate contamination of ground water in the mid-Columbia Basin. Washington State Interagency Ground Water Committee Publ. 96-17.

Curry, A.S. 1938. Consumptive use of water by alfalfa in tanks. New Mexico Coll. Agric Mech. Arts and Agric. Exp. Stn. Press, Las Cruces.

Dabney, S.M., G.V. Wilson, K.C. McGegor, and G.R. Foster. 2004. History, residue, and tillage effects on erosion of loessial soil. Trans. ASAE 47(3):767–775.

Duriancik, L.F., D. Bucks, J.P. Dobrowolski, T. Drewes, S.D. Eckles, L. Jolley, R.L. Kellogg, D. Lund, J.R. Makuch, M.P. O'Neill, C.A. Rewa, M.R. Walbridge, R. Parry, and M.A. Weltz. 2008. The first five years of the Conservation Effects Assessment Project. J. Soil Water Conserv. 63:185A–197A.

Fawcett, R., and D. Towery. 2002. Conservation tillage and plant biotechnology: How new technologies can improve the environment by reducing the need to plow. Available at http://croplife.intraspin.com/Biotech/papers/35%20Fawcett.pdf (verified 187 Dec. 2009). Conservation Tillage Information Center, Purdue Univ., West Lafayette, IN.

Gill, T.E., and T.A. Cahill. 1992. Playa-generated dust storm from Owens Lake. p. 63–73. In C.A. Hall, Jr. (ed.) The history of water: Eastern Sierra, Owens Valley, White-Inyo Mountains. Proc. of the Fourth White Mountain Research Station Symp., Bishop, CA.

Gugino, B.K., O.J. Idowu, R.R. Schindelbeck, H.M. van Es, D.W. Wolfe, B.N. Moebius, J.E. Thies, and G.S. Abawi. 2007. Cornell soil health assessment training manual. Cornell Univ., Ithaca, NY.

Hansen, L., and M. Ribaudo. 2008. Economic measures of soil conservation benefits. USDA-ERS Tech. Bull. 1922.

Hanson, B.R., D. Putnam, and R. Snyder. 2009. Drip irrigation provides the salinity control needed for profitable irrigation of tomatoes in the San Joaquin Valley. Calif. Agric. 63:131–136.

Hanson, B.R., L.J. Schwankl, K.F. Schulbach, and G.S. Pettygrove. 1997. A comparison of furrow, surface drip, and subsurface drip irrigation on lettuce yield and applied water. Agric. Water Manage. 33:139–157.

Haufler, J.B. 2005. Fish and wildlife benefits of Farm Bill conservation programs: 2000–2005 update. Wildlife Society Technical Review 05-2. Available at http://www.nrcs.usda.gov/Technical/nri/ceap/review.html (verified 17 Dec. 2009). Wildlife Society, Bethesda, MD.

Haufler, J.B. 2007. Fish and wildlife response to Farm Bill conservation practices. Wildlife Society Technical Review 07-1. Available at http://www.nrcs.usda.gov/Technical/nri/ceap/review.html (verified 17 Dec. 2009). Wildlife Society, Bethesda, MD.

Hewes, L., and P.E. Frandson. 1952. Occupying the wet prairie: The role of artificial drainage in Story County, Iowa. Ann. Assoc. Am. Geogr. 42:24–50.

Hubbs, M.D., M.L. Norfleet, and D.T. Lightle. 2002. Interpreting the soil conditioning index. p. 192–196. In E. v. Santen (ed.) Making conservation tillage conventional: Building a future on 25 years of research. Proc. of 25th annual southern conservation tillage conference for sustainable agriculture. Spec. Rep. 1. Alabama Agric. Exp. Stn. and Auburn University, Auburn.

Jelinek, L.J. 1979. Harvest empire: A history of California agriculture. Boyd & Fraser, San Francisco, CA.

Johnson, J.M.-F., R.R. Allmaras, and D.C. Reicosky. 2006a. Estimating source carbon from crop residues, roots, and rhizodeposits using the national grain-yield database. Agron. J. 98:622–636.

Johnson, J.M.F., M.D. Coleman, R.W. Gesch, A.A. Jaradat, R. Mitchell, D.C. Reicosky, and W.W. Wilhelm. 2007. Biomass-bioenergy crops in the United States: A changing paradigm. Am. J. Plant Sci. Biotechnol. 1:1–28.

Johnson, J.M.F., D.C. Reicosky, R.R. Allmaras, D. Archer, and W. Wilhelm. 2006b. A matter of balance: Conservation and renewable energy. J. Soil Water Conserv. 63:121–125.

Kanwar, R.S., R.M. Cruse, M. Ghaffarzadeh, A. Bakhsh, D.L. Karlen, and T.B. Bailey. 2005. Corn/soybean and alternate farming systems effects on water quality. Appl. Eng. Agric. 21:181–188.

Karl, T.R., J.M. Melillo, and T.C. Peterson. 2009. Global climate change impacts in the United States. Available at http://downloads.globalchange.gov/usimpacts/pdfs/climate-impacts-report.pdf (verified 17 Dec. 2009). Cambridge Univ. Press, Cambridge, UK.

Karlen, D.L., S.S. Andrews, B.J. Wienhold, and T.M. Zobeck. 2008a. Soil quality assessment: Past, present and future. J. Integr. Biosci. 6:3–14.

Karlen, D.L., D.L. Dinnes, and J.W. Singer. 2010. Midwest soil and water conservation: Past, present, and future. p. 131–162. *In* T.M. Zobeck and W.F. Schillinger (ed.) Soil and water conservation advances in the United States. SSSA Spec. Publ. 60. SSSA, Madison, WI.

Karlen, D.L., E.C. Hurley, S.S. Andrews, C.A. Cambardella, D.W. Meek, M.D. Duffy, and A.P. Mallarino. 2006. Crop rotation effects on soil quality at three northern corn/soybean belt locations. Agron. J. 98:484–495.

Karlen, D.L., M.J. Mausbach, J.W. Doran, R.G. Cline, R.F. Harris, and G.E. Schuman. 1997. Soil quality: A concept, definition, and framework for evaluation. Soil Sci. Soc. Am. J. 61:4–10.

Karlen, D.L., M.D. Tomer, J. Neppel, and C.A. Cambardella. 2008b. A preliminary watershed scale soil quality assessment in north central Iowa, USA. Soil Tillage Res. 99:291–299.

Kaspar, T.C., D.B. Jaynes, T.B. Parkin, and T.B. Moorman. 2007. Rye cover crop and gamagrass strip effects on NO_3 concentration and load in tile drainage. J. Environ. Qual. 36:1503–1511.

Kemper, W.D., W.H. Heinemann, D.C. Kincaid, and R.V. Worstell. 1981. Cablegation: 1. Cable controlled plugs in perforated supply pipes for automatic furrow irrigation. Trans. ASAE 24(6):1526–1532.

Kjelgaard, J.F., D.G. Chandler, and K.E. Saxton. 2004. Evidence for direct suspension of loessial soils on the Columbia Plateau. Earth Surf. Processes Landforms 29:221–236.

Laflen, J.M. 1998. Understanding and controlling soil erosion by rainfall. p. 1–20. *In* F.J. Pierce and W.W. Frye (ed.) Advances in soil and water conservation. Ann Arbor Press, Ann Arbor, MI.

Lascano, R.J., and R.E. Sojka (ed.) 2007. Irrigation of agricultural crops. 2nd ed. Agron. Monogr. 30. ASA, CSSA, and SSSA, Madison, WI.

Lemunyon, J.L., and R.G. Gilbert. 1993. Concept and need for a phosphorus assessment tool. J. Prod. Agric. 6:483–496.

Liebig, M.A., M.E. Miller, G.E. Varval, J.W. Doran, and J.D. Hanson. 2004. AEPAT: Software for assessing agronomic and environmental performance of management practices in long-term agroecosystem experiments. Agron. J. 96:109–115.

Liebig, M.A., and G.E. Varvel. 2003. Effects of western Corn Belt cropping systems on agroecosystem functions. Agron. J. 95:316–322.

Locke, M.A., D.D. Tyler, and L.A. Gaston. 2010. Soil and water conservation in the Mid-South United States: Lessons learned and a look to the future. p. 201–236. *In* T.M. Zobeck and W.F. Schillinger (ed.) Soil and water conservation advances in the United States. SSSA Spec. Publ. 60. SSSA, Madison, WI.

Lubowski, R.N., M. Vesterby, S. Buchkoltz, A. Baez, and M.J. Roberts. 2006. Major uses of land in the United States, 2002. Econ. Info. Bull 14. Available at http://www.ers.usda.gov/publications/EIB14/eib14.pdf (verified 17 Dec. 2009). USDA-ERS.

Lucas, R.E. 1982. Organic soils (Histosols) formation, distribution, physical and chemical properties and management for crop production. Res. Rep. 435, Farm Science. Michigan State Univ. Agric. Exp. Stn., East Lansing, MI.

Madden, N.M., R.J. Southard, and R.M. Mitchell. 2008. Conservation tillage reduces PM10 emissions in dairy forage rotations. Atmos. Environ. 42:3795–3808.

Madden, N.M., R.J. Southard, and J.P. Michell. 2009. Soil water content and soil disaggregation by disking affects PM10 emissions. J. Environ. Qual. 38:36–43.

Mausbach, M.J., and A.R. Dedrick. 2004. The length we go—Measuring environmental benefits of conservation practices. J. Soil Water Conserv. 59:96A–103A.

McGregor, K.C., J.D. Greer, and G.E. Gurley. 1975. Long-term no-till cropping practices. Trans. ASAE 18:918–920.

Moebius, B.N., H.M. van Es, R.R. Schindelbeck, O.J.O. Idowu, D.J. Clune, and J.E. Thies. 2007. Evaluation of laboratory-measured soil properties as indicators of soil physical quality. Soil Sci. 172:895–912.

Montgomery, J.A., D.K. McCool, A.J. Busacca, and B.E. Frazier. 1999. Quantifying tillage translocation and deposition rates due to moldboard plowing in the Palouse region of the Pacific Northwest, USA. Soil Tillage Res. 51:175–187.

Mutchler, C.K., and J.D. Greer. 1984. Reduced tillage for soybeans. Trans. ASAE 27:432–436.

National Research Council. 2009. Liquid transportation fuels from coal and biomass: Technological status, costs, and environmental impacts. America's Energy Future Panel on Alternative Transportation Fuels, National Academy of Sciences, National Academy of Engineering, and National Research Council. The National Academies Press, Washington, DC.

Nearing, M.A., F.F. Pruski, and M.R. O'Neal. 2004. Expected climate change impacts on soil erosion rates: A review. J. Soil Water Conserv. 59(1):43–50.

O'Geen, A.T., M.J. Singer, and W. Horwath. 2010. Soil and water conservation for California and the desert Southwest: Past, present, and future trends. p. 237–262. *In* T.M. Zobeck and W.F. Schillinger (ed.) Soil and water conservation advances in the United States. SSSA Spec. Publ. 60. SSSA, Madison, WI.

Papendick, R.I. 2004. Farming with the wind. II: Wind erosion and air quality control on the Columbia Plateau and Columbia Basin. Spec. Rep. by the Columbia Plateau PM_{10} Project. Rep. XB 1042. Washington Agric. Exp. Stn., Pullman, WA.

Pettigrew, W.T., and M.A. Jones. 2001. Cotton growth under no-till production in the lower Mississippi River Valley alluvial flood plain. Agron. J. 93:1398–1404.

Pruski, F. F., and M. A. Nearing. 2002. Climate-induced changes in erosion during the 21st century for eight U.S. locations. Water Resour. Res. 38(12), 1298, doi:10.1029/2001WR000493.

Raper, R.L., D.W. Reeves, J.N. Shaw, E. van Santen, and P.L. Mask. 2007. Site-specific subsoiling benefits for cotton production in Coastal Plains soils. Soil Tillage Res. 96:174–181.

Reheis, M.C. 2009. Owens (dry) Lake, California: A human-induced dust problem. Available at http://geochange.er.usgs.gov/sw/impacts/geology/owens/ (verified 17 Dec. 2009).

Renard, K.G., G.R. Foster, G.A. Weesies, and J.P. Porter. 1991. RUSLE: Revised universal soil loss equation. J. Soil Water Conserv. 46:30–33.

Schillinger, W.F., R.I. Papendick, and D.K. McCool. 2010. Soil and water challenges for Pacific Northwest agriculture. p. 47–80. *In* T.M. Zobeck and W.F. Schillinger (ed.) Soil and water conservation advances in the United States. SSSA Spec. Publ. 60. SSSA, Madison, WI.

Schindelbeck, R.R., H.M. van Es, G.S. Abawi, D.W. Wolfe, T.L. Whitlow, B.K. Gugino, O.J. Idowu, and B.N. Moebius-Clune. 2008. Comprehensive assessment of soil quality for landscape and urban management. Landsc. Urban Plan. 88:73–80.

Schneider, A.D., G.W. Buchleiter, and D.C. Kincaid. 2000. LEPA irrigation developments. p. 89–96. *In* R.G. Evans et al. (ed.) Proc. 4th Decennial Symp., National Irrigation Symp. ASAE, St. Joseph, MI.

Schnepf, M., and C. Cox. 2006. Environmental benefits of conservation on croplands: The status of our knowledge. Available at http://www.nrcs.usda.gov/Technical/nri/ceap/review.html (verified 19 Dec. 2009). Soil and Water Conservation Society, Ankeny, IA.

Schoups, G., J.W. Hopmans, C.A. Young, J.A. Vrugt, W.W. Wallender, K.K. Tanji, and S. Panday. 2005. Sustainability of irrigated agriculture in the San Joaquin Valley, California. Proc. Natl. Acad. Sci. USA 102:15352–15356.

Soil and Water Conservation Society. 2008. Beyond T: Guiding sustainable soil management. A report of an expert consultation. Soil and Water Conservation Society, Ankeny, IA.

Sporcic, M., T. Keep, and L. Nelson. 1998. WEQ management period method wind erosion model worksheet. Available at http://www.nm.nrcs.usda.gov/technical/tech-notes/agro/ag55.xls (verified 17 Dec. 209).

Soil Survey Staff. 1999. Soil taxonomy: A basic system of soil classification for making and interpreting soil surveys, 2nd ed. USDA-NRCS, USDA Agric. Handb. 436. U.S. Gov. Print. Office, Washington, DC.

Stewart, B.A., R.L. Baumhardt, and S.R. Evett. 2010. Major advances of soil and water conservation in the U.S. southern Great Plains. p. 103–130. *In* T.M. Zobeck and W.F. Schillinger (ed.) Soil and water conservation advances in the United States. SSSA Spec. Publ. 60. SSSA, Madison, WI.

Sullivan, P. 2003. Overview of cover crops and green manures: Fundamentals of sustainable agriculture. Appropriate Technology Transfer for Rural Areas, National Sustainable Agric. Info Serv. ATTRA Publ. IP024. Available at http://attra.ncat.org/attra-pub/PDF/covercrop.pdf (verified 17 Dec. 2009).

Tanaka, D.L., D.J. Lyon, P.R. Miller, S.D. Merrill, and B.G. McConkey. 2010. Soil and water conservation advances in the semiarid northern Great Plains. p. 81–102. *In* T.M. Zobeck and W.F. Schillinger (ed.) Soil and water conservation advances in the United States. SSSA Spec. Publ. 60. SSSA, Madison, WI.

Torbert, H.A., K.N. Potter, and J.E. Morrison. 2001. Tillage system, fertilizer nitrogen rate, and timing effect on corn yields in the Texas Blackland Prairie. Agron. J. 93:1119–1124.

Trimble, S.W., and P. Crosson. 2000. U.S. soil erosion rates: Myth and reality. Science, New Series 289:248–250.

U.S. Dep. of the Interior, USGS. 2007. High Plains regional ground water study. Available at http://co.water.usgs.gov/nawqa/hpgw/SETT.html (verified 17 Dec. 2009).

USDA-ARS. 2009. About RUSLE2 technology. Available at http://fargo.nserl.purdue.edu/rusle2_dataweb/About_RUSLE2_Technology.htm (verified 17 Dec. 2009).

USDA-NAL. 2009. CEAP bibliographies and literature reviews. Available at http://www.nrcs.usda.gov/Technical/nri/ceap/review.html (verified 17 Dec. 2009).

USDA-NASS. 2007. The census of agriculture. Available at http://www.agcensus.usda.gov/Publications/2007/Full_Report/index.asp (verified 17 Dec. 2009).

USDA-NASS. 2008. 2008 state agriculture overview—Florida. Available at http://www.nass.usda.gov/Statistics_by_State/Ag_Overview/AgOverview_FL.pdf (verified 17 Dec. 2009).

USDA-NRCS. 2002. National agronomy manual. 3rd ed. Available at http://www.nrcs.usda.gov/technical/agronomy.html (verified 17 Dec. 2009).

USDA-NRCS. 2003. Interpreting the soil conditioning index: A tool for measuring soil organic matter trends. Soil Quality-Agron. Tech. Note 16. Available at http://soils.usda.gov/sqi/concepts/soil_organic_matter/som_sci.html (verified 17 Dec. 2009).

USDA-NRCS. 2006a. Land resource regions and major land resource areas of the United States, the Caribbean, and the Pacific Basin. USDA Agric. Handb. 296. USDA-NRCS, Washington, DC.

USDA-NRCS. 2006b. Model simulation of soil loss, nutrient loss, and change in soil organic carbon associated with crop production. Available at http://www.nrcs.usda.gov/technical/nri/ceap/croplandreport/ (verified 17 Dec. 2009).

USDA-NRCS. 2007. National Resources Inventory 2003. Available at http://www.nrcs.usda.gov/technical/NRI/2003/SoilErosion-mrb.pdf (verified 17 Dec. 2009).

USDA-NRCS. 2008. Digital General Soils Map (GSM) version 2. Continental United States. December 2008 ed. Available at http://soildatamart.nrcs.usda.gov (verified 17 Dec. 2009). USDA-NRCS Soil Data Mart Source.

USDA-NRCS. 2009. Revised Universal Soil Loss Equation, Version 2 (RUSLE2). Available at http://fargo.nserl.purdue.edu/rusle2_dataweb/RUSLE2_Index.htm (verified 17 Dec. 2009).

van Es, H.M. 2010. Historical and emerging soil and water conservation issues in the Northeastern USA. p. 163–182. *In* T.M. Zobeck and W.F. Schillinger (ed.) Soil and water conservation advances in the United States. SSSA Spec. Publ. 60. SSSA, Madison, WI.

van Es, H.M., K.J. Czymmek, and Q.M. Ketterings. 2002. Management effects on N leaching and guidelines for an N leaching index in New York. J. Soil Water Conserv. 57:499–504.

Wienhold, B.J., J.L. Pikul, M.A. Liebig, M.M. Mikha, G.E. Varvel, and J.W. Doran. 2006. Cropping systems effects on soil quality in the Great Plains: Synthesis from a regional project. Renewable Agric. Food Syst. 21:49–59.

Wikipedia. 2009. Climate zones of the continental United States. Available at http://en.wikipedia.org/wiki/File:Climatemapusa2.PNG (verified 17 Dec. 2009).

Wilhelm, W.W., J.M.F. Johnson, D.L. Karlen, and D.T. Lightle. 2007. Corn stover to sustain soil organic carbon further constrains biomass supply. Agron. J. 99:1665–1667.

Wischmeier, W.H., and D.D. Smith. 1978. Predicting rainfall-erosion losses—A guide to conservation farming. Agric. Handb. 537. USDA, Washington, DC.

Zobeck, T.M., J. Crownover, M. Dollar, R.S.V. Pelt, V. Acosta-Martinez, K.F. Bronson, and D.R. Uchurch. 2007. Investigation of soil conditioning index values for southern High Plains agroecosystems. J. Soil Water Conserv. 62:433–442.

Zobeck, T.M., A.D. Halvorson, B.J. Wienhold, V. Acosta-Martinez, and D.L. Karlen. 2008. Comparison of two soil quality indexes to evaluate cropping systems in northern Colorado. J. Soil Water Conserv. 63:329–338.

Index

Aasheim, Torleif, 89
Adaptive nitrogen management, 177–178
Agricultural Act of 1956, 215
Agricultural Adjustment Act of 1933, 87
Agricultural Appropriations Bill of 1929, 214
Agricultural dust. *see also* Dust emissions
   air quality standards for, 60–63
Agroecosystem Performance Assessment Tool (AEPAT), 283
Air quality
   California, 245–246
   Pacific Northwest region, 59–63
   standards for agricultural dust, 60–63
Air temperature. *see* Mean annual air temperature
Akron, Colorado study, 114–116
Alabama and Mississippi Blackland Prairie, 210
Alfalfa, 69, 250
Alfisols, 132, 270
Alternate furrow irrigation, 118
Alternate irrigated–dryland cropping, 30
Animal production, Midwest region, 138, 151
Annual grain legumes, 92, *93*
Annual precipitation. *see* Mean annual precipitation
Arkansas, 206–207
Arkansas River, 106
Arkansas River Alluvium, 209
Arkansas Valley and Ridges, 207
Artificial drainage, Midwest region, 136–137
Atlantic and Gulf Coast Lowland Forest and Crop Region, 210
Atmospheric carbon dioxide, 32–33

Bennett, Hugh Hammond, 6, 108, 136, 187, 188, 213
Billion Ton Report, 152
Biochar, 196
Bioenergy, woody biomass, 171–172
Biofuel production
   future concerns, 286
   issues for water conservation, 34–35
   Mid-South region, 227
   Midwest region, 151–154
Biogas, 173
"Black alkali," 243
Boll Weevil Monument, *188*
Boll weevils, 187

Boston Mountains, 206
Brassica juncea, 69
Buchanan Amendment, 214
"Bull tongue scooter," 6
Burnoff, 141
Bushland, Texas studies, 112–114, 117–121

Cablegation, 268
Calhoun, John C., 105
California
   conservation tillage, 251–252, 256
   cover crops, 252, 253
   farmland protection programs, 256–257
   irrigation, 240–241, 249–251
   land evaluation and reclamation, 241–243, 254
   land use changes, 244, *245*, 257
   residue management, 254
   salinity and sodicity, 243
   soil conservation, 256
   urban expansion, 244–245, 257
   water conservation, 255
California Irrigation Management Information System, 246
California Land Conservation Act of 1965, 244, 256–257
Campbell, H. W., 81, 83–84, 107–108, 110
"Campbell's Soil Culture," 107–108
Capillarity, 4
Carbon policy, Northern Great Plains region, 96
Carbon sequestration, 171
Carey Land Grant Act, 116
Cascade Mountains, 50
"Catch crops," 253
Cattle grazing, soil compaction and, 151
Cellulosic biofuel production, 34–35
Center pivot sprinkler system, 116, 269
Central Valley Water Project (California), 241
Cereal–pulse cropping, 94–95
Chain diking, 20, *21*
Checks, 251
Chemical fallow, 89
Chesapeake Bay, 165, 169–170, 176
Chicago Fire, 131, 132
Chisel plows, 110
Climate change. *see* Global climate change
Climate zones, *265*
Clump planting, 124
Coastal estuaries, 168–170, *272*

293

Coastal Plains region. *see also* Southeast region
 climate, 183–184
 conservation concerns, 273
 farming trends, 185
 plant water availability, 190
 soils, 184, 274
 tillage, 190–191
Columbia Basin. *see also* Pacific Northwest region
 soils, 52
 water erosion, 267
 wind erosion, 267–268
Columbia Basin Project, 53
Columbia Plateau, 52. *see also* Pacific Northwest region
Columbia Plateau PM_{10} Project, 61–62, 74
Compaction, 274, 285
Conservation bench terraces (CBTs), 14–15
Conservation districts, 196–197
Conservation Effects Assessment Project (CEAP), 225, 280, *281*, 288
Conservation organizations, Southeast region, 196–197
Conservation Reserve Program (CRP), 150, 215, 256, 275
Conservation Security Program, 281
Conservation tillage
 California, 256
 defined, 9
 Mid-South region, 275
  agronomic studies, 223–224
  contemporary studies on, 222–223
  cover crops, 220–222
  early efforts, 216–217
  early-stage transition to, 220
  effects on soil properties, 224
  effects on water quality, 224–225
 Midwest region, 147, 150
 Northern Great Plains region, 88–89, 92–93
 Southeast region, 191–193, 274
 Southwest region, 251–252
Contour-balk method, 6
Contour hedging, 20–22
Contour tillage, 11–13
Contouring, 216
Controlled traffic, 179–180
Corn
 Midwest region, 139, 145
 Piedmont region, 186
 tillering, 123
Corn stover
 in biofuel feedstock production, 152–153
 winter grazing in the Midwest region, 151
Cornell Soil Health Test, 173–174, 283
Corn–soybean rotation, 139, 145, 151
Cotton production
 California, 246
 Piedmont region, 187

Cover crops
 future concerns, 287
 Mid-South region, 217–218, 220–222
 Midwest region, 150
 Northeast region, 178
 overwintering, 67
 Southeast region, 192, 274
 Southwest region, 252–253
 water conservation and, 22
 water retention and, 26–27
Cretaceous Western Coastal Plain, 210
Crimson clover, 6
Crop residues. *see also* Corn stover
 biofuel production and, 286
 in control of erosion, 5–6
 management in the Southwest region, 253–254
 reducing decomposition of, 33
 water capture and, 4–6
 in water retention, 23–24
Crop Sequence Calculator, 95
Crop water use, Bushland, Texas studies, 119
Crop water use efficiency. *see* Water use efficiency

Deep percolation, 27–28, 247
Deep tillage
 Coastal Plains region, 190–191
 in snow management, 15–16
 Southeast region, 195–196, 274
 in water conservation, 10–11
Donahue, J. L., 108
Draft animals, 189
Drinking water, 168, 272
Drip irrigation. *see also* Microirrigation
 in salt-affected regions, 250
 Southern Great Plains region, 120
 Southwest region, 247–248, 276
Droughts. *see also* Dust Bowl
 Southern Great Plains region, 109
Dry Farming Congresses, 108
Dryland cropping
 Pacific Northwest region
  land devoted to, *48*
  soil and water conservation advances, 70–74
  water erosion, 57–59
 Southern Great Plains region, 109–110
 water capture and, 3
Duley, F. L., 111
Dust Bowl, 5, 108, 110, 136
Dust emissions
 air quality standards for, 60–63
 California, 245–246
Dust mulch fallow, 85
Dust mulching, 22–23, 60
Dust storms, *270*
Dynamic cropping systems, 95

Index 295

E Horizon, 190–191
East Cross Timbers area, 210
Efficient water use
  alternate irrigated–dryland cropping, 30
  atmospheric carbon dioxide levels and, 32–33
  avoiding long fallow periods, 32
  crop selection, 29
  irrigation management, 29–30
  opportunity cropping, 31
  overview, 28–29
Electrical conductivity, 248
Entisols, 132
Environmental Policy Integrated Climate (EPIC) model, 154
Environmental Quality Incentives Program (EQIP), 57
Erosion. *see* Soil erosion; Water erosion; Wind erosion
Estuaries, *272*
Ethanol production, 34, 151–154
Eutrophication
  Chesapeake Bay, 169–170
  freshwater lakes, 170
Evaporation, soil water retention and, 22
Evapotranspiration, 119

Fallow efficiency, 87, 88
Fallowing. *see also* Summer fallow
  efficient water use and, 32
  water capture and, 18–20
Farm Bill of 2002, 280
Farm Security and Rural Investment Act of 2002, 281
Farmland Mapping and Monitoring Program (California), 244
Farmland protection programs, 256–257
Fertilizers
  guano, 165
  in Midwest crop production, 142
  wheat production costs and, 96
Fires, 131–132
"Fixed-cropping systems," 93
Flood Control Act of 1944, 136
Flooding irrigation, 16
Florida, 274
Florida Subtropical Fruit, Truck Crop, and Range Region, 274
Floridan Aquifer, 194
Food, Agriculture, Conservation, and Trade Act of 1990, 91, 94
Food Security Act of 1985, 91, 166, 215
Forage, salt-tolerant, 250
Forests, California, 245
Freeman silt loam, 27
Freshwater lakes, 170
Froelich, John, 139
Fuel costs, deep tillage and, 195–196
Furrow diking, 13, *14*, 120

Furrow irrigation
  Bushland, Texas studies, 118
  overview, 16
  Pacific Northwest region, 53
  Southwest region, 246–247, 250–251

Geib, H. V., 108
Genetically modified crops, 227
Gettel, Arnold, 89
Global climate change
  future concerns, 286
  Midwest region, 154
  Northeast region, 171
  Northern Great Plains region, 96–97
  soil quality and, 174, 176
Glyphosate, 92, 93
Glyphosate-resistant weeds, 93
Gowder, J. Mack, 6
Graham, W. T., 110
Graham-Hoeme plow, 110, 112
Grain sorghum, 121, *122*
Grand Prairie area, 210
Grass production, 173
Grazing, soil compaction and, 151
Great Depression, 134
Great Plains region. *see also* Northern Great Plains region; Southern Great Plains region
  areas of, 103, *104*
  climate, 268
  conservation concerns, 269
  cropping systems, 268
  irrigation, 268–269
Green manures, 69, *70*
  legume, 91
Guano, 165
Gulf of Mexico, 219
Gypsum, 193

Halophytes, 249
Hand hoeing, 217
Hardy, R. Luther, 6
Hatch Act, 258
Herbicides
  in no-tillage, 9, 217
  in weed control and water capture, 8
  in weed control and water retention, 26
Hezel soil, 27
High Plains. *see* Southern Great Plains region
High Plains Aquifer, 105–106, 268, *269*
High pressure sprinklers, 248
Hilgard, Eugene, 243
Histosols, 132, 140–141, 270, 274
"Hobby farms," 143
Hoeing, 217
Hoeme, Fred, 110
Homestead Act of 1862, 134
Howell, Terry, 119

"Improvers," 165
"In place" mulch, 24
Inceptisols, 132–133
Indigo, 187
Indigofera hirsuta, 187
Infiltration, 3–4
"Infiltration excess," 177
Irrigated–dryland cropping, alternate, 30
Irrigation
   efficient water use and, 29–30
   Great Plains region, 268–269
   Pacific Northwest region
      land devoted to, *48*
      major projects, 52–54
      soil and water conservation advances, 66–69
      water erosion, 57
   research programs at Bushland, Texas, 118–121
   Southern Great Plains region, 105–107, 116, 125
   Southwest region
      concerns and advances, 276–277
      drip, 247–248
      history of, 240–241, 250–251
      improving surface irrigation, 246–247
      regulated deficit irrigation, 255
      in salt-affected environments, 248–250
      scheduling, 246
   water capture and, 16–17

James, Edwin, 105

Koole brothers, 88

Lake Champlain, 170
Land Grant Universities, 258
Landscape-scale management, Midwest region, 154–156
Legumes
   annual grains, 92, *93*
   green manures, 91
Lettuce production, *271*
Levees, 243
Linder's Pasture, 213
Lister tillage, 12–13
Livestock production, Midwest region, 138, 151
Llano Estacado, 106
Long, Stephen Harriman, 105
Long Island, New York, 166
Low Energy Precision Application (LEPA) irrigation, *16*, 17, 120

Mackay, Angus, 83
Madison, James, 165
Management System Evaluation Areas (MSEA), 225
Manure
   Midwest region, 144–145
   Southeast region, 193
Marek, Tom, 119
Marginal lands, Mid-South region, 227
Mass failure erosion, *51,* 57
Mean annual air temperature, 263, *264*
Mean annual precipitation, 263, *264*
Merino sheep, 165
Methane capture, 173
Microirrigation, 120, 269. *see also* Drip irrigation
Mid-South region
   area of, 203
   average farm size, *205*
   climate, 203, 274
   conservation concerns, 274–275
   conservation tillage
      agronomic studies, 223–224
      contemporary studies on, 222–223
      cover crops, 220–222
      early efforts, 216–217
      early-stage transition to, 220
      effects on soil properties, 224
      effects on water quality, 224–225
   cover crops, 217–218, 220–222
   demographics, 203–204
   future efforts in soil and water conservation, 226–228
   geology and topography, 205–211
   major land resources areas, *202*
   overview, 201–203
   soil conservation
      1900-1980, 211–218
      1980 to present, 218–225
   soil erosion
      early efforts to reduce, 216–218
      historical overview, 211–215
   soils and land resource areas, 206–211, 274
   total number of farms, *204*
   water erosion reduction, 218–219
   water quality problems, 219
Midwest region
   1945 to the present, 139–149
   animal production systems, 138
   artificial drainage effects, 136–137
   biofuel feedstock production, 151–154
   boundaries, 133–134
   climate, 131, 270
   conservation concerns, 271
   crop production, 141–142
      in the future, 149–150
   crop yield response, 145
   cropping systems, 137–138, 139, 151, 270–271

environmental issues, 145–149
fires, 131–132
global climate change and, 154
hydrologic changes, 140–141
land tenure, 134–135, 142–143, *144*
landscape-scale management, 154–156
livestock production, 138, 151
manure and livestock effects, 144–145
mechanization, 139
natural resource conditions, 135–136
public conservation policy, 156–157
recent land use changes, *149*
settlement patterns, 133
soil erosion, 135–136
soil orders, 132–133, 270
Miscanthus, 227
Mississippi Delta Cotton and Feed Grains Region, 209
Mississippi Delta MSEA, 225
Mississippi Embayment, 205
Modeling, 226–227
Moldboard plowing
  Midwest region, 135
  water erosion and, 58–59
Mollisols, 132, 270
"Mucks," 140–141
Mulching
  dust mulching, 22–23, 60
  water capture and, 17–18
  water retention and, 23–24
Mules, 189
Mustard green manure, 69, *70*

National Ambient Air Quality Standard (NAAQS), 60–63
National Association of Conservation Districts, 196
National Resources Inventory (NRI), 278–279, 288
National Soil Information System (NASIS), 254
Native Americans, 186–187, 240
Natural Events Policy (NEP), 62
Natural Resources Conservation Service, 87
Nebraska Tractor Tests, 190
New Hampshire, 165–166
New York City, 168, 176, 284
New York State, 166
Nitrate leaching, 57
  Midwest region, 145, 271
Nitrogen fertilizer, wheat production costs and, 96
Nitrogen management
  adaptive, 177–178
  risk-based, 177
No-tillage
  biofuel feedstock production and, 153
  future concerns, 287

Mid-South region, 275
  agronomic studies, 223–224
  cover crops, 220–222
  early efforts, 217
  early-stage transition to, 220
  effects on water quality, 224
Midwest region, 147
Northern Great Plains region, 88–89, 92–93
Pacific Northwest region, 71, *72*
poultry litter treatment and, 193
water capture and, 9–10
Noble, Charles, 111
Noble plows, 111
NO_3-N contamination, 145–146
Northeast region
  adaptive nitrogen management, 177–178
  agricultural production in, 163–164, 272
  agriculture and land use history, 164–166
  area of, 163, 271
  bioenergy and greenhouse gas emissions, 171–173
  climate, 163, 271–272
  coastal estuaries, 168–170
  conservation concerns, 272
  cover crops, 178
  restricted tillage systems, 179
  risk-based management of nutrients, 177
  soil and nutrient management tools, 170–171
  soil and water conservation programs, 166–167
  soil and water erosion costs, 167–168
  soil compaction issues and controlled traffic, 179–180
  soil quality/health management, 173–176
  soils, 272
  water conservation concerns, 284
  water quality concerns, 168, 176
Northern Great Plains region
  climate, 81–82
  conservation tillage, 88–89
  cultivated soils, 82
  future outlook, 95–98
  increased cropping intensity in, 89–91
  overview, 81
  recent advances, 91–95
  summer fallow, 82–88
Nutrient management, risk-based, 177

Object Modeling System (OMS), 66
Off-farm landlords, 143
Office of Dry Land Agriculture, 109
Ogallala Aquifer, 105–106, 268
Onion production, *69*
"Open field" rotation, 164

Opportunity cropping, 31
Organic material, deep percolation and, 28
Organic soils, Midwest region, 140–141
Organization of Petroleum Exporting Countries (OPEC), 116
Oriental mustard, 69
Oryza sativa, 187
Ouachita Mountains, 207
Owens Valley, California, 276
Ozark Highlands, 206

Pacific Northwest Direct Seed Association (PNDSA), 72–73
Pacific Northwest region
  climate, 50, 52, 265
  combined wind and water erosion modeling, 66
  conservation issues, 266–267
  cropping systems, 266
  dryland cropping areas, 265
    available water and wheat grain yield, 56–57
    high precipitation zone, 55
    intermediate precipitation zone, 55
    land devoted to, *48*
    low precipitation zone, 54
    winter wheat in, 55–56
  future research needs, 74–76
  grants for erosion control research, 74
  historical overview, 47
  irrigated cropping areas
    land devoted to, *48*
    major projects, 52–54
  soil and water conservation
    challenges in, 47, 49, 50, *51*
    dryland cropland, 70–74
    irrigated cropland, 66–69
  soil types, 52, 262
  water erosion
    modeling, 63–65, 66
    off-site damages, 57–59
  wind erosion
    air quality and, 59–63
    modeling, 65–66
Palliser, John, 81
Palouse Conservation Experiment Station, 70
Panicum virgatum, 227
Paraquat, 9
Paratilling, 192
Pea, 91
Peconic Estuary Program, 176
Perennial wheat, 75
Peshtigo Fire, 131–132
Pesticides, in Midwest crop production, 142
Phosphogypsum, 20
Phosphorus
  eutrophication of freshwater lakes and, 170

risk-based management in the Northeast, 177
Piedmont region. *see also* Southeast region
  climate, 183–184
  conservation concerns, 273
  farming trends, 186
  historical overview of agriculture in, 187–189
  soils, 184–185, 274
Pisum sativum, 91
Plant density, water use efficiency and, 123
Plastic film mulching, 17, 24
Plowing
  California, 242–243
  deep, 11
  defined, 5
  in dry farming, 3
  erosion and, 4–5
  Midwest region, 135
  water erosion and, 58–59
  water infiltration and, 3–4
PM_{10}, 60–63, 256
Polyacrylamide (PAM), 20, 67, 196, 266–267
Potato-based cropping, 69, *70*
Poultry litter, 193
Prairie Farm Rehabilitation Administration, 87
Precipitation. *see* Mean annual precipitation
Precipitation use efficiency (PUE), 88
Preemption Act of 1841, 134
Pressurized sprinklers, 248
Profile modification, 11
Pullman soil, 11
Pulse crops
  cereal–pulse cropping, 94–95
  Northern Great Plains region, 92, *93*, 97

Radish production, *141*
Real-time kinematic (RTK) satellite navigation, 180
Red River Alluvium, 209
Reduced tillage
  Southeast, 191–193
  water capture and, 8–9
Regulated deficit irrigation, 255
Rented farmland, 143
Reservoirs, 176
Residues. *see* Crop residues
Revised Universal Soil Loss Equation, Version 2 (RUSLE2), 64, 71, 75, 282
Revised Universal Soil Loss Equation (RUSLE), 64, 170, 278
Rice, 187
Ridge tillage, 180
Rill erosion, 57–58
Ripping, 15–16, 242
Rodweeder, 60

Rolled rye cover crop, *178*
Roosevelt, Franklin Delano, 196
"Rotation effect," 94
Rural Investment Act of 2002, 280
Russell, J. C., 111
Russian thistle, 60

Sacramento–San Joaquin Delta, 243, 254
Safe Drinking Water Act of 1989, 168
"Safener-treated" seed, 26
Salix, 172
Salsola iberica, 60
Salt-affected environments, 277
 irrigation and, 248–250
 Southwest region, 243
San Joaquin Valley, 249, 250, 256
Sand soils, deep percolation and, 27–28
"Saturation excess," 177
Sheep production, 165, 173
Simulation modeling, 226–227
Sinapis alba, 69
Siphon tubes, 116
"Slip-plowing," 242
Slot mulching, 16, 18
Smith–Lever Act, 258
Snow management, 15–16
Sodicity, 243
Sodium, 243
Sodium adsorption ratio (SAR), 248
Soil amendments, soil productivity in the Southeast and, 193
Soil Bank Program, 215
Soil carbon, 253
Soil compaction, 151, 179–180, 274, 285
Soil Conditioning Index (SCI), 281–282, 284, *285*, 288
Soil Conservation Act of 1935, 214
Soil Conservation and Domestic Allotment Act of 1936, 214
Soil Conservation Service (SCS), 87, 136, 188, 215
Soil Culture Manual (Campbell), 107–108
Soil erosion
 defined, 278
 evaluating, 288
 future concerns, 286
 Mid-South region
  early efforts to reduce, 216–218
  historical overview, 211–215
 Midwest region, 135–136, 146–147
 Northeast region, 167–168, 272
 plowing and, 4–5
Soil Erosion Service, 136
Soil health, 173
Soil loosening, 10–11. *see also* Plowing
Soil loss. *see* Soil erosion
Soil management assessment, 277–284
Soil Management Assessment Framework (SMAF), 282, 283, 284, *285*, 288

Soil organic matter (SOM)
 Bushland, Texas studies, 113
 cover crops in the Southwest and, 252–253
 estimating changes in, 281–282
 Southeast region, 194–195
Soil quality
 climate change and, 174, 176
 defined, 173, 281
 overview, 173–174, *175*
Soil quality indexes, 281–284
Soil quality management, Northeast region, 173–176
Soil slip, *51*, *57*, *267*
Soil subsidence, *271*, 274
Soil surveys, 241
Soil water storage efficiency, Northern Great Plains region, 90
Soils
 Mid-South region, 206–211, 274
 Midwest region, 132–133, 270
 Northeast region, 272
 Northern Great Plains region, 82
 Pacific Northwest region, 52
 salt-affected, 277
  irrigation in, 248–250
 soil orders of the United States, *266*
 Southeast region, 184–185
 Southern Great Plains region, 103–104
 Southwest region, 238, *239*, 276
Solutions to Environmental and Economic Problems (STEEP), 74
Sorghum
 no-tillage, *9*
 tillering, 123
 Tribune, Kansas studies, 121, *122*
Sorsby, Nicholas, 212
South Atlantic and Gulf Slope Cash Crops, Forest, and Livestock Region, 209
Southeast region. *see also* Coastal Plains region; Piedmont region
 climate, 183–184, *185*
 conservation concerns, 274
 conservation organizations, 196–197
 cropland area, 185
 deep tillage and fuel costs, 195–196
 farming trends, 185–186
 Florida, 274
 historical overview of agriculture in, 183, 186–190
 soil amendments and soil productivity, 193
 soil organic matter, 194–195
 soils, 184–185, 274
 tillage management, 190–193
 water storage, 194
Southern Coastal Plain, 209
Southern Great Plains region
 climate, 104–105

Southern Great Plains *continued.*
  early farming systems, 107–109
  increasing water use efficiency, 122–125
  irrigation in, 105–107, 116, 125
  overview, 125
  research studies
    1900–1940, 109–110
    1940–1975, 110–116
    1975 to present, 116–121, *122*
  soils of, 103–104
Southern Mississippi River Alluvium, 209
Southern Mississippi Terraces, 209
Southern Mississippi Valley Loess, 209–210
Southwest region
  agricultural landscape, 237–238
  area of, 275
  climate, 238, 275–276
  conservation concerns, 276–277
  conservation tillage, 251–252
  cover crops, 252–253
  crop diversity in, 276
  cropland areas, 276
  farmland protection programs, 256–257
  future outlook, 257–258
  land capability classification, *239*
  land evaluation and reclamation, 241–243, 254
  physiography, 237
  residue management, 253–254
  salinity and sodicity, 243
  soil conservation, 250–254, 256
  soils, 238, *239*, 276
  urban expansion, 244–245
  water conservation, 246–250, 255
  water supply, 240–241
  wind and water erosion, 245–246
Southwestern Prairies Cotton and Forage Region, 210
Soybean production, 139, 145, 151
Spodosols, 133
Spring wheat–fallow rotation, *85*
Sprinkler irrigation, 16–17, 120, 248
SQ indicators, 282
State Water Project (California), 241
Stockton Gang Plow, 242
Storie Index, 254
Stream channelization, 136–137
Strip cropping, 13, 88, 216
Strip tillage
  Midwest region, 147, *148*
  Northeast region, 179
  Pacific Northwest region, 67–68, *69*
  Southern High Plains region, 26–27
Stubble-mulch tillage
  Bushland, Texas study, 112–114
  origin of, 111–112
  water capture and, 6–8
Subsidence, *271*, 274
Subsoiling, 195–196
Subsurface drip irrigation, 250, 269

"Subsurface packer," 107
"Summer culture," 83–84
Summer fallow, 82–88
Surface residues, 4–6
Surface sealing, 251
Surge flow, 269
Surge irrigation, 16, 247
Susquehanna River Basin, 169
Sustainable agriculture, Northern Great Plains region, 91–92
Swamp Land Acts, 136
Sweep plows, *112*
Switchgrass, 227

Temperature. *see* Mean annual air temperature
Terracing, 14–15, 216
Texas Blackland Prairie, 210
Texas Claypan Area, 211
Texas Panhandle, 106, 120
"Three sister" cropping system, 164
Tillage erosion, 59, 267
Tillage management
  Midwest region, 147–149
  Northeast region, 179
  Southeast, 190–193
  in weed control and water retention, 26
Tillage reduction. *see* Reduced tillage
Tillering, 123
Tobacco, 164
Tomato production, 250
Total Maximum Daily Load (TMDL), 176
Tractors
  development of, 139
  Southeast region, 189–190
"Trash farming," 6
Tree biomass, 171–172
Tribune, Kansas studies, 121, *122*
Trifolium incarnatum, 6
Triplett, Glover, 147

Ultisols, 133
Undercutter system, 71, *73*
Universal Soil Loss Equation (USLE), 63–64
Urban expansion, 244–245, 257

Van Doren, Dave, 147
Vegetable industry, 186
Vermont, 170
Vertical mulching, 17–18
"Vertical tillage," 179
Verticillium dahliae, 69
Vineyards, 252

Water capture
  deep soil loosening, 10–11

Index

in dry farming, 3
fallowing, 18–20
infiltration, 3–4
irrigation method, 16–17
mulching, 17–18
no-tillage, 9–10
other practices, 20–22
snow management, 15–16
soil surface alterations, 11–15
stubble-mulch tillage, 6–8
surface residues, 4–6
tillage reduction, 8–9
weed control, 8
Water conservation
efficient water use, 28–33
future challenges and opportunities, 33–35
importance of, 1–2
Northeast region, 284
overview, 35–36
research on, 2
water capture (see Water capture)
water retention, 22–28
wind erosion control and, 60
Water erosion
estimating, 278
Great Plains region, 269
Midwest region, 271
on-site versus off-site costs in the Northeast, 167–168
Pacific Northwest region, 50, 51, 266–267
dryland farming, 57–59
irrigated farming, 57
modeling, 63–65, 66
Southwest region, 245, 251
Water Erosion Prediction Project (WEPP), 64–65
Water infiltration, 3–4
Water quality
Mid-South region, 219
Northeast region, 272
Water retention
crop termination time, 28
deep percolation, 27–28
dust mulching, 22–23
evaporation, 22
other mulches, 23–24
weed control, 25–27
Water storage, Southeast region, 194
Water supply, Southwest region, 240–241
Water use efficiency (WUE), 94, *115*
atmospheric carbon dioxide levels and, 32–33
Bushland, Texas studies, 118–119
defined, 29
increasing in the Southern Great Plains, 122–125
Waterloo Gasoline Traction Engine Company, 139

Watersheds
artificial drainage effects in the Midwest region, 136–137
protection, 284
Weed control
water capture and, 8
in water retention, 25–27
Weeds, glyphosate resistance, 93
Wells, nitrogen contamination, 57
Western Coastal Plain, 209
Wetlands
artificial drainage in the Midwest region, 136–137
Mid-South region, 227–228
Wheat grain yield, available water and, 56–57
Wheat production
California, 242
N fertilizer costs and, 96
Wheat straw, decomposition rates, 75
Wheat–fallow (WF) system, 18, *19*, 31, 85, 113–114
Wheat–grain sorghum–fallow (WSF) system, 18–19, 30, 31, 114
White mustard, 69
Williamson Act (California), 244, 256–257
Willows, 172
Wind energy, 173
Wind erosion
Florida, 274
Great Plains region, 269
Pacific Northwest region, *49*, 59–63, 267–268
modeling, 65–66
Southwest region, 245–246, 251, 277
water conservation and, 60
Wind Erosion Equation (WEQ), 65, 279
Wind Erosion Prediction System (WEPS), 65–66, 74, 75
Wind farms, 173
Winter cover crops, 67
Winter triticale, 150
Winter wheat
Pacific Northwest dryland areas, 54–56, 57
strip-till, *69*
Winter wheat–fallow rotation, 85
Winter wheat–summer fallow (WW–SF) system, 54, 55, 71, 73
Woody biomass, 171–172
World War I, 134

XIT Ranch, 109

Yakima River Basin, 267–268
Yakima River Basin Project, 53

Zone tillage, 179
Zybach, Frank, 116, 269